Ubiquitous Developments in Ambient Computing and Intelligence:

Human–Centered Applications

Kevin Curran
University of Ulster, Northern Ireland

Information Science
REFERENCE

Senior Editorial Director:	Kristin Klinger
Director of Book Publications:	Julia Mosemann
Editorial Director:	Lindsay Johnston
Acquisitions Editor:	Erika Carter
Development Editor:	Michael Killian
Production Coordinator:	Jamie Snavely
Typesetters:	Jennifer Romanchak & Michael Brehm
Cover Design:	Nick Newcomer

Published in the United States of America by
Information Science Reference (an imprint of IGI Global)
701 E. Chocolate Avenue
Hershey PA 17033
Tel: 717-533-8845
Fax: 717-533-8661
E-mail: cust@igi-global.com
Web site: http://www.igi-global.com/reference

Library of Congress Cataloging-in-Publication Data

Ubiquitous developments in ambient computing and intelligence: human-centered applications / Kevin Curran, editor.
    p. cm.
  Includes bibliographical references and index.
  Summary: "This book provides a comprehensive collection of knowledge in cutting-edge research in fields as diverse as distributed computing, human computer interaction, ubiquitous computing, embedded systems, and other interdisciplinary areas which all contribute to ambient computing and intelligence"--Provided by publisher.
  ISBN 978-1-60960-549-0 (hardcover) -- ISBN 978-1-60960-550-6 (ebook) 1. Ubiquitous computing. 2. Ambient intelligence. 3. Electronic data processing--Distributed processing. I. Curran, Kevin, 1969-
  QA76.5915.U264 2011
  004--dc22
                                        2011009954

British Cataloguing in Publication Data
A Cataloguing in Publication record for this book is available from the British Library.

Table of Contents

Preface xix

Detailed Table of Contents

Section 1

Smart environments support the activities of individuals by enabling context-aware access to pervasive information and services. This chapter presents the iTransIT framework for building such context-aware pervasive services in Smart Cities. The iTransIT framework provides an architecture for conceptually integrating the independent systems underlying Smart Cities and a data model for capturing the contextual information generated by these systems. The data model is based on a hybrid approach to context-modelling that incorporates the management and communication benefits of traditional object-based context modelling with the semantic and inference advantages of ontology-based context modelling. The iTransIT framework furthermore supports a programming model designed to provide a standardised way to access and correlate contextual information from systems and ultimately, to build context-aware pervasive services for Smart Cities. The framework has been assessed based on a prototypical realisation of an architecture for integrating diverse intelligent transportation systems in Dublin and by building context-aware pervasive transportation services for urban journey planning and for visualising traffic congestion.

This chapter describes last improvements made on ALZ-MAS; an Ambient Intelligence based multi-agent system aimed at enhancing the assistance and health care for Alzheimer patients. The system makes use of several context-aware technologies that allow it to automatically obtain information from users and the environment in an evenly distributed way, focusing on the characteristics of ubiquity, awareness, intelligence, mobility, etc., all of which are concepts defined by Ambient Intelligence. Among these context-aware technologies we have Wireless Sensor Networks. In this sense, ALZ-MAS is currently being improved by the use of a new platform of ZigBee devices that provides the system with new telemonitoring and locating engines.

Chapter 3
    Jesus Favela, CICESE, Mexico
    Mónica Tentori, CICESE and Universidad Autónoma de Baja California, Mexico
    Daniela Segura, CICESE, Mexico
    Gustavo Berzunza, CICESE, Mexico

Sentient computing can provide ambient intelligence environments with devices capable of inferring and interpreting context, while ambient displays allow for natural and subtle interactions with such environment. In this chapter we propose to combine sentient devices and ambient displays to augment everyday objects. These sentient displays are aware of their surroundings while providing continuous information in a peripheral, subtle, and expressive manner. To seamlessly convey information to multiple sentient displays in the environment, we also propose an approach based on abstract interfaces which use contextual information to decide which display to use and how the information in the display changes in response to the environment. Our approach is illustrated through a hospital monitoring application. We present the design of two sentient displays that provide awareness of patient's urine outputs to hospital workers, and how contextual information is used to integrate the functionality of both displays.

Chapter 4
    Christian Tchepnda, Orange Labs-France Telecom Group, France
    Hassnaa Moustafa, Orange Labs-France Telecom Group, France
    Houda Labiod, Institut Telecom–Telecom ParisTech, France
    Gilles Bourdon, Orange Labs-France Telecom Group, France

This chapter provides a panorama on the security in vehicular networks' environments. The special characteristics of these environments are presented and a general classification for the different types of attacks illustrated by some relevant attacks examples is introduced. Consequently, some key security requirements and security challenges are derived, considering Intelligent Transportation System (ITS) or Safety services as well as non-ITS or non-Safety services. Finally, some existing contributions in this subject are presented, and their deployment feasibility is discussed.

Chapter 5

Felix Villanueva, University of Castilla-La Mancha, Spain
Francisco Moya, University of Castilla-La Mancha, Spain
Fernando Santofimia, University of Castilla-La Mancha, Spain
David Villa, University of Castilla-La Mancha, Spain
Jesus Barba, University of Castilla-La Mancha, Spain
Fernando Rincon, University of Castilla-La Mancha, Spain
Juan Lopez, University of Castilla-La Mancha, Spain

Ubiquitous computing, pervasive computing, ambient intelligence, etc. are research lines that, with slight differences, emphasizes their efforts in improving everyday life of users. However, all these approaches share a common set of requirements, for the underlying IT infrastructure, devoted to support advanced services. A key component of these, sometimes called "new paradigms", is the fact that technology is found embedded in the environments were we live. In this chapter we are going to propose a comprehensive vision for modelling this type of environments from a practical point of view. This work cover form HW developments, which seamless integrate in the environment, to automatically generated services based on user needs. In the last decade, authors of this work have been proponents of a unified approach, based on the distributed object abstraction, allowing synergies to be better exploited. Remote device management, wireless sensor and actuator networks, hardware components and now even reconfigurable hardware platforms and service platforms are considered as part of a large evolving system sharing a common middleware and a single design methodology.

Chapter 6

Lidia Fuentes, University of Malaga, Spain
Nadia Gamez, University of Malaga, Spain
Pablo Sanchez, University of Cantabria, Spain

The development of Ambient Intelligence (AmI) software applications implies dealing with a wide variety of devices, which runs in different environments. These applications also target a wide range of end-users, with different needs and requirements. Software Product Lines are a relatively modern software paradigm whose main goal is to offer techniques and mechanisms to the systematic development of applications belonging to a domain with a high degree of variability. Therefore, the application of a Software Product Line for the construction of a family of middleware platforms for AmI applications should help to deal with the variability inherent to this domain. The first step when constructing a Software Product Line (SPL) is to create some sort of model which specifies the variability of the domain the SPL targets. This model is then used as basis for configuring and automatically creating specific products. The aim of this chapter is to highlight the complexity of managing different types of variability during the development of applications for AmI environments. A generic process for automatically generating a custom configuration of a middleware variant is also presented.

Chapter 7

    Andreas Schaller, Motorola, Germany
    Katrin Mueller, Motorola, Germany

The Internet of Things will enable connectivity for virtually any physical object that potentially offers a message, and will affect every aspect of life and business. This chapter looks at the concepts and technologies in three application areas that Motorola is contributing to now and in the coming years.

Section 2

Chapter 8

    William R. Hazlewood, Indiana University Bloomington, USA
    Lorcan Coyle, University College Dublin, Ireland

The rise of the Internet, the ever increasing ubiquity of data, and its low signal-to-noise ratio have contributed to the problem of information overload, whereby individuals have access to more data than they can assimilate into meaningful and actionable information. Much of the success of Web 2.0 has been achieved after an effective tackling of this problem. Ambient Information Systems take the battle into the physical world by integrating information into the physical environment tin a non-intimidating and non-overloading fashion. After two international workshops on Ambient Information Systems, we outline our vision for the field, consolidate a new definition, identify the key concerns of the research community, and issue a call to arms for future research.

Chapter 9

    Fabian Hemmert, Deutsche Telekom Laboratories, Germany

The work reported in this chapter is concerned with the relationship of the user to his mobile phone, especially with the habit of checking the mobile phone for missed events. We present two qualitative studies that have been conducted with mobile phones, symbolizing their status through life-like movements - breath and pulse. It was to be determined whether a continuous, rhythmic and life-like signal would be eligible to ambiently express the phone's state. The results of the studies were mixed, as some users were simply annoyed by the permanent actuation, while others appreciated the functionality. The response times to occured events seem to be appropriate for an ambient display. The studies raised further questions, regarding the psychological and physiological consequences of such technology.

Chapter 10

    Bernhard Wally, Research Studio Pervasive Computing Applications, Austria
    Alois Ferscha, Research Studio Pervasive Computing Applications, Austria

Media façades, realized through projection systems, could be a promising technology for scalable public displays in urban spaces. With low requirements regarding the infrastructure and virtually no influence on the buildings' fabric, projected façades offer exceptional flexibility and extensibility as well as easy maintenance. As cities are increasingly confronted with digital signage products besides other public display systems, a projector-based system offers the possibility to be switched off and restore the screen to its previous state in the blink of an eye. We present the prototypical implementation of a "Staged Façades Framework" leveraging a façade's structure and ornamentation for dynamically adapting pieces of multimedia content.

Chapter 11

This work reports on the findings of a case study examining the use of ambient information displays in an indoor academic setting. Using a questionnaire-based survey, we collect experiences and expectations of the viewers who are based on different floors of the same building. Based on the survey feedback, we offer some design principles to avoid the underutilization of peripheral displays and make the most of their potential in indoor environments.

Chapter 12

With the recent emergence of a wide range of information displays that reach beyond the traditional graphics-based computer screen, it seems that the original definition of ambient display, and its focus on user attention and aesthetics, has become diluted. Instead, we propose a taxonomy of alternative information displays that is mainly based on context, in terms of the data it represents and the environment it is located in. The resulting model described three different categories: visualization as translation, visualization as augmentation and visualization as embodiment. This model aims support visualization designers and developers in considering the correct visualization as well as display medium.

Chapter 13

Presence is an important part of our day-to-day lives. Often we will have a sense of who is around us and what they are doing by the sounds of doors closing, cupboards banging, footsteps on floors, voices vaguely heard through walls, etc. In digital spaces, such as GUI desktops, presence enhances our sense of connection with geographical separate friends and colleagues. In this chapter we report on Ambient Jewelry, which is a project exploring the intersection of individual and user generated customization with ambient presence displays. With this research we are seeking techniques that enable people to invent, discover and find new forms of ambient presence visualizations.

A changing computing landscape is expected to sense the physical world yet remain concealed within its very infrastructure to provide virtual services which are discreetly networked, omnipresent yet non-intrusive. Ambient Information Systems (AIS), permit a mode of expression that can easily exist at the level of subconscious realisation. This research focuses on the development of an Ambient Communication Experience (ACE) system. ACE is a synchronisation framework to provide co-ordinated connectivity across various environmentally distributed devices via sensor data discovery. The intention is to facilitate location-independent and application-responsive screening for the user, leading to the concept of technologically integrated spaces. The aim is to deliver contextual information without the need for direct user manipulation, and engagement at the level of peripheral perception.

This chapter is motivated by two evaluation case studies of ambient information displays. Firstly, an intrusive evaluation of a display called MoneyColor concentrates on the relationship between "distraction" and "comprehension". This revealed that the comprehension is in direct proportion to display-distraction, but there is no clear relationship between comprehension and self-interruption. Secondly, a non-intrusive evaluation of a display called Fisherman described a quantitative measurement of user "interest" and applied this measurement to investigate "evaluation time" issue. These experiments give some insight into number of issues in evaluation of ambient displays.

Social interactions among a group of friends will typically have a certain recurring rhythm. Most people interact with their own circle of friends at a range of different rates, and through a range of different modalities (by email, phone, instant messaging, face-to-face meetings and so on). When these naturally recurring interactions are maintained effectively, people feel at ease with the quality and stability of their social network. Conversely, when a person has not interacted with one of their friends for a longer time interval than they usually do, a situation can be identified in that relationship which may require action to resolve. Here we discuss the opportunities we see in using ambient information technology to effectively support a user's social connectedness. We present a social network visualisation which provides a user with occasional recommendations of which of their friends they should contact soon to keep their social network in a healthy state.

Section 3

Chapter 17

Interactive architecture bridges in itself two design traditions, i.e. design of interactive systems on the one hand, and architecture as the tradition of designing our built environment on the other hand. This chapter reports from our ongoing project focused on the design and implementation of an interactive environment for public use. The chapter describes the project, reviews and outlines the main design challenges as pinpointed in the literature on interactive architecture, and describes the practical challenges identified in this particular project. This chapter then presents the participatory design approach adopted in this project to overcome these challenges, and describes and analysis the methodological implications from this project. These implications include the lessons learned from the coordination of a geographically distributed design team, "role gliding" as the reinterpretation of the designers as users in the participatory design process, and a shift from communities of practices to mixtures of professions.

Chapter 18

In Opportunistic Networks (OppNets), mobile devices transmit messages by exploiting the direct contacts, without the need of an end-to-end infrastructure. Disconnections of nodes and high churn rates are normal features of opportunistic networks. Hence, routing is one of the main challenges in this environment. In this chapter, we provide a survey of the main routing approaches in OppNets and classify them into three classes: context-oblivious, mobility-based, and social context-aware routing. We emphasize the role of context information in forwarding data in OppNets, and evaluate the relative performance of the three routing techniques. Finally, we present how context-based information is used to route data in a specific subclass of OppNets: Sensor Actor Networks (SANETs).

Embedded systems within home appliances are not usually manufactured to operate in a networked environment; connecting supplementary hardware/software systems through a wireless, PC-controlled medium is necessary to enable full, efficient control of their functions from a remote location. Access to the home's central PC may be gained via a local web server, giving Internet-based control from almost anywhere in the world. The proposed system constitutes a significant improvement over those discussed in the literature to date, and reviewed here. It enables complex-appliance control in a secure and reliable portable-wireless environment, and was developed using ASP.Net. The system was assessed for Received Signal Strength (RSS) in an environment more radio-hostile than that found in a typical household. The minimum RF level found at a transfer rate of 9.6 kbps was 8 dB above the receiver's quoted sensitivity of -103 dBm; this fading margin will increase in a normal household environment.

In this work we present a middleware developed for Ambient Intelligence environments. The proposed model is based on the blackboard metaphor, which is logically centralized but physically distributed. Although it is based on a data-oriented model, some extra services have been added to this middle layer to improve the functionality of the modules that employ it. The system has been developed and tested in a real Ambient Intelligence environment.

Advancements in sensor technology, wireless communications and information technology has enabled the success of new types of dynamic computing systems. However designing systems which are flexible and can adapt to the changing needs of the user remains a major research challenge. Flexibility and adaptability are fundamental requirements for Ambient Intelligent (AmI) systems. The complexity involved in designing applications and devices which change and adapt their behaviour automatically based on their context or situation is well recognised. Providing technology which meets the changing needs of the user is heavily reliant on the appropriate infrastructure design. This work outlines the development of an Ambient Middleware framework for Context-Aware systems. The framework will integrate with sensor technologies, intelligent algorithms and the semantic web.

Section 4

The development of infrastructures enabling dynamic and automated composition of IT systems is a big challenge. This chapter addresses a new idea of allowing component-based systems to reconfigure themselves. Therefore, we propose DAiSI - a Dynamic Adaptive System Infrastructure for dynamic integration of components as well as their reconfiguration during runtime. Thereby, one of the features of the infrastructure is, that it is capable of binding components based on their availability. In this chapter we concentrate on presenting how resource constrained sensor nodes can be integrated into a system using this infrastructure.

Ambient display is a display, which sits on the peripheral of user's attention. Currently, the research on ambient displays is still in initial stage, so few evaluation styles are available to evaluate ambient displays. Our previous research (Shen, Eades, Hong, & Moere, 2007) proposed two evaluation styles for ambient displays: Intrusive Evaluation and Non-Intrusive Evaluation. In this journal, we focus on the first style by applying two intrusive evaluation case studies. The first case study compares the performance of three different peripheral display systems on both large and small displays. Our results indicate there is a significant difference on a primary task performance and a peripheral comprehension task between large and small displays. Furthermore, we have found that distraction may be composed by display-distraction and self-interruption, and that animation may only influence the display-distraction. In addition, a measurement of efficiency derived from cognitive science is proposed. The second case study focuses on exploring the correct disruptive order of visual cues (animation, color, area and position). Our results show that the correct disruptive order of visual cues in ambient displays is: animation, color, area and position. Furthermore, we also revealed how display-distraction influences the comprehension of ambient display. In addition, this case study further amended the measurement of efficiency, which was proposed in previous case study, to improve its accuracy.

    Michael P. Poland, University of Ulster, Northern Ireland
    Chris D. Nugent, University of Ulster, Northern Ireland
    Hui Wang, University of Ulster, Northern Ireland
    Liming Chen, University of Ulster, Northern Ireland

Smart Homes are environments facilitated with technology that act in a protective and proactive function to assist an inhabitant in managing their daily lives specific to their individual needs. A typical Smart Home implementation would include sensors and actuators to detect changes in status and to initiate beneficial interventions. This chapter aims to introduce the diversity of recent Smart Home research and to present the challenges that are faced not only by engineers and potential inhabitants; but also by policy makers and healthcare professionals.

    Mehdi Najjar, University of Moncton, Canada & University of Sherbrooke, Canada
    François Courtemanche, University of Montreal, Canada
    Habib Hamam, University of Moncton, Canada
    Alexandre Dion, University of Sherbrooke, Canada
    Jérémy Bauchet, TELECOM-SudParis, France
    André Mayers, University of Sherbrooke, Canada

The chapter presents a novel modular adaptive artful intelligent assistance system for cognitively and/ or memory impaired people engaged in the realisation of their activities of daily living (ADLs). The goal of this assistance system is to help disabled persons moving/evolving within a controlled environment in order to provide logistic support in achieving their ADLs. Empirical results of practical tests are presented and interpreted. Some deductions about the key features that represent originalities of the assistance system are drawn and future works are announced.

    Kevin Curran, University of Ulster, Northern Ireland
    Stephen Norrby, University of Ulster, Northern Ireland

The ability to track the real-time location and movement of items or people offers a broad range of useful applications in areas such as safety, security and the supply chain. Current location determination technologies, however, have limitations that heavily restrict how and where these applications are implemented, including the cost, accuracy of the location calculation and the inherent properties of the system. The Global Positioning System (GPS), for example, cannot function indoors and is useful only over large-scaled areas such as an entire city. Radio Frequency Identification (RFID) is an automatic identification technology which has seen increasingly prominent use over the last few decades. The technology uses modulated Radio Frequency signals to transfer data between its two main components, the reader and the transponder. Its many applications include supply chain management, asset tracking, security clearance and automatic toll collection. In recent years, advancements in the technology have allowed the location of transponders to be calculated while interfacing with the reader. This chapter documents an investigation into using an active RFID based solution for tracking.

Preface

INTRODUCTION

Ambient Intelligence refers to computing environments which are aware and responsive to the presence of human interaction. The aim is to use the space surrounding us in the form of movement, shape and sound recognition and create a system that will be able to recognize all the different scents that are in the environment. Ambient Intelligence has been influenced by user centered design which is an approach to design which regards the user's needs as the most important determinant of the content and structure of the design (Friedewald et al., 2005). Ambient Intelligence builds upon ubiquitous computing and user-centric design. Ubiquitous computing (calm technology) is the shift, where technology becomes virtually invisible in our everyday life or rather - embedded in our environment whereas it is made typically invisible (Weiser, 1999). There are of course many definitions of Ambient Intelligence (AmI) (de Man, 2003). To add another, we could say that Ambient Intelligence has the awareness of specific characteristics of human presence and personality dealing in turn with user needs, responding intelligently and all the while remaining invisible to the user (unless necessary) and striving to ensure that any interactions should be of minimal effort, easy to understand and ultimately enjoyable. Now, if you really think about that statement and the checklist of aspects which need to be satisfied – then you could be forgiven for thinking that it is a fantasy. Of course, the vision of Ambient Intelligence is difficult but here in this book is where we can expect to read about the vision becoming a reality.

Ambient Intelligence also builds upon Moore's Law which stated that the number of transistors on a chip will double approximately every two years. Electronics are now so small and powerful that they can be adapted to fit into almost every possible type of object no matter what the shape or size. The key to delivering ambient intelligence to users is being able to provide what is wanted, when, where and how it is wanted so that users receive the exact information, at the right time and in the right manner (Basten et al., 2003).

THE PAST

The Roots of Ambient Intelligence Ambient intelligence originated at Philips where in 1998, the board of management of Philips commissioned a number of internal workshops to study different scenarios that would transform the high-volume consumer electronic industry. The vision was of people living easily in digital environments in which the electronics are sensitive to needs, personalized to requirements, anticipatory of behavior and responsive to a person's presence (Aarts and Marzano, 2003). Philips then xx

joined the Oxygen alliance, an international consortium of industrial partners within the context of the MIT Oxygen project, in 1999 where the focus was to develop technology for the computer of the 21st century. Therefore in 2000, plans were put into action when a feasible and usable facility dedicated to Ambient Intelligence was built (Riva et al., 2005). The Ambient Intelligence Space was introduced by ISTAG Information Society Technologies Advisory Group. A few of the characteristics that will help in the social acceptance of an Ambient Intelligence system are that it should facilitate human contact, should be easily controllable by users, it should help build up techniques and skills as well as knowledge which in turn will ensure that the quality of work that is produced will be to a higher standard and people should be able to trust the system fully confident that it works correctly (Weber et al., 2005). Due to the complexity and importance of ambience intelligence, teams designing interfaces will need to create systems that are more responsive to people's needs and actions, whereas the systems become true assets for expanding our minds. The convergence of computing with telecommunications and multimedia resources will ensure that the means of communicating will increase and help to bring form to the Ambient Intelligence scenarios.

In computing, ambient intelligence refers to electronic environments that are sensitive and responsive to the presence of people. Ambient intelligence is a vision on the future of consumer electronics, telecommunications and computing. It was originally developed in the late 1990s for the time frame 2010–2020 where we shall be surrounded by electronic environments which are sensitive and responsive to people. In an ambient intelligence world, devices work in concert to support people in carrying out their everyday life activities, tasks and rituals in easy, natural way using information and intelligence that is hidden in the network connecting these (Curran & Norrby, 2009). As these devices grow smaller, more connected and more integrated into our environment, the technology disappears into our surroundings until only the user interface remains perceivable by users. Ambient Intelligence technologies are expected to combine concepts of ubiquitous computing and intelligent systems putting humans in the centre of technological developments. It calls for the development of multi-sensorial interfaces which are supported by computing and networking technologies present everywhere and embedded in everyday objects. It also requires new tools and business models for service development and provision and for content creation and delivery

The field of *Ambient Intelligence* endeavours to provide an understanding of the complexities in interacting more naturally with computers. Fields from distributed computing, human computer interaction, ubiquitous computing, embedded systems and other interdisciplinary areas all contribute to this science. Ambient Intelligence researchers in the field often share a common interest in gaining greater insights into the convergence of pervasive computing, intelligent systems research and context awareness, independent of research methods. Watch this space!

THE STATE OF PLAY AT PRESENT

To predict the future for Ambient Intelligence, I guess we can do worse than to look at the past and current uses of Ambient Intelligence. Therefore, some of the ways ambient intelligence has been applied has been through entertainment, advertising and home-automation. Philips have created some wonderful experiences through colours that change whilst watching a movie to intensify the mood of the scene such as Ambilight. Another ambient technology known as AmBX took the concept of the Ambilight lighting and added more multi-sensory to the experience through adding a new type of surround sound, vibration, air movement and some other effects such as delivering an immersive experience for gaming through the integration of games and peripherals working in harmony together.

Ambient intelligence because of it interactivity with the user is an attractive medium to advertisers. One such Intelligent Advertising project is AdSwitch which is designed to change when someone approaches the advert as their gender and age will be determined to evaluate an advertisement suitable to the user. For instance, as the elderly woman moves to the head of the queue, she is shown the advert for retirement homes and when the teenage boy heads the queue, some computer games adverts will play. This could be a large step forward for the advertising industry as not all adverts are able to reach their potential customers and now advertisers can target the correct market as the advert will adapt to the changing environment. The application of Ambient Intelligence in the Home Automation field is likely to continue as it can be simply allowed to disappear into the environment without home owners having to notice it carrying out the complex instructions that would make lives easier. It is also likely that newer methods of interacting with the interfaces will be a hot area for some time to come as speech and touch have specific limitations. It can be argued that one of the main reasons that ambient intelligence has not been implemented widely today is due to the constraints that come with it. For instance, to have every object made intelligent requires mass produced nano components yet nanotechnology is complex and hard to work with, the time it takes to develop devices with nano technology is much longer due to the fact that everything that is in the design must be built on a very small. There is also the aspect of security with Ambient Intelligence and if people are not willing to trust the ambient technology then it will fail (Wright et al., 2008). In Ambient Intelligent environments, information not only resides in one node but is distributed between many therefore every single node within the system needs to be protected (Espiner, 2008).

Ambient intelligence is beginning to have an influence on the market place today. Some of these products are at early stages and some are in niche markets. Take for instance, the award winning 'Philips Wake-Up Light' (see Figure 1). This alarm clock with a 300 lux light bulb can be used by anyone to help them wake up more naturally (by dawn simulation - so replicating waking up as nature intended - by sunlight). This means people feel more refreshed and ready to hit the day rather than being woken abruptly by a loud, sudden beeping. In fact you can set it to 3 natural sounds (morning birds, seashore, pond) or your favorite digital FM radio station. What is the relationship with Ambient Computing and an alarm clock? Well the clue may be in the manufacturers of this product ....Philips.

Earlier, l make it clear how indebted the field of ambient intelligence should be to the pioneers such as Emile Aarts of Philips. Remember, Philips had a clear focus in the early days of developing a fully networked, anytime-anywhere pervasive-computing technology. They had a clear visions of changing our everyday objects – from microwaves to heating consoles, even vacuum cleaners – into mini-computers that could 'talk' remotely to communication servers. Well, items such as the above award winning wake up light are a direct result of the initial AmI prototypes in their labs. Is this what they set out to do? Of course not but this is just possibly one of the nice revenue earners along with their other excellent ambient lights which show you that it does pay to conduct R&D.

Similarly, the Mist Clock Radio is a product which attempts to eliminate complexity from a bedside and replace it with intuitive access to clock and alarm functions, along with a 2-day weather forecast from AccuWeather.com. It has an FM radio with RDS (Radio Data System), and an InTouch messaging service that allows the sending of up to 140 character messages directly to a compatible Ambient product. One scenario that the company offer is where a school cancel notification is sent directly to the product so you know when you can sleep in before you get out of bed... Or send a "Happy Birthday" message

Figure 1. Philips Wake-up Light

Figure 2. Mist Clock Radio

to someone special... Or set notifications for special events, such as "don't forget, flight at 6am". Of course there are gaps in such a product but you can see where the future may lead us in such a hybrid communications/household device. (see Figure 2)

Another product on the market is the Ambient Umbrella (see Figure 3). The goal of this umbrella is to let one know when rain or snow is in the forecast by illuminating its handle. Light patterns intuitively indicate rain, drizzle, snow, or thunderstorms. If rain is forecast, the handle of this umbrella glows so you should not forget it. The Ambient Umbrella continuously displays forecast data for 150 locations. Embedded in the handle is a wireless data-radio chip which receives accuweather.com data and pulses when rain is forecast

The Philips Ambilight TV is best described as a flat panel TV with built-in ambient lighting effects (see Figure 4). It differs from other similar products due to its Ambilight 'surround colour experience'. It strives to immerse the viewer in the action by making the screen seem larger and simultaneously relaxing the viewer's eyes. The idea of this came from the research Philips carried out where they discovered that when people watch TV, they naturally and subconsciously take in their surroundings without thought. Therefore by projecting a corresponding light onto the background where the TV is placed provides a more relaxing and engaging viewing experience.

In fact the Ambilight TV fits into the market area where many people expect Ambient Intelligence to have a major impact – and that is Home Automation. Technology has been available for some time to create a fully automated home, but the cost benefit ratio was much too high to mass-produce these products and sell to Joe Public. Again, the reason for the excitement in this space is that the overall goal for ambient technology is to disappear into the environment surrounding us. This then allows it carry out complex (and tedious) instructions that would make our lives easier on a Friday or Saturday night.

Figure 3. Ambient Umbrella Handle (left) and Full View of Ambient Umbrella (right)

Figure 4. Philips Ambilight (In Orange)

Of course, this technology will only be presented to us in the home through intelligent user-friendly interfaces. These may be touch screen mobile control panels or the voice recognition systems which work through miniature microphones installed in the home that respond to instructions rather than users carrying the panel around. People can then speak instructions to execute preset 'Movie' settings that have already been customized to close the curtains/blinds, dim the lights, apply climate control (heating, moisture) and increase volume.

Another area of daily life where ambient intelligence research has led to innovative products is in flexible digital displays. There are numerous different flexible display technologies on the market, some made with plastic substrate and electronics. The days of newspaper being shipped across countries in the dead of night to peoples doorsteps may be a thing of the past for wireless digital flexible displays may be able to download in real-time breaking stories and sport updates whilst at the same time offering the reader a similar if nor improved reading experience as paper. Anecdotal evidence in fact suggests that flexible displays (or e-paper) are more comfortable to read than conventional displays. This is due to the stable image, which does not need to be refreshed constantly, the wider viewing angle, and the fact that it reflects ambient light rather than emitting its own light.

It has become more apparent that our lives will become more digitalised in the future with more embedded devices, network devices, location tracking and general increased public surveillance. This has led to a growing concern from segments of society (Wright et al., 2008). One concern is that Ambient Intelligence driven systems may hold too much information about individuals leading to invasions of privacy. They highlight the potential exploitation of those with lesser education and mental stability. There are others who feel that society will become more isolated as a result of not communicating via more traditional face-to-face means - but rather through computer online. There are those who worry about terrorist seizing information on populations especially in the case of war. Less dramatic but nonetheless a concern is this information being used in fraud and identity theft.

THE FUTURE

Levitt and Dubner in the best selling *SuperFreakonomics* (....sequel to the best-selling *Freakonomics*) outline a real-world scenario concerning incentives where insurance companies introduce Pay As You Drive (PAYD) schemes. This is where insurance companies offer discounts based on restrained mileage usage. It generally works by having the drivers who sign up install a wireless device in their cars that transmits to the insurance company not just how many miles they drive but also when those miles are driven and, to some extent, how they are driven. The small wireless device measures the car's speed every second, from which insurance companies can derive acceleration and braking behaviour so not only will the insurance company be able to charge drivers for the actual miles they consume but they will also be better able to assess the true risk of each driver.

One question people may ask is that "if Pay As You Drive is so great, then why has it taken so long to implement?" Well, there are a number of answers to that. Firstly, the tracking technology has only recently become affordable, secondly, insurers were anxious about drivers' privacy concerns (believe it or not) and finally, there was a substantial risk for whichever company was first to offer PAYD on a large scale (Dubner and Levitt, 2008).

As with most incentive changes, there will be winners and losers and the biggest winners here may be those who can drive the same distance they previously drove but now pay less. However the bigger goal for society — and the wild card in this or any incentive shift — is to create real behaviour change. It may just happen that PAYD can induce some of its high-mileage customers to drive less and especially to drive more safely, resulting in smaller claims payouts for the insurance companies and fewer negative externalities for everyone leading to added benefit for all of society.

Why stop there however, what if we can deploy sensors to modify human behaviour in all spheres of life? Let us imagine the world in a very short time where activity monitors are common place, all products have inbuilt location sensing and modifiable displays? (Just remember that technology costs are spiralling downwards). Then imagine for instance, sensors in shoes which record walking activity and thus offer tax breaks or shopping vouchers. What about incentives for those who used public transport? What about incentives for those who picked up litter and actually placed it in rubbish bins? Here in the last scenarios, the government incentives are to reduce healthcare and local council costs therefore incentives can indeed be cost effective. The key here is that we should perhaps adopt a paradigm shift in our thinking regarding surveillance and intrusion and adopt a more radical view and see it as perhaps a key actor to enforcing motivation for 'good deeds in society'. In some ways, we are encouraging people to 'play games in daily life'. The difference here, from say a poster campaign to warn people of the dangers of not washing your hands after visiting the bathroom, is that we can use technology to detect if they actually do wash their hands, and then award points (as described earlier) in the knowledge that we correctly detected a good deed for humanity. Of course there will be cheaters and workarounds/backdoor scams to earn unwarranted points in the 'game of life' but what technological innovation does not have? and do the benefits for mankind outweigh the negatives? You bet they do!

One particular interesting (or scary) vision of the future is the inherent traceability of our lives. It may not be unusual for our descendants to 'Google' much of our current daily behaviour. OK, imagine the scenario where all CCTV, banking data, shop purchases by credit card, car park entries etc are logged and archived online for preservation purposes. Also imagine, that this information becomes publically available at a later date due to new laws. Then, someone would be able to sit down, use image recognition software to trawl through gigantic CCTV footage for regions, gather related credit card purchases, access Google search archives for IP addresses, access IPTV programmes watched, access home automation records etc (Curran & Hubrich, 2009). In effect, try to imagine that every action which leaves a digital audit trace being cross-referenced with many other audit trails to zoom in on daily activities of loved ones during a specific period. Let us not stop there, what is to stop our live web chat sessions being retrieved? Our emails which were archived by the good people in the IT department? surely no-one will find their privacy violated when these 'old' emails get thrown out into the public domain in the future. Of course, none of us should have to worry if we didn't include any incriminating evidence with these emails.....but who among us still feel that complacent that we would expose our emails to the world?

Of course, there are many positives. What about those who wish perhaps to see an image of a parent whom they never knew. They may have knowledge that on the 5th of June, they went to London to the Natural History Museum. Here perhaps public archive footage of visitors that day could lead to nice high resolution of their parent entering and walking around the museum. Perhaps new DNA evidence leads to the finger of suspicion pointing to an individual - well perhaps publically well preserved audit trails of payments, CCTV footage and mobile phone usage will help in the case. Again, we simply have to imagine the exponential increase in processing power leading to simply unbelievable data mining queries over gigantic data sets of multimodal data.

Of course, the goal is always to have the computing power blend seamlessly into the background. A research project in this area (Hegarty et al., 2008) that I am currently involved with focuses on moving the current 'session' with the user. So imagine the scenario where someone is in a meeting. They are working with their smartphone. So on the smartphone, they are viewing the BBC website, they also have a PDF document opened (and have last looked at page 10 of the document before switching to BBC website) whilst also starting to download a video. Once the meeting finishes, they return to their office. Now in the perfect world, their session should seamlessly move of the phone and onto their desktop. Therefore, the user should have the BBC pages loaded, video resumed and PDF document opened at exact page as previously on the phone. In essence, a shifting of the previous 'session' to the more suitable device. An impossible task? Perhaps......but welcome to the world of research - no one said it was easy.

Talking of mobile devices, it is now agreed that mobile devices offer convenient communication capabilities and have the potential to create intermediary support for ergonomically challenged users (Mushcab & Curran, 2009). With the global proliferation of increasing longevity, assisting the elderly and those living with impediments through human engineering and computing technology is pivotal to biotechnological attainment. To remain independently empowered, seamless integrations through efficient affable interfaces are required to provide sedulous location-independent and appliance-sensitive media viewing for the user (Traynor et al., 2010). There are Ambient Systems such as the Ambient Interface Design (AID) system aimed at improving our lives. AID for instance seeks to assist with finding personal preferences and provides a synchronisation framework, coordinating connectivity across various environmentally distributed devices via sensor data mapping (Hegarty et al., 2009). Cooperative interface communication coupled with context awareness are abstracted to a representation that facilitates optimisation and customisation to these displays. To overcome personal challenges in the efficient selection and acquisition of online information, AID mediates between the needs of the user and the constraints of the technology to provide a singular customised encapsulation of 'ability preference and device' for each authenticated member. A particular emphasis is the application of a human-centered design ethos (Hegarty et al., 2009).

Therefore is seems that technologically integrated spaces may change our perception of information and our behavioural interactions associated with its provision. Here a system delivers contextual user preferences without the need for direct user manipulation in overcoming age or disability related issues in providing for ergonomics. In recognising individual capabilities and needs an enhancement of satisfaction, speed and performance should be experienced. Ubiquity and seamless access through Internet services will assist in providing adaptive personal interfaces in mixed mode modality and media. Proactive collaboration between the possible devices aims to capture and simplify tasks for the elderly and those with disability in a sensitive, secure and intuitive environment endorsing efficient support in tailoring to the user requirements. This will help to ensure seamless continuity between components providing usability and maximum user convenience. An Ambient Intelligent system like AID can act as a prerequisite for 'Personalised Interfaces' which aim to mediate between the needs of the user and the technology to help reduce personal challenges and provide a customised user experience for the efficient selection and acquisition of online information customised to preference, ability and chosen device (Dong et al., 2002). In so doing a mobile persistent browsing experience will be filtered to the user as they roam untethered keeping data and communications ubiquitous. Citizens on the move are becoming networks on the move as individuals carrying devices are integrated into a framework of networks supporting a dynamic experience (Carbonell, 2006). These are the areas of society where Ambient Intelligence can lead to a brighter, more intuitive, more helpful future in our everyday lives. As a wise man once said "And in the end, it's not the years in your life that count. It's the life in your years.".

CONCLUSION

Ambient Intelligence (AmI) involves the convergence of several computing areas. The first is ubiquitous computing which focuses on the development of various ad hoc networking capabilities that exploit highly portable or else numerous, very-low-cost computing devices. The second key area is intelligent systems research, which provides learning algorithms and pattern matchers, speech recognition and language translators, and gesture classification and situation assessment. The final element is context awareness which attempts to track and position objects of all types and represent objects' interactions with their environments. Finally, an appreciation of the social interactions of objects in environments is essential.

Ambient Intelligence is an emerging paradigm for knowledge discovery, which originally emerged as a design language for invisible computing and smart environments. Since its introduction in the late 1990's, AmI has matured and evolved, having inspired the development of new concepts for information processing, as well as multi-disciplinary fields including computer science, interaction design, mobile computing, and cognitive science. This means that computers suited with intelligent and user friendly interfaces will be integrated into the world around us without being obtrusive such as a self-cleaning house or a vacuum cleaner which can sense where there's still dirt or where you haven't cleaned for a long time and point this out. It's understandable that people might worry that a situation could arise where the computer would be running their life and taking all decisions, but the goal of AmI is only to support people.

In a broad sense, Ambient Intelligence is perceptual interaction, involving common sense, serendipity, analogy, insight, sensory fusion, anticipation, aesthetics and emotion all modalities that we take for granted in human interaction but have normally been considered out of reach in the computational world. We discover knowledge through the windows of our senses: sight, sound, smell, taste and touch, which not only describe the nature of physical reality but also connect us to it. Our knowledge is shaped by the fusion of multidimensional information sources: shape, colour, time, distance, direction, balance, speed, force, similarity, likelihood, intent and truth. Ambient Intelligence is not only interaction but also perception. We do not simply acquire knowledge but rather construct it with hypotheses and feedback. Many difficult discovery problems become solvable through interaction with perceptual interfaces that enhance human strengths and compensate for human weaknesses to extend discovery capabilities. For example, people are much better than machines at detecting patterns in a visual scene, while machines are better at detecting errors in streams of numbers.

Ambient Intelligence aims to make technology much smarter so that they will be able to interact and change to suit immediate requirements through intelligent user-friendly interfaces. Predicting the technologies that will shape the future ambient intelligence world is difficult however, it is expected that Ambient Intelligent technology will develop considerably. We have a certain amount of confidence in this as technology trends certainly have momentum and due to this have paved a way for Ambient Intelligence through such elements as computing, communication, software, sensors and displays. In accordance to Moore's law, data density on integrated circuits is continuing to double every eighteen months and related disciplines such as storage and CPU speeds also show substantial rates of change. The concept of Ambient Intelligence requires severe technological advances in sensor technology, communications, micro actuator technology, ultra-low power radio and in smart materials to create the adaptiveness and responsiveness to the environment. All of the elements have to be integrated into the architectural framework of an Ambient Intelligent System and these will then form a library of building blocks for general Ambient Intelligent System architectures.

Kevin Curran
University of Ulster, Northern Ireland

REFERENCES

Aarts, E., & Marzano, S. (2003) The New Everyday: Visions of Ambient Intelligence. 010 Publishing, Rot-terdam, Netherlands, 2003.

Basten, T., Geilen, M. and de Groot, H. (2003) Ambient Intelligence: Impact on Embedded System Design.

Carbonell, N. (2006). Ambient Multimodality: towards Advancing Computer Accessibility and Assisted Living. *International Journal on Universal Access in the Information Society (UAIS)*, 18-26.

Curran, K., & Hubrich, S. (2009). Optimizing Mobile Phone Self-Location Estimates by Introducing Beacon Characteristics to the Algorithm, Journal of Location Based Services, Vol. 3, No. 1, pp: March 2009, ISSN: 1748-9725, Taylor & Francis

Curran, K., & Norrby, S. (2009). RFID-Enabled Location Determination within Indoor Environments. International Journal of Ambient Computing and Intelligence, Vol. 1, No. 4, pp:63-86, October-December 2009, ISSN: 1941-6237, IGI Publishing

de Man, H. (2003). Foreword . In Basten, T., Geilen, M., & de Groot, H. (Eds.), *Ambient Intelligence: Impact on Embedded System Design* (p. vii). New York: Kluwer.

Dong, H., Keates, S., & Clarkson, P. J. (2002). Accommodating older users' functional capabilities . In Brewster, S., & Zajicek, M. (Eds.), *HCI BCS London* (pp. 10–11).

Dubner, S., & Levitt, S. (2008) *Not-So-Free Ride,* New York Times, April 20, 2008

Espiner, T. (2008) Privacy Experts Warn of 'Ambient Intelligent' Risks, ZDNet.co.uk, February 2008 http://news.zdnet.co.uk/security/0,1000000189,39292582,00.htm?r=2

Friedewald, M., Da Costa, O., Punie, Y., Alahuhta, P., & Heinonen, S. (2005, August). Perspectives of ambient intelligence in the home environment . *Telematics and Informatics, 22*(Issue 3), 221–238. doi:10.1016/j.tele.2004.11.001

Hegarty, R., Lunney, T., Curran, K., & Mulvenna, M. (2008) Ambient Intelligent Mobile Persistent Browsing Experience (AIMPBE): Seamless Session Browsing Experiences across Heterogeneous Devices using Sensors. PGNET 2008 - The 9th Annual Postgraduate Symposium: The Convergence of Telecommunications, Networking and Broadcasting 2008, Liverpool, John Moores University, UK, 23rd-24th June 2008, pp:27-32

Hegarty, R., Lunney, T., Curran, K., & Mulvenna, M. (2009) Ambient Communication Experience (ACE) International Journal of Ambient Computing and Intelligence, Vol. 1, No. 2, pp:53-59, April 2009, ISSN: 1941-6237, IGI Publishing

Kluwer Academic Publishers. Boston, 2003

Mushcab, H. A., & Curran, K. (2009) An Investigation into the Variance of Activity Monitor Measurements at Different Sites on the Human Body. International Journal of Adaptive and Innovative Systems, Vol. 1, No. 2, December 2009, ISSN: 1740-2107, Inderscience

Riva, G., Vatalaro, F., & Davide, F. And Alcaniz, M. (2005) Ambient Intelligence: The Evolution of Technology, Communication and Cognition, IOS Press, US, 2005

Traynor, D., Xie, E., & Curran, K. (2010) Context-Awareness in Ambient Intelligence. International Journal of Ambient Computing and Intelligence, Vol. 2, No. 1, pp:13-24, January-March 2010, ISSN: 1941-6237, IGI Publishing

Weber, W., Rabaey, J. M., & Aarts, E. (2005). *Ambient Intelligence* (1st ed.). Springer. doi:10.1007/b138670

Weiser, M. (1999, July). The Computer for the 21st Century, ACM SIGMOBILE Mobile . *Computer Communication Review*, *3*(3).

Wright, D., Gutwirth, S., Friedewald, M., Vildjiounaite, E., & Punie, Y. (2008) Safeguards in a World of Ambient Intelligence, Vol. 1, 2008, ISBN: 978-1-4020-6661-0

Section 1

Chapter 1
Context–Aware Pervasive Services for Smart Cities

René Meier
Trinity College Dublin, Ireland

Deirdre Lee
National University of Ireland, Ireland

ABSTRACT

Smart environments support the activities of individuals by enabling context-aware access to pervasive information and services. This article presents the iTransIT framework for building such context-aware pervasive services in Smart Cities. The iTransIT framework provides an architecture for conceptually integrating the independent systems underlying Smart Cities and a data model for capturing the contextual information generated by these systems. The data model is based on a hybrid approach to context-modelling that incorporates the management and communication benefits of traditional object-based context modelling with the semantic and inference advantages of ontology-based context modelling. The iTransIT framework furthermore supports a programming model designed to provide a standardised way to access and correlate contextual information from systems and ultimately, to build context-aware pervasive services for Smart Cities. The framework has been assessed based on a prototypical realisation of an architecture for integrating diverse intelligent transportation systems in Dublin and by building context-aware pervasive transportation services for urban journey planning and for visualising traffic congestion.

INTRODUCTION

Current advances in information and communication technology, where a variety of networked

DOI: 10.4018/978-1-60960-549-0.ch001

sensor-based systems and devices are deployed on the scale of towns, cities, and even countries, represent an excellent opportunity to support everyday life activities. Such smart environments are based on the vision of ubiquitous computing where everyday entities communicate and collaborate to provide information and services to users. They will lead to *Smart Cities* that can support the activities of their inhabitants to improve quality of life and ensure sustainability. Smart Cities will support activities ranging from transportation, to healthcare, to sports and entertainment, to professional and social activities. They will support people in smart workplaces, in smart cars, in smart homes, and in large geographical areas, for example, outlined by a shopping mall, by a road, or by city limits.

Smart Cities are inherently heterogeneous, as they likely will consist of a multitude of sensors, devices, networks, and ultimately systems, especially, with increasing geographical scale. People living and moving in Smart Cities may use integrated devices, such as on-board computers in a vehicle, or handheld devices, such as mobile phones, Personal Digital Assistants (PDAs), and laptop computers to interact with the environments and to use the services they provide. These devices will provide access in a pervasive manner, that is anywhere and at any time, to the contextual information and the context-aware services available in Smart Cities, ranging from personal and professional information services, to environmental monitoring and control, to social services, to city-wide information systems (Abowd et al., 1997; Cheverst, Davies, Mitchell, Friday, & Efstratiou, 2000), to traveller assistance (Kjeldskov et al., 2003; Sivaharan et al., 2004; Wong, Aghvami, & Wolak, 2008), to optimised urban traffic control (Dowling, Cunningham, Harrington, Curran, & Cahill, 2005; Dusparic & Cahill, 2009).

Transportation is one obvious domain for providing the foundation of Smart Cities since services can be built to exploit the very many heterogeneous sensor-rich systems that have already been deployed on metropolitan scale and along national road networks to support urban traffic control and highway management. Such environments might enable people to access information ranging from places of interest, to prevailing road and weather conditions, to expected journey times, to up-to-date public transport information. It might also enable suitably privileged users to interact with the infrastructure, for example, to request a change to a traffic light or to reserve a parking space.

This article presents a framework for building context-aware pervasive services for Smart Cities. Particularly important for the provision of such context-aware pervasive services is the seamless integration of the individual systems associated with Smart Cities into comprehensive platforms. The iTransIT framework (Meier, Harrington, Beckmann, & Cahill, 2009; Meier, Harrington, & Cahill, 2005, 2006) proposes an architecture for the conceptual integration of the individual systems and their information deployed in a Smart City. This enables information integration and sharing across independent systems and context-aware pervasive services. The framework also proposes an extensible and layered data model to facilitate data exchange between systems and services with diverse data sets and quality of service requirements. Data layers are defined within a common context model along the primary context dimensions of space, time, quality and identity, and may be distributed across multiple systems. The data model is based on a hybrid approach to context modelling that combines the management and communication benefits of traditional object-based context modelling with the semantic and inference advantages of ontology-based context modelling. The Primary-Context Model and Primary-Context Ontology have been designed with a strong emphasis on primary context, which is used to access other system context and to correlate context from independent systems, making them particularly suitable for large-scale smart computing environments. And finally, the framework proposes a spatial programming model designed to provide a standardised way for pervasive services to access context information that is provided by independent systems by exploiting the overlapping primary context attributes of the information maintained by these systems. This enables services to use and act upon information from a variety of deployed (and novel) systems as well as to share information between them. The spatial programming model hides the complexity and diversity of the underlying systems and their data sources and provides services with a common view on the available information and its context. For example, a service might use the spatial programming model to retrieve public transport information, which might be provided by an underlying system, and then access relevant weather information provided by another system using the temporal and spatial primary context of this information.

The iTransIT framework has been motivated by the transportation needs of Dublin City in the Republic of Ireland and has been designed to enable information integration and sharing across independent Intelligent Transportation Systems (ITS) and context-aware pervasive user services. It has been developed in cooperation with the Traffic Office of Dublin City Council and detailed framework requirements were informed by a comprehensive audit of existing and planned future intelligent transportation systems and services in the Dublin City area.

The framework has been realised in the form of a proof-of-concept prototype that captures a variety of real transportation information derived from systems currently deployed in Dublin City. The framework's support for pervasive services has been assessed by building context-aware services for multi-modal urban journey planning and for visualising traffic congestion. Such traveller and driver information services can be considered canonical services of Smart Cities since they exploit information generated by a variety of underlying heterogeneous systems in a context-aware manner. The prototype is based on transportation information relevant to and derived from a real metropolitan environment and demonstrates how our framework facilitates the emergence of truly pervasive services for Smart Cities.

The remainder of this article is structured as follows: Section 2 surveys related work. Section 3 presents an overview of the architecture for integrating independent transportation systems in Smart Cities. Section 4 introduces the hybrid context model and outlines the spatial programming model for building context-aware pervasive services. Section 5 describes our prototypical realisation of the framework and of the context-aware pervasive services for Smart Cities. Finally, section 6 concludes this article by summarising our work.

RELATED WORK

There is significant ongoing work in the area of ITS architectures (European Commission, URL accessed in 2008; U.S. Department of Transportation, URL accessed in 2007). The Keystone Architecture Required for European Networks (KAREN) project is of particular interest to European ITS developers while the National ITS Architecture is being promoted by the U.S. Department of Transportation. These frameworks essentially promote a common, system-wide organization based on standardised functions. They are similar to the iTransIT framework in that they enable integration of a collection of individual systems. However, they are not concerned with building context-aware pervasive services for Smart Cities and hence, they support neither information-specific integration requirements nor a means for pervasive services to access context information provided by a wide variety of systems.

Temporal, spatial and quality of service attributes represent types of meta-data that may be integrated into a context model to provide more intelligent and focused use of data (Hönle, Käppeler, Nicklas, Schwarz, & Grossmann, 2005). This approach has been applied in the Nexus framework (Grossmann et al., 2005; Lehmann, Bauer, Becker, & Nicklas, 2004) which provides a common context model infused with spatial infor-

3

mation to build world models that are distributed across environments possessing rich context data sources, known as Augmented Areas. The context model is presented as a global object-based ontology for developing interoperable world models. This interoperability is ensured through the use of a common but large data schema, the Standard Class Schema, to define various world models. The authors have defined a simple spatial query language that can be used to interact with objects representing an Augmented Area. An interface known as an Augmented World model provides a federated global view on all compliant local models. The focus of our framework has been to support a more constrained yet expressive set of context abstractions which are used to both facilitate data modelling and to provide the basis for building services for Smart Cities. Using such a constrained set of context abstractions simplifies management and maintenance in light of continuously evolving Smart Cities as novel services are expected to use combinations of existing abstractions.

Gaia (Roman et al., 2002) is a canonical example of a middleware infrastructure to enable active or smart spaces in ubiquitous computing habitats that emphasises the notion of space programmability. Gaia extends the notion of traditional operating systems to ubiquitous computing environments by providing components such as the Context File System and an event manager to track active space state information. Gaia focuses on managing resources contained in physical spaces. User data and applications are abstracted into a user virtual space and can be mapped dynamically to the resources located in the current environment. Applications developed for a Gaia active space use a comprehensive set of services at runtime. The iTransIT framework adopts a different approach in that it uses a set of context abstractions exposed through the spatial programming model to provide an interface to a smart environment populated by heterogeneous systems. Aside from calls to the spatial applica-

tion programming interface, systems may operate independently of the iTransIT framework.

Other related work includes systems that have focussed on addressing specific aspects of building context-aware smart spaces in transportation environments rather than on providing a common context-based integration platform as proposed by the iTransIT framework. TOPAZ (Kim, Lee, Munson, & Tak, 2006) is a service-oriented framework that promotes a business-level application model. TOPAZ envisions a global marketplace of telematics services where infrastructure providers and application providers are independent business entities. TOPAZ provides an open platform and a Web-service-based portal for managing applications, infrastructure and users. While the platform provides a range of core services for service metering, service monitoring, service diagnostics, and for displaying services, especially, through in-vehicle user interfaces (Munson & Tak, 2007), it does not support an explicit common context model that enables the use of overlapping context information across independent applications.

INTEGRATING INDEPENDENT SYSTEMS

The basis for the provision of context-aware pervasive services is the conceptual integration of the individual systems associated with Smart Cities into comprehensive platforms. As illustrated in Figure 1, the iTransIT architecture for integrating independent transportation systems and services in Smart Cities structures legacy systems, iTransIT systems, and context-aware pervasive services into three tiers. These tiers define the relationships between systems and services and provide a scalable approach for integrating systems and their context information as individual components can be added to a specific tier without direct consequences to the components in the remaining tiers.

The legacy tier provides for the integration of legacy systems and describes existing as well as

Figure 1. iTransIT ITS architecture framework overview

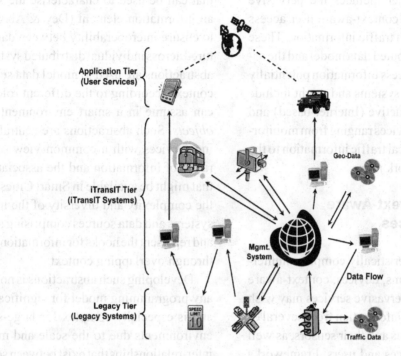

future transportation systems that have not been developed to conform to the iTransIT system architecture and layered data model. Such legacy systems often feature a form of persistent data storage and might include systems for traffic and motorway management that have commonly been deployed in many urban environments.

The purpose of the iTransIT tier is to integrate transportation systems that model contextual information and implement the spatial programming model. This tier therefore comprises a federation of transportation systems that implement the layered data model. The data model is distributed across these iTransIT systems (Meier, Harrington, Beckmann, & Cahill, 2009), with each system implementing the subset of the overall model that is relevant to its operation. iTransIT systems maintain their individual information, which is often gathered by sensors or provided to actuators, by populating the relevant part of the data model. However, some of the information maintained in an iTransIT system specific part of the data model

may actually be provided by underlying legacy systems. Most significantly, traffic information captured in this tier is maintained with its temporal, spatial, quality, and identity context; persistently stored data is geo-coded typically by systems exploiting a database with spatial extensions.

The systems that may exist in the iTransIT tier can be classified according to the paradigms they exploit when interacting with other legacy or iTransIT systems (Meier, Harrington, Beckmann, & Cahill, 2009). Such iTransIT systems may be purpose built and therefore optimized to accommodate service or user-specific requirements or may be general purpose. As shown in Figure 1, the framework may incorporate a general-purpose iTransIT Management system. The iTransIT Management system is the canonical application of this domain and is expected to implement a major part of the data model. It typically serves as a main repository for geo-coded data generated and used by connected legacy and iTransIT systems.

The application tier includes the pervasive services that provide context-aware user access to and interaction with traffic information. These services use the distributed data model and the associated context to access information potentially provided by multiple systems and might include a wide range of interactive (Internet-based) and embedded control services ranging from monitoring of live and historical traffic information to the display of road network maps.

Facilitating Context-Aware Pervasive Services

Smart Cities characteristically comprise numerous sensor-rich systems, devices, context-aware services, and users. Pervasive services may wish to acquire contextual information from several of the underlying systems and their sensors, as well as from related services and users. Frameworks supporting Smart Cities must provide support for locating these entities and their information, for accessing specific information, and for managing the context of information. The iTransIT framework proposes a layered data model that is based on a hybrid approach to modelling context for abstracting information and context and a spatial programming model to use such contextual information. The spatial programming model provides a standardised way for pervasive services to access and use information and context that is distributed across independent systems and related services. The spatial programming model provides common access to such distributed information based on overlapping context thereby enabling services in Smart Cities to exploit and act upon information from a variety of systems and other services as well as to share information between them.

Abstracting Information and Context

The iTransIT data model proposes a small set of predefined abstractions for composing information and context, where context is any information that can be used to characterise the situation of an information element (Dey & Abowd, 2000), to ensure interoperability between data sets captured across individual distributed systems. These abstractions are used to model data sets and their context according to the different roles data sets can assume in a smart environment as *spatial objects*. Such abstractions are central to providing services with a common view on the wide range of information and the associated context that might be available in Smart Cities. They hide the complexity and diversity of the independent systems and data sources comprising such spaces and represent the hooks for information integration through overlapping context.

Developing such abstractions is non trivial for any programming model for significant systems and is especially complex for large-scale smart environments due to the scale and multitude of inter-relationships that exist between sensors, systems, services, users, and their data sets. Lehman et al. (Lehmann, Bauer, Becker, & Nicklas, 2004) suggest an exhaustive ontology for defining how context information can be shared between applications in augmented areas. However, based on our experience with a real smart environment in the transportation domain, we have found that a relatively small number of abstractions suffices to decompose a Smart City domain model. Using a small set of (coarse-grain) abstractions rather than attempting to model the entire world in detail simplifies management and maintenance in light of continuously evolving environments. Novel systems or services are expected to be modelled using combinations of existing abstractions whereas an exhaustive model might have to be expanded to capture the specific characteristics of novel systems.

Primary-Context Model (PCM)

The PCM (Lee & Meier, 2007) is an object-oriented context model that defines our spatial object abstractions for modelling information and associated Primary Context (PC) and ultimately, for information access and information correlation through primary context. As summarized in Figure 2, spatial objects have been designed as a series of abstract object types and include three main types for modelling global information, which are *system object, real world object and data object*, as well as types for modelling primary context including identity, time, quality and location. Spatial objects represent information and context as a series of parameters structured as name-type-value triples. Name and type of context parameters are predefined to enable spatial object correlation based on context.

The three main types model the different roles that objects can assume within a smart environment and a Smart City. System objects represent general information describing the operational status of software components, including systems and services, while real world objects represent physical entities. In a smart transportation environment, for example, system objects might capture the operational status of a car parking system or a journey time estimation service whereas real world objects might model vehicles,

roads or traffic signals. Data objects represent non-physical entities and model any static or dynamic information regarding, or generated by, real world object or systems objects, such as public transport timetables or the number of available car parking spaces.

Identity PC uniquely describes spatial objects and consists of the spatial object type and an identifier. The identifier is unique within a certain spatial object type, implying that the combination of type and identifier distinctively identifies any spatial object within a smart environment. *Time PC* models the temporal context of data objects enabling pervasive services to access and correlate information based on time relevance. *Quality PC* defines a set of quality requirements associated with a data object. Although quality is not typically considered as primary context, we argue that quality is essential for accessing and correlating information. Quality PC allows pervasive services to identify information that may provide certain service guarantees and enables management of deficient or erroneous context.

Location PC is arguably the most important primary context of the PCM and uses geometric

Figure 2. Spatial object abstractions

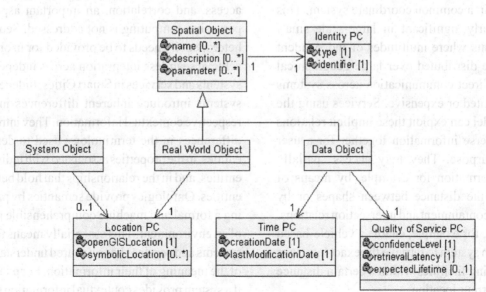

shapes to model the relevant special context of sensors, systems, services and even users. Location PC supports a topographical approach (Bauer, Becker, & Rothermel, 2002) to modelling space implying that shapes explicitly represent spatial context derived from the real world. Shapes may reflect the physical appearances of spatial objects modelling occupied space or may describe areas of interest that specify the regions covered by services. For example, a city-wide car parking system might use the spatial model to define the physical locations occupied by its car parks whereas a road weather service might use the spatial model to outline the locations occupied by weather stations as well as the areas to which reports from individual stations apply. Using a topographical approach to modelling space enables systems and services to independently define and use potentially overlapping spatial context in a consistent manner. Unlike topological approaches (Bauer, Becker, & Rothermel, 2002), in which geographical relationships between spatial objects are described explicitly, topographical models define relationships between spatial objects implicitly and without explicit interactions between objects. The relations between spatial objects (and ultimately systems, services and users) are defined by the position of their respective shape within a common coordinate system. This is particularly significant in large-scale smart environments where multitudes of independent systems are distributed over large geographical areas and direct communication across systems may be limited or expensive. Services using the spatial model can exploit these implicit relations to link diverse information together for a user specific purpose. They may access spatially related information for example, by means of exploiting the distance between shapes or by exploiting containment and intersection relations. This might, for example, enable a vehicle-based information system to retrieve the exact locations of car parking facilities within a certain distance from its current location.

The iTransIT framework supports the model for defining geometric shapes defined by the OpenGIS standard (Open GIS Consortium Inc, 1999). Spatial objects can be represented by various geometry types. Points might be used to define the location of a specific traffic signal or an individual user while polygons might represent the spatial context of a car park or an area of interest. As pointed out above, geometric shapes are specified using a common coordinate system. The selection of such a system depends on the domain of the smart environment for which the spatial objects are used. Coordinates derived from third party location sensors, such as Global Positioning System (GPS) receivers, are mapped onto the chosen reference system if they are based on another system. For example, GPS coordinates may need to be converted into a regional reference system chosen for a specific space. The Irish national grid reference system, a system of geographic grid references commonly used in Ireland, has been chosen as the coordinate system in our prototype.

Primary-Context Ontology (PCOnt)

While adopting an object-oriented approach to modelling context facilitates context management, access, and correlation, an important aspect of pervasive computing is not addressed. Semantic heterogeneity needs to be provided for in order to achieve seamless integration across independent systems and services in Smart Cities. Independent systems introduce inherent differences in their respective contextual information. They introduce differences in the terminology used to describe entities, in the properties associated with individual entities, and in the relationships that hold between entities. Ontologies provide semantics by providing a formal and machine comprehensible model of an environment. This essentially means that all systems and services have a shared understanding of the meaning of their information. For example, if a system provides contextual information (in the form of a spatial object) describing a bus, another system or a pervasive service can recognise the semantic meaning of the term 'bus', as a public transport vehicle, which in turn is a real world spatial object, and therefore must have associated Location PC and Identity PC.

Our hybrid approach to modelling context (Lee & Meier, 2009) introduces, in addition to the PCM, the PCOnt. The PCOnt is an ontology-based context model built using the OWL Web Ontology Language (Smith, Welty, & McGuinness, 2004) that facilitates machine interpretability of content through the provision of additional vocabulary along with a formal semantics. The PCOnt is divided into the *Upper PCOnt* and *Extended PCOnts*. As shown in Figure 3, the Upper PCOnt formally defines the spatial objects of the PCM and the primary context they must be associated with. Extended PCOnts are sub-ontologies of the Upper PCOnt and provide a formal representation of specific sub-domains within a smart environment, for example, in a smart transportation environment, Extended PCOnts might describe the weather sub-domain or the public transport sub-domain. The division of the PCOnt into the Upper PCOnt and the Extended PCOnts facilitates

extensibility as it allows for the accommodation of new systems and services into a Smart City.

Recent research (Khedr & Karmouch, 2005; Strimpakou, Roussaki, & Anagnostou, 2006) argues that it is unfeasible to reach consensus on a single global context-ontology that formally defines all possible contextual concepts and their relationships. Even in a contained environment, such as a single pervasive computing domain, it is difficult to create a single ontology for encompassing the semantics of every system. Moreover, maintaining such an ontology, especially, in terms of storage, distributed access and consistency in light of likely extensions, raises further non-trivial issues. We argue that the division of the PCOnt into the Upper PCOnt and the Extended PCOnts facilitates extensibility as it allows for the accommodation of new systems and services into a pervasive environment without a need for domain wide consensus. Also, Extended PCOnts enable distributed management of (sub-)ontologies and alleviate the burden of systems and services having to maintain a single, possibly very large ontology.

While the Upper PCOnt captures the basic context concepts of a Smart City, the extended PCOnts

Figure 3. The Upper PCOnt.

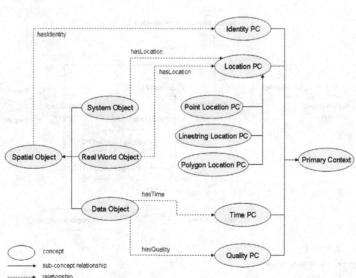

are sub-ontologies of the Upper PCOnt and provide a formal, semantic representation of specific sub-domains. For example, our Extended PCOnts represent sub-domains of the transportation domain, including a traffic congestion sub-domain and a road network sub-domain. As previously outlined, this approach offers extensibility and alleviates the burden of having to conform to a single, possibly very large ontology. Moreover, it supports efficient context processing and reasoning as a small number of Extended PCOnts is required by a system at any one time. Similarly, for pervasive services to benefit from ontological features, they only require the Extended PCOnts of the systems that provide the contextual information used by a particular service rather than of all systems in the Smart City domain. For example, a pervasive service advising drivers of possible routes might use context from a road network system and from a traffic congestion system. Such a service depends on the PCOnts of these two sub-domain systems only to infer the best route a driver might take, considering prevailing congestion levels. Figure 4 illustrates an Extended PCOnt of a traffic congestion system that serves as a canonical example of

how to construct an Extended PCOnt based on the Upper PCOnt. Two new concepts are defined in this Extended PCOnt for the congestion area and for the congestion record. The congestion record represents the current traffic congestion data and the congestion area represents the geographical area to which the record applies. Congestion area is a sub-concept of the real world object concept, meaning that it must be associated with location PC. The hasLocation relationship to a location PC is overwritten with a hasLocation relationship to a polygon location PC. This still satisfies the Upper PCOnt as polygon location PC is a sub-concept of location PC. The congestion record is a sub-concept of the data object concept, meaning that it must be associated with both time PC and quality PC. The relationship appliesToArea is also defined between a congestion record and a congestion area, stating that a congestion record must be associated with a congestion area.

Such a formal specification of data enables the correlation and merging of context from multiple sources in a Smart City. The following use-case further highlights the benefits of a shared understanding of context. Traffic congestion on

Figure 4. The Extended PCOnt for a traffic congestion system

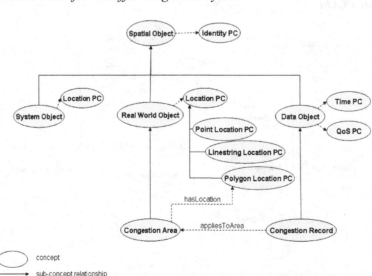

the west side of a Smart City is recorded using a road-sensor system, while traffic congestion on the east side of the Smart City is recorded using a modern camera system. However, both systems model their context in terms of the PCOnt, using a 'pcont-traffic:congestion' concept. Therefore, a web application that provides a graphical interface of all traffic congestion in the Smart City can retrieve congestion context from both systems, using the spatial programming model, and merge the context based on the PCOnt concepts used. Context from both systems are displayed homogenously to the web user, regardless that the information was sourced from distinct, heterogeneous congestion systems.

Using the Spatial Model

Systems use spatial objects to model their contextual information and implement a common interface, called the Application Programming Interface (Spatial API) (Meier, Harrington, Termin, & Cahill, 2006), to provide access to these objects. Each system models the subset of the spatial objects that is relevant to its respective purpose and context-aware pervasive services exploit the Spatial API to integrate and share

information in a common way regardless of the specifics of the system implementing a particular part of the spatial model.

As illustrated in Figure 5, the operations of the Spatial API provide a means for systems and services to locate, access and manage spatial objects. A set of select() operations is available for locating spatial objects using primary context queries (including geometric queries) and queries based on the typed parameters of objects. Real world and system spatial objects can be located using a combination of Location PC, spatial object type and parameter value. For example, real world spatial objects of type "bus stop" might be located based on their location and based on the bus route they serve. Spatial objects representing data can be located by combining Time PC and Quality PC with the object type and a parameter value. For example, the data associated with a weather station might be selected using the value of a measurement in combination with the temporal occurrence and quality of the measurement. Such queries may identify zero, one or more spatial objects. For example, selecting the bus stops of a certain bus route in a particular area might identify multiple suitable stops. The Identity PC resulting from such selection operation may then

Figure 5. The spatial application programming interface

	<<Interface>> Spatial API
IdentityPC[]	select (type : String)
IdentityPC[]	select (type : String, pq : ParameterQuery)
IdentityPC[]	selectData (type : String, tq : TimeQuery, qq : QualityQuery, pq : ParameterQuery)
IdentityPC[]	selectRealOrSystem (type : String, lq : LocationQuery, pq : ParameterQuery)
Parameter	getParameter (identity : IdentityPC, parameterName : String)
Parameter[]	getParameters (identity : IdentityPC, parameterNames : String[])
Parameter[]	getAllParameters (identity : IdentityPC)
LocationPC	getLocation (identity : IdentityPC)
TimePC	getTime (identity : IdentityPC)
QualityPC	getQuality (identity : IdentityPC)
void	updateParameter (identity : IdentityPC, updatedParameter : Parameter)
void	updateAllParameters (identity : IdentityPC, updatedParameters : Parameter[])

be used to either retrieve or update the parameters of spatial objects.

Significantly, the spatial programming model allows services to exploit primary context along a combination of the spatial, temporal, quality and type dimensions. This might enable a road-user information system to use the location and time primary context of an accident to retrieve the prevailing weather conditions at the accident site and subsequently to advice drivers of dangerous road conditions. Furthermore, the spatial programming model enables a federation of independent systems to model their respective information and context *locally* as spatial objects. Each of these systems implements the Spatial API to provide access to its respective set of spatial objects. This enables systems and services in a Smart City to use, share, locate and correlate these distributed objects using a common set of context operations irrespective of the complexities of the systems accommodating the objects and without the need for an overall close integration of the systems. This mapping of the PCM and its programming interface onto individual systems therefore provides for truly pervasive and context-aware services in large-scale and heterogeneous smart environments.

As previously discussed, the Identity PC encapsulates an identifier and a spatial object type and is used to uniquely identify spatial objects in a Smart City. The spatial object type also corresponds to a concept defined in the PCOnt. This augments each spatial object with semantics that may be used for consistency checking and inference purposes. The Upper PCOnt represents the high-level ontology capturing our general context concepts and needs to be available at any system or service that wishes to avail of the semantics of a spatial object. In contrast, Extended PCOnt are system-specific sub-ontologies and as such, are collocated with the respective systems they describe and from where they can be obtained. This distributed approach to maintaining Extended PCOnts allows pervasive services to retrieve only those Extended PCOnts that are relevant to their purpose. Once Extended PCOnts are available, they may be used to facilitate advanced reasoning over information, enabling deduction of further context from the context that is directly available from underlying systems.

Realising Context-Aware Pervasive Services

We have realised a proof-of-concept smart transportation environment for a Smart City based on a prototypical realisation of our iTransIT framework. The prototype implements an iTransIT Management system that captures a variety of real static and dynamic transportation information derived from systems currently deployed in Dublin City. We have built pervasive services for multi-modal urban journey planning and for visualising traffic congestion demonstrating how our framework can facilitate context-aware pervasive services.

Figure 6 illustrates the prototype and the systems and services that compose this proof-of-concept smart environment. The core of the prototype is the iTransIT Management system that implements the Spatial API and uses spatial objects to model information concerning a range of transportation systems currently deployed in Dublin City. The spatial data model of the Management system has been realised using a MySQL database with spatial extension and models the road network comprising intersections, roads, lanes, traffic counts, traffic volumes, and congestion levels as well as the public transport network consisting of bus and tram routes, stops, timetables, bus and tram locations, and bus lanes. This PCM integrates static and dynamic data provided by real legacy systems including the main traffic management system, a public transport information service, and a congestion level application.

Two legacy systems emulate the real interface of existing transportation systems and use real data from these systems to populate the data model

Figure 6. The iTransIT framework prototype

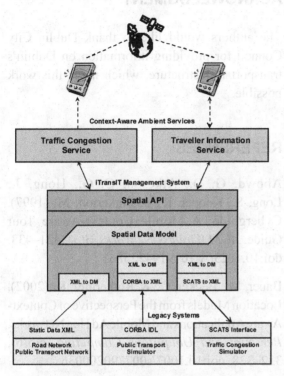

with dynamic information on public transport, including timetables and vehicle locations, and on road network traffic congestion. These two legacy systems connect to the Management system using different communication technologies. Information received by the Management system is initially converted into an XML-based format before being translated into SQL statements for populating the data model. In addition to ensuring realistic information exchange, this approach of using real legacy interfaces and real data is expected to enable a transparent switch over from our prototypical legacy system simulators to the real systems without changes to either the Management system or the pervasive services. A third legacy system simulator populates the spatial data model with static information on the road network and on the public transport network.

The prototype Smart City includes two context-aware pervasive services for providing information to users through mobile devices, a service for multi-modal urban journey planning (Brennan & Meier, 2007) and a service for visualising traffic congestion in the road network. Both services use the Spatial API to access the data model and ultimately, to transparently correlate and use the information provided by the underlying independent legacy systems. The Smart Traveller Information Service enables travellers to plan journeys involving multiple forms of transportation including walking, public transport, cycling, and private vehicles thereby bridging the coordination gap between these modes of transportation by suggesting journey routes according to traveller preference and availability of transportation means. The Traffic Congestion Service overlays intersection-specific congestion information over a road network map displaying up-to-date congestion levels. Such information enables travellers to adjust their journey routes and to avoid high-congestion areas depending on context such as the time of day. Such traveller and driver information services can be considered canonical pervasive services of a Smart City since they exploit information generated by a variety of underlying heterogeneous systems in a context-aware manner.

SUMMARY AND CONCLUSION

This article presented a framework designed to provide a standardised way to build context-aware pervasive services for Smart Cities using information that is distributed across independent systems and their devices. The iTransIT framework provides an architecture for integrating independent intelligent transportation systems and supports a spatial programming model that uses a small set of predefined types to model distributed context information as spatial objects. This provides a common view on such information and enables pervasive services in a Smart City to exploit, act upon and share information based on overlapping identity, temporal, quality and spatial aspects.

The spatial programming model supports a topographical location model in which spatial context derived form the real world is explicitly represented by shapes that reflect occupied space or describe areas of interest. This enables systems distributed in large smart environments to independently define and use spatial context in a consistent manner. The spatial programming model is supported by a data model that explicitly captures the relationships between information provided by separate underlying systems and allows individual systems to maintain parts of the overall data model. The data model is based on a hybrid approach to modelling context combining the advantages of object-oriented and semantics-based modelling techniques. The Primary-Context Model provides object types for modelling global information and introduces the management and communication benefits of traditional object-based context modelling. The Primary-Context Ontology augments these object types with semantic concepts providing the semantic and inference advantages of ontology-based context modelling. Both, the Primary-Context Model and the Primary-Context Ontology have been designed with a strong emphasis on primary context, which is used to access other system context and to correlate context from independent systems, making them particularly suitable for large-scale smart computing environments such as Smart Cities.

The framework has been realised in the form of a proof-of-concept prototype that captures a variety of real transportation information derived from systems currently deployed in Dublin City. The framework's support for pervasive services has been assessed by building context-aware services for multi-modal urban journey planning and for visualising traffic congestion. The prototype is based on transportation information relevant to and derived from a real urban smart environment and demonstrates how our framework facilitates the emergence of truly pervasive context-aware services in Smart Cities.

ACKNOWLEDGMENT

The authors would like to thank Dublin City Council for providing information on Dublin's transport infrastructure, which made this work possible.

REFERENCES

Abowd, G. D., Atkeson, C. G., Hong, J., Long, S., Kooper, R., & Pinkerton, M. (1997). Cyberguide: A Mobile Context-Aware Tour Guide. *ACM Wireless Networks*, *3*(5), 421–433. doi:10.1023/A:1019194325861

Bauer, M., Becker, C., & Rothermel, K. (2002). Location Models from the Perspective of Context-Aware Applications and Mobile Ad Hoc Networks. *Personal and Ubiquitous Computing*, *6*(5/6), 322–328. doi:10.1007/s007790200036

Brennan, S., & Meier, R. (2007). STIS: Smart Travel Planning Across Multiple Modes of Transportation. In *Proceedings of the 10th International IEEE Conference on Intelligent Transportation Systems (IEEE ITSC 2007)* (pp. 666-671). Seattle, Washington, USA: IEEE Computer Society Press.

Cheverst, K., Davies, N., Mitchell, K., Friday, A., & Efstratiou, C. (2000). Experiences of Developing and Deploying a Context-aware Tourist Guide: The GUIDE Project. In *Proceedings of the Sixth Annual International Conference on Mobile Computing and Networking (MobiCom 2000)* (pp. 20-31). Boston, Massachusetts, USA: ACM Press.

Dey, A., & Abowd, G. (2000). Towards a Better Understanding of Context and Context-Awareness. In *the Workshop on The What, Who, Where, When, and How of Context-Awareness, as part of the 2000 Conference on Human Factors in Computing Systems (CHI 2000)* (pp. 1 - 12). The Hague, The Netherlands.

Dowling, J., Cunningham, R., Harrington, A., Curran, E., & Cahill, V. (2005). Emergent Consensus in Decentralised Systems using Collaborative Reinforcement Learning. In *Post-Proceedings of SELF-STAR: International Workshop on Self-* Properties in Complex Information Systems* (pp. 63-80): Springer-Verlag.

Dusparic, I., & Cahill, V. (2009). Distributed W-Learning: Multi-Policy Optimization in Self-Organizing Systems. In *Proceedings of the Third IEEE International Conference on Self-Adaptive and Self-Organizing Systems (SASO'09)* (pp. 1-10): IEEE Press.

European Commission. (URL accessed in 2008). The KAREN European ITS Framework Architecture.

Grossmann, M., Bauer, M., Hönle, N., Käppeler, U.-P., Nicklas, D., & Schwarz, T. (2005). Efficiently Managing Context Information for Large-scale Scenarios. In *Proceedings of the Third IEEE International Conference on Pervasive Computing and Communications (PerCom 2005)* (pp. 331-340). Kauai Island, Hawaii, USA: IEEE Computer Society.

Hönle, N., Käppeler, U.-P., Nicklas, D., Schwarz, T., & Grossmann, M. (2005). Benefits of Integrating Meta Data into a Context Model. In *Proceedings of the 2nd IEEE PerCom Workshop on Context Modeling and Reasoning (CoMoRea 2005)* (pp. 25-29). Kauai Island, Hawaii, USA: IEEE Computer Society.

Khedr, M., & Karmouch, A. (2005). ACAI: agent-based context-aware infrastructure for spontaneous applications. *Journal of Network and Computer Applications, 28*(1), 19–44. doi:10.1016/j.jnca.2004.04.002

Kim, J. H., Lee, W. I., Munson, J., & Tak, Y. J. (2006). Services-Oriented Computing in a Ubiquitous Computing Platform. In *Proceedings of the Fourth International Conference on Service Oriented Computing (ICSOC 2006)* (pp. 601-612). Chicago, USA: Springer Verlag.

Kjeldskov, J., Howard, S., Murphy, J., Carroll, J., Vetere, F., & Graham, C. (2003). Designing TramMateña Context-Aware Mobile System Supporting Use of Public Transportation. In *Proceedings of the 2003 Conference on Designing for User Experiences* (pp. 1-4). San Francisco, California, USA: ACM Press.

Lee, D., & Meier, R. (2007). Primary-Context Model and Ontology: A Combined Approach for Pervasive Transportation Services. In *Proceedings of the First IEEE International Workshop on Pervasive Transportation Systems (IEEE PerTrans 2007)* (pp. 419-424). White Plains, New York, USA: IEEE Computer Society.

Lee, D., & Meier, R. (2009). A Hybrid Approach to Context Modeling in Large-Scale Pervasive Computing Environments. In *Proceedings of the Fourth International Conference on COMmunication System softWAre and middlewaRE (COMSWARE 2009)* (pp. 1-12). Dublin, Ireland: ACM Press.

Lehmann, O., Bauer, M., Becker, C., & Nicklas, D. (2004). From Home to World - Supporting Context-aware Applications through World Models. In *Proceedings of Second IEEE International Conference on Pervasive Computing and Communications (Percom'04)* (pp. 297-308). Orlando, Florida: IEEE Computer Society.

Meier, R., Harrington, A., Beckmann, K., & Cahill, V. (2009). A Framework for Incremental Construction of Real Global Smart Space Applications. *Elsevier Pervasive and Mobile Computing, 5*(4), 350–368. doi:10.1016/j.pmcj.2008.11.001

Meier, R., Harrington, A., & Cahill, V. (2005). A Framework for Integrating Existing and Novel Intelligent Transportation Systems. In *Proceedings of the 8th International IEEE Conference on Intelligent Transportation Systems (IEEE ITSC'05)* (pp. 650-655). Vienna, Austria: IEEE Computer Society.

Meier, R., Harrington, A., & Cahill, V. (2006). Towards Delivering Context-Aware Transportation User Services. In *Proceedings of the 9th International IEEE Conference on Intelligent Transportation Systems (IEEE ITSC 2006)* (pp. 369 - 376). Toronto, Canada: IEEE Computer Society.

Meier, R., Harrington, A., Termin, T., & Cahill, V. (2006). A Spatial Programming Model for Real Global Smart Space Applications. In *Proceedings of the 6th IFIP International Conference on Distributed Applications and Interoperable Systems (DAIS 06)* (pp. 16-31). Bologna, Italy: Springer-Verlag.

Munson, J., & Tak, Y. J. (2007). The XVC Framework for In-Vehicle User Interfaces. In *Proceedings of the First IEEE International Workshop on Pervasive Transportation Systems (IEEE PerTrans 2007)* (pp. 435-442). White Plains, New York, USA: IEEE Computer Society.

Open GIS Consortium Inc. (1999). *OpenGIS Simple Features Specification for SQL, Revision 1.1* (OpenGIS Project Document 99-049,).

Roman, M., Hess, C., Cerqueira, R., Ranganathan, A., Campbell, R., & Nahrstedt, K. (2002). Gaia: A Middleware Infrastructure to Enable Active Spaces. *IEEE Pervasive Computing / IEEE Computer Society [and] IEEE Communications Society, 1*(4), 74–83. doi:10.1109/MPRV.2002.1158281

Sivaharan, T., Blair, G., Friday, A., Wu, M., Duran-Limon, H., Okanda, P., et al. (2004). *Co-operating Sentient Vehicles for Next Generation Automobiles.* Paper presented at the The First ACM International Workshop on Applications of Mobile Embedded Systems (WAMES'04), Boston, Massachusetts, USA.

Smith, M. K., Welty, C., & McGuinness, D. L. (2004). OWL Web Ontology Language Guide [Electronic Version]. *W3C Recommendation.* Retrieved 2008.

Strimpakou, M. A., Roussaki, I. G., & Anagnostou, M. E. (2006). A context ontology for pervasive service provision. In *Proceedings of the Twentieth International Conference on Advanced Information Networking and Applications (AINA '06)* (pp. 1-5). Vienna, Austria: IEEE Computer Society. U.S. Department of Transportation. (URL accessed in 2007). The National ITS Architecture Version 5.0. from http://itsarch.iteris.com/itsarch/index.htm

Wong, W. S., Aghvami, H., & Wolak, S. J. (2008). Context-Aware Personal Assistant Agent Multi-Agent System. In *Proceedings of the 19th IEEE International Symposium on Personal, Indoor and Mobile Radio Communications (PIMRC 2008)* (pp. 1-4).

Chapter 2
Improving an Ambient Intelligence Based Multi-Agent System for Alzheimer Health Care using Wireless Sensor Networks

Dante I. Tapia
Universidad de Salamanca, Spain

Ricardo S. Alonso
Universidad de Salamanca, Spain

Juan M. Corchado
Universidad de Salamanca, Spain

ABSTRACT

This paper describes last improvements made on ALZ-MAS; an Ambient Intelligence based multi-agent system aimed at enhancing the assistance and health care for Alzheimer patients. The system makes use of several context-aware technologies that allow it to automatically obtain information from users and the environment in an evenly distributed way, focusing on the characteristics of ubiquity, awareness, intelligence, mobility, etc., all of which are concepts defined by Ambient Intelligence. Among these context-aware technologies we have Wireless Sensor Networks. In this sense, ALZ-MAS is currently being improved by the use of a new platform of ZigBee devices that provides the system with new telemonitoring and locating engines.

INTRODUCTION

The continuous technological advances have gradually surrounded people with a wide range of electronic devices and information technology. In this regard, it is necessary to develop intuitive interfaces and systems with some degree of intelligence, with the ability to recognize and respond to the needs of individuals in a discrete and often

DOI: 10.4018/978-1-60960-549-0.ch002

invisible way, considering people in the center of the development to create technologically complex and intelligent environments. This paper describes ALZ-MAS; an Ambient Intelligence based multi-agent system aimed at enhancing the assistance and health care for Alzheimer patients in geriatric residences. Furthermore, this paper includes new changes made to this system regarding previous publications (Tapia & Corchado, 2007), including the integration of new wireless sensor devices to improve the system with new and better locating techniques.

Ambient Intelligence (AmI) is an emerging multidisciplinary area based on ubiquitous computing, which influences the design of protocols, communications, systems, devices, etc., proposing new ways of interaction between people and technology, adapting them to the needs of individuals and their environment (Weber, *et al.* 2005). AmI offers a great potential to improve quality of life and simplify the use of technology by offering a wider range of personalized services and providing users with easier and more efficient ways to communicate and interact with other people and systems (Weber, *et al.*, 2005; Corchado, *et al.*, 2008b). However, the development of systems that clearly fulfill the needs of AmI is difficult and not always satisfactory. It requires a joint development of models, techniques and technologies based on services. An AmI-based system consists of a set of human actors and adaptive mechanisms which work together in a distributed way. Those mechanisms provide on demand personalized services and stimulate users through their environment according to specific situation characteristics (Weber, *et al.*, 2005).

One of the most important characteristics of ALZ-MAS is the use of intelligent agents. Agents have a set of characteristics, such as autonomy, reasoning, reactivity, social abilities, pro-activity, mobility, organization, etc. which allow them to cover several needs for Ambient Intelligence environments, especially ubiquitous communication and computing and adaptable

interfaces. Agent and multi-agent systems have been successfully applied to several Ambient Intelligence scenarios, such as education, culture, entertainment, medicine, robotics, etc. (Corchado, *et al.*, 2008b; Sancho, *et al.*, 2002; Schön, *et al.* 2005; Weber, *et al.* 2005). The characteristics of the agents make them appropriate for developing dynamic and distributed systems based on Ambient Intelligence, as they possess the capability to adapt themselves to the users and environmental characteristics (Jayaputera, *et al.*, 2007). The continuous advancement in mobile computing makes it possible to obtain information about the context and also to react physically to it in more innovative ways (Jayaputera, *et al.*, 2007). The agents in ALZ-MAS are based on the deliberative Belief, Desire, Intention (BDI) model (Jennings & Wooldridge, 1995) (Bratman, *et al.*, 1988; Pokahr, *et al.*, 2003), where the agents' internal structure and capabilities are based on mental aptitudes, using beliefs, desires and intentions (Bratman, 1987; Erickson, *et al.*, 1995; Geogeff & Rao, 1998). Nevertheless, Ambient Intelligence developments need higher adaptation, learning and autonomy levels than pure BDI model (Bratman, *et al.*, 1988). This is achieved by modeling the agents' characteristics (Wooldridge & Jennings, 1995) to provide them with mechanisms that allow solving complex problems and autonomous learning. An essential aspect in this work is the use of a set of technologies which provide the agents with automatic and real-time information about the environment, and allow them to react upon it. In this sense, most of the context information can be collected by distributed sensors throughout the environment and even over the users themselves. It is possible to distinguish between two types of sensor networks: wired and wireless. Wireless Sensor Networks (WSNs) are more flexible and require less infrastructural support than wired sensor networks (Sarangapani, 2007). Although there are plenty of technologies for implementing WSNs (*e.g.*, ZigBee, Wi-Fi or Bluetooth), it is not easy to integrate devices from different technologies into a single network (Marin-Perianu, *et al.*, 2007).

In the next section, the problem description that motivated the development of ALZ-MAS is presented. Then, it is described the basic components of ALZ-MAS and the most important technologies currently used to provide the agents in ALZ-MAS with improved context-aware capabilities. After that, it is explained some experiments of the system applied to a real scenario, as well as the results obtained, comparing the previous version of ALZ-MAS and the new release presented in this paper. Finally, conclusions and future lines of work are depicted.

PROBLEM DESCRIPTION

Dependence is a permanent situation in which a person needs important assistance from others in order to perform basic daily life activities such as essential mobility, object and people recognition, and domestic tasks (Costa-Font & Patox, 2005). There is an ever growing need to supply constant care and support to the disabled and elderly, and the drive to find more effective ways of providing such care has become a major challenge for the scientific community (Nealon & Moreno, 2003). The World Health Organization has determined that in the year 2025 there will be 1 billion people in the world over the age of 60 and twice as many by 2050, with nearly 80% concentrated in developed countries (WHO, 2007). Spain will be the third "oldest country" in the world, just behind Japan and Korea, with 35% of its citizens over 65 years of age (Sancho, *et al.*, 2002). In fact, people over 60 years old represent more than 21% of the European population (WHO, 2007), and people over 65 are the fastest growing segment of the population in the United States of America (Anderson, 1999). Furthermore, over 20% of those people over 85 have a limited capacity for independent living, requiring continuous monitoring and daily assistance (Erickson, *et al.*, 1995). The importance of developing new and more reliable ways of providing care and support for the elderly is underscored by this trend, and the creation of secure, unobtrusive and adaptable environments for monitoring and optimizing health care will become vital. Some authors (Nealon & Moreno, 2003) consider that tomorrow's health care institutions will be equipped with intelligent systems capable of interacting with humans. Multi-agent systems and architectures based on intelligent devices have recently been explored as supervision systems for medical care for dependent people. These intelligent systems aim to support patients in all aspects of daily life (Cesta, *et al.*, 2003), predicting potential hazardous situations and delivering physical and cognitive support (Bahadori, *et al.*, 2003).

Ambient Intelligence based systems aim to improve quality of life, offering more efficient and easy ways to use services and communication tools to interact with other people, systems and environments. Among the general population, those most likely to benefit from the development of these systems are the elderly and dependent persons, whose daily lives, with particular regard to health care, will be most enhanced (Corchado, *et al.*, 2008a; Van Woerden, 2006). Dependent persons can suffer from degenerative diseases, dementia, or loss of cognitive ability (Costa-Font & Patox, 2005). In Spain, as an example, dependency is classified into three levels (Costa-Font & Patox, 2005): Level 1 (moderated dependence) refers to all people that need help to perform one or several basic daily life activities, at least once a day; Level 2 (severe dependence) consists of people who need help to perform several daily life activities two or three times a day, but who do not require the support of a permanent caregiver; and finally Level 3 (great dependence) refers to all people who need support to perform several daily life activities numerous times a day and, because of their total loss of mental or physical autonomy, need the continuous and permanent presence of a caregiver.

Agents and multi-agent systems in dependency environments are becoming a reality, especially in health care. Most agent-based applications are related to the use of this technology in the monitoring of patients, treatment supervision and data mining. Lanzola *et al.* (1999) present a methodology that facilitates the development of interoperable intelligent software agents for medical applications, and propose a generic computational model for implementing them. The model may be specialized in order to support all the different information and knowledge-related requirements of a hospital information system. Meunier (1999) proposes the use of virtual machines to support mobile software agents by using a functional programming paradigm. This virtual machine provides the application developer with a rich and robust platform upon which to develop distributed mobile agent applications, specifically when targeting distributed medical information and distributed image processing. While an interesting proposal, it is not viable due to the security reasons that affect mobile agents, and there is no defined alternative for locating patients or generating planning strategies. There are also agent-based systems that help patients to get the best possible treatment, and that remind the patient about follow-up tests (Miksch, *et al.*, 1997). They assist the patient in managing continuing ambulatory conditions (chronic problems). They also provide health-related information by allowing the patient to interact with the on-line health care information network. Decker & Li (1998) propose a system to increase hospital efficiency by using global planning and scheduling techniques. They propose a multi-agent solution that uses the generalized partial global planning approach which preserves the existing human organization and authority structures, while providing better system-level performance (increased hospital unit throughput and decreased inpatient length of stay time). To do this, they use resource constraint scheduling to extend the proposed planning method with a coordination mechanism that

handles mutually exclusive resource relationships. Other applications focus on home scenarios to provide assistance to elderly and dependent persons. RoboCare presents a multi-agent approach that covers several research areas, such as intelligent agents, visualization tools, robotics, and data analysis techniques to support people with their daily life activities (Pecora & Cesta, 2007). TeleCARE is another application that makes use of mobile agents and a generic platform in order to provide remote services and automate an entire home scenario for elderly people (Afsarmanesh, *et al.*, 2004). Although these applications expand the possibilities and stimulate research efforts to enhance the assistance and health care provided to elderly and dependent persons, none of them integrate intelligent agents, distributed and dynamic applications and services approach, or the use of reasoning and planning mechanisms into their model.

An Ambient Intelligence Based Multi-Agent System for Alzheimer Health Care

ALZ-MAS (*ALZheimer Multi-Agent System*) (Corchado, *et al.*, 2008a; 2008b; Tapia & Corchado, 2009) is a distributed multi-agent system designed upon Ambient Intelligence and aimed at enhancing the assistance and health care for Alzheimer patients living in geriatric residences. The main functionalities in the system include reasoning and planning mechanisms (Glez-Bedia & Corchado, 2002) that are embedded into deliberative BDI agents, and the use of several context-aware technologies to acquire information from users and their environment. As can be seen in Figure 1, ALZ-MAS structure has five different deliberative agents based on the BDI model (BDI Agents), each one with specific roles and capabilities:

- *User Agent*. This agent manages the users' personal data and behavior (monitoring,

Figure 1. ALZ-MAS basic structure

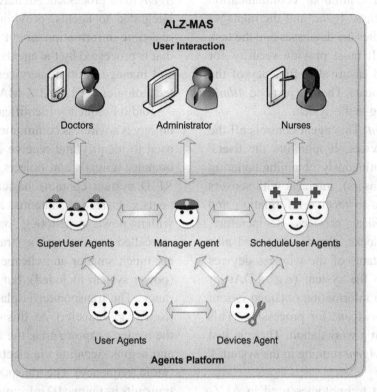

location, daily tasks, and anomalies). The *User Agent* beliefs and goals applied to every user depend on the plan or plans defined by the super-users. *User Agent* maintains continuous communication with the rest of the system agents, especially with the *ScheduleUser Agent* (through which the scheduled-users can communicate the result of their assigned tasks) and with the *SuperUser Agent*. The *User Agent* must ensure that all the actions indicated by the SuperUser are carried out, and sends a copy of its memory base (goals and plans) to the *Admin Agent* in order to maintain backups. There is one agent for each patient registered in the system.

- *SuperUser Agent*. It also runs on mobile devices (PDAs) and inserts new tasks into the *Admin Agent* to be processed by a reasoning mechanism (Corchado, *et al.*, 2008b). It also needs to interact with

the *User Agents* to impose new tasks and receive periodic reports, and with the *ScheduleUser Agents* to ascertain the evolution of each plan. There is one agent for each doctor connected to the system.

- *ScheduleUser Agent*. It is a BDI agent with a planning mechanism embedded in its structure (Corchado, *et al.*, 2008b). It schedules the users' daily activities and obtains dynamic plans depending on the tasks needed for each user. It manages scheduled-users profiles (preferences, habits, holidays, etc.), tasks, available time and resources. Every agent generates personalized plans depending on the scheduled-user profile. There is one *ScheduleUser Agents* for each nurse connected to the system.

- *Admin Agent*. It runs on a workstation and plays two roles: the security role that monitors the users' location and physical building status (temperature, lights, alarms, etc.) through continuous communication with the *Devices Agent*; and the manager role that handles the databases and the task assignment. It must provide security for the users and ensure the efficiency of the tasks assignments. There is just one *Admin Agent* running in the system.

- *Devices Agent*. This agent controls all the hardware devices. It monitors the users' location (continuously obtaining/updating data from sensors), interacts with sensors and actuators to receive information and control physical services (temperature, lights, door locks, alarms, etc.), and also checks the status of the wireless devices connected to the system (*e.g.*, PDAs or laptops). The information obtained is sent to the *Admin Agent* for processing. This agent runs on a workstation. There is just one *Devices Agent* running in the system.

Next, the main technologies used in ALZ-MAS to provide the agents with context-aware capabilities are presented.

Technologies Used in ALZ-MAS for Context-Awareness

The agents in ALZ-MAS collaborate with context-aware agents that employ Radio Frequency Identification, Wireless Sensor Networks and automation devices to provide automatic and real-time information about the environment, and allow the users to interact with their surroundings, controlling and managing physical services (*i.e.*, heating, lights, switches, etc.). All the information provided is processed by the agents, specially the *Devices Agent* which is a BDI agent that runs on a workstation. The *Devices Agent* monitors the users' location, interacts with the ZigBee devices to receive information and control physical services, and also checks the status of the wireless devices connected to the system (*e.g.*, PDAs). The information obtained is sent to the *Admin*

Agent to be processed. All hardware is someway integrated to agents, providing automatic and real-time information about the environment that is processed by the agents to automate tasks and manage multiple services. Next, the main technologies used in ALZ-MAS are presented.

Radio Frequency Identification (RFID) technology is a wireless communications technology used to identify and receive information about humans, animals and objects on the move. An RFID system contains basically four components: tags, readers, antennas and software. Tags with no power system (*e.g.*, batteries) integrated are called *passive tags* or "transponders", these are much smaller and cheaper than *active tags* (power system included), but have shorter read range. The transponder is placed on the object itself (*e.g.*, bracelet). As this object moves into the reader's capture area, the reader is activated and begins signaling via electromagnetic waves (radio frequency). The transponder subsequently transmits its unique ID information number to the reader, which forwards it to a device or a central computer where the information is processed and showed. This information is not only restricted to the location of the object, but also can include specific detailed information concerning the object itself. The most use is in industrial/manufacturing, transportation, distribution, etc., but there are other growth areas including health care. The configuration used in the previous version of ALZ-MAS (Tapia & Corchado, 2009) consists of a transponder mounted on a bracelet worn on the users' wrist or ankle, several sensors installed over protected zones with an adjustable capture range up to 2 meters, and a central workstation where all the information is processed and stored. Nevertheless, current version of ALZ-MAS uses ZigBee devices to obtain both users' location and other context information.

Wireless Sensor Networks, and more specifically, ZigBee, is another important technology used in ALZ-MAS.

AmI-based developments require the use of several sensors and actuators strategically distributed throughout the environment. This provides the systems with context-aware capabilities to change its behavior automatically. It is possible to make a difference between sensor networks: wired and wireless. There are several technologies for creating wired sensors networks, such as X10, LonWorks or KNX. However, wired networks are not so flexible as wireless sensors networks and require more infrastructural support (Ahmed, *et al.*, 2007). On the other hand, wireless technologies enable easier deployments than the wired ones, avoiding the need of wiring homes or hospitals and decreasing the costs and drawbacks of the setup phase. ZigBee is a low cost, low power consumption, wireless communication standard, developed by the ZigBee Alliance (ZigBee Standards Organization, 2006). It is based on IEEE 802.15.4 protocol, and operates at 868/915MHz & 2.4GHz spectrum. ZigBee is designed to be embedded in consumer electronics, home and building automation, industrial controls, PC peripherals, medical sensor applications, toys and games, and is intended for home, building and industrial automation purposes, addressing the needs of monitoring, control and sensory network applications (ZigBee

Standards Organization, 2006). ZigBee allows star, tree or mesh network topologies. Devices can be configured to act as: network *coordinator* (control all devices); *router* (send/receive/forward data to/from coordinator,,end devices and other routers); and *end device* (send/receive data to/from coordinator). Figure 2 (left) shows the ZigBee devices currently used in ALZ-MAS to control heating, lights, door locks, alarms, etc. These devices, called n-Core Sirius-A, have both 2.4GHz and 868/915MHz versions and have several communication ports (GPIO, ADC, I2C and UART through USB or DB-9 RS-232) to connect to distinct devices, including almost every kind of sensor and actuator (n-Core, 2010). This way, it is deployed a mesh of these devices to control all these services. n-Core Sirius-A devices form part of the n-Core platform (http://www.n-core.info), which offers a complete API (Application Programming Interface) to access all its functionalities, including some telemonitoring and locating engines. Thus, it can be used different locating techniques using Sirius A devices as readers and Sirius B devices, showed in Figure 2 (right), as tags carried by patients and medical personnel.

Wireless LAN (Local Area Network) also known as Wi-Fi (Wireless Fidelity) networks,

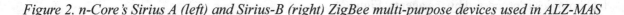

Figure 2. n-Core's Sirius A (left) and Sirius-B (right) ZigBee multi-purpose devices used in ALZ-MAS

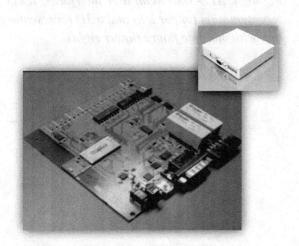

increase the mobility, flexibility and efficiency of the users, allowing programs, data and resources to be available no matter the physical location. These networks can be used to replace or as an extension of wired LANs. They provide reduced infrastructure and low installation cost, and also give more mobility and flexibility by allowing people to stay connected to the network as they roam among covered areas, increasing efficiency by allowing data to be entered and accessed on site (Hewlett-Packard, 2002). New handheld devices facilitate the use of new interaction techniques, for instance, some systems focus on facilitating users with guidance or location systems (Corchado, *et al.*, 2005) by means of their wireless devices. ALZ-MAS incorporates "lightweight" agents that can reside in mobile devices, such as cellular phones, PDAs, etc., and therefore support wireless communication, which facilitates the portability to a wide range of devices. Figure 3 shows the user interface executed in a PDA emulator. The Wi-Fi infrastructure in ALZ-MAS supports a set of PDAs for interfaces and users' interaction; a workstation where all the high demanding CPU tasks (planning and reasoning) are processed; and several access points for providing wireless communication between distributed agents.

All information obtained by means of these technologies is processed by the agents. Figure 4 shows the main user interface of ALZ-MAS. Depending on the system requirements, several interfaces can be executed. The interfaces show basic information about nurses and patients (name, tasks that must be accomplished, schedule, location inside the residence, etc.) and the building (outside temperature, specific room temperature, lights status, etc.).

EXPERIMENTS AND RESULTS

ALZ-MAS is an Ambient Intelligence based multi-agent system aimed at enhancing the assistance and health care for Alzheimer patients. ALZ-MAS takes advantage of the cooperation among autonomous agents and the use of context-aware technologies providing a ubiquitous, non-invasive, high-level interaction among users, system and environment.

One of the most important features in ALZ-MAS is the use of complex reasoning and planning mechanisms. These mechanisms dynamically schedule the medical staff daily tasks. Figure 5 (left) shows a window with the general planning process result. It contains the date, time to initiate the task, task description, priority of the task, length of the task, and the patient associated with

Figure 3. ALZ-MAS' PDA user interface showing different situations. From left to right: the location of patients and nurses; the list of tasks scheduled by the planning mechanism; and the login dialog for registering in the system

Figure 4. ALZ-MAS main user interfaces: a 2D representation (upper left) and a 3D representation with multiple floors (lower right)

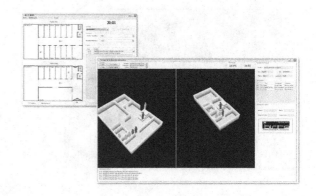

each task. To generate a new plan, a *Schedule User Agent* (running on a PDA) sends a request to the *Agents Platform*. The request is processed by the *Manager Agent* which decides creating a new plan. Then, the solution is sent to the platform which delivers the new plan to all *Schedule User Agents* running. The planning mechanism creates optimal paths and scheduling in order to facilitate the completion of all activities defined for the nurses connected to the system. As can be seen in Figure 5 (right), the information is provided to all nurses and doctors in a user-friendly format using mobile devices (PDA) to see their corresponding tasks.

Several tests have been done to demonstrate the efficiency of ALZ-MAS which consisted of collecting data regarding the time spent by the nurses on routine tasks and the number of nurses working simultaneously. The prototype of ALZ-MAS, using both RFID and ZigBee devices, was adopted at first on June 12th, 2007 (Tapia & Corchado, 2009). Likewise, on August 2th, 2010 a new release of ALZ-MAS using n-Core ZigBee devices (n-Core, 2010) for both locating and telemonitoring tasks were adopted and compared with previous version. As in the previous experiment (Tapia & Corchado, 2009), the tasks executed by nurses were divided into two categories, direct action tasks and indirect action tasks. Direct action tasks are those which require the nurse acting directly on the patient during the whole task (medication, posture change, toileting, feed-

ing, etc.). In the indirect action tasks the nurses do not need to act directly on the patients all the time (reports, monitoring and visits). We focused on indirect tasks because ALZ-MAS can handle most of them, so nurses can increase their productivity and the quality of health care.

Figure 6 shows the average time spent on indirect tasks by all nurses before implementation, with the previous release of ALZ-MAS and finally the release presented in this paper. ALZ-MAS continues reducing the time spent on indirect tasks. For example, the average number of minutes spent by all nurses on monitoring patients has been reduced from more of 150 daily minutes (before ALZ-MAS implementation) to approximately 90 daily minutes. Furthermore, this new release of ALZ-MAS performed considerably better than the previous release, with just 64 average daily minutes.

Figure 7 shows the average number of nurses working simultaneously each hour of a day before the implementation of ALZ-MAS, with the previous release of ALZ-MAS and with the new version here presented. In these set of tests, there were selected 50 patients and 12 nurses. According to the times spent by the nurses carrying out their tasks before the implementation, it can be seen how ALZ-MAS facilitates the more flexible assignation of the working shifts. The number of nurses working simultaneously before and after the implementation of the system is reduced substantially, especially at peak hours in which the indirect action tasks are more prone to overlap with the direct action tasks. For instance, from 13:00 to 15:00 there is a reduction of 5 nurses working simultaneously. This is achieved because there is an optimal distribution of tasks using ALZ-MAS. Moreover, with the new version of ALZ-MAS, it can be slightly reduced the number of nurses, especially because of the better detection of accesses to restricted areas, next described.

The security of the center has also been improved in two ways: the system monitors the patients and guarantees that each one of them is

Figure 5. Interface window showing the result of a general planning

Figure 6. Average time (minutes) spent on indirect tasks

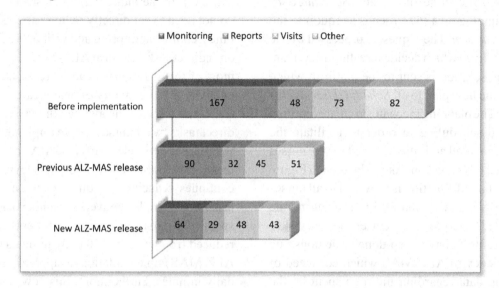

in the right place, and secondly, only authorized personnel can gain access to the residence protected areas. Figure 8 shows the number of accesses to restricted zones detected before the implementation of ALZ-MAS, with the previous release of ALZ-MAS and with the release presented in this paper. As can be seen, with the previous release there were detected almost twice unauthorized accesses than before. This is an important data because it can be assumed that several accesses were not detected in the past and most of them could lead to risky situations. Moreover, with the new release of ALZ-MAS using new ZigBee devices and more accurate locating

Figure 7. Number of nurses working simultaneously

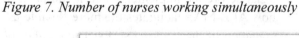

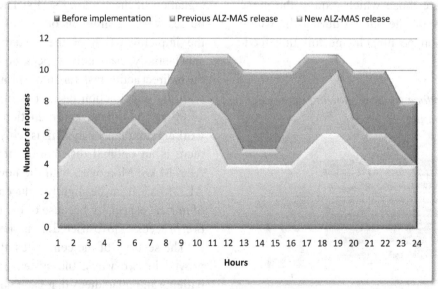

Figure 8. Number of detected accesses to restricted areas

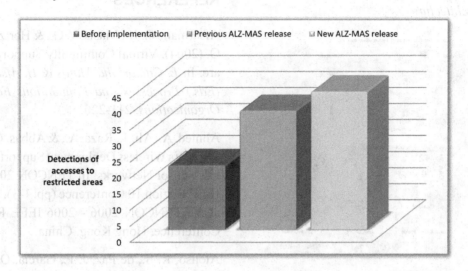

techniques, there is an improvement regarding the previous ALZ-MAS version, increasing from 37 to 43 daily detections.

CONCLUSION AND FUTURE WORK

It is demonstrated that ALZ-MAS can improve the security and health care efficiency through monitoring and automating medical staff's work and patients' activities, facilitating working shifts organization and reducing time spent on routine tasks. RFID, Wi-Fi and ZigBee technologies supply the agents with valuable information about the environment, contributing to a ubiquitous, non-invasive, high-level interaction among users, system and the environment. Future work consists of improving ALZ-MAS by adding more features and increasing its performance. Currently, the BISITE Research Group of the University of Salamanca (http://bisite.usal.es) is working on the improvement of ALZ-MAS through different but related lines of work.

First of them consists of releasing a new version of ALZ-MAS using a new SOA-based multi-agent architecture (Tapia, *et al.*, 2009), known as FUSION@ (Flexible and User Services Oriented

Multi-agent Architecture). FUSION@ is a SOA-based multi-agent architecture that facilitates the integration of distributed multi-agent systems and heterogeneous wireless sensor networks. The FUSION@ model has also been designed to develop Ambient Intelligence based systems. FUSION@ exceeds existing architectures and frameworks, such as JADE or RETSINA, by adding new layers, and facilitating the distribution and management of resources (*i.e.,* services). FUSION@ can be used to develop any kind of complex systems because it is capable of integrating almost any service and application desired, without depending on any specific programming language. Because the architecture acts as an interpreter, the users can run applications and services that can be programmed in virtually any language. The architecture of FUSION@ is depicted in Figure 9, where can be seen its main blocks: Agent Platforms, Services, Applications and Communication Protocols.

A further line, and closely related to FUSION@, is HERA (Hardware-Embedded Reactive Agents) (Alonso, *et al.*, 2010), which facilitates agents, applications and services communication in FUSION@ through of using dynamic and self-adaptable heterogeneous WSNs. The agents in HERA are directly embedded on the WSN nodes

Figure 9. Integration of HERA platform into FU-SION@ architecture

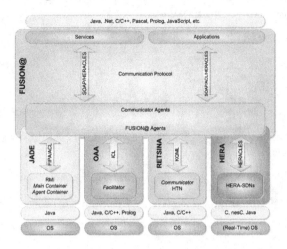

and their services can be invoked from other nodes in the same network or another network connected to the former one. HERA is an evolution of SYLPH (Services laYers over Light PHysical devices) (Corchado, *et al.*, 2010) The SYLPH platform follows a SOA model for integrating heterogeneous WSNs in AmI-based systems. As SYLPH, HERA focuses specifically on devices with small resources in order to save CPU time, memory size and energy consumption. HERA allows the agents to be directly embedded in the WSN nodes and invoked from other nodes either in the same network or another network connected to the former. Furthermore, as shown in Figure 9, HERA can be integrated into FUSION@, allowing to create Ambient Intelligence based systems where there is no distinction between a software and a hardware agent.

ACKNOWLEDGMENT

This project has been supported by the Spanish Ministry of Science and Technology project TIN 2009-13839-C03-03: *Organizaciones Virtuales Adaptativas: Mecanismos, Arquitecturas y Herramientas* (OVAMAH).

REFERENCES

Afsarmanesh, H., Masís, V. G., & Hertzberger, L. O. (2004). Virtual Community Support in Telecare. In *L. Camarinha-Matos & H. Afsarmanesh (Eds.) Processes And Foundations For Virtual Organizations*, 211-220.

Ahmed, A., Ali, J., Raza, A., & Abbas, G. (2006). Wired Vs Wireless Deployment Support For Wireless Sensor Networks. In TENCON 2006 - 2006 IEEE Region 10 Conference (pp. 1-3). Presented at the TENCON 2006 - 2006 IEEE Region 10 Conference, Hong Kong, China.

Alonso, R. S., de Paz, J. F., García, Ó., Gil, Ó., & González, A. (2010). HERA: A New Platform for Embedding Agents in Heterogeneous Wireless Sensor Networks. In Hybrid Artificial Intelligence Systems []. Springer Berlin / Heidelberg.]. *Lecture Notes in Computer Science, 6077*, 111–118. doi:10.1007/978-3-642-13803-4_14

Anderson, R. N. (1999). A Method for constructing complete annual U.S. life tables. Vital Health Statistics. *National Center for Health Statistics, 2* (129), 1-28.

Bahadori, S., Cesta, A., Grisetti, G., Iocchi, L., Leonel, R., Nardi, D., et al. (2003b). RoboCare: Pervasive Intelligence for the Domestic Care of the Elderly. *AI*IA Magazine Special Issue*.

Bratman, M. E. (1987). *Intentions, plans and practical reason*. Cambridge, MA, USA: Harvard University Press.

Bratman, M. E., Israel, D., & Pollack, M. (1988). Plans and resource-bounded practical reasoning. *Computational Intelligence, 4*, 349–355. doi:10.1111/j.1467-8640.1988.tb00284.x

Cesta, A., Bahadori, S., Cortellesa, G., Grisetti, G., & Giuliani, M. (2003). The RoboCare Project, Cognitive Systems for the Care of the Elderly. *In Proceedings of International Conference on Aging, Disability and Independence (ICADI'03)*. Washington, DC, USA.

Corchado, J. M., Bajo, J, & Abraham, A. (2008a). GERAmI: Improving the delivery of health care. *IEEE Intelligent Systems, Special Issue on Ambient Intelligence* - Mar/Apr '08. Vol. 23(2). pp. 19-25.

Corchado, J. M., Bajo, J., de Paz, Y., & Tapia, D. I. (2008b). Intelligent environment for monitoring Alzheimer patients, agent technology for health care. *Decision Support Systems, 44*(2), 382–396. doi:10.1016/j.dss.2007.04.008

Corchado, J. M., Bajo, J., Tapia, D. I., & Abraham, A. (2010). Using Heterogeneous Wireless Sensor Networks in a Telemonitoring System for Healthcare. *Information Technology in Biomedicine. IEEE Transactions on, 14*(2), 234–240.

Corchado, J. M., Pavón, J., Corchado, E., & Castillo, L. F. (2005). Development of CBR-BDI agents: A tourist guide application. *In Proceedings of the 7th European Conference on Case-based Reasoning 2004, Lecture Notes in Artificial Intelligence (LNAI). 3155*, pp. 547-559. Springer-Verlag.

Costa-Font, J., & Patxot, C. (2005). The design of the long-term care system in Spain: Policy and financial constraints. *Social Policy and Society, 4*(1), 11–20. doi:10.1017/S1474746404002131

Decker, K., & Li, J. (1998). Coordinated hospital patient scheduling. *In Proceedings of the 3rd International Conference on Multi-Agent Systems (ICMAS'98)* (pp. 104-111). IEEE Computer Society.

Erickson, P., Wilson, R., & Shannon, I. (1995). Years of Healthy Life. *Statistical Notes* (7).

González-Bedia, M., & Corchado, J. M. (2002). A planning Strategy based on Variational Calculus for Deliberative Agents. *Computing and Information Systems Journal, 10*, 2–14.

Hewlett-Packard. (2002). *Understanding Wi-Fi.* Hewlett-Packard Development Company.

Jayaputera, G. T., Zaslavsky, A. B., & Loke, S. W. (2007). Enabling run-time composition and support for heterogeneous pervasive multi-agent systems. *Journal of Systems and Software, 80*(12), 2039–2062. doi:10.1016/j.jss.2007.03.013

Jennings, N. R., & Wooldridge, M. (1995). Applying agent technology. *Applied Artificial Intelligence, 9*(4), 351–361. doi:10.1080/08839519508945480

Lanzola, G., Gatti, L., Falasconi, S., & Stefanelli, M. (1999). A Framework for Building Cooperative Software Agents in Medical Applications. *Artificial Intelligence in Medicine, 16*(3), 223–249. doi:10.1016/S0933-3657(99)00008-1

Marin-Perianu, M., Meratnia, N., Havinga, P., de Souza, L., Muller, J., & Spiess, P. (2007). Decentralized enterprise systems: a multiplatform wireless sensor network approach. *Wireless Communications, IEEE, 14*(6), 57–66. doi:10.1109/MWC.2007.4407228

Meunier, J. A. (1999). A Virtual Machine for a Functional Mobile Agent Architecture Supporting Distributed Medical Information. *In Proceedings of the 12th IEEE Symposium on Computer-Based Medical Systems (CBMS'99).* IEEE Computer Society, Washington, DC.

Miksch, S., Cheng, K., & Hayes-Roth, B. (1997). An intelligent assistant for patient health care. *In Proceedings of the 1st international Conference on Autonomous Agents (AGENTS'97)* (pp. 458-465). California, USA: ACM, New York. n-Core: A Faster and Easier Way to Create Wireless Sensor Networks. (2010). Retrieved October 15, 2010, from http://www.n-core.info

Nealon, J. L., & Moreno, A. (2003). *Applications of Software Agent Technology in the Health Care domain* (Vol. 212). (A. Moreno, & J. L. Nealon, Eds.) Basel, Germany: Birkhäuser Verlag AG, Whitestein series in Software Agent Technologies.

Pecora, F., & Cesta, A. (2007). Dcop for smart homes: A case study. *Computational Intelligence, 23*(4), 395–419. doi:10.1111/j.1467-8640.2007.00313.x

Pokahr, A., Braubach, L., & Lamersdorf, W. (2003). Jadex: Implementing a BDI-Infrastructure for JADE Agents. *In EXP - in search of innovation (Special Issue on JADE)*, 76-85.

Sancho, M., Abellán, A., Pérez, L., & Miguel, J. A. (2002). *Ageing in Spain. Second World Assembly on Ageing*. Madrid, Spain: IMSERSO.

Sarangapani, J. (2007). *Wireless Ad hoc and Sensor Networks: Protocols, Performance, and Control* (1st ed.). CRC.

Schön, B., O'Hare, G. M., Duffy, B. R., Martin, A. N., & Bradley, J. F. (2005). Agent Assistance for 3D World Navigation. *Lecture Notes in Computer Science, 3661*, 499–499. doi:10.1007/11550617_50

Tapia, D. I., Bajo, J., & Corchado, J. M. (2009). Distributing Functionalities in a SOA-Based Multi-agent Architecture. In *7th International Conference on Practical Applications of Agents and Multi-Agent Systems (PAAMS 2009)* (pp. 20-29).

Tapia, D. I., & Corchado, J. M. (2009). An Ambient Intelligence Based Multi-Agent System for Alzheimer Health Care. *International Journal of Ambient Computing and Intelligence, 1*(1), 15–26. doi:10.4018/jaci.2009010102

van Woerden, K. (2006). Mainstream Developments in ICT: Why are They Important for Assistive Technology? *Technology and Disability, 18*(1), 15–18.

Weber, W., Rabaey, J. M., & Aarts, E. (2005). *Ambient Intelligence*. Springer-Verlag New York, Inc. doi:10.1007/b138670

WHO. (2007). *Global Age-friendly Cities: A Guide*. World Health Organization.

Wooldridge, M., & Jennings, N. R. (1995). Intelligent Agents: Theory and Practice. *The Knowledge Engineering Review, 10*(2), 115–152. doi:10.1017/S0269888900008122

ZigBee. (2006). *ZigBee Specification Document 053474r13*. ZigBee Standards Organization. ZigBee Alliance.

Chapter 3
Adaptive Awareness of Hospital Patient Information through Multiple Sentient Displays

Jesus Favela
CICESE, Mexico

Mónica Tentori
CICESE and Universidad Autónoma de Baja California, Mexico

Daniela Segura
CICESE, Mexico

Gustavo Berzunza
CICESE, Mexico

ABSTRACT

Sentient computing can provide ambient intelligence environments with devices capable of inferring and interpreting context, while ambient displays allow for natural and subtle interactions with such environment. In this paper we propose to combine sentient devices and ambient displays to augment everyday objects. These sentient displays are aware of their surroundings while providing continuous information in a peripheral, subtle, and expressive manner. To seamlessly convey information to multiple sentient displays in the environment, we also propose an approach based on abstract interfaces which use contextual information to decide which display to use and how the information in the display changes in response to the environment. Our approach is illustrated through a hospital monitoring application. We present the design of two sentient displays that provide awareness of patient's urine outputs to hospital workers, and how contextual information is used to integrate the functionality of both displays.

INTRODUCTION

Sentient computing is an approach that allows users to naturally interact with the physical envi-ronment by becoming aware of their surroundings and by reacting upon them (López de Ipiña & Lai Lo, 2001). Awareness is achieved by means of a sensor infrastructure that helps to maintain a model of the world which is shared between users

DOI: 10.4018/978-1-60960-549-0.ch003

and applications – referred as Sentient artifacts (Hopper, 1999). Indeed, sentient artifacts have the ability to perceive the state of the surrounding environment, through the fusion and interpretation of information from possibly diverse sensors (Addlesee et al., 2001). However, it is not sufficient to make Ambient Intelligence (AmI) environments aware of the user's context, they must be able to find a way to communicate this information to users while becoming a natural interface to the environment (Shadbolt, 2003).

Ambient displays could be embedded in everyday objects already known and used, thus becoming the user interface of the AmI environment. This vision assumes that physical interaction between humans and computational devices will be less like the current keyboard, mouse, and display paradigm and more like the way humans interact with the physical world. For instance, a mirror augmented with infrared sensors and an acrylic panel could detect human presence and act as a message board to display relevant information when a user faces the mirror. Hence, AmI environments could be augmented with such displays that unobtrusively convey information to users without requiring their full attention, while at the same time, allowing an implicit and natural interaction. Indeed, the notion of what constitutes a computer display is changing. No longer is a display confined to the typical CRT monitor with a single user paying focused attention while interacting with virtual objects on the screen (Lund & Wilberg, 2007). Rather, computer displays are found in such diverse forms as small screens in mobile phones or handheld computers, to ambient displays that provide peripheral awareness to the presence and status of people, objects or information.

In this article, by binding the ideas of sentient computing and ambient displays we propose the concept of sentient displays to define a new and appropriate physical interaction experience with an AmI environment. Such sentient displays will be capable of monitoring users' context, promptly notify relevant events and provide users with continuous information in a subtle, peripheral and expressive manner without intruding on our focal activity. Moreover, multiple such displays could be integrated in an AmI environment, with a decision of which one to use dependent on contextual circumstances, such as the user's location, the presence of other people or the activity being performed by the user. Thus, we also discuss an approach to develop contextual interfaces for a variety of sentient displays located throughout the intelligent environment. Our approach is based on the use of abstract interfaces that are specialized to specific devices once a decision is made as to which sentient display(s) should be used. This approach facilitates the progressive integration of new sentient displays.

To illustrate the concept of sentient displays we draw upon scenarios related to hospital work. Mobility and frequent task switching cause hospital workers to occasionally miss important events, such as a catheter being disconnected due to the patient movement or the need to change a urine bag that has been filled-up (Moran et al., 2006). Consequently, hospital workers have been held liable for their failure to monitor and promptly respond to patients needs (Smith & Ziel, 1997). Sentient displays located throughout hospital premises could be used for a diverse number of hospital applications, such as notifying hospital workers of a crisis or just provide continuous awareness of the health status of patients.

SENTIENT DISPLAYS: AUGMENTING NATURAL OBJECTS WITH AMBIENT DISPLAYS AND SENTIENT TECHNOLOGIES

Research in pervasive computing has included the development of ambient devices that can become part of the background while acting as a digital interface to ambient information. As stated by Mankoff: "Ambient displays are aesthetically pleasing displays of information which sit on the periphery of a user's attention. They generally support the monitor of information and have the ambitious goal of presenting information without distracting or burdening the user" (Mankoff et al., 2003). For instance, the artist Natalie Jermijenko at Xerox Parc augmented a string with a motor and spin to convey the traffic's status to a user –the Dangling String (Weiser & Brown, 1995). The device rotates at a speed that depends on the amount of traffic in the highway captured through analog sensors. During periods of intense traffic, the string's movements are slightly audible as well. Thus, ambient displays are, unlike ordinary computer displays, designed not to distract people from their tasks at hand, but to be subtle reminders that can be occasionally noticed. In addition to presenting information, the displays also frequently contribute to the aesthetics of the locale where they are deployed (Lund & Wilberg, 2007). For instance, as part of the AmbientRoom project, several displays using light, sound or motion have been developed to augment a user's office (Ishii et al., 1998). Undeniably, ambient displays need computing devices capable of perceiving our surroundings by seeing or hearing the entities in the environment, what these entities are doing and where they are. To this aim, research in sentient computing has focused on the development of sensors that attached to today's computing and communication technology are capable of perceiving a range of contextual information such as location, traffic status, user's presence and so on (Abowd & Mynatt, 2002). The most popular sentient devices are indoor location systems (Addlesee et al., 2001; Werb & Lanzl, 1998).

While ambient displays provide a different notion of what constitutes an interface to the AmI environment, sentient technologies allow such displays to be reactive and perceptive to dynamic changes in the environment. In this article we propose the concept of sentient displays combining the ideas of ambient displays and sentient computing. Sentient displays are our everyday

artifacts augmented with digital services capable of perceiving information from the environment and then using this information to extend the capabilities of such artifact. We envision a sentient artifact as an object that encapsulates the information perceived and then provides users with a new form of interaction with the environment. This interaction could be either by offering continuous, subtle and peripheral awareness or by allowing users to change the status of such object in order to affect an AmI environment.

OPPORTUNITIES FOR THE DEPLOYMENT OF SENTIENT DISPLAYS IN HOSPITALS: A CASE STUDY

For nine months, we conducted a field study in a public hospital's internal-medicine unit, observing the practices of the hospital staff, who attended patients with chronic or terminal diseases (Moran et al., 2006). Such patients are often immobile and incapable of performing the activities of daily living (ADL) by themselves. The study was conducted to understand: (1) the type of patients' information being monitored by hospital workers and (2) the problems faced by hospital workers when monitoring patients.

Hospital workers are responsible for providing integral and specialized care for patients. As part of this, nurses monitor patient's activities of daily living (ADL), such as, if a patient has taken his medicine, if he has walked, eaten, felt from the bed, evacuated, etcetera. As a part of specialized care, nurses need to monitor the behavioral patterns in the activities that put at risk the patients' health or that indicate an internal failure which might evolve into a more serious disease (e.g., pneumonia, an apoplexy or a stroke), such as, if a patient is agitated, if a patient is bleeding or if the patient has respiratory insufficiency. These behavioral patterns associated to risk activities (RA) are monitored through the vital signs. To illustrate the problems faced by hospital workers when monitoring patients we present a real-scenario that was observed in the hospital:

Nurse Rita is informed, at the beginning of her working shift, that the attending physician has changed Pedro's medication to include cyclosporine. Pedro is a 56 years old man, who has a chronic renal failure and just had a renal transplant. So, to monitor Pedro's reaction to the new kidney and to the medicine being administered to him, Rita needs to supervise the frequency and quantity of Pedro's urine. Nurse Rita starts her shift by taking care of Juan –the patient in bed 226. While she is inserting a catheter to Juan, Pedro's urine bag fills up. Unaware of Pedro's status, Rita continues taking care of Juan. After several minutes another nurse informs Rita that Pedro's urine bag spilled up. Rita moves to Pedro's room to clean him.

The problem illustrated in the scenario could be avoided if Rita knows when Pedro's urine bag is almost full. This, and similar examples, helped us identify major issues faced by hospital workers when monitoring patients. In particular, issues related to hospital workers being on the move include maintaining awareness of their patients' status, being easily accessible when an emergency occurs, and prioritizing patient care on the basis of the patient's health condition. In addition, nurses must manage the tradeoff between having expressive versus silent awareness. While nurses want to be aware of the status of all the patients they are taking care off, they don't want this awareness to intrude in their focal activity. Finally, nurses need to interpret ambient information over time and at different levels of detail. This poses interesting challenges related to how contextual information influences the importance of the information presented. For instance, while to monitor Pedro's health it is significant for Rita to know the frequency and quantity of his urine

outputs, for those patients with other diseases this information might not be relevant for her. This need to monitor the status of patients in an environment already saturated with information and with hospital workers constantly on the move and switching from one task to another, inspired us to design sentient displays for the hospital.

THE ADL MONITOR: A MOBILE SENTIENT DISPLAY

The ADL Monitor is a sentient display aimed at creating a wearable ambient connection between patients and nurses (Tentori & Favela, 2008). The ADL Monitor is composed of one sentient artifact and two ambient displays. The first ambient display is a two-layered vinyl bracelet containing five buttons with embedded lights (see figure 1a). Each button represents a patient under the nurse's care. The lights turn on when a patient is executing an activity, when particular actions occur, or after a series of events take place. Nurses can press the button to consult information associated to the activity a particular patient is executing. This information is shown by the ADL assistant that runs on the nurse's smartphone (see figure 1b) –the second ambient display. Nurses can also use the ADL assistant to assign priorities by selecting colors (figure 1c) or to set contextual information to act as a trigger for the activities being monitored (figure 1d). To notify patient's urine habits the mobile ADL Monitor uses the WeightScale. The WeightScale is a sentient artifact attached to the urine bag and measures its weight.

Going back to our scenario: Rita uses ADL assistant in her smart phone to specify that the light representing Pedro in her bracelet should turn yellow when Pedro evacuates, and red if he evacuates more than five times in six hours (Figure 1d).

Later, while Rita is preparing medicines, Pedro's light turns yellow. Rita presses the button,

Figure 1. The mobile ADL Monitor. (a) A nurse uses the bracelet; (b) the mobile ADL assistant shows information related to an activity being executed by a patient; (c) a nurse uses her smartphone to configure the bracelet; and (d) a nurse associates contextual information with an activity

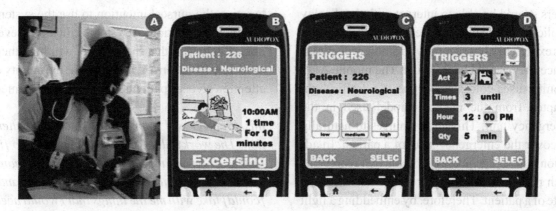

and her smart phone indicates what Pedro is doing (Figure 1b). Rita learns that Pedro has urinated approximately 10 milliliters (this information is calculated though the weight sensor attached to Pedro's urine bag). Rita goes to Pedro's room to update his liquid balance.

Throughout the night, Pedro's light in Rita's bracelet constantly turns yellow. A couple of hours later, while Rita is talking to Dr. Perez, her bracelet turns red. Rita consults her smart phone and realizes that Pedro has urinated seven times in six hours. She discusses this with Dr. Perez, who then decides to change Pedro's medication to avoid damaging the new kidney.

The system uses a client-server architecture as a basis for its implementation. When a nurse presses a button on the bracelet, a message is sent back to the server, specifying a patient and bracelet ID. This ID is used by the server to determine which patients' status should be displayed on which smart phone. We developed our own components to communicate the bracelet with the server. A transmitter is responsible for sending and receiving messages from the bracelet at frequencies under 27 Mhz. This transmitter is internally connected to the CPU and embeds a receptor circuit that manages the radioelectrical

signals from the bracelet and translates them into pulses. In contrast, the bracelet has embedded a receptor circuit that converts radioelectrical signals into electrical pulses. In the following lines we described how the components work to support the services just described.

Providing Perceptible and Silent Awareness

The idea of this service is to adequately manage how the information will be presented to the user. An ambient display that changes too fast can distract the user whiles a display that changes too slowly can pass unnoticed (Johan et al., 2000). To balance this tradeoff, the mobile ADL Monitor modulates the information shown to the user. While the bracelet only displays the status of a patient and his identity, the smartphone shows more information, such as the quantity and frequency of urine outputs. This will allow a nurse to explicitly extend the information shown by the bracelet with the one shown in the smartphone binding both displays while unrestricting their usefulness by presenting just enough information –how much a patient has urinated.

Enabling Simple, Effortless and Seamless Interaction

Users should be able to interact with the display implicitly and naturally. Users do not have previous experience interacting with ambient displays; hence they should be intuitive. The mobile ADL Monitor uses colors analogous to a traffic light adapted from the medical model used in the emergency unit. This allows nurses to naturally discover the emergency state of a patient. In addition, nurses can press the button that represents each patient to consult more information of the state of a patient. Therefore, by embedding a light in each button of the bracelet we are extending the capabilities of an artifact without altering the traditional means of interaction with it. This will result in a reduction of the cognitive load by learning how displays work and increasing the amount of attention on content (Gross, 2003).

Enabling Unobtrusive Information Sensing

The mobile ADL Monitor requires to monitor the weight of a urine bag wore by a patient. For this, we developed a sentient artifact that measures the amount of urine in a bag and communicates this information wirelessly through a mote –the weightScale. This weightScale is attached to a urine bag wore by a patient allowing thus an unnoticeable sensing. The weightScale is made of two acrylic pieces which are separated through a spring and a push button. We calibrated the required separation between both pieces. When the urine reaches a threshold (i.e., when the urine has filled 80% of the urine bag) the button is pressed. Once the button gets pressed, the sensor generates an electronic pulse. This pulse is read by the mote that is responsible for the transmission of this information wirelessly. When the bag is replaced the button goes back to its normal position. We use motes to avoid saturating the rooms with wires that could be obtrusive to nurses and patients.

To evaluate the ADL Monitor we interviewed seven nurses, each for 30 to 60 minutes, to evaluate the bracelet's design, the system's core characteristics, the nurses' intention to use the system, and their perception of system utility. All seven nurses indicated that the bracelet will help them save time, avoid errors, and increase the quality of attention given to patients. One nurse commented,

this bracelet will improve the quality of attention. The work will be the same, but I will do [it] faster. ...For instance, if a patient has evacuated ... I would promptly know the patient needs and I [could] take with me the things that I would need.

In addition, nurses noticed that the system will help them prioritize events and patients:

Something that we currently cannot do is identify which patient has to be attended first; a system like this one [would] help me identify the urgency with which each of my patients needs to be attended.

Overall, the staff viewed the application as useful, efficient, and generally appealing. Nurses repeatedly expressed that this system would solve many of the problems they face and improve their work, saying that it directly assists with "patient care" rather than merely supporting "secondary tasks," as they say current systems do. Nurses validated both scenarios and provided us with additional insights and opportunities for applying our technology. For instance, nurses explained that they are used to have the technology directly attached to the patient to avoid problems and errors. Nurses explained that having the information in the smart phone might cause problems, because they might confuse the patient they are attending with another one. For instance a nurse explained:

I prefer for the bracelet to only function as an indicator, rather than consulting the information of the patient in my cell phone I would prefer to consult this information in the room of the patient.

In this case I would be sure that the problem I am handling corresponds to such patient.

Indeed, fixed monitoring systems that allow patients to place a call to a nurse at the nurse pavilion have been successfully adopted in hospitals. What we need is to allow our sentient display to be seamlessly integrated with fixed monitoring systems.

THE FLOWERBLINK: A FIXED SENTIENT DISPLAY

In this section we describe a fixed sentient display that notifies nurses the patients' urine outputs and the status of their urine bag to be integrated with the ADL Monitor–the Flower Blink (Segura et al., 2008). The FlowerBlink is a wooden box containing twenty four artificial flowers: twelve emergency flowers with stems and twelve situation stemless flowers (Figure 2). The flowers are composed of a two-layered felt that enclose pistils covered with insulating tape. In each pistil a red or yellow led is embedded. The emergency flowers have stems with an embedded yellow light in their pistils (Figure 2a). All emergency flowers blink whenever an event or an emergency occur with a urine bag wore by a patient –if a urine bag

is full. In contrast, situation flowers are flowers without stems that have a red light embedded in their pistils. These situation flowers are arranged in a matrix to represent patients' location in the unit. Each column in the matrix represents a room while a row represents a patient's bed (Figure 2b) –each room has three beds for patients. This arrangement allows nurses to quickly discover which patients' bag is about to spill. Situation flowers turn on whenever a nurse approaches the FlowerBlink or if the emergency flowers are blinking. While emergency flowers are blinking a situation flower turns on, indicating to a nurse the location of the patient related to that event.

The FlowerBlink includes two sentient artifacts and one ambient display. The first sentient artifact is the WeightScale, described in section 4. The other sentient artifact is the PrescenceDetector that is a card carried out by a nurse that detects her presence when she is in front of the Flower-Blink. The ambient display is the flower vase with a set of flowers that display the status of the urine bag of the patient. We embedded in the box of the ambient display a communication interface which directly controls the flowers light. When the base station receives the information, it identifies the sensor that sent it, thereby identifying the location of the patient, and then turning on the red light of the corresponding flower. We use the phidgets

Figure 2. The FlowerBlink placed in the nurse pavilion. (a) The flowers that notify of emergency events (b) The flowers that personalized their color based on the nurse's presence

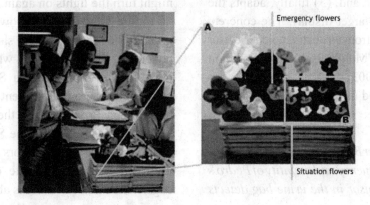

toolkit (Greenberg & Fitchett, 2001) to implement the FlowerBlink.

One of the main challenges in integrating the FlowerBlink and the ADL Monitor is content adaptation. Binding both sentient displays will involve choosing on which device to display the information. This decision must take into account the device capabilities and its user's context. For instance, while the FlowerBlink can show patients' status, their location, their urine bag status and their frequency of urine outputs; the bracelet is only capable of displaying patients' identity and their status. Moreover, the smartphone can show a more complex representation of content because a complex interface can be displayed in such device. Adding more information in the FlowerBlink or in the bracelet could cramp both displays confusing the user on how to use them. This mismatch between rich content and constrained devices capabilities presents a main challenge in integrating multiple sentient displays (Lum & Lau, 2002).

SUPPORTING MULTIPLE SENTIENT DISPLAYS TO MONITOR PATIENT STATUS

In this section we describe our approach to seamlessly convey patient status information to multiple sentient displays. Based on contextual information our approach: (1) selects the sentient display to be responsible for showing ambient information, (2); defines a concrete interface for the selected display; and, (3) finally, adapts the information in the target display. The concrete interface is derived from an abstract, generic user interface (Braun & Mühlhäuser, 2004; Souchon & Vanderdonckt, 2003).

This is illustrated through the following version of our scenario:

Rita uses the FlowerBlink and the ADL Monitor to supervise the frequency and quantity of Pedro's urine outputs. A sensor in the urine bag detects

the presence of new liquid. At this time, Rita, the nurse responsible for monitoring the patient, approaches the nurse pavilion. Thus, the system decides to notify her through the FlowerBlink sentient display located in this area. The description of the abstract notification interface is sent to the agent that acts as a proxy for the sentient display. The agent calls its interpreter to transform the abstract interface to a concrete interface that it then sends to the FlowerBlink. Rita notices that the flower base is blinking and realizes that the information relates to one of her patients. She consults her smartphone to learn that Pedro has urinated for the third time this morning and his urine bag might soon need to be replaced. The interface in the FlowerBlink will turn all lights off as its proxy agent becomes aware that Rita has consulted the information in her smartphone.

As the scenario shows, contextual information is used by the system in two stages. First, location information is used to decide which sentient display will be the most suitable to use. Since Rita is in the nurse pavilion the FlowerBlink located there would be the best display to notify the status of her patients. Once the concrete interface is executing on the sentient display it will be adapted when it is informed that the users notices the information. In the example when the sentient display realizes that Rita has become aware of the patient status it adapts its interface by turning off the lights. The presence of another person for which the information is relevant, for instance, the head nurse, might turn the lights on again.

Figure 3 and Figure 4 show the sequence diagram of the scenario. These show the main components of the architecture, which are described next. In the architecture a Server application communicates to the different sentient displays, trough their Proxy Agents, the changes notified by the Sensor Solicitor. The Sensor Solicitor is connected to a set of sensors which update the information about the state of patients' urine bags. When a notification is about to be sent the

Server requests the Composer for the generic user interface to be used to inform the patient's status (patient, disease, time, urine bag level, and so on). This interface will be interpreted for each sentient display depending of its own resources. The Server decides to notify the nurse through the FlowerBlink because she is at the nurse pavilion, thus the generic user interface is sent to the FlowerBlink Proxy Agent. This agent updates the FlowerBlink state in response to the interpretation of the generic interface given by the Proxy Agent's

Interpreter. In this case, the lights are turned on, to inform that the urine bag is almost full.

When the nurse notices that the FlowerBlink is blinking, she consults her smartphone for detailed information about her patient. The smartphone's Proxy Agent requests the information to the Server. This information is delivered using the same generic interface sent to the FlowerBlink. Then, the Proxy Agent invoques its interpreter to translate it to the capabilities of the smartphone, so the Agent can render the information in the

Figure 3. Sequence diagram of the scenario, showing how the notification is sent through the FlowerBlink

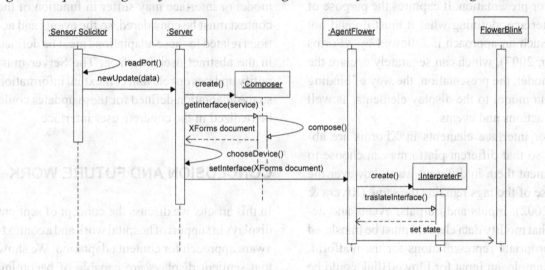

Figure 4. Sequence diagram of the scenario, showing how the FlowerBlink is turned off when its Agent becomes aware that the nurse has consulted the information in her smartphone

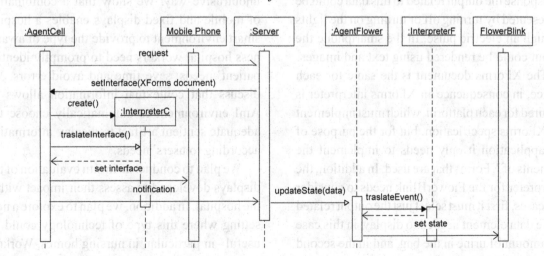

smartphone using text and images. This acts as a trigger to notify the FlowerBlink that the nurse has become aware of the patient's status, so it must turn off the lights. The Server is responsible for sending to the FlowerBlink Agent the event, which in turn is passed to the Interpreter to adapt the information in the user interface. The interpreter indicates to the FlowerBlink Proxy Agent the adaptation to be performed in the display, in this case, to turn the lights off.

The generic user interface is described using a User Interface Declarative Language because it does not assume any specific interaction modality or presentation. It captures the purpose of the interface, defining what it must do and not how. Such an approach is followed by XForms (Boyer, 2007), which can separately declare the data model, the presentation, the way of binding the data model to the display elements, as well as the actions and events.

User interface elements in XForms are abstract, so that different platforms can choose to implement them in different ways, however the purpose of the tags remains the same (Rivera & Len, 2002). Inputs and outputs, events and actions that modify data element must be translated to appropriate representations for the platform. For example, an input for FlowerBlink could be given by a sensor sensitive to the light, another example is when the data model is changed and in response the output related to this data could be represented by turning off or turning on the lights through an electric pulse. In the smartphone the output could be rendered using text and images.

The XForms document is the same for each device, in consequence an XForms interpreter is required for each platform, which must implement the XForms specification, but for the purpose of the application it only needs to implement the elements of XForms that are used. In addition, the interpreter for the FlowerBlink needs to consider two cases, first it must select just the output related to the data element needed to display, in this case the amount of urine in the bag, and in the second

case the amount of urine in the bag at three state alerts depending on a predefined threshold. This kind of consideration goes beyond the XForms specification, since this is specific to the application and platform. For the cell phone it is possible to display all the data in the model.

The XForms composer defines the abstract user interface in an XForms document, it contains the information related to the patient defined in the data model, an XML structure, the generic outputs bind to the data model, and the actions to perform adaptations in the data model and the user interface. All possible adaptations that data model or interface may suffer in function of the context must be considered, so the events and actions related to these adaptations must be defined in the abstract user interface. The Server must notify updates on relevant contextual information so the adaptation defined for these updates could be realized in the concrete user interface.

CONCLUSION AND FUTURE WORK

In this article, we discuss the concept of sentient displays in support of hospital work and a context-aware approach for content adaptation. We show that sentient displays are capable of becoming aware of users' context and then present continuous and expressive information in a subtle and unobtrusive way. We show that a combination of mobile and fixed displays enables a hospital smart environment to provide the type of awareness hospital workers need to promptly identify patient' needs, save time and avoid errors. We discuss that contextual information allows an AmI environment to automatically choose the adequate sentient artifact to display information according to users' needs.

We plan to conduct an in situ evaluation of the displays developed to assess their impact within the hospital. In addition, we plan to explore a new setting where this type of technology could be useful –in particular, in nursing homes. Workers at nursing homes specialized in the care of elders with cognitive disabilities face working conditions that are similar to those in hospitals. Such workers also use common strategies to monitor patients' status. This monitoring is done manually, making it time consuming and error prone. This is another healthcare scenario in which sentient displays can prove useful.

ACKNOWLEDGMENT

This work was partially funded by CONACYT through scholarships provided to Monica Tentori, Daniela Segura and Gustavo Berzunza.

REFERENCES

Abowd, G., & Mynatt, E. (2002). The humen experience. *IEEE Pervasive, 1*(1), 48–57. doi:10.1109/MPRV.2002.993144

Addlesee, M., Curwen, R., Hodges, S., Newman, J., Steggles, P., & Ward, A. (2001). Implementing a sentient computing system. *IEE Computer, 34*(8), 50–56.

Boyer, J. (2007). Xforms 1.0 (third edition). Http://www.W3.Org/tr/2007/rec-xforms-20071029/.

Braun, E., & Mühlhäuser, M. (2004, May 25-28). Extending xml uidls for multidevice scenarios. Paper presented at the Workshop on Developing User Interfaces with XML of the Advanced Visual Interfaces Conference, Gallipoli, Italy.

Greenberg, S., & Fitchett, C. (2001, November 11-14). Phidgets: Easy development of physical interfaces through physical widgets. Paper presented at the 14th annual ACM symposium on User interface software and technology, Orlando, Florida.

Gross, T. (2003, June 22-27). Ambient interfaces: Design challenges and recommendation. Paper presented at the International Conference on Human-Computer Interaction, Crete, Greece.

Hopper, A. (1999). The cliord paterson lecture: Sentient computing. Philosophical Transactions of the Royal Society of London, 358(1773), 2349-2358.

Ishii, H., Wisneski, C., Brave, S., Dahley, A., Gorbet, M., Ullmer, B., et al. (1998). Ambientroom: Integrating ambient media with architectural space. Paper presented at the Conference on Human Factors in Computing Systems (CHI), Los Angeles, US.

Johan, R., Skog, T., & Hallnäs, L. (2000, January 22-24). Informative art: Using amplified artworks as information displays. Paper presented at the Designing augmented reality environments, Elsinore, Denmark.

López de Ipiña, D., & Lai Lo, S. (2001, September 17-19, 2001). Sentient computing for everyone. Paper presented at the The Third International Working Conference on New Developments in Distributed Applications and Interoperable Systems, Kraków, Poland.

Lum, W., & Lau, F. (2002). A context-aware decision engine for content adaptation. *IEEE Pervasive Computing / IEEE Computer Society [and] IEEE Communications Society, 1*(3), 41–49. doi:10.1109/MPRV.2002.1037721

Lund, A., & Wilberg, M. (2007). Ambient displays beyond conventions. Paper presented at the British HCI Group Annual Conference.

Mankoff, J., Dey, A. K., Hsieh, G., Kientz, J., Lederer, S., & Ames, M. (2003). Heuristic evaluation of ambient displays. Paper presented at the Conference on Human Factors in Computing Systems, Lauderdale, Florida, USA.

Moran, E. B., Tentori, M., González, V. M., Martinez-Garcia, A. I., & Favela, J. (2006). Mobility in hospital work: Towards a pervasive computing hospital environment. *International Journal of Electronic Healthcare, 3*(1), 72–89. doi:10.1504/IJEH.2007.011481

Rivera, J., & Len, T. (2002). Get ready for xforms. Http://www.Ibm.Com/developerworks/xml/library/x-xforms/.

Segura, D., Favela, J., & Tentori, M. (2008). Sentient displays in support of hospital work. Paper presented at the UCAMI, Salamanca, Spain.

Shadbolt, N. (2003). Ambient intelligence. *IEEE Intelligent Systems, 18*(2), 2–3. doi:10.1109/MIS.2003.1200718

Smith, K. S., & Ziel, S. E. (1997). Nurses' duty to monitor patients and inform physicians. *AORN Journal, 1*(2), 235–238.

Souchon, N., & Vanderdonckt, J. (2003, June 4-6). A review of xml-compliant user interface description languages. Paper presented at the International Conference on Design, Specification, and Verification of Interactive Systems, Funchal, Portugal.

Tentori, M., & Favela, J. (2008). Activity-aware computing for healthcare. *IEEE Pervasive Computing / IEEE Computer Society [and] IEEE Communications Society, 7*(2), 51–57. doi:10.1109/MPRV.2008.24

Weiser, M., & Brown, J. S. (1995). Designing calm technology. *PowerGrid, 1*(1), 10.

Werb, J., & Lanzl, C. (1998). Designing a positioning system for finding things and people indoors. *IEEE Spectrum, 35*(9), 71–78. doi:10.1109/6.715187

Chapter 4
Vehicular Networks Security:
Attacks, Requirements, Challenges and Current Contributions

Christian Tchepnda
Orange Labs-France Telecom Group, France

Hassnaa Moustafa
Orange Labs-France Telecom Group, France

Houda Labiod
Institut Telecom–Telecom ParisTech, France

Gilles Bourdon
Orange Labs-France Telecom Group, France

ABSTRACT

This article provides a panorama on the security in vehicular networks' environments. The special characteristics of these environments are presented and a general classification for the different types of attacks illustrated by some relevant attacks examples is introduced. Consequently, some key security requirements and security challenges are derived, considering Intelligent Transportation System (ITS) or Safety services as well as non-ITS or non-Safety services. Finally, some existing contributions in this subject are presented, and their deployment feasibility is discussed.

INTRODUCTION

Vehicular communication is an emerging class of mobile communication enabling mobile users in their vehicles to communicate to the road and to each other. Currently, Inter-Vehicle Communication Systems (IVCS) are widely discussed, attracting considerable attention from the research

community as well as the automotive industry. In fact, vehicular networks are expected to be massively deployed in the near future, driven by navigation safety requirements and by the investments of car manufacturers and Public Transportation Authorities. New standards are emerging for vehicular communications. Dedicated Short Range Communications (DSRC) is a block of spectrum in the 5.850 to 5.925 GHz

DOI: 10.4018/978-1-60960-549-0.ch004

band allocated by the US Federal Communications Commission (FCC) to vehicular communications (5.9 GHz DSRC). Consensus around the world is emerging around a customized version of IEEE 802.11 in the 5GHz band also known as 802.11p or WAVE (Wireless Access for the Vehicular Environment). Vehicular networks have special behavior and characteristics, distinguishing them from other types of ad-hoc networks. The nodes' (vehicles') mobility in these networks is high and may reach up to 200Km/h, these networks may experience frequent disconnections and impaired propagation channel resulting in a highly bandwidth constrained environment, these networks performance and motion patterns are closely interdependent, these networks topologies are dynamic but constrained by roads' topologies, these networks may scale to a very large number of nodes (vehicles) according to the traffic condition and finally these networks probably have a potentially heterogeneous administration. We can assume that vehicular communications, opposing the wireless mobile communications, are not resource constrained (energy, CPU, memory, etc.) as vehicles are not tiny nodes and are capable of providing large resources.

Although, vehicular networks are considered as one of the promising concrete applications of ad hoc networks, their special behavior and characteristics create some communication challenges (for network operators and service providers), which can greatly impact the future deployment of these networks. An important research and development aspect in vehicular communication concerns the development of security mechanisms that allow trust among the communicating parties (whether vehicles or infrastructure elements) and guarantee only authorized users' access to network resources and services offered by the provider as well as secure data transfer. In fact, security requirements differ according to the type of applications/services, where different security levels are needed. We notice that vehicular communication security is a young research domain,

showing few contributions and lacking concrete security solutions.

This article gives a panorama on vehicular communication security. We discuss the different types of attacks in this environment and present from a deployment perspective the security requirements that should be satisfied, taking into consideration safety applications and commercial applications expected in the future. The remainder of this article is organized as follows: Section 2 figures out services and potential architectures in vehicular networks. Section 3 presents a classification for potential attacks giving some attacks examples. Section 4 introduces our view of the main security requirements and security challenges for vehicular communications deployment. In Section 5, we give an overview on the related work discussing the main contributions and mentioning their limitations as well as some open issues. Finally, the article is concluded in Section 6.

SERVICES AND ARCHITECTURES

Services

Vehicular communications are expected to provide a wide set of useful services to drivers and passengers. We classify these services into two main classes: i) Intelligent Transportation System (ITS) or Safety services, ii) non-ITS or non-Safety services. ITS was the main objective in the emergence of vehicular communications, where the primary works aimed at providing ITS solutions. ITS target is to minimize accidents and improve traffic conditions through providing drivers and passengers with useful information, e.g. road conditions alarms, congestions alarms, fire alarms, accident-ahead warnings, speed limit reminder, and traffic messages' exchange that is useful in avoiding collision at intersection, optimizing traffic flows, and avoiding crash situations.

On the other hand, non-ITS services aim at providing commercial, leisure and convenience services. Non-ITS services have taken recent attention in vehicular communications, being a target of some recent research contributions in this domain. Such services should guarantee data transfer between vehicles and are expected to provide passengers and drivers with Internet connections facility exploiting an available infrastructure in an "on-demand" fashion. Examples of useful non-ITS services are: electronic tolling system, multimedia services (*e.g.* interactive video games, VoIP, streaming, etc.), web browsing, email access, file sharing, and discovery of local services in the neighborhood (*e.g.* restaurants, bars, movie theatres, etc.). We notice that the messages' transmission model in vehicular networks depends on the type of provided services (ITS or non-ITS), where broadcast transmission is mostly relevant for ITS/Safety services and unicast or multicast transmission is used for non-ITS/non-Safety services.

Architectures

Vehicular communications are expected to take place in urban zones, rural zones and highways through providing some network functionalities, protocols and integration strategies for services' delivery to users. Vehicular networks can be provided by network operators, service providers or through integration between operators, providers and a governmental authority. The recent advances in wireless technology as well as the new ad hoc scenarios defined within the Internet Engineering Task Force (IETF) allow several possible vehicular network architectures. Three deployment alternatives, that could be mutual, include: i) a pure wireless Vehicle-to-Vehicle ad hoc network (V2V) allowing standalone vehicular communication with no infrastructure support, ii) a wired backbone with wireless last hops, iii) and a hybrid Vehicle-to-Road (V2R) architecture that does not rely on a fixed infrastructure in a constant manner, but can exploit it for improved performance and service access when it is available. In addition,

the Car-to-Car Communication Consortium (C2C-CC) specified some architectural considerations for vehicular networks deployment, including: i) Road-Side Units (RSUs) existing along the road, and ii) vehicle equipment with an On Board Unit (OBU), and potentially multiple Application Units (AUs) executing a single or a set of applications while using the OBU communication capabilities. Vehicles' OBUs and RSUs can form ad hoc networks, where communication can be: i) V2V taking place directly between OBUs via multi-hop or single-hop without involving any RSU, or ii) Vehicle-to-Infrastructure (V2I), in which OBUs communicate with RSUs in order to connect to the infrastructure.

ATTACKS IN VEHICULAR NETWORKS

In this section we discuss the most relevant vehicular communications attacks through providing a classification and some concrete examples.

Attacks Classification

An important key in securing vehicular communications is determining the types of attacks threatening the communication in such environment. Different types of attacks may exist according to the type of environment as well as the usage scenario. Based on the taxonomy provided by Raya et al. (2005) with few enhancements, these attacks are classified as follows:

- **Internal or External:** An internal attack can be mounted by an authenticated member of the vehicular network. In other words, this member is identified by other members as a legitimate member. This type of attack is probably the most critical one. On the other hand, an external attack can be mounted by a non authenticated entity that is hence considered as an intruder by legitimate members. Unlike an internal attacker, an external attacker is limited in the diversity of attacks he can mount.

- **Intentional or Unintentional:** An intentional attack is mounted by an entity aiming voluntarily to disrupt the network operation. Conversely an unintentional attack is mostly due to potential transmission or network operation errors.

- **Active or Passive:** An active attack is mounted by an attacker who generates or modifies the network traffic. In contrast, a passive attack is mounted by an attacker who will only eavesdrop the wireless channel for later unauthorized use.

- **Independent or Coordinated:** An independent attack is caused by a unique attacker whereas a coordinated attack is caused by a group of attackers sharing the same interest.

Attacks Examples

Since it is hardly possible to give an exhaustive list encompassing all attacks in vehicular networks, we have rather chosen to derive a general classification of attacks. In the following subsections, we only introduce some important and relevant attacks examples that have been identified.

- **Privacy attack:** This is considered as the Big Brother case where an attacker actively monitors the network traffic in order to disclose vehicles identities and trace them. Some examples of traceable identifiers are IP addresses, MAC addresses, certificates IDs, etc. Even if individual messages do not contain such identifiers, a particular string that does not in itself identify the vehicle could appear in a series of messages. If an attacker ever unambiguously observes the vehicle emitting that string, they

can use the string as an identifier for the vehicle. Moreover, using radio fingerprinting (*i.e.* a physical layer attack) is another way to identify and trace vehicles. Figure 1 illustrates an identity disclosure example. Considering the attacks classification given in the previous subsection, this attack is characterized as: (*Internal or External, Intentional, Passive, and Independent*).

- **Information inconsistency:** In this case the attacker injects wrong information in the network in order to affect the behavior of other vehicles. An example scenario is a vehicle cheating with positioning information in order to alter its perceived position, speed, direction, itinerary, etc. By doing so, the attacker can divert the traffic from a given road and hence free that road for himself. Figure 2 and Figure 3 illustrate this case. In Figure 2, the attacker diffuses bogus traffic information and in Figure 3, we have some attackers cheating with positioning information. In Figure 2 the attack is characterized as: (Internal, Intentional, Active, and Independent) whereas in Figure 3 the attack is characterized as: (*Internal, Intentional, Active and Coordinated*).

- **Impersonation/Masquerading:** In this case, the attacker uses a false identity pretending to be another vehicle. More generally, the attacker uses a false credential in order to be granted another vehicle privileges. Figure 4 shows an example of such attack. This specific attack example is characterized as: (*Internal or External, Intentional, Active and Independent*).

- **Denial of Service (DoS):** In this case the attacker prevents legitimate vehicles to access the network services. This can be done by jamming the wireless channel, overloading the network or having a non

Figure 1. Identity disclosure

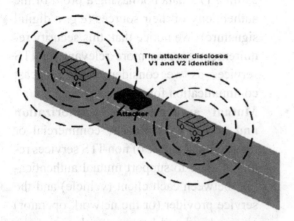

Figure 2. Bogus traffic information injection

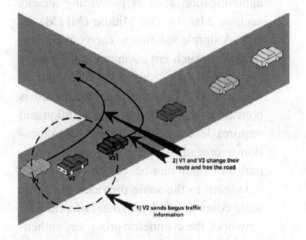

Figure 3. Cheating with positioning info

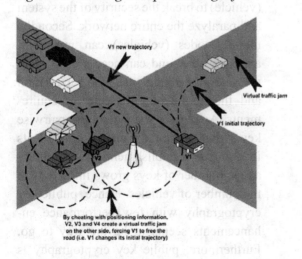

Figure 4. Masquerading

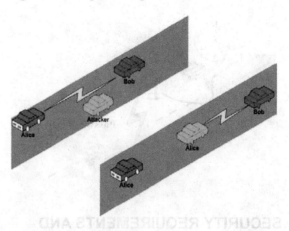

Figure 5. DoS - channel jamming

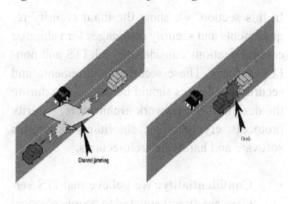

cooperative behavior (*e.g.* dropping packets). Figure 5 illustrates an attack example where the attacker causes a crash by preventing legitimate vehicles to exchange critical traffic information. This attack is characterized as: (*Internal or External, Intentional, Active and Independent or Coordinated*).

- **Eavesdropping:** In this case, the attacker monitors the network traffic in order to extract any sensitive information. Figure 6 shows the case where an attacker eavesdrops and extracts a commercial transaction password. This attack is characterized as: (*Internal or External, Intentional, Passive and Independent*).

Figure 6. Eavesdropping a commercial transaction

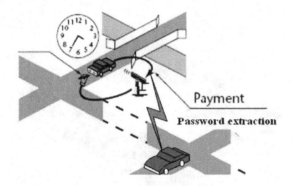

SECURITY REQUIREMENTS AND SECURITY CHALLENGES

In this section, we show the main security requirements and security challenges for vehicular communications considering both ITS and non-ITS services. These security requirements and security challenges should be considered during the design of the network architecture, security protocols, cryptographic algorithms as well as software and hardware architectures.

- **Confidentiality:** We believe that ITS services are directly related to people physical safety. If a vehicle that is not authenticated (*i.e.* an illegitimate vehicle) is in accident, authenticated vehicles (*i.e.* legitimate vehicles) may also be affected. Consequently, to efficiently achieve the main goal of ITS services which is mainly peoples' safety, every vehicle (legitimate and illegitimate) should be capable of receiving and processing ITS data. Thus, unlike non-ITS services which may require confidentiality due to their commercial nature, ITS services should not require protection against eavesdropping.

- **Source authentication:** In ITS services, the only restriction lies in avoiding illegitimate vehicles to generate ITS data. This is simply implemented through dis-

carding ITS data not having a proof of the authenticity of their sources (*e.g.* a digital signature). We notice that, this security requirement appears more relevant for ITS services as we consider only broadcast communication for these services.

- **Mutual authentication, authorization and access control:** The commercial or transactional nature of non-ITS services requires them to support mutual authentication between each client (vehicle) and the service provider (or the network operator) on one hand and between each communicating vehicles on the other hand. Mutual authentication aims at preventing attacks such as Man In The Middle (MITM) attack. A simple solution to carryout authentication in such environment is to employ a symmetric key shared by all nodes in the network. Although this mechanism is considered as a *plug and play* solution and requires less processing and communication overhead, it is limited to closed scenarios of small number of vehicles, mostly belonging to the same provider. For wide scale commercial deployment of vehicular networks, the symmetric group key authentication has two main pitfalls: firstly, an attacker only needs to compromise one node (vehicle) to break the security of the system and paralyze the entire network. Secondly, mobile nodes (vehicles) can impersonate each other and can access each other messages breaking the non-repudiation and the confidentiality security requirements. As regards the symmetric pairwise key authentication, the main problem is its inherent key establishment non-scalability as the number of keys grows linearly with the number of vehicles. Hence, public key cryptography with few performance enhancements seems to be the way to go. Furthermore, public key cryptography is a robust security primitive for implementing authorization and access control which are important counter-attack measures in vehicular networks deployment allowing only authorized mobile nodes to be connected and preventing adversaries to sneak into the network disrupting the normal operation or service provision.

- **Non repudiation:** Vehicles causing accidents or injecting malicious data must be reliably identified. Hence, a vehicle should not be able to deny the transmission of a message. If used carefully, digital signatures can provide the non-repudiation property. However, the main reason for using signatures is not to provide non-repudiation but to allow authentication between two entities who have not previously encountered each other, without having to make an online query to a third party. Although non repudiation security requirement is mostly critical for ITS services, it may be desirable to also have it for some sensitive non-ITS services especially those involving online payments.

- **Privacy:** As people increasingly worry about the Big Brother enabling technologies, private individuals' anonymity and non-traceability should be guaranteed. It should be noted however that anonymity and non-traceability are strictly conditional as non-repudiation must also be enforced. Although traceability is a legitimate process for governmental authorities and networks operators, the non-traceability is an important security requirement in order to assure peoples' privacy. Thus a complex problem arises in this issue. In fact, a tough requirement in vehicular networks environments is to manage traceability in terms of allowing this process for the concerned authorities and at the same time assuring the non-traceability between mobile clients (vehicles) themselves. Nevertheless, the latter is difficult to achieve and so far

no promising solutions exist to resolve this issue in the vehicular networks dynamic and open environment. It is noticed that the traceability can include: i) who is talking to who, ii) what one is sending, iii) which site one is accessing or which application one is using, and iv) where is the mobile client now (his location) and where is he going to be after a while. In fact, the privacy security requirement applies to both ITS and non-ITS services.

- **Real-time constraints:** A critical feature in ITS services is their time sensitiveness, where ITS data are mostly real-time data with about 100ms critical transmission delay (Yang et al., 2004). ITS services are expected to carry out much more signature verification than signature generation. So, an important challenge, achieving real-time constraints, is choosing the fastest public key cryptosystem in signature verification which at the same time performs well in signature generation. Also, the selected cryptosystem should be as compact as possible. In any case, any security mechanism for ITS services should take into consideration these real-time constraints.

- **Data Consistency / Liability:** This is also an important security issue for ITS services as even authenticated vehicles could become malicious by sending bogus information in order to gain an undue advantage, and thus can cause accidents or disturb the network operation. As a mechanism example ensuring data consistency or liability, we can quote verification by correlation which consists in correlating, through a reputation-based or a recommendation-based system, data received from a given source with those received from other sources. Some other approaches consist in enabling any node to search for possible explanations for the data it has collected based on the fact that malicious nodes may be present. Explanations that are consistent with the node's model of vehicular networks are scored and the node accepts the data as dictated by the highest scoring explanations (Golle et al., 2004).

- **Integrity:** This security requirement applies to ITS and non-ITS services as it protects against altering a message in transit. In practice, authenticity and integrity go together since there's no point correctly identifying a message origin if the message content is altered.

- **Availability:** Denial of Service (DoS) attacks due to channel jamming, network overloading or non cooperative behaviors may result in network unavailability. Hence, a continuous network operation should be supported by alternative means. The non-availability risk can be mitigated by exploring the numerous security mechanisms (*e.g.* monitoring, reputation-based systems, etc.) which can be used for non-cooperative nodes detection or by exploring channel and technology switching and cognitive radio techniques which can be used against jamming attacks. The availability security requirement applies to any vehicular service.

- **High mobility support:** This is a crucial challenge in designing vehicular networks security system. We assume that the vehicles' computing platforms have the same computational capability and energy supply as wired clients such as desktop PCs. However they significantly differ in their mobility support and their resulting throughput capability. These factors result in a mismatch between security protocols execution time in vehicular networks and their execution time in wired networks. This security execution gap is an important issue that must be faced by vehicular network designers. An attempt to lower

this gap is making vehicular security protocols and their inherent cryptographic algorithms, lightweight and fast (without loosing security robustness). For instance, it has been demonstrated that by implementing only a subset of security protocols' features, it is possible to reduce the overhead and the execution time. This goal can also be achieved by selecting optimal software or hardware implementations for cryptographic algorithms and adapting the encryption policies based on the content of the data that is being encrypted (*e.g.* video encryption). An important scheme reducing the execution time and adapting high mobility is the low complexity security algorithms. For example, the current security protocols such as SSL/TLS, DTLS, WTLS, etc. generally use RSA-based public key cryptography for authentication. The security of the basic RSA algorithm is derived from the integer factorization which is NP-hard. Hence, RSA can provide high security if the modulus is a large integer (*e.g.* 1024 or 2048 bits) whose factoring is extremely complex. This means that the basic computation for decrypting data is performed using large keys, making it computationally and time expensive. We can take advantage of alternative public key cryptography standards (PKCS) that provide security robustness while requiring less execution time. Elliptic Curve Cryptosystems (ECC) and lattice-based cryptosystem NTRU are examples of such alternative public key cryptosystems that are increasingly being used in wireless security software toolkits. For bulk data encryption/decryption, a protocol such as AES is preferred since older ones like DES or 3DES appear less attractive due to security limitations or computational and time expensiveness.

An additional way helping to lower the security execution gap is to carefully choose the transport layer over which security protocols are implemented when securing transactions over IP. For example, Transport Layer Security (TLS) which secures application-layer traffic over TCP/IP is discouraged for mobile use as it operates over TCP. Conversely, Datagram TLS (DTLS) which secures application-layer traffic over UDP/IP is better accepted as it operates over a connectionless transport layer (*i.e.* UDP). A protocol like IPSec which secures IP traffic, should be avoided as its secure connections (known as Security Associations or SAs) are cumbersome to set up, requiring too many messages. However, when vehicles are not in motion (*e.g.* in a parking space), protocols like Internet Protocol Security (IPsec) or TLS might become appropriate.

Although high mobility support is a global challenge for any vehicular service security, we however conclude that ITS services security requirements are a little bit different from non-ITS services security requirements. In Figure 7, we highlight the main security requirements of both services, showing the commonality and the difference between them.

ANALYSIS OF RELATED WORKS

Main Contributions

Vehicular communications security is a young research domain, showing few research contribu-

tions and lacking real solutions development. The existing contributions mainly focus on securing ITS services without providing general security architectures considering both ITS and non-ITS services. Zarki et al. (2002) address ITS services security in vehicular environment. They consider that there is no routing and no hand-over in their scenario as they use a broadcasting communication model that is one way with the Base Station (BS). They show that through providing efficient PKI and digital signatures mechanisms, the confidentiality and key distribution do not need to be considered. These mechanisms are required to have acceptable delay with respect to the ITS services real-time constraints. Since this contribution does not support privacy issues, and more importantly does not consider non-ITS services security requirements, this limits the possibility of its wide scale deployment, as ITS services show far less potential compared to non-ITS services when it comes to the possibility of services' commercialization. Privacy issues for ITS services are more specifically tackled by Hubeaux et al. (2004). They introduce the concept of entropy anonymity metric, recommending the use of PKI and some location verification tools to implement ITS security. The main advantage of this work is that privacy mechanisms which are introduced can also be considered for non-ITS services. Blum et al. (2004), present a secure communication architecture for Inter Vehicles Communication (IVC) which comprises a PKI, a distributed IDS (Intrusion Detection System) and a virtual network infrastructure. Although this work is enough gen-

Figure 7. Main security requirements and security challenges for ITS and non-ITS services

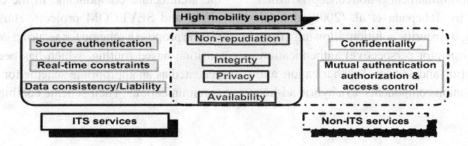

eral for securing ITS and non-ITS services, it is extremely restrictive in considering a stand-alone vehicular ad-hoc network which does not show any great interest for the envisioned business model of network operators where services delivery are mainly done through access points or base stations. Golle et al. (2004) propose a general approach to evaluate the validity of ITS data in vehicular networks, focusing on artificial intelligence issues in such environment. A more network-oriented work introducing a threat analysis and a security architecture for ITS services is presented in by Raya et al. (2005, 2007). They provide a set of security protocols making use of PKI, digital signatures, anonymous public keys implementing privacy and secure positioning among other points. Nevertheless, the security architecture is strictly relevant for vehicular networks running ITS services. An approach considering a real deployable solution from a network operator perspective is presented by Moustafa et al. (2006). This solution aims at securing ITS and non-ITS services based on EAP-Kerberos using public key certificates at entry points of highways. Actually this solution needs to support the continuous access to infrastructure services, as vehicles must always re-authenticate whenever they change their Access Points (APs). To enhance vehicular networks ubiquitous secure access from a network operator perspective, a novel architecture and security mechanisms are proposed by Tchepnda et al. (2006) taking advantages of: i) the ad hoc multi-hop authentication concept, ii) the smart card-based authentication allowing authentication before the V2R communication, and iii) the grid paradigm for security resources' aggregation. The ad-hoc multi-hop authentication concept is further developed by Tchepnda et al. (2008) through introducing a security solution allowing (from a network operator perspective) authentication, access control and services' authorization and featuring 4 main components: a) a hybrid ad-hoc

vehicular network architecture, b) a trust and security infrastructure, c) an authentication and credential delivery protocol and d) an authentication transport protocol for supporting EAP (Extensible Authentication Protocol) transport over layer-2 in multi-hop networks. The authors' authentication messages transport scheme is based on 3 main features: the stateless broadcast based geographic transport of authentication messages, the opportunistic relay of these messages (*i.e.* any node can relay a packet if relaying is relevant in order to reach the destination) and their multi-path transport (*i.e.* packet can reach the destination through more than one path). Also, the authors' approach tends to increase the protection of IP and upper layers services as access to those services is denied until the authentication with the network operator is successfully completed at layer 2. Although this solution proves to provide a robust and pervasive authentication between vehicles and the network operator authentication server, a security association derivation with access points in such a multi-hop architecture, is still to be designed. In the Now (Network On Wheels) project context, Matthias Gerlach et al. (2007) introduce a security architecture integrating existing individual solutions for vehicle registration, data integrity, data assessment, authentication, pseudonyms, certification, revocation and so on. They distinguish in their architecture the high-level views i.e. the functional layers and the organizational structure describing how the overall security system should look like and the implementation-near views describing an implementation design for the security system in the vehicle's on-board unit and presenting the information flow among the architecture components. In the context of NOW and SEVECOM projects, Harsch et al. (2007) propose a scheme for securing geographic position-based routing, which has been widely accepted as an appropriate scheme for vehicular communications. Their scheme combines digital signatures, plausibility checks, and rate limitation. Indeed, digital signatures are based on a combination of hop-by-hop signature and end-to-end signature thus providing a strong authentication, integrity and non-repudiation. On the other hand, plausibility checks (*e.g.* on velocity, on timestamp, on transmission range, etc.) reduce the impact of false positioning information on the routing protocol. Finally, the rate limitation reduces the effect of massive packet injections from malicious nodes that aim to overload the network. Although the authors' objective to enhance the network robustness can be met when using their solution in a pure ad-hoc vehicular network, their approach can hardly meet the network operators deployment requirements as there seems to be no hierarchy neither in the network architecture nor in the security roles among the network's nodes. Coronado et al. (2007) depict a trusted authority architecture including a governmental authority and private authorities aiming to offer reliable communications on top of which services can be deployed. These authorities are in charge of providing pseudonyms, key distribution and key management for on-demand requesters namely users and services providers. Single-hop and multi-hop secure service provisioning scenarios are illustrated although not sufficiently detailed to be thoroughly analyzed.

We had in the past many industrial projects on vehicular communications in Europe, Asia and USA (e.g. CarTalk, Chauffeur1, Chauffeur2, Fleenet, PATH, etc.) but unfortunately these projects didn't take security issues into consideration. However some efforts are made to address this limitation through ongoing projects or consortiums such as Car2Car Communication Consortium (C2C-CC), SEVECOM (SEcure VEhicular COMmunications) project, NoW (Network On Wheels) project and the DSRC-based IEEE P1609.2 project (2006) aiming to specify safety applications security mechanisms based on public key cryptography.

SUMMARY AND OUTLOOK

From our investigation to the existing contributions, we notice that most of them focus on securing ITS services and/or pure ad-hoc vehicular communications, neglecting the tremendous potential of non-ITS services and infrastructure or hybrid ad-hoc vehicular networks in driving the development and deployment of vehicular networks. Although extensively tackling security of ITS services, some of these contributions fail in considering some peculiarities of such services like broadcast transmission and its resulting effect on security requirements. All these limitations fuel the motivation in providing a broader and a more complete view of vehicular communications security challenges.

In summary the future security mechanisms of vehicular networks should comply with the special characteristics of these networks *i.e.* high mobility, constrained bandwidth, large resources (CPU, energy, memory), dynamic topologies constrained by roads' topologies, large number of nodes, heterogeneous administration, etc. Moreover, these security mechanisms should be transparent for non-ITS applications in order to serve network operators and services providers business needs, and should allow vehicles (in infrastructure or hybrid ad-hoc network architectures) not to re-authenticate from scratch whenever they move. To sum up, the main open issue here lies in designing multi-purpose security architectures complying with vehicular networks characteristics and meeting all the respective requirements of ITS and non-ITS services in a single framework. This type of framework can be depicted as a context-aware or a service-aware security framework for vehicular communications.

CONCLUSION

Security is one of the significant challenges impacting mobile ad-hoc networks and vehicular networks specifically. A point that complicates this issue is that securing vehicular communication is service-related. For instance, safety-related services should be granted to every vehicle in order to as much as possible minimize accidents on the roads whereas non-safety-related services should be only granted to vehicles which have subscribed for them. In this article, we illustrate vehicular networks applications and potential architectures, addressing the main security requirements and challenges in this specific environment. We noticed that the existing contributions are not general for all vehicular networks' environments and are restricted mostly to ITS services and/or standalone ad-hoc vehicular networks. Moreover these contributions hardly comply with the main security requirements that are important in designing security solutions for real deployments of vehicular networks. Thus, those solutions can restrict vehicular networks potential, ignoring its importance in providing ubiquitous communications. Consequently, appropriate security mechanisms are required allowing trust and secure transmission, while taking into consideration the dynamic and non-fully centralized nature of vehicular networks as well as the different types of applications and their specific requirements.

REFERENCES

59 GHz DSRC, http://grouper.ieee.org/groups/scc32/dsrc/index.html

Blum, J. & Eskandarian, A. (2004). The Threat of Intelligent Collisions. *ITProfessional (IEEE Computer Society periodical)*.

Coronado, E., & Cherkaoui, S. (2007). Secure Service Provisioning for Vehicular Networks. *International Workshop on ITS for Ubiquitous ROADS (UBIROADS)*.

Gerlach, M., Festag, A., Leinmüller, T., Goldacker, G., & Harsch, C. (2007). Security Architecture for Vehicular Communication. *International Workshop on Intelligent Transportation (WIT)*.

Golle, P., Greene, D., & Staddon, J. (2004). Detecting and Correcting Malicious Data in VANETs. *ACM International Workshop on Vehicular Ad Hoc Networks (VANET)*.

Harsch, C., Festag, A., & Papadimitratos, P. (2007). Secure Position-Based Routing for VANETs. *IEEE Vehicular Technology Conference (VTC-Fall)*.

Hubeaux, J.-P., Capkun, S., & Luo, J. (2004). *The Security and Privacy of Smart Vehicles*. IEEE Security & Privacy Magazine.

IEEE. P1609.2 (2006) - Standard for Wireless Access in Vehicular Environments - Security Services for Applications and Management Messages. IEEE 802.11p (status of the project), IEEE Task Group TGp, http://grouper.ieee.org/groups/802/11/Reports/tgp_update.htm

Moustafa, H., Bourdon, G., & Gourhant, Y. (2006). Providing Authentication and Access Control in Vehicular Network Environment. *International Information Security Conference (IFIP SEC)*.

Raya, M., & Hubaux, J. (2005). The Security of Vehicular Ad Hoc Networks. A*CM Workshop on Security of Ad Hoc and Sensor Networks (ACM SASN)*.

Raya, M. & Hubaux, J.-P. (2007), Securing Vehicular Ad Hoc Networks. *Journal of Computer Security (JCS) - special issue on Security on Ad Hoc and Sensor Networks*.

Tchepnda, C., Moustafa, H., Labiod, H., & Bourdon, G. (2006). Securing Vehicular Communications: An Architectural Solution Providing a Trust Infrastructure, Authentication, Access Control and Secure Data Transfer. *IEEE AutoNet - Global Communications Conference (Globecom)*.

Tchepnda, C., Moustafa, H., Labiod, H., & Bourdon, G. (2008). Performance Analysis of a Layer-2 Multi-hop Authentication and Credential Delivery Scheme for Vehicular Networks. *IEEE Vehicular Technology Conference (VTC-Spring)*.

Yang, X., Liu, J., Zhao, F., & Vaidya, N. (2004). A vehicle-to-vehicle communication protocol for cooperative collision warning. *International Conference on Mobile and Ubiquitous Systems (MobiQuitous)*.

Zarki, M., Mehrotra, S., Tsudik, G., & Venkatasubramanian, N. (2002). *Security Issues in a Future Vehicular Network*. European Wireless.

This work was previously published in International Journal of Ambient Computing and Intelligence (IJACI), Volume 1, Issue 1, edited by Kevin Curran, pp. 39-52, copyright 2009 by IGI Publishing (an imprint of IGI Global).

Chapter 5
A Comprehensive Solution for Ambient Intelligence:
From Hardware to Services

Felix Villanueva
University of Castilla-La Mancha, Spain

Jesus Barba
University of Castilla-La Mancha, Spain

Francisco Moya
University of Castilla-La Mancha, Spain

Fernando Rincon
University of Castilla-La Mancha, Spain

Fernando Santofimia
University of Castilla-La Mancha, Spain

Juan Lopez
University of Castilla-La Mancha, Spain

David Villa
University of Castilla-La Mancha, Spain

ABSTRACT

Ubiquitous computing, pervasive computing, ambient intelligence, etc. are research lines that, with slight differences, emphasizes their efforts in improving everyday life of users. However, all these approaches share a common set of requirements, for the underlying IT infrastructure, devoted to support advanced services. A key component of these, sometimes called "new paradigms", is the fact that technology is found embedded in the environments were we live. In this paper we are going to propose a comprehensive vision for modelling this type of environments from a practical point of view. This work cover form HW developments, which seamless integrate in the environment, to automatically generated services based on user needs. In the last decade, authors of this work have been proponents of a unified approach, based on the distributed object abstraction, allowing synergies to be better exploited. Remote device management, wireless sensor and actuator networks, hardware components and now even reconfigurable hardware platforms and service platforms are considered as part of a large evolving system sharing a common middleware and a single design methodology.

DOI: 10.4018/978-1-60960-549-0.ch005

INTRODUCTION

Ambient intelligence (AmI) focused on users and their needs. It provides services to users anticipating their actions and modifying the environment, facilitating their everyday tasks. In 2001 the ISTAG published the work entitled "Scenarios for Ambient Intelligence in 2010". That work described a set of scenarios showing interaction among users and the information and communication technologies. Nowadays it can be affirmed that maybe they were too optimistic. Nevertheless, the Ambient Intelligence vision described in that document is still valid. Furthermore, the described scenarios can be used as guidelines for research purposes. This chapter is devoted to deal with a recurrent problem in Ambient Intelligence as it is the integration of heterogeneous devices, technologies and services, that are to be deployed in an Ambient Intelligence environment.

In the same line, Ubiquitous Computing (UC) is all about heterogeneity, it deals with heterogeneity in heterogeneous ways. Some authors identify different areas of UC leading to different approaches to the development of Ubiquitous Computing environments (Endres, 2005). Sometimes there is an explicit distinction between Ubiquitous Computing and Pervasive Computing (Gaber, 2007) to differentiate the main focus. Pervasive Computing deals with providing adaptive or emerging services to fit user needs in a given context, whereas Ubiquitous Computing would be mainly focused on globally accessible services (anytime, anywhere).

Additionally, most research topics in UC must also deal with the fact that the target systems are inherently distributed. Therefore UC environments have much in common with distributed heterogeneous object platforms developed in the nineties (CORBA, EJB, DCOM,...) and also with current grid computing platforms (Globus, gLite,...). Our research tries to leverage the achievements of those platforms by defining a unified middleware with the capability to interact with standard middlewares although specially suited to UC needs.

One major source of heterogeneity is the wide variety of devices connected by means of different networking technologies in almost every UC or AmI environment. The concept of residential gateway was coined in the field of residential services as an analogy to a concentrator that is to say, a device with multiple network interfaces used to interconnect all the device networks available in a given scenario. Middlewares like OSGi (OSGi, 2004) or Amigo (Georgantas, 2005) took advantage of this mediating device so as to provide a whole service management platform. Implicit to this approach is the fact that most services will be running in the residential gateway. On the one side, this is positive from the point of view of manageability. The residential gateway may be controlled by the service provider or even by the telecommunication operator. But this device also constitutes a single point of failure which makes impractical the implementation of critical or very simple services (door opening, lighting,...).

With more and more candidate technologies being integrated in Ubiquitous Computing environments it is increasingly hard to design a residential gateway, at a reasonable cost, behaving as a single device with all required interfaces. From a business point of view, service providers are using residential gateways as a way to control the distribution of new services, limiting users' freedom to choose alternative service providers. While a mature market would see this as a competitive advantage, an emerging market such as the residential services sees a reduction of the perceived utility and consequently a slowdown in the rate of new deployments.

Currently DVB set-top-boxes, mobile phones, or public WiFi networks constitute alternative technologies for the interconnection of residential networks or device networks with an external service provider (e.g. through Internet). Therefore, the overall architecture of an ubiquitous environment is evolving from a star topology centred on a residential gateway to a fully distributed mesh network where several devices provide some capabilities traditionally associated to a residential gateway.

As a conclusion, nowadays no single device will be able to support all the features required to provide services in a given scenario. Instead, an increasing number of devices will need to cooperate in order to provide transparent gateway services among the different technologies.

This decentralized model also influences the design of the middleware:

- Management tasks (e.g. version control, start/stop commands, installation and removal of services, etc.) are distributed among a set of devices.
- The proper operation of services in a UC environment does not depend on a single device. We may provide service replication procedures in order to increase the reliability.
- Security mechanisms will need to take into account the availability of several broadband and/or WAN interfaces (e.g. Internet).
- Service configuration is becoming increasingly complex.
- Device and software deployment is highly dynamic.
  Here, it is believed that object-oriented distributed middlewares include an attractive set of features to enable next generation ubiquitous computing environments. Eight years ago we proposed an architecture based on the distributed object abstraction (Moya, 2002) to overcome the limitations of OSGi, based on large-scale residential services. This initial architecture has been significantly enhanced in recent years to support highly dynamic environments:
- Integrating embedded low cost devices with limited resources (Villa, 2006) (Moya, 2007)

- Simplifying configuration procedures by mean service discovery protocols (Villa, 2007)
- Providing common steps for HW/SW interoperability (Villanueva, 2007)
- Providing a taxonomy of services, devices and events for building a model information system in order to establish a common vocabulary for service development (Villanueva, 2009)
- Integrating multimedia platforms like OpenMax (Barba, 2010)

Current work on this evolving architecture is mainly concerned with the remote deployment of distributed applications to low-end heterogeneous devices such as eight-bit microcontrollers (microcomponents), and high-level support for service composition from semantic descriptions. Once again we focus on minimalism in order to allow a certain degree of dynamic service discovery, aggregation and composition even for the smallest computing devices.

In figure 1 overall structure of Distributed Object Based Services (DOBS) is depicted. DOBS is the resulting framework after several iterations carried out by the ARCO Research Group at University of Castilla-La Mancha. DOBS aims at providing a full framework for Ubiquitous Computing, built on top of standard distributed objects. Our main design goals were:

- Basic services should be easy to implement on any computing platform, no matter how small they are. Moreover, they have to be able to be implemented in hardware.
- Support for remote service management has to be available.
- The maximum resource usage efficiency is sought, in terms of memory consumption, required bandwidth, etc.

Figure 1. Distributed Object Based Services

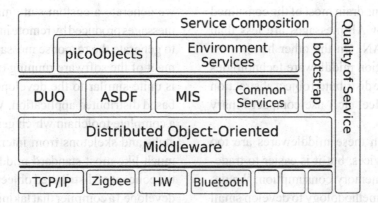

- It should allow easy interoperability mechanisms in order to integrate third party services.
- It should provide a complete set of tools for ubiquitous computing application development and a set of templates for basic services. It should not rely on a specific implementation language or a particular operating systems.

The remainder of this paper is structured as follows. Next section describes the issues related to the lowest level of the architecture, built on wireless sensor and actuator networks. Services and service composition section introduces the service concept as the core element of a middleware architecture aimed at supporting ubiquitous and pervasive computing. This section also outlines some of the key concepts involved in service composition, emphasizing the semantic model used to describe the application domain. Actions and events in Ambient Intelligence section is devoted to the specific considerations about providing intelligence to ubiquitous and pervasive services. Finally, the last section exposes the designed workflow to generate hardware objects dedicated to those highly demanding tasks in terms of computational resources.

SENSING AND MODIFYING THE REAL WORLD

Besides the gradual transformation of infrastructures using residential gateways to fully distributed deployments, wireless sensor networks are also playing an important role in Ubiquitous Computing and influencing the overall middleware design.

Wireless Sensor and Actuator Networks (WSANs) are becoming attractive for monitoring and small device control (door locks, windows, lighting, switches, etc.) due to their flexibility and reduced cost. Ambient Intelligence could be the killer application WSANs are looking for.

Unit cost for WSAN devices as a great impact on the success of the technology, and the resources required for a middleware are directly translated into an increase of such unit cost. Therefore we feel that most of the middleware technologies, specifically those used in Ubiquitous Computing, made a wrong decision when they chose either the Java platform or Web Services (e.g. (Eisenhauer,2009)) to deal with the heterogeneity issue. In our opinion, these were made at the expenses of large resource requirements for target devices or application specific gateways.

Similar considerations could be argued for textual message encodings, such as XML, as used in traditional Web Services or UPnP. Unlike conventional Ethernet or WiFi networks, devices in a WSAN are usually battery-powered and wireless communications drain most of the consumed power. Standard SOAP messages are less than efficient in a WSAN. On the other hand, most of the communication middleware technologies that are based on the distributed object abstraction (CORBA, ZeroC Ice, etc.) use compact binary protocols.

Obviously, even these middlewares are too big for WSAN devices, but it is easier to trade-off flexibility for memory consumption. We designed a complete methodology to develop small distributed objects able to interact with standard middlewares (Moya, 2007). In spite of the other approach efforts, aimed at embedding the middleware technology in resource constrained devices, by removing features from a standard middleware (e.g. (Subramonian, 2004)), we took the opposite approach, by building the minimum set of features to emulate the standard behaviour.

For the simplest case (8-bit microcontrollers) we generate a custom state-machine to analyze messages produced by remote invocations and also to generate the response messages. The development of the software running on WSAN devices is quite similar to the development of any RMI based distributed application. We are developing a complete toolchain which generates simplified stubs and skeletons from interface descriptions, much like most standard middlewares based on the concept of distributed object. We have already developed a compiler that taking an object distributed scenario, modelled with a specific language (IcePick), together with the interface definition (in ICE interface definition language SLICE) of languages, we can generate the communication infrastructure for TinyOS (the most used WSN operating system). In Figure 2 we can see this developing process for ZeroC ICE middleware.

Figure 2. Design flow for DOBS objects on WSN devices

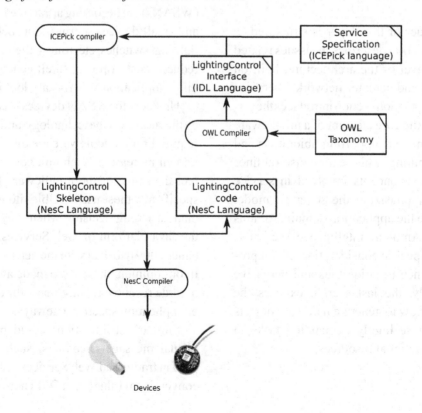

SERVICES AND SERVICE COMPOSITION

In DOBS, services are considered as the basic element of the system architecture. Furthermore, Ubiquitous and Pervasive Computing are service oriented, and so, they have to deal with the way services are deployed, managed, or supported. In this context, services are not considered in an isolated manner, but in conjunction with the rest of services provided by the existing devices. In this regard, service composition provides the foundations for orchestrating existing services into composite ones.

Manual and semiautomatic composition, conversely to automatic composition, depends on user actions for accomplishing the composition task. Therefore, in an UC context where user interaction tends to be minimized, automatic composition is the best solution to this end.

Automatic service composition can be achieved by means of web services and ontologies. These two approaches, however, lack of the capabilities to deal with the high dynamism implicit in WSN, where devices are continuously appearing and vanishing, and so are the services.

DOBS considers the combination of intelligent agents and ontologies as a mean for providing the middleware with reasoning capabilities. Among the existing solutions (Wooldridge, 2000) to implement intelligent agents, the Belief-Desire-Intention (BDI) (Rao,1991) model has proved to be a powerful framework to build rational agents. Furthermore, Jadex (Pokahr, 2003) provides an agent-oriented reasoning engine that once adapted to work on top of the middleware, provides the reasoning capabilities for the service composition mechanism in a dynamic context. In this regard, the ontology support is essential to understand and effectively react to changes and new requirements by means of automatic service composition.

Taxonomy Representation

In order to define a common vocabulary and a basic set of services, which both developers and manufacturers may find in any UC environment, we use a custom taxonomy with the following characteristics:

- Service names, their attributes and types are defined in a semi-formal way, and also the set of allowed values for the attributes.
- A common vocabulary is made available for any purpose. For example, it may be used to perform a search using the service discovery mechanisms with a set of attribute-value pairs.
- Relationships among services are described without limitations of simple tree-like structures.

We chose ontologies as the representation approach to our taxonomy, basically because of the availability of convenient tools and because it provides a flexible way of representing knowledge. Our application domain is limited to Ambient Intelligence services though it may be extended easily.

The standardized set of services with known interfaces, names, attributes and allowed values for those attributes enables the development of advanced services.

The basic set of services described in the ontology was modelled after other common vocabularies from different sources, such as Bluetooth profiles, UPnP service templates, OMA Mobile Location Service, or OMG multimedia streaming service (AVStreams).

The ontology was developed in OWL language using the Protegé tool. Services are modelled as classes and each class contains a set of attributes. An attribute has a type and, in some cases, a set of allowed values. The ontology by itself constitutes a valuable tool for a developer to get a quick understanding of the basic services.

Besides, a compiler has been built to simplify the development even more (figure 2). The ontology compiler generates interface descriptions for any service from the OWL description. Therefore, the service developer is mainly concerned with the functional aspects of the service, with minimal considerations about remote interaction.

Place & Play Philosophy

In Ubiquitous Computing environments, devices and services appear and disappear continuously. It may be because some of them are mobile devices or simply because devices and services may be turned on and off dynamically. Reducing configurations procedures is a key requirement for any practical environment. Assuming we have different devices using different remote services, it becomes clear that we will need gateways distributed around the environment in order to enable interoperability among services using heterogeneous technologies. But there are some additional requirements:

- A common addressing scheme for the services. Traditionally IP addresses fulfill this requirement but not every WSAN support a TCP/IP stack (not even for IP stacks with minimal resource requirements). Heterogeneous gateways are more conveniently handled with a routing component at the application layer.
- A service discovery protocol providing lookup and announce services. This service discovery protocol (SDP) must be available even for the smallest services and there must be interoperability procedures with other SDP since it is not feasible to impose a unique SDP. In DOBS we provide a minimum set of primitives which may be implemented even in a WSAN device. DOBS service discovery service may implement either a push or a pull mode and

it is already being integrated with different SDP (UPnP SSDP, and Bluetooth).
- A bootstrap service used to initialize a device and integrate it in the environment. Most of the services to be integrated in a ubiquitous computing environment will need other basic services. The bootstrap service may be used to get initial references for such basic services. For example, the DOBS SDP uses an event-oriented model to announce services or to search services. Therefore one of the first tasks needed to integrate a service in a DOBS enabled ubiquitous computing is getting a reference to the event channel service.

Standards

The lack of standards in ubiquitous environments is an obstacle that prevents these applications from leaving the research labs and reaching the mass market. In DOBS we follow existent standards, as much as, possible applying systematic rules when these standards need to be adapted somehow. Systematic translation of standard interfaces allows easier integration with third-party implementations of the standard. For example, we use OMG standards but the interface descriptions are translated into the DOBS interface description language. Currently we use the following service standards:

- For Audio and Video streams we use OMG AVStreams specification.
- For position related services we adopted the Mobile Location Protocol from OMA and a partial OpenLS specification from the OpenGIS Consortium.
- For basic device services the taxonomy was designed after UPnP templates and Bluetooth profiles.

ACTIONS AND EVENTS IN AMBIENT INTELLIGENCE: AUTOMATIC SERVICE COMPOSITION

The strong coupling between the action and event theory and planning has given birth to the concept of *action planning*. Commonly, actions and events have been equivalently treated, or with the slight difference of considering actions as events intentionally generated (Hommel, 2001). On the contrary, there are some other theories that support the opposite believe, for instance, the work in (Bach, 1990) argues that actions are not events. The main argument supporting this dissociation lays on considering actions and their agents as inseparable or correlative (Hyman, 2006). The theory of action for multi-agent planning (Georgeff, 1988) also advocates for this distinction, although hinting that actions are accomplished by agents in their endeavor to achieve a goal. Despite agreeing in considering agents along with actions, this work does not consider actions in terms of the targeting goals, but as justified later on, in terms of requirements preceding the action and consequences of it.

Davidson's theories, specially the philosophy of action, also identifies actions with events, as argued in (Davidson, 1963). Actions are described as a combination of two views. On the one hand, actions can be seen as causal explanations of body movements and on the other hand, actions can also be seen as the justifying reason that leads the action to take place. Davidson considers events equivalent to actions. The only difference is that when an action is considered as an event, it is re-described in terms of its effects.

It has to be highlighted that Cyc, through its language CycL, represents actions and events using a Davidsonian approach. Therefore, actions are described as events but carried out by an agent. This works beliefs that actions differs from events, with some slight hints. This position is grounded on a mixture of the aforementioned theories, adopting those aspects that better fit the application domain, Ambient Intelligence, where actions and events are to be considered.

The planning problem has been traditionally stated in terms of a world description or initial state, the goal to be achieved and the available actions. Needless to say, actions are specified in terms of prerequisites that are to be satisfied so as to perform the action, and the effects of executing the action. Nevertheless, the planner strategy proposed here differs from this traditional approach in considering actions, in opposite to states of the world, as the primary elements. Planning problems under this perspective are now stated in terms of a goal action, so called non-feasible action, to be performed on an object, and the list of doable actions that provide the means to accomplish this goal action. The following section will take care of the planning strategy details. In the mean time, this section introduces the semantic model underlying the Ambient Intelligence architecture, and the knowledge representation at the knowledge base.

The beliefs about what is an action and the features that differ it from an event are combined in a semantic model for actions and events in Ambient Intelligence. However, what does a semantic model stand for? From a computing perspective, it is considered to be an agreement on how to interpret the knowledge represented in the knowledge base. Furthermore, semantic models assure common interpretations to shared knowledge. It is also an essential requirement when there are different instances handling the same knowledge. Every holder is expected to extract the same meaning or conclusions from the represented knowledge.

Proposing **a semantic model** for actions and events for Ambient Intelligence is the main contribution of this work. It is also the cornerstone where the rest of the involved technologies are grounded on. For instance, the planning algorithm expects actions to cause events, where the agent might be a relevant element of the causal explanation. In a concise manner, actions either precede or come after events, but are not events.

The proposed semantic model is depicted in figure 3. Apart from the concept of action and event, there are some other relevant entities whose semantics have to modeled. It is obvious that Ambient Intelligence cannot conceive existence without services. For this reason, the service concept exhibits a core position in the proposed model. Services can be described in terms of the actions that they can undertake and the objects or things receiving such actions. As defended in this work, actions are not events, and so is reflected in the semantic model. Events involve actions in the sense that actions are required either for the event to take place or as result of the event occurrence, or both of them. In any case, an event description is made in terms of actions.

It is evident the simplicity of the model in comparison to some other semantic models (Bandara, 2008; Chen, 2003; Preuveneers, 2004). This simplicity is the result of reducing Ambient Intelligence to those concepts that cannot be avoided, in other words, those that compose the quintessence of Ambient Intelligence. This simple semantic model can be used to model the domain knowledge, independently of the application context. Moreover, this simplicity easy the implementation of the semantic model in those technologies involved in devising systems for Ambient Intelligence.

HARDWARE NODES

Within the framework of WSNs, there is a wide variety of nodes that conforms the system. The use of DOBS within WSNs is primary intended to encapsulate the nodes with less computational and memory requirements into an object-like appearance. Due to technological restrictions, those applications that needs of high computational resources to achieve hard time deadlines must move on to a hardware implementation.

For example, imagine a special node that must perform some kind of image processing algorithm to detect movement in a secure environment. This node must notify the object controller when a possible security breach is taking place.

Along with the automation of software embedded objects for small microcontrollers, we have developed a parallel design flow to easily create, integrate and interoperate with hardware objects. A hardware object (from now on HwO) is a custom integrated circuit that will perform a complex task in a WSNs.

Figure 4 shows the workflow of the proposed HwO generation process. The input to this process is an object interface description, written in an interface description language, just like the other objects will see the hardware component in the system. As we will see below, a hardware object

Figure 3. Entities and relationships for the semantic model

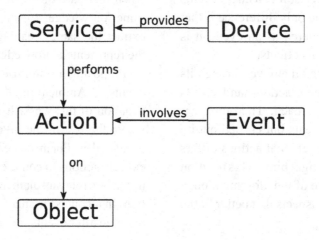

exhibits a distinctive interface that determines how its functionality is accessed (object access protocol). This information is used to generate: (1) the on-chip communication infrastructure and (2) the final hardware object implementation. This HwO implementation can be the result of a integration process, reusing existing designs implementing the required functionality. A new, hand coded chip implementation is needed when no reuse opportunities are present for the current application. Notice that this process is completely automatic. Finally, the resulting VHDL (a hardware description language) code is then synthesized.

A WSN is modeled as a set of objects that communicates through message passing. Concepts as attributes, method, parameters are mature in the software community since they have been widely applied in the development of any kind of projects for decades; this is not the case in hardware. It is then mandatory to establish a hardware object model so as to reduce the existing gap between the two worlds (hardware and software).

The benefits of viewing hardware components as objects is twofold since (1) it leaves invariable the system model making transparent the integration of software and hardware components and (2) it enables the automatic generation of the interconnection infrastructure because of the introduction of semantics in the communication into and out of the chip.

To implement logical objects as physical hardware components, we define: (1) a standardized interface in order to automatize the generation of wrappers and (2) a method invocation mechanism that must be understood by it. A hardware object exhibits a distinctive physical interface:

- Common system signals (clock, reset, etc.).
- One input signal per method to activate it.
- One output signal per method to indicate the end of an operation. This is used for synchronization purposes.
- Several input/output data ports.

Figure 4. Design flow for hardware objects

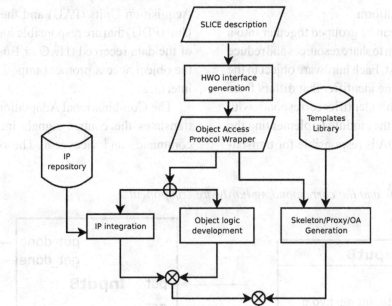

65

Our hardware object model uses the same data type system as the software implementation in order to define the inter-component communication semantics. At the time of writing this paper, all basic types (bool, short, int, float, etc.) plus structures, sequences (vectors) of a fixed size and any combination of them are supported by HwOs.

Figure 5 illustrates the module interfaces for a object implementing a data buffer of integers. We developed the HwO Access Protocol (HAP) tool that generates (1) scheduling information about the hardware method invocation protocol and (2) VHDL code of the finite state machine (FSMs) that understands the remote invocation protocol.

Hardware Object Platform

A HwO only implements the functionality it was designed for. We intentionally decoupled communication from behavior to make HwO modules reusable in future designs. By isolating HwOs from communication implementation details we make them immune to unforeseen changes in the communication infrastructure. To make HwOs accessible from outside the chip, we define a hardware object platform.

Several HwOs can be grouped together into a single HwO platform to share resources and reduce implementation cost. Each hardware object in the system has an unique identifier that differs from the OID. Actually, this identifier corresponds with the base address of the module implementing the skeleton. The HwOA is responsible for translat-ing external OID to internals valid bus addresses. Both proxies and skeletons agree in how method invocations translate in a sequence of low level actions over the bus to activate the execution of the operation. The data encoding/decoding rules are the same as in software. Therefore a method call is decomposed into write and read primitives. Read and write are basic services offered by most of the buses so that we do not limit the platform implementation to a concrete technology.

Interconnection Infrastructure Generation

The generation of skeletons (the hardware object wrappers) and the HwOA which implies the generation of proxies is a critical step in the hardware design flow. The final implementation must be highly optimized to fit the low-cost requirements while keeping the process automatic to save design time. We defined two interface templates which will be specialized according to the number and kind of methods to be interpreted. Figure 6 shows the general architecture of a proxy.

The most important modules are the Port Acquisition Units (PAU) and the Port Delivery Unit (PDU) that are responsible for the adaptation of the data received (HwO or Bus) according to the object access protocol imposed by the HwO interface.

The Combinational Adaptation Logic (CAL) translates the control signals into specific bus commands and viceversa. The correspondence

Figure 5. UML view and the corresponding hardware component

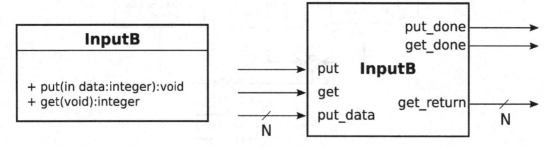

between FSM control signals and bus control signals is defined separately in system configuration files. The Control Logic implements the FSM doing the local (object access) and remote protocol (bus communication) adaptation. Eight parameterized VHDL design modules has been developed (one for each case and actor in the communication).

A skeleton is only produced for those hardware objects exporting at least one method. Only methods remotely invoked by the client, using a proxy to the target is generated. This reduces the logic used in the proxy since there is no implementation for unused methods.

An additional optimization introduced in this process is the reutilization of logic when two method definitions not necessary belonging to the same object/class match (identical physical hardware object interface).

ENVIRONMENT SIMULATOR

Other of our current works is a modular plugin-based environment simulator. Due the lack of real environments we found difficult to evaluate (and compare) different approaches for different problems (middleware, automatic service composition, etc.). Meanwhile other more mature areas, usually have simulators for these tasks (e.g. NS2 or Omnet for computers networks), there is a lack of this type of valuable tools for modeling UC environments. Our intention is to model different layers in order to provide a generic environment simulator useful for research community. Taking discrete event simulators as the starting point, our intention is to model, at least the following items:

- Physical layer: for the modeling of physical rooms with doors, windows, etc., and physics event propagation like noise, light, together with physical objects states (e.g.

Figure 6. Internal architecture of a hardware proxy

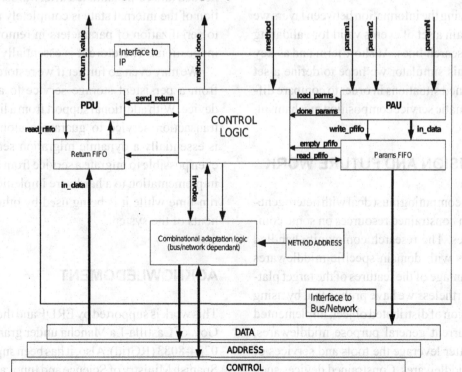

door open/close). We build this layer by simplifying the physics event propagation, so by now, avoiding aspects such as attenuation, reflection, etc.

- Device layer: for specifying the devices present in the environment, is attached to the physical models and it models devices like sensors, actuators, microphones, cameras, etc. Sensors and actuators can sense and modify the physical layer whereas microphones and cameras can reproduce previously attached files (in simulation configuration phase) with the audio and video as if they were in a real environment.
- Services layer: Attached to those devices deployed in the simulation scenarios, simple services are modeled. At this layer, the simulator starts to be useful since we can build simple services for reacting to events provided by device layer.
- Human layer: This layer models user behaviors and actions (room entries, talk with other users, acting over the lights, etc.)

Simplifying the information between layers we hope to obtain a set of events valid for validating different research lines. At short-term and as key results of this simulator we hope to define a set of well defined situations in order to compare different automatic service composition mechanism.

CONCLUSION AND FUTURE WORK

Ubiquitous computing must deal with heterogeneity and with constrained resources on some computing nodes. The research community handled these issues with domain specific middlewares taking advantage of the features of the target platform. Nevertheless we have probed that by using the abstraction of distributed object, implemented in many current general purpose middlewares, we may better leverage the tools and services of standard middlewares. Constrained devices such

as WSN nodes or hardware modules may use an adaptation of the standard design flow with minimal impact on the application programmer.

While the application-level interface is completely uniform across the whole system this is not made at the expense of preventing customized behaviour for optimum performance. Users may provide additional transport protocols for new communication technologies or they may even implement critical services on custom hardware. Location transparency is preserved as much as possible.

Besides, the distributed object model makes some advanced services a feasible goal. Two specially important examples are object persistency and object migration. Object persistency is the ability to store the internal state of the object in a persistent store and restore it when needed. This is extremely useful to decouple the life-time of a service from the life-time of the program implementing it. Services, even a small sensor service, may be frozen in a storage device (e.g. a battery powered memory, a flash memory, etc.) when not needed and re-instantiated afterwards. Serialization of the internal state is completely analogous to serialization of parameters in remote method invocations. Therefore it is essentially free.

We may even go further if we restore an object from a persistent storage service to a different device. With additional support from a lightweight transaction service to guarantee atomicity this is essentially a dynamic migration service. It is even possible to migrate a service from a software implementation to a hardware implementation at run-time while it is being used by other components of the system.

ACKNOWLEDGMENT

This work is supported by ERDF and the Regional Gov. of Castilla-La Mancha under grants PAI08-0234-8083 (RGrid). Also, it has been supported by Spanish Ministry of Science and Innovation under grants CEN-20091048 (Energos) and TEC2008-06553 (DAMA).

REFERENCES

Bach, K. (1990). Actions Are Not Events, Mind. *Oxford Journals, 89*(353), 114–120.

Bandara, A., Payne, T., De Roure, D., Gibbins, N., & Lewis, T. (2008). A pragmatic approach for the semantic description and matching of pervasive resources. *International Journal of Pervasive Computing and Communications, 6*(1), 434–446.

Barba, J., de la Fuente, D., Rincón, F., Sánchez, F., & López, J. C. (2010). OpenMax Hardware Native Support for Efficient Multimedia Embedded Systems. *IEEE 2010 International Conference on Consumer Electronics.* (pp. 433-434).

Chen, H., & Joshi, A. (2004). An Ontology for Context-Aware Pervasive Computing Environments, *Special Issue on Ontologies for Distributed Systems. The Knowledge Engineering Review, 18*(3), 197–207. doi:10.1017/S0269888904000025

Davidson, D. (1963). Actions, Reasons, and Causes. *The Journal of Philosophy, 60*(23), 685–700. doi:10.2307/2023177

Eisenhauer, M., Rosengren, P., & Antolin, P. (2009). A Development Platform for Integrating Wireless Devices and Sensors into Ambient Intelligence Systems. *Sensor, Mesh and Ad Hoc Communications and Networks Workshops, 2009. SECON Workshops '09. 6th Annual IEEE Communications Society Conference.* (pp. 1-3).

Endres, C., Butz, A., & MacWilliams, A. (2005). A Survey of Software Infrastructure and Frameworks for Ubiquitous Computing. *Mobile Information Systems, IOS Press, 1*(1), 41–80.

Gaber, J. (2007). *Spontaneous Emergence Model for Pervasive Environments* (pp. 1–4). IEEE Proceedings of Globecom Workshops.

Georgantas, N., Mokhtar, S. B., Bromberg, Y. D., Issarny, V., Kalaoja, J., Kantarovitch, J., et al. (2005). The Amigo Service Architecture for the Open Networked Home Environment, *IEEE Proc. of 5th Working IEEE/IFIP Conference on Software Architecture,* (pp. 295-296).

Georgeff, M. P. (1984). A Theory of Action for MultiAgent Planning, *Proceedings of 1984 conference of the American Association for Artificial intelligence.* (pp. 121-125).

Hommel, B., Musseler, J., Aschersleben, G., & Prinz, W. (2001). The theory of event coding (TEC): A framework for perception and action planning. *The Behavioral and Brain Sciences, 24*(5), 849–878. doi:10.1017/S0140525X01000103

Hyman, J. (2006). Three fallacies about action. *In Proceedings of the 29th International Wittgenstein Symposium.* (pp. 137-163).

Moya, F., & Lopez, J. C. (2002). SENDA: An Alternative to OSGi for Large Scale Domotics. *In proceedings of IEEE Networks Conference.* (pp. 165-176).

Moya, F., Villa, D., Villanueva, F. J., Barba, J., Rincon, F., Lopez, J. C., & Dondo, J. (2007). Embedding Standard Distributed Object-Oriented Middlewares in Wireless Sensor Networks. *Wireless Communications and Mobile Computing Journal, 12*(3), 315–327.

OSGi Alliance. (2006). OSGi Service Platform: Core Specification, version 4.0.1, www.osgi.org.

Pokahr, A., Braubach, L., & Lamersdorf, W. (2005). Jadex: A BDI Reasoning Engine, R. *Multi-Agent Programming, 3*(3), 149–174. doi:10.1007/0-387-26350-0_6

Preuveneers, D., Jan, V. B., Wagelaar, D., Georges, A., Rigole, P., & Clerckx, T. (2004). Towards an Extensible Context Ontology for Ambient Intelligence. *In proceedings of second european symposium in ambient. Intelligence,* 148–159.

Rao, A. S., & Georgeff, M. P. (1991). Modeling rational agents within a BDI-architecture, *Proceedings of the 2nd International Conference on Principles of Knowledge Representation and Reasoning (KR'91)*.10 (3), (pp. 473-484).

Subramonian, V., & Xiang, G. (2004). Middleware Specification for Memory-Constrained Networked Embedded Systems, *In proceedings of IEEE Real-Time and Embedded Technology and Applications Symposium (RTAS)*. (pp. 306-313).

Villa, D., Villanueva, F. J., Moya, F., Rincon, F., Barba, J., & Lopez, J. C. (2006). Embedding a Middleware for Networked Hardware and Software Objects. *In proceedings of Advances in Grid and Pervasive Computing.*(pp. 567-576).

Villa, D., Villanueva, F. J., Moya, F., Rincon, F., Barba, J., & Lopez, J. C. (2007). Minimalist Object Oriented Service Discovery Protocol for Wireless Sensor Networks. *In proceedings of Advances in Grid and Pervasive Computing.* (pp. 472-483).

Villanueva, F. J., Villa, D., Moya, F., Rincon, F., Barba, J., & Lopez, J. C. (2007). *Lightweight Middleware for Seamless HW-SW Interoperability, with Applications to Wireless Sensor Networks, In proceedings of IEEE Design* (pp. 1042–1047). Automation and Test in Europe.

Villanueva, F. J., Villa, D., Moya, F., Santofimia, M. J., & Lopez, J. C. (2009). A Framework for advanced home service design and Management. *IEEE Transactions on Consumer Electronics*, *55*(3), 1246–1253. doi:10.1109/TCE.2009.5277984

Wooldridge, M. (2000). *Reasoning about Rational Agents. Intelligent robotics and autonomous agents series 16*. The MIT Press.

Chapter 6
Variability in Ambient Intelligence:
A Family of Middleware Solution

Lidia Fuentes
University of Malaga, Spain

Nadia Gamez
University of Malaga, Spain

Pablo Sanchez
University of Cantabria, Spain

ABSTRACT

The development of Ambient Intelligence (AmI) software applications implies dealing with a wide variety of devices, which runs in different environments. These applications also target a wide range of end-users, with different needs and requirements. Software Product Lines are a relatively modern software paradigm whose main goal is to offer techniques and mechanisms to the systematic development of applications belonging to a domain with a high degree of variability. Therefore, the application of a Software Product Line for the construction of a family of middleware platforms for AmI applications should help to deal with the variability inherent to this domain. The first step when constructing a Software Product Line (SPL) is to create some sort of model which specifies the variability of the domain the SPL targets. This model is then used as basis for configuring and automatically creating specific products. The aim of this article is to highlight the complexity of managing different types of variability during the development of applications for AmI environments. A generic process for automatically generating a custom configuration of a middleware variant is also presented.

INTRODUCTION

Ambient Intelligence (AmI) represents a new generation of computing environments equipped with a wide range of small devices and appliances present everywhere, available for everyone and at all times (Weiser, 1991). AmI technologies are mainly based on the combination of concepts from ubiquitous and pervasive computing

DOI: 10.4018/978-1-60960-549-0.ch006

(Pervasive, 2003) and the production of software embedded in everyday objects and devices. AmI applications have to deal with a wide variety of devices ranging from mobile phones and PDAs with medium capacities to sensors, actuators, consumer electronics and wearable devices (Pervasive, 2003) with critical resource limitations. These devices are networked and operate across highly heterogeneous computing environments in terms of network access types, typically consisting of wireless (e.g. WiMAX, WBRO, etc.), cellular (e.g. UMTS, GSM, GPRS, etc.) and short/medium range (e.g. Bluetooth, Wifi, UMB, etc.) systems. Middleware platforms could play a key role in hiding the complexity and heterogeneity of lightweight devices connected via high-speed networks, by providing specific services (e.g. location, context-awareness, security, etc.) to support and to facilitate AmI applications development.

The large number of heterogeneous devices and the diversity of communication technologies and AmI application requirements make it unfeasible to construct a single middleware platform, using traditional single software engineering techniques, which can be deployed and configured on all kind of devices and providing services that fulfil the requirements of all AmI applications. Instead, the developer of a middleware platform for AmI applications should create *families* of middleware platforms that can be instantiated and customised according to the different hardware and software constraints imposed by both devices and applications. Thus, the application of a Software Product Line (SPL) approach would be very useful to deal with the different requirements of either devices or applications in terms of commonalities and variabilities defining a family of AmI middleware platforms (Apel & Böhm, 2005). Since device resource constraints (e.g. in memory, processor throughput, etc.) is an important consideration in AmI, only a specific middleware platform configuration that is suitable for the device capacities must be installed. Resource limitation is not the only variable dimension that AmI developers have

to deal with however. Other factors can be identified relating to the communication protocols supported, the kind of interfaces or the high diversity of operating systems as well as the different APIs available for each operating system delivered for specific devices. Not all the devices support the same version of a given operating system, and not all the APIs are available for all kinds of devices. Middleware for AmI should benefit from the SPL approach in terms of configurability, reusability and evolution management (White & Schmidt, 2008). AmI applications will benefit from a highly-optimized and custom middleware, which will offer appropriate services consistent with device configuration and resource constraints.

In a family of middleware for AmI, the product-line architecture (PLA) is common for all the product members. The PLA of the middleware is composed of different fine-grained services creating domain (AmI) specific features, either common or variable features. So, a first step towards the definition of a middleware for AmI product line consists of specifying the feature model specific for the AmI domain. Feature modeling analyzes commonality and variability from a domain perspective (Lee, 2002). Then, a feature model allows specifying where the variability is in independently of the core asset, and enables reasoning about all the different possible configurations. A feature model for the AmI domain will help to specify and automatically derive different configurations of middleware tailored according to a high diversity of constraints (e.g. device capacities or application requirements).

The aim of this paper is to highlight the complexity of managing different types of variability during the development of applications for AmI environments. The inherent variability of the AmI domain will be characterized by feature models. These feature models will enable different versions of a specific middleware for AmI to be generated, with the minimum number of services being required either by the devices and/or applications. A generic process for automatically generating a custom configuration of a middleware variant is also presented. Several benefits are obtained using an SPL to define a family of middleware for AmI. The responsibility of device users to carry out device and application configuration is drastically reduced, decreasing user headaches and runtime errors. Moreover, since the management of the intrinsic variability of the AmI domain is tackled at the middleware level, it can be ensured that only the correct version of middleware services will be invoked by final applications. Hence, the development and deploying tasks of AmI applications is also simplified, since the middleware hides the device variability complexity and provides custom-made services.

CHARACTERIZING THE VARIABILITY OF THE AMI DOMAIN

A Software Product Line aims to create the infrastructure for the rapid production of software systems for a specific market segment. These software systems are similar and therefore share a subset of common features, but variations may also be present. The main goal of a Software Product Line is to construct, as automatically as possible, specific products after a set of choices and decisions have been adopted, specifying which variants must be included in a specific product.

Product Line Software Engineering (PLSE) exploits commonality and manages variability among products from a domain perspective (Lee, 2002). Consequently, adopting this approach seems to be appropriate in order to encompass all the variability that we found in middleware for AmI applications. In the feature-oriented approach, commonalities and variabilities are analyzed in terms of features. A feature is any prominent and distinctive concept or characteristic that is visible to various stakeholders (Lee, 2002). The features can be organized into a feature model that represents all possible products of a software product line. Feature model-

ing analyzes commonality and variability from a domain perspective. Commonalities are modelled as mandatory features and variabilities are modeled as variable features which are classified as alternative or optional features. Furthermore, for each variable feature, feature dependency analysis can identify dependencies between features.

As we mentioned before, a feature model can be used as input for generating an architectural representation of a product line. Thus, in this section firstly, we detail the feature model that will be used as input for the middleware product family architecture later depicted in the last subsection.

AmI Middleware Feature Model

In order to instantiate a particular product of the middleware family it is necessary to know all the features that influence the specific configuration of the middleware that fits the specific characteristics of each device. Nevertheless not only device capacities, especially the limited hardware and software resources, affect the configuration and instantiation of a middleware. The next list describe the main groups of features that must be considered when configuring a deploying a specific instance of a middleware platform for Ambient Intelligence.

- **Device driven features**. As already mentioned, the distinctive characteristics of each device strongly influence the size and the implementation version of the middleware services, in view of the hardware and software technologies available for a given device.
- **Applications driven features**. Final applications may require only a subset of the available middleware services. Considering the resource limitations of AmI devices, only those services that will be invoked by final applications will be part of a specific middleware configuration.

- The **Network Driven Features**. These features include the logical topologies used to organize the nodes and specific protocols used to exchange data and control information inside the network.

Our middleware feature model is designed using a feature modeling tool we have constructed, called Hydra (2009), which also provides a constraint solver to automatically infer the minimum set of low-level features that must be selected to obtain a specific middleware.

Since the idea is to define a highly flexible configuration process, the middleware for AmI must be structured in fine-grained components (Services in Figure 1) decoupled from a base infrastructure (Microkernel in Figure1). The basic services are a mandatory feature but the extra services are optional. The lookup of remote applications and the discovery of distant devices are examples of basic services. Extra services will be instantiated only when required by an application (e.g. coodination, topology control, data fusion, etc.).

Regarding the device driven features, the type of device, and the radio technology are all hardware resources, and operating system and APIs are software features. In this case, the user must specify, before deploying the middleware platform in a specific device, the following features:

- The type of device where the middleware will be instantiated.
- The operating system used by the device.
- The APIs that can be used develop particular services of the middleware, for a specific device with a certain operating system.
- The radio technology defines the communication interfaces and protocols available for each device.

The Device Type feature defines the different types of devices that are normally used in AmI environments. The list of devices is very heterogeneous and will continue to evolve, so this feature must to be updated to incorporate new types of devices. As part of the device type, a set of attributes is defined to store the resource constraints characteristic of each device (e.g. memory, processor, battery, etc.). Since these kinds of devices are very limited in capacity, the configuration process will consider the device resource values of these attributes to instantiate the configuration middleware minimum size.

AmI devices can be classified into three categories, as show in Figure 2: high capacity devices, sensors and embedded devices (or consumer electronics, those found in objects such in an intelligent washing machine.). Furthermore, within each of these categories there are many types of devices. High capacity devices are, for

Figure 1. Middleware Feature Model

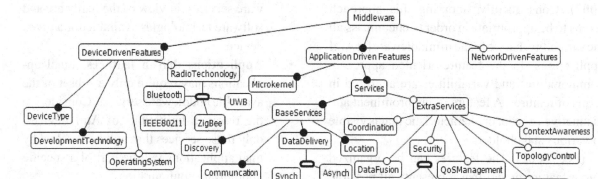

instance, Smartphones, GPS devices or PDAs. In sensors we can distinguish between several categories of nodes, as the TinyOS motes or the spots of Sun Microsystems. Also the sensors can be classified by means of their provided sensing units, their mobility capacities and their roles. The role denotes the responsibility of a node and has influence in the middleware configuration process: ordinary (source nodes), cluster-head and sinks.

Another very important feature that has a strong influence on selecting the correct implementation of middleware services is the operating system. There is considerable variability in the operating systems available, which makes the developer's task more difficult, since different versions of the same service must be delivered and the correct one must be selected for a given device and op-

erating system. Different operating systems, with their respective distribution and versions, are suitable for different devices. In the feature model are shown the most representative systems (Figure 3), with some distributions (Symbian, Windows Mobile, Android, Tiny OS, …).

Like the operating system, another important software feature is the development technology, which captures the variability of the available APIs for every version of each distribution of an operating system. In the partial feature model shown in Figure 4, only a subset of the existing possibilities of programming languages is depicted: Java, Symbian C++ and the two different ways of implementing applications in the Windows Mobile operating system: the "managed" mode in .NET and the native mode in C++. In all current

Figure 2. Device Type Sub-Features

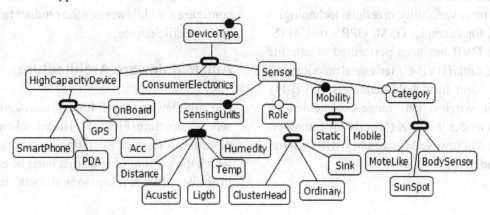

Figure 3. Operating System Sub-Features

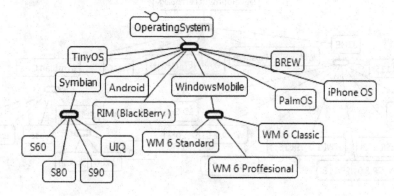

operating systems the applications can be implemented using Java (J2ME), in which case each API can be different depending on the device distributor (Nokia, Sony, ...) with the variability that this involves. J2ME has many libraries available, for example MIDP, PDA or Bluetooth. In the case of Symbian, the applications can be implemented using several programming languages. In the case of Symbian C++ APIs do not depend on the device distributor as happens with J2ME.

Finally, another feature where the variability is very high is in the radio technologies that can be used in the device. We can distinguish between short or medium range communications and long range. The first are mainly wifi, infrared, bluetooth, rfid, zigbee and UWB. In long range communication, we distinguish between cellular technologies, Digital Video Broadcast (DVB), and wireless long range communications. Within these categories we found more variability, in cellular technologies we have, for example, GSM, GPRS or UMTS. Also, the DVB has been performed in satellite (DVB-S), cable (DVB-C), terrestrial broadcasting (DVB-T), and hand held terminals (DVB-H). Finally, in wireless long range communication we can consider WiMAX (Worldwide Interoperability for Microwave Access) and WiBRO (Wireless Broadband).

Of course, the different features identified may not be free of dependencies and interactions between them. Typical constraints between features are: (1) *dependencies*, the selection of a feature implies that one or more features must also be selected. For instance, if a wireless communication system is selected as a service, at least one protocol for wireless communication must also be selected); (2) *mutual exclusion;* the selection of one feature means that other features can not be selected. For instance, if a device with low memory is selected, this would automatically disable all the features that imply high memory consumption, such as security service. The elicitation and specification of these constraints is crucial if we want to avoid ill-formed configurations of specific products being created.

After developing the feature model we can observe that the variability of AmI devices can not be neglected and it is not an easy task to configure a middleware of the product family for each specific device.

AmI Middleware Architecture

Our middleware will follow a microkernel plus services structure (Figure 5). The microkernel term describes a form of operating system design in which the amount of code that must be executed in privileged mode is kept to an absolute minimum

Figure 4. Development Technologies Sub-Features

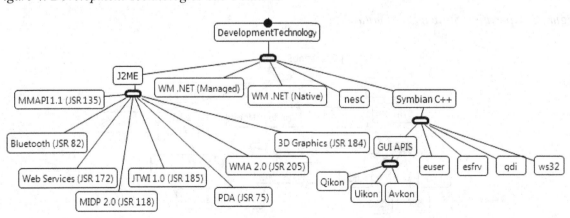

(Greenwood, 2008). As a consequence, the rest of the services are built as independent modules that are plugged and executed by the kernel. In this way, we obtain a more modular and reusable system. Furthermore, we distinguish between mandatory base services and the rest of the optional extra services that will be added according to the applications requirements.

Using the feature model as input, we will design the architecture of our middleware product family. One of the most suitable paradigms that give support to a high degree of configurability in the middleware family, is the event-based composition (Pohl, 2007; Wang, 2008). Our middleware follows an event driven composition scheme that decouples services from the microkernel, and also from the applications. Similarly to other well-known event-based platforms (Heinzelman, 2004) we have chosen the publish/subscribe communication scheme. Using this scheme the applications will subscribe to events that will be published by the services. Since in AmI standardization is important, we have followed the Data Distribution Service (DDS) specification (OMG, 2008). DDS is a specification that OMG standardizes to publish/subscribe middleware. DDS defines a set of standard interfaces for event subscription and publication. These standard interfaces are implemented as part of our microkernel. So, the services and the applications use these interfaces to publish and subscribe

events, which in the case of DDS are identified as topics.

Furthermore, before running an application, during the middleware instantiation process, the properties and constraints about the device, application and networks requirements have to be known. With this information and with the architectural description of the application, the particular middleware architecture of the middleware family must be instantiated.

As mentioned previously, due to resource limitations the particular middleware instantiated has to be the minimum possible that fits the constraints. For example, if the device type is a sensor, only the middleware services which are really needed must be instantiated. In this case, the encryption service may not be necessary, so the specific middleware will not provide this service. Furthermore, only the correct implementation of the services, considering either the hardware and software infrastructure has to be instantiated. For example, a traditional encryption algorithm, such RSA, does not work in sensor networks, so another type of algorithms will be instantiated instead. Additionally, many sensor networks work with TinyOS, and all the middleware components, the microkernel and services that have to be instantiated must run with TinyOS. So, the correct versions of the microkernel, and each service is chosen during the automatic generation of one middleware configuration (e.g. the TinyOS version).

Figure 5. AmI Middleware Architecture

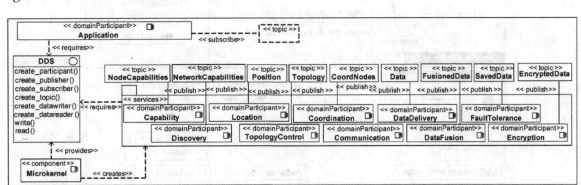

INSTANTIATING THE AMI MIDDLEWARE FOR SPECIFIC DEVICES AND APPLICATIONS

A Software Product Line Engineering process is comprised of two phases: *Domain Engineering* and *Application Engineering* (see Figure 6) (Pohl, 2005). Domain Engineering deals with the creation of the infrastructure or Product-Line Architecture, which will enable the rapid, or even automatic, construction of specific software systems within the family of products an SPL covers. Application Engineering is concerned with the engineering of specific products or single software systems using the infrastructure previously created at the Domain Engineering level. Ideally, Application Engineering should be as automated as possible, i.e. the user should only specify which features want to include in a specific product, then a tool would validate it is possible to construct a correct and safe product with this selection of features, and after that, the specific product would be automatically generated using the software assets created during domain engineering.

Figure 6 shows the application of an SPL Engineering process to the development of middleware platforms for AmI applications. The different elements of this process are described below:

1. First of all, variability of the family of products to be developed is analysed and specified using a feature model (Czarnecki, 2005). In our case, the feature model presented in a previous section specifies the different kinds of variations that can exist between different middleware platforms due to: (1) the platform being deployed in devices with different characteristics; and (2) if there are more or less services included in the middleware platform. The feature model for middleware platforms plus the constraints between features (i.e. dependencies and interactions between features) represent the 'variability specification', or, using SPL terminology, the *problem space*.

2. Once variability of a family of products has been identified, engineers must design and develop a system that supports this variability, i.e. software engineers and architects must design and implement a flexible architecture that enables its customisation,

Figure 6. SPL Engineering process applied to AmI middleware platforms

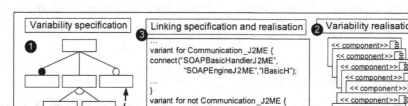

including and excluding functionality and components as required. Different mechanisms are available for this purpose, from low-level mechanisms such as conditional compilation or the use of parameterisation or generics to more high-level mechanisms, such as the decomposition of a middleware platform into a microkernel structure plus a set of pluggable components that may be optional or variable services. As a result of this process, a reference architecture and implementation are obtained. This reference implementation contains all the components that are required for implementing any product covered by the SPL family. It should be noticed that this reference implementation is not runnable per se, i.e., it must configured and instantiated before it can be executed. The unique required task for obtaining a specific product from this reference implementation would be to appropriately instantiate and connect these components according to the features that must be included in such a specific product. This step represents 'variability realisation', or, using SPL terminology, the *solution space*.

3. The connection between a feature model and a reference architecture is rarely a trivial one-to-one mapping. For instance, the feature *Operating System* that appears in Figure 3 will probably influence all components of the SPL implementation, because a different version of each component will be most likely to be created for each operating system and API. Thus, when a specific operating system is selected (e.g. Symbian), we must ensure that the Symbian compliant version of each component is used to build the product (e.g. a specific middleware service). Different SPL tools and languages, such as pure::variants (Beuche, 2003), Gears (Krueger, 2007), fmp2rsm (Czarnecki, 2005b) or VML (Loughran, 2008; Sánchez,

2008) support the definition of mappings between a feature model and a reference architecture/implementation, often called *family model*. In Figure 3 we can see a piece of VML code. This mapping usually specifies which actions must be performed when a certain feature is selected. These actions range from generating a certain part of the code of a component to the setting of certain parameters or inclusion/exclusion of certain components from a compilation unit.

For instance, if the tinyOS mote is selected as device type, this means that generating a middleware platform with a small size is necessary. In this way, a precompiler directive called *binarySize* might be set to *MINIMUM* in order to exclude, by conditional compilation, all the non-strictly required parts of the implementation component. This kind of rule represents the mapping between *problem space* and *solution space*, and is the basis for the automatic derivation of specific products at the application engineering level, as is explained in the next two points.

4. Once the domain engineering infrastructure or SPL infrastructure has been created, specific products, i.e. middleware platforms for specific devices with a customised number of services, can be automatically derived. The first step in this process is the creation of a well-formed configuration that specifies which features must be included in the specific product being engineered. In our case, the selection of features will be firstly influenced by the device where the middleware platform is going to be deployed.

For instance, if the device only has a textual interface, then the features related to the Graphical User Interface will be automatically disabled. If the device only supports a specific operating system, the corresponding feature is automatically selected. Then, different features are selected according to the application requirements. This feature will be most likely to be related with the services to be included in the middleware. It should be noticed that the feature selection imposed by the device and the feature selection demanded by the application that uses the middleware, or even by the user, may conflict. For instance, a device with limited processor capabilities would not be able to run security services that imply complex encryption algorithms. This kind of conflict involves trade-offs that must be negotiated depending on whether end-users prefer to use better and probably more expensive devices or they prefer to use cheaper devices but at the expense of certain application requirements. Different techniques can be used for creating configurations, from using a simple feature modelling tool, such as fmp (Czarnecki, 2005b) to creating dedicated wizards or even Domain-Specific Languages (DSLs) (Santos, 2008).

5. Finally, using the configuration created in the previous step, and the mapping created in Step 3, SPL tools, such as *pure::variants*, are able to automatically generate the specific product that corresponds to the desired configuration. This is achieved by interpreting and executing the rules that specify the mapping between the feature model and the reference implementation. As a result of executing these rules, the components that will comprise the specific middleware platform, plus their appropriate instantiation, initialisation, configuration and compilation files are automatically obtained.

DISCUSSION

Recently a systematic review about SPL applied to mobile middleware has been published (Morais, 2009). Some of our previous works (Fuentes, 2005; Fuentes, 2006; Fuentes, 2008) have been selected for inclusion in this review. This review demon-

strates that the idea of applying a SPL approach to the development of middleware platforms for AmI applications is a novel and interesting idea, since the goal of the authors is to construct a family of middleware platforms for mobile devices using a SPL approach. Nevertheless, few approaches have been found for this systematic review and many of them are in the very early (developmental) stages.

Apart from our previous work, they have selected four different approaches, which we summarize here. In (Lee, 2007) a SPL process for the configuration of specific products using feature models is presented. The goal and the function of the process are similar to ours, but Lee (2007) presents a systematic process, i.e. products must be manually constructed after configuration following a set of well-defined rules. Instead, we aim to construct an automatic one where these rules are automatically executed by a computer. Furthermore, the middleware and the process are only applied to the different roles that node sensors can play, so it would be a small and particular case of our approach.

Apel and Bohm (2005) share our objective of designing a lightweight, device-independent and customizable family of middleware platforms, which is able to run on heterogeneous hardware and software. They use mixins as design and implementation mechanism for building flexible architectures and they work focuses on variability realisation or *solution space*. Instead, we address all the SPL process, paying special attention to the configuration process, in order to automate it as much as possible. In Apel and Bohm, the construction of specific middleware platforms according to a given configuration would be the responsibility of the application programmer, which is in charge of selecting the adequate components and mixins and customizing, instantiating initializing and connecting them. In our approach, this process is completely automatic. Finally, Apel and Bohm (2005) focus exclusively on the communication services, proposing to add services such as security or fault tolerance as future work, being them already considered in our work.

PLIMM (Zhang, 2007) is a *Product Line enabled Intelligent Mobile Middleware*, in which Frame based on SPL techniques is applied to help manage the contexts. In PLIMM the context modelling is performed using ontologies and the authors propose an SPL process for the evolution of the ontology. Nevertheless, they do not propose a process to configure and customize the middleware as we do. The variability of the services and devices that an AmI middleware has to deal with is simply not considered.

Finally, in (Krishna, 2006) the authors present how context-specific techniques can be applied to the design of AmI middleware whose architecture is based on product lines, but they do not design a family of middleware platforms using a SPL approach. They show a toolkit for automating context specific specializations, allowing already developed middleware to be customized; but they do not propose a new middleware as we do. This process is based on some code annotations that indicate the variations points of the middleware platform. These annotations have to be specified by hand. They only automate the delivery of specialization but not the identification of specializations suitable for the PLA of a system. With our process however, given only the application restriction,

device constraint and the network characteristics can automatically generate the minimum valid configuration that works properly.

Table 1, shows a summary of the comparative study of the related works appearing in the systematic review previously commented. The most relevant advantages of our approach is the complete automatic process for the configuration and instantiation of a particular customized middleware and the implementation of the services that this middleware provides in several platforms as Android, TinyOS, Java Sun Spot and J2ME. However, new or different platforms may be included. In order to do that our process and tools help to add new features for the new platform but obviously, this task must to be realized by a developer with some knowledge about SPL and feature modelling.

CONCLUSION

In conclusion, the adoption of an SPL engineering approach for the development of middleware platforms for AmI applications requires a considerable investment for creating the Product-Line Architecture, or domain-engineering infrastructure. However, as the development effort of specific middleware platforms is drastically reduced

Table 1. Summary of Software Product Lines Applied to Mobile Middleware.

	Configuration Process	Variability Managed	Services Developed	Variability Technology	Implementation State
Lee	Systematic manual method	Node sensor roles	None	Feature models	None
Apel and Bohm	Configuration phase steps defined	All kind of variability	Communication related services	Mixins	Ful implementation in C++
Zhang	Process for evolution	All kind of variability	Adaptation related services	Frame based	Early stage
Khrisna	Toolkit for Automating Context-Specific Specializations	All kind of variability	None	Feature oriented	None
Our Approach	Automatic configuration process	All kind of variability: Applications, Networks and Device variability	Location, Monitoring, Context-Aware, Data Fusion,...	Feature models	Implementation of many of the services in several platforms: Android, TinyOS, Sun Spot, J2ME

(practically just a configuration is required), as soon as more and more middleware platforms are instantiated, the construction of the SPL will become cost-effective and generate benefits. Since each device used in an AmI application is most likely to require its own version of the middleware platform, the adoption of an SPL Engineering approach for the construction of these middleware platforms is clearly justified.

REFERENCES

Apel, S., & Böhm, K. (2005). Towards the Development of Ubiquitous Middleware Product Lines. In ASE'04 SEM Workshop, volume 3437 of LNCS.

Beuche, D. (2003). Variant management with pure::variants. Technical report, pure-systems GmbH.

Czarnecki, K. et al (2005b). Fmp and fmp2rsm: eclipse plug-ins for modeling features using model templates. OOPSLA Companion 200-201.

Czarnekci, K. (2005). Staged Configuration through Specialization and Multi-Level Configuration of Feature Models. Software Process Improvement and Practice, special issue on. *Software Variability: Process and Management*, *10*(2), 143–169.

Fuentes, L., et al. (2005). An Aspect-Oriented Ambient Intelligence Middleware Platform, In Proc. 3rd Int. Work. on Middleware for Pervasive and Ad-Hoc Computing.

Fuentes, L., et al. (2006). Combining Components, Aspects, Domain Specific Languages and Product lines for Ambient Intelligent Application Development, Proc. of International Conference on Pervasive Computing, Ireland.

Fuentes, L., & Gámez, N. (2008). A Feature Model of an Aspect-Oriented Middleware Family for Pervasive Systems, In Proc. AOSD Workshop on Next Generation Aspect Oriented Middleware, 11-16, Belgium.

Greenwood, P. et al (2008). Reference architecture. AOSDEurope NoE Public Documents (AOSD-Europe-ULANC-37).

Heinzelman, W. B. (2004). Middleware to support sensor network applications. *IEEE Network*, *18*(1), 6–14. doi:10.1109/MNET.2004.1265828

Hydra (2009). Hydra Feature Modelling. http://caosd.lcc.uma.es/spl/hydra

Krishna, A. (2006). Context-Specific Middleware Specialization Techniques for Optimizing Software Product-Line Architectures. *ACM SIGOPS Operating Systems Review*, *40*(4), 205–218. doi:10.1145/1218063.1217955

Krueger, C. W. (2007). Biglever Software Gears and the 3-tiered SPL Methodology. In OOPSLA '07: Companion to the 22nd ACM SIGPLAN conference on Object oriented programming systems and applications companion, 844–845, New York, NY, USA, ACM.

Lee, K., et al. (2002). Concepts and guidelines of feature modeling for product line software engineering. Number 2319 in LNCS, 62–77. Springer-Verlag.

Lee, W., et al. (2007). Product Line Approach to Role-Based Middleware Development for Ubiquitous Sensor Network, In Proc. 7th IEEE Int. Conf. on Computer and Information Technology, 1032-1037, Japan.

Loughran, N., et al. (2008). Language Support for Managing Variability in Architectural Models. Proc. of the 7th International Symposium on Software Composition, LNCS 4954:36-51, Budapest.

Morais, Y., et al. (2009). A Systematic Review of Software Product Lines Applied to Mobile Middleware, In Proc. 6th Int. Conf. on Information Technology: New Generations, USA.

OMG (2008). OMG Data Distribution Service (DDS) for real-time systems, v1.2.

Pervasive (2003). Centre for Pervasive Computing. http://www.pervasive.dk.

Pohl, C. et al (2007). Survey of existing implementation techniques with respect to their support for the practices currently in use at industrial partners, AMPLE Project deliverable D3.1.

Santos, A. L., et al. (2008). Automated Domain-Specific Modeling Languages for Generating Framework-Based Applications. Proc. of the 12th Int. Software Product Line Conference, Limerick.

Wang, M. M. (2008). Middleware for wireless sensor networks: A survey. *Journal of Computer Science and Technology.*, *23*(3), 305–326. doi:10.1007/s11390-008-9135-x

Weiser, M. (1991). The computer for the Twenty-First Century. *Scientific American*, 165.

White, J., & Schmidt, D. C. (2008). Model-Driven Product-Line Architectures for Mobile Devices, Proceedings of the 17th Annual Conference of the International Federation of Automatic Control, Seoul.

Zhang, W., et al. (2007). Product Line Enabled Intelligent Mobile Middleware, In Proc. 12th IEEE Int. Conf. on Engineering Complex Computer Systems, 148-160.

Chapter 7
Motorola's Experiences in Designing the Internet of Things

Andreas Schaller
Motorola, Germany

Katrin Mueller
Motorola, Germany

ABSTRACT

The Internet of Things will enable connectivity for virtually any physical object that potentially offers a message, and will affect every aspect of life and business. This article looks at the concepts and technologies in three application areas that Motorola is contributing to now and in the coming years.

MOTOROLA'S POSITION IN THE INTERNET OF THINGS

In just 20 years, the Internet has fundamentally changed the way we live, learn, do business and entertain ourselves. What makes the Internet so revolutionary is that it provides a standard way for people to connect anywhere around the world. Today's Internet connects people to people, providing information in text, video, sound and other formats intended for use by people. The next step is to Internet-enable physical objects—connecting

people with things and even things with things. The Internet of Things will enable connectivity not just between people and their computing devices, but between actual, everyday things. By enabling connectivity for virtually any physical object that can potentially offer a message, the Internet of Things will affect every aspect of life and business in ways that used to be the realm of fantasy—or even beyond fantasy (Bullinger et al., 2007). This article looks at the concepts and technologies in three application areas that Motorola is contributing to now and in the coming years.

DOI: 10.4018/978-1-60960-549-0.ch007

THE RETAIL SPACE

Overview of Motorola's Activities

Motorola's Enterprise Mobility group is addressing the Retail Space from three different directions: Supply Chain efficiency, associate effectiveness, and customer experience. Especially personalized shopping experience is converting browsing into buying customers by delivering tailored products and promotional information.

Motorola's Enterprise Mobility solutions transform the customer experience by leveraging personalized information and creating new shopping experiences by connecting customers and products seamlessly while increasing sales and brand loyalty for the retailer.

The goal is to provide the customer with (Motorola, 2008):

- Instant access to price and availability data via personal shopping systems
- Cross-sell and up-sell opportunities through target promotions (Micro Kiosks)
- Payment systems to put your customers in control of the checkout process to utilities checkout performance.

Figure 1. Future payment vision to utilities checkout performance

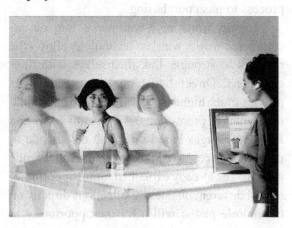

Things to Things Technologies

To increase the customer shopping experience "person to things" (P2T) communication and therefore the P2T interaction has to be improved. This can be achieved by leveraging any kind of data capturing technologies. Most of these technologies are already available in devices used in B2B application, such as 1D, 2D barcode scanning or RFID reading. For generating new kind of customer services in retail it will be necessary to transfer these technologies in mass markets devices. To ensure a fast adoption rate it is necessary to start with low hanging fruit technologies like barcode scanning by camera, which will become a "free" feature for mobile devices morphing into high end camera phones. The drawback for this approach is that traditional laser scanning of barcodes displayed on mobile devices can not be used due to incompatibility with the phone displays properties.

Another data capturing technology is near field communication (NFC), which is build on existing smart card technology used for loyalty, access, and payment contact less cards. In addition to the checkout service improvements, this technology can provide the customer with the opportunity to

Figure 2. Motorola SLVR NFC

85

Figure 3. Motorola PSA MC 17

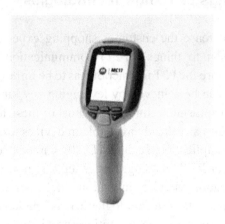

interact with different objects inside of the retail store by a simple touch. Therefore it will be possible for the customer to identify themselves in front of a micro kiosk or any kind of future e-paper display, which allows the retailer to offer a selection of new services like coupons downloading to the handset or personalized advertisement based on historic or current shopping.

The mayor difference between the barcode and the NFC approach is that in the barcode based scenario the personalized data are stored in the customer phone whereas in the NFC scenario a retail application managing the coupons is hosted on the phone. The pros of the second scenario are obvious as the retailer now owns a section of its customer e-wallet which can be adapted anytime to the customers needs over the air.

For many other data capturing technologies the infrastructure as well as the devices has to be established. The well known example for this technology is UHF RFID tagging. Whereas in the B2B space pallet and box tagging is increasing step by step and EPC B2B services and platforms are in the focus of many companies, it is still a long way to go to see enough item level tagging to allow handset makers to enlarge the integration of UHF readers from enterprise specific to customer mass market devices. In additional the business case for the future flat rate period

in the mass market driven wireless industry has not been clearly identified so far. As a result the telecom providers will not sponsor the UHF reader integration and the customer would have to pay a higher priced phone to purchase the UHF feature compared to a camera phone where the barcode feature scanning will be for free.

In addition to the data capturing technologies the wireless technologies used to transfer the information have to be mass market capable, too. In Europe these are primarily GSM, UMTS, BT, and finally WiFi based communication protocols. Most of the retailers require a penetration rate of 60+% to be used in retail. Therefore only GSM, BT, and SMS are currently available ubiquitous technologies to be built on. Especially as data flat rates are currently just appearing on the market, which offers internet connectivity opportunities for each customer inside of the retail store. Retailers can avoid creating complex databases and rely on publicly available information published by the manufacturer of the product.

New Benefits Opportunities and Next Steps

Motorola's retail customers have seen different benefits implementing MC 17 like self scanning approaches. In addition to the opportunity to completely dissolve queuing at cashiers for the people using self scanning devices, product information can be provided at any time during the shopping process to push purchasing.

Moving from an e-commerce into an m-commerce world, wireless technology allows the retailers to stronger link themselves with their customers. Direct 1-to-1 marketing campaigns provide much higher success rates than traditional mass market promotions. As a result SMS and PUSH messages based on RFID or barcode to personal devices have a positive impact on revenue growth. The already explained future opportunity to host different business applications directly on the mobile phone will offer the opportunity to

Figure 4. New shopping process flow in retail shops

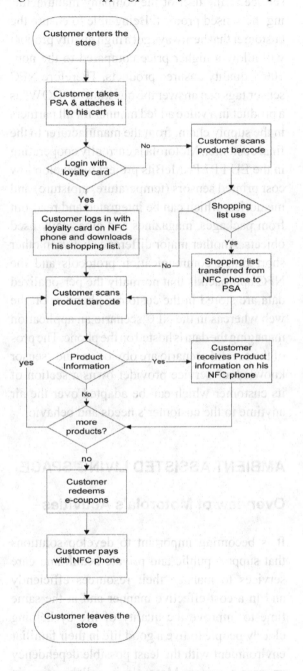

dramatically increase customer attention. Wireless push technology will be able to update the retailers' space on the mobile phone based on customers' behavior or other events like children's birthdays etc. In the future loyalty programs will be able to offer coupons for children which might be linked directly to specific products e.g. books

and cannot be used by the child to purchase e.g. a new video games. Finally contactless payment methods integrated into mobile devices will allow new check-out procedures in the retail floor. Especially for micro payments not requiring a printed receipt new concepts have to be developed for the different kind of retail shops e.g. apparel, supermarket, convenience store or petrol station.

To further define the next needs of the retail industry Motorola has joined the EU FP6 StoLPaN project, where a special retail track is focusing on the benefits of retailers using new wireless and in particular NFC technology. Despite the fact that some requirements of the retail industry are not quite in line with wireless providers' point of view, the targeted customer applications are common and wireless providers are eager to get into the B2C market. Upcoming visions will not only be based on over the air configurable smart cards integrated into the phone, but they also will be leveraging new mobilized wireless infrastructure integrated into different objects, e.g. point of sales terminals for loyalty payment integrated into shopping cart bars.

Cheap mass market data capturing technologies are a key for success in the retail industry. Therefore it will be interesting if low cost printed and disposable RFID tags will be drifting into the retail space. Not to replace UHF RFID tags in the supply chain but to offer customer services based on low cost, large area sensing data on item level. EPC numbers and sensor data access-able by millions of users will change the way people interact with perishable food and plants as well as with moisture or pressure sensitive goods.

Therefore the next-next application area for RFID tags will be driven by very low cost sensor networks. Whereas EPC identification tags are providing static content, sensor tags have a dynamic content based on the sensed environment. As printed electronics are especially useful for large area and disposable sensing a complete printed NFC sensor tag could be a game changer in many industries, as there is cold chain, e-health and

Figure 5. Wireless interactions in the retail shop (Stolpan, 2008)

Figure 6. Customer checking food quality

ambient assisted living or wellness applications. It is obvious that the sensing applications have to target non historical tracking use cases and focus on boundary or limit driven sensing solutions. As a sensing value depends always on the location or the object it is attached to, every sensing solution need to be wireless connected to provide the user with a correct answer based on the sensed value. This fact provides to opportunity to run different wireless service for analyzing the sensing world. The revenue in this scenario will be driven by the people access the sensor advisor and not by the tag and sensor cost. As printed NFC sensor tag will be available at the price lower than a SMS it might make more sense in the future to give the RFID sensor tags away for free and charge the advisory

service to the user or the company manufacturing the sensed product. Being able to ensure the customer that he always got a high quality product will allow a higher price compared to the non-100% quality ensured products. Therefore NFC sensor tags can answer the question of "HOW" is a product in a value added manner for all partners in the supply chain, from the manufacturer to the final customer. Motorola is currently cooperating in the EU FP7 PriMeBits project to develop low cost printed sensors (temperature, moisture) and memories, which can be integrated and read-out from packages, magazines and other daily used objects. Another major difference between other short range communication protocols and the NFC approach is that normally the personalized data are stored in the customer phone or on the web whereas in the NFC scenario an application managing the data is hosted on the phone. The pros of the second scenario are obvious as the "sensor knowledge" service provider owns a section of its customer which can be adapted over the air anytime to the customer's needs and behavior.

AMBIENT ASSISTED LIVING SPACE

Overview of Motorola's Activities

It is becoming important to develop solutions that support public and private health and care services to manage their resources efficiently and in a cost-effective manner and at the same time to improve the quality of life by helping elderly people to live a good life in their familiar environment with the least possible dependency on care services. Motorola is collaborating in the EU funded project PERSONA on a scalable open standard technological platform to enable a broad range of AAL Services for social inclusion, for support in daily life activities, for early risk detection, for personal protection from health and environmental risks and for support in mobility and displacements within the neighborhood/town.

Things to Things Technologies

ICT offers important means to address the challenges of independent living and inclusion by, for example, extending the time during which elderly people can live independently in their preferred environment and by providing a basis for a new generation of inclusive products and services that will help integrate people who are at risk of exclusion.

Relevant technologies supporting this trend are:

- Low cost printed sensors for environmental and user condition monitoring
- Smart textiles and other un-intrusive devices for user state monitoring
- User state discovery and interpretation based on history, activity and context
- Anticipation and forecast of user intention based on user state, needs, desires, daily work flow and interaction
- User state based content delivery, service composition and security
- Seamless service access
- Multi-protocol gateways and multi-radio communication management
- Multimodal interface and interaction

Technologies to be developed shall consider the health, psychological & well-being status of the elderly, needs, preferences, fears and concerns as well as the role in a social environment. In order to make the environment and services reactive to user needs, it is necessary that further research is addressed to intelligent and adaptable user profiling, user motivation and adaptable support, user's behavior learning and prediction.

New Benefits Opportunities and Next Steps

PERSONA targets four spaces to provide AAL services: the person, the home, the neighborhood

Figure 7. AAL spaces in PERSONA

and the village (Figure 7). Users live in spaces, many of which are enabled with AAL technology. These AAL Spaces render personalized AAL Services to each individual user (Müller et al., 2008).

The PERSONA project identified different scenarios and use cases and related business opportunities considering the user needs in the four spaces. Process has been supported by an intensive involvement of stakeholders at pilot sites in three European countries. In a refinement process 19 AAL services have been defined and specified out of 34 services:

1. Videoconference
2. Videochatting
3. Neighborhood virtual community
4. Personal Agenda
5. Shopping assistant
6. Cooking assistant
7. Nutritional Advisor
8. Home access control
9. Emergency assistance
10. Fall detection service (see Figure 8)
11. Remote rehabilitation Service
12. Personal Health Management
13. Teleconsultation
14. Outdoor Activity Monitorization Service
15. Assist abnormal situations
16. Behavioural Trends Risks
17. Plan a Journey
18. Guide to use transport
19. Outdoor user location tracking

The AAL services offer an atomic functionality to the user to cover a specific need. However

Figure 8. AAL service "fall detection" – illustration (PERSONA, 2008)

the services can be bundled to service packages. This modular approach provides flexibility.

For example, the service "Remote Rehabilitation" has a number of benefits for the elderly and the welfare organization contributing to the general concept of health and social integration of an elderly, as well as considering cost and quality aspects of the welfare system and therapies applied to elderly people. The PERSONA system is able to recognize any healthy risk during the rehabilitation and to inform the therapist. The PERSONA system ensures that more patients can be served at the same time using remote connections and control providing a potential for cost reduction. PERSONA helps the therapists to monitor the patients remotely to ensure the high quality standard in providing instruction and individual feedback to the patients. The personal real time feedback improves the customer relationship and the compliance to the therapy.

Backbone is the PERSONA architecture enabling the seamless integration and interaction between different spaces and the access on demand to services and their personalization. PERSONA proposes a physical and a logical architecture for AAL spaces (Furfari and Tazari, 2008). The abstract physical architecture treats an AAL space as a dynamic ensemble of networked nodes and the logical architecture abstracts all functionality not leading to context, input, or output events (or the direct processing of such events) as service. The proposed architecture is service oriented. The explicit distinction between context events, input

events, output events, and service requests and responses, the coherence of the resulting system is guaranteed based on a modeling of the basic data flow, which leads to the identification of a set of four communication buses, namely a context bus, an input bus, an output bus, and a service bus (Figure 9). The I-publisher and O-subscriber enable the interaction between the user and the environment. Die interaction can be voice based, visual, haptic or gesture. The context publisher provides environmental, personal based, temporary, spatial and social parameter to describe the user and activity situation.

A possible sort of context publisher is a synthesizer/reasoner that delivers aggregated/derived context events in terms of the context ontology. Such reasoners normally register to the context bus as both subscriber and publisher in order to use context events from lower levels and produce context events on a higher level. Apart from special-purpose reasoners that act as "experts" for deriving a specific (set of) context event(s), there can also be a general-purpose reasoner that can derive high-level context events from low-level ones based on a rule repository. Services and context are available on all system levels and nodes. The communication buses are realized by the PERSONA middleware. The input, output, and context buses work event-based and the service bus works call-based. The middleware enables the orchestration of the ensemble based on a set of specified ontologies, protocols, and strategies. The middleware is divided into three basic layers: the abstract connection layer (ACL), the SodaPop layer, and the PERSONA-specific layer.

In a next evaluation cycle the use cases illustrated in mock-ups and demonstrated to end user and welfare organizations as well as stakeholders. The feedback will be used to refine the services and interaction flow and result in an exemplary implementation of the references architecture. In a final step the implementation will be demonstrated in trials at pilot sites involved in the project.

Figure 9. PERSONA architecture

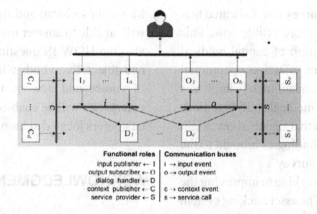

THE HOSPITAL SPACE

Overview of Motorola's Activities

Motorola T2TRC has developed a real-time asset tracking system to improve operation efficiency of modern workplaces by tracking mobile assets in real-time by applying wireless sensor networks (WSN). The real-time asset tracking system has been tried out in a real hospital environment to test out its effectiveness and how users accept the new ways of working using the system. The system reduces time to locate assets, and can as-

Figure 10. Hospital space

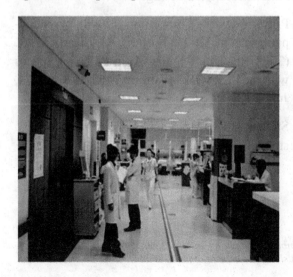

sist patient in times, and ultimately it improves quality of service by medical staff and improved utilization of the high-priced medical equipments. Further, we prove the effectiveness of WSN. These asset tracking technologies can also be deployed in heavy industry, shipyards, and logistics by locating parts or packages in time.

Things to Things Technologies

The major things-to-things technologies to aid hospital operation in tracking medical equipments are designing and implementing low-power and low-cost wireless sensor networks, location algorithms, software middleware and back-end applications. Motorola's asset tracking system systems uses 802.15.4 based MAC and ZigBee-like network protocols. To support low-power operation, the system utilizes low-power MAC and network protocols, and conserves power as much as possible. The asset only updates its location when there are meaningful movements. The sensor node itself filters all the transient movements.

New Benefits Opportunities and Next Steps

The asset tracking system brings many benefits to medical staff and hospital's administration. From post-trial survey, nurses stated that it takes less time to locate assets, and they can spend more time with patients. The survey also indicated that medical equipments are more visible now. This translates to high utilization of capital medical equipments, brings more effective operational efficiency to the hospital and ultimately improves the quality of service by medical staff. One finding worth mentioning is that nurses show slight resistance to the new technologies brought to the hospital in the post-trial survey.

Motorola T2TRC is working to improving the system in the two ways. The asset tracking system does not interface/communicate with medical equipments the nodes are tracking. The value of the system can greatly improve if nodes and medical equipments are communicating. However, there are many obstacles to accomplish. One of them is to standardize sensor nodes' interfaces to medical equipment, and we are currently working with medical equipment manufacturers to collect consensus on this interface issue. The other thing we are planning on doing is to extract valuable information by mining the movement pattern and utilization of the medical devices. As the hospital administration states, the mined information can give us and hospital administration information they have never seen before, such as patients' movement patterns, operational efficiency of each medical device, and so on.

SUMMARY

These are just three examples of what the Internet of Things could bring in the foreseeable future. The reality will likely become even more amazing as the Internet of Thing world evolves. New wireless solutions will upraise in the areas of ambient assisted living, retail and in the enterprise

space. The Internet of Things is one component of Motorola's vision, and future wireless solutions will be able to answer not only the WHAT IS but also the HOW IS questions about each product and object. Everybody will gain a higher freedom of choice and new business opportunities for enterprises will be enabled to provide services to customers located at home, on the go or at work.

ACKNOWLEDGMENT

Finally the authors would like to thank Byung-Yong Sung, South Korea, for his contribution to the hospital space.

REFERENCES

Bullinger, H.-J., & ten Hompel, M. (Eds.). (2007). *Internet der Dinge*. Berlin: Springer. doi:10.1007/978-3-540-36733-8

Motorola (2008) Motorola Inc, Payment Trends and Emerging Technologies for Retailers, Whitepaper, USA, 2008

Müller, K., Rumm, P., & Wichert, R. (2008). *PERSONA – ein EU-Projekt für Unabhängigkeit und Lebensqualität im Alter*. Berlin: Proceedings Ambient Assisted Living.

PERSONA EU Consortium. (2008), www.aal-persona.com, 2008. Furfari, F.; Tazari, M.-R. (2008) Realizing Ambient Assisted Living Spaces with the PERSONA Platform ERCIM News, 74, July 2008.

Stolpan (2008) StoLPaN EU Consortium., www.stolpan.com, Budapest, 2008.

Section 2

Chapter 8
On Ambient Information Systems:
Challenges of Design and Evaluation

William R. Hazlewood
Indiana University Bloomington, USA

Lorcan Coyle
University College Dublin, Ireland

ABSTRACT

The rise of the Internet, the ever increasing ubiquity of data, and its low signal-to-noise ratio have contributed to the problem of information overload, whereby individuals have access to more data than they can assimilate into meaningful and actionable information. Much of the success of Web 2.0 has been achieved after an effective tackling of this problem. Ambient Information Systems take the battle into the physical world by integrating information into the physical environment in a non-intimidating and non-overloading fashion. After two international workshops on Ambient Information Systems, we outline our vision for the field, consolidate a new definition, identify the key concerns of the research community, and issue a call to arms for future research.

INTRODUCTION

Various multimedia and Internet technologies have fueled strong cravings for information within our culture. Today the average American spends more time using various information communication technologies (ICTs), such as personal computers,

DOI: 10.4018/978-1-60960-549-0.ch008

cell phones, iPods, television, radio, etc., than any other activity throughout the day (Papper, 2005). About 30% of the day is spent with such ICT usage as the *sole* activity versus 20.8% spent on work activities, while an additional 39% of the day is spent using ICTs along with some other activity (ibid.). Such frequent use of ICT stems from an emergent desire to be constantly informed, and always aware of what is occurring around us.

Rhetorical reports supporting both the pros and cons of this hunger for information have been discussed, with some touting the advantages of being always connected versus others claiming a pseudo-attention deficit disorder emerging among the populace (Richtel, 2003). Regardless of the possible benefit or determent, the world is moving toward greater and greater quantities of information being made available; the real question is *how* we are going provide this level of information without overloading people's senses. Similar problems have been addressed on the Internet using information filtering, aggregation, and personalization (cf. Brusilovsky et al. 2007), but since Ambient Information Systems (AIS) are deployed physically in the world around us they require new thinking about how to handle information overload.

Recently there has been a distinct shift in the medium that people use to interact with broadband information from the exclusive domain of the desktop computer to the laptop, phone, and handheld video game console. As display and computing technology continue to become widely available, it is inevitable that users will be able to interact with information on everyday household devices that up to now have not had this capability. However, it is apparent that if broadband information is allowed to constantly interrupt in all aspects of our daily existence, our lives could become much more confusing and difficult. Smoothly integrating this overwhelming abundance of information into the environment around us in such a way that it is available in a calm, non-overwhelming, ambience is the central goal of AIS research. Successful AIS require consideration of information modeling and filtering techniques, the societal impact of information technology, the psychology of human attentiveness, user experience, and emerging technologies and materials. AIS is inspired by a number of earlier movements, and overlaps with many paradigms, including *ambient displays* (Wisneski et. al., 1998), *peripheral displays* (Matthews, 2007), *slow technology* (Hallnäs, 2001),

glanceable displays (Stasko, 2007), *informative art* (Holmquist, 2003), *unremarkable computing* (Tolmie, 2002), and *calm technology* (Weiser, 1995). AIS make use of existing artifacts and physical spaces to deeply integrate information so that is minimally distracting, but in some way perceivable even when not being directly concentrated upon. The classification of AIS are not restricted to the application of visual displays (as with peripheral displays), a particular level of efficiency (as with glanceable displays), scale of implementation (i.e. a single artifact vs. a large system of artifacts), or any particular type of hardware or software platform. Some recent AIS research investigates delivering information beyond the visual sense, using smell (Kaye, 2004), touch (Hemmert 2009), and sound (Hazlewood, 2008).

After two successful workshops on Ambient Information[1], with twenty oral presentations, two half-day discussion sessions, and engagement with a growing community of researchers, we have decided that it is time to consolidate the recent work of the community in this journal special issue. Our goal in this work is to use our engagement with the community to refine a definition of AIS, examine the issues that arise in terms of design and evaluation, and provide a set of challenges for furthering research in this domain. In the following sections, we structure our definition by stating and elaborating on the essential qualities of AIS. We follow by describing particular issues in both designing and evaluating this form of information delivery. We finish by laying out a series of grand challenges, which we feel are essential to further AIS research.

REFINING A DEFINITION OF AMBIENT INFORMATION SYSTEMS

It is tempting to try to understand AIS technologies by thinking about possible information devices that could exist exclusively in the periphery of attention, but in daily life our focus of attention shifts frequently and there is no clear distinction between the periphery and non-periphery. Various information sources are constantly competing and shifting in and out of our field of attention, so it is misleading to consider any artifact as being exclusively ambient or non-ambient. Instead, AIS distinguish themselves in that they are designed in such a way that they may facilitate at least some degree of *ambient interaction*. More specifically, ambient interaction is a *property*, which allows some technologies to continue to provide at least some level of information transfer when not in the center of a person's awareness. This property may, or may not, be expressed within a particular artifact's design. Accommodating ambient interaction requires that information be integrated into the environment in such a way that it blends in, and does not cause unmanageable amounts of distraction. The degree to which an information source can facilitate interaction from the periphery is tied directly to its ability to be non-intrusive, intuitive, and easily ignorable when more important matters need addressing.

Levels of Attention

Artifacts can facilitate ambient interaction at varying levels depending on their relationship with the environment and the perceiver. In terms of interaction, a person's field of perception can be broken down into three realms of attention: primary, secondary, and tertiary (shown in Figure 1), and different designs can facilitate interaction differently within these fields. For example, let us imagine an author writing a piece of text with a word processor. The word processor is designed to exist exclusively in the *primary* realm of attention while in use – it has no overt ambient character. By comparison, an instant messaging application, which might also be active, has some ambient capabilities and may facilitate interactions in the *secondary* realm of attention. As the instant messenger application sits on the edge of the screen one can subtly perceive the animations caused by

people logging in and out. From the state of the avatar associated with each of those people, one can gain a low-level understanding of the status of all the contacts. These cues can be perceived indirectly, and one does not have to break attention from the primary focus of the word processor to access some of its information. In this scenario, the *tertiary* realm of activity occurs away from the screen. There are people walking the halls, doors opening and closing, vehicle traffic outside, the smell of coffee, cold air from the vent, and the sunlight shining brightly through the window. These sensations provide information (useful or not) about the overall environment.

One of the goals of AIS research is to better understand these secondary and tertiary realms of attention so that we may make better use of them in the AIS design process. In order to reduce ambiguity over the concept of ambience we prefer not to consider AIS as existing exclusively in any one of these realms of attention. We prefer to think of good *ambientness* in a technology as its ability to shift forwards and backwards between these realms of attention. Some implementations may have features that enhance or reduce this ability. For example, the instant messenger application has a *limited* ambient capability. It can

Figure 1. Artifacts can facilitate different levels of ambient interaction, allowing them to exist in different realms of attention

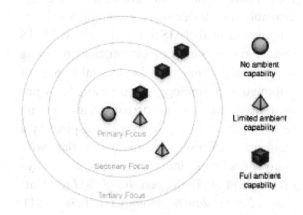

be used directly in the primary realm of attention, and can shift into the secondary realm and still provide a level of information. However, it is not clear that it can offer anything from the tertiary realm.

Integrated vs. Embedded

We believe it is important to understand a distinction between *embedding* information into, and *integrating* information with, the environment. Embedding involves attaching a new information artifact on, in, or next to an existing space or artifact. For example, Samsung has proposed a smart-fridge, which combines a tablet computer and a refrigerator. The tablet has been *embedded* into the refrigerator, and can provide useful information, but does not constitute *integration* since the original components can still be fully considered separately. In contrast, Figure 2 illustrates a project entitled "Open Source", which exemplifies full integration between information and the surrounding environment (Mehin et. al., 2004). The designers propose the use of a special color-changing concrete impregnated with a thermo-reactive pigment that reacts to digitally controlled heating elements hidden inside. This project suggests using this concrete to create a large community space that changes based on the activities taking place. In such a space it is

difficult for people to distinguish the community space from the information it delivers. From a person's perspective, the information is the space and vice versa.

Non-Invasive, Ignorable, and Low Cognitive Load

One of the major goals of AIS is to saturate the environment with pieces of potentially useful information without overwhelming people with more information than they can handle. To avoid overload, the information must be designed to be noticeable only when it is relevant to the observer, and nearly imperceptible otherwise. As an example, consider the History Tablecloth (Figure 3), which is an electronically enhanced tablecloth designed to cover a kitchen or dining room table and provide a since of how the space is utilized by illuminating in the places where objects are placed (Gaver et. al, 2006). When an object is placed on the tablecloth a visual halo appears that expands very slowly, and when items are removed the halo begins to fade away. The effect is that people are now able to see not only where things are, but also where they were, and people using the table over time can begin to understand more deeply how they make use of this particular surface in their home. The effect of the tablecloth is that people may notice the patterns it displays when they are

Figure 2. Open Source². A conceptual design for a community square in which color changing concrete is used to display information based on the activities taking place

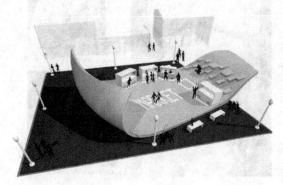

considering their use of their dining room table, but people are still able to carry on their typical dinner activities, and ignore the tablecloth's information if they do not find it of any use.

Another good example where information is provided at minimal cognitive cost to the observer can be found with Solestrom's SmartSwim UV Intensity Bikini (SmartSwim, 2008). This is a typical bikini adorned with special beads that turn dark based on the mount of UV rays they are subjected to. UV rays are the major factor that leads to harmful sunburns, not the brightness of the sun, as some may believe. In this example, the bikini wearer and those around her can be constantly aware of their risk of acquiring sunburn, with no distraction.

THE DESIGN OF AMBIENT INFORMATION SYSTEMS

The design of AIS is highly complex due to the large number of different dimensions (cultural, spatial, aesthetic, technical, etc.) that have to be accounted for when presenting information ambiently. The ambient property of an AIS is

not "used" so much as simply perceived and digested in the background of our awareness, and the experience of an ambient display is largely a result of its interaction with its surroundings and its references to cultural practices and preconceptions (Offenhuber, 2008). If information is successfully delivered in an ambient way, we do not expect that anyone would consider the information provided for longer – or any more deeply – than a sign on the road as it passes by. However, the way the information is presented is paramount to its plausibility as an ambient source. The success is in the details, in this case, the design of the medium in which the information is presented.

In the context of AIS, the value of proper design goes beyond simply making the information functional or beautiful, and contributes to both the *integration* of information into the environment (so as to be ambient), as well as one's *interpretation* of the information (so that it is perceived and digested appropriately). As discussed earlier, integration requires a blending between an existing artifact or physical space, and a new information medium. Any artifact or physical space has an existing set of inherent aesthetic attributes. The ways in which we can manipulate and appropriate

Figure 3. The History Tablecloth[3] (left) has a pattern of embedded electroluminescent material that begins to glow when objects are placed upon the surface. When objects are removed the pattern begins to fade slowly. The SmartSwim UV Intensity Bikini[4] (right) uses UV sensitive materials to warn against excessive exposure to the sun.

  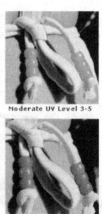

these attributes have been studied at length in the disciplines of design and architecture, but are new territory for most technology centric disciplines.

Forlizzi, et al. (2001) alludes to the growing necessity for deeper analysis of information aesthetics by pointing out that the value of information technology is measured less exclusively in terms of its functionality in solving problems of interest. Now that computational technology is being applied beyond the – mostly utilitarian – business environment, we have begun to see traits such as *desirability* become just as relevant as *usefulness* (p. 141). Technologists have to consider not only whether their implementation works, but also whether it "goes with the couch" (ibid.). Without appropriate aesthetic considerations the technology will always "stick-out," making true ambience more difficult.

Proper design considerations are also important in determining how information is perceived, and simply presenting information as-is is not a sufficient condition for the success of an AIS. There is a symbiotic relationship between information and the medium used to deliver the information (McLuhan, 1967). McLuhan posits that the aesthetic characteristics of a particular information medium will have a significant effect on one's understanding (or interpretation) of the information presented. This relationship between information content and media means that the design attributes for a particular information technology (i.e. AIS) are not necessarily trivial or subjective, and have a serious impact on the success or failure of a particular implementation. However, the proper use of such attributes in terms of ambient information design has not been thoroughly explored. As an example where different design strategies have been applied to convey the same information, consider Dima Komissarov's Flashbag (Figure 4, right) and Didigo's SmartDrive (Figure 4, left), two flash storage devices that advertise their free capacity. The 00 Flashbag is surrounded by a small rubber bladder that inflates as it "fills up" with data (Kormissarov, 2006). The designer states that

the purpose of the Flashbag is to allow people to perceive how much space is left on their drive by sight and touch. In contrast, the SmartDrive provides similar functionality through the use of an E-ink display that shows a pie chart representing the available storage space (Didigo, 2006). Both devices convey how much storage space is available, but their choice of information presentation gives the products different levels of ambientness. We would argue that the design attributes of the Flashbag allow it to facilitate ambient interaction on more levels and in a more intuitive manner with lower cognitive load of interpretation than the SmartDrive. The Flashbag allows one to be aware of data storage capacity simply by the way it feels inside the pocket, or by glancing at it from across the room, where the SmartDrive requires a specific, intentional, visual inspection of the embedded display.

THE EVALUATION OF AMBIENT INFORMATION SYSTEMS

In an HCI laboratory, any kind of measured task completion has some confounding effect on what is being measured. With typical information technologies, researchers are able to account for the effects of artificial environments, or tasks, by separating out the effects of the lab setting from the valuable bits of information that are independent of the simulated environment. For example, a researcher can single out a particular research problem (e.g. sharing information between two people), develop a solution for solving that problem (e.g. a new data sharing paradigm), and measure how well people are at applying the solution to successfully evaluate the solution (e.g. time taken to discover a function or feature, awareness that a file has transferred, ease of accepting/viewing an incoming file). The researcher can construct a set of tasks for the user to complete, and if the results are good, the researcher knows that when a person needs to share information

Figure 4. Comparison of the "SmartDrive[5]" (left) and "Flashbag[6]" (right)

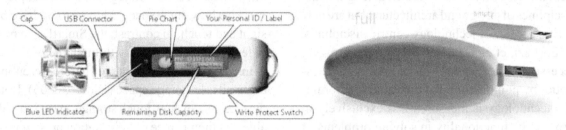

with another person using the provided software, there is a strong possibility that the person will know what to do. With AIS technologies however, we cannot understand their effects until we can be sure that the observer is in no way perceiving them directly. To perform an HCI lab study on an AIS implementation, a participant would have to be introduced to the AIS so as to understand its function, and then asked to conduct a separate task that would distract them enough to *force* the AIS into their peripheral attention. But what exactly do the results from such a study tell an AIS researcher other than that people are *capable* of detecting some level of ambient information? The ability of such a study to inform researchers as to how AIS integrate into the environment, and whether or not people can make good use of them, is questionable since *having the distractions of one task obscure an information channel is not the same thing as having that information live naturally in the periphery*. The lab scenario is akin to asking if one is capable of concentrating on two conversations at the same time, but this is a very different proposition to asking whether or not they can or will make use of extra information transmitted to them by an AIS that is embedded into the environment (such as the ability to process and use SmartSwim's UV levels). Traditional HCI user interface evaluation methodologies can tell us about the quality of a specific AIS implementation (i.e. *could* it work), but because AIS are designed to be subtle, and primarily used indirectly in everyday environments, these methodologies do not give enough insight to help predict how one

of these technologies is experienced in an actual context of use (i.e. *does* it really have any effect).

This is not to say that typical usability methods are unnecessary. Usability studies tell us whether or not certain features are possible, for example, whether a person is at all capable of detecting subtle changes in movement, shape, or color, of a particular design. However, by their very nature, these technologies cannot function as intended until they have properly blended into the fabric of the observer's everyday environment, and to say anything meaningful about AIS will require researchers to go beyond simple usability by moving out of the lab and conducting studies in-situ. In order to progress research in this domain, new frameworks and evaluation methods which focus on studying the use of AIS in the wild have to be constructed to give researchers deeper insights on how people make use of the information provided. Some good examples of existing in-situ research on studies of AIS include (Stasko, 2005), where highly personalized information displays were observed in participant's offices, (Hsieh and Mankoff, 2004), where a usability/distraction/awareness framework was used to evaluate an AIS developed to filter email, and most recently, Matthew's thesis (2007), which provides a great deal of useful information regarding the design and evaluation of peripheral displays. However, this area of study still suffers from an overall lack of research due in part to the difficulty involved in creating user studies for this class of technology (Carter and Mankoff, 2004).

FUTURE DIRECTIONS FOR AMBIENT INFORMATION SYSTEMS

From our engagement with the community, we can see that furthering research in AIS requires several challenges be addressed in both designing and evaluating implementations.

Challenges for AIS Design

Even though we have many of the tools necessary for building AIS implementations, including sensors, smart materials, and communication protocols, a greater understanding of the issues specific to *design* needs to be developed so that we can understand how these tools can be applied to construct technologies that facilitate ambient interaction. We propose the following challenges be tackled in order to expand our thinking about AIS technology:

- Analyze the relationships between design attributes (i.e. the visual mechanisms, tactical qualities, sounds, smells, metaphors, cultural aspects, etc.) used to present information, and their use in the development of different AIS implementations. For example, in what ways might tactile sensation facilitate an ambient awareness of storage capacity as with the FlashBag?
- Develop new AIS design methods derived from perspectives and approaches employed by different academic disciplines. The development process conducted by an industrial designer may be very different from how an HCI researcher, or a digital artist, but these different processes may inform each other if the knowledge and processes could be successfully shared across disciplines.
- Experiment with novel types of content in everyday living. On the beach it might

be useful to know the current UV level, as with the UV Sensitive Bikini; likewise AIS seems ideally placed to provide for the growing public awareness and demand for information about personal carbon footprints and energy consumption.
- Discover new applications of ambient information. AIS that inform us about weather, stocks, and email traffic have obvious utility, but new forms of information may also be useful if presented in an ambient fashion. For instance, the History Tablecloth allows people reflect on the use of a table within the home (i.e. eating, studying, socializing, etc.). This information may be drawn upon when people are deciding how to rearrange their home, plan a party, or remember where their spouse usually keeps their keys.

Challenges for AIS Evaluation

Currently there are few widely accepted metrics for evaluating the success of AIS. As we have discussed, these technologies are unusual in their use, and typical HCI evaluation methodologies do not tell us all that we need to know to adequately judge the success of AIS. It is important not only to know if information is perceived, but we also need to know whether people appropriate the information at all. We suggest that AIS researchers focus the development of evaluation methodologies that can:

- determine if onlookers perceive information provided by an AIS as intended, and whether they are able to make use of the information provided
- describe how, and to what extent, people are being influenced by the information provided by an AIS

- measure the level of distraction produced by an AIS in different circumstances
- characterize the effects of a given AIS in terms of user experience

CONCLUSION

We envision a world in which every object and surface is capable of providing at least some additional layer of information. The only way this will be acceptable is if the information can be presented without overwhelming or annoying the people we are trying to inform. In this work we have developed a definition of Ambient Information Systems, and discussed issues in both the design and the evaluation of such technologies. We have issued a set of challenges that we believe must be undertaken to further the growth of AIS research. However, it is clear that this list is not exhaustive and in time new challenges will be exposed. We hope that more researchers will see that AIS are a viable and important technology that will become increasingly necessary in a society with growing appetites for information, and step up to the challenges we have set forth.

ACKNOWLEDGMENT

We would like to thank all of those who helped organize, and participated in, the Ambient Information Systems workshops in Toronto in 2007 and South Korea in 2008, as well as those who participated in the program committees.

REFERENCES

Brusilovsky, P., Kobsa, A., & Nejdl, W. (Eds.). (2007): The Adaptive Web, Methods and Strategies of Web Personalization. LNCS 4321 Springer, ISBN 978-3-540-72078-2

Didigo, (2006). Didigo SmartDrive USB Key. Retrieved December 1, 2008, from Ubergizmo, The Gadget Blog Web site: http://www.ubergizmo. com/15/archives/2006/01/didigos_smartdrive_ usb_key_with_led_display.html

Gaver, W., Bowers, J., Boucher, A., Law, A., Pennington, S., & Villar, N. (2006). The history tablecloth: illuminating domestic activity. In *Proceedings of the 6th conference on Designing Interactive systems* (pp. 199-208). University Park, PA, USA: ACM

Hallnäs, L., & Redström, J. (2001). Slow Technology: Designing for Reflection. *Personal and Ubiquitous Computing, 5*(3), 201–212. doi:10.1007/ PL00000019

Hazlewood, W. R., & Knopke, I. (2008). Designing Ambient Musical Information Systems. In Proceedings of the *8th International Conference on New Interfaces for Musical Expression* (pp. 281-285) Genoa, Italy: ACM

Hemmert, F. (2009). Life in the Pocket. *International Journal of Ambient Computing and Intelligence (IJACI)* on Ambient Information Systems 2009.

Holmquist, L. E., & Skog, T. (2003). Informative art: information visualization in everyday environments. In Proceedings of the *1st international Conference on Computer Graphics and interactive Techniques in Australasia and South East Asia* (pp. 229-235) Melbourne, Australia. ACM, New York, NY

Hsieh, G., & Mankoff, J. (2003). A Comparison of Two Peripheral Displays for Monitoring Email: Measuring Usability, Awareness, and Distraction. UC Berkeley, EECS Department. Technical Report No. UCB-CSD-03-1286.

Jafarinaimi, N., Forlizzi, J., Hurst, A., & Zimmerman, J. (2005). Breakaway: an ambient display designed to change human behavior. In *CHI '05 extended abstracts on Human factors in computing systems* (pp. 1945-1948). Portland, OR, USA: ACM.

Kaye, J. (2004). Making Scents: aromatic output for HCI. *Interaction*, *11*(1), 48–61. doi:10.1145/962342.964333

Komissarov, D. (2006). plusminus design: flashbag. Retrieved December 1, 2008, from plusminus design by Dima Komissarov Web site: http://www.plusminus.ru/flashbag.html

Matthews, T. L. (2007). *Designing and evaluating glanceable peripheral displays*. PhD Thesis. University of California at Berkeley.

Mcluhan, H. M. (1967). *Understanding Media: The Extension of Man*. New American Library.

Mehin, A., Rosen, T., & Glaister, C. (2004). *Open Source*. Retrieved December 1, 2008, from Afshin Mehin's Design Portfolio Web site: http://afshinmehin.com/open_source.htm

Mynatt, E. D., Back, M., Want, R., & Frederick, R. (1997). Audio aura: light-weight audio augmented reality. In *Proceedings of the 10th annual ACM symposium on User interface software and technology* (pp. 211-212). Banff, Alberta, Canada: ACM.

Offenhuber, D. (2008). The Invisible Display - Design Strategies for Ambient Media in the Urban Context. In *Proceedings of 2nd Workshop on Ambient Information Systems*. Colocated with Ubicomp 2008, Seoul, South Korea 2008.

Papper, R. A., Holmes, M. E., Popovich, M. N., & Bloxham, M. (2005). Middletown Media Studies II: The media day. Muncie, IN: Ball State University Center for Media Design (report available online www.bsu.edu/cmd/insightandresearch).

Richtel, M. (2003). The Lure of Data: Is It Addictive? Retrieved December 1, 2008, from The New York Times Web site: http://query.nytimes.com/gst/fullpage.html?res=9502E3D81E3AF935A35754C0A9659C8B63

SmartSwim. (2008). SmartSwim UV Intensity Bikini. Retrieved December 1, 2008, from Impact Lab: A laboratory of the future human experience Web site: http://www.impactlab.com/2008/10/02/smartswim-uv-intensity-bikini/

Stasko, J., McColgin, D., Miller, T., Plaue, C., & Pousman, Z. (2005). Evaluating the InfoCanvis Peripheral Awareness System: A Logitudinal, In Situ Study. Technical Report GIT-GVU-05-08, GVU Center/Georgia Institute of Technology, Atlanta, GA, USA

Tolmie, P., Pycock, J., Diggins, T., MacLean, A., & Karsenty, A. (2002). Unremarkable computing. In *Proceedings of the SIGCHI conference on Human factors in computing systems: Changing our world, changing ourselves* (pp. 399-406). Minneapolis, Minnesota, USA: ACM.

Weiser, M., & Brown, J. S. (1995). *Designing Calm Technology*. Xerox PARC.

Wisneski, C., Ishii, H., Dahley, A., Gorbet, M. G., Brave, S., Ullmer, B., et al. (1998). Ambient Displays: Turning Architectural Space into an Interface between People and Digital Information. In Proceedings of the *First International Workshop on Cooperative Buildings, Integrating Information, Organization, and Architecture* (pp. 22-32).

ENDNOTES

[1] The Ambient Information Systems workshop website is here: http://ambientinformation.org

[2] http://afshinmehin.com/open_source.htm

3 http://www.equator.ac.uk/var/uploads/pro-
   posals_tablecloth.gif
4 http://infosthetics.com/archives/uvbikini2.
   jpg

5 http://www.ubergizmo.com/photos/2006/1/
   didigo-smartdrive.jpg
6 http://www.plusminus.ru/flashbag1.jpg

Chapter 9
Life in the Pocket –
The Ambient Life Project:
Life–Like Movements in Tactile Ambient Displays in Mobile Phones

Fabian Hemmert
Deutsche Telekom Laboratories, Germany

ABSTRACT

The work reported in this article is concerned with the relationship of the user to his mobile phone, especially with the habit of checking the mobile phone for missed events. We present two qualitative studies that have been conducted with mobile phones, symbolizing their status through life-like movements - breath and pulse. It was to be determined whether a continuous, rythmic and life-like signal would be eligible to ambiently express the phone's state. The results of the studies were mixed, as some users were simply annoyed by the permanent actuation, while others appreciated the functionality. The response times to occured events seem to be appropriate for an ambient display. The studies raised further questions, regarding the psychological and physiological consequences of such technology.

INTRODUCTION

Nowadays, mobile phones are seamlessly integrated into our everyday lives. Being of high relevance for both social and individual needs, this form of

DOI: 10.4018/978-1-60960-549-0.ch009

telecommunication has brought along a series of implications for our daily routines, one of them is the need to *check* our phone occasionally (see Figure 1). Currently, in mobile phones, the state of *silence* is ambiguous: It does tell its user that 'nobody is calling right now', but it does not make a distinction between 'no missed events' and '2 missed calls and 1 missed text message'. As this information is often only shown on the phone's display, the phone needs to be visually checked. Certainly, the phone may ring and vibrate when an event is occurring, but most users are likely to miss one of these occasionally – a circumstance that often leads them into the habit of repeatedly checking their phones.

This draws an interesting parallel to the 1990s, when mobile phones were less widespread, and *Tamagotchi*™ digital pets resided in the pockets of their caretaking owners. Simulating pet-like needs (e.g. eating, being cleaned or playing), they also required to be checked at least occasionally. Nowadays, some mobile phones seem to receive even more care and attention than their egg-shaped predecessors: They are given names, adorably customized and placed into custom-made mobile phone chairs. They also often rest next to their owners' sleeping places – just in case. But where is the turning point between information and annoyance? Notification systems and status displays are an active research field of rapid development and high potential, especially with regard to these major issues of the information age: distraction and interruption. Projects in this area are concerned with the ideal timing for an interruption, (Adamczyk & Bailey, 2004) its effects on performance

Figure 1. Life in the pocket

and anxiety (Bailey, Konstan, & Carlis, 2001) and context-specific notification styles (McCrickard & Chewar, 2003).

Various other projects have investigated the field of non-intrusive, ambient information in mobile contexts so far, including surface- and shape-based devices like the Tactophone (Horev, 2006) and the Dynamic Knobs phone (Hemmert, Joost, Knörig, & Wettach, 2008) and excitatory displays like Shoogle (Williamson, Smith, & Hughes, 2007). Mobile phones recently launched, such as the NEC Mobile FOMA 904i, feature a button for a 'tactile echo' of the phone: When the button is pressed, the phone will vibrate in a certain pattern, depending on its state (short vibration = nothing happened, two short vibrations = text message, one long vibration = missed call, etc.). While the principle itself is very efficient, as the phone can be checked through the pocket, the cognitive effort to 'decode' the vibration pattern is still considerably high. Other devices, such as some phones from the Motorola RAZR product range, offer periodical beeping after a missed event. Recently, novel psychosomatic syndromes have been reported, describing the erroneous perception of incoming calls: 'phantom vibration' and 'ringxiety'. The Ambient Life project is concerned with the creation of an ambient display for the mobile phone's status, in order to investigate possible solutions for the problems of mobile phone status display and notification.

RHYTHMIC LIFE-LIKE MOVEMENTS

Developing a permanent tactile display on a mobile phone is strongly tied to an appropriate design of the 'information – annoyance' trade-off of the system. In the Ambient Life project, a status display was sought that would ideally be easy to check, easy to ignore, and easy to notice upon a change. It seemed to be a promising approach to blend a system into the user's perception by making it as inherently familiar as possible, basing it on two of the most basic and omnipresent signs of life: Breath and heartbeat (see Figure 2).

A number of projects has researched the inclusion of these into HCI before, including several concerned with telepresence, i.e. *imPulse* and *united-pulse* (Gilad & Christian, 2007; Werner, Wettach, & Hornecker, 2008), and such that investigate the awareness of one's own body, such as *AtemRaum* (Zingerle, Wagner, & Heidecker, 2006). A term that might soon be considered the spanning word for these approaches might be *Instinctive Computing*, as mentioned by Cai recently (Cai, 2007). Spillers argues in his work on rhythmic interaction design (Spillers, 2008) that *rhythm* may actually be one of the central elements in HCI. Li recently presented his work about *Tapping and Rubbing*, which explores the simulation of human touch through voice-coil motors (Li, Baudisch, Griswold, & Hollan, 2008).

It might be hypothesized that a touch is never ambient, as being touched might just always attract our attention, and that a phone that imitates a living being – or even a social counterpart – can only call for more attention than a dead object. Nonetheless, the idea of giving users a permanent feeling about their phones, similar to a pregnant woman's feelings about the condition of a baby in

her womb, was a concept that required practical investigation.

THE AMBIENT LIFE PROJECT

A series of prototypes was built. The first object of our research was the phone's breath. We employed an Arduino board to drive a servo in a thorax-like way, and experimented with various materials and shapes of a possible breathing mobile phone, among them plush, plastic, and textiles (see Figure 3).

In later prototypes, a heartbeat was added by driving a vibration motor in short impulses, which resulted in a 'bump' feeling. Later, Java software was written to implement the functionality on existing mobile phones. Here, the built-in vibration motor was used to create continuous heartbeat-like 'bump' actuations. This was repeated for every heartbeat, resulting in the classing 'du-dum' rhythm. Even though the continuous vibrations reduced the phone's battery lifetime to 6 hours, using an actual mobile phone as the prototype allowed the conduction of a series of studies, in which the system could be evaluated in actual mobile contexts. The basic concept here was a simple two-state system, involving a 'no missed

Figure 2. a) Normal mobile phone notification, b) calm and excited pulse, c) calm and stopped pulse

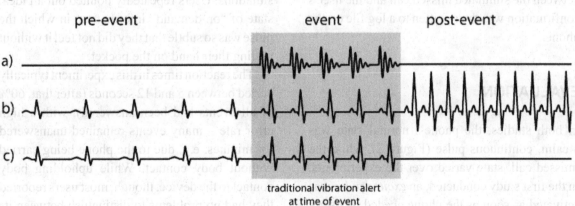

Figure 3. Prototype evolution

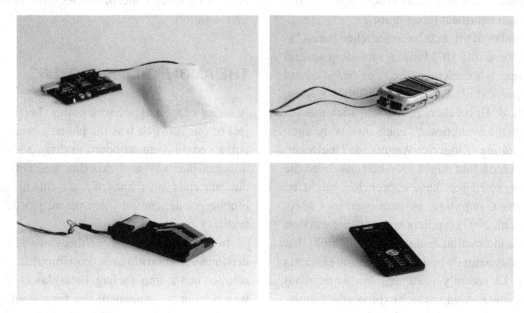

calls' (normal) state and a 'missed call' state, in which the phone would need the user's attention. In both studies, the participants were asked to wear the phone for two days and adjust the vibration's intensity to their needs. They were given diaries to record their experiences and asked to carry the phone as much as possible. While the phones did not use the user's SIM cards, a missed call was simulated every 10-15 minutes from 9:00am to 9:00pm. The users were asked to confirm the missed call by pressing 'OK' on the phone as soon as they noticed it. The time difference between the simulated missed call and the user's confirmation was then written to a log file on the phone.

EVALUATION

In both studies, the phone's normal state was a calm, continuous pulse (Figure 2), while the 'missed call' state varied over the experiments. In the first study conducted, an *excited pulse* was activated as soon as the phone needed its user's attention, and it was of interest whether the user

would take notice of the changed pulse, and how long it would take him to do so. A qualitative user study with 7 users (3f, 4m, 20-33 yrs.) was conducted using filmed interviews and user observation through log files on the phones as the means of inquiry. In this study, many users were simply annoyed by the continuous pulse. The annoyance was reportedly stronger in some situations than in others; the users stated that the pulse was annoying especially in situations of silence, focused attention, or rest; the proposed feature seemed to be more adequate for noisy situations. Users repeatedly pointed out an ideal state of "on demand" information, in which the pulse was so subtle that they did not feel it without putting their hand on the pocket.

The reaction times in this experiment typically varied between 5 and 12 seconds (after that, 60% of all events had been answered), with a high error rate – many events remained unanswered for minutes, e.g. due to the phone being carried without body contact. While upholding body contact to the device, though, most users reported they had no problems to distinguish between its 'calm' and 'excited' states.

One of the most striking findings was the 'gap' the phone left when taken out of the pocket, as some users reported. This may underline the question of which consequences accompany permanently being informed about one's mobile phone: Already, users report that "something is missing" when they leave the house without their mobile phone (James & Drennan, 2005), and a permanent tactile stimulus might eventually even amplify this feeling. The 'gap' of a missing pulse served as a basis for the second study: Would users take notice of a suddenly stopped pulse? While this might simply add another dimension of notification (normal pulse; excited pulse; missing pulse) it might also help users to detect instantly when they had left their phone somewhere.

We conducted another qualitative user study with 6 users (3f, 3m, 22-33 yrs.), all of which had been participating in the first study, too. Again, we used video interviews and user observation through log files on the phones as our methods of inquiry, and the experiment lasted again two days, in which missed calls were simulated every 10-15 minutes from 9:00am to 9:00pm. The difference was that upon a simulated missed call, the phone would no longer switch from 'calm' to 'excited', but from 'calm' to 'dead': The heartbeat would suddenly stop. Again, the users liked the functionality in some situations, while they found it annoying in others. Some also reported a 'phantom vibration', times when they felt a vibration even though it had stopped. One user particularly liked the permanent reassurance that the phone was 'present and active'. In this experiment, 19% of the responses occurred within the first 10 seconds, 44% within the first 30 seconds. 55% of the responses to a stopped beat occurred in the first minute after the event. After 10 minutes, 90% of the events were confirmed. The results of this study indicated that a suddenly stopped pulse is indeed taken note of, even though not as fast and accurately as a suddenly excited pulse.

The two studies raise a number of questions: How does the subjective relationship to one's phone change, when it is constantly beating? What are the psychological implications of the constant rhythm? What are the bodily consequences of a heartbeat, different from one's own, permanently present? Clearly, the questions raised in the preliminary Ambient Life studies, require a long term study. Currently, such a study is conducted, utilizing the user's SIM cards; the functionality will be tested in real situations, with real mobile phone usage and over a longer period of time.

CONCLUSION

Is what we have seen the future? It is still unclear whether phones that simulate a life of their own are desirable, useful or even potentially dangerous. Furthermore, it is yet to be determined what the input for such a system would be. Possibly, the transition of machines to social actors is inevitable in times of increasing device smartness. While our relationship to the mobile phone seems to have changed already since its offspring in the 1990s, it will be interesting to see where this development goes.

REFERENCES

Adamczyk, P., & Bailey, B. (2004). *If not now, when?: the effects of interruption at different moments within task execution*. In CHI '04: Proceedings of the SIGCHI conference on Human factors in computing systems.

Bailey, B., Konstan, J., & Carlis, J. (2001). *The Effects of Interruptions on Task Performance, Annoyance, and Anxiety in the User Interface*. In Proceedings of INTERACT '01.

Cai, Y. (2007). Instinctive Computing. In Artifical Intelligence for Human Computing, LNAI 4451.

Gilad, L., & Croft, C. (2007). *imPulse*. In CHI '07: Extended Abstracts of the SIGCHI conference on Human factors in computing systems.

Hemmert, F., Joost, G., Knörig, A., & Wettach, R. (2008). *Dynamic knobs: shape change as a means of interaction on a mobile phone*. In CHI '08: Extended abstracts on Human factors in computing systems.

Horev, O. (2006). *Tactophone*.

James, D., & Drennan, J. (2005). *Exploring Addictive Consumption of Mobile Phone Technology*. In Proceedings of ANZMAC 2005.

Li, K. A., Baudisch, P., Griswold, W. G., & Hollan, J. D. (2008). *Tapping and rubbing: exploring new dimensions of tactile feedback with voice coil motors*. In UIST '08: Proceedings of the 21st annual ACM symposium on User interface software and technology.

McCrickard, D., & Chewar, C. (2003). *Communications of the ACM 46, 3 (March. 2003)*. Attuning Notification Design to User Goals and Attention Costs.

Spillers, F. (2008). *Synch with me: Rhythmic interaction as an emerging principle of experiential design*. Paper presented at the 6th Conference on Design & Emotion 2008.

Werner, J., Wettach, R., & Hornecker, E. (2008). *United-pulse: feeling your partner's pulse*. In Mobile HCI 2008: Proceedings of the 10th international conference on Human computer interaction with mobile devices and services.

Williamson, J., Smith, R., & Hughes, S. (2007). *Shoogle: excitatory multimodal interaction on mobile devices*. In CHI'07: Proceedings of the SIGCHI conference on Human factors in computing systems.

Zingerle, A., Wagner, T., & Heidecker, C. (2006). *AtemRaum*.

This work was previously published in International Journal of Ambient Computing and Intelligence (IJACI), Volume 1, Issue 2, edited by Kevin Curran, pp. 13-19, copyright 2009 by IGI Publishing (an imprint of IGI Global).

Chapter 10
Staged Façades:
Peripheral Displays in the Public

Bernhard Wally
Research Studio Pervasive Computing Applications, Austria

Alois Ferscha
Research Studio Pervasive Computing Applications, Austria

ABSTRACT

Media façades, realized through projection systems, could be a promising technology for scalable public displays in urban spaces. With low requirements regarding the infrastructure and virtually no influence on the buildings' fabric, projected façades offer exceptional flexibility and extensibility as well as easy maintenance. As cities are increasingly confronted with digital signage products besides other public display systems, a projector-based system offers the possibility to be switched off and restore the screen to its previous state in the blink of an eye. We present the prototypical implementation of a "Staged Façades Framework" leveraging a façade's structure and ornamentation for dynamically adapting pieces of multimedia content.

INTRODUCTION

At times in which computers appear to be everywhere while at the same time – due to miniaturization and rigorous embedding – physically appear nowhere, where tiny computing devices are continuing to pervade into everyday objects, users presumably do, and increasingly will not notice them anymore as separate entities. Ap-

pliances, tools, clothing, accessories, furniture, rooms, machinery, cars, buildings, roads, cities, even whole agricultural landscapes increasingly embody miniaturized and wireless, thus invisible information and communication systems. Information technology rich systems and spaces are being created, radically changing the style of how we perceive, create, think, interact, behave and socialize as human beings, but also how we learn, work, cultivate, live, cure, age as individuals or in societal settings. A major issue in such

DOI: 10.4018/978-1-60960-549-0.ch010

technology rich settings is how we perceive information, how we interact with digital media, how we manage to sustain attentive to information of interest, how we stay aware of the dynamics and changes of information, or how we manage perceptual complexity and information overload.

In an attempt of relating the understanding of science and the understanding of art, (Vogel and Balakrishnan, 2004) postulates scientists to see only the "observed in the material world", while the artist sees the "spiritual": "While the scientist describes and predicts, the artist distils and presents. Interpreting science […] means balancing the desire of scientists to spew data with the artistic urge to create a transcendent experience." In quintessence, "Informative Art" (Holmquist and Skog, 2003) is art with electronics, with content and presentation being primary, while technology, form and function is fused and secondary. Following Buckminster Fuller's belief, that as technology advances, art begins to resemble science, we here addresses the process of "creating an (urban) experience" from "data spews" by means of artful display installations, often referred to as informative art or ambient displays, or ambient information systems. Here, in this work, we refer to such systems as "Peripheral Interfaces" or "Peripheral Displays", stressing the fact that these interfaces aim at not overloading human attention, but rather deliver information to the periphery of perception, mostly in an aesthetically pleasing way.

Of particular interest in this work are peripheral displays in cities. According to the most recent U.N. estimates, by the end of 2008, half the world's population will live in urban areas and about 70 percent will be city dwellers by 2050. Thus, cities are becoming increasingly the most relevant places bringing together people from many areas of culture and life, acting as important opinion leaders, initiators of change, or providers of new opportunities. Expressions of communication among citizens in urban settings are public displays, addressing and delivering information to crowds, rather than individuals. Contemporary public displays, designed to raise attention (for e.g. commercial purposes like advertisement), have started to aggressively pollute the visual appearance of a city, and paradoxically, by that continuously distracting attention. Aggressive public display installations and settings hence fail to achieve their purpose, encouraging a new style of city displays, seamlessly and unobtrusively embedded into the architectural appearance of city.

PERIPHERAL DISPLAY CONCEPTS

Peripheral interfaces were proposed to provide users with information considered relevant at arbitrary points of work or living engagement, originating from many different – mostly geographically dislocated – sources and presented at the periphery of human perception. Particularly, and most importantly, if visual perception is concerned, and if the flow of information is unidirectional from the display to the user, we thus use the term "Peripheral Displays". Having the displays operate in the periphery of a user's awareness allows other user tasks to sustain primacy. Much like the information presented by clocks, posters, paintings or windows, peripheral displays move to the centre of attention only when appropriate and desirable. Computational counterparts of such displays have been designed to support group awareness in work groups in virtual space settings, for knowledge dissemination in enterprises, for users of instant messaging systems, for deaf users, to keep in touch with family members, or to display a cities health information in public places – to name a few. In peripheral display systems, usually abstract art has been proposed to serve as the visualization paradigm for contextual information, design principles and guidelines have been developed, upon which software frameworks and development toolkits have been built. Evaluation guidelines have been developed and assessment studies have been conducted, e.g. relating comprehension of peripheral displays (i.e. how well a user understands and uses such artefacts) to the time span of their use.

A variety of definitions for peripheral displays, informative art, ambient information systems etc., have been proposed in the literature, using slightly different characterizations. Their common core is the aim to deliver information through visuals that are quickly and easily perceived while doing other tasks (Elliot and Greenberg 2004). As an example, "ambient displays" are understood as "aesthetically pleasing displays of information which sit on the periphery of a user's attention. They generally support monitoring of non-critical information" (Mankoff and Dey 2003). Ambient displays have been proposed to provide users with information considered relevant at arbitrary points of work or living engagement, originating from many different – mostly geographically dislocated – sources, and presented at the periphery of human (visual) perception. Monitoring the display should cause minimal distraction from the user's focus of attention (Ishii and Ulmer 1997) (Mankoff et al., 2003). The display and its delivered experience move to the focus of attention only if desired or appropriate in a certain situation, hence justifying the synonym "peripheral display". Addressing the aspect of attention, the definition by Mankoff et al. (2003) appears representative: Peripheral Displays "[Ambient displays] are *aesthetically pleasing displays* of information which sit *on the periphery of a user's attention*. They generally support monitoring of non-critical information." To summarize, peripheral displays integrate information visualization into everyday environments according to the following aspects: (i) amplified, aesthetic art objects act as abstract information displays, (ii) displays use the of periphery of a human's attention, (iii) displays represent "slow technology" and are attempting to cope with information overload, and (iv) displays do not attempt to provide the user with exact information. The potential gain (and subtle hope) of peripheral displays are reflected as follows:

- **Intuitive Awareness:** information can be perceived at quick, opportunistic glances
- **Decrease Anxiety/Stress:** displays prevent form actively having to find information
- **Distraction free:** the user can remain focussed with his primary task
- **Reduce Cognitive Load:** load is reduced at both the preattentive, as well as at the interpretative phase of perception
- **Time Saving:** convenient perception prevents from time costly querying the environment
- **Learnability:** metaphoric encoding helps to define intuitive information to symbol mappings

A comprehensive taxonomy of the meanwhile rich body of literature for peripheral displays has recently been developed by (Tomitsch et al., 2007).

PERIPHERAL DISPLAYS IN CITIES

Urban environments are, amongst other things, a fertile ground for the out of home (OOH) advertisement market. In areas of high population density, lots of people can be reached by placing a simple billboard at crowded places such as railway stations or along the main traffic routes. In the past decades the number of public signage products increased dramatically and introduced innovative solutions for urban settings including branded tramways, buses and stations, coated buildings and digital signage. However, the current excrescence of OOH advertisement sites has even reached the ceiling in some parts of the world: in São Paulo, the city's mayor decided in 2006 (successfully, as of January 2008) to get rid of what he called "visual pollution", referring to the vast amount of billboards, electronic ads, shop signs and street banners (Downie, 2008). OOH is just one of the examples of how we are increasingly surrounded by devices that try to get as much of our attention as possible. The municipalities for urban development are facing hard times, as public displays are more and more fed with dynamic content – with a presumed impact on urban safety, e.g. through distracted drivers and pedestrians or stimulus satiation. Ambient information systems try to lower the potential of distraction and overloading by means of a cautious but efficient usage of attention. While public displays are mostly used for advertisement, there are many more application scenarios that get more and more explored as the enabling technologies get cheaper and offer better quality. One of the scenarios in a cultural field is presented as one of the application domains of our general-purpose event framework in the section "Staged Façades Framework".

Gellersen et al. (1999) has broadened the concept of ambient media to "the use of our surroundings for information display", which represents a key concept of what we think of ambient displays: integration into our lives by either imitating commonplace objects or by extending existing objects with somewhat smart behaviour. In (Ames et al., 2003) a city-sensitive ambient display is described which displays the city's health status by calculating electricity usage from light pollution sensed by using cameras and by incorporating recycling information. This information is then used as an overlay to a map of the city and presented on a screen to users. An early mobile city guide considering UMTS is presented in (Kreller et al., 1998) using a personal display for location based services – in the work presented in this article we are moving away from handheld solutions to displays that are a vital part of the city: façades.

A possible method for interacting with public displays is shown in (Balagas et al., 2004), where a mobile phone is used as a pointing device to a public display using the integrated camera. Multimedia content on public displays is investigated by (Churchill et al., 2004): plasma screens are used to display "user generated content", e.g. announcements, calendars, images, movies in order to share this information with co-workers

in a laboratory setting using different interaction techniques. Later, this installation was installed in various locations, such as a governmental building. An overview regarding research in large displays and interaction therewith is given in (Czerwinski et al., 2006), focussing on large displays' effects on productivity as well as usability issues and interaction techniques.

In (Ferscha, 2007a) a general purpose software framework for informative art display systems is presented and some general aspects of typical ambient displays are depicted, including themes, symbols and connotations. On the basis of real paintings, methods for integrating information therein are proposed and implemented in the peripheral display framework. Subsequent research led to the proposal of more user-oriented, participatory design process for ambient displays (Ferscha, 2007b), by letting the user decide on the specific theme a peripheral display is operated at. Different elements of various artworks are manipulated to resemble sensor data or abstract context information thus leaving the decision for the concrete piece of painting used for displaying ambient information to the user.

One of the rather seldom seen examples of (really) large public displays is presented in (Peltonen et al., 2008), explaining a detailed observation of the multi-touch display called City Wall. While the emphasis of this project lies on the multi-user interaction possibilities, it also shows some interesting aspects of how people approach public displays. Depending on the current usage of the display, people need to wait for a free slot if too many people are interacting already, or they can start interacting immediately if nobody is using the display. The empirical data shows however, that there are usually at least two steps involved: (1) noticing that there is a display, (2) interacting with the display. One conclusion of Peltonen et al. (2008) is that "City Wall's large physical size appeared to support making interactions visible". During eight days of operation 1199 people interacted with the system.

With regards to digital media façades, Schoch (2006) classified them into "add-on displays" (degrading buildings to being brackets for the screens), "media façades" (take the buildings proportions into consideration) and "buildings designed with media technology as a main element". This classification resembles more or less the evolution of media façades and doesn't distinguish between techniques or technologies. For our work, add-on displays are usually aesthetically unpleasant and do not support the paradigm of unobtrusiveness. Especially designed "multimedia buildings" are a very nice playground for many applications; however in existing urban environments such buildings are rare if existing at all, mostly due to regulations such as the protection of historical monuments. Of the three categories the second one "media façades" best matches our own current R&D focus, because "media facades do take the buildings proportions into consideration" (Schoch, 2006). In our work we distinguish between two types of media façades: active and passive façades (see section "Enabling Technologies").

A very good overview of the development of interactive media façades is given by Mignonneau and Sommerer (2008), starting with Jean Nouvel in 1988 and ending with an interactive urban installation in 2007. One of the key findings of the authors is that "interactive art and interface design are now mature enough to be used in the public space on a large scale within cities and public buildings".

STAGED FAÇADES

Media façades have become an established component in modern architecture, highly supported by the respective technological improvements regarding outdoor display systems. The usage of a building's façade as an ambient urban display opens highly flexible ways for creative applications.

Enabling Technologies

The installation and operation of a media façade can be rather expensive and clearly depends on the technologies used – but besides cost, there are other challenges that influence the technology decision. There are two basic types of media façades: (1) façades that are "active" screens, i.e. the visual pixels are generated from "within" the façade and presented thereon and (2) façades as "passive" screens, i.e. the pixels are generated elsewhere but displayed on the façade. Active façades can be implemented by using e.g. LCD or LED displays that are integrated or belatedly mounted, or by using mechanical components that can be controlled in order to visualize digital content, while passive façades are based on projection systems.

While both types of media façades have their respective (dis-)advantages, we believe that projections offer a wider variety of possible applications due to the following properties:

- **Ease of installation:** A projector and a spot (this is the probably most tricky part) where it can be placed is all that is needed. If the projector is situated outdoors, an appropriate housing is required.
- **Flexibility:** If only parts of a façade are turned into a media façade, it only requires slight rearrangements to enlighten another part of the façade.
- **Extensibility:** In order to increase the size of the media façade, either add another projector or change the zoom level of the current projector. Alternatively, a steerable mirror could be used to project the digital content onto (very) dislocated façades/objects.
- **Unobtrusiveness:** The façade is not manipulated. No components need to be fixed into the fabric of the building – during daylight the façade looks as usual.

- **Acceptability:** Only the projector and its optional housing are physically present components. When the projector is switched off, the façade remains unaltered.
- **Single point of failure:** There is only the projector that may fail. And if it does, the façade simply looks the way it was originally built. In multi projector systems this advantage might get lost, however it is possible to have fallback projectors in case of critical applications.

Content and Presentation

One of the key aspects of our understanding of media façades is the renunciation of a visible 4:3 rectangular screen that is typically imposed by current projecting technologies. Luckily, projectors offer to only lighten up selected parts of a façade, thus enabling arbitrarily shaped fragments of content without the visual clutter of a rectangular frame.

We have investigated two kinds of shapes in a demo setup: static and dynamic fragments. With static fragments we mean preconfigured two-dimensional shapes that can display still or moving images and text within certain boundaries (cf. Figure 1.c). Dynamic fragments are floating elements that are able to move freely within a predefined area but obstacles can be declared which can be hit by the elements and let them bounce back. Separate words of a sentence could e.g. "drop" into the façade and virtually interact with window borders or ornamentations.

STAGED FAÇADES FRAMEWORK

We have implemented a staged façades framework prototype to get an impression of the efficiency of urban façades as large-scale public displays. The two visualization metaphors static fragments and dynamic fragments were projected onto the façade of a theatre in Linz, Austria during a late evening performance of La Traviata.

Technical Implementation

We have implemented our framework as a two-dimensional OpenGL application with the ability to render simple still image textures as well as recorded videos and live video streams acquired through a USB webcam. Fragments can be assigned different z-values thus enabling a certain layer control. Static fragments are simply correctly arranged textured polygons that stay at a certain position and show a movie clip or any other texture, while dynamic fragments are

Figure 1. Segmentation of (a) a building's façade using (b) edge detection and (c) subsequent labeling of different areas. In our prototype this process is done manually, however an automated segmentation is the next step towards a truly flexible framework

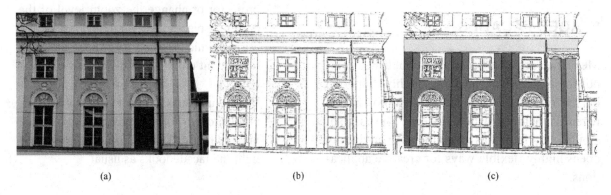

(a)   (b)   (c)

convex polygons with arbitrary textures that are registered at a dynamics engine which calculates their movements based on simulated physical properties such as gravity, elasticity and weight of different objects. Windows and other ornamentation are defined as obstacles, which bounce back the dynamic fragments and thus define "closed areas" that cannot be entered.

One important aspect is to exclude windows to be projected onto, in order to not distract people working in the respective rooms behind those windows. In the same way that obstacles can be defined (by manually marking the shape of these objects using a computer mouse, directly on the façade), areas with black content can be added to the OpenGL scene on an "always-on-top" layer, thus preventing static and dynamic fragments to be visibly projected within these areas.

Live Demonstration

We set up a live demonstration at the Theatre Linz in order to test the visual appearance of our framework under real life conditions. In our lab environment we already created impressive effects by letting fragments physically interact with doors, light switches and even people; however it was not clear what impression a dynamic façade would have. We used a large venue projector with 12.000 ANSI lumens to project on an area of about 4.5 x 6 square meters from a distance of approximately 18 meters. The effect of both static and dynamic fragments was very good regarding both the "technical" (brightness, resolution) and the "subjective" appearance (overall look and feel), regarding to the statements of present viewers (cf. Figure 2).

CONCLUSION

Our first prototype showed that the technology used for the projection is suitable for urban media façade setups. The overall impression of the displayed content was very good; especially the dynamic fragments and their virtual physical interactions with the façade's structure were perceived as entertaining and funny. Since this installation was designed to run for a short time in order to give an impression to the development team as well as to representatives of the Theatre Linz, we did not generate a survey or other formalized process to gather quantitative data on the installation. The informal response of the involved persons and our own impression however have both caused us to continue our work on media façades as a main research task in a follow-up research pro-

Figure 2. (a) simulation of gravity affected dynamic fragments on a Viennese building, (b) live demonstration at the Theatre Linz – static fragments and (c) dynamic fragments falling down the façade and bouncing off windows

(a)   (b)   (c)

gramme focussing on pervasive display systems in public spaces.

ACKNOWLEDGMENT

We would like to thank Bernadette Emsenhuber, Heinrich Schmitzberger and Dominik Hochreiter of University Linz who helped us with the preparation of the live demonstration at the Theatre Linz, as well as Thomas Königstorfer, commercial chairman of the Theatre Linz, for his support regarding the live setup and encouragement for further development.

REFERENCES

Ames, M., Bettadapur, C., Dey, A., & Mankoff, J. (2003). Healthy Cities Ambient Displays. *In Extended Abstracts of UbiComp 2003.* http://guir.berkeley.edu/pubs/ubicomp2003/healthycities.pdf

Churchill, E. F., Nelson, L., Denoue, L., Helfman, J., & Murphy, P. (2004). Sharing Multimedia Content with Interactive Public Displays: A Case Study. *In Proceedings of the 5th conference on Designing Interactive Systems* (pp. 7-16). New York: ACM.

Czerwinski, M., Robertson, G., Meyers, B., Smith, G., & Robbins, D. (2006). Large Display Research Overview. In *CHI '06: Extended Abstracts on Human Factors in Computing Systems* (pp. 69–74). New York: ACM. doi:10.1145/1125451.1125471

Downie, A. (2008). São Paulo Sells Itself. In *Time Magazine, US Edition*, 172:22. New York: Time Warner.

Elliot, K., & Greenberg, S. (2004). Building Flexible Displays for Awareness and Interaction. In *Proceedings of the UbiComp '04 Workshop on Ubiquitous Display Environments*, Nottingham, U.K.

Ferscha, A. (2007a). Informative Art Display Metaphors. In Stephanidis, C. (Ed.), *Universal Access in HCI, Part II* (pp. 82–92). Berlin, Heidelberg: Springer.

Ferscha, A. (2007b). A Matter of Taste. In Schiele, B. (Eds.), *Ambient Intelligence* (pp. 287–304). Berlin, Heidelberg: Springer. doi:10.1007/978-3-540-76652-0_17

Gellersen, H. W., Schmidt, A., & Beigl, M. (1999). Ambient Media for Peripheral Information Display. *Personal and Ubiquitous Computing, 3*(4), 199–208. doi:10.1007/BF01540553

Holmquist, L. E., & Skog, T. (2003). Informative art: information visualization in everyday environments. *Proceedings of the 1st international conference on Computer graphics and interactive techniques* (pp. 229-235). New York: ACM.

Ishii, H., & Ullmer, B. (1997). Tangible Bits: Towards Seamless Interfaces between People, Bits and Atoms. In *Proceedings of the Conference on Human Factors in Computing systems* (pp. 234-241). New York: ACM.

Kreller, B., Carrega, D., Shankar, J. P., Salmon, P., Böttger, S., & Kassing, T. (1998). A Mobile-Aware City Guide Application. In *Proceedings of ACTS Mobile Communications Summit* (pp. 60-65), Rhodes, Greece.

Mankoff, J., & Dey, A. K. (2003). From conception to design: a practical guide to designing ambient displays. In Ohara, K., & Churchill, E. (Eds.), *Public and Situated Displays*. Amsterdam: Kluwer.

Mankoff, J., Dey, A. K., Hsieh, G., Kientz, J., Lederer, S., & Ames, M. (2003). Heuristic Evaluation of Ambient Displays. In *Proceedings of the Conference on Human Factors in Computing Systems (CHI 2003)* (pp. 169-176). New York: ACM.

Mignonneau, L., & Sommerer, C. (2008). Media Facades as Architectural Interfaces. In Sommerer, C., Lakhmi, C., & Mignonneau, L. (Eds.), *The Art and Science of Interface and Interaction Design* (pp. 93–104). Berlin, Heidelberg: Springer. doi:10.1007/978-3-540-79870-5_6

Peltonen, P., Kurvinen, E., Salovaara, A., Jacucci, G., Ilmonen, T., Evans, J., et al. (2008). It's Mine Don't Touch!: Interactions at a Large Multi-Touch Display in a City Centre. In *Proceeding of the 26th Annual SIGCHI Conference on Human Factors in Computing Systems* (pp. 1285-1294). New York: ACM.

Schoch, O. (2006). My Building is my Display. In *Proceedings of the 24th Annual eCAADe Conference* (pp. 610-616).

Tomitsch, M., Kappel, K., Lehner, A., & Grechenig, T. (2007). Towards a Taxonomy for Ambient Information Systems. In *Workshop at Pervasive 2007: Designing and Evaluating Ambient Information Systems. 5th International Conference on Pervasive Computing* (pp. 42-47). Toronto, Canada.

Vogel, D., & Balakrishnan, R. (2004). Interactive Public Ambient Displays: Transitioning from Implicit to Explicit, Public to Personal, Interaction with Multiple Users. In *Proceedings of the 17th Annual ACM Symposium on User Interface Software and Technology* (pp. 137-146). New York: ACM.

This work was previously published in International Journal of Ambient Computing and Intelligence (IJACI), Volume 1, Issue 2, edited by Kevin Curran, pp. 20-30, copyright 2009 by IGI Publishing (an imprint of IGI Global).

Chapter 11
Ambient Displays in Academic Settings:
Avoiding their Underutilization

Umar Rashid
University College Dublin, Ireland

Aaron Quigley
University College Dublin, Ireland

ABSTRACT

This work reports on the findings of a case study examining the use of ambient information displays in an indoor academic setting. Using a questionnaire-based survey, we collect experiences and expectations of the viewers who are based on different floors of the same building. Based on the survey feedback, we offer some design principles to avoid the underutilization of peripheral displays and make the most of their potential in indoor environments.

INTRODUCTION

Ambient information displays have emerged as an effective way of disseminating information in an unobtrusive and low effort manner. They have found their use in indoor such as classrooms, workplaces, megachurches (Huang et al. 2003, McCarthy et al. 2001, Wyche et al. 2007, Zhao et al. 2002) as well as outdoor settings such as shopping malls, city squares, airports, and train stations (Huang et al., 2008). In spite of their deployment and evaluation in various settings, a sound understanding of factors that may cause underutilization of their potential remains lacking. A comprehensive case study about the use of ambient displays in public settings was reported in (Huang et al., 2008). However, there is no counterpart of this study for ambient displays in indoor academic environments.

This work investigates the current use of ambient displays in the Complex & Adaptive Systems Laboratory (CASL) at University College Dublin

DOI: 10.4018/978-1-60960-549-0.ch011

(UCD), Ireland. We report on the results of a questionnaire-based survey that was conducted among 59 members of CASL. We explain the survey methodology, experiences and expectations of the viewers we collected from the survey. Based on the survey findings, we present some design guidelines that may help the designers tackle the factors responsible for underutilization of ambient displays in an indoor academic setting.

SURVEY METHODOLOGY

The Complex and Adaptive Systems Laboratory (CASL) is a collaborative research laboratory at University College Dublin, Ireland. It is situated in a five-story building and hosts members from various disciplines. These include academic staff, post-doctoral researchers, postgraduate students as well as human resource staff. In addition, there are also undergraduate students based here for 3-months long internship during the summer. At present, there are five large displays installed in the CASL, one on each floor of the building. Each display is of size 32" and shows, among other information, the profiles of staff members (i.e. their university web pages), research images, and a news feed, as shown in Figure 1(a), in a repeated loop of 10-seconds duration.

We conducted a questionnaire-based survey to explore the ways in which CASL members are currently using the displays in the building. The survey involved 59 participants in the age group of 17-50 who were based on different floors of the building. Among the participants, 28 were postgraduate students, 3 academics, 11 post-doctoral fellows, 8 undergraduate students and 9 administration staff. Before completing the questionnaire, each participant was given an overview on the purpose of survey. The participants were first asked to draw the design and layout of the display from memory without looking at it akin to the diagram show in Figure 1(b). The next section of questionnaire was aimed at collecting their current experiences with the displays followed by their expectations and suggestions for improving these experiences. After completing the questionnaire, the first author held a 5-10 minutes long discussion with each participant to get a better understanding of their views. On average, each participant spent 20-25 minutes with the questionnaire and post-questionnaire discussion. The survey lasted for seven days and all participants were given a candy as a gratuity.

It needs to be mentioned that there is a trade-off when asking participants to remember things from memory, as opposed to observing them in context as reported in (Huang et al., 2008). In

Figure 1. (a) Ambient display in CASL (b) design and layout of the display

the former approach, the possibility of recall bias on the part of participants cannot be ruled out. At least two participants failed to draw some contents from the memory but after looking at the questions in the next section of the questionnaire, they immediately determined the contents on the display. However, using this approach, we are able to collect quantitative data about what and where people look at the displays.

SURVEY FINDINGS: EXPERIENCES

The following section describes the experiences of participants with the displays in CASL.

Drawing the Design and Layout of the Display

Most participants were able to recall the photos and profile details of staff members on the display. In contrast to that, less than half could recall news feeds, research images, UCD and CASL logos, and the clock. The results of this exercise are shown in Table 1(a).

Surprisingly perhaps, we did not encounter any correlation between the ability of participants to recall the contents of the display and the time duration for which they had been based in CASL. Moreover, while they were able to recall the profiles of staff members, very few participants were able to identify all the profile details (e.g. contact info, bio, links) on the displays. This concurs with the observation pointed out in (Huang

Table 1. (a) Displayed contents recalled by participants (b) Displayed contents considered useful by participants (c) Spots in CASL where participants looked at the displays

Contents on displays	Participants who recalled	Contents on displays	Participants who considered it most useful	Spots	Participants who look at displays
Staff member Photo	50 (85%)	Profiles	22 (37%)	Canteen	32 (54%)
Profile details	49 (83%)	Clock	9 (15%)	Canteen + Reception	8 (13.6%)
News feed	28 (47%)	News feed	8 (13.5%)	Floor where cubicle is	7 (12%)
Peripheral research image	23 (39%)	Clock + profiles	6 (10%)	Canteen + Floor where cubicle is	6 (10%)
CASL logo	20 (34%)	Profiles + news	3 (5%)	Reception	4 (7%)
Clock (time and date)	20 (34%)	Clock + profiles + news	3 (5%)	Photocopier (1st floor)	1 (1.7%)
UCD logo	14 (24%)	Clock + news	3 (5%)	Canteen + Reception + floor where cubicle is	1 (1.7%)
Top research image	7 (12%)	Nothing	2 (3.3%)		
		News + research images	1 (1.7%)		
		Clock + profiles + news + research images	1 (1.7%)		
		Clock at reception + profiles at canteen	1 (1.7%)		
(a)		(b)		(c)	

et al., 2008) that people pay very brief attention to the large displays and are rarely likely to stop and go through the whole content in detail.

Most Useful Contents on the Displays

Among the contents currently being shown on displays, most participants regarded the profiles of academic and research staff to be the most useful information, followed by the clock and news feed. However, there was one participant who considered time to be the most useful content on the display near the reception desk while profiles of staff members on the display in the canteen. Table 1(b) shows the results of what participants regarded to be the most useful contents on the display.

Places Where they Looked at the Displays

We discovered that participants were most likely to glance at the display in the canteen on the 4th floor, as shown in Table 1(c). The canteen is where most members of the CASL gather during their lunch break every weekday. Moreover, there is a weekly tea party there at 4pm every Thursday. In addition to that, other social events such as birthday, farewell, and graduation parties are also held there.

Perceived Purpose of the Displays

As part of a qualitative evaluation of the displays, we asked the participants what purpose, in their perception, these displays served in the CASL. Their responses led us to conclusions as follows:

Visual Appeal

Most participants were of the opinion that the displays served an aesthetic purpose and made the environment visually appealing. Some were

of the opinion that the presence of the displays gives the impression of working in a "technological environment".

Community Awareness

The displays enabled the viewers to get to know staff members of the CASL. They were able to associate names with faces of members in a relatively effortless manner, i.e. without browsing the CASL/UCD website and visiting the web page of individual members.

Motivation

The displays show the profiles of academic and research staff members in a repeated loop. Undergraduate students who arrived few weeks ago on summer internship found it quite motivating and inspirational. Here is how an undergrad internee remarked:

I realized that it takes hard work and dedication to be on these displays.

SURVEY FINDINGS: EXPECTATIONS

The final part of the questionnaire consisted of open-ended questions designed to provoke the participants to divulge what changes they expected to be brought about with the displays in the CASL. These included the questions about the type of information to be shown on displays, positioning of displays in the CASL, and changes in interaction mode with displays. The results of this section of questionnaire are explained below.

Content of the Displays

Participants in general were of the view that instead of profiles of staff members, news and events should be given more prominence on the display. They pointed out that the web pages being shown were not tailored to public display. For example, it makes no sense to show the "Links" section of a web page on a non-interactive public display.

Currently, news appears in a ticker at the bottom of the display. Many participants wanted this section of display to be made more prominent. Moreover, to their dismay, the news displayed was quite static and not updated regularly. They wanted to see news about upcoming conferences, seminars, and award announcements, along with auxiliary information such as weather forecast, intermittent traffic.

Change in Position of the Displays

Participants wanted displays to be placed in the areas of the building where most people linger. These areas include elevators, places outside the elevators, besides the stairs, or seating areas.

Making the Displays Interactive

Inspired by the case studies of Plasma Poster (Churchill et al., 2004), Opinionizer (Brignull at al., 2003) and Dynamo (Brignull at al., 2004), we proposed to the participants the possible option of making the CASL displays interactive and allowing them to upload content of their choice. Most of them were apathetic to the proposed feature, but a few of them found this idea exciting. Although, they still preferred a moderated control over the user-uploaded content lest it undermine the professional look and feel of the displays.

Presence/Absence Information

As a way of enhancing collaboration, we proposed to the participants the option of displaying their presence/absence information. Most participants expressed strong opposition to the idea of displaying their presence/absence information on displays. They considered such information to be quite private and not something to be shared with other than their immediate colleagues. This proposal of displaying presence/absence information was inspired by applications such as In/Out Board (Salber et al., 1999) and Active Portrait (Huang et al., 2003). However, in the case of aforementioned applications, the information was accessible to only the close colleagues rather than people from other research groups, not to mention non-academic staff, e.g. human resource staff, as in the case of the displays in the CASL.

UTILIZE THE POTENTIAL TO FULLEST: DESIGN GUIDELINES

Based on the collected experiences and expectations of our survey participants about displays in the CASL, we offer some design guidelines to utilize the full potential of ambient displays in academic setting.

Content Type: "Core" and "Auxiliary" Contents

Contents of ambient displays should be customized to the site and the users (Brewer, 2004). In academic setting, "core contents" on ambient displays should be focused on relevant event and news, rather than profiles of academic staff. It is more inspirational to see events such as recent awards, patents and publications of colleagues on ambient displays rather than their profiles. Researchers seem more interested in dynamic and up-to-date content rather than static ones.

In addition to "core" contents, to further evoke the interest of viewers, some auxiliary contents may be added such as latest news about weather forecast, and intermittent traffic.

Contextualization of Content

Ambient displays should display information relevant to different audiences in different settings. In our case, most participants were of the view that the content on the display near reception desk should be more general and appealing to visitors. One administration staff member who joined CASL a few weeks ago was particularly perplexed to notice the content on the said display did not show to the visitors any introductory information about the vision and activities of the CASL.

Positioning of the Displays

Ambient displays should be placed considering the movement flow of people in the building. Before conducting the survey, we assumed that almost every member of CASL looked at the display near the reception desk. However, we found out that many people used the car park and entered the building using an elevator from the underground basement to reach their floor, thus bypassing the reception desk on the ground floor. Most people viewed the display in the canteen followed by the reception desk, and quite a few of them looked at them at the floor where their cubicles were. That indicates that 3 out of 5 displays in the building were hardly, if ever being viewed by the occupants. Moreover, a place that was used by all members of CASL had no display, i.e. the elevator. There were also suggestions to place the displays near printers, photocopiers, and water-coolers. These observations signify the importance of identifying the movement flow of people and congestion spots within the building before positioning ambient displays.

Privacy Concerns

Information displayed on ambient displays should not infringe upon the privacy of members. Considering the strong opposition to the public display of presence/leave information we encountered in the survey, designers of ambient display systems must be sensitive to privacy concerns of viewers. This issue becomes critical when, unlike the cases (Salber et al. 1999, Huang et al. 2003), many viewers do not happen to be their immediate colleagues.

CONCLUSION AND FUTURE WORKS

In this article, we reported on the findings of a questionnaire-based survey of the current use of ambient displays in an indoor environment of a research lab. We collected the experiences and expectations of the viewers, along with highlighting the limitations of our survey methodology. Based on survey findings, we formulated some design principles to minimize the underutilization of ambient displays in indoor settings. We plan to implement the proposed changes in the design, layout and positioning of the displays in CASL and collect the subsequent feedback from the users.

ACKNOWLEDGMENT

This research is supported by Irish Research Council for Science, Engineering and Technology (IRCSET): funded by the National Development Plan, and co-funded by IBM.

REFERENCES

Brewer, J. (2004). Factors in Designing Effective Ambient Displays. Poster in Ubicomp 2004.

Brignull, H., et al. (2004). The Introduction of a Shared Interactive Surface into a Communal Space. In Proc. CSCW 2004, 49-58.

Brignull, H., & Rogers, Y. (2003). Enticing People to Interact with Large Public Displays in Public Spaces. In Proc. Interact 2003, 17-23.

Churchill, E. F., et al. (2004). Sharing Multimedia Content with Interactive Public Displays: A Case Study. In Proc. DIS 2004, 7-16.

Huang, E. M., et al. (2008). Overcoming Assumptions and Uncovering practices: When Does the Public Really Look at Public Displays? In Proc. Pervasive 2008, 228-243.

Huang, E. M., & Mynatt, E. D. (2003). Semi-public displays for small, co-located groups. In Proc. CHI 2003, 49-56.

McCarthy, J., et al. (2001). UniCast, OutCast & GroupCast: Three Steps Toward Ubiquitous, Peripheral Displays. In Proc. Ubicomp 2001, 332-345.

Salber, D., et al. (1999). Designing for Ubiquitous Computing: A Case Study in Context Sensing. GVU, Technical Report GIT-GVU-99-29, July 1999.

Wyche, S. P. (2007). *2007, 2771-2776.* Exploring the Use of Large Displays in American Mega-churches. In Extended Abstracts CHI.

Zhao, Q. A., & Stasko, J. T. (2002). What's Happening?: Promoting Community Awareness through Opportunistic, Peripheral Interfaces. In Proc. AVI 2002, 69-74.

This work was previously published in International Journal of Ambient Computing and Intelligence (IJACI), Volume 1, Issue 2, edited by Kevin Curran, pp. 31-38, copyright 2009 by IGI Publishing (an imprint of IGI Global).

Chapter 12
Beyond Ambient Display:
A Contextual Taxonomy of Alternative Information Display

Andrew Vande Moere
The University of Sydney, Australia

Dietmar Offenhuber
Ludwig Boltzmann Institute of Media Art Research, Austria

ABSTRACT

With the recent emergence of a wide range of information displays that reach beyond the traditional graphics-based computer screen, it seems that the original definition of ambient display, and its focus on user attention and aesthetics, has become diluted. Instead, we propose a taxonomy of alternative information displays that is mainly based on context, in terms of the data it represents and the environment it is located in. The resulting model described three different categories: visualization as translation, visualization as augmentation and visualization as embodiment. This model aims support visualization designers and developers in considering the correct visualization as well as display medium.

INTRODUCTION

Since its conception about 15 years ago, most discussions in the field of information visualization have focused on the graphical representation of data on screen-based output media. The use of traditional screens (including light projections) for the purpose of presenting information graphically

possesses several obvious qualities, including: 1) its dynamic frame-rate to update the displayed content quickly and frequently, 2) its huge, detailed display resolution to convey a large amount of visual objects simultaneously, and 3) its capability to "immerse" people within the presentation, in particular for applications that require user interaction. Due to the evolving character of modern technology, the very nature of digital screens is in constant flux. A wide spectrum exists between

DOI: 10.4018/978-1-60960-549-0.ch012

the ultra-bright LED screens as large as (and non-conventionally proportioned) as skyscrapers, and e-paper displays as thin, light and flexible as real paper. For all the obvious qualities such displays enjoy, they still generally require dedicated flat surfaces, brightly illuminate their surrounding environments, are less perceivable in daylight, tend to obtrude everyday tasks by grabbing visual attention, and often remind users of advertising and work-related tools rather than an informational medium that encourages contemplation, analysis or reflection of the content being shown.

Therefore, the question can be asked whether displays, and in particular those displays located in public or environmental contexts, should mimic the inherent discrete nature of computing by utilizing pixel-based graphics. Instead, we propose that such displays should be inspired by how our everyday physical environment is able to communicate meaning and functionality by natural and easily understood affordances. By considering what exists "beyond the screen", novel display techniques might emerge that are less disruptive, but more enjoyable, in conveying information in meaningful and effective ways. Naturally, an inherent trade-off exists between the communication bandwidth and the obscurity of the physical embodiment (in the sense of providing material shape) of information. However, we claim that what a non-graphic pixel-less display might lose in information resolution, it could make up in a richer, more intriguing and memorable experience that nonetheless is able to communicate insight and contemplation.

The concept of displaying information in alternative, non-screen based ways is not new. In particular, the field of ambient display (sometimes also labeled as *peripheral display* (Matthews, Dey, Mankoff, Carter, & Rattenbury, 2004), *ambient visualization* (Skog, Ljungblad, & Holmquist, 2003), *informative art* (Redström, Skog, & Hallnäs, 2000), (Skog et al., 2003), *ambient awareness device* (Brewer, Williams, & Dourish, 2005) or *ambient information system* (Pousman

& Stasko, 2006)) has focused on representations that primarily target the periphery of human awareness. However, with the recent emergence of a wide spectrum of alternative information displays, as overwhelming as architectural facades (ChaosComputerClub, 2001), and as subtle as electronic jewelry (Fajardo & Vande Moere, 2008), it seems that the original definition of ambient display has become diluted, in spite of various existing models (Pousman & Stasko, 2006), (Tomitsch, Kappel, Lehner, & Grechenig, 2007) and heuristic evaluations (Mankoff et al., 2003). This article therefore reaches beyond the concept proposed by ambient display and its main focus on functionality, user attention and aesthetics, by presenting a concise taxonomy of alternative information displays that is instead based on the notion of context. It merges and builds upon previous models on Physical Data Visualization (Vande Moere, 2008) and the Invisible Display (Offenhuber, 2008), in capturing the essence that drives most, if not all, approaches towards conveying information beyond the traditional screen.

THE DEFINITION OF CONTEXT

In academic literature, the discussion of ambient displays is mainly limited to their intrinsic qualities. Displays are regarded as solitary objects - only the relationship between observer and display is taken into account. Yet, the relationship between a display and its context is equally important for the experience, especially when the display is seamlessly embedded into the public, architectural environment. In the scope of this article, we approach the notion of context from a data oriented (i.e. internal context) and an environmentally oriented (i.e. external context) point of view.

The internal context emerges from the relationship between the data and its representation. This relationship involves 1) the denotations - the literal meaning of the data, its quantities and patterns; 2) connotations or suggestive meanings evoked by the design of the display, its aesthetic or persuasive qualities, and 3) interactions with external sources of information. For example, the interpretation of presented information might change, if other displays with conflicting messages are placed next to it.

In turn, the external context refers to the environmental setting of a display – its social, physical, and informational background. Existing cultural codes of representation, as well as the social inscriptions of a place, time or situation form the social context of the display. Environmental influences, such as light situation or ambient noise, as well as the display's architectural setting and visibility are examples of the physical context. Information and messages presented in the display's vicinity make up the informational context (i.e. whether a display is placed in the solitude of a country road or in a highly information-saturated environment).

Internal and external context form the background of our proposed taxonomy. We classify alternative visualization displays based on their relationship with the data they represent, as well as their apparent relationship to their environment. One should note, however, that the term "context", remains undefined. While several aspects have been described above, its conclusive assessment is not possible a priori. Context is not to be understood as a stable representation of a setting, but rather, as Paul Dourish puts it, it is actively constructed as "an emergent feature of the interaction, determined in the moment and in the doing" (Dourish, 2004).

ALTERNATIVE DISPLAY MODEL

In this section, we present three different categories of alternative displays, based on the context of how the information is represented: through translation, augmentation or embodiment. These are not meant to be exclusive, and examples of overlapping exist.

Visualization as Translation – The display *without* context. Many information displays exist that have no contextual relationship with the data that is shown, where it is shown and whom it is shown to. Most traditional information visualization approaches, for instance, are inherently context-less, due to their motivation towards evaluating and optimizing effectiveness and efficiency considerations. For such applications, data sets are treated objectively, neutral and emotionless. The focus is on how to best represent the patterns "within" the data, regardless of what the data stands for. Accordingly, an identical bar graph technique can be used for depicting food ingredients as well as to denote the catastrophic effects of climate change. Most traditional ambient displays also exist in this realm. While aesthetically fully adapted to "dissolve" within their physical environment, there is generally no relationship between the representation and the data, or its meaning. Accordingly, the Mondrian style used in the informative art project (Skog et al., 2003) has the ability to represent a bus time table, as well as the weather around the world. The colors of the Ambient Orb (Ambient_Devices, 2002) might equally reflect the stock market, sailing conditions or football match scores. Here, context is purposively ignored to obscure the fact that the display is a visualization, what is visualizes or how it visualizes the data (Holmquist, 2004). Accordingly, information and display dissolve their relationship and thus exist independently, in that even without knowing that the display in fact is a visualization, users still enjoy its existence in different context, such as artistic or architectural.

The display becomes a direct translation of the data into an abstract language, which must be "learned", often over a relatively long period of time, in order to be understood. The connection between the information (and its meaning), and its representation on the display is relatively arbitrary. However, translated techniques retain their intrinsic meaning, even without the displayed information: the Mondrian painting can be enjoyed

Figure 1. From left to right: Ambient Orb (Ambient Devices), Domestic Shoe Production 1960-1998 (J. Salavon), Heatsink (Arroyo et al.), Nuage Vert (HeHe), PingPongPixel (J. Breejen, M. Deenstra), Of all the people in all the world (Stan's Cafe).

as piece of computer art, while the Ambient Orb remains a calm, beautiful light object. However, the potential realm of what data can be translated into is infinite, as any known human stimulus can ultimately be driven by some sort of real-time or historical data source. Accordingly, some "data art" designers and artists have explored the boundaries of our visual sense (e.g. Jason Salavon's "Shoes, Domestic Production 1960-1998 (Salavon, 2008)), as well as the possibilities of alternative sensorial modalities, such as sound, touch, smell, or taste, to represent information (Vande Moere, 2008). Due to the immense realm of opportunities, this field is still in an explorative state, even while there exists the more functional goal to use alternatively sensorial channels to free and augment our visual sense for parallel activities.

Visualization as Augmentation – The display *within* context. Other forms of alternative information displays are specifically designed within the functionality of a specific physical context, making use of the physical affordances provided by the physical object they are directly embedded within. A tension exist between the object, which exists independently from the display, and its secondary use as a display: both object and display are perceived as one as the natural affordances provide sufficient cues to steer and focus the process of understanding the displayed content. However, the display requires both the existence and functionality of the object to exist; by separating display and object, the display looses

its meaning. From color-coded water streams (Arroyo, Bonanni, & Selker, 2005) to data-driven illuminated clouds (HeHe, 2008), such information augmented objects might have the particular quality to be more "ambient" and "peripheral" than many existing displays that claim to fall within the traditional definition of ambient visualization, due to the tight coupling between information and the environment, so that the display becomes less obtrusive and more intuitively understandable.

Another field in this category, so-called wearable visualizations, are based on representing information within the context of a person "wearing" the display. Wearable visualizations are thus "performed" by a wearer, and the fact that it is perceived as being worn provides the meaning to the display. Similar to the difference whether a slogan is printed in a book or on a T-shirt, wearable data-driven electronic fashion pieces receive meaning through the relationship to the person wearing it, as well as through the situation in which it is worn (Fajardo & Vande Moere, 2008).

Due to its unique characteristics, visualization augmentation has a huge potential to accomplish the vision of the ubiquitous computer (Weiser, 1991) as well as that of the original ambient display (Wisneski et al., 1998). However, its development is mainly hampered by the constraints to represent information within the physical affordances of everyday objects.

Visualization as Embodiment – The display *is* context. Some information displays fully determine the contextual systems by their own existence. For instance, pixel sculptures, physical installations that utilize matrices of small, repeated objects to simulate text and objects, draw their aesthetic effect from the complexity and sophistication involved in materializing, and dynamically transforming, physical pixels. Although all pixel sculptures communicate specific content, very few go beyond addressing the physical medium of the display itself: often, the display medium overwhelms the meaning of the content, and in fact, the message "is the medium". The "pixel material", ranging from ping-pong balls (Breejen & Deenstra, 2007) to well synchronized water drops (Rayner, 2007), is rarely chosen in accordance to a contextually relevant factor, and these sorts of displays are mainly driven by factors of originality (to be the first in implementing a specific sort of display) or effects (overwhelming users with the technical or visual quality of the display). However, even with a disconnection between information and medium, it is unlike the translation category. The display cannot exist without the information: a pixel sculpture's "raison d'être" is representing information, and without information, the pixel sculpture becomes a collection of dynamic items without unity or meaning. More outspokenly, the emerging field of data sculptures addresses the materialization of information into three-dimensional form. Such sculptures often play with the distance between sign (the information) and object (the materialization of the information) in that their metaphorical distance plays an important role in how the information is interpreted. The representation of people as grains of rice (Stan's_Cafe, 2008) forms such as an example: the sheer magnitude of rice grains might well impress the audience, but only because each of the mountains of rice have a small, informational label to denote their meaning.

Overlapping categories. The boundaries between the categories of translation and embodiment are fluid. While in the first category the emphasis is set on the representational language, it is the materiality of the display's components that make up the second category. However, some examples combine both aspects. For instance, a single Ambient Orb (Ambient_Devices, 2002) highlights the translation of data into color, while a matrix of nine Ambient Orbs driven by an appropriate data-set shifts the emphasis to its materiality as a pixel sculpture. Yet, even in this borderline case, the experience is determined by display's relationship to its context. While one orb shows no such relationship, the spatial arrangement of many orbs establishes a network of relationships between its components, thus creates its own context. Table 1 further exemplifies the distinctions between the three categories. It differentiates between: 1) Shape, the correspondence between the physical manifestation of the display and the information it conveys (e.g. does the shape still makes sense without the information represented?); 2) Functionality, the question whether the display fulfills other purposes (i.e. artistic or utilitarian) without its secondary function of conveying information; and 3) Environment, the connection between the display and its environment (e.g. does the display change its meaning significantly in a different physical environment?).

CONCLUSION

In the current age of rapid experimentation by artists, designers and developers, information visualization is increasingly moving towards becoming a medium in its own right. Accordingly, the traditional definition of ambient display, with its main focus on cognitive issues like peripherality and aesthetic value, seems to have become insufficient to capture the current developments towards more explorative ways of representing information. By focusing on three different contextual approaches by which the information is represented, we present a concise model that aims to capture the main research

Table 1. Alternative information display model

CATEGORY	Mapping	Augmentation	Embodiment
Design fields.	*Ambient Display Alternative Modality*	*Object Augmentation Wearable Visualization*	*Data Sculpture Pixel Sculpture*
Shape. Display's shape dependent from information?	No.	No.	Yes.
Functionality. Display functionality dependent from information?	Yes.	Yes.	No.
Environment. Display dependent from environment?	No.	Yes.	No.
Negative Issues.	Learning information mapping rules required.	Limited possibilities of physical affordances.	Complexity of display. Medium is more important than message.
Potential Applications Focus.	Traditional information visualization. Focus on patterns within data.	Focus on functionality of information augmented object. Data must be conceptual connected to object.	Focus on communication medium. Reinterpretation of data.

directions, and to inform the design decisions of future display developers.

REFERENCES

Ambient_Devices. (2002). Ambient Orb.

Arroyo, E., Bonanni, L., & Selker, T. (2005). Waterbot: exploring feedback and persuasive techniques at the sink. Paper presented at the SIG-CHI conference on Human factors in computing systems (CHI'05).

Breejen, J. d., & Deenstra, M. (2007). Ping Pong Pixel.

Brewer, J., Williams, A., & Dourish, P. (2005). Nimio: An Ambient Awareness Device. Paper presented at the European Conference on Computer-Supported Cooperative Work (ECSCW'05).

ChaosComputerClub. (2001). Project Blinkenlights.

Dourish, P. (2004). What we talk about when we talk about context. *Personal and Ubiquitous Computing*, *8*(1), 19–30. doi:10.1007/s00779-003-0253-8

Fajardo, N., & Vande Moere, A. (2008). External-Eyes: Evaluating the Visual Abstraction of Human Emotion on a Public Wearable Display Device. Paper presented at the Conference of the Australian Computer-Human Interaction (OZCHI'08), Cairns, Australia.

HeHe. (2008). Nuage Vert.

Holmquist, L. E. (2004). Evaluating the Comprehension of Ambient Displays. Paper presented at the Conference on Human Factors in Computing Systems - Extended Abstracts (CHI'04), Vienna, Austria.

Mankoff, J., Dey, A. K., Hsieh, G., Kientz, J., Lederer, S., & Ames, M. (2003). Heuristic Evaluation of Ambient Displays. Paper presented at the SIG-CHI conference on Human factors in computing systems (CHI'03), Ft. Lauderdale, Florida, USA

Matthews, T., Dey, A. K., Mankoff, J., Carter, S., & Rattenbury, T. (2004). A toolkit for managing user attention in peripheral displays. Paper presented at the Symposium on User Interface Software and Technology (UIST'04), Santa Fe, US.

Offenhuber, D. (2008). The Invisible Display - Design Strategies for Ambient Media in the Urban Context. Paper presented at the International Workshop on Ambient Information Systems, Co-located with Ubicomp 2008, Seoul, South Korea.

Pousman, Z., & Stasko, J. (2006). A taxonomy of ambient information systems: four patterns of design. Paper presented at the Advanced Visual Interfaces (AVI'06), Venezia, Italy.

Rayner, J. (2007). Aquascript - Information Waterfall.

Redström, J., Skog, T., & Hallnäs, L. (2000). Informative art: using amplified artworks as information displays. Paper presented at the Designing Augmented Reality Environments (DARE 2000).

Salavon, J. (2008). Jason Salavon. Shoes, Domestic Production 1960 - 1998.

Skog, T., Ljungblad, S., & Holmquist, L. E. (2003). Between Aesthetics and Utility: Designing Ambient Information Visualizations. Paper presented at the Symposium on Information Visualization (Infovis'03).

Stan's_Cafe. (2008). Of all the people in all the world.

Tomitsch, M., Kappel, K., Lehner, A., & Grechenig, T. (2007). Towards A Taxonomy For Ambient Information Systems. Paper presented at the Pervasive 2007 Workshop on the Issues of Designing and Evaluating Ambient Information System, Toronto, Canada.

Vande Moere, A. (2008). Beyond the Tyranny of the Pixel: Exploring the Physicality of Information Visualization. Paper presented at the IEEE International Conference on Information Visualisation (IV'08), London, UK.

Weiser, M. (1991). The computer for the 21st century. *Scientific American, 265*, 66–75. doi:10.1038/scientificamerican0991-94

Wisneski, C., Ishii, H., Dahley, A., Gorbet, M., Brave, S., Ullmer, B., et al. (1998). Ambient Displays: Turning Architectural Space into an Interface between People and Digital Information. Paper presented at the International Workshop on Cooperative Buildings (CoBuild '98).

This work was previously published in International Journal of Ambient Computing and Intelligence (IJACI), Volume 1, Issue 2, edited by Kevin Curran, pp. 39-46, copyright 2009 by IGI Publishing (an imprint of IGI Global).

Chapter 13
Meaning Makers:
User Generated Ambient Presence

Germán Lado Insua
National University of Distance Education, Spain, and University College Dublin, Ireland

Mike Bennett
University College Dublin, Ireland

Paddy Nixon
University College Dublin, Ireland

Lorcan Coyle
University College Dublin, Ireland

ABSTRACT

Presence is an important part of our day-to-day lives. Often we will have a sense of who is around us and what they are doing by the sounds of doors closing, cupboards banging, footsteps on floors, voices vaguely heard through walls, etc. In digital spaces, such as GUI desktops, presence enhances our sense of connection with geographical separate friends and colleagues. In this article we report on Ambient Jewelry, which is a project exploring the intersection of individual and user generated customization with ambient presence displays. With this research we are seeking techniques that enable people to invent, discover and find new forms of ambient presence visualisations.

INTRODUCTION

Ambient Jewelry is a work-in-progress project that explores the intersection of individual and user generated customization with ambient presence. Awareness of presence is an important part of our day to day lives. Often we have a sense of who is around us and what they are doing by

the sounds of doors closing, cupboards banging, footsteps on floors, voices vaguely heard through walls, etc. As of yet presence representations, such as in Instant Messaging clients or on social networks such as Facebook, rarely enable us to control how our presence is represented. We cannot design colourful Jewels rather than virtual flowers (ambient presence avatars) that spin on our friend's desktops or webspace to show how fast we're typing. Nor can we create the relationships

DOI: 10.4018/978-1-60960-549-0.ch013

between arbitrarily designed presence avatars and how transforms of the avatars encode actions.

The designers of the presence systems specify the representation of presence. Within the project we took an open design approach. That is we acknowledge that users may be better suited to inventing presence representations to suit their needs, social status and social connectedness. There are two different roles for users to design and personalise Ambient Jewelry presence:

1. **The Creator of an Ambient Jewel:** They design an Ambient Jewel to fit their likes, e.g. they create the initial graphical design of a Jewel from a family photograph (static content). Then they make the Jewel dynamic by setting up how the graphical look of the Jewel changes based on their actions, e.g. type fast and Jewel blinks fast. Once a Creator has made a new Jewel they may share it with their friends. When a Jewel is shared with friends it is sent to the friend's remote desktop GUIs. When a Jewel is shown on a desktop it continues changing based on the Creators remote actions.

2. **The User of Ambient Jewels:** The User is the person who receives the Jewel and who sees it visually changing on their desktop. The design process still continues with the User because the User is able to use their friends' Jewels to decorate their desktop. A User with more Jewels has more options to arrange them into aesthetically and artistically appealing patterns, shapes and clusters.

By introducing sharing of the ambient displays we are indirectly forcing Users to reflect on Jewel meanings. Will groups of friends converge and create the same style of Jewels, almost forming a shared ambient display graphical language that is specific to their group or community? Or will certain graphical representations and Jewel transforms emerge across all Users, because they make "sense" in an ambient display? Will users

tend to create disturbing effects, e.g. blinking and spinning jewels? Or will a social consensus emerge with the implicit agreement not to use disturbing effects?

In this article we outline our framework for and approach to enabling Users to become designers of their ambient presence displays. We are especially interested in understanding how the Users of a Jewel perceive the Jewel Creators actions.

AMBIENT JEWELRY

Presence and Ambient Displays have been explored in many innovative research projects (Dey & de Guzman, 2006; Streitz, Röcker, Prante, Stenzel & van Alphen, 2003). For example InfoCanvas is an implementation of a user customizable ambient display where users can design the contents of the ambient display as part of information art (Stasko, Miller, Pousman, Plaue & Ullah, 2004). Another similar display is Scope (van Dantzich, Robbins, Horvitz & Czerwinski, 2002), which consists of small iconic representations based on notifications.

There are numerous different approaches to digital presence awareness. Prior, Arnott & Dickinson (2008) tell us about an interface they created based on metaphors of the real world to help older adults understand the concept of Instant Messaging. While Kranz, Holleis & Schmidt (2006) created a novel physical device to share our on-line status. BuddyBeads (Kikin-Gil, 2006) is an example of research into creating physical Jewels that represent different emotions as nonverbal messages. Another interesting example is Ambient Furniture that connects two geographically separated family tables, e.g. place a cup on one table and a vague outline of the cup appears on the other table (Patel & Agamanolis, 2003).

Ambient Jewelry consists of a cross-platform framework that easily lets people create and share their presence avatars. These avatars, which we have called Jewels, consist of small shaped windows of approximately 20-100 pixels. The Jewels allow the display of people's actions on their friends and colleagues' computers. So if a friend of mine has my Jewel, he will know if I am connected, typing, or moving the mouse about by watching what my Jewel does on his desktop. For example, I could design my Jewel to visually fade while changing color to red in order to indicate that I'm really busy typing with my keyboard, or change colour from blue to black to show I'm at the coffee machine.

Interface

The main Ambient Jewelry program consists of:

- **Jewels (Figure 1a)** Shaped display windows that represent other people's presence. They are placed on the desktop. This is the part of the Ambient Jewelry software with which the User of Ambient Jewels interacts. Each Jewel has its own window.
- **Jewel Manager (Figure 1b)** Displays the list of Jewels available in the system. The Jewel Manager allows a User to carry out management tasks such as the installation of new Jewels, or adding Jewels to or removing Jewels from the desktop.
- **Design Tool (Figure 1c):** Allows the Creator to build, customize and modify their Jewels. In this window they can design a Jewel or assign the actions to the

graphical transformations applied to a Jewel. In order to achieve this, the window consists of different options such as sliders to control the amount of time, color and different movements (transformations, rotations, shakes, etc.) applied to graphics that represent actions.

- **Jewel Desktop Layout (Figure 1):** A major feature of Ambient Jewelry is that it enables Users with Jewels on their desktops to create formations, patterns and designs with them. By doing this the User can create their own form of ambient display consisting of other people's customized Jewels (ambient displays). The idea of aggregating customization of others customization opens another facet of user customization. We are expanding Ambient Jewelry to allow the User to personalize his own actions with other people's Jewel based formations. This can be thought of as an Object Orientated style inheritance of ambient displays.

Example of Using Ambient Jewelry

1. The Creator creates their Jewel by using the Design Tool by setting up the following effects on their Jewel: Mouse-movement = Jewel Rotation, Number-of-Windows-Opened = Sparkling Jewel, Away-From-

Figure 1. (a) Jewels; (b) Jewel manager; (c) Design tool

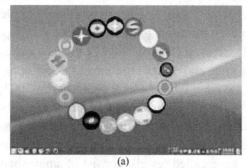

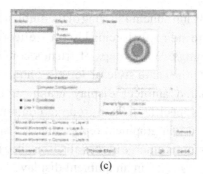

(a)   (b)   (c)

Computer = Fade Jewel, Keyboard-Typing = Smooth-Blinking Jewel.

2. When finished designing the Jewel the Creator saves the creation to a *.GEM file that stores all the data. The Creator sends the GEM file to one of their friends via email, instant messaging, or through the network communication layer between Ambient Jewelry clients.

3. User of Ambient Jewels: Receives the *.GEM file and chooses to install it into their Ambient Jewelry software using the Jewel Manager window. When installed a new Jewel appears in the list of Jewels - with the static representation as an icon. Once installed the User activates the Jewel, causing it to appear on their desktop. Then the Jewel connects to the remote Ambient Jewelry server and starts to act following its script of actions when receiving the action data from the remote host (Creator's Ambient Jewelry client).

CONCLUSION

How will Users of the Jewels understand what changes in a Jewel mean? This raises an important aspect of our research - does Ambient Jewelry lead to discussions about Jewel meanings (encouraging back channel communication and socialization)? Also as was mentioned in the Introduction will a shared ambient display graphical language emerge? If so how much of that will be due to the expressiveness or limitations of the range of Jewels people can create with our software?

Users may need help in understanding what their friends Jewel transforms mean. In order to examine this learning curve issue we are considering having two control User groups. The first group would have small tags as part of the Jewels, which show keywords about the actions performed, while the second group would have no textual information about what Jewel changes mean.

When considering the business applications of Ambient Jewelry we realize that the core functionality may not be enough. In order to broaden the use of Jewels in professional applications we may need to take a different approach to the actions grabbed. Multiple actions may need to be mapped to a single graphical transform, for example displaying the rhythm of work in a shop by making the Jewel move faster when more people come into the shop and buy milk. If we use this approach, we would create a Jewel linked to a business, not a person, so the Jewel would display the status of the shop. A potential issue with this approach is granularity of the ambient display - too many actions and too much information about actions may be impossible to meaningfully display in the small display space of a Jewel. This leads to the question: How can we measure or quantify the graphical expressiveness of an ambient display?

ACKNOWLEDGMENT

Thanks to support from the School of Computer Science & Informatics, University College Dublin. Thanks to ODCSSS, which is part funded by an Undergraduate Research Experience and Knowledge grant (UREKA) from the Science Foundation Ireland (SFI). This work is partially supported by SFI under grant number 04/RPI/1544 "Secure and predictable pervasive computing".

REFERENCES

Dey, A. K., & de Guzman, E. (2006). From awareness to connectedness: the design and deployment of presence displays. In *Proceedings of the CHI'06*, 899–908

Kikin-Gil, R. (2006). Buddybeads: techno-jewelry for non-verbal communication within teenager girls groups. *Personal and Ubiquitous Computing*, 10(2-3), 106–109. doi:10.1007/s00779-005-0015-x

Kranz, M., Holleis, P., & Schmidt, A. (2006). Ubiquitous presence systems. In *SAC '06: Proceedings of the 2006 ACM symposium on Applied computing*, 1902–1909.

Patel, D., & Agamanolis, S. (2003). Awareness of life rhythms over a distance using networked furniture. In *Adjunct Proceedings of UbiComp 2003*. Habitat.

Prior, S., Arnott, J., & Dickinson, A. (2008) Interface metaphor design and instant messaging for older adults. In *CHI '08: CHI '08 Extended Abstracts*, 3747–3752.

Stasko, J., Miller, T., & Pousman, Z. Plaue, C., & Ullah, O. (2004). Personalized peripheral information awareness through information art. In *Proceedings of UbiComp '04*, 18–35.

Streitz, N. A., Röcker, C., Prante, T., Stenzel, R., & van Alphen, D. (2003). Situated interaction with ambient information: Facilitating awareness and communication in ubiquitous work environments. In *Tenth International Conference on Human-Computer Interaction (HCI International 2003)*, 133–137.

van Dantzich, M., Robbins, D., Horvitz, E., & Czerwinski, M. (2002). Scope: Providing awareness of multiple notifications at a glance. In *Proceedings of AVI 2002*, 157–166.

This work was previously published in International Journal of Ambient Computing and Intelligence (IJACI), Volume 1, Issue 2, edited by Kevin Curran, pp. 47-52, copyright 2009 by IGI Publishing (an imprint of IGI Global).

Chapter 14
Ambient Communication Experience (ACE), Information Interaction in Design Space

Rosaleen Hegarty
University of Ulster, Northern Ireland

Tom Lunney
University of Ulster, Northern Ireland

Kevin Curran
University of Ulster, Northern Ireland

Maurice Mulvenna
University of Ulster, Northern Ireland

ABSTRACT

A changing computing landscape is expected to sense the physical world yet remain concealed within its very infrastructure to provide virtual services which are discreetly networked, omnipresent yet non-intrusive. Ambient Information Systems (AIS), permit a mode of expression that can easily exist at the level of subconscious realisation. This research focuses on the development of an Ambient Communication Experience (ACE) system. ACE is a synchronisation framework to provide co-ordinated connectivity across various environmentally distributed devices via sensor data discovery. The intention is to facilitate location-independent and application-responsive screening for the user, leading to the concept of technologically integrated spaces. The aim is to deliver contextual information without the need for direct user manipulation, and engagement at the level of peripheral perception.

INTRODUCTION

Mankoff and Anind (2003) define the development of ubiquity as relying on the concept of user

periphery; as any individual's full attention can only be factored to a few applications at any given time. Ambient Information Systems (AIS) enable a classification of communication that can easily exist at a level of subliminal perception. Principles of cognition are usually aggregated under the main

DOI: 10.4018/978-1-60960-549-0.ch014

auditory, visual and often innovative tactile sensory impetus. AIS are designed principally for the aesthetic transmission of non-critical information. Several definitions for ambient information systems have been suggested in the relevant literature and they embody concepts such as glanceable displays, slow technology, calm technology through to ambient and peripheral displays and informative art systems (IAS) (Hazelwood, Coyle, Pousman & Lim, 2008). These descriptive terms have as a common theme *'information,'* information that is delivered and displayed effortlessly, without distracting the user from a primary task (Streitz, Rocker, Prante, Alphen, Stenzel & Magerkurth, 2005). Issues that have arisen in this area of AIS research concerning the user's psychological attitudes towards displays and their opinions towards technologically rich spaces include the observer's primary concern over the perception of the information, or the perception of the complexity of the information. There exists a fear of information processing overload and a concern over sensitivity of information especially in public space. In addition to the aforementioned there is a regard for ones capability to maintain awareness of dynamic changes, in facilitating human computer interactions that are socially acceptable (Ferscha, 2007). Ishii affirms that the information that is provided to these displays is relevant only at arbitrary points in time originating from disparate geographically distributed locations (Ishii & Ullmer, 1997).

Principles of interpretive cognition and the success of ambient displays, or ambient information systems are characterised as having the capacity to modify the awareness of the user. In turn these systems have the potential to adapt the behaviour of individuals based on the embodied information of the display. Often ambient information bears relevance to only a few individuals, at any given time; therefore the consideration of aesthetics is elementary to such designs, especially when incorporated in work spaces. Ferscha, Emsenhuber,

Schmitzberger and Thon (2006) place critical importance on the values of 'purpose', 'contextual relevance' and 'perceivable cohesion' in the conceptual structuring of awareness information. Ambient systems should remain secondary to the primary work assignment, yet still be easily comprehendible. Within the context of moving information from the periphery to the centre, another important factor is that of user cognitive state (Mankoff & Anind, 2003). Cognitive state is reflective of the users' in situ and the systems ability to augment their consciousness through sensory perception and cognitive behavioural interactions. System activity is operating on users' multimodal senses below the threshold of consciousness, requiring only subconscious recognition (Baars & Mc Govern, 1996). Screen based media and associated physical architectural space provide the medium for investigative studies in this area. The behavioural characteristics (as defined by Pousman & Stasko, 2006) of ambient information systems rely on the presentation of non-critical information and the successful transmission of its intended message, though subtle. The flow of information and the concentration of the user must be fluid in that what was once peripheral can become central and can glide on this property within the AIS schema as the content is reflected implicitly at the periphery of human focus. Real objects and tangible architectural space provide the medium for this message of ambient information. AIS should provide non-distracting subtle changes reflecting information updates. In essence AIS systems should be aesthetically pleasing and environmentally suitable (Pousman & Stasko, 2006).

Pousman and Stasko, (2006) postulate further on this seamless and transparent design space based on the work of Ferscha et al., (2006) by defining the dimensions that create it: (i) reflecting on the information capacity of the system; (ii) the possible notification level of the design; (iii) representational fidelity from within the product; (iv) the aesthetic emphasis of the presentation. Finally they propose an evaluation framework based on these dimensions (see Pousman & Stasko, 2006). Direct user inputs it would seem will be replaced by implicit interaction services that are context aware and acknowledging at the level of peripheral awareness for the user. This vision will provide the computing landscape that is expected to sense the physical world yet remain concealed within its very infrastructure to provide the virtual services that will be discreetly networked, omnipresent yet non-intrusive and are borne from the ubiquitous and pervasive paradigm. Technologically integrated spaces have the potential to change our perception of information and our behavioural and social interactions associated with their provision advocating this imperative paradigmatic shift in information and communication technology.

MOTIVATION

The main motivation for this research is to provide sensor-activated communication. This will enable contextualised content viewing. Mobile devices offer convenient communication capabilities and have the potential to create intermediary support for the user and their environment enhancing an intelligent space. The ACE system's function is in the autonomous realisation of a user's presence through Radio Frequency IDentification-RFID readings with the expected objective of delivering contextual personal preferences permitting implicit interaction within the system. This communication will permit a one to many (1:n) exchange via shared distributed devices utilised in smart architectural space enabling the creation of surround and fluid protean displays.

The 'ambientROOM' project is an example of such, but incorporating a broad range of various interactions from light patches, soundscapes and water ripples. The aim of 'ambientROOM' is to extend and augment Human Computer Interaction

beyond computer screens (Wisneski, Ishii, Dahley, Gorbet, Brave, Ullmer & Yarin, 1998). Carbonell (2006) reflects on ambient interface interactions as having to be reconfigured for throughput to output terminals of varying media and screen dimensions. This concept is reflected in the ACE system components of PC, PDA, flat screen and smart mobile phone, and possibly further mobile devices and stationary artefacts. A one to many (1:n) configuration is substantiated when a user's tag reading activates a within range device display. Implementation of these constraints gives rise to 'interface plasticity' and 'adaptive multimodality' (Calvary, Thevenin, & Coutaz, 2003). However maintaining simplicity whilst asserting notions of 'calm' remains the consummation in these phenomena and a reflection of the technology we seek (Weiser, 1991).

The classic AIS example is Jeremijenko's Display Installation entitled 'Live Wire', which attracts either aural or visual attention as the incitement requires. More recent ambient displays include 'The Kandinsky system', which generates aesthetic information collages converting textual input to image output (Fogarty, Forlizzi & Hudson, 2001). 'IMPACT' monitors daily physical activity and provides feedback through detailed and abstracted displays (Forlizzi, Li, & Dey, 2007). 'Ambient Orb' presents ambient information through wireless configurations to track personal portfolio interests such as market shares. 'Hello.wall' uses a large ambient display coupled with a hand-held device exploiting the ability to perceive information via codes (Vogel & Balakrishnan, 2004). Consistently the purpose is to refine knowledge to a symbolic representation requiring little cognitive effort. An ethical issue that arises is that the abstracted notation of information is reliable and consistent for the initiated users specified; otherwise it could lose all purposeful functionality. Privacy related data for example may need to be tagged as 'sensitive' and filtered away from any public audience.

Architecture

The key components of ACE collaborate to ensure continuity of the user experience and include a sensor network, web server, session server, and user session client (to store user history, cookies, current web page state and bookmarks amongst other user facilities) to different displays as illustrated in Figure 1. Physical space as shown in Figure 2 a, is our normal space where we enter and actively and explicitly make things happen. Ambient space (Figure 2 b) is illustrated with the parameters of sensing, profiling, movement and devices to capture and provide implicit and ambient information for the user.

The system will utilise the Supple toolkit (Gajos, 2008) application, which implements 'decision-theoretic optimization' in automati-cally generating user interfaces. We are working on implementing a Grails web based Java framework that will utilise a database for authentication and preference elicitation, and automated interface optimisation and customisation. This information will be used to optimise user preferences at run time over all currently connected device displays. The ACE system (Figure 3) will take as input the preference elicitation information along with the associated device constraints and customise the interface accordingly.

Contextualised content viewing is required for the automated provision of services based on the users profile and preference. Adaptability to a user's situation is enabled by context awareness, *"Context is any information that can be used to characterise a situation of an entity"* (Dey & Abowd, 2000). This entity can be a person, place

Figure 1. Interface integration across 1:n displays

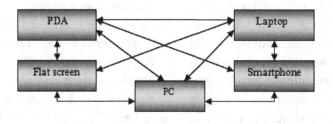

Figure 2. Physical Space →Ambient Space

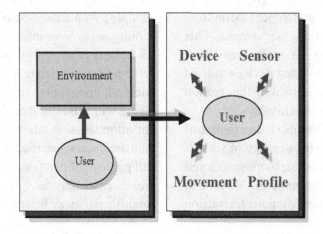

or computational device, with real existence and can change dynamically. Schmidt et al., say *"context can give meaning to something else* (Schmidt, 2005). The sources available to contextualise information in this research include sensors in mobile devices, RFID tags, network servers and application servers among others. Generally context will refer to the identification of users, tasks and their objectives that can be exploited and adapted by the system.

The server side can act as a coordinator to manage the data, and facilitate screen resizing before exporting content to a newly activated device. The client side component will have the necessary functionality to manage session synchronisation. The server must also maintain a user's personal profile and orchestrate this profile to heterogeneous devices within dynamic environments. In addition the server will also be responsible for carrying out routine authentication

and authorisation and provide session state and mobility handling within the system.

Amongst the challenges for this system, there exists the requirement to work in real-time and to cope with varying levels of ambiguity, such as changes in user predilection, user idiosyncratic actions and weak sensor signals. Adaptability to new heterogeneous devices and amended environments will result in readjustment to meet user specification and compensate for device failure supporting integration and interoperability. Whilst dynamically adapting to user requirements through reconfiguration, 'trust,' 'security' and 'safety' standards must also be adhered to, and integrated into the system design. The core of the application architecture is to provide natural interactions and hence requires abstraction of the underlying technical communication infrastructure; hiding complexity, whilst enhancing experience and confidence. Successful ubiquity however, requires

Figure 3. High-level architecture of the ACE system

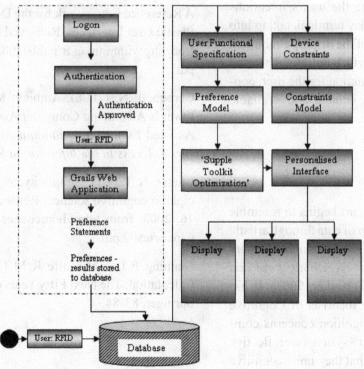

appropriate transparency integrated into the ecology of ones environment facilitated through peripheral interfacing.

The ability to capture the context of the user in state, application and service requires interpretation of 'W6'; the 'Who?,' 'What?,' 'Why?,' 'Where?,' 'When?' and 'hoW?' and is central to the design and profile of the user. Context is argued to be a feature of interaction in any human-computer symbiosis (Dourish, 2004). It is based on the premise that intelligence is action orientated and context can be used to bring order and clarity to unclear situations in order to deliver appropriate actions. Therefore context is seen as a tool for action selection. Within ACE providing device interchange while sustaining the capabilities and resources of the current screening is part enabled by context awareness. Location information is another form of context aware information within ACE. A migration theory associated with user perception may also be incorporated further into the design of ACE as a means to capture key information concerning the user. This modelling may need to encapsulate the user's intentions towards a particular display terminal, taking into account the capabilities of the display equipment and the surrounding interface options. This will provide additional information for the user, concerning the information content and available screen display real estate.

CONCLUSION

As technology advances, art begins to resemble science; the interpretation of data through artistic creations reflects a form of compression. *"Content and presentation become everything; form and function must be fused"* (Walker, 2003). It has been noted amongst the theorists of Cognitive Science that much of cognition concerns compression (Wolff, 1982). AIS systems are reflective of cognitive systems in that they unite cognitive economy and principles of information compres-

sion, where the main goal is in the concentration and computation of data and the encoding to a form that is later retrieved and comprehended (Chater, 2002; Wolff, 2006). Many aspects of cognition, from perception, language acquisition, to high-level cognition involve finding patterns that provide the simplest explanation of available data enabling categorisation and causal relations. The emphasis is on simplicity, and ease of use. Denning and Metcalfe (1998) affirm, *"to become attuned to more information is to attend to it less,"* this is where the design of AIS resides, and is the context of this research.

REFERENCES

Baars, B. J., & Mc Govern, K. (1996). Cognitive views of consciousness, What are the facts? How can we explain them?" In *The Science of Consciousness* (eds.)M. Veldmans Routledge Press, 69.

Calvary, G., Thevenin, D., & Coutaz, J. (2003). A Reference Framework for the Development of Plastic User Interfaces. Retrieved May 20, 2008, from http://iihm.imag.fr/publs/2003/MuiBook03.pdf

Carbonell, N. (2006). Ambient Multimodality: towards Advancing Computer Accessibility and Assisted Living. *International Journal on Universal Access in the Information Society*, 18-26.

Chater, N. (2002). Simplicity: A unifying principle in cognitive science. Retrieved November 16, 2008, from http://homepages.cwi.n/~paulv/papers/tcs02.pdf

Denning, P. J., & Metcalfe, R. M. (1998). Beyond Calculation: The Next Fifty Years of Computing, Springer, 83-84.

Dey, A. K., & Abowd, G. D. (2000) "Towards a Better Understanding of Context and Context Awareness," In *Proceedings-Conference Human Factors In Computing Systems*, The Hague, The Netherlands.

Displays. In T. Pfeifer et al. (eds.): *Advances in Pervasive Computing2006Adjunct Proceedings of Pervasive*, books@OCG.at Vol. 207, ISBN 3-85403-207-2.

Dourish, P. (2004). What we talk about when we talk about context. *Personal and Ubiquitous Computing*, *8*(1), 19–33. doi:10.1007/s00779-003-0253-8

Ferscha, A. (2007) A Matter of Taste. *Workspace Awareness in Mobile Virtual Teams*, In *Proceedings of the 9th IEEE International Workshop on Enabling Technologies*. Retrieved September 14, 2010 from portal acm.org/citation.cfm?id=1775424

Ferscha, A., Emsenhuber, B., Schmitzberger, H., Thon P. (2006). Aesthetic Awareness

Fogarty, J., Forlizzi, J., & Hudson, S. E. (2001). Aesthetic Information Collages: Generating Decorative Displays that Contain Information. *Proceedings, ACM Press*, 141-150.

Forlizzi, J., Li, I., & Dey, A. (2007). Ambient Interfaces that Motivate Changes in Human Behaviour. Retrieved May 20, 2008, from http://ftp.informatik.rwth-aachen.de/Publication/CEUR-WS/Vol-254/paper02.pdf

Gajos, K. Z. (2008) "Automatically Generating User Interfaces," In: Ph.D.Dissertation, Retrieved July 30, 2009, from http://www.cs.washington.edu/ai/puirg/papers/kgajos-dissertation.pdf

Hazelwood, W., Coyle, L., Pousman, Z., & Lim, Y.-K. (2008). Ambient Information Systems. In

Ishii, H., & Ullmer, B. (1997). Tangible Bits, Towards Seamless Interfaces between People, Bits and Atoms. In Proceedings *of the Conference on Human Factors in Computing Systems*. ACM Press, New York 234-241.

Mankoff, J., & Dey, A. K. (2003). From conception to design: a practical guide to designing ambient displays. In *K. Ohara & E. Churchill* (eds.), *Public and Situated Displays*. Kluwer. Retrieved November 15, 2008, from http://www.intelresearch.net/Publications/Berkeley/072920031038_155.pdf

Pousman, Z., & Stasko, J. (2006). A taxonomy of ambient information systems: four patterns of design. In *Proceedings of the working conference on advanced visual interfaces*, 67-74.

Proceedings of the 2nd Workshop on Ambient Information Systems. Colocated with Ubicomp 2008, Seoul, South Korea.

Retrieved November 13, 2008, from http://www.cc.gatech.edu/~john.stasko/papers/avi06.pdf

Schmidt, A. (2005). Interactive Context-Aware Systems Interacting with Ambient Intelligence. In Riva, G., Vatalaro, F., Davide, F., & Alcaniz, M. (Eds.), *Ambient Intelligence,The Evolution of Technology, Communication and Cognition, Towards the Future of Human-Computer Interaction* (p. 164). IOS Press.

Streitz, N. A., Rocker, C., Prante, T., Alphen, D. V., Stenzel, R., & Magerkurth, C. (2005). Designing Smart Artifacts for Smart Environments. *Computer*, *38*(3), 41–49. doi:10.1109/MC.2005.92

Vogel, D., & Balakrishnan, R. (2004). *Interactive Public Ambient Displays: Transitioning from Implicit to Explicit, Public to Personal, Interaction with Multiple Users*. Retrieved May 20, 2008, from http://www.dgp.toronto.edu/~ravin/papers/uist2004_ambient.pdf

Walker, K. (2003). Interactive and Informative Art. In *D. Duncan Seligman* (eds.), *Artful Media. IEEE Xplore*. Retrieved November 12, 2008, from http://ieeexplore.iee.org/stamp/stamp.jsp?arnumber=1167916&isnumber=26330

Weiser, M. (1991). The Computer for the Twenty-First Century, In *Scientific American,* 94- 104.

Wisneski, G., Ishii, H., Dahley, A., Gorbet, M., Brave, S., Ullmer, B., & Yarin, P. (1998). Ambient display: turning architectural space into an interface between people and digital Information. In *N.A. Streitz, S. Konomi & H-J. Burkhardt* (eds), Cooperative buildings. In *Proceedings of the First International Workshop on Cooperative Buildings*. Lecture Notes in Computer Science 1370; Springer-Verlag, Heidelberg; 22-32.

Wolff, J. G. (1982). Language acquisition, data compression and generalization. *Language & Communication, 2,* 57–89. doi:10.1016/0271-5309(82)90035-0

Wolff, J. G. (2006). Information Compression by Multiple Alignment, Unification and Search as a Unifying Principle in Computing and Cognition. Retrieved 16 November 2008, from http://www.citebase.org/fulltext?format=application/pdf&identifier=oai:arXiv.org:cs/030705

Chapter 15
Issues for the Evaluation of Ambient Displays

Xiaobin Shen
University of Melbourne, Australia

Andrew Vande Moere
University of Sydney, Australia

Peter Eades
University of Sydney, Australia

Seok-Hee Hong
University of Sydney, Australia

ABSTRACT

This article is motivated by two evaluation case studies of ambient information displays. Firstly, an intrusive evaluation of a display called MoneyColor concentrates on the relationship between "distraction" and "comprehension". This revealed that the comprehension is in direct proportion to display-distraction, but there is no clear relationship between comprehension and self-interruption. Secondly, a non-intrusive evaluation of a display called Fisherman described a quantitative measurement of user "interest" and applied this measurement to investigate "evaluation time" issue. These experiments give some insight into number of issues in evaluation of ambient displays.

INTRODUCTION

In this article, the term "ambient display" is used generically to denote a subfield in information visualization research that investigates the presentation of information through the periphery of user attention. It has its roots in the ubiquitous computing dream of Weiser (Matthews, T., et al.,

2003). Related terminologies include peripheral displays (Matthews, T., et al., 2003), informative art (Future-Application-Lab), notification systems (McCrickard, D. S., et al., 2003), and even ambient information systems (Pousman, Z., & Stasko, J., 2006). The differences between these terms are not immediately obvious, and perhaps the subtle disparities are not significant.

The functional relationship between ambient displays and more generally, information

DOI: 10.4018/978-1-60960-549-0.ch015

visualization, has not been clearly defined. This article treats ambient displays as a specific type of information visualization characterized by two design principles: *attention* and *aesthetics*. Mainstream information visualization demands *full*-attention (*e.g.* users explore, zoom and select information mainly in the primary focus of their attention [Somervell, J., et al., 2002]), while ambient displays only require *partial* attention, in that human attention can also be committed to other tasks at hand. Also, the use or consideration of visual aesthetics is at most a secondary concern in the design of most information visualization applications (versus the currently more dominant focus on measuring and optimizing the effectiveness and efficiency of visualizations [Lau, A., & Moere, A. V., 2007]). However, aesthetics is a key issue in the development of ambient displays, which generally require being visually unobtrusive but still needing to draw user interest by way of enticing and maintaining human curiosity through visual theatrics, even over longer periods of time.

To date, many ambient displays have been designed and some have been commercialized (*e.g.* ambient orb [Ambient-Device, 2008], ambient umbrella [Ambient-Device, 2008], ambient football scorecast [Ambient-Device, 2008]). Furthermore, most ambient display design approaches use vision, audio and tactile senses. *InfoCanvas* (Plaue, C., Miller, T., & Stasko, J., 2004) is a typical visual example, which uses a beach scene to depict multiple pieces of real-time information. Other similar examples include: the *Digital Family Portrait* (Mynatt, E. D., et al., 2001) (which uses the density of icons in a band to represent a measurement for one habit of a user); the *Kandinsky system* (Fogarty, J., Forlizzi, J., & Hudson, S. E., 2001) (provides an artistic collage of images to represent email notes and news articles); and the *Interactive Poetic Garden* (White, T., & Small, D., 1998).

Lumitouch (Chang, A., et al., 2001) is a tactile example, which can transmit emotional content when the picture frame is touched. Other similar

systems include: *Vispad* (Weissgerber, D., Bridgeman, B., & Pang, A., 2004) (a new haptic data display), *Water lamp* and *Pinwheel* (Dahley, A., Wisneski, C., & Ishii, H., 1998), *Dangling String* (Weiser, M., & Brown, J. S.), *Information Percolator* (Heiner, J. M., Hudson, S. E., & Tanaka, K., 1999), *BusMobile* (Mankoff, J., et al., 2003), *Daylight Display* (Mankoff, J., et al., 2003), *Personal Ambient Display* (Wisneski, C., et al., 2006), and *Haptic shoes* (Fu, X., & D. Li., 2005). *Non-speech audio glance* (Hudson, S. E., & Smith, I., 1996) is an example of an ambient audio display, which represents important properties of a message as a concise sound. *Musicbox* (Ullmer, B., & Ishii, H., 2006) is a wooden box which glows and plays music in response to light, movement and live music around a remote piano.

Unfortunately, little progress has been made in defining evaluation methodologies for ambient displays, in comparison to the design. Mankoff et al. (2003) proposed a heuristic evaluation for ambient displays. Pousman et al. (2006) proposed a four dimensional guide for the evaluation of ambient information systems. McCrickard (2003) proposed a so-called IRC framework (I-Interruption, R-Reaction, C-Comprehension) to evaluate the notification system. Shami et al. (2005) proposed the CUEPD (Context of Use Evaluation of Peripheral Displays) evaluation method to capture context of use through individualized scenario building, enactment and reflection. In this article, we also adapt a DECIDE framework from Preece (2002) (originally used for interaction designs) to guide the evaluation of ambient displays (Shen, X., 2006).

Despite the lack of attention paid to it, evaluation is one key research challenge for ambient displays. We believe that future research into evaluation should be a priority for ambient display researchers. Effective evaluation methods have the capability of judging the quality of the design to provide a basis for making future improvements and further development of the field. Our interest is motivated by two experiments, first described in (Shen, X., et al., 2007; Shen, X., et al., 2008).

In this article, we discuss issues based on these two ambient evaluation case studies. Firstly, an intrusive evaluation of a display called *Money-Color* aims to discover the relationship between "distraction" and "comprehension". Secondly, a non-intrusive evaluation of a display called *Fisherman* aims to describe a quantitative measurement of user "interest". In these case studies, ethical issues arise. Overall, the experiments lead to a discussion of issues in the evaluation of ambient displays.

Case Study 1: Intrusive Evaluation of *Moneycolor*

An intrusive evaluation of *MoneyColor* was introduced in (Shen, X., et al., 2007). *MoneyColor* represents stockmarket price and volume data in an aesthetically pleasing watercolor painting of the Australian Outback. A screen-shot of *MoneyColor* and some experimental environment are shown in Figure 1.

The experiment was conducted in a laboratory. Two monitors were used in this experiment. The "primary" monitor was sited in front of subjects and the "peripheral" monitor was mounted on the wall (subjects need to raise their heads to see the peripheral monitor). Eighteen subjects participated in the study (9 female, 9 male; 7 subjects knew nothing about ambient displays;

and the reminder had some knowledge; none were experts). There were two user tasks. The primary task for participants was to play a specially designed game for two minutes on the "primary" monitor (see Figure 1). Subjects were also required to glance information from the "peripheral" monitor. Each subject had 15 tests, based on information displayed in the peripheral monitor. The entire experiment lasted about 1.5 hours for each subject. Testing of all 18 subjects was conducted within three weeks. Standard HCI ethical procedures were followed, with standard consent forms.

A within-subject experimental design was used with non-fixed ordering of the experimental tests.

Our previous paper (Shen, X., et al., 2007) revealed that *distraction* can be further divided into two parts: *display-distraction* and *self-interruption*. Here, we want to discover the relationship between "distraction" and "comprehension".

Three parameters were analyzed:

- *Mean Comprehension Rate* (MCR) is derived from the answers given in the questionnaire; it measures the correctness of the information that subjects recalled about the information on the peripheral display. A larger MCR indicates better understanding of the ambient display.

- *Mean Self-Interruption* (MSI) counts the number of focus shifts to the peripheral screen prompted by the subjects them-

Figure 1. Mephor and experimental setting of MoneyColor

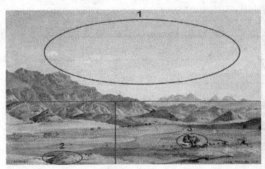

selves; a larger MSI denotes a more curious or nervous subject.

- *Mean Display-Distraction* (MDD) counts the number of focus shifts to the peripheral screen caused by display distraction; a lower MDD denotes a calmer ambient display.

A statistical correlation method was used to compute relationships between MCR, MSI and MDD. The results (see details in Figure 2) showed that MCR is indirectly proportional to MDD. However, there is no significant relationship between MCR and MSI.

Case Study 2: Non-Intrusive Evaluation of *Fisherman*

The *Fisherman* display and its environment are illustrated in Figure 3. More specifically, the display was located in a purpose-built frame, which also enclosed an IR sensor and a video camera. The evaluation study lasted five months. Every single person passing by *Fisherman* was a subject of this experiment, as it was based on the assumption that an effective evaluation study of a publicly accessible ambient display should be derived from actual use of the display in a real-

life environment. The *Fisherman* visualization metaphor was described on an A4 sheet on the frame, for all passers-by to see (see Figure 3).

The camera and the IR sensor independently counted the number of people who passed by the display. The count was done twice as an error control. The face detection system counted the number of times that a person faced the display for more than 10 seconds. Further, a face recognition program was used to determine how many different subjects visited our display within one day. A participant was counted as taking a second visit if he/she left the display for more than 1 minute.

Note that the state of the art in face detection and recognition is currently not precise in non-laboratory conditions (i.e. it is strongly affected by lighting conditions, camera pose angle limitations, etc.). Tests showed an error rate of about 30% in face detection; while this was high, it was partially corrected by the IR sensor and the results were adequate for our needs. Face recognition error rates were higher, and the quality of our data on the number of different viewers of *Fisherman* is questionable.

As well as the sensor-based data collection, we used 3 questionnaire/interviews to determine other factors, including the *comprehension* level

Figure 2. Relationship between MCR, MDD and MSI

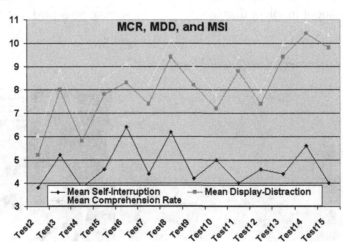

Figure 3. Implementation of Fisherman

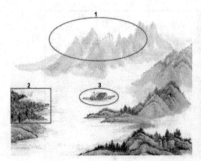

of the users. This was a measure of how much information users understood from the display.

Ethical issues become important for non-intrusive evaluations. In our experiment, we were using a video camera in a semi-public space. In Australia, this comes under a variety of state and federal laws, as well as institutional ethics guidelines (see Human-Resource-Committee for an example). Altogether, there are a large variety of principles and guidelines that constrain video capture, recording, access and storage.

To address these issues, we modified the face detection and recognition program systems so that our system only recorded the *events* of faces looking at the display (versus storing the actual video). The face recognition was used to distinguish between different subjects, but did not associate faces with names. Furthermore, to meet state government requirements, a paper notice for continually running a web camera was mounted on the built frame (see Figure 3).

Fisherman represents stock price movements in a traditional Chinese watercolor. Our non-intrusive evaluation of the *Fisherman* display measured a number of parameters (Shen, X., et al., 2007; Shen, X., et al., 2008). Here we describe how we measured the "user interest" of participants, defined as the ratio of the total number of participants *passing by* the display to the total number of participants *looking at* the display.

In other words,

$$\text{Interest} = \text{TSL/TSP} \qquad (1)$$

where *TSL* is the total number of subjects looking at the display, and *TSP* is the total number of subjects passing by the display. Our hypothesis is that the more interest an ambient display can attract, the more participants will be disrupted in the normal activity (e.g. passing by) and look directly the display.

Figure 4 shows the mean value of user *interest* over the 20 weeks of the experiment. (Note: weeks 16 and 17 were during a holiday period). The main result is that the interest decreases at the beginning then it starts to stabilize. This can be explained that as a novelty at the start of the experiment. We also noted from the face recognition data that some participants went to check the display a couple of times a day; this shows that some participants retained interest. Further results, including a discussion of the correlation between interest and other parameters from the questionnaires (such as comprehension of the display), are described in (Shen, X., et al., 2007).

DISCUSSION

In summary our intrusive evaluation of *Money-Color* reveals a relationship between comprehension and distraction; results in the non-intrusive evaluation of *Fisherman* describe a quantitative measurement of "user interest". In this section,

Figure 4. Mean value of "interest" in each week

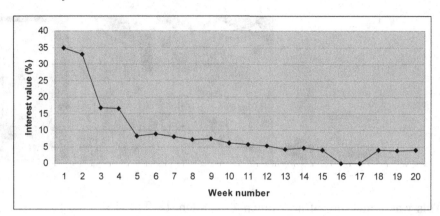

we discuss further issues arising from these two case studies.

Relationship Between "Comprehension" and "Distraction"

In (Shen, X., 2006) we divide the distraction parameter in two parts: *display-distraction* and *self-interruption*. Display distraction is caused by the display itself and can be divided into five levels based on different data and tasks (Matthews, T., et al., 2004). Self-interruption occurs when subjects decide to look at the peripheral screen themselves. Self-interruption is mostly affected by the characteristics of subjects themselves (e.g. personality, curiosity). It is difficult to decrease the level of distraction by self-interruption because this is under the control of subjects, however it is possible to decrease the level of distraction by display distraction (e.g. using slow or smooth animation).

The intrusive evaluation of *MoneyColor* further indicates that the relationship between *display-distraction* and *comprehension* is in direct ratio (the more display-distraction in ambient displays, the better performance in comprehension). On the other hand, there is no obvious relationship between *self-interruption* and *comprehension*. Part of the reason is that display-distraction is caused by the changing data source whereas self-interruption

is caused by the personality of the subjects. Thus, subjects have a better chance identifying changes in ambient displays by display distraction than by self-interruption.

User Interest

We propose a quantitative measurement of user interest as the ratio of the number of participants passing by the display to the total number of participants looking at the display. User interest in *Fisherman* peaked at the beginning, then decreased, and finally stabilized. This can be explained as a novel display in a work place can easily draw user interest. Later a number of users may quickly lose interest (e.g. not useful, don't like display; can't understand). Some participants may remain their interests (display is useful to them), which can be proved by our actual collected data (Shen, X., et al., 2007). For example, we noted from the face recognition data that some participants went to check the display a couple of times a day, indicating that some participants retained interest, which in turn can explain the stabilized interest curve after a couple of weeks.

We believe that the ratio of the number of participants passing by the display to the total number of participants looking at the display gives a reliable quantitative measurement of user interest.

Evaluation Timeline

Given the change in user interest over time, a natural question is raised: "When a test should be conducted?" Many researchers answer this question based on their past experience, but from our experiments we suggest that the evaluation of an ambient display should be delayed until the value of user interest becomes stable. This is because a stable user interest value means that the display itself integrates into the environment and will not draw unusual attention from users; this meets Mankoff's (2003) principles of ambient displays that the ambitious goal of ambient displays is to present information without distracting or burdening users.

Ethical Issues

Standard ethics issue can be well protected in intrusive evaluation, as most intrusive evaluation is conducted in a closed environmental laboratory. On the other hand, it is a challenging task to well protect ethics in non-intrusive evaluations. This is because non-intrusive evaluation is usually conducted in a public or semi-public site, and automatically collects information through video and audio devices. Since ambient evaluators cannot control the experimental environment, it is easy to transgress privacy standards. Privacy concerns arise, mainly due to the unobtrusive setting in an everyday environment (e.g. we embed sensors in the workplace and automatically collect experimental data). Legal concerns arise from many laws, principles and guidelines regarding video camera collecting information in Australia, the state of New South Wales, and local authorities. For example, the Australian *Office of the Privacy Commissioner* clearly requires that all cameras mounted inside of a building can only be used for security purposes, while 11 additional principles are listed to guide actual video capture, recording, access and storage.

Two steps can be taken to resolve these two concerns. In order to resolve privacy concerns, we used a modified face detection and recognition program (based on Intel OpenCV) so that our system only recorded the *number* of faces (versus storing the actual image or video files). In order to solve legal concern (meet the New South Wales state government legislation), a paper notice announcing a continually running a web camera was mounted on the built frame (see Figure 3). Detailed settings for video camera and IR sensor are available in (Shen, X., et al., 2008).

Intrusive vs. Non-Instrusive

There was a major difference between two evaluations described in this article. The intrusive evaluation of *MoneyColor* has a higher user involvement. Intrusive evaluation is ideal in the quantitative measurement of parameters. Intrusive evaluations are mostly task-oriented, and ethical issues can be well-protected. Most existing evaluation methods in information visualization are intrusive. In contrast, the non-intrusive evaluation of *Fisherman* relies on tracing users by video/image processing or alternative sensors to collect results (that require less or no user interruption). However, ethical issues are a major concern. Furthermore, many potentially useful techniques are still under development (*e.g.* it is difficult to robustly distinguish two different faces in non-laboratory environments).

Of course, the downside of intrusive evaluation is that it may lack so-called *ecological validity*. Ecological validity concerns how the environment in which an evaluation is conducted influences or even distorts the results (Preece, J., Sharp, H., & Rogers Y., 2002). The laboratory environment of an intrusive evaluation can affect the performance of subjects because of the higher mental effort required (e.g. fear and nervousness, for example, they may concentrate on specific tasks poorly). Furthermore, intrusive evaluation may have some scenarios which may never happen in real life or, on the other hand, they miss some scenarios which do happen in real life. In contrast, non-intrusive evaluation is conducted in general environmental and mainly collects results by observation. Thus, the environment has less impact on results. Furthermore, subjects also have lower cognitive load under this style, which also benefits results.

A final remark is that the boundary between intrusive and non-intrusive evaluation styles is not necessarily well defined. These are extreme end-points on a continuous range rather than separate buckets. Thus, it is possible that an experiment that was planned to be conducted in non-intrusive evaluation style becomes intrusive in some way. For example, our questionnaire interview can result in unintended attention being paid to the *Fisherman* experiment itself.

In general, we conclude that non-intrusive evaluation is a better way to conduct the evaluation of ambient displays, but it may be limited by current evaluation technologies and ethical constraints.

CONCLUSION

This article describes issues for evaluation of ambient displays, motivated from two evaluation case studies. Intrusive evaluation of *MoneyColor* discovered the relationship between "distraction" and "comprehension". Non-intrusive evaluation of *Fisherman* proposed the quantitative measurement of user "interest". Further, this quantitative measurement has been used to solve the "evaluation time" issue (when a test should be conducted). We also discussed ethical issues.

Our conclusions are based on our two case studies, but may be more broadly valid. Our future plans include conducting more experiments to further validate these conclusions.

REFERENCES

Chang, A., et al. (2001). *Lumitouch: An emotional communication device*. In *CHI'01 Extended Abstracts on Human Factors in Computing Systems*, (pp. 313-314). ACM Press.

Dahley, A., Wisneski, C., & Ishii, H. (1998). Water lamp and pinwheels: Ambient projection of digital information into architectural space. In *CHI'98 Conference Summary on Human Factors in Computing Systems* (pp. 269-270). ACM Press.

Fogarty, J., Forlizzi, J., & Hudson, S. E. (2001). *Aesthetic information collages: Generating decorative displays that contain information*. In *UIST '01: Proceedings of the 14th Annual ACM Symposium on User Interface Software and Technology* (pp. 141-150). ACM Press.

Fu, X., & Li, D. (2005). *Haptic Shoes: Representing Information By Vibration*. in *In Proc. Asia Pacific Symposium on Information Visualisation*. Sydney: CRPIT.

Future-Application-Lab. *Informative Art*. http://www.viktoria.se/fal/projects/infoart/. Accessed on 3 April, 2006; Online Resources.

Heiner, J. M., Hudson, S. E., & Tanaka, K. (1999). *The information percolator: Ambient information display in a decorative object*. In *Proceedings of the 12th Annual ACM Symposium on User Interface Software and Technology*. ACM Press.

Hudson, S. E., & Smith, I. (1996). *Electronic mail previews using non-speech audio*, in *Proceeding of the Conference Companion on Human Factors in Computing Systems: Common Ground* (pp. 237-238). ACM Press: Vancouver, British Columbia, Canada.

Human-Resource-Committee (2008). *National statement on ethical conduct in research involving humans: Part 18-Privacy of information*. accessed on 10 Oct.

Intel, *Intel Open CV,*www.intel.com/research. Accessed on 11 August, 2008, Online Resources.

Lau, A., & Moere, A. V. (2007). Towards a Model of Information Aesthetics in Information Visualization. In *Proceedings of the 11th International Conference Information Visualization*. 2007. Ambient-Device. (2008). *Ambient Device Information at a glance*. Accessed on 18 Dec., 2008 http://www.ambientdevices.com/cat/index.html, Online Resources.

Mankoff, J., et al. (2003). Heuristic evaluation of ambient displays. *Proceedings of the Conference on Human Factors in Computing Systems*, (pp. 169-176).

Matthews, T. (2003). *A peripheral display toolkit. EECS Department*. Berkeley: University of California.

Matthews, T., et al. (2004). A toolkit for managing user attention in peripheral displays. In *Proceedings of the 17th annual ACM symposium on User interface software and technology*. 2004: ACM.

McCrickard, D. S. (2003). A model for notification systems evaluation-assessing user goals for multitasking activity. *ACM Transactions on Computer-Human Interaction*, 10(4), 312–338. doi:10.1145/966930.966933

Mynatt, E. D., et al. (2001). Digital family portraits: Supporting peace of mind for extended family members. *In Proceedings of the SIGCHI Conference on Human Factors in Computing Systems* (pp. 333-340). ACM Press.

Office-of-the-privacy-commissioner. *Privacy in Australia*. http://www.privacy.gov.au/ Accessed on 20 Dec., 2008, Online Resources.

Plaue, C., Miller, T., & Stasko, J. (2004). Is a picture worth a thousand words?: an evaluation of information awareness displays. In *Proceedings of the 2004 Conference on Graphics Interface, Canadian Human-Computer Communications Society* (p. 117-126). Ontario, Canada.

Pousman, Z., & Stasko, J. (2006). A Taxonomy of Ambient Information Systems: Four Patterns of Design. *In Proceedings of the working conference on Advanced visual interfaces*. Venezia, Italy: ACM.

Preece, J., Sharp, H., & Rogers, Y. (2002). *Interaction Design: Beyond HumanComputer*. 3rd edition ed. John Wiley & Sons Ltd.

Shami, D., Leshed, G., & Klein, D. (2005). Context of Use Evaluation of Peripheral Displays (CUEPD). *In INTERACT 2005, LNCS*, 579-587.

Shen, X. (2006). Design and Evaluation of Ambient Displays. In *School of Information Technology*. Sydney: University of Sydney.

Shen, X., et al. (2007). Intrusive and Non-ntrusive Evaluation of Ambient Displays. In *Workshop at Pervasive'07 Design and Evaluating Ambient Information Systems*. Toronto, Canada.

Shen, X., et al. (2008). An Evaluation of Fisherman in a Partial-Attention Environment. In *Proceedings of ACM CHI'08 BELIV workshop*.

Somervell, J., et al. (2002). An evaluation of information visualization in attention-limited environments. In *Proceedings of the symposium on Data Visualisation 2002*. Barcelona, Spain.

Ullmer, B., & Ishii, H. (2006). *Musicbox in tangible bits*. Accessed on 15 January, 2006 http://tangible.media.mit.edu/projects/musicbox/, Online Resources.

Weiser, M., & Brown, J. S. (n.d.). Designing calm technology. *PowerGrid Journal, 1*(1), 1-5.

Weissgerber, D., Bridgeman, B., & Pang, A. (2004). *Vispad: A novel device for vibrotactile force feedback*, in *Proceedings of HAPTICS'04* (pp. 50-57). IEEE Computer Society.

White, T., & Small, D. (1998). *An interactive poetic garden.* In *In Preceedings of CHI'98: CHI 98 Conference Summary on Human Factors in Computing Systems* (pp. 335-336). ACM Press.

Wisneski, C., et al. (Accessed on 2 December, 2006). *Personal ambient display in tangible media group.* http://tangible.media.mit.edu/projects/pad Online Resources.

This work was previously published in International Journal of Ambient Computing and Intelligence (IJACI), Volume 1, Issue 2, edited by Kevin Curran, pp. 59-69, copyright 2009 by IGI Publishing (an imprint of IGI Global).

Chapter 16
Using Ambient Social Reminders to Stay in Touch with Friends

Ross Shannon
University College Dublin, Ireland

Eugene Kenny
University College Dublin, Ireland

Aaron Quigley
University College Dublin, Ireland

ABSTRACT

Social interactions among a group of friends will typically have a certain recurring rhythm. Most people interact with their own circle of friends at a range of different rates, and through a range of different modalities (by email, phone, instant messaging, face-to-face meetings and so on). When these naturally recurring interactions are maintained effectively, people feel at ease with the quality and stability of their social network. Conversely, when a person has not interacted with one of their friends for a longer time interval than they usually do, a situation can be identified in that relationship which may require action to resolve. Here we discuss the opportunities we see in using ambient information technology to effectively support a user's social connectedness. We present a social network visualisation which provides a user with occasional recommendations of which of their friends they should contact soon to keep their social network in a healthy state.

INTRODUCTION

When modelling the social interactions among a group of friends, certain recurring rhythms are identified between participants. Within this

DOI: 10.4018/978-1-60960-549-0.ch016

group, a single person may have a range of different rhythms with each of their friends, due to the similarity of their schedules, the differing strengths of those friendships, and a range of other social factors (Viegas et al., 2006). When these rhythms are maintained well—that is, the person interacts with each friend at the regularity that they normally do—the health of that friendship will feel natural. If on the other hand the friendship falls out of rhythm, through neglect or unfortunate circumstance, and the two people do not see each other or otherwise interact, this gap will be felt, though perhaps not always understood.

We refer to this as a person's social rhythm, and it describes the rate and regularity with which they interact with the various people they know. It is an intuitive, fuzzy metric; if asked how often you interact with a certain friend of yours, you may reply with "about twice a week" or "most days", not something more specific like "once every 37 hours." These frequencies will differ among subgroups of a social network: interactions with family members may have a different regularity than with work colleagues, and some friends may have special significance and be seen much more often. Still others may have a very low level of engagement—only being seen at annual events like birthdays or academic conferences.

A person's ability to effectively regulate their own social rhythm relies on their perception of time running like clockwork, but the human mind's perception of the passage of time is capricious at best (Harrison et al., 2007). Numerous studies have pointed to the fallibility of this ability, due to stress, anxiety, caffeine intake and a range of other factors (Chavez, 2003). Without external prompts, keeping up with friends—especially peripheral friends, who are not part of one's close social circle—can become a matter of chance and circumstance. Because social interactions are inherently vague and intuitive, there is no single point in time at which one is motivated to rekindle a relationship in decline. We believe that explicit cues based on historically observed rhythms will help alleviate this problem, just as they have been shown to support a user's health in other studies (Consolvo et al., 2008). We will discuss these issues in depth in the next section.

Intuitively, you may have experienced a digital or physical artefact that you come across arbitrarily which spurs you into thinking of a friend and then contacting them. For example, seeing a photograph of you and a friend may prompt you to send them a message to talk about a shared experience. Similarly, hearing a friend's name or reviewing past correspondences with them may remind you to contact them (Viegas et al., 2004). It is along these lines that we seek to provide subtle reminders of a friend at the right time, to induce a user into re-establishing contact. We have developed a visualisation for this purpose, which we present in section 4.

Attention and Awareness in Social Networks

One aspect of human memory is the remembrance of past experiences, known as "retrospective memory." A second form of memory, "prospective memory", works in the opposite direction and can be thought of as remembering to remember something (a task or object) at a certain time in the future (Winograd, 1988). For example, remembering to call a friend after work at 6 o'clock, or remembering to bring a book you have borrowed with you when going to visit a colleague.

Though the workings of prospective memory are not yet fully understood, the cognitive process is thought not to require external artefacts to trigger a memory (Meier et al., 2006), but can certainly be aided by such objects, like shopping lists. Setting an alarm on a phone or other device that is triggered at a certain time of the day is also effective, as it takes the burden of remembering when to do a task off the person's mind.

Facebook, a prominent social networking website[1], offer a feature they call a "news feed", which is a way to keep track of activity within your network of friends. The news feed presents a reverse-chronological list of events, such as photos being uploaded, public messages being exchanged, or status messages being updated. This gives the user a constant stream of activity and information about the members of their social network, though as the number of friends in your network increases, this list offers a view of a decreasing subset of your friends' activity on the website.

The first problem this brings up is that at any time, a user watching the activity on their news feed are mostly kept updated on the latest and loudest of their friends. Those friends who post status updates about every detail of their day will be featured much more frequently than those friends who broadcast information about themselves less frequently or not at all, even though it is quite likely that it is these quiet friends that are most likely to fall off a user's mental radar.

Second, none of the popular online social networks implement any concept of a friendship's inherent strength. All friends are presented equally, despite some presumably being more important than others to the person at the centre of the network. With many people having identified hundreds of friends on the website (Ellis et al., 2006), many of whom may be peripheral to them in everyday life (Fogg et al., 2008), it is easy for some more important friends to be lost among the throng. Indeed, a user may end up receiving many updates from friends whom they would be happy to hear from much less frequently.

Together, these factors have the effect of selectively emphasising a person's friends in proportion to their engagement with the social networking website, rather than in proportion to how frequently a user personally interacts with that friend. The phrase "out of sight, out of mind" describes the deleterious effects of this vicious cycle: as a friend is remembered less frequently, they become less likely to be contacted in future.

Previous studies have analysed social rhythms in socio-technical systems, although the focus of these studies was on the general trends of social rhythms apparent on a very large scale. Golder et al. studied interactions between college students on Facebook, and found that students' social calendars were heavily influenced by their school schedule (Golder et al., 2007). Leskovec et al. analysed all conversations conducted over Microsoft's Mes-

senger instant messaging service in the month of June 2006, and concluded that users of similar age, language and location were most likely to communicate frequently (Leskovec et al., 2007).

Online social networking sites are used in part to maintain social connections which were originally forged offline (Ellison, 2007). "Dunbar's number" is a proposed upper bound to the number of people an individual can maintain stable social relationships with. Though we may suppose that this number would be a function of our circumstances and available free time, it is in fact related to the size of the neocortex. Among humans, this bound stands at approximately 150, and is due to the cognitive overheads involved in remembering and being able to meaningfully interact with others (Dunbar, 1992). Although social networking applications have long allowed users to have many more than this number of "friends" identified within the system (Boyd, 2007), it is unlikely that a user would report that they are friends with all of these people in the traditional sense (Boyd, 2006).

Despite the large number of friends identified by the average Facebook user, a person's social network cannot be described by data from any one source. Though the majority of a user's friends may indeed be present in an online social networking website, they will also have friends that they interact with purely offline, or mostly by phone or email. These ongoing social interactions are equally valid in characterising a user's circle of friends.

Because of the range of communication options available to us, reactivating links between people is relatively easy, if we are prompted at the right time. These social networking websites in particular present a low-cost way for people to evolve, maintain and reinforce a wide network of friends and acquaintances. The issue becomes one of identifying which friends are core to the network, and capturing information about the historical regularity of contact with all friends, so that we can accurately deliver helpful recommendations to the user.

Our application provides the user with suggestions of actions they can take to maintain the stability of their social network through a visual interface. This encourages users to contact their friends regularly, but also helps them to identify problems with certain friends early, so that they can take steps to correct a deviation before it becomes more pronounced. Thus, if a user tends their network well, they will have stronger ties with a wider and more diverse set of friends.

Visualising Social Interactions

There have been many visualisations generated of social networks, particularly since the rise of social networking websites and the rich data sets they present. Many visualisations use a familiar node-link diagram of a graph (Heer et al., 2005). Visualisations in this style will often present the graph from an "ego-centric" perspective, where the user being analysed is shown at the centre of the view, with their friends arrayed around them. In this project, because we are not interested in the network links that exist among friends, we can dispense with this network view, and focus on the strength of the connections between a user and their immediate network of friends, and therefore allow them to answer questions about the health of their network at a glance.

As with the social networking websites, a weakness we have identified with existing social network visualisations is that they frequently treat all edges in the network as being weighted identically. That is, an edge is either present or not present; there is no gradation to the strength of each link, and all links are drawn with equal length. In real life, we know that friendships do not behave like this. The social links between people become weaker over time and grow stronger through positive interactions. Representing this dynamism requires additional sources of data.

Data Sources

Ambient systems can leverage the vast amounts of data available from the physical and virtual worlds. We now leave digital traces of most of our social interactions: all of our email is archived on a server somewhere, our instant messages are logged locally and remotely, posts to social network profiles are publicly visible, and so on. Even co-location data can be recorded if the users have a capable mobile device, allowing the identification of events like two people meeting in a bar or at a sports event.

Though all of this data is attractive, for this initial version of our application, we decided to focus on records of mobile phone interactions, which we are able to download as a spreadsheet from our telecommunication provider's website. These records gave us access to traces of a user's incoming and outgoing phone calls, as well as SMS text messages for the preceding month. We manually relate each phone number in the records to the corresponding friend from the user's Facebook network, which allows us to refer to each friend by name in the display.

The software has been built to be agnostic to the nature of the interactions, so adding support for emails in future, for example, is a matter of writing a client to connect to the user's inbox and find mails that they have sent or received from their friends. These, along with other discrete interactions like instant messaging conversations or comments left on eachother's Facebook pages, can then be entered into the system.

Visualisation of Social Rhythms

Figure 1 shows a visualisation that we generated from the phone data combined with the user's Facebook network information. Each row represents the social interactions a person has engaged in with one of their friends via their phone: blue dots indicate phone calls, with the size of the dot reflecting the length of the call, while red dots indicate text messages and are uniformly-sized. Weeks are delineated by differing background colours to provide users with an indication of their longer-term habits at a glance. Our visualisation is built using Processing (Reas et al., 2003), a Java-based visualisation framework.

The current day is highlighted, and the next week is visible on the right of the display. Cues for future interactions are displayed in this area as hollow circles. Their colour and size indicate the type of interaction suggested, based on a prediction algorithm that we have written for this purpose.

Predicted social interactions are drawn on the day that our algorithm has calculated to be most likely for them to occur, but the user can see them a week in advance. This gives the user several opportunities to act on the information being presented to them at an appropriate time. The intent is not to interrupt the user, but simply to plant the seed of memory so that they can act upon it when it is convenient.

If the user does not interact with their friend in any way before the suggested interaction, an "X"

is marked at this position and this is counted as a "miss." The prominent marking of these events (or non-events, if you will) serve to draw the user's attention to these more critical cues. If the user then contacts the friend in question within a week of this event, the marker is removed and a regular blue or red marker is placed at this point.

Properties of Ambient Information

Neely et al. have previously explored their hypothesis that some context sources are more applicable to being presented in an ambient manner than others (Neely et al., 2007). The reasons they described are precision, criticality, periodicity, interpretability and self-descriptiveness.

In addition, we propose three aspects of the reminders in our visualisation which make them appropriate for delivery by ambient information systems: they are passive, dynamic and simple. Passive means that changes in the information do not always require immediate attention; users can take note of reminders but choose not to act on them until later. Dynamic means that the data

Figure 1. Our visualisation of a single user's social network, showing a record of their interactions with a subset of their friends over the course of six weeks. Blue circles are phone calls; the size of the circle reflects the length of the call. Red circles are SMS text messages. Suggested future social interactions are indicated by hollow circles on the right, giving the user time to act on those suggestions when it is convenient.

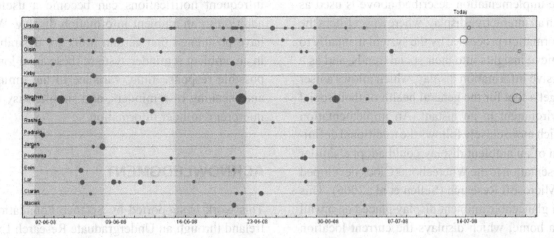

changes over time; if the display remains at the periphery of a person's attention, they can monitor for changes while concentrating on other activities. Simple means that the information can be digested easily; at a basic level, a reminder simply consists of the name of a friend whom they should contact soon. Other information may be present, such as a suggested contact time or medium, but this only serves to augment the primary information.

These three properties correspond well to the interaction, reaction and comprehension model proposed by McCrickard et al. (2003). Not all notification systems are as well-suited to an ambient implementation. Consider as a counterpoint the visualisation an air-traffic controller uses to direct planes at an airport, which satisfies none of the above criteria: the information requires immediate response, as planes must be given clearance to land or take off as quickly as possible; must be monitored constantly; and there are typically a huge number of variables to take into account for each notification, such as the plane's location, scheduled departure/arrival time, current velocity, etc. It would of course be possible to create an ambient display which delivers information about planes arriving and leaving an airport; while passengers might find this interesting and informative, air-traffic controllers would have no use for it.

Ambient Applications

The implementation described above is used as both an interactive display, where a user filters the information processed by the system manually to achieve insights into their social trends, and as a passive information display, which allows a user to get a feel for the general health of their social environment in an instant. An implementation which more closely follows the traditional definition of an ambient display could adopt a similar presentation to the Whereabouts Clock developed at Microsoft Research (Sellen et al., 2006). This is a glanceable ambient display placed on a wall in a home, which displays the current location of all members of the family. A similar display which displays a collection of avatars representing some of the user's friends which harnesses the information traces we discussed previously would have an ideal marriage of these properties.

Since the critical information for the user—reminders indicating when a friendship is stagnating—is atomic and relatively simple, it could be used in conjunction with a number of lo-fi data delivery methods. The user could subscribe to receive suggestions as text messages on their mobile phone, or through email or twitter tweets, informing them of the person they need to catch up with.

One can imagine a future scenario where all devices in the home are connected, and digital photo frames could be updated on a frequency predicated by the requirement of the user to update that friendship. Facebook-enabled photo frames have already been released—it is simply the randomisation algorithm that needs to be more intelligent.

CONCLUSION

We have presented a visualisation of a user's interactions with members of their social network, and describe how this kind of information can help a user to keep their social network in a healthy state. Given sufficiently careful treatment, infrequent notifications can become a useful addition to an ambient information display. We have postulated that certain traits are desirable in an ambient reminder system; these are a long possible response time, variance in the timing and meaning of reminders, and simple, easy to interpret reminder information.

ACKNOWLEDGMENT

This work is supported by Science Foundation Ireland through an Undergraduate Research Experience and Knowledge grant (UREKA), and under grant number 03/CE2/I303-1, "LERO: the Irish Software Engineering Research Centre."

REFERENCES

boyd, d., & Ellison, N. B. (2007). Social network sites: Definition, history, and scholarship. Journal of Computer-Mediated Communication, 13(1), 11.

boyd, d. (2006). Friends, Friendsters, and MySpace Top 8: Writing community into being on social network sites. First Monday, 11(12).

Chavez, B. R. (2003). Effects of Stress and Relaxation on Time Perception. Masters thesis, Uniformed Services University of the Health Sciences, Bethesda, Maryland.

Consolvo, S., Klasnja, P., McDonald, D. W., Avrahami, D., Froehlich, J., LeGrand, L., et al. (2008). Flowers or a robot army?: encouraging awareness & activity with personal, mobile displays. In UbiComp '08: Proceedings of the 10th international conference on Ubiquitous computing, NY, USA, 2008 (pp. 54–63). ACM.

Ellison, N. C. S., & Lampe, C. (2006). Spatially Bounded Online Social Networks and Social Capital: The Role of Facebook. In Annual Conference of the International Communication Association, Dresden, Germany, 2006.

Fogg, B., & Iizawa, D. (2008). Online Persuasion in Facebook and Mixi: A Cross-Cultural Comparison. *Persuasive Technology*, *2008*, 35–46. doi:10.1007/978-3-540-68504-3_4

Golder, S. A., Wilkinson, D., & Huberman, B. A. (2007). Rhythms of Social Interaction: Messaging within a Massive Online Network. In 3rd International Conference on Communities and Technologies (C&T 2007).

Harrison, C., Amento, B., Kuznetsov, S., & Bell, R. (2007). Rethinking the progress bar. In UIST '07: Proceedings of the 20th annual ACM symposium on User interface software and technology, New York, NY, USA, 2007 (pp. 115–118). ACM.

Heer, J., & boyd, d. (2005). Vizster: Visualizing Online Social Networks. In IEEE Symposium on Information Visualization (InfoVis 2005). Minneapolis, Minnesota, October 23-25.

McCrickard, D. S., Chewar, C., Somervell, J. P., & Ndiwalana, A. (2003). A model for notification systems evaluation- assessing user goals for multitasking activity. *ACM Transactions on Computer-Human Interaction*, *10*(4), 312–338. doi:10.1145/966930.966933

Meier, B., Zimmermann, T., & Perrig, W. (2006). Retrieval experience in prospective memory: Strategic monitoring and spontaneous retrieval. *Memory (Hove, England)*, *14*(7), 872–889. doi:10.1080/09658210600783774

Neely, S., Stevenson, G., & Nixon, P. (2007). Assessing the Suitability of Context Information for Ambient Display. In Workshop on Designing and Evaluating Ambient Information Systems at Pervasive 2007.

Reas, C., & Fry, B. (2003). Processing: a learning environment for creating interactive Web graphics. In SIGGRAPH '03: 2003 Sketches & Applications, NY, USA, 2003 (p. 1). ACM.

Sellen, A., Eardley, R., Izadi, S., & Harper, R. (2006). The whereabouts clock: early testing of a situated awareness device. In CHI '06: extended abstracts on Human factors in computing systems, New York, NY, USA, 2006 (pp. 1307–1312). ACM.

Viegas, F. B. boyd, d., Nguyen, D. H., Potter, J., & Donath, J. (2004). Digital artifacts for remembering and storytelling: posthistory and social network fragments. Proceedings of the 37th Annual Hawaii International Conference on System Sciences, IEEE Computer Society.

Viegas, F. B., Golder, S., & Donath, J. (2006). Visualizing email content: portraying relationships from conversational histories. In CHI '06: Proceedings of the SIGCHI conference on Human Factors in computing systems, New York, NY, USA, 2006 (pp. 979–988). ACM.

Winograd, E. (1988). Some observations on prospective remembering. Practical aspects of memory: Current research and issues, 1, 348–353.

ENDNOTE

[1]   www.facebook.com

Section 3

Chapter 17
Designing Interactive Architecture:
Lessons Learned from a Multi-Professional Approach to the Design of an Ambient Computing Environment

Mikael Wiberg
Umeå University, Sweden

ABSTRACT

Interactive architecture bridges in itself two design traditions, i.e. design of interactive systems on the one hand, and architecture as the tradition of designing our built environment on the other hand. This article reports from our ongoing project focused on the design and implementation of an interactive environment for public use. The article describes the project, reviews and outlines the main design challenges as pinpointed in the literature on interactive architecture, and describes the practical challenges identified in this particular project. This article then presents the participatory design approach adopted in this project to overcome these challenges, and describes and analysis the methodological implications from this project. These implications include the lessons learned from the coordination of a geographically distributed design team, "role gliding" as the reinterpretation of the designers as users in the participatory design process, and a shift from communities of practices to mixtures of professions.

INTRODUCTION

Interactive architecture (Bullivant, 2005) bridges in itself two design traditions, i.e. design of interactive systems (e.g. Benyon, et al., 2004) on the one hand, and traditional architecture (e.g. Ching, 1943) as the tradition of designing our built environment on the other hand. As such, this emerging area, in which digital technologies are used as one design material (Vallgårda & Redström, 2007) amongst others in the creation of new built environments, challenges the traditional approach to systems design, as well as the methods applied to arrive at well-grounded

DOI: 10.4018/978-1-60960-549-0.ch017

digital solutions. More specifically, interactive architecture as an emerging design practice calls for an architectural approach to interactive systems design, and for an interactive systems design approach to the design of our built environment. As formulated by Sengers, et al. (2004) the recent movement forwards ubiquitous computing calls for such a bridge between architecture and interactive systems design:

Imagine a world without architects, where only engineers construct buildings. With a keen eye towards functionality, these engineers would make sure buildings were sound, but something would be lacking. People would miss the richness of architecture – the designed connection to their lives, history, and culture. The designed experience of these buildings would be irrelevant to their social and personal concept of buildings. Yet this is the world researchers are inadvertently creating with ubiquitous computing *(Sengers, et al. 2004, p. 14)*.

Most recently this challenge has been addressed in a number of papers in the area of participatory design and related design approaches including e.g. reports on design of immersive environments for public use (Robertson, et al., 2006), design of co-creative media environments (Watkins & Russo, 2005), and design of museums as interactive public places for cultural engagement (Watkins, 2007), exhibition design (Taxén, 2004) and educational programs (e.g. Roussou et al., 2007). While these studies document the design cases and the methods applied in these projects there is still a need for new studies that explicitly sets out to address this seemingly gap between architecture and interactive systems design and to contribute with new knowledge and specific insights related to methodological approaches to design in the area of interactive architecture.

In this article we report from our ongoing project focused on the design and implementation of a unique interactive environment for public use, with the specific purpose of gaining new knowledge on how to further develop the participatory

design approach to address development projects in the area of interactive architecture.

The rest of the article is structured as follows. We first outline and review the related research in this area, followed by a description of the main design challenges as pinpointed in the literature on interactive architecture. We then present the project at hand and the practical challenges identified in this particular project followed by a description of the participatory design approach adopted in this project to overcome these challenges, and describes and analysis the methodological implications from this project. Based on the observations made in this project and the implications drawn from these observations, the article ends with the outlining of a number of conclusions related to participatory design in the area of interactive architecture.

Related Research

Research on methods and design for interactive architecture spans across several areas including approaches like ambient intelligence and ubiquitous computing from the interactive systems field, and a turn towards digital materials in the field of architecture. Below I will outline some of the most recent attempts made to bridge the areas of interactive systems design and architecture to create a knowledge base, and point of departure for research into interactive architecture.

Reviewing current research on this topic within the field of interactive systems design we find documented research on design of ambient information systems (Pousman & Stasko, 2006) ambient intelligence (Ruyter & Aarts, 2004) i.e. computerized environments, and its use in everyday life (e.g. Cai & Abascal, 2006), and research into intelligent architecture and design of interactive places for architecture and entertainment (e.g. Sparacino, 2008).

From the field of architecture we find a similar movement into the area of interactive architecture including e.g. reviews and application of innovative digital materials and technologies in the creation of built environments under the notion of "living systems" (Margolis & Robinson, 2007), intellectual essays written on architecture from the perspective of virtual and real spaces (Grosz, 2001), reviews of new digital materials for architecture (Matério, 2007), i.e. partly digital fabrics and materials sometimes referred to as "transmaterials" (Brownell, 2005, 2008), or "smart materials" (Addington & Schodek, 2005). If moving further into the architectural research community we find examples of documented projects in the area of interactive architecture under the label of "disappearing architecture" (Flashbart & Weibel, 2005) in which the notion of "nonlocation" has been introduced to discuss how digital technologies not only adds to the construction, form and function of a place, but at the same time makes the place dislocated through the geography-spanning character of digital technologies.

If reviewing the work done in-between these two strands of research, i.e. work specifically conducted to address interactive architecture we find some good examples including Bullivant´s work on responsive environments (Bullivant, 2006), interactive architecture (Bullivant, 2005), interactive design environments (Bullivant, 2007), Spiller´s work on reflexive architecture (Spiller, 2002) and Kolarevic & Malkawi´s work on performative architecture (2005). Taken together, this strand of literature provides a very detailed overview of the practical and concrete initiatives taken right now in terms of design of interactive environments.

Another source of inspiration can be found in the intellectual work by Oosterhuis (2007) on the components and nature of interactive architecture including his statement that "interactive architecture is not about communication between people, it is defined as the art of building relationships between built components in the first place, and building relations between people and the built components in the second place". Further on, McCullough´s (2004) theoretical conceptualiza-

tion of this movement in terms of the establishment of a new digital ground, and Greenfield´s (2006) reinterpretation of pervasive computing, ubiquitous computing, and ambient informatics into the proposed notion of "everyware" serves as an important and fundamental point of reference for further research into this area.

If also looking into current research on methods and design approaches to realize interactive architecture we find some good support in the area of participatory design as outlined in the introduction above, including research conducted by e.g. Robertson (2006), Watkins & Russo (2005), Taxén (2004) and Roussou et al. (2007). Having this said, however, we still lack some documented research that takes on an architectural approach to interactive systems design, and an interactive systems design approach to the design of our built environment, i.e., and approach that takes into account the broad range of "users" that an interactive environment includes. While this has been acknowledged in the area of participatory design as the need for a multi-voiced approach to design, and the acknowledging of the importance of diverse application of PD (Törpel, 2005) it has not yet been applied in the area of interactive architecture. In this article we therefore sets out to report from one such project in which we have adopted an architecturally situated participatory design approach to the design of an interactive environment. Given this methodological interest this article also ends with the outlining of a number of conclusions related to participatory design in the area of interactive architecture.

Given this background we took as a design challenge for this project to adopt a multi-voiced approach to participatory design in which we wanted to be careful about who we considered to be a "user" of this interactive environment, as well as who we considered to be included as a "designer" in this development project. As the following case will illustrate we acknowledged this as a grand design challenge and we observed several interesting aspects of this challenge as we initiated our design process.

DESIGN CASE: THE ICEHOTEL X INTERACTIVE ARCHITECTURE

In our ongoing project focused on interaction design in extreme environments we have a long-term collaboration with the company ICEHOTEL located in the very north part of Sweden. In fact. ICEHOTEL is situated in the village Jukkasjärvi, 200 kilometres north of the Arctic Circle in Sweden and 17 kilometers from Kiruna, the nearest town.

The original company "Jukkas" (present day ICEHOTEL) has been a tourist operator in the northern region of Sweden since the 1970s. For many years the company focus was on the summer season and the magnificent outdoor experiences including hiking, fishing, and river tours. However, during the dark winter the river was frozen and the people of the small village of Jukkasjärvi went into hibernation.

By the end of the 1980s it was decided to turn things around. Instead of viewing the dark and cold winter as a disadvantage, the unique elements of the arctic were to be regarded an asset. Inspired by the work of visiting Japanese ice artists, in 1990 the French artist Jannot Derit was invited to have the opening of his exhibition in a specially built igloo on the frozen Torne River. This first version of the ICEHOTEL measured 60 square metre. The building were named "Artic Hall" and it attracted many curious visitors to the area. Since then the company have grown and today it has a turnover above 200 milj SEK per year and it attracts many tourist from allover the world to come and experience the wilderness and the exotic

Although ICEHOTEL has many local attractions to offer including attractions like the uniqueness of sleeping in a hotel made of just snow and ice filled with art and interior decorations also made of this simple but still elegant material, combined with hiking tours, hunting activities, ice

fishing, snow mobile rentals, the Saab ice driving experience, and of course, the natural northern light to offer visitors from allover the world they also do several things to reach out and address an international audience. Today, ICEHOTEL is a player at an international arena through their collaboration with Absolut (http://www.absolut. com/) around the Absolut ICEBAR concept with ice bars nowadays located in Stockholm, London, Tokyo and Copenhagen and through bigger media events made together with international brands including e.g. Hugo Boss, Saab, Yves saint Lauren, Montblanc, etc.

Through the realization of the Absolut ICE-BAR concept ICEHOTEL discovered the possibility of extending the spirit of ICEHOTEL in Jukkasjärvi to other locations as well, i.e. from a shorter extension down to Stockholm in Sweden, to Tokyo as a more distant location.

Right now ICEHOTEL is taking its next step to strengthen its position as a player on an international arena. This time through a project with an explicit focus on interactive architecture. Together with Umeå university and Philips as a technology partner ICEHOTEL is exploring how the design materials of ice and digital material could be composed, or completely blended to create a unique interactive and entertaining environment that could communicate the spirit of ICEHOTEL across the globe to several new locations. This whole development project called ICEHOTEL X has as its goal to be a forerunner in interactive architecture through the unique combination of two materials that normally does not go well together, i.e. digital technology and water, in any form or state.

The design concept of ICEHOTEL X is however not a purely technologically driven project, and it is not intended to work as a technology showroom for the technology partner Philips. Instead, the guiding idea is that it should be an interactive environment totally designed inline with the vision of ubiquitous computing as stated by Mark Weiser:

For ubiquitous computing one of the ultimate goals is to design technology so pervasive that it disappears into the surrounding [...] The most profound technologies are those that disappear. They weave themselves into the fabric of everyday life until they are indistinguishable from it. (Weiser, 1991, p. 66)

In order to reach this goal we realized quite early on in the project that we needed to address this challenge from two different perspectives. One of which we needed to focus on the environment as a whole and how it needed to be configured to support some unique experiences for its visitors, i.e. in the words of Oosterhuis (2007) how the relationships between the components of this environment (including the ice walls, art pieces, food, drinks, activities, etc) should be defined and linked together to then "build relations between people and the built components in the second place" Oosterhuis (2007), i.e. to create an unique experience of the spirit of ICEHOTEL. Thus, we needed to address this design challenge from multiple viewpoints including professional perspectives from architects, artists, chiefs and food designers, interaction designers, ice designers, computer engineers etc.

From the second perspective we needed to address several specific requirement related to the location and character of the environment. Since the vision was to create an ice-based environment similar to the Absolut ICEBAR we needed to have in mind the cold climate in the environment (minus 5 degrees celcius) and how to adjust the technology installations according to this requirement. Further on, we needed to plan for the activities in this environment given a floor space of about 100 square meters and a low ceiling (2,40 meters from floor to inner ceiling, and then another 60 centimeters for the cooling systems, ventilation etc.). Further on, the floor needed to be designed to carry the weight of the ice walls and for the trucks that bring the ice inside the environment each time the place is changing its theme (typically

every 6-9 month). This idea of frequently updating the environment with a new interior also calls for another technical requirement, i.e. to design a flexible installation, or general platform that easily can be re-configured every 6-9 month to support new interactive themes, activities, events and experiences.

In general we envisioned an interactive environment rather than a reactive/responsive environment, i.e. the visitors should be able to interact with the walls, floors, things and the ceiling and not just passively watch it like an animated installation. In other words, we wanted to support the visitors' active exploration of, and interaction with the ICEHOTEL X environment.

From a technological viewpoint we opted for a design goal of a general flexible platform rather than a specific installation (compare the "general computer" vs. "information appliance" discussion a couple of years ago, e.g. Bergman, 2000). And in this vision we aimed for something like a "WIMP-standard" (see e.g. Marcus, 1998) for an interactive physical, and social environment.

METHOD & PROCESS

As the case description has illustrated the realization of an interactive architecture like ICEHOTEL X is confronted with several design challenges. Amongst others, 1) to design the environment as a whole with the visitors unique experience in focus, 2) to design this whole environment as an exercise into the composition of materials (both physical and digital) as to make them appear as one integrated environment, and 3) to move away from a technology snowroom into a design solution in which the digital technology is so tightly integrated in the environment that it, in Weisers' vocabulary "disappears" and becomes one design material amongst others in the creation of this environment.

Designing the Participatory Design Team: A Mixture of Distributed Professions

To get the design process going we needed to overcome several methodological challenges. Below we summarize and present the three main challenges that we ran into related to designing a participatory design team.

Challenge No #1: Who is the User?

To start up the design process, and to start addressing the design challenges as outlined in the case description we decided to adopt a multiple-voices participatory design approach. However, in terms of participants we were not sure about whom to invite as a "user" in this process although this is a fundamental corner stone of any participatory design process where "participatory" typically means, "participating users". Different from many other participatory design projects in which the use context is more easily recognized in terms of e.g. an existing organization, existing users, and an existing workplace in need of a new information system we could not easily recognize the "user" in our project. We didn't have a user organization to pick users from (since the environment should be designed for any visitor interested in a unique interactive experience on some theme that could communicate "the spirit of ICEHOTEL"), neither was there a workplace nor any similar location to observe and study. Nor did we have a preset "staff" or group of users to pick from. Instead, our project was focused on the design of the whole environment including which target group to address in the design, to the form of the physical space and the design of a support organization for this installation. So, our first challenge was to start off with some thinking on how to view as a representative for the user of ICEHOTEL X.

While an easy answer to this question could have been to e.g. construct a couple of persona descriptions (Benyon, et al., 2004) of typical ICEHOTEL X visitors we wanted to take the issue of "who is the user of this environment" one step further. In the interactive architecture literature (e.g. Bullivant, 2007) it is argued that people do not "use" an interactive environment in the sense of "using a computer" but instead they are "inhabitants" of a location. While this could have been just a matter of which label to put on these prospected visitors of this interactive environment it inspired us to continue our thinking on the notion of a "user" of this environment. In parallel with this process we were also puzzled by several questions like "How easy will it be to keep this high-tech environment up and running on a daily basis?", "How easily, and how often can we change the theme for this environment?", "Can we re-configure the environment for special occasions or events?", etc, i.e. what will be the possibilities and limitations, i.e. in what way can <u>weuse</u> it? Through this thinking we realized that the actors and designers involved in this project were in fact users of this environment themselves. In synonym with a computer where a user might ask how he/she will be able to use it, re-configure it, and install new programs on it, and so on, we realized that the users of this environment would not only be the visitors, but also the staff that should keep this system running, as well as the designers that should continuously develop new interactive themes for this interactive environment. So, in our project we experienced a "role gliding" process in which the "designers" were reinterpreted as "users" in the participatory design process, and the typically users, i.e. the visitors were seen as inhabitants of this space to be created.

Challenge No #2: A Team of Distributed Professions: So Where do we Start?

Having discovered the role gliding process in our project from viewing the visitors as users to begin viewing them as inhabitants, and to view the designers as users of the environment we then faced the next methodological challenge in our project, i.e. to start to develop the environment as a whole through a multiple voices participatory design approach inspired by (Törpel, 2005). To create a sense of wholeness in the design (Nelson & Stolterman, 2003) we wanted several voices to be heard in the design phase of the project. To do this we invited an art director and a project manager from a design and PR bureau, an architect, a project manger, a food designer, and an artist from ICEHOTEL, and a marketing chief and a light designer from Philips to join us in our creative design team. Through this constellation we were able to put together a team of people that could represent multiple roles, perspectives and goals, i.e. a team with unique competences distributed across a wide set of professions.

Somewhat different from the notion of "communities of practice" (CoPs) typically referring to "design communities increasingly characterized by a *division of labor* comprising individuals who have unique experiences, varying interests, and different perspectives" (Fisher, 2008) and which consist of "practitioners who work as a community in a certain domain undertaking similar work" (Wenger, 1998), we arranged our design team as a "mixture of professions" as a notion for a design teams consisting of individuals from a wide and dispersed set of professions with a design-orientation as the only common factor across these various disciplines, thus creating a very unique design team with design competences ranging from e.g. food design to lightening design, or from architectural design to interaction design. With this mixture of professions we did not only manage to create an interesting mix of people, but also a group capable of viewing each other, i.e. the other designers in this group, as users of the environment to be created. As such, we managed to arrange a design team with a mixture of professions capable of "designing for designers as users" of a unique interactive architecture, in this case the ICEHOTEL X environment. From an academic viewpoint, this initiative also added a new dimension to distributed participatory design,

i.e. a distribution of the design competence in the group across several design disciplines.

Having the design team in place we still had to overcome the challenge of how to start up the design process. Given a multitude of design perspectives and design orientations in our project it was not easy to agree upon a method to follow, or a common point of departure for the project. If the design team would have consisted of just engineers or interaction designers, i.e. people belonging to the same "community of practice" as described above, we could have started off with e.g. an ethnographic pre-study followed by e.g. some task analysis and requirement identification as a start for the development work. But here we needed to tackle the interactive environment to be produced as a whole, and from a multiple set of viewpoints directly at the start of the project (including e.g. an interaction design perspective, a food design perspective, an architectural perspective, and so on). To find a solution to this we decided to organize the project group with two project managers, one project manager from ICEHOTEL with an overall responsibility for the complete environment including a responsibility for everything from the activities that the environment should be able to support to the interior design and the different interactive themes to be supported by the environment. A second project manager from academia were then chosen as a technical project manager responsible for coordinating the designers related to the design and implementation of any digital technology in the ICEHOTEL X environment. This responsibility covered anything from discussing novel interaction modalities with the interaction designers to coordination meetings with the general project manager for ICEHOTEL X. With this set-up we could initiate the design process in two ways in parallel including one track devoted to the overall character and "packaging" of the ICEHOTEL X concept, its activities and physical layout, and one track devoted to the digital and interactive design of the interactive environment.

Challenge No #3: A Temporally and Spatially Distributed Design Team!

Having the mixture of professions set for the design team as well as an idea of the management of the whole project we still had to face the fact that the design team would be distributed both temporally and spatially.

Those two dimensions of distributed participatory design has been highlighted by Fisher (2008) in which he states for the spatial dimension of distributed participatory design that even though communication technology enables profoundly new forms of collaborative work it can still be difficult to support collaborative design processes at a distance when it comes to critical issues such as dealing with ill-defined problems, or establishing mutual trust without face-to-face interaction. Further on, Fisher (2008) continues to argue that "by bringing spatially distributed people together by supporting computer-mediated communication allows the shift that *shared concerns* rather than shared location becomes the prominent defining feature of a group of people interacting with each other" (Fisher, 2008, p.3).

For our particular project the project members would be geographically distributed with locations of designers up at ICEHOTEL in Jukkasjärvi in the North of Sweden, at Umeå university in the middle of Sweden, in Stockholm in the south part of Sweden, and in Eindhoven in the Nederlands. Further on, this design team would be spatially distributed over a couple of years from the first launch of the first ICEHOTEL X environment in January 2009 and for several coming years.

This spatial distribution of the design process has also been described by Fisher (2008) in which he argues that design process often take place over many years, with initial design followed by extended periods of evolution and redesign. Here, we view our ongoing project as a practical illustration of this theory in practice.

A Digital Playground: Technical Explorations

Having arranged the design team we then started off with a series of face-to-face meetings in Stockholm in order to establish a shared understanding of the technical possibilities for the creation of a unique interactive environment. These efface-to-face meetings were, in line with the arguments made by Fisher (2008), crucial to build a common ground in the design team and to create a shared point of departure for the coming design and development phase.

In these meetings we reviewed several existing technologies for creating digital interactive environments ranging from simple technologies like video projectors and LED-lights to more advanced technologies like OLED-displays, various dynamic transmaterials, 3D screens, hologram technologies, digitally controlled fans and servomotors, surround sound systems, active & passive RFID-tags, motion- gesture- and position tracking systems, technologies for multi touch-screens, ultra sound systems, etc.

These technology reviews were made in order to get an overview of the latest developments in the area of novel interaction technologies and to get a feeling for the "digital playground" at hand for this particular project.

A Series of Design Workshops

To get the distributed design team together in face-to-face interaction we decided to arrange a number of design workshops in which the whole design team met in Stockholm to discuss, share ideas, and develop the concept of ICEHOTEL X.

In the first workshop much focus were directed to crave out the brand values of ICEHOTEL and discuss how these values could be transferred to another location. As a results from this workshop it was decided that a feeling of "The spirit of ICEHOTEL" should be the goal for any ICEHOTEL X environment, and this goal should be reached through the development of themes related to the ICEHOTEL in which "momentary escapades" should be a guiding visionary concept for the experiences and activities to be supported in this unique environment.

In our second workshop the focus were set on arriving at a first theme to be explored and manifested in the first iCEHOTEL X installation. While we had many different suggestions we quickly decided to go for "wilderness" as a theme. This, because the very concept of "wilderness" is closely related to the spirit of ICEHOTEL as a very special and exotic environment located in the wilderness above the arctic circle. The concept of "wilderness" were also chosen since it was a concept broad enough to give room for some creative thinking in terms of unique food to be served in this environment, snow storm projections on some walls, and other interactive installations with some dramatic effects suitable to create some unique experiences for any visitor to this first ICEHOTEL X environment.

In our third workshop we wanted to return to questions related to how to realize all this in technological terms. Here, much effort were spent on questions related to modes of interacting with the environment, which surfaces to digitalize, and to what extent the whole environment should be

not only made of ice but also interactive from a digital point of view.

In this workshop an artist, an art director, a project manager from ICEHOTEL, an IT expert, a light designer and a market manager from Philips participated in this whole-day event.

Through simple sketches as illustrated below we worked through the whole range of scenarios from only supporting one single user´s interaction with only one digital interactive wall (see the upper left sketch below), via scenarios for "single-user, multiple walls"," single user, multiple walls + interactive floor", "single user, multiple walls + interactive floor + interactive ceiling", "multiple users, multiple walls + interactive floor + interactive ceiling", "multiple users, multiple walls + interactive floor + interactive ceiling + interaction via the environment with distributed friends", and finally "multiple users, multiple walls + interactive floor + interactive ceiling + interaction via the environment with distributed friends all equipped with tagged or digital objects + the environment equipped with tagged objects as well".

The development of the simplest scenario was quite straight forward whereas the last scenario were inspired by the extended perspective on mobility proposed by (Kakihara & Sorensen, 2002) in which mobility is discussed in terms of the mobility of not only people, but also of

Figure 1. Sketches on the scenarios explored in design workshop No 3

symbols or signs (i.e. communication) and objects. Similarly, we wanted to explore not only a scenario with one person interacting with a single interactive object or wall, but explore the whole range of scenarios from that rather simple scenario to a "fully interactive scenario" in which several persons and objects interact with each other and with and via a fully interactive environment. This, to outline a sketch of the whole design space for the project at hand.

To bring some extra dimensions into this already complex picture we added the dimension of possible modes or degrees of interaction with the environment ranging from a *passive* environment that demands no activity from the visitor, but instead broadcasts some animations or information to the people in the environment, via design of *ambient* information displays which demands some attention from the visitor to acknowledge subtle changes in the environment, to more *interactive* installations that demand some action taken of a visitor to show some information or respond in any other way.

Here, we arranged this session as a typical brain storming exercise in which we started with an exercise in divergent thinking in which any idea that came up should be stated explicitly without any critique from any other design team member, followed by a session directed towards more convergent thinking in which we tried to sort out the best ideas and decide which ideas to move forward with in the design process.

Profession Mixing for Distributed Participatory Design

While the on-site design workshops were quite easy to arrange and to carry out it was much harder to find good ways of dealing with the in-between workshop activities for a fruitful, creative, and effective design process.

In order to combine different design perspectives and to continue the convergent process towards a concrete design small two party meetings were arranged over phone, via email, and through the exchange of sketches, drawings and Powerpoint illustrations. Via these meetings the profession could be mixed but with a much more specific agenda than in the larger design workshops. E.g. a meeting between the lightening designer and the interaction designer were arranged to discuss if a wall display could be realized with a grid of OLED lights and what kind of resolution one such display could deliver. Another meeting were arranged between the artist and the market manager to discuss activities to be held in the environment. Through these multiple design meetings over a distance several new links were made within the design team, which created a network of personal relations within the design team.

DISCUSSION

In this article we have presented our work on "designing a design team" to realize an interactive architecture capable of communicating the spirit of ICEHOTEL. We have described our participatory design process as applied in this project and we have outlined the specific challenges needed to be addressed in this work, both in terms of the environment to be created, but also in terms of challenges identified when working in a distributed participatory design project. It is now time to summarize, analyze and to discuss the main implications and methodological contributions from this study.

If looking into the direct observations made in our research project we can find at least five distinct characteristics of this project in relation to a participatory design approach to interactive architecture.

First of all, we have described and characterized the constellation of the project members in terms of a spatially and temporally distributed design team. As such, our project serves as a good illustration of these two dimensions of distributed participatory design as suggested by Fisher (2008). Secondly, our project illustrate a movement from interactive systems design processes to an interactive environment design process which calls for another take on the putting together of a functioning design team. Here, and thirdly, we have illustrated how we could move from a focus on "communities of practices" to "mixtures of professions" to design a design teams capable of addressing an interactive architecture as a whole. Further on, and as a forth character of our project we have discussed and elaborated upon the notion of who the user is of an interactive environment through a discussion of users vs. inhabitants. While this discussion is not unique in itself we have on the other hand further extended this discussion to its implications for a participatory design to interactive architecture, that is, if the users are not really users but rather inhabitants, then who should be invited to the participatory design process? Here, we have also addressed this in terms of a "role gliding process" in which users are viewed as inhabitants of interactive environments, and typical designers are reinterpreted as "users" of the environment they are creating. While this could be seen as a little bit awkward, it is in fact just the case in any participatory design project, i.e. that the users becomes designers of an environment they are thereafter users and redesigners of. Our main conclusion in relation to this last aspect of this participatory design project is that the notions of "users" and "designers" are quite stereotypic labels that we put on people. Labels that binds us to a certain way of looking upon a problem, and with a certain solution in mind.

In terms of the focus on " interactive architecture" as put forward in this article we must admit that it is in itself a design perspective, i.e. a label on the project that calls for a design-orientation in the project agenda. We do not say that it is wrong, but we should be aware of our own point of departure for this project and keep in mind that the ordinary visitors to the ICEHOTEL X environment will probably label it in more relaxed ways and maybe even come up with funny labels

like: "A cool place"! No matter what the labels will be we are totally convinced that a distributed participatory design approach, with a mixture of design professionals simultaneously viewed as users and designers in the process, is a key factor to successful design of interactive architecture.

CONCLUSION

In this article we have presented our ongoing research and development project focused on the realization of an interactive architecture for unique experiences of the spirit of ICEHOTEL. The article has presented how the area of interactive architecture in itself bridges two design traditions, i.e. design of interactive systems on the one hand, and architecture as the tradition of designing our built environment on the other hand. In this article we have also pinpointed and summarized the main design challenges as discussed in the literature on interactive architecture.

More specifically we have in this article reported from our ongoing project focused on the design and implementation of an interactive environment for public use. The article has describes the project at hand, and presented the practical design challenges identified in this particular project. In this article we have also presented the participatory design approach adopted in this project to overcome the design challenges identified, and we have shown how we specifically needed to put together a participatory design team from a wide range of professional, i.e. a distributed design team in terms of professional competence, but also a distributed design team in terms of the multiple geographical locations of the design team members.

We have also presented and analyzed the methodological implications from this project. These implications include the lessons learned from the coordination of a geographically distributed design team, "role gliding" as the reinterpretation of the designers as users in the participatory design process, and a shift from "communities of practices" to "mixtures of professions" as particular contributions to the current strand of research on distributed participatory design.

REFERENCES

Addington, M., & Schodek, D. (2005). *Smart materials and etchnologies for the architecture and design professions*. Elsevier, Architectural Press.

Bergman, E. (2000). *Information Appliances And Beyond, Paperback*. UK: Elsevier Science & Technology.

Brownell, B. (2005). *Transmaterial: A Catalog of Materials That Redefine our Physical Environment*. Princeton Architectural Press.

Brownell, B. (2008). *Transmaterial 2: A Catalog of Materials That Redefine our Physical Environment*. Princeton: Architectural Press.

Bullivant, L. (2005). *4dspace: Interactive Architecture, Architectural Design*. Wiley-Academy.

Bullivant, L. (2006). *Responsive environments – Architecture, art and design*. V & A Contemporary Publications.

Bullivant, L. (2007). *4dsocial: Interactive Design Environments*. Architectural Design, Wiley-Academy.

Cai, Y., & Abascal, J. (2006). *Ambient intelligence in everyday life*. Springer-Verlag.

Fisher, G. (2008. April 5-10). Challenges and Opportunities fro Distributed Participatory Design (DPD). In *proceedings of CHI 2008*, Florence, Italy, ACM Press.

Flachbart, G., & Weibel, P. (2002). *Disappearing architecture – From real to virtual to quantum*. Birkhäuser.

Greenfield, A. (2006). *Everyware – The dawning age of ubiquitous computing*. New Riders.

Grosz, E. (2001). *Architecture from the outside – Essays on virtual and real space*. MIT Press.

Kakihara, M., & Sorensen, C. (2002). Mobility: an extended perspective. In *Proceedings of the 35th Annual Hawaii International Conference on System Sciences* (pp. 1756–1766).

Kolarevic, B. (2003). *Architecture in the digital age – Design and manufacturing*. Taylor & Francis.

Kolarevic, B., & Malkawi, A. (2005). *Performative Architecture – Beyond instrumentality*. Spon Press.

Marcus, A. (1998). Metaphor design for user interfaces. In *Proceedings of - CHI 98 – the ACM conference on Human factors in computing systems*. ACM Press. doi:10.1145/286498.286577

Margolis, L., & Robinson, A. (2007). *Living Systems – Innovative materials and technologies for landscape architechture*. Birkhäuser.

Materio (2007). *Material World 2: Innovative Materials for Architecture and Design*. Birkhäuser.

McCullough, M. (2004). *Digital Ground – Architecture, Pervasive Computing, and Environmental Knowing*. MIT Press.

Muller, M., Blomberg, J., Carter, K., Dykstra, E., Halskov, K., & Greenbaum, M. (1991). Participatory design in Britain and North America: responses to the "Scandinavian Challenge. In *Proceedings of CHI'91 - the SIGCHI conference on Human factors in computing systems: Reaching through technology*. ACM Press.

Nelson, H., & Stolterman, E. (2003). *The Design Way: intentional change in an unpredictable world*. Educational Technology Publications.

Oosterhuist, K. (2007). *iA #1 Interactive Architecture*. Paperback, Episode publishers, Rotterdam.

Pousman, Z., & Stasko, J. (2006). A taxonomy of ambient information systems: four patterns of design. In *proceedings of AVI '06 - the working conference on Advanced visual interfaces*. ACM Press.

Robertson, T., Mansfield, T., & Loke, L. (2006, August). Designing an immersive environment for public use. In *Proceedings Participatory Design Conference*, Trento, Italy, ACM Press.

Ruyter, B., & Aarts, E. (2004). Ambient intelligence: visualizing the future. In *Proceedings of AVI '04 - the working conference on Advanced visual interfaces*. ACM Press.

Sengers, P., et al. (2004). Culturally Embedded Computing. *Pervasive Computing, 3*(1).

Sparacino, F. (2008). Natural interaction in intelligent spaces: designing for architecture and entertainment. *Multimedia Tools and Applications, 38*, 307–335. doi:10.1007/s11042-007-0193-9

Spiller, N. (2002). *Reflexive architecture. Architectural Design*. Wiley-Academy.

Taxén, G. (2004). Introducing participatory design in museums. In *Proceedings Participatory Design Conference 2004*, Toronto, Canada.

Törpel, B. (2005). Participatory design: a multi-voiced effort. In *Proceedings of CC '05 - the 4th decennial conference on Critical computing: between sense and sensibility*. ACM Press.

Vallgårda, A., & Redström, J. (2007). Computational composites. In *Proceedings of CHI '07 - the SIGCHI conference on Human factors in computing systems*. ACM Press.

Watkins, J. (2007, November). Social Media, Participatory Design and Cultural Engagement. In *proceedings of OzCHI 2007*, Adelaide, Australia.

Watkins, J., & Russo, A. (2005, April 12-15). Digital Cultural Communication – Designing co-creative new media environments. *C & C '05*, London, UK.

Weiser, M. (1991, September). The computer of the 21st century. *Scientific American, 265*(3), 66–75. doi:10.1038/scientificamerican0991-94

Wenger, E. (1998). *Communities of Practice – Learning, Meaning, and Identity*. Cambridge, UK: Cambridge University Press.

Zhou, C., Frankowski, D., Ludford, P., Shekhar, S., & Terveen, L. (2007). Discovering personally meaningful places: An interactive clustering approach. [TOIS]. *ACM Transactions on Information Systems, 25*(3).

This work was previously published in International Journal of Ambient Computing and Intelligence (IJACI), Volume 1, Issue 3, edited by Kevin Curran, pp. 1-18, copyright 2009 by IGI Publishing (an imprint of IGI Global).

Chapter 18
Routing in Opportunistic Networks

Hoang Anh Nguyen
University of Applied Sciences (SUPSI), Switzerland

Silvia Giordano
University of Applied Sciences (SUPSI), Switzerland

ABSTRACT

In Opportunistic Networks (OppNets), mobile devices transmit messages by exploiting the direct contacts, without the need of an end-to-end infrastructure. Disconnections of nodes and high churn rates are normal features of opportunistic networks. Hence, routing is one of the main challenges in this environment. In this article, we provide a survey of the main routing approaches in OppNets and classify them into three classes: context-oblivious, mobility-based, and social context-aware routing. We emphasize the role of context information in forwarding data in OppNets, and evaluate the relative performance of the three routing techniques. Finally, we present how context-based information is used to route data in a specific subclass of OppNets: Sensor Actor Networks (SANETs).

INTRODUCTION

In the last decade, mobile ad hoc networking has been suggested as a technology for realizing the ubiquitous computing vision. However, after more than ten years of research in this field, this promising technology has not yet entered the mass market. One of the main reasons for this is the lack of a pragmatic approach to the design of in-

frastructure-less multi-hop ad hoc networks (Conti et al., 2007: The Theory). In current networks, the network layer has become the interface (and thus the bottleneck) between a growing multitude of applications and an increasing number of technologies. In terms of mobile ad hoc networks, this has resulted in the exponential grow of complexity at the network layer, which has further complicated practical realization. Opportunistic networking tries to simplify this aspect by removing the assumption of physical end-to-end connectivity

DOI: 10.4018/978-1-60960-549-0.ch018

while providing connectivity opportunities to pervasive devices when no direct access to the Internet is available. Pervasive devices, equipped with different wireless networking technologies, are frequently out of range from a network but are in the range of other networked devices, and sometimes cross areas where some type of connectivity is available (e.g. Wi-Fi hotspots). Thus, they can opportunistically exploit their mobility and contacts for data delivery (Conti et al., 2007: The Reality).

The elimination of the need to build paths drastically simplifies the routing in opportunistic networks; however, challenges remain that are distinct from those of conventional network routing methods. A routing scheme in OppNets has to provide data with some reliability[1] (ideally with full reliability) even when the network connectivity is intermittent or when an end-to-end path is temporally nonexistent. Moreover, since "contacts" in an opportunistic network may appear arbitrarily without prior information, neither scheduling routing nor mobile relay approaches can be applied. In such environments, flooding-based routing protocols appeared for some time to be popular design choice. However, this approach tends to be very costly in terms of traffic overhead and energy consumption. Routing performance improves when knowledge regarding the expected topology, the behavior of the participants, and the information about the participants themselves in the networks can be exploited: that is, the context information of the networks.

Context information can cover various ranges, depending on the specific routing protocols. It could be the workplace, home address, profession, and email address, the mobility pattern of nodes, or the communities that the nodes belong to, and so on. All information that aids in making decisions to route messages is context information. For example, to identify those hops best suited for communication towards the eventual destination, the home address of a user is a valuable piece of context information.

In the following section, we provide a brief description of the primary routing approaches in OppNets available in the literature, from "naïve" approaches to "intelligent" ones. Specifically, we emphasize the role of context information as well as social aspects in routing messages, where the classification of routing approaches is based on the amount of context information used as given in (Conti et al, 2008). Based on the context information exploited we classify routing in OppNets into three classes: context-oblivious, mobility-based and social context-aware protocols. Finally, we present the context-based routing protocols in Sensor Actor Networks (SANETs).

Context-Oblivious Routing

Flooding-based routing algorithms belong to the context-oblivious routing group, from "blindly" flooding techniques to controlled flooding solutions. In flooding techniques, a source node sends out a request packet on its entire outgoing links. Each node receives a request packet and forwards the packet on its entire outgoing links except the one corresponding to the incoming link on which the packet arrives. Each request packet may reach the destination node along a different route at a different time. The advantage of flooding-based routing is its simplicity in finding a route[2], in particular, a minimum delay ratio for a connection request because it doesn't require any global information about network topology, or any context information. However, flooding causes a huge number of control packets in control channels, which can result in network congestion. Moreover, this kind of technique floods all the nodes in the network, and is thus very costly in terms of energy consumption and memory. Network performance is particularly important in OppNets because of the device constraints.

One way to address this problem is to use a hop counter in the header of each packet and decrement it at each hop; when the counter of a packet reaches zero, the packet is discarded.

Another approach is to set Time-To-Live (TTL) for each packet as in Epidemic routing (Vahdat et al., 2000). Epidemic routing customizes traditional flooding to mobile opportunistic networks. It is one of the first schemes proposed to enable message delivery in such networks. Each node maintains a list of all messages it carries, whose delivery is pending. Whenever it encounters another node, the two nodes exchange all messages that they do not have in common, and in this way, all messages are eventually spread to all nodes. The packet is delivered when the first node carrying a copy of the packet meets the destination. The packet will keep on getting copied from one node to the other node till its *TTL* expires.

Network coding based routing schemes for OppNets can also be classified as flooding based techniques. In network coding based routing schemes, a message (or group of messages) is transformed into another format prior to transmission (Widmer et al., 2005; Wang et al., 2005). The design principle of coding based schemes is to embed additional information within the coded blocks such that the original message can be successfully re-constructed with only a certain number of the coded blocks. More precisely, differing from replication based schemes which rely on successful delivery of each individual data block; coding based schemes consider a block successfully delivered when the necessary number of blocks is received to reconstruct the original data, which can be just a small portion of the total number of the blocks transmitted. As a result, coding based schemes tend to be more robust than replication based schemes when network connectivity is extremely poor (this is considered as the worst delay performance case). However, coding based schemes are less efficient when the network is well connected (this is considered as the very small delay performance case), which is simply due to additional information embedded in the code blocks.

Another approach to route packets in sparse networks is that of controlled replication or spray-ing – Spray and Wait (Spyropoulos et al., 2005). A small, fixed number of copies are distributed to a number of distinct relays. Then, each relay carries its copy until it encounters the destination or until the *TTL* of the packet expires. By having multiple relays looking independently and in parallel for the destination, this protocol creates enough diversity to explore the sparse network more efficiently while keeping the resource usage per message low. Spray and wait is one of the simplest spraying schemes proposed in the literature. Specifically, the source node forwards all the copies (let the number of copies being sprayed be labeled as L) to the first L distinct nodes it encounters. (In other words, no other node except the source node can forward a copy of the packet.) And, once these copies are distributed, each copy performs direct transmission. The analytical model derived in (Spyropoulos et al., 2005) shows that L can be chosen based on a target average delay. The spray phase may be performed in many ways. Under the assumption that nodes movements are independent and identically distributed, the Binary Spray and Wait policy is the best in terms of delay. Any node (including the sender) holding n copies ($n > 1$) of the message hands over ($n/2$) copies to the first encountered node, and keeps the remaining copies for itself. When a node is left with only one copy of the message, it switches to direct transmission and only transmits the message to the final destination node when (and if) it is met.

Mobility-Based Routing Protocols

Routing protocols that lie in the mobility-based category exploit more context information to make forwarding decisions, such as the mobility information of nodes. Node mobility impacts the effectiveness of routing in Opportunistic Networks, and Grossglauser et al. (2002) proved that it increases the performance of ad hoc networks, especially in the routing of messages when efficient routing techniques are deployed. When network mobility departs from the well-known random way-point mobility model, Camp et al. (2002) and Hong et al. (1999) have shown that the overhead carried by epidemic and/or flooding based routing schemes can be further reduced by taking into account the knowledge of node mobility. The Probabilistic Routing scheme - PRoPHET (Lindgren et al., 2003) calculates the delivery predictability from a node to a particular destination node based on the observed contact history, and forwards a message to its neighboring node if and only if that neighbor node has a higher delivery predictability value. PRoPHET uses "History of past Encounters and Transitivity" to estimate each node's delivery probability for each other node. The delivery predictability is the probability of a node encountering a certain destination. It increases when the node frequently meets the destination and decreases (according to an aging function) in the contrary.

The context information used in PRoPHET is the frequency of meetings between nodes, as is also seen in the MV (Meeting and Visits) and MaxProp protocols (Burns et al., 2005; Burgess et al., 2006). A node uses MaxProp to schedule packet transmission to its peers and determines which packets should be deleted when buffer space is almost full. Packets are scheduled based on path likelihoods to peers according to historical data. In addition, several complementary mechanisms, including acknowledgments, a head-start for new packets, and lists of previous intermediaries are used in this approach. The MV routing protocol (Burns, 2005) also takes into account the frequency of meetings between nodes. The nodes remember their path (visits) and the other nodes they met on the way. Each node stores variables for all the nodes so far encountered, describing the likelihood of a successfully delivery to this node. When node A and B meet directly, they set the delivery probability to each other to 1, and synchronize their set of variables. These delivery probabilities degrade in time and are refreshed periodically by meeting with nodes with high delivery probability. If A meets B again, they synchronize again and reset the delivery probability between them to 1. However, the MV protocol introduces a more sophisticated method to select the messages to forward to an encountered node. Basically, the choice depends on the probability of encountered nodes to successfully deliver messages to their eventual destinations. The delivery probability relies on recent-past observations of both the meetings between nodes and the visits of nodes to geographical locations.

This scheme has been revised by Leguay et al. (2006) - MobySpace by taking the mobility pattern into account. In MobySpace, the mobility pattern is the context information that the source node uses to route the message. It relies on the notion that a node is a good candidate for taking a message if it has a mobility pattern similar to that of the destination. Routing is done by forwarding messages toward nodes that have mobility patterns that are more and more similar to the mobility pattern of the destination. To deal with the mobility patterns of node, a virtual Euclidean space is used where each axis represents a possible contact between a couple of nodes and the distance along an axis measures the probability of that contact to occur.

Ghosh et al. (2007) propose routing based on the predefined infrastructure, such as the places that device holders often visited; they call them "solar-hub". This takes the advantage of user mobility profiles to perform "hub-level"-based routing. With "solar-hub", the message from the sender to the receiver is routed to one or more hubs frequently visited by the receiver, called destination hubs, where the receiver can retrieve the message when it visits the same hubs again. In this scenario, it is necessary to know about the places visited by the receiver (hubs).

Unlike Spray and Wait (Spyropoulos et al., 2005), in the second phase ("focus" phase) in Spray and Focus (Spyropoulos et al., 2007) rather than waiting for the destination to be encountered, each relay can forward its copy to a potentially more appropriate relay, using a carefully designed utility-based scheme. The potential relays are selected based on a set of timers that record the time since two nodes last saw each other. This last encounter timer criterion is also present in Grossglauser et al.'s scheme (2003). Here, node mobility is exploited to disseminate destination location information. Each node maintains a local database of the time and location of its last encounter with every other node in the network. This database is consulted by packets to obtain estimates of their destination's current location. As a packet travels towards its destination, it is able to successively refine an estimate of the destination's precise location, because node mobility has "diffused" estimates of that location.

The context information in Bubble Rap (Hui et al., 2008) is the social communities that nodes belong to. Communities are automatically defined and labeled based on the patterns of contacts between nodes. When a node wants to send a message to other node it looks for nodes belonging to the same community of the destination. If such nodes are not found, it forwards the message to increasingly sociable nodes, which have more chance of getting in touch with the community of the destination. The sociable level of a node is defined by the set of peers that the node is usually in touch with. Exploiting context information related to the social behavior of people is one of the most promising research directions in the area.

CAR-Adaptive Routing for Intermittently Connected Mobile Ad hoc Networks (Musolesi et al., 2005) uses Kalman filters to combine and evaluate the multiple dimensions of the context in order to take routing decisions. The context is made of measurements that nodes perform periodically, which can be related to connectivity, but not necessarily. The connectivity happens inside MANET clouds, to reach nodes outside the cloud; a sender looks for the node in its cloud with the highest probability of successfully delivering the message to the destination. Then this node temporarily stores the message, waiting either to get in touch with the destination itself, or to enter a cloud with other nodes with higher probability of meeting

the destination. Therefore, nodes in context-aware routing compute delivery probabilities proactively, and disseminate them in their ad hoc cloud. Note that context information is exploited to evaluate probabilities just for the destinations that each node is aware of (i.e. that happen to have been co-located in the same cloud at some time). The main focus of context-aware routing is on defining algorithms to combine context information (which is assumed to be available in some way) to compute delivery probabilities. Specifically, a multi-attribute utility-based framework is defined in CAR. The framework is general enough to accommodate different types of context information. Context information in CAR consists of the logical connectivity of nodes, such as the rate of connectivity change, the delivery probability of the neighbor nodes to the destination, and device information, such as residual battery life. However, the social context information is not taken into consideration as in social context-based category (described in the next section). Thus, from this point of view, CAR can be seen as a conjunction between mobility-based protocols and social context-based protocols.

Social Context-Based Protocols

The main difference between social context-based protocols and mobility-based protocols is that the context information in the mobility-based protocols is about the mobility patterns of the nodes, the information of the devices themselves, or the encounter history between nodes. Social context-aware protocols not only exploit such kinds of context information as in the mobility-based protocols, but also take into account the "social aspect" of the nodes as an important parameter to route the messages. This is motivated from the fact that in most cases, the mobility of nodes is decided by the carriers (e.g. human, animals, and vehicles). Hence, the social relationship of the carriers plays an important role in how they encounter each other. The advantage of this approach is that it is more general than mobility-based approaches. Indeed, these routing protocols can be used with *any* set of context information, and thus they can be easily customized to best suit the particular environment. To the best of our knowledge, there are two protocols that fall in this category: HiBOp (Boldrini et al., 2007), and Propicman/SpatioTempo (Nguyen et al., 2007; Nguyen et al., 2008).

The context information in HiBOp (Boldrini et al., 2007) is a set of information that describes the node profile, and the history of social relationships among nodes. At each node, the information used to build the context can be personal information about the user (e.g. name, residence, workplace, profession). Nodes share their own data during contacts, and thus learn the context they are interested in. HiBOp assumes that each node locally stores an *Identity Table (IT)* that contains personal information on the user that owns the device. Nodes exchange *ITs* when getting in touch. At each node, its own *IT*, and the set of current neighbors' *ITs*, represent the *Current Context*, which provides a snapshot of the context the node is currently in.

The second context information in HiBOp is the information of encounter history. Even if a node is not currently a good forwarder because of its current context, it still can be a good forwarder because of its habits and past experiences. Under the assumption that humans are most of the time 'predictable', it is important to collect information about the context data seen by each node in the past, and the recurrence of these data in the node's current context. To this end, each context attribute seen in the current context (i.e. each row in neighbours' *ITs*) is recorded in a *History Table*, together with a continuity probability index that represents the probability of encountering that attribute in the future.

The main idea of HiBOp forwarding is looking for nodes that show an increasing match with the known context attributes of the destination. A high match means a high similarity between node's and destination's contexts and, therefore, a

high probability for the node to bring the message in the destination's community (possibly, to the destination). Therefore, a node wishing to send a message through HiBOp specifies (any subset of) the destination's *IT* in the message header. Any node in the path between the sender and the destination asks encountered nodes for their match with the destination attributes, and hands over the message if an encountered node shows a greater match than its own. HiBOp uses CMM – Community based Mobility Model (Musolesi et al., 2006) – in the simulation to compare the performance with Epidemic and Prophet routing techniques. In this model, every node belongs to a social community. Nodes in the same community are friends, while those in different communities are none-friends. Among nodes, there are the social links with different weight. These social links will attract the movement of a node in the testbed. In CMM, testbed is in the form of grid, each community is initially randomly placed in a square of a grid. Node selects the target cell based on the social attraction of the cell to the node. This attraction is measured as the sum of the social links' weights between the node and the nodes currently moving in or toward the cell. CMM allows one to model specific scenarios, where communities are workplaces, residence places, etc.

In Propicman (Nguyen et al., 2007) the context information of each node is represented by means of a *node profile* with evidence/value pairs. To each evidence is associated a weight that represents the importance of this evidence in the network. For security reasons, each node profile also contains the hashed values of evidences and values, for instance, as following node profile in Table 1.

When a node S wants to send a message M to the destination D, it sends to its neighbors M's header h_M. This header contains the information the sender knows about the destination (part of destination's node profile). h_M is forwarded to the two-hop neighbors of S. Based on this information and their node profiles, the neighbor (and the two-hop neighbor) nodes compute their delivery

Table 1. A node profile

	Evidence name(E)	Value(V)	Hashed values
Personal Information	Name	Alessandro	H(Name, Alessandro)
	Nationality	Italy	H(Nationality, Italy)
	Profession	IT researcher	H(Profession, IT researcher)
Residence	Street	Nosedo	H(Street, Nosedo)
	City	Lugano	H(City, Lugano)
	Country	Switzerland	H(Country, Switzerland)
Workplace	Street	Cantonale	H(Street, Cantonale)
	City	Manno	H(City, Manno)
	Organization	SUPSI	H(Organization, SUPSI)
Hobbies	Name	Football	H(Name, Football)
	Association	Supsi club	H(Association, Supsi club)

probability (*DP*). *S* then sends the message *M* only on the two-hop route(s) with the highest delivery probability, and only if this is higher than its own. After sending the message content, *S* keeps the message for the next eventual encounter.

The message header h_M is the concatenation of all the hashed pairs of evidences/values as follows:

$$h_M = \underset{i=1}{\overset{n}{Concatenation}} (H(E_{Di}, V_{Di}), MAC_S, SN)$$

(1)

It includes the MAC address of *S* (*MAC_S*) and the sequence number of *M* (*SN*) used to avoid duplicated messages; the unknown values are left blank.

When the neighbor *N* receives h_M, it compares its own node profile with the information of the destination hashed in the message header (see Figure 1).

From the matched fields, it computes its delivery probability DP_N to the destination as follows:

Figure 1. Local matching - Propicman

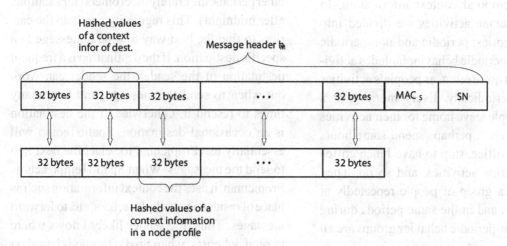

$$0 \leq DP_N = \frac{\sum Matched(W_i)}{\sum W_{Mi}} \leq 1 \qquad (2)$$

where $\sum Matched(W_i)$ is the sum of the weights of the evidences in N, which (non empty) hashed values matched the ones in h_M, and $\sum W_{Mi}$ is the sum of the weights of all the evidences that S knows about D (not empty in h_M).

From N, h_M continues to be sent to N's neighbor nodes. These neighbor nodes compute their *DPs* as in (2) and send the results back to N. N will select the highest second hop node's *DP* and send the result of DP_N*max$\{DP_{second\ hop}\}$ to S. Thus, S is able to compute the two-hop route(s) with the highest *DP*, and forward the message to the destination through this route.

SpatioTempo (Nguyen et al., 2008) is derived from Propicman, and also uses context information as node profiles to compute the delivery probability of nodes to destinations. The forwarding process is performed as in Propicman: the sender sends a message header that contains some information about the destination, the two-hop neighbors compute their own delivery probability based on their matching context information with the destination and send the results back to the sender. The sender will select the highest two-hop route(s) to forward the message content.

SpatioTempo is the first scheme that takes into account temporal context information. In this scheme, human activities are divided into two main categories: periodic and non-periodic behaviors. The periodic behavior includes activities that happen quite often, as people's activities are repeated periodically. Every morning at a given time, people leave home for their activities (work, school, etc.); perhaps spend some hours working in the office, stop to have lunch/coffee or other recreation activities, and so on. They probably meet a group of people repeatedly at the same places and in the same periods during the day. The non-periodic behavior groups are all the other activities: for example, when a person goes on holiday this activity is not frequent and not repeated.

Furthermore, the authors consider in depth the social relationship between users. They observe that most people have some frequent contact persons and other occasional contact persons in their social relationships. The occasional contact persons are those that they rarely send messages to, whereas they often send messages to the frequent contact persons. For their frequent contact people, they may have some knowledge of these individuals' periodic behavior. Thus they know *when* and *where* to send out messages in order to have a higher delivery probability. Thus in Spatio-Tempo, they classify two classes of destinations: Frequent destinations and Occasional destinations.

For occasional destinations, the authors propose to use Propicman (Nguyen et al., 2007) as this scheme is efficient in those cases where there is no support information on when and where to send the message to this type of destination. For frequent destinations, SpatioTempo introduces the concept of *cycles* and *periods* of a carrier's activities, as they observe that the activities of carriers are different at the different periods in a day. In some periods, they often meet some specific people (for example, colleagues in the office during the working hours, friends in the bar, family members at night), whereas, in some other periods, they rarely meet others (for example, after midnight). This regularity can help the carriers to find the best way to send a message to a specific destination. If the destination is a frequent destination of the sender, the sender can work out when to send the message, and how many times to resend it. Otherwise, if the destination is an occasional destination, SpatioTempo will essentially use Propicman to select the next hop to send the messages. When SpatioTempo acts as Propicman, it uses the context information such as place of residence, workplace, bars, etc. to forward messages. Thus, the sender likely knows where to send, whereas, when SpatioTempo is based on the periodical behavior of nodes and hence it will probably know when to send.

In other words, if the sender has a message to send to one of its frequent destinations, it will know in which period of a cycle (a working day, for instance) it should increase the number of broadcastings of the message header to have the highest delivery probability of delivering the message to the destination. Likewise, it knows in which period of a cycle not to broadcast the message header. Hence, SpatioTempo reduces the excess network traffic while keeping the average end-to-end delay of messages reasonable.

EVALUATION

In this section, we present the preliminary analyses and comparison of the delivery cost between the three routing classes introduced above. If the constraints of devices and network bandwidth are not important issues, context-oblivious routing techniques are suitable candidates as they are simple to implement and very good in terms of delivery ratio. Whereas, context-based routing protocols are useful when device constraints and network traffic are taken into account.

Let us assume a network with N nodes, with transmission rate λ, and average path length $\sqrt{N}$ (Santivanez, 2001). In the context-oblivious routing schemes, after a certain time, each packet is flooded to all nodes (or some fraction of them), thus we have $(\lambda * N)$ transmissions that "flood" the whole network for each node. Therefore, the cost of those schemes for the whole network with N nodes is $\theta(\lambda * N^2)$.

When mobility information is used to limit the distribution, then each packet reaches $\alpha * N$, with $1 \geq \alpha > 0$, where α depends on the network mobility and how we handle the mobility information. Thus, in the mobility-based routing techniques, the cost for transmission is

$$\theta\left[(\lambda * N)(\alpha * N)\right] = \theta(\lambda * \alpha * N^2)$$

As the mobility information can not be sufficient to radically discriminate between the nodes N, we have the case that most of the nodes are reached by each packet and $\alpha \cong 1$. For example, in Spray and Focus (Spyropoulos et al., 2007) and Last Encounter (Grossglauser et al., 2003), nodes select the next candidates to forward the message based on a set of timers that record the time since two nodes last saw each other. This record can vary by time, thus the message can be widely forwarded to almost every other node.

When the mobility information is used in more advanced way, $\alpha \Rightarrow 1/$, as the nodes reached are above the average path. Thus, in this case, $\alpha * N \rightarrow \sqrt{N}$ and the cost is $\theta(\lambda * N^{1.5})$(average path) but the delay ratio increases.

In the social context-aware protocols, the cost for transmission is of the order of $\theta(\lambda * N^{1.5})$, as only nodes matching context information are flooded. As they are selected with social criteria, the delay ratio is higher than in flooding based techniques, lower than in mobility-based schemes, whilst with the overhead parameter; social context-aware routing protocols appear to be the best choice since only the nodes that match context information with a certain percentage are flooded.

A simulative comparison between three protocols representative of these three routing classes is presented in (Nguyen et al., 2007). This confirms our preliminary analytical study. Clearly, in terms of delay, if the network congestion is not an issue, a flooding based technique is the best choice, followed by social context-aware protocols, as seen in Figure 2. Mobility-based routing techniques show lower performance. If we consider the network traffic evaluation, as seen in Figure 3, flooding-based techniques are obviously very costly, as data is flooded to all the nodes in the network. Here again, social context-based routing protocols obtain the best performance as only some nodes with certain matching rate of context information are involved in the transmission process. Furthermore, as short delay is not the main requirement of OppNets, the result of social context-based routing protocols can be considered very satisfactory.

In addition to the analytical and simulative comparison between three types of routing techniques, we are currently performing experimental studies with actual devices within the Haggle project[3].

SANETS

A Wireless Sensor Network (WSN) (Akyildiz et al., 2002) is a special type of ad hoc network composed of a large number of nodes equipped with different sensor devices. WSNs are emerging as an important computer class based on a new computing platform and networking structure that will enable novel applications that are related to areas such as environmental monitoring, industrial and manufacturing automation, health-care, and

Figure 2. Delay in Epidemic, Prophet, and Propicman schemes

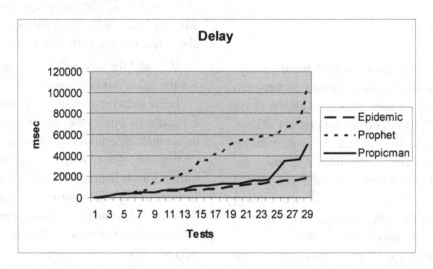

Figure 3. Network overhead in Epidemic, Prophet, and Propicman schemes

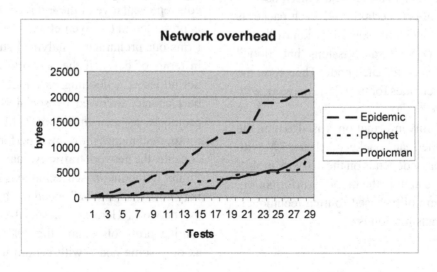

the military. Commonly, wireless sensor networks have severe constraints regarding power resources and computational capacity.

A WSN may be designed with different objectives. It may be designed to gather and process data from the environment in order to have a better understanding of the behavior of the monitored entity. It may also be designed to monitor an environment for the occurrence of a set of possible events, so that proper action can be taken whenever necessary. A fundamental issue in WSNs is the way the collected data is processed. Technological advancements in hardware and wireless networking have recently raised the potential for wireless sensor networks (WSN) with much effort concentrated on collecting vast amounts of sensed information at a single, powerful base station. Although a variety of applications can exploit this setup, the network algorithms developed for it have limited use in Sensor-Actuator Networks (SANETs) that exploit data inside the network. In such scenarios, actuator devices are physically dispersed beside the sensors where they collect and act on sensor data. Exploiting a traditional, centralized approach requires collecting information at a base station and re-sending it to the actuators. This, however, increases unnecessarily both the amount of data transmitted and the latency between data collection and actuation. Some other works in this direction (Jain, 2006; Shah, 2003; Zhao, 2004) where special nodes are moving and transport the information within the sensed area. However, in those solutions, mobility is confined to the special nodes that move with a predefined trajectory. For mobile sensor data gathering, there are different techniques. One can be to only allow data delivery when sensors are in direct proximity of the sinks, a technique that involves very little communication overhead. However, the delivery ratio might be very poor. Epidemic-based techniques, on the other hand, have very good delivery ratios if buffers are sufficiently large, however the overhead in terms of communication and, therefore, energy is quite high.

In sensor networks where energy and communication overhead is an issue, the spreading of the message needs to be very carefully controlled and there is a trade off with respect to the delivery ratio. Thus there is a need for routing techniques that meet all demands in terms of the energy and communication overhead as well as the delivery ratio.

Context-based routing protocols for SANETs obtain good performance in comparison with conventional routing techniques. SCAR - Sensor Context-Aware Routing Protocol (Mascolo et al., 2006) and PROSAN - Probabilistic ROuting in SANets (Nguyen et al., 2007) are two of the first routing techniques that can be considered as context-based routing protocols. The scenario that is envisaged in these routing algorithms is one where the mobile sensor nodes (e.g., animals, vehicles, humans) route data through each other in order to reach sink nodes, which can be either fixed or mobile.

SCAR (Mascolo et al., 2006) is derived from CAR (Musolesi et al., 2005) and uses the Kalman filter and prediction techniques from context information of the sensor nodes (such as previous encountered neighbors, battery level...) to determine which of the sensor neighbors are the best carriers to forward the messages.

Specifically, in this scheme, mobile sensor nodes try to send their data to sinks, scattered over the field. Each sensor node tries to deliver its data in bundles to a number of neighbors which seem to be the best carriers to reach a sink. The decision process by which nodes select the best carriers is based on prediction of the future evolution of the system. It relies on the analysis of the history of the movement pattern of the nodes and their co-location with the sinks and on the evaluation of the current available resources of the sensors. In particular, each node evaluates its change rate of connectivity, co-location with sinks, and battery level. The forecasted values of the context attributes describing the context are then combined to define a delivery probability for each sensor to deliver bundles to sinks. While moving, the sensors will transfer their data to other sensors only if these have a higher probability to deliver the data to sinks (i.e., they are better carriers). The calculation of the delivery probability is local and it does not involve any distributed computation. Nodes exchange information about their current delivery probability and their available buffer space with the neighbors only periodically.

PROSAN (Nguyen et al., 2007), is derived from Propicman (Nguyen et al., 2007). The carrier's information, or node profile, is used to predict the subsequent moves of the (sensor) nodes. This is based on the consideration that the device carriers move in a predictable fashion based on repeating behavioral patterns at different timescales (day, week, and month). And the same observation applies also to vehicles, as they are either used for personal mobility (i.e. a person that drives a car) or serve several people (e.g. bus service). In the first case, they are also related to human behavioral patterns. In the second case, they have a strictly repeating deterministic pattern by their nature.

As in Propicman, a sensor node forwards information only to the nodes with the highest probability of delivering the message toward the destination (delivery probability), which can be considered quasi-static information. This has the double advantage of reducing significantly the number of nodes involved in the forwarding process, and of minimizing the delay. The delivery probability (DP) is computed based on the context-information of nodes, more specifically the pairs of evidences/values. Differently from Propicman, as sensor nodes have low power and memory, single hop routing computation of DP is used instead of two-hop.

Context information describes the profile of sensor node's carriers. It also gives indications about the sensor node application, as they are mainly intended for enabling the information exchange for a given application. When a node S has some information I to deliver to the actuator(s) A, it sends to its neighbors I's header

h_I. This header is composed by the part of the node profile of the destination that S knows as in (1). Thus, the neighbor nodes compute their delivery probability as the sum of weights of matching values with actuator(s) as indicated in (2) and (if above the threshold T) sends it back to S, which is then able to derive the best neighbor(s). The threshold T is set in PROSAN to make explicit as the selection is on a single hop, and in this way to avoid responses from nodes that will not be then considered. The selection can be for more than one neighbor if there is a reliability requirement, or if the delay is an issue.

Another notable feature of PROSAN is that only the source node can forward messages. The intermediate nodes can store messages and only forward them to destinations (actuators) when they meet. The destination can be either a specific actuator or a group if the action can be performed by more than one actuator.

A second scheme is derived from the original in PROSAN, called *hybrid P-MULE* (Prosan-MULE). In this approach, some nodes act as mules, even if they use the probabilistic approach of PROSAN. These p-mules nodes are nodes with higher capacities (memory, power, CPU) and move around in the network along a fixed trajectory.

The introduction of this model was motivated by the fact that we wanted to understand how much nodes with higher capacity could increase network performance. Furthermore, in some special cases, for example when the actuators are static, there is some benefit in having nodes with deterministic behavior. In this case we will know with certainty when a p-mule is going to meet the actuator(s). However, this meeting, as well as the one with the sender S, could happen with some delay, and in this case a hybrid approach can have better results.

Therefore, in order to meet both reliability and delay constraints, each sender will have a timer t for any information it wants to deliver to an actuator. If, when S has information I to send, a p-mule is able to collect it, S will give it to the p-mule, but, as it is also able to compute the time when *I* will be delivered to actuators, for a period *t*, it will continue to use PROSAN to try to deliver *I* with less delay to other nodes. Similarly, if *S* encounters a p-mule after it has already delivered *I* to other nodes, it will deliver it to the p-mule as well, in order to have more reliability. In the case of static actuators, we have a deterministic way of computing *t* as function of the time a p-mule needs to go on a trajectory to the position of the actuators. In the case of mobile actuators, this time *t* is statistically computed with times the p-mule encountered the actuators in the past.

Note that, from the probabilistic point of view, when actuators are static, a p-mule has delivery probability equal to one.

Unlike Ferry and Data Mules (Shah, 2003; Zhao, 2004), SCAR and PROSAN (Mascolo et al., 2006; Nguyen et al., 2007) exploit context information to route data. Only the sensor nodes with high delivery probability to the destinations (sinks, actuators) are intermediate nodes in the routing process. Thus, less sensor nodes are involved to route data, and accordingly, there is less energy consumption and memory storage required. Meanwhile, context-based routing techniques maintain the delay in data transmission at an acceptable rate in comparison with Ferry and Data Mules. Moreover, PROSAN (Nguyen et al., 2007) can also deal with the situation where there are no nodes acting as actuators or mules. In this case, context information is efficiently exploited to route data.

CONCLUSION

Opportunistic networking is a very promising technology for realizing the ubiquitous vision. Based on the increasing pervasiveness of our world, and on releasing end-to-end connectivity constraint, it can better exploit social characteristics via context awareness. We presented here a classification of routing schemes in OppNets based on the types of information they use and how this is handled.

We then sketched an analytical comparison of the three routing classes and showed that our preliminary results are confirmed by simulation. Future works include a refined analytical and experimental study for reinforcing our results.

ACKNOWLEDGMENT

This work was partially funded by the European Commission under the HAGGLE FET-SAC Project (EU FP6).

REFERENCES

Akyildiz, I. F. (2002). Wireless sensor networks: A survey. *Computer Networks*, *38*(4), 393–422. doi:10.1016/S1389-1286(01)00302-4

Boldrini, C., Conti, M., Jacopini, I., & Passarella, A. (2007, June). *HiBOp: A History Based Routing Protocol for Opportunistic Networks*. Paper presented in the Proceedings of the WoWMoM 2007, Helsinki.

Burgess, J., Gallagher, B., Jensen, D., & Levine, B. N. (2006, April). *Maxprop: Routing for vehicle-based disruption-tolerant networking*. Paper presented in the Proceedings of the IEEE INFOCOM, Barcelona.

Burns, B., Brock, O., & Levine, B. N. (2005, March). *MV Routing and capacity building in disruption tolerant networks*. Paper presented in the Proceedings of the IEEE INFOCOM 2005, Miami, FL.

Camp, T., Boleng, J., & Davies, V. (2002). A survey of mobility models for ad hoc network research. *Wireless Communication and Mobile Computing Journal*, *2*(5), 483–502. doi:10.1002/wcm.72

Conti, M., Crowcroft, J., Giordano, S., Hui, P., Nguyen, H. A., & Passarella, A. (2008). Minema. H. Miranda, L. Rodrigues, & B. Garbinato (Ed.), *Routing issues in Opportunistic Networks*. Springer

Conti, M., & Giordano, S. (2007). Multihop Ad Hoc Networking: The Theory. *IEEE Communications Magazine, 45*(4), 78–86. doi:10.1109/MCOM.2007.343616

Conti, M., & Giordano, S. (2007). Multihop Ad Hoc Networking: The Reality. *IEEE Communications Magazine, 45*(4), 88–95. doi:10.1109/MCOM.2007.343617

Ghosh, J., Sumesh J. Philip, & Chunming, Q. (2007, March). Sociological Orbit aware Location Approximation and Routing (SOLAR) in MANET. *ELSEVIER Ad Hoc Networks Journal, 5*(2), 189-209.

Grossglauser, M., & David, N. C. T. (2002). Mobility Increases the Capacity of Ad hoc Wireless Networks. *IEEE/ACM Transactions on Networking, 10*(4). doi:10.1109/TNET.2002.801403

Grossglauser, M., & Vetterli, M. (2003, March). *Locating nodes with EASE: last encounter routing in ad hoc networks through mobility diffusion*. Paper presented in the Proceedings of the *22nd IEEE Annual Joint Conference of the IEEE Computer and Communications Societies (IEEE INFOCOM 2003)*, San Francisco.

Hong, X., Gerla, M., Bagrodia, R., & Pei, G. (1999, August). *A group mobility model for ad hoc wireless networks*. Paper presented in the Proceedings of the ACM International Workshop on Modeling, Analysis and Simulation of Wireless and Mobile Systems (MSWiM), Seattle, Washington.

Hui, P., Crowcroft, J., & Yoneki, E. (2008, May). *Bubble rap: Social-based forwarding in delay tolerant networks*. Paper presented in the Proceedings of the 9th ACM international symposium on Mobile ad hoc networking & computing (MobiHoc'08).

Jain, S., Shah, R. C., Brunette, W., Borriello, G., & Roy, S. (2006). Exploiting Mobility for Energy Efficient Data Collection in Wireless Sensor Networks. *Mobile Networks and Applications*, 11.

Leguay, J., Lindgren, A., Scott, J., Friedman, T., & Crowcroft, J. (2006, September). *Opportunistic content distribution in an urban setting*. Paper presented in the Proceedings of the 2006 SIGCOMM Workshop on Challenged Networks (CHANTS 2006), Pisa, Italy.

Lindgren, A., Doria, A., & Schelen, O. (2003, July). Probabilistic routing in intermittently connected networks. *ACM SIGMOBILE Mobile Computing and Communications Review, 7*(3), 19–20. doi:10.1145/961268.961272

Mascolo, C., & Musolesi, M. (2006, July). *SCAR: Context-aware Adaptive Routing in Delay Tolerant Mobile Sensor Networks*. Paper presented in the Proceedings of the Delay Tolerant Mobile Networks Symposium of Int. Wireless Communications and Mobile Computing Conference (IWCMC 2006). Vancouver, Canada.

Musolesi, M., Hailes, S., & Mascolo, C. (2005, June). *Adaptive Routing for Intermittently Connected Mobile Ad Hoc Networks*. Paper presented in the Proceedings of the 6th International Symposium on a World of Wireless, Mobile, and Multimedia Networks (WoWMoM), Taormina - Giardini Naxos.

Musolesi, M., & Mascolo, C. (2006). *A Community Based Mobility Model for Ad Hoc Network Research*. Paper presented in the Proceedings ACM/Sigmobile Realman.

Nguyen, H. A., & Giordano, S. (2007, September). *PROSAN: Probabilistic Opportunistic Routing in SANETs*. Paper presented in the Proceedings of the ACM MobiCom/SANETs, Montreal.

Nguyen, H. A., & Giordano, S. (2008, June). *Spatiotemporal Routing Algorithm in Opportunistic Networks*. Paper presented in the Proceedings of the IEEE WoWMoM/AOC, California.

Nguyen, H. A., Giordano, S., & Puiatti, A. (2007, June). *Probabilistic Routing Protocol for Intermittently Connected Mobile Ad hoc Networks (PROPICMAN)*. Paper presented in the Proceedings of the IEEE WoWMoM/AOC 2007, Helsinki.

Santiváñez, C. A., Ramanathan, R., & Stavrakakis, I. (2001, October). *Making link-state routing scale for ad hoc networks*. Paper presented in the Proceedings of the 2nd ACM international symposium on Mobile ad hoc networking & computing, Long Beach, CA, USA

Shah, R. C., Roy, S., Jain, S., & Brunette, W. (2003, May). *Data MULEs: Modeling a three-tier architecture for sparse sensor networks*. Paper presented in the Proceedings of the IEEE workshop on Sensor Network Protocols and Applications (SNPA), 2003.

Spyropoulos, T., Psounis, K., & Raghavendra, C. S. (2005, August). *Spray and wait: Efficient routing in intermittently connected mobile networks*. Paper presented in the Proceedings of the ACM SIGCOMM workshop on Delay Tolerant Networking (WDTN), Philadelphia, PA.

Spyropoulos, T., Psounis, K., & Raghavendra, C. S. (2007, March). *Spray and Focus: Efficient mobility-assisted routing for heterogeneous and correlated mobility*. Paper presented in the Proceedings of the IEEE PerCom Workshop on Intermittently Connected Mobile Ad Hoc Network, NY.

Vahdat, A., & Becker, D. (2000, April). *Epidemic Routing for Partially Connected Ad hoc Networks* (Tech. Rep. CS-200006). Duke University.

Wang, Y., Jain, S., Martonosi, M., & Fall, K. (2005, August). *Erasure-Coding Based Routing for Opportunistic Networks*. Paper presented in the Proceedings of the ACM SIGCOMM WDTN-05, Philadelphia, PA.

Widmer, J., & Le Boudec, J. (2005, August). *Network coding for efficient communication in extreme networks*. Paper presented in the Proceedings of the ACM SIGCOMM 2005, Workshop on Delay Tolerant Networking (WDTN 2005), Philadelphia, PA.

Zhao, W., Ammar, M., & Zegura, E. (2004, May). *A Message Ferrying Approach for Data Delivery in Sparse Mobile Ad Hoc Networks*. Paper presented in the Proceedings of the 5th ACM International Symposium on Mobile Ad Hoc Networking and Computing (MobiHoc), Tokyo, Japan.

ENDNOTES

[1] We notice that the traditional concept of reliable routing, as in legacy networks here does not apply. OppNets are really best effort, and a message could be lost or experience a long delay.

[2] Note that also the traditional concept of route does not apply in OppNets. In fact, as a physical connection does not exist, a message eventually reaches the destination with a sequence of independent hops.

[3] Haggle project (EU FP6-2004-IST-4)

This work was previously published in International Journal of Ambient Computing and Intelligence (IJACI), Volume 1, Issue 3, edited by Kevin Curran, pp. 19-38, copyright 2009 by IGI Publishing (an imprint of IGI Global).

194

Chapter 19
Online Remote Control of a Wireless Home Automation Network

John Wade
University of Ulster, Northern Ireland

Jose Santos
University of Ulster, Northern Ireland

Noel Evans
University of Ulster, Northern Ireland

ABSTRACT

Embedded systems within home appliances are not usually manufactured to operate in a networked environment; connecting supplementary hardware/software systems through a wireless, PC-controlled medium is necessary to enable full, efficient control of their functions from a remote location. Access to the home's central PC may be gained via a local web server, giving Internet-based control from almost anywhere in the world. The proposed system constitutes a significant improvement over those discussed in the literature to date, and reviewed here. It enables complex-appliance control in a secure and reliable portable-wireless environment, and was developed using ASP.Net. The system was assessed for Received Signal Strength (RSS) in an environment more radio-hostile than that found in a typical household. The minimum RF level found at a transfer rate of 9.6 kbps was 8 dB above the receiver's quoted sensitivity of -103 dBm; this fading margin will increase in a normal household environment.

INTRODUCTION

As the cost of electronics components and microprocessors decrease, they are embedded increasingly into every day household items,

e.g. microwave ovens, toasters, televisions and washing machines. Unfortunately it is still not possible to communicate with these appliances via a network, be that from within or outside the home. Although the appliances have embedded microprocessors to help control their onboard systems, they do not have the capability to com-

DOI: 10.4018/978-1-60960-549-0.ch019

municate with a network of any kind. This is because there are no communication devices pre-installed and as yet no clear leader exists in home automation network protocols. Until this happens, true home automation networks cannot be fully realised. This, however, does not limit the ability to remotely control appliances in the home. To do this, domestic appliances can be grouped as:

1. Appliances that can only be turned on and off (Group 1).
2. Appliances that can be controlled in a more functional manner, such as televisions, DVD players and HiFi equipment (Group 2).

There are many reasons why the ability to remotely control the home is an advantage. In modern times, security and time management have become important issues. Houses may give an impression of occupation through controlled lighting and have their alarm system monitored; kitchen tasks may be started remotely from a work location, saving time after the daily commute. A control network could also give the elderly and disabled a more independent way of life.

In section two, a background review of previous research into this topic is presented. Section three discusses the hardware design for the system investigated. Section four explores the software design for both the Internet interface and the firmware for the microprocessors. Section five discusses the testing protocol and results obtained from the system. Finally, section six presents conclusions and suggestions for future work.

Computer Controlled Home Automation

There have been several approaches to computer controlled home automation: what follows is a review of the most significant and recent contributions.

Al-Ali A.R. & Al-Rousan M. (2004) developed a system built from a Java based user interface that was accessible through the World Wide Web. The system allowed the user to turn a cooker, light bulb or a fan on and off. This system used direct wiring from the computer to the appliances to exercise control over them: this approach is very costly due to the amount of cable needed to connect all the appliances found in a modern house. Also, appliances that fall into Group 2 could not be implemented in this system and introduction of new appliances into the household will result in further integration costs.

Sriskanthan N., (2002), proposed a system that controlled home appliances from a PC using Bluetooth as the communications technology. As before, there was no consideration for those appliances that fall into Group 2 and could not be controlled over the Internet. By using Bluetooth there is also a limit to the number of appliances that can be controlled. According to Stallings (2002), up to eight devices can communicate in a small network called a piconet, and up to ten piconets can coexist in the same coverage range of a Bluetooth radio. This permits up to 80 appliances to be connected. Although a significant number at present, in the future this may become a limitation on the system. Another disadvantage of Bluetooth is that it allows ad-hoc networking. This enables an appliance that is Bluetooth enabled to establish an instant connection with another Bluetooth enabled appliance in the network when it comes into range. The main implication of this statement is that as new appliances are introduced into the home, the PC software has to be able to identify the appliance and either accept it or reject it automatically.

Bigio P. & Cucos A. & Corcoran P & Chahil C & Lusted K. (1999) designed and implemented a non-standard means of wireless networking suitable for home automation. Their system consisted of a low-power RF network broadcasting on 433 MHz, which again is license-free as it falls in the Industrial Scientific & Medical (ISM) band according to the European Radio Commission Committee (2005).

The system is based on a master/slave topology and is composed of a base station, relay units, and slave units. The base distinguishes between application requests and functions: application requests remain transparent to the radio system and therefore only the function of the appliance is broadcast. These broadcasts consist of frames/packets which have headers, body, trailer and a block/frame check for error checking. The relay units are used to extend the range of the base station, which has a range of 150 m. This range is sufficient in most homes and therefore the relay units are not normally needed. The slave units are used to relay the information provided by the base station to their appliance. The network manager software controls all communications of the Radio Frequency (RF) network; it runs as a background service on the PC and is also responsible for granting or denying access to recently arrived slave units, depending on the unit being a legal part of the network. This system, whilst providing clear advantages over those previously proposed, still does not provide support for control over the Internet. However, it does show how useful and powerful using a non-standard RF network for the communications medium can be, by allowing the designer full flexibility over the communications protocol.

Thomas R. (2000) designed a system that could decode signals from remote control units using the RC5 protocol, which is used by Philips, and the SIR C protocol used by Sony. This work highlights the problems that arise when trying to capture, decode and recreate remote control protocols. This system only dealt with two of the more common protocols; there are numerous others from a variety of manufacturers. Trying to produce a system that can recreate all protocols is not feasible, for two reasons. Firstly, from an economic point of view, a very wide range of remote controls from various manufacturers would need to be available so that signals may be captured and recreated. Secondly, the time needed to do this accurately is problematic; other workers dedicate

much effort in this area [ref: Innotech Systems]. Therefore, it was considered more practical here to adopt a pre-designed universal remote control in the design.

Guan R. & Pruehsner WR & Enderle JD (2000) designed a system which used a GUI (Graphical User Interface) running on a PC to address the control problem presented by appliances that fall into Group 2. User input from a graphical representation of a remote control in the GUI sent data wirelessly to a PIC microcontroller via the serial port of the PC. This data was then transformed into special control commands forwarded to a PP4001 universal remote control IC; this is pre-programmed to control most brands of appliances that have Infra Red (IR) remote controls. Although this approach negates the need to design a custom decoder, again there was no facility for control over the Internet and the PP4001 is expensive.

By extending the elements discussed above, it became possible to implement a system that is capable of controlling both groups of appliances over the Internet, thus providing a reliable and secure connection to all appliances within a wireless home network from almost anywhere in the world.

Home Automation Network Hardware Implementation

The Home Automation Network is broken into 3 different sub-systems: the control unit (Base Unit), the Group 1 receiver units (GP1 Units), and the Group 2 receiver units (GP2 Units).

Base Unit

As shown in Figure 1, the Base unit is the main control center for the system; it communicates with the host PC (home PC) via a serial port connection. The main computational element that controls communications is a PIC 16F877 microcontroller, which has a USART (Universal Synchronous Asynchronous Receiver Transmitter) built in. This receives data from the PC and is also responsible for RTS (Request to Send) handshaking between the Base unit and the PC. This ensures that no data is lost during communications due to buffer over-runs. All communications between the microcontroller and the PC use a MAX233 as an intermediate signal level converter.

Once data has been received by the microcontroller, it verifies that a full packet is present and the data is correct; data and packet structure will be discussed further in section 4. Once deemed correct, the microcontroller decides which group of appliances the data is intended for and processes it accordingly, either passing it to the Group 1 encoders or sending it through the USART to the Group 2 encoder, and on to the transmitter.

If the microcontroller decides that the data is intended for the Group 1 appliances, it firstly selects the appropriate input line of a digital multiplexer (Mux); this ensures that only data from the Group 1 encoders is sent to the transmitter. Then the data is output on ports A and C of the microcontroller, which are connected to the Group1 Manchester encoders (RF600E). These communicate with 4 decoders (RF600D), one on each GP1 unit. Matching the encoders to the decoders ensures that no other appliances outside of the system can be activated unintentionally and aids system security. The new encoded data is then sent via the Mux to the RTFQ1 (433 MHz FSK transmitter) [rfsolutions]; this has an estimated radiated

power of 5 dBm when using a λ/4 antenna. The companion receiver has a sensitivity of -103 dBm for 9.6 kbs operation. This implies that a maximum path loss of 108 db may be tolerated.

If the microcontroller decides that the data is intended for the Group 2 appliances, then once again the correct input line to the Mux is chosen and the data is relayed via the USART to a serial encoder (RF600T). This is a serial version of the previous encoder which also uses Manchester encoding. The Encoder encapsulates the data into its own transmission packet, which consists of a 76 bit preamble, a 4-bit sync pattern, 1 start bit, 8 command bits, the data bits (size depends on the data sent from the microcontroller), and 8 checksum bits. This ensures that all data is received correctly by the decoder (RF600T) on the GP2 unit. This new encoded data is then sent to the FSK transmitter.

GP1 Units

The GP1 unit block diagram is shown in Figure 2. Each of the units is responsible for receiving control information from the Base unit and controlling the Group 1 appliances connected to them. Each GP1 unit can control 1 appliance.

When data is received by the FSK receiver the RF600D decodes it; if the data is intended for that unit then the decoder activates or deactivates an isolating relay, which in turn controls the relevant

Figure 1. Base unit block diagram

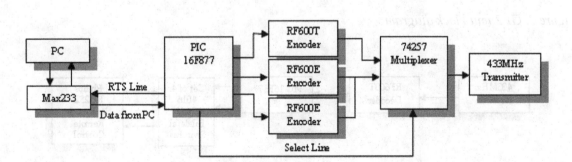

Figure 2. GP1 unit block diagram

AC mains-connected appliance. The decoder has two modes of operation, momentary and latched: here the latter mode is used. Each time data is received and verified for that specific decoder the output of the decoder is switched to the opposite state, i.e. if it was 'on' then it will be switched to 'off', and vice-versa. This implies that the same data is transmitted for on and off. This element is part of the software design and will be discussed in section 4.

GP2 Units

Figure 3 shows a GP2 unit, responsible for receiving control information from the Base and controlling the appropriate Group 2 appliance remote control. Each GP2 unit can control one remote.

When data is received by the FSK receiver the decoder (RF600T) ensures steering to that particular unit, and on to a PIC 16F877 microcontroller for further verification that it originated from the registered Base. If this is so, the PIC outputs the data on ports B and D. These are connected to 4 separate 4016 quad bilateral switch

banks. These switches are in turn hardwired to a Philips RU252 Universal Remote Control, which has the ability to control both televisions and VHS/DVD players/recorders from a wide number of manufacturers: up to 16 buttons on the remote may be controlled. In the prototype 15 were used for proof of concept. All 32 remote switches could be controlled with a few changes to the software and the addition of another 4 4016 devices.

Home Automation Network Software Implementation

The software required to control the system was broken down into three different programs: to enable communications to the home server via a website, to control the microcontroller on the Base unit, and to control the microcontroller on the GP2 units.

Website Software

The website used to access the system from a remote location is programmed in ASP.Net which

Figure 3. GP2 unit block diagram

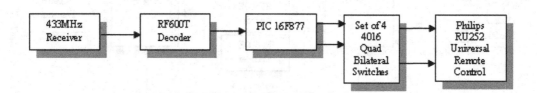

forms part of the Visual Studio.Net package and the.Net framework. It allows the creation of Web applications and services that run under IIS (Internet Information services). IIS host Web applications on the Windows server, which in this case was based on the home PC. It manages the application, passes requests from clients to the application, and returns the applications responses to the client. ASP.Net is one of the most complete platforms for developing Web applications, making creation, debugging and deployment straightforward, as noted in Webb J. (2002).

When the user first accesses the website the Login screen is presented. Here the user is required to enter a user name and password; authorized user information is stored in a configuration file on the server. If the user is verified he / she is redirected to the home page, shown in Figure 4. When the Home page is loaded it accesses a database on the server that contains the current state of the Group 1 appliances on the system and displays this information under the Current State check

boxes. If a check box is ticked then the appliance is "on" and vice-versa. The user can then update the state of the appliances by making adjustments to the New State check boxes. Once the user is satisfied with the changes the Update Appliances button is pressed; this sends the New State check boxes information back to the server, which then calculates two sets of data from this information.

Firstly, the New State information needs to be converted into two numbers, each set ranging from 0 to 16 i.e. a 4-bit nibble. This is carried out as follows: appliances 1 to 4 represent the first set of data where appliance 1 is the least significant bit and appliance 4 is the most significant bit. If an appliance is set to "on" then the corresponding bit is set, otherwise it is cleared. The same procedure is carried out for appliances 5 to 8. Once this set of data has been generated it is the necessary to produce another two numbers from the Current State check boxes. The two sets of data are then XOR'ed with one another and the result stored as Function bytes 0 and 1. This

Figure 4. System home page

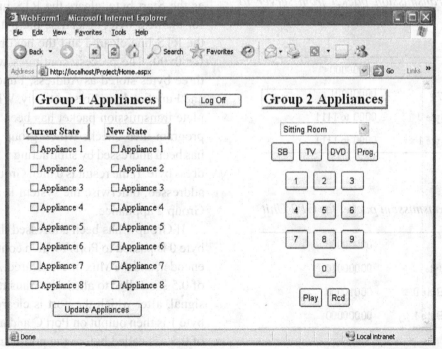

ensures that if an appliance changes state then the corresponding bit for output will be set, allowing the Base unit to drive the encoders correctly, as discussed in section 3.1.

This data is then sent to the serial port where it is added to the transmission packet and transmitted to the base. This packet is made up of a start byte = 0, address byte = 1 and the two function bytes as shown in Figure 5. The database is updated with the New State checkbox information and display in the Current Status check boxes on the refreshed page.

The user also has the option of controlling a Group 2 appliance via the onscreen remote control, by firstly selecting the area where the remote control is located from a dropdown list box. The address of the remote is defined by adding two to the index of the area selected in the list and is stored. When the user presses a button the address is sent to the serial port and forms part of the transmission packet. Each button has its own function defined for controlling the remote control and the two function bytes are exclusively defined

Figure 5. Transmission packet from server to base unit

Start Byte	00000000
Address Byte	00000001
Function Byte 0	0000 to 1111
Function Byte 1	0000 to 1111

Figure 6. Transmission packet for GP2 Unit

Start Byte	00000000
Address Byte	00000010
Function Byte 0	00010000
Function Byte 1	00000000

within these functions. The Function 0 byte controls the first 8 switches and the Function 1 byte controls the next 8 switches. The screen is then refreshed. The transmission packet is similar to the transmission packet for the Group one appliances. Figure 6 shows an example of the sitting-room remote control being accessed with the number 1 button pressed. Figure 7 shows the two function bytes and the corresponding switches that each bit controls.

If the Program button is pressed then buttons 1 and 3 are simultaneously accessed on the remote control; this allows the remote to enter program mode where a new device number may be added and hence allow the remote to control a new appliance. On completion, 'Log off' permits a return to the Login screen.

Base Unit Microcontroller Firmware

When the microcontroller is started it clears the Request to Send (RTS) line leaving it ready for reception and waits until a byte has been received. The RTS line is then set, stopping all transmission from the PC. If this byte is 0x00 then it stores it as the Start byte, clears the RTS line and waits for the next byte, otherwise the byte is ignored, the RTS line cleared and the next byte checked for 0x00. The process continues with the next three bytes stored as Address, Function byte 0, and Function byte 1 respectively. When the complete transmission packet has been received the program then checks which group of hardware has been addressed by subtracting 1 from the Address byte. If the result is 0 then Group 1 has been addressed, otherwise the system is addressing a Group 2 appliance.

If Group 1 has been addressed then Function byte 0 is passed to Port A which controls the first encoder, and the Mux line is cleared. A short delay of 0.5 s is called to allow the transmission of the signal, after which the port is cleared. Function byte 1 is then output on Port C and another delay of 0.5 s is called before the port is cleared.

Figure 7. Function bytes and their corresponding switches

	Bit 0	Bit 1	Bit 2	Bit 3	Bit 4	Bit 5	Bit 6	Bit 7
Function Byte 0	SB	TV	DVD	0	1	2	3	4
Function Byte 1	5	6	7	8	9	Play	Record	NA

If Group 2 has been addressed then the Mux line is set, the Start byte, Address byte, System Identification Number (SID) and the two function bytes are transmitted via the onboard USART to the serial encoder chip and then onto the RF transmitter. The SID number is pre-programmed into the microcontroller and consists of 4 bytes that provides up to 2^{32} different combinations. It is used as a unique system identifier for all the Group two remote controls. This ensures that only GP2 units registered with the same SID number as the base unit can be controlled by that base unit, thus preventing another system from accessing the GP2 units.

GP2 Unit Microcontroller Firmware

The start of the GP2 microcontroller program is similar to that in the Base unit, but with 4 extra bytes of data to be received before a complete transmission packet is collected: these are stored as SID 0 to 3. When the full packet has been received the microcontroller verifies that it has been addressed by subtracting the pre-programmed address from the address received. If the result is 0 its carries on, otherwise the packet is ignored and the microprocessor resets, ready for another transmission.

The next step is to verify that the SID number received matches the pre-programmed SID in memory: if so it continues, otherwise it again resets ready for another transmission. Once it has verified that the data is intended for the GP2 unit it checks if the program button was pressed on the website. This is done by subtracting the

function 0 byte from 0x50. The result of pressing the program button is that Function byte 0 = 0x50. If the result is 0 then it enters the Program routine. Here Function byte 0 is passed to Port B and a delay of 3 s is called before clearing the port. This activates buttons 1 and 3 on the remote control and makes it enter programming mode. If the result is not 0 then "Function 0" byte is passed to Port B for 0.5 s, and the port cleared. This is followed with Function byte 1 being passed to port D for 0.5 s before the port is cleared. Ports B and D are connected to quad bilateral switches that are hardwired to the remote control. In total, 253 GP2 units can be addressed by the Base unit.

System Testing

Hardware tests were carried out using a program written in VB6 that allowed the Start, Address, and Function bytes to be explicitly entered as numbers before accessing the serial port. Transmission range in a hostile radio envonment was evaluated and software tests were carried out on the website.

Transmission Characteristics Test

Transmission range was tested by locating the transmitter and receiver units along different paths with a variety of obstacles, giving a significantly more radio-hostile environment than that found in a typical household, and measuring the Received Signal Strength (RSS) in each case. Figure 8 shows the location of the transmitter and receivers, along with the relevant obstacles in the path. The walls and columns are made of reinforced concrete with metal platting. The floor and ceilings are made of concrete, the overhang ceiling is made of mineral fiber tiles, the stud wall is made of a wooden frame covered in gypsum plaster board, and the elevator shaft wall is a red-brick construction.

As noted in Figure 9, the received input level never fell below -94.2 dBm, giving an 8.8 dB margin above the manufacturer's quoted sensitivity of -103 dBm, for a transfer rate of 9.6 kbps. The fading margin in a normal domestic situation (with thinner concrete absorbers) is expected to be significantly greater.

Hardware Test & Software Tests

To test the hardware, a prototype system was constructed. Three GP1 units were implemented using two encoders; the first encoder addressed 2 units, and the second addressed one unit. The intention was to prove that more than 1 decoder could be addressed by the same encoder and operated independently, and that the signal from

the two encoders were separate, i.e.: if the first appliance was operated by the first encoder then the first appliance on the second encoder should not be operated at the same time as the signals should be different. The GP1 units were operated individually and then simultaneously by sending the appropriate commands from the test program.

During testing, the only problem that occurred was that if two sets of packets were sent one immediately after the other, one of the two encoders would lock up; this resulted in the base unit needing to be reset to correct the problem. However this will not represent a problem when the system is controlled through the website as it provides adequate time between packet transmissions due to page loading and refreshing.

The prototype also included a single GP2 unit. Correct operation was confirmed using a test program and the unit was also tested to verify that it would not respond to an address that was different to that stored in memory and that it would not respond to a packet with the incorrect SID number. This last test was achieved by replacing

Figure 8 Transmitter and receiver locations for RSS evaluations

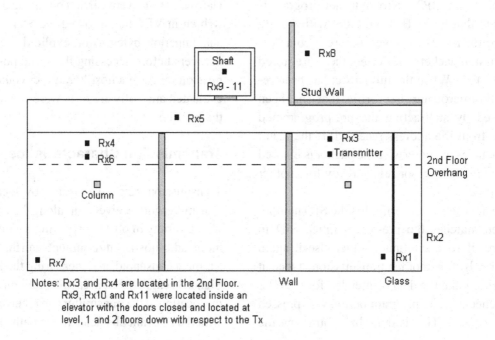

Notes: Rx3 and Rx4 are located in the 2nd Floor.
Rx9, Rx10 and Rx11 were located inside an elevator with the doors closed and located at level, 1 and 2 floors down with respect to the Tx

Figure 9. Received signal strength measurements

Rx No	RSS (dBm)	Propagation Path	Direct Path Length
1	-57.52	Around Square Column (x m^2)	9 m
2	-52.75	Through Glass Panel (direct Line of Sight)	10 m
3	-53.32	Through Overhang Ceiling	3 m
4	-88.09	Overhang Ceiling and 2 Walls	17 m
5	-65.15	Through Wall	11.5 m
6	-72.89	Through 2 Walls	19 m
7	-85.75	Through 2 Walls	23 m
8	-66.80	Through 2 Stud Walls	10 m
9	-93.30	Elevator Shaft	13.5 m
10	-93.38	Elevator Shaft – 1 Floor Down	14.2 m
11	-94.20	Elevator Shaft – 2 Floors Down	16.2 m

the microcontroller in the base unit with another one with a different SID number.

The web-based application program was first tested in a stand-alone mode for access security and for correct updating of the database with the "New States" when the "update" button was pressed on the application; then the prototype was fully connected to the host-PC and full control was achieved from the web-server.

CONCLUSION

The system developed is a very powerful home automation network that can be accessed from remote locations through the World Wide Web and operates in a wireless environment within the home. It consists of a website which is located on a home server and associated hardware, also connected to the server. The hardware is comprised of a Base unit that receives signals from the website and relays them on to the receiver units which are connected to the appliances. At present the system can control 8 appliances that can be turned on and off (GP1) and 253 appliances that are accessed via a remote control (GP2). Only minor software changes are needed to permit significant expansion. The system can operate in radio-hostile environments while maintaining a data rate of 9.6 kbps.

Although the system as described is not a fully-definitive home automation solution, it does serve as useful prototype. There are many improvements that could be made e.g.: the implementation of duplex communications between the Base and receiver units. The receivers could then inform the Base, and ultimately the user via the Web, that commands have been received and executed. This negates the need for the database as the receiver units could relay their status when the website is accessed. A related improvement is to grant users local control of the Group 1 appliances, with duplex links updating their Current State resulting from local switch changes within the home. The website program might also be enhanced to include a plan/layout of the home where each controlled appliance is shown in its proper physical location; this decreases search time on user access by eliminating the need to search through check boxes and dropdown lists.

Finally, the system developed can save time, help improve home security, and in general bring a better way of life to the end user.

REFERENCES

Al–Ali, A. R., & Al-Rousan, M. (2004). Java-Based Home Automation System. *IEEE Transactions on Consumer Electronics, 50*(2), 498–504. doi:10.1109/TCE.2004.1309414

Bigioi, P., Cucos, A., Corcoran, P., Chahil, C., & Lusted, K. (1999, August). Transparent, Dynamically Configurable RF Network Suitable For Home Automation Applications. *IEEE Transactions on Consumer Electronics, 45*(3), 474–480. doi:10.1109/30.793529

European Radio Commissions Committee. (2005) Frequencies and Standards. (on-line) http://www.ero.dk/doc98/official/pdf/ REP083. PDF#433050000. Accessed 5th July 2005.

Guan, R., Pruehsner, W. R., & Enderle, J. D. (2000, April). The Computerized Environmental Remote Control. *Proceedings of the IEEE 26th Annual Northeast Bioengineering Conference* (pp. 147–148).

RFSolutions. (2006) *RTFQ1 Data Sheet.* (on-line) http://www.rfsolutions.co.uk/acatalog/DS069-7.pdf

Sriskanthan, N., & Tan, K. (2002). Bluetooth Based Home Automation Systems. *Journal of Microprocessors and Microsystems, 26*, 281–289. doi:10.1016/S0141-9331(02)00039-X

Stallings, W. (2002). *Wireless Communications and Networking.* New Jersey, USA: Prentice-Hall.

Thomas, R. (2000, September). Remote Control IR Decoder. *Everyday Practical Electronics, 29*(9), 698–701.

Webb, J. (2002). *Developing Web Applications With Microsoft Visual Basic. Net and Microsoft Visual C#. Net.* Washington, USA: Microsoft Press.

This work was previously published in International Journal of Ambient Computing and Intelligence (IJACI), Volume 1, Issue 3, edited by Kevin Curran, pp. 39-52, copyright 2009 by IGI Publishing (an imprint of IGI Global).

Chapter 20
Distributed Schema-Based Middleware for Ambient Intelligence Environments

Javier Gómez
Universidad Autónoma de Madrid, Spain

Germán Montoro
Universidad Autónoma de Madrid, Spain

Pablo Haya
Universidad Autónoma de Madrid, Spain

Manuel García-Herranz
Universidad Autónoma de Madrid, Spain

Xavier Alamán
Universidad Autónoma de Madrid, Spain

ABSTRACT

In this work we present a middleware developed for Ambient Intelligence environments. The proposed model is based on the blackboard metaphor, which is logically centralized but physically distributed. Although it is based on a data-oriented model, some extra services have been added to this middle layer to improve the functionality of the modules that employ it. The system has been developed and tested in a real Ambient Intelligence environment.

INTRODUCTION

The Ubiquitous Computing term was coined by Mark Weiser in 1991 (Weiser, 1991). From that moment on, many problems and opportunities have arisen from that vision of a world rich in

DOI: 10.4018/978-1-60960-549-0.ch020

information and interaction. Ambient intelligence environments (also called intelligent environments) are one of the fields where Ubiquitous Computing can be naturally applied. We can define an active environment as a space limited by physical barriers, which is capable to sense and interact with its inhabitants.

The definition leads to the necessity of some kind of physical infrastructure for sensing and acting into the real world. However, as we will show below, these environments present some particular problems beyond hardware issues. For instance, the environment configuration changes dynamically and client applications should be notified of these changes. Thus, a software infrastructure is also needed to solve these problems.

The approach that we present in this work tries to solve these issues, making easier the developing task and the interaction among applications. For this, it employs a common, normalized and formalized definition of the reality. This definition, and the information that it stores, should be accessible and shared by clients and applications.

Moreover, some extra features have been added to the system to provide additional services, such as an historical registry, which shows all the activity carried out by the system or a rule-based service, which changes the behavior of the environment under some circumstances.

Another interesting feature is one that adds a description of the representation of the elements that compose the environment. This feature facilitates the definition and development of interfaces to interact with the environment. User Interfaces are becoming an important subject in the Ambient Intelligence field, because computers usually keep hidden from users and system services are obtained by means of context awareness interaction. Moreover, this interaction must be adapted to the task, the environment, its occupants and the available resources (Paterno & Santoro, 2002; Rayner et al., 2001). The integration of this description with the rest of the elements of the model helps to fulfill this task.

Finally, as an important aspect of our development, this model and its services have been tested in a real intelligent environment.

MOTIVATION

Any intelligent environment is composed by a heterogeneous set of software and hardware components (Haya, et al. 2001). This involves some challenges:

- **Bounded environment**. Human activities are usually taking place in a discrete and bounded environment. As Kindberg and Fox (2002) pose in their *boundary principle*, designers should be aware of this distribution. In this respect, each smart space partitions the whole domain in isolated management areas. That is, in a house environment, in example, management resource policies are spatially limited to the home extension, and homeowners should decide them. This is particularly true for privacy concerns since humans consider home as a private space and they would like to manage it following their own criterions.

- **Heterogeneous components**. Smart homes are populated by a heterogeneous set of numerous components that can be either software or hardware. So it is needed to integrate and manage different kind of technologies. This leads to a more complex development process. This complexity affects to every component of the smart home. In particular, the final user would like to interact with the environment using different modes (such as voice, gestures, tactile, etc.) This implies, practitioners have to deal with very different user interaction techniques. Besides, the distribution of the information required to choose among different communication networks depending on several factors such as bandwidth constraints, mobility or deployment cost.

- **Highly distributed components**. Both sensors, whose task is to catch information from the environment, and actuators, which are the devices that make changes in the real world, are located in different places. New extra impediments appear during the developing process of a distributed system. Some particular tasks, such as configuration and debugging, are more complicated in a distributed framework.

- **Dynamic configuration**. Smart home environments are highly dynamic. It cannot be possible to predict when users go in or leave the environment, and also, when devices are attached or detached. The system has to be always running. For instance, home's inhabitants consider inadmissible periodically failures of their homes. This implies that the management of new components has to be done at run-time.

The process of developing applications for intelligent environments requires a software infrastructure to deal with these problems. Programmers require both being able to obtain the information from an individual component, and accessing to the global state of the environment. This also includes information from non-computational elements (users, objects, time, etc.) and the relations between them.

An abstraction layer is required to allow the management of the information relative to the environment. Therefore, we propose an improvement of a previously developed middleware (Haya, et al. 2004) that allows accessing to the information that comes from either hardware or software elements, and that provides them with additional features.

The process of developing applications for intelligent environments requires a software infrastructure to deal with these problems. Programmers require both being able to obtain the information from an individual component, and accessing to the global state of the environment. This also includes information from non-compu-

tational elements (users, objects, time, etc.) and the relations between them.

RELATED WORK

Much taxonomy can be found in literature to classify middle layers. On the one hand, attending to its programming model, we can classify them in:

- **Service oriented**: Based on the client – server model. Client applications access to the context by means of a standard communication interface.
- **Data oriented**: They are centered in context representation. The distribution is carried out by a reduced operations set. The mechanism the middle layer uses to distribute information can be classified regarding the spatial and temporal coupling level:
- **Temporarily and spatially coupled**: A process communicates with a known receptor only if they coincide with each other in time.
- **Temporarily coupled and spatially uncoupled**: Process group temporarily to transmit information, but they do not have to know each other.
- **Temporarily uncoupled and spatially coupled**: The emitter process needs to know the receptor(s) of the data it is sending, but they do not have to coincide in time.
- **Temporarily and spatially uncoupled**: Transmitter processes do not know the receptors(s) and they do not have to coincide in time.According to the technology employed in its implementation, we can divide them into:
- **Distributed Objects**: The basic unit is the object (active or passive). Active objects are contextual information sources and can be queried by object remote calls.

- **Infrastructure**: It is based on an infrastructure of known, reliable and public servers that provide a set of services.
- **Blackboard**: It is a centralized mechanism in which context aware applications store and get information back from a common, known and accessible repository. o Finally, regarding to its purpose:
- **Acquisition and processing of context**: They provide mechanisms to standardize the communication with the different technologies. In some situations, they can process some of the data to obtain a more abstract representation
- **Distribution oriented**: They want to get an effective context distribution

Middle Layers for Intelligent Environments

Accord (Akesson, 2000): This tool allows configuring the devices of a house environment in a flexible way. Each device publishes its state in a common shared space. The editor is oriented to configure the environment by the final user.

- **Aware Home** (Kidd, 1999): This project aims to build a house to be used as an ubiquitous computing lab to support life in that house
- **Beach** (Tandler, 2004): (Basic Environment for Active Collaboration) It is a platform developed in SmallTalk that makes the creation of hypermedia collaborative applications easier
- **DOBS** (Villanueva, 2009): Poses a framework oriented to distributed objects to design services. It is composed of a set of modules, as interfaces, audio and video services, common and integration platform services and an information model.
- **EmiLets** (de Ipiña, 2006): Presents a middle layer that tries to facilitate the creation of spaces with intelligent objects and sup-

ports the mobile phone as the remote control of all of that devices.

- **Gaia** (Román, 2001): On the one hand, it is based on distributed objects. On the other hand, it similar to a classical distributed operating system. It is composed of a collection of services that provides a programming interface. This way, the environment and the resources that composes it as if they were a unique and programmable entity.
- **ICrafter** (Ponnenkanti, 2001): This system focuses on a flexible services composition. It looks for facilitating the creation of user interfaces from the available services in a moment. A service can be either a device or an application
- **InConcert** (Brumitt, 2000): This is the middle layer that was used in the Easy Living Project (Microsoft Research division). The communication mechanism is asynchronous, XML-based and it uses a machine-independent addressing.
- **IDP** (Choi, 2006): This middle layer provides in-home services based on biometric information and context. The middle layer receives biometric information, such as heart rhythm, facial expressions, body temperature, location and person movements, from the sensors deployed in the environment.
- **Metaglue** (Phillips, 1999): Provides a coordination mechanism for big groups of software agents. Some facilities were added to the system, such as new services discovering, resources acquiring policies, etc. It is an extension of the Java programming language.
- **OSGi** (Gong, 2001): This approach tries to standardize the connections between devices (inside or outside of the house) to facilitate VoIP, TV on demand, remote control services, etc.

- **Plan-B** (Ballesteros, 2006): This work proposes a new approach. Instead of using a middleware, it is based on a virtual file system in which all of the elements of the environment are organized.
- **Semantic Space** (Wang, 2004): This infrastructure for intelligent environments is based in context. There are three key aspects: An explicit knowledge representation (in RDF and OWL), a search engine (based on RDQL) and a reasoner that allows inferring new situations from the information stored in the knowledge base
- **SmartOffice** (Le Gal, 2001): This work presents an integration resource-oriented protocol. Every module communicates with the resource server supervisor.

MIDDLEWARE LAYER: THE BLACKBOARD

The blackboard metaphor poses that all information exchange is done through a logically centralized module, where producers publish their output without knowing who will consume them.

In our case, the blackboard is a physically distributed middle layer between elements of the environment and applications. It presents multiple characteristics, oriented to solve the problems presented previously. It can be studied under three points of view: from a data model point of view, an application model point of view and a communication model point of view.

Data Model

The data model is a representation of the information relative to the world, which is independent from the source that generates it and the abstraction level. It is divided into two clearly different but narrowly related parts: The schema model and the repository. The schema model contains the description of the world, in terms of classes,

their properties, capabilities and the relations that can appear between them, that is, an ontological model. On the other hand, the repository stores entities that are the realizations of the classes of the schema. Entities can represent physical objects, such as computers, people, etc. or virtual objects, such as pictures, personal information, songs, etc. Regardless of the nature of the entities, all their information is accessible through the global information structure.

This representation allows combining both abstract concepts and information from sensors. Some of the advantages of this data model are:

- **Functionality and data are separated**. This allows developing each part individually. A data oriented middle layer can be the base of a service oriented middle layer, so the data layer can be reused by several services.
- **Uncoupled communication**. The components of the architecture are more independent thanks to a decoupled communication mechanism. The blackboard model (see forward sections) makes the coordination between applications that interact with the environment easier, since they do not have to be synchronized either temporally or spatially. The fact that two applications do not have to be synchronized temporally involves that to communicate them, it is not necessary to run both at the same time. On the other hand, the lack of space synchronization produces that two applications do not have to know each other to interchange information. This is possible because the blackboard stores all the information of the environment. This kind of communication makes the reconfiguration process more efficient in dynamic environments, since the procedure to follow when a new component appears or disappears is transparently carried out.

- **Multiple and heterogeneous information sources are allowed**. The information of the environment may come from sensors and also be deduced. Following the data-oriented paradigm, we have defined a common schema that establishes the representation of the data stored in the blackboard. This schema has been designed to reflect a universal description of the environment components, independent of any particular technology. In doing so, many different applications can reuse the same information. This implies, on the one hand, that system the functionality emerges from the different use that distinct modules do of the same information and, on the other hand, that producers may improve their acquisition procedures while the data model remains unalterable. For instance, location information is obtained using different levels of abstraction (i.e. room level or spatial coordinates). Consumers choose which level of detail is desired, and subscribe to changes on the pertinent variables. An improvement in the location mechanism does not affect to the consumers, since the measured variables remain the same.

- **Straightforward creation of user interfaces.** Our blackboard approach makes easier to keep only one application model that can be reused in several personalized interfaces. Thus, the MVC (Model-View-Controller) pattern (Reenskaug, 1979) that has been used in the user interface implementation is transferred easily because the separation between the three components arises naturally. Moreover, the information represented in the common schema makes possible to automatically generate different and adapted interfaces (Gómez, et al., 2008).

A data oriented approach does not exclude the middle layer to provide other services. For example, to store an historical register of the contextual information could be an interesting service since lots of applications can demand it.

Application Model

Blackboard architectures are considered a classic paradigm (Engelmore & Morgan, 1988) that has been proved to be used in control systems (Hayes-Roth, 1985). Blackboard architectures were used to solve non-deterministic problems (Erman, et al., 1980). The solution was found by making some modules to cooperate; each one specialized in one specific task. Every process stored partial results in a blackboard. There was also a centralized coordinator whose task was to choose, reject or merge those partial results. Each module only knew the blackboard and did not know any extra information about the rest of the system. So, a data-centered view is considered, instead of one centered in the process. System components do not communicate each other directly, but they sent requests to a central repository. To take information from the system, these components can subscribe to changes on the blackboard or access to it directly. Some characteristics of our architecture are:

- **Common data model.** The information stored in the blackboard follows a common model. As it was said in previous sections, this model separates data and functionality, allows applications to be uncoupled both spatially and temporally and the MVC pattern makes the implementation of interfaces easier.

- **Logically central repository.** The middleware allows accessing all the environment information as it was stored in a unique repository. On the application developer side there is only one blackboard. But it is composed by distributed set of spaces that manage a part of the global information. This solution was proposed to make easier the implementation task, without losing the scalability of the whole system.

- **Communication mechanism.** There are two types of protocols. On the one hand, there is a polling-based protocol, which allows obtaining the information directly from the blackboard. On the other hand, there is a publish-subscribe protocol, where the sources of information publish on the blackboard changes in the context, and consumers subscribe to these changes to receive them.

Communication Model

As we mentioned above, the collection of devices, people, relations, etc., which establishes the model of the world, is available for developers through the blackboard. Classical implementations are based on a shared tuples spaces (Gelernter, 1985). Nevertheless, our blackboard implementation is based on a directed graph composed by entities and relations. This representation fits better with the organization of the real world than the model based on tuples. Another advantage of this model is that navigation through the instances of the model is easier.

Applications can access the blackboard by means of a set of operations that has been defined to allow asking the blackboard for instances or updating them. It also allows discovering new instances or relations, and subscribing to their changes.

For a better understanding of the communication model we have established a division between the different kinds of modules that can interact with the blackboard. This classification establishes two axes: virtual-real world and publisher-consumer of information. Thus, we distinguish between five types of clients:

- **Sensors.** Information sources linked to the real world are included here. Sensors

measure information from the real world directly, in a low level of abstraction.

- **Actuators.** They make changes in the real world from the modifications in the blackboard. As Sensors, they are physical entities but virtually represented in the blackboard.

- **Interpreters.** These components subscribe to changes in the blackboard. They can be classified in two subcategories, depending on how they process the information: They can turn the information from sensors to high-level information or they can divide a complex task in simpler actions.

- **Consumers.** They are the final receptors of the changes produced in the blackboard. User Interfaces and autonomous event-based applications are included here.

- **Producers.** This group is formed by applications that update the model stored in the blackboard. These changes can be received by a Consumer or alter the real world.

Figure 1 summarizes the interaction between these five types of clients. As it is shown, the blackboard acts as a "meeting point" for the components of the system. Arrows in broken line show events generated by changes in the model. These arrows recover information about entities and relations. On the other hand, arrows in solid line show two different operations: look up information or updates. These arrows modify the value of a property or add/remove entities or relations to the model. When producers/sensors/interpreters need to communicate new changes, they modify the information in the blackboard. When consumers/actuators need the information, they can either ask the blackboard directly to see if any modification has happened or subscribe to the modifications and, when a modification happens, be notified.

One of the advantages that the blackboard paradigm provides is that clients do not have to know the existence of the rest of the components;

Figure 1. Communication model used in a blackboard-based architecture

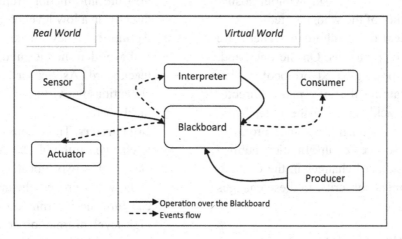

each client only knows about the existence of the blackboard and the part of the model in which it is interested. This approximation let clients be uncoupled either temporally, spatially and functionally.

To be uncoupled spatially and temporally involves that processes do not know the receiver of their messages and do not have to share the same time frame. The communication is carried out using a sharing mechanism in which emitters leave the information that would be gathered by receptors when it is needed.

To be functionally uncoupled means that producers do not have to know how consumers will use the information. These three uncoupling levels mean an advantage in dynamical environments, since the system do not have to be reconfigured after adding/removing components.

Architecture

We divide the whole space into domains in order to improve scalability. Each domain, as it will be shown below, is composed of a set of servers and drivers. These domains could be, in turn, distributed in a network.

While the schema model is shared by all the elements of the domain, the repository can be divided into parts. There are also additional modules: an authorization server, an entity name solver server and drivers. These drivers are responsible for allowing the correct access to the physical device or even to memory data. A diagram of a domain is shown in Figure 2.

- **BBAUTH**: This server manages user authentication in the blackboard system. It also acts as a DNS that resolves the access to the rest of servers that compose the domain.

- **BBENS**: It is a DNS focused on entities, i.e., it resolves an entity request by returning the information needed to connect to the specific repository that contains the entity.

- **BBSCH**: This is the schema model. It is unique for the whole domain, so all the repositories share the information that this server provides. Whenever a new element is added to the blackboard, the schema server must be checked for model agreement.

- **REPOSITORIES**: There can be more than one repository. They are composed of two servers: the repository itself and another one dedicated to notify applications about changes made over the set of entities of the specific repository to which it is as-

Figure 2. Architecture of the System: Repositories, modules and drivers

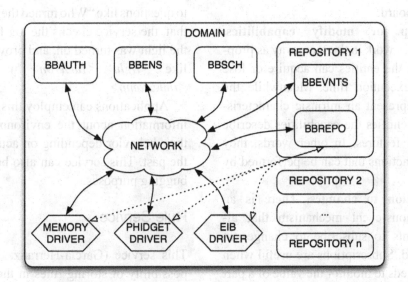

Basic Operations

sociated (event triggering and the publish/subscribe mechanism will be explained in the next section).

- **DRIVERS**: They are responsible for allowing access to the physical device or to memory-stored data. They connect through the network to the repository they are associated to. We have developed three kind of drivers until now:
  - **Memory**: provides access to memory-stored data
  - **Phidget**: enables access to Phidget devices.
  - **EIB**: allows access to elements that communicate through an EIB Bus.

Basic Operations

We have defined a set of basic operations that support the communication model described above. It can be summarized in the following five operations:

- **Look up or modify properties**. The blackboard provides a standard set of functions

that give access to the property. Properties whose values are measurements of physical devices are treated in a special way. This is, the value of the property is not stored in the blackboard. Instead, the blackboard works as an intermediate. When the value is required the blackboard asks directly the device for it.

- **Look up or modify relations.** The blackboard has the capability to add or remove relations between entities. Relations are used as a mechanism to show the connections between the elements of the environment at any moment. For example, relations are used to represent locations or memberships.

- **Look up or modify entities.** Like relations, entities can be added or removed as they become a part or are removed from the environment. When a new entity is added, its representation is inserted in the blackboard. This representation includes the name of the entity, its type, properties and capabilities. If an entity is removed, all its information is not longer available in the blackboard.

- **Look up or modify capabilities.** Capabilities work in the same way as properties, but the entities can acquire or lose them in execution time. Meanwhile the entities represent an intrinsic characteristic of the entities the capabilities describe functional features. In other words, they represent actions that can be performed by an entity.

- **Subscription to changes.** There is an asynchronous-event mechanism that allows clients to subscribe to changes in blackboard. Subscriptions are useful when a client needs to monitor the value of a part of the data model throughout the time.

With this set of operations, the system provides clients a simple and common mechanism to access the information. They do not have to worry about how the blackboard gets the value from a sensor or deduce it.

Blackboard Services

As it was mentioned before, a data-oriented approach does not exclude a service-oriented approach. There are some basic services that are widely requested by the clients. These have been included as an integrated part of the middleware.

Three of the services developed so far are: a "log service", which keeps an historical registry of all the operations invoked in the blackboard; a "rule service", which specifies common behaviors for indirect control; and an "interface service", which makes easier the labor of developing interfaces for direct control.

Log Service

This extra information source for clients is an historical registry that stores the actions that took place and the actors that took part on them.

Thanks to this service the blackboard can answer to questions like "Who turned the light on?" After that, the service checks the log for the last time the light was turned on, and provides something like *"<light> <turn on> by <whoever> at <timestamp>"*.

Applications can employ this service to infer information about the environment or change their behavior depending on actions realized in the past. This service can also be useful for debugging purposes.

Rule Service

This service (García-Herranz, 2008) adds the possibility of storing rules in the blackboard to specify the behavior of the environment under some specific conditions. It is based on ECA Rules (Events-Conditions-Actions) that are composed by:

- **Events**. The reason why the rule should be triggered.
- **Conditions**. The context state that needs to be satisfied for detonating the action.
- **Actions**. The task that has to be accomplished.

This ECA rules can be used to express both reaction and transformation rules. The reaction rules are the ones that produce changes in the world as a reaction to a condition. The use of reaction rules allows modeling behaviors like user preferences. For example, a user can personalize the noise level of the environment. A rule can express that when the telephone rings if the user is in the environment and the TV is on, the TV should mute.

Transformation rules allow producing new information from other information. For example, a door is represented in a graphical interface by an icon that transforms depending on the state of the door. A rule can be used so that if it is opened, the image will show an open door and if it is closed, the image will show a closed door.

Interface Service

The information stored in the blackboard can be also used by applications to provide interaction interfaces between users and the environment.

Since these environments provide new possibilities of interaction (Weiser, 1994), designers of the interfaces have to face new challenges (Shafer, et al., 2001). This interaction could be in different ways, oral interactions, gestures, tangible, etc. and also in many different devices, such as a PC, mobile devices (Eisenstein, J., et al. 2000), etc.

To allow the interaction, people who use the environment and the environment itself must share the same knowledge (Brujin, 2003). This common knowledge can be employed to obtain multiple and dissimilar interfaces.

Implementing an adaptive interface for each environment is an awkward task. This is solved by automatically generating the interfaces form the information stored in the blackboard. Since it is possible to monitor the changes of the environment, the interfaces reflect this transformation dynamically.

This service relates a description of the different ways of direct control to each element of the blackboard. Specifically, the direct controls of the interfaces are associated to the capabilities of the elements. This description of the interfaces is divided in three parts: one describing general properties of the representation, another one adding information related to the graphical interface and a third one that stores information for the oral interface.

- **General representation information**. This includes properties that are common for both oral and graphical interfaces.
- **Graphical representation information**. It describes the graphical interface: imag-

es, positions and sizes, interaction objects (button, slider bar, etc.)

- **Oral representation information**. Linguistic information is defined here, such as lexical and grammatical information.

We use this information to generate both graphical and oral interfaces (Montoro et al., 2006), although it could be used to deploy other kind of interfaces. As an illustrating example, the "hasStereoVolume" capability has two properties: volume level for the left speaker and the volume level for the right speaker. An audio source entity, or any other element with this capability, will have, among others, two interface descriptions, one for each property. From these two descriptions the graphical interfaces shows a slider in the audio source and the oral interface generates the dialogue to dim up and down the volume.

CONCLUSION

In this paper we have presented a middleware developed for ambient intelligence. Since developers have to deal with the problems that an intelligent environment presents, such as distributed and different nature technologies, hardware and software integration, different kinds of networks, new elements that appear in the system at any time, interface adaptation, etc.; a middle layer helps them to overcome them. Some of the characteristics of this system are:

- **From the data model point of view**. It separates functionality and data, letting applications to be spatially, temporally and also functionally uncoupled. The data-model remains unaltered, while applications may change. To develop adapted user interfaces becomes a straightforward task.
- **From the application model point of view**. The stored information follows a common data-model that acts as a logi-

cally central repository. It allows clients access the required information, regardless its nature.

- **From the communication model point of view**. There are two protocols to communicate with the blackboard. The first of them is a polling based protocol that allows retrieving information directly. The other one is based on a publish-subscribe mechanism, where the sources of information publish the changes and the consumers subscribe to those changes to receive the related information.

The system provides a set of operations to allow the communication with the clients. They do not have to worry about how the blackboard obtain or deduce any information or to know the internal structure of the whole system (shown in Figure 2).

We also consider that scalability is a critical characteristic of this middle layers. It has been guaranteed by the use of domains. A domain can exist by itself or can compound a bigger one, so the scalability is carried out automatically.

Finally, some services have been added to provide additional functionalities. Among them, a log service in charge of registering all the actions performed by the blackboard, a rule service to define rules that modify the behavior of the environment under some conditions and an interface service that adds information relative to the description of the user interfaces.

The work presented in this paper has been developed and tested in a real intelligent environment. We have adapted a laboratory furnishing as a living room and a workspace. It currently integrates a heterogeneous set of devices from different technologies (such as KNX, X10 or Phidget). Among them, we can find lights and switches, an electronic lock mechanism, speakers, microphones, a radio tuner, a TV set, RFID cards, etc.

Following the "Build what you use, use what you build", the laboratory is used in a daily basis by their members as a test bench for developed and new technologies. It allows direct control of its elements by means of manual control, a graphical user interface and a spoken dialogue interface and indirect control by means of a set of behavioral rules. We have also developed graphical user interfaces for mobile devices (iPhone and Android platforms), so a user can interact with the environment anywhere and at any time.

It also allows external collaborators and new members to develop new applications and interfaces that will be easily integrated in the environment. Among them we can find a gestural interface associated to a multi-touch table or new location and people recognition modules.

ACKNOWLEDGMENT

This work was partially funded by ASIES (Adapting Social & Intelligent Environments to Support people with special needs), Ministerio de Ciencia e Innovación – TIN2010-17344, e-Madrid (Investigación y desarrollo de tecnologías para el e-learning en la Comunidad de Madrid) S2009/TIC-1650 and Vesta (Ministerio de Industria, Turismo y Comercio, TSI-020100-2009-828) projects.

REFERENCES

Åkesson, K.-P., Bullock, A., Greenhalgh, C., Koleva, B., & Rodden, T. (2000). A toolkit for user re-configuration of ubiquitous domestic environments. In *Proceedings of the 15th Annual ACM Symposium on User Interface Software and Technology*, Paris. ACM Press.

Ballesteros, F., Soriano, E., Leal, K., & Guardiola, G. (2006). Plan b: An operating system for ubiquitous computing environments. In *Proceedings of the Fourth Annual IEEE International Conference on Pervasive Computing and Communications*, pages 126–135. IEEE Computer Society.

Brumitt, B., Meyers, B., Krumm, J., Kern, A., & Shafer, S. A. (2000). Easyliving: Technologies for intelligent environments. In *Handheld and Ubiquitous Computing, 2nd Intl. Symposium*, pages 12–27.

Choi, J., Shin, D., & Shin, D. (2006). Intelligent pervasive middleware based on biometrics. *Lecture Notes in Computer Science, 4159*, 157. doi:10.1007/11833529_16

de Bruijn, J. (2003). Using ontologies. enabling knowledge sharing and reuse on the semantic web. Technical report, Technical Report DERI-2003-10-29, DERI, 2003.

de Ipiña, D. L., Vazquez, J., Garcia, D., Fernandez, J., García, I., Sainz, D., & Almeida, A. (2006). A middleware for the deployment of ambient intelligent spaces. *Lecture Notes in Computer Science, 3864*, 239. doi:10.1007/11825890_12

Eisenstein, J., Vanderdonckt, J., & Puerta, A. (2000). Adapting to mobile contexts with user-interface modeling. In *wmcsa*, page 83. Published by the IEEE Computer Society.

Engelmore, R., & Morgan, T. (1988). *Blackboard systems*. MA: Addison-Wesley Reading.

Erman, L., Hayes-Roth, F., Lesser, V., & Reddy, D. (1980). The hearsay-ii speech-understanding system: Integrating knowledge to resolve uncertainty. [CSUR]. *ACM Computing Surveys, 12*(2), 213–253. doi:10.1145/356810.356816

García-Herranz, M., Haya, P. A., Esquivel, A., Montoro, G., & Alamán, X. (2008). Easing the smart home: Semi-automatic adaptation in perceptive environments. *J. UCS, 14*(9), 1529–1544.

Gelernter, D. (1985). Generative communication in linda. [TOPLAS]. *ACM Transactions on Programming Languages and Systems, 7*(1), 80–112. doi:10.1145/2363.2433

Gómez, J., Montoro, G., & Haya, P. A. (2008). ifaces: Adaptative user interfaces for ambient intelligence. In *Proceedings of IADIS International Conference Interfaces and Human Computer Interaction*, pages 133 – 140.

Gong, L. (2001). A software architecture for open service gateways. *IEEE Internet Computing, 5*(1), 64–70. doi:10.1109/4236.895144

Haya, P. A., Alamán, X., & Montoro, G. (2001). A comparative study of communication infrastructures for the implementation of ubiquitous computing. *UPGRADE. The European Journal for the Informatics Professional, 2*, 5.

Haya, P. A., Montoro, G., & Alamán, X. (2004). A prototype of a context-based architecture for intelligent home environments. In *International Conference on Cooperative Information Systems (CoopIS 2004)*.

Hayes-Roth, B. (1985). A blackboard architecture for control. *Artificial Intelligence, 26*(3), 251–321. doi:10.1016/0004-3702(85)90063-3

Kidd, C., Orr, R., Abowd, G., Atkeson, C., Essa, I., & MacIntyre, B. (1999). The aware home: A living laboratory for ubiquitous computing research. *Lecture Notes in Computer Science*, 191–198. doi:10.1007/10705432_17

Kindberg, T., & Fox, A. (2002). System software for ubiquitous computing. *Pervasive Computing, IEEE, 1*(1), 70–81. doi:10.1109/MPRV.2002.993146

Le Gal, C., Martin, J., Lux, A., & Crowley, J. (2001). Smartoffice: Design of an intelligent environment. *IEEE Intelligent Systems*, 60–66. doi:10.1109/5254.941359

Montoro, G., Haya, P. A., Alamán, X., López-Cózar, R., & Callejas, Z. (2006). A proposal for an xml definition of a dynamic spoken interface for ambient intelligence. In Computer Science (LNCS), L. N., editor, *International Conference on Intelligent Computing (ICIC 06)*, volume 4114, pages 711–716.

Paternó, F., & Santoro, C. (2002). One model, many interfaces. In Kolski, C., & Vanderdonckt, J. (Eds.), *Computer-Aided Design of User Interfaces III* (pp. 143–154). Dordrecht: Hardbound. CADUI, Kluwer Academic Publishers.

Phillips, B. (1999). *Metaglue: A Programming Language for Multi-Agent Systems*. PhD thesis, MIT.

Ponnekanti, S. R., Lee, B., Fox, A., Hanrahan, P., & Winograd, T. (2001). Icrafter: A service framework for ubiquitous computing environments. *Lecture Notes in Computer Science, 2201*, 56–77. doi:10.1007/3-540-45427-6_7

Rayner, M., Lewin, I., Gorrell, G., & Boye, J. (2001). Plug and play speech understanding. In *Proceedings of the Second SIGdial Workshop on Discourse and Dialogue-Volume 16*, pages 1–10. Association for Computational Linguistics.

Reenskaug, T. (1979). Thing-model-view-editor, an example from a planningsystem. 12.

Román, M., Hess, C. K., Ranganathan, A., Madhavarapu, P., Borthakur, B., Viswanathan, P., et al. (2001). Gaiaos: An infrastructure for active spaces. Technical Report UIUCDCS-R-2001-2224 UILU-ENG-2001-1731, University of Illinois, Urbana-Champaign.

Shafer, S., Brumitt, B., and Cadiz, J. (2001). Interaction issues in context – aware intelligent environments. *Human – Computer Interaction*.

Tandler, P. (2004). The beach application model and software framework for synchronous collaboration in ubiquitous computing environment. [Special issue: Ubiquitous computing.]. *Journal of Systems and Software, 69*(3), 267–296. doi:10.1016/S0164-1212(03)00055-4

Villanueva, F., Villa, D., Santofimia, M., Moya, F., & López, J. (2009). A framework for advanced home service design and management. *IEEE International Conference on Consumer Electronics, Las vegas, EEUU, January*, 26.

Wang, X. H., Dong, J. S., Chin, C., & Hettiarachchi, S. R. (2004). Semantic space: an infrastructure for smart spaces. *IEEE Pervasive Computing / IEEE Computer Society [and] IEEE Communications Society, 3*(3), 32–39. doi:10.1109/MPRV.2004.1321026

Weiser, M. (1991). The computer for the twenty-first century. *Scientific American, 265*(3), 94–104. doi:10.1038/scientificamerican0991-94

Weiser, M. (1994). The world is not a desktop. *Interaction, 1*(1), 7–8. doi:10.1145/174800.174801

Chapter 21
Proactive Context–
Aware Middleware

Karen Lee
University of Ulster, Northern Ireland

Tom Lunney
University of Ulster, Northern Ireland

Kevin Curran
University of Ulster, Northern Ireland

Jose Santos
University of Ulster, Northern Ireland

ABSTRACT

Advancements in sensor technology, wireless communications and information technology has enabled the success of new types of dynamic computing systems. However designing systems which are flexible and can adapt to the changing needs of the user remains a major research challenge. Flexibility and adaptability are fundamental requirements for Ambient Intelligent (AmI) systems. The complexity involved in designing applications and devices which change and adapt their behaviour automatically based on their context or situation is well recognised. Providing technology which meets the changing needs of the user is heavily reliant on the appropriate infrastructure design. This work outlines the development of an Ambient Middleware framework for Context-Aware systems. The framework will integrate with sensor technologies, intelligent algorithms and the semantic web.

INTRODUCTION

Recent advances in wireless networking technologies and the growing success of mobile computing devices are enabling new classes of applications which present challenging problems for designers.

Devices face temporary and unannounced loss of network connectivity when they move from one cell to another and are frequently required to react to changes in the environment, such as a change in context or a new location. The concept of context and context-awareness has been central issues in Ambient Intelligent research for the last decade (Oh et al., 2007). Context-

DOI: 10.4018/978-1-60960-549-0.ch021

awareness has emerged as an important idea for achieving automatic behaviours' in pervasive and predictive systems. For example, a system that senses a user's condition, location or physical actions and adapts to maximise user convenience is utilising context awareness. Initial research began by looking at context-aware systems more generally and independently of specific applications, including context middleware and toolkits from Dey et al., (1999). Building upon this work, ontology's describing context for building different context-aware applications were researched by Chen et al., (2004). The need for middleware to seamlessly bind the required hardware and software components together is well recognised; middleware improves maintainability and also promotes reuse (Henricksen et al., 2005). Middleware for ubiquitous and context-aware computing entails several challenges, including the need for balance between heterogeneity, transparency and awareness, while maintaining the requirement for a certain degree of autonomy (Soldatos, 2007). Mobile devices need to be aware and adapt themselves to highly dynamic environments therefore adding momentum to research into context and location aware middleware.

AMBIENT INTELLIGENCE AND CONTEXT

The following sections provide a background to the research by reviewing literature relevant to the focus of our research.

Ambient Intelligence

Ambient Intelligence (AmI) refers to a vision of the future information society where intelligent interfaces enable people and devices to interact with each other and the environment. The technology operates in the background while computing capabilities are everywhere connected and always available (Weiser 1991). This intelligent environ-

ment is aware of the specific characteristics of human presence and preferences and can adapt context parameters such as location, proximity, light, temperature and contextual information in accordance with people's wishes and needs. The report published by IST Advisory Group states that Ambient Intelligence is all about 'human-centred computing', user friendliness, user empowerment and the support of human interaction (ISTAG, 2001; Ducatel et al, 2001). Key technological requirements identified for AmI with the year 2010 in the horizon are:

- very unobtrusive hardware
- a seamless mobile/fixed communication infrastructure
- dynamic and massively distributed device networks
- natural feeling human interfaces
- dependability and security

Ambient Intelligence offers many new possibilities in providing convenience for the user and acting as an invisible interface for driving the behaviour of the device or system.

Pervasive Computing

The traditional notion of pervasive computing is a digitally-enhanced habitat where physical and digital devices are seamlessly integrated (Al-Muhtadi et al., 2004). In his seminal paper Weiser (1991) envisaged the concept of pervasive or ubiquitous computing, describing an invisible, embedded technology to serve users in a seamless and unconscious interaction. Pervasive technology can be location and context aware and therefore conscious of the presence of other devices and available resources. The term pervasive also encompasses many mobile technologies which, largely driven by Moore's law lead to the development of dynamic and diminutive devices. Another example is the European success of the Global System for Mobile communications, (GSM). Pervasive devices include Global Positioning Satellite (GPS) receivers, Radio Frequency Identification (RFID) tags and scanners, mobile phones, Personal Digital Assistants (PDAs), smart homes equipped with autonomous self-aware sensors and Telematic systems such as intelligent vehicle technologies. A large body of worldwide research in pervasive computing exists today within projects such as the distraction free ubiquitous Project Aura[1] and other related projects from Carnegie Mellon University, the human-centered Project Oxygen[2] from MIT and IBM's Planet Blue[3] project which aims at providing a technology-assisted immersive environment.

Context and Context-Awareness

The terms context and context-awareness can be difficult to elucidate; many definitions have been used since research started in this area. In the work that first introduced the term 'context-aware,' Schilit and Theimer (1994) refer to context as location, identities of nearby people and objects, and changes to those objects. In a similar definition, Brown (1996) adds to the previous definition and describes context as location, identities of the people around the user, the time of day, season and temperature. Ryan et al., (1998) use a combination of these definitions. Dey and Abowd (1999) add physical or computational objects to the list of context definitions. They also define context-awareness or context-aware computing as the use of context to provide task-relevant information and/or services to a user while Chen and Kotz (2000) state that *"Context is the set of environmental states and settings that either determines an application's behaviour or in which an application event occurs and is interesting to the user"*. Context can be implicit or explicit. To date the main challenges identified in this area are in the building of infrastructures to promote the design, implementation and evolution of context-aware applications and the acquisition of contextual

information, in particular location technologies and sensor networks (Dey and Abowd, 1999).

Imagine a scenario where a group of people are in a meeting with existing pervasive devices such as Smartphone's or PDA's and the chair of the meeting no longer has to remind attendees to silence their phones as each device can dynamically adapt their current state to an appropriate setting such as silent mode and possibly accept or reject situation dependent text messages from a partner or children. A user's context can be dynamic and when using devices in these settings, a user has much to gain by the effective use of implicitly sensed context. It allows a device's behaviour to be customised to the user's current situation which requires it to be aware of its environment, therefore fulfilling the requirements of Ambient Intelligence identified by the IST Advisory Group (ISTAG. 2001; Ducatel et al., 2001) and the invisible computer as discussed by Weiser (1991).

Middleware

In a distributed computing system, middleware is defined as the software layer that lies between the operating system and the applications on each site of the system (Krakowiak, 2003). The role of middleware is to provide an additional layer of abstraction suitable for each specific type of application. In traditional distributed systems, the goal of the middleware has been to hide heterogeneity and distribution by providing ways of treating remote resources as if they were local. This proves an additional challenge in dynamic ambient environments as objects and components often need to base decisions on information about distribution and the environment. Middleware for Pervasive computing focuses on providing suitable abstractions for dealing with heterogeneity and distribution without hiding them, therefore providing information such as context information regarding the devices or objects (Kjaer, 2007).

Context-aware middleware can be categorised into a taxonomy of system capabilities (Kjaer

2007). Categories include the environment whereby a middleware system makes explicit or implicit assumptions about the environment it is to be used in. Systems can also rely on external communication services, thus this middleware is said to be self-contained. Middleware can have the capability to reason about and act upon itself and therefore is reflective in nature (Capra et al., 2001). Middleware systems must also be flexible due to different elements of the system by using context in different ways.

Middleware Intelligence

Uncertainty always exists as an unavoidable factor in any pervasive context-aware system. The issue of uncertainty within pervasive computing has provoked much research into addressing and modelling context information (Truong et al., 2005). With a view to designing the proposed context-aware middleware framework, Bayesian networks and Swarm Intelligence will be researched and investigated as a potential mechanism for addressing uncertain reasoning for context-awareness and dynamic discovery of context sources. Context-aware systems rely mainly on sensors or external sources to capture the context, (location, activity, time). This information is often unreliable due to the inaccuracy and lack of precision of sensors interpreting the environment (Dobson et al., 2007). Current research also looks at hybrid approaches which incorporate the use of semantic web technologies such as ontology's for modelling and acquiring context (Clear et al., 2007).

To date researchers have good reasons to find swarm intelligence appealing for solving problems within the multidisciplinary areas of neurophysiology, cognitive science, mathematics, physics, electrical engineering, and computer science (Bonabeau et al., 1999). This discipline is mostly inspired by the behaviour of social insect colonies such as swarms of ants, termites, bees, wasps, as well as fish schools and bird flocks. In general,

this is done by mimicking the behaviour of these swarms. Swarm intelligence offers an alternative way of designing "intelligent" systems, in which autonomy, emergence and distributed functioning replace control, programming and centralisation (Eberhart et al., 2001).

Middleware for Context-Awareness

To date much research has been carried out in the area of semantic web techniques for the creation of pervasive computing scenarios where devices and objects communicate using these technologies. Traditional web technologies such as HTTP, HTML and XML[4] have been used for providing presentation and control mechanisms in pervasive computing environments. Additional properties such as context-awareness, intelligence and decentralisation are required for ambient computing environments therefore entailing a further investigation and research effort in this area. Dey et al., (1999) carried out some of the first work in this area by exploring the use of semantic web languages for building context-aware architectures. They developed the Context Toolkit which is based around the notion of widgets[5]. This model is simple and uses widgets for sensory capture. Context is shared between components as streams of XML over HTTP. Chen et al., (2004) developed the Context Broker Architecture (CoBrA) architecture using SOUPA (Standard Ontology for Ubiquitous and Pervasive Applications) which employ the semantic web languages Resource Description Framework (RDF) and (OWL) to support context reasoning within Ambient Intelligence. This research provides several experimental initiatives in the integration of semantic web technologies in ubiquitous and ambient intelligent computing to support context awareness.

THE AMICA FRAMEWORK

Within the scope of the proposed project, extensive research associated with the efficient design and implementation of Ambient Middleware framework for Context-Awareness (AMiCA) will be conducted. Figure 1 outlines the basic components of the overall system interacting with pervasive devices. The key components within the layered middleware architecture are the context management module and the intelligent reasoning module for modelling and addressing context gathered both implicitly and explicitly. The inputs and outputs will be the main source of information for context determination by the middleware, this interaction can be provided in the form of sensor networks or other locally acting communicating pervasive device. A combination of techniques to provide this functionality will be researched. The potential techniques for reasoning under uncertainty will also be investigated further before a definitive decision is made on the design of the middleware.

RELATED WORK

Table 1 compares several middleware initiatives which integrate semantic web technologies and intelligence for context-aware ubiquitous and ambient intelligence in recent years. In the table, a taxonomy of characteristics are listed, with a tick ($\sqrt{}$) indicating if the characteristics are present for each of the architectures. As illustrated in the table Dey and Abowd (2001) developed the Context Toolkit which is based around the notion of widgets[6]. This model is simple and uses widgets as sensory capture. Context is shared between components as streams of XML over HTTP. The Cooltown project (Barton et al., 2001) is intended to support wireless, mobile devices to interact with a web-enabled environment through sensors. Autonomy is provided by updates received from the sensors. Gaia from Roman et al., (2002) is intended to be a meta-operating system. It builds on the notion of active space which coordinates heterogeneous devices in physical space. Gaia self-senses context through its infrastructure. Project Aura (Garlan et al., 2002) is a task oriented system for infrastructural environments, however it does not support building applications. CARMEN is a project which uses proxies as mobile agents to handle resources in wireless settings. Context is achieved through migration of proxies with users. CARMEN implements user profiles to retrieve the context from the proxies (Bellavista et al.,

Figure 1. Basic components of Ambient Middleware for Context-Awareness (AMiCA)

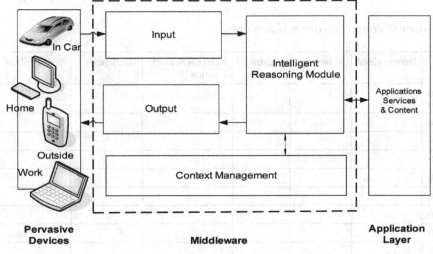

2003). Gu et al., (2003) base the Service-Oriented Context-Aware Middleware or SOCAM architecture on the idea of using Web Ontology Language (OWL) to model context. The model is then used by an interpreter to reason about context with rules. SOCAM also incorporates a service discovery mechanism. Chen et al (2004) developed the Context Broker Architecture (CoBrA) architecture using SOUPA (Standard Ontology for Ubiquitous and Pervasive Applications) which employ the semantic web languages Resource Description Framework (RDF) and (OWL) to support context reasoning within Ambient Intelligence.

CONCLUSION

The focus at this preliminary stage of the project has been an investigation into the area of context-aware middleware for Ambient Intelligent systems and applications. Everyday objects are being enhanced with sensing, processing and communication abilities and as a result our everyday living/working is moving towards a higher degree of complexity. The goal of Ambient Middleware for context-awareness is to continuously and implicitly adapt the environment to meet evolving user expectations. Up-to-date valid context information is the key requirement for successful transparent interaction. A review of various existing experimental initiatives has given an insight into the recent advances in distributed and heterogeneous context-aware middleware. Due consideration is also given to the various existing methods of representing context awareness, context modelling and acquisition techniques, all of which will be of critical importance in the development of Ambient Middleware for Context-Awareness. Semantic technologies represent a very promising approach to solving many problems in ambient applications. Using semantic technologies in conjunction with reasoning algorithms based on Swarm Intelligence/Bayesian networks offers a potential unique contribution. Another contribution is having the system web enabled which makes it accessible worldwide.

REFERENCES

Al-Muhtadi, J., Chetan, S., Ranganathan, A., & Campbell, R. (2004) Super spaces: A middleware for large scale pervasive computing environments. In: *Workshop on Middleware Support for Pervasive Computing (PerWare), PerCom'04 Workshop Proceedings,* Orlando. 198–202

Aura (2002) *Distraction-free Ubiquitous Computing.* http://www.cs.cmu.edu/~aura/

Table 1: Summary of context-aware middleware

Middleware	Decentralised	Autonomy	Lightness	External Sensory Capture	Intelligence	Web Enabled	Context-Aware
Context toolkits (2001)				√			√
Cooltown (2001)	√	√	√	√		√	√
Gaia (2002)	√	√	√		√		√
Aura (2002)		√					√
CARMEN (2003)	√	√	√		√		√
SOCAM (2004)		√		√	√		√
CoBrA (2004)		√		√	√		√
SoaM (2007)		√	√	√	√		√
AMiCA (2008)	√	√	√	√	√	√	√

Barton, J. and Kindberg. T. (2001) *The Cooltown user experience.* Technical report, Hewlett Packard, February 2001.

Bellavista, P., Corradi, A., Montanari, R., & Stefanelli, C. (2003). Context- aware middleware for resource management in the wireless internet. *IEEE Transactions on Software Engineering, 29*(12), 1086–1099. doi:10.1109/TSE.2003.1265523

Blue, P. *IBM project* (2004) http://researchweb.watson.ibm.com/compsci/brochure2001/PlanetBlue.pdf

Bonabeau, E., Dorigo, M., & Théraulaz, G. (1999). *Swarm intelligence: from natural to artificial systems.* Oxford University Press.

Brown, P. J. (1996) The Stick-e Document: a Framework for Creating Context-Aware Applications. In: *Proceedings of Electronic Publishing '96.* Page(s): 259-272

Capra, L., & Emmerich, W. and Mascolo. C. (2003) Carisma: Context-aware reflective middleware system for mobile applications. *IEEE Transactions on Software Engineering, 29*(10):929 – 45, 2003/10/. doi:10.1109/TSE.2003.1237173

Capra, L., Emmerich, W., & Mascolo, C. (2001). Reflective middleware solutions for context-aware applications. *Lecture Notes in Computer Science, 2192,* 126–133. doi:10.1007/3-540-45429-2_10

Chen, G., & Kotz, D. (2000) A Survey of Context-Aware Mobile Computing Research, *Dartmouth Computer Science Technical Report TR2000-381,* Department of Computer Science, Dartmouth College, November 2000.

Chen, H. Perich. F., Finin, T. and Joshi. A. (2004) SOUPA: Standard Ontology for Ubiquitous and Pervasive Applications. *Proceedings of Mobiquitous 2004: International Conference on Mobile and Ubiquitous Systems: Networking and Services,* Boston, USA.

Chen, H. (2004) *An Intelligent Broker Architecture for Pervasive Context-Aware Systems,* PhD Thesis, University of Maryland, Baltimore County.

Clear, A. K. Dobson. S. and Nixon. P. (2007) An approach to dealing with uncertainty in context-aware pervasive systems. In: *Proceedings of the UK/IE IEEE SMC Cybernetic Systems Conference 2007. IEEE Press.*

Context Aware Computing Group Blog, (2006) http://context.media.mit.edu/press/

Dey, A.K., Salber, D., Futakawa, M. and Abowd, G.D. (1999) An Architecture to Support Context-Aware Computing. *Submitted to UIST '99.*

Dobson, S., Coyle, L., & Nixon, P. (2007). *Hybridising events and knowledge as a basis for building autonomic systems.* IEEE TCAAS Letters.

Ducatel, K., Bogdanowicz, M., Scapolo, F., Leijten, J. and Burgelma, J.C. (2001) *ISTAG: Scenarios for ambient intelligence in 2010. ISTAG 2001 Final Report.*

Eberhart, R. C., Shi, Y. and Kennedy, J. (2001) *Swarm Intelligence.* Morgan Kaufmann; 1st edition, 978-1558605954

Engelbrecht, A. P. (2007). *Computational Intelligence, An Introduction.* John Wiley & Sons.

Gaia Project. (2005) *Active Spaces for Ubiquitous Computing* http://gaia.cs.uiuc.edu/

Gu, T., Pung, H. K., & Zhang, D. Q. (2004) A Bayesian approach for dealing with uncertain contexts", In *the Proceeding of the Second International Conference on Pervasive Computing (Pervasive 2004),* Vienna, Austria, April 2004.

Gu, T., Pung, H. K., & Zhang, D. Q. (2004a) A middleware for building context-aware mobile services, *Proceedings of IEEE Vehicular Technology Conference* (VTC), Milan, Italy.

Henricksen, K., Indulska, J., McFadden, T., & Balasubramaniam, S. (2005) Middleware for Distributed Context-Aware Systems, *Proc. of the International Symposium on Distributed Objects and Applications (DOA'05)*, Cyprus, October 2005, *Lecture Notes in Computer Science*, LNCS 3760, Page(s): 846-863.

Kjaer, K. E. (2007) A survey of context-aware middleware SE'07: *Proceedings of the 25th conference on IASTED International Multi-Conference* 2007.

Krakowiak, S. (2003) *What is Middleware?* http://middleware.objectweb.org/

Oh, Y., Schmidt, A. and Woo, W. (2007) Designing, Developing, and Evaluating Context-Aware Systems, *MUE2007, IEEE Computer Society*, 2007, Page(s): 1158-1163.

OWL. (2008) *Web Ontology Language Primer* http://www.w3.org/TR/owl-ref/

Oxygen, M. I. T. Project (2004) *Pervasive Human Centered Computing*, http://oxygen.csail.mit.edu/Overview.html

Primer, R. D. F. (2008) *Resource Description Framework* http://www.w3.org/RDF/

Román, M., Hess, C. K., Cerqueira, R., Ranganathan, A., Campbell, R. H., & Nahrstedt, K. (2002). Gaia: A Middleware Infrastructure to Enable Active Spaces. [Oct–Dec]. *IEEE Pervasive Computing / IEEE Computer Society [and] IEEE Communications Society*, 74–83. doi:10.1109/MPRV.2002.1158281

Ryan, N., & Pascoe, J. (1998) Adding Generic Contextual Capabilities to Wearable Computers. In: *Proceedings of 2nd International Symposium on Wearable Computers*. Page(s) 92-99

Schilit, B., Adams, N., & Want, R. (1994) Context-Aware Computing Applications. *1st International Workshop on Mobile Computing Systems and Applications*. Page(s): 85-90

Schilit. B. and Theimer. M. (1994) Disseminating active map information to mobile hosts. *IEEE Network*, Page(s):22–32.

Sousa, J. P., & Garlan, D. (2002) Aura: An architectural framework for user mobility in ubiquitous computing environments. In WICSA 3: *Proceedings of the IFIP 17th World Computer Congress - TC2 Stream /3rd IEEE/IFIP Conference on Software Architecture*, pages 29–43, Deventer, The Netherlands, The Netherlands, 2002. Kluwer, B.V.

Truong, B. A. Lee. Y. K. and Lee. S. Y. (2005) Modeling uncertainty in context-aware computing. *Fourth Annual ACIS International Conference on Computer and Information Science*, 2005. Volume, Issue, 2005 Page(s): 676 - 681

Vazquez J.I., López de Ipiña D. and Sedano I. (2007) SOAM: A Web-Powered Architecture for Designing and Deploying Pervasive Semantic Devices. *International journal of web information systems - ijwis*, 2007.

Weiser, M. (1991) The Computer for the 21st Century, in: *The Scientific American*, vol. 265, no. 3, 1991, Page(s): 66-75.

ENDNOTES

[1] Distraction free ubiquitous computing, http://www.cs.cmu.edu/~aura/
[2] http://oxygen.lcs.mit.edu/Overview.html
[3] http://www.research.ibm.com/compsci/planetblue.html
[4] Hypertext Transport Protocol, Hypertext Markup Language and Extensible Markup Language

[5] A widget is a software component which provides an application with information about its environment, thereby separating the application logic from the low-level details of the sensors.

[6] A widget is a software component which provides an application with information about its environment, thereby separating the application logic from the low-level details of the sensors.

Section 4

Chapter 22
Integrating Sensor Nodes into a Middleware for Ambient Intelligence

Holger Klus
TU Clausthal, Germany

Dirk Niebuhr
TU Clausthal, Germany

ABSTRACT

The development of infrastructures enabling dynamic and automated composition of IT systems is a big challenge. This paper addresses a new idea of allowing component-based systems to reconfigure themselves. Therefore, we propose DAiSI - a Dynamic Adaptive System Infrastructure for dynamic integration of components as well as their reconfiguration during runtime. Thereby, one of the features of the infrastructure is, that it is capable of binding components based on their availability. In this paper we concentrate on presenting how resource constrained sensor nodes can be integrated into a system using this infrastructure.

INTRODUCTION

The vision of Ubiquitous Computing or Ambient Intelligence aims towards supporting people in their daily life at home or at work. In recent years more and more embedded components have become available trying to make this vision come true. Unfortunately these components rarely work together allowing the formation of dynamic systems with emerging capabilities. Building infrastructures for dynamic and automated composition of these components to exchange data and

form new systems is a big challenge. For allowing components to work in an ambient manner, these components have to be bound. Moreover, Ubiquitous Computing or Ambient Intelligence systems have to be dynamically adaptive since some components are mobile and may appear suddenly during runtime. The dynamic integration of components into a system at runtime therefore is crucial for these kind of systems (Bartelt et al., 2005). For simplicity we will refer to those systems as Dynaptive[1] Systems in the following. This paper addresses a new idea of allowing Dynaptive Systems to reconfigure themselves and

DOI: 10.4018/978-1-60960-549-0.ch022

introduces an approach for integrating resource constraint sensor nodes.

We propose the Dynamic Adaptive System Infrastructure DAiSI. It is an infrastructure for component reconfiguration and dynamic integration. The heart of DAiSI is a Configuration Component which manages the automatic binding of components based on their required and provided services. We present the general component model and the DAiSI Configuration Component. Moreover we show how a specific sensor node can be integrated in such a self-configuring system.

Context

The work presented in this paper was (partially) carried out in the BelAmI (Bilateral German-Hungarian Research Collaboration on Ambient Intelligence Systems) project (Bilateral German–Hungarian Collaboration Project on Ambient Intelligence Systems, 2009), funded by the German Federal Ministry of Education and Research (BMBF), the Fraunhofer-Gesellschaft and the Ministry for Science, Education, Research and Culture of Rhineland-Palatinate (MWWFK). DAiSI has initially been developed to serve as basis for binding components of the BelAmI project. The application domain of the BelAmI project is assisted living, where a demonstrator for elderly care has been built (Nehmer, Becker, Karshmer,&Lamm, 2006). In this demonstrator multiple embedded sensors collect data within an intelligent home environment. The goal was to aggregate this sensor information to probabilistically gather results about the constitution of elderly people and to support them in various manners. One application, we realized within the BelAmI project, was an intelligent fridge running on top of DAiSI (Klus, Niebuhr, & Rausch, 2007). This fridge was able to detect spoilt food or provide recipes based on its contents.

In the following we further evolved DAiSI in order to achieve dependable dynamic adaptive systems by binding only components, which are semantically compatible. This extended version of DAiSI has been elaborated within the Resist project funded by Siemens. Together with Siemens we applied for a patent on our approach to Dependable Dynamic Adaptive Systems using Behavior Equivalence Classes to (re-)evaluate semantical Compatibility of Component Bindings (Niebuhr, Rausch, Klus, Appel, Klein, Reichmann, & Schmid, 2010).

We exhibited an application demonstrator from the emergency management domain at CeBIT 2009 visualizing the benefits of our approach (Niebuhr, Schindler, & Herrling, 2009). This demonstrator will also serve as application example within this paper.

Paper Outline

The paper is structured as follows: First of all we distinguish our middleware platform from related work. Then we continue with a short description of the application example which will be used to explain our concepts in the following. Afterwards, we describe how DAiSI is structured, how DAiSI application components are integrated into a system, and how they are configured automatically. Finally we sketch a concept how resource constrained sensor nodes can be integrated into DAiSI and end up with conclusions we derived from this work.

RELATED WORK

The core of DAiSI is the Configuration Component, which enables the automatic reconfiguration of a component landscape. In the following we present a selection of technologies, both state of the art and state of the practice that deal with automatic reconfiguration.

STATE OF THE ART

There are several middleware solutions from the research community supporting proactive and reactive system adaptability (Sadjadi, Survey, & Exam, 2003). These can be further categorized in component and system adaptation frameworks. DAiSI falls into the category of reactive system adaptation. In other words it supports changing the configuration of a system without (a) the necessity of knowing all possible types of components in advance and (b) without knowing the explicit description of the reconfiguration behavior. In (Oreizy, Medvidovic, & Taylor, 1998) reactive system adaptation is also supported. The C2 (Taylor, Medvidovic, Anderson, Whitehead, & Robbins, 1995) architectural style comes into play when one sees architectural connectors as well as components as first class entities. The authors have developed an infrastructure that allows adding and removing components and connectors at runtime by using a special scripting language. Moreover, they support modifying associations between connectors and components. Finally, a special validator component checks whether the modifications are valid. The motivation is different than for DAiSI in this case. The authors aim to support manual reconfiguration for runtime system maintenance instead of automated reconfiguration which is offered by DAiSI. In (Trapp, 2005) proactive system and component adaptation is described. A special-purpose executable modeling language enables the explicit description of the adaptation behavior of embedded systems. By contrast, DAiSI provides for less expressive and implicit description of adaptation. This is achieved by different configurations available for each application component. The surrogate architecture (The Jini™ Technology Surrogate Architecture Overview, 2009) exists for integration of ressource-constrained nodes into Jini networks. The Device Bay approach presented in this paper is based on this surrogate architecture which we applied to our underlying CORBA middleware.

STATE OF THE PRACTICE

Dynamic Loading (e.g. Java Class Loading), Serviceoriented Architectures (e.g. Web Services) and Dependency Injection (Martin Fowler's web page on dependency injection, 2009) are widespread technologies that support the dynamic integration of components and offer some reconfiguration facilities. Regarding Dynamic Loading and Service Orientation, the main differences between them and DAiSI are (a) the instantiation of types that usually takes place for every imported type and (b) the active service lookup. Dependency Injection features the most similarities to the DAiSI Configuration Component, since the main idea of Dependency Injection is that service requestors are passive. They do not look up services; they only define needed services, which are delivered by the infrastructure. DAiSI works in that way; it analyzes component interdependencies, looks up available component services and returns the required references automatically and asynchronously in terms of a callback mechanism. One important difference of DAiSI is the reconfiguration support. DAiSI updates the component binding in the event of modification of the component landscape (i.e. component appearance, failure, update). Another main difference lies in the multiple configurations of component: A DAiSI application component registers a series of different configurations, each one contains provided and required services. In other words there is not only one set of dependencies that must be resolved but an ordered collection of alternative dependency configurations.

In the following we will introduce a small application scenario used in this paper to explain DAiSI and the integration of sensor nodes into it.

APPLICATION EXAMPLE

Imagine a huge disaster like the one, which occurred during an airshow in Ramstein in 1988. Two planes collided in air and crashed down into the audience. In cases of such a disaster with a huge amount of seriously injured casualties, medics need to get a quick overview of the whole situation. The medics do a quick triage (Manchester Triage Group, 2005), classifying the casualties regarding the severity of their injury, in order to treat casualties with serious injuries first.

In our scenario, medics are supported by an IT system, enabling them to get a quick overview of the overall situation and to keep track of the physical situation of the previously classified casualties. Each medic is equipped with a bunch of casualty units. The casualty unit stores data regarding the specific casualty like the casualty's name, gender, or current position. Medics equip each casualty they discover with such a unit.

For serious injured casualties vital data sensors, like a pulse rate sensor or a blood pressure sensor, can be attached to a casualty unit in order to keep the triage class of a casualty up to date if his condition changes over time. These sensors enable medics and an incident command to capture and monitor a casualty's physical condition without needing to be physically present at his place. So an incident command can quickly send a nearby medic to a casualty, whose situation became critical.

Hence, the described system is a typical component-based dynamic adaptive system. It consists of a vast array of casualty units, biosensors, medic units, and an incident command component, which are bound during runtime. The overall system is evolving during runtime as new casualties may be integrated via their casualty unit as well as casualty units may leave the system as casualties are transported to hospitals for further treatment. The components involved in the scenario which the following sections will focus on are depicted in Figure 1.

Figure 1. Overview about the different components within the application example

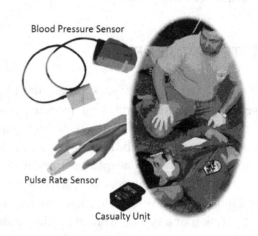

INFRASTRUCTURE ARCHITECTURE

DAiSI is a service-oriented middleware architecture. For the addressed Dynaptive Systems we identified four logical layers. On the top level we have the Application Layer, where application components are placed. The binding of these components for the exchange of data is done via the Middleware Layer. This layer contains infrastructure components like a Node Component or the Configuration Component described in the next subsection. Where the Configuration Component deals with component binding at runtime, the Node Component is responsible for life cycle management of infrastructure and application components on the physical hardware nodes. Additionally the middleware layer provides a so-called Device Bay, which integrates resource-constrained nodes. The bottom two layers (Communication Layer and Physical Layer) are out of the scope of this paper, since we focus on available standards for their implementation. In the following part we begin with a detailed introduction of DAiSI's Configuration Component. Afterwards we describe the component model which is used by the Configuration Component.

Figure 2. The type view of an example component

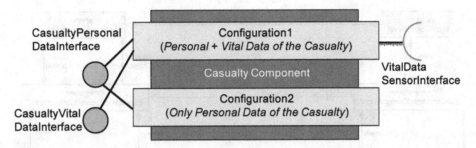

Configuration Component

One important concept of DAiSI is that all components may offer different configurations like shown in Figure 2. Considering the example introduced before, you can think of the casualty component, which has two configurations: One needing a service which provides sensor data like blood pressure and pulse rate, and another configuration, which does not require any external service. In the first configuration it may offer personal information like the casualty's gender or name as well as a history of the vital data and a calculated triage class. In the second configuration it can only offer the personal information, since it has no access to vital data of the casualty. Each of these configurations is specified by the component services which it provides (e.g. CasualtyPersonalDataInterface or CasualtyVitalDataInterface) and requires (e.g. VitalDataSensorInterface). The main task of the Configuration Component is to determine, which components can form a Dynaptive System and how they can be bound. Therefore, all components have to register at the Configuration Component. The Configuration Component checks for all registered components, whether they contain a runnable configuration and which services this configuration provides. By runnable configuration we mean that all component service references can be set to component services of other runnable component configurations. According to these runnable component configurations the Configuration Component binds components

that have requested to run with other components, sets the current configuration, and finally lets the component run. Moreover, it does the same for all components that are bound to those components that initially requested to run. In order to enable the Configuration Component to configure the Dynaptive System, all application components have to be compliant with the component model introduced in the following. This is necessary since the Configuration Component has to extract all configuration relevant information from the components at runtime.

Application Component Model

Components within Dynaptive Systems can be seen from two different levels: the instance view and the type view. You can see the component model in Figure 3 containing the instance view on the right hand side whereas the type view is depicted on the left hand side. The Configuration Component uses the type information, in order to decide which system configuration has to be established. It then selects specific component instances for this configuration and binds them.

The instance view describes a concrete component implementation. This implementation may support several configurations, which can be selected by the Configuration Component depending on the available component instances in the specific environment. The supported configurations moreover are ordered enabling the Configuration Component to decide which configura-

Figure 3. The Component Model proposed by DAiSI

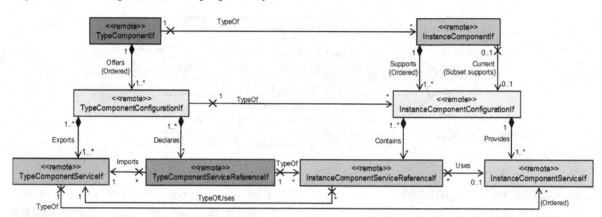

tion is the best if multiple configurations are runnable. The first configuration is considered to be the best one, therefore the Configuration Component will consider Configuration1 as the best one in our example depicted in Figure 2. Finally when running, a component instance contains a reference to the currently running configuration enabling the Configuration Component to decide, whether a newly runnable configuration is better than the active configuration.

The type view describes which types of configurations are supported by a component implementation type and which types of Component Service References and Component Services are declared, respectively, exported by a component configuration as it had been depicted in Figure 2. This information has to be derived from the instances by reflection at runtime or defined separately in advance. The Configuration Component manages all the type information and uses it for calculating the dynamic configuration of the system.

Configuration Process

As already stated in (Bartelt et al., 2005) configuring Dynaptive Systems is a three step process. The following subchapters explain, how each of these steps is enacted by DAiSI.

Discovering components regarding their functional requirements. The new idea of DAiSI is to turn this around, since components now specify what they need in their different configurations and do not look up other components themselves. They get component services which are syntactically equivalent to their specified required component services delivered directly by the Configuration Component, if they are available. They are therefore only passive components within the configuration process.

Selecting the best components depending on the current context. The Configuration Component selects the best runnable configuration for each component that requested to run. This is calculated depending on all components which are known to the Configuration Component. Further context adaptivity is currently under development, since in the near future components should not only be able to specify what kind of component service they need, but also which quality of service they require. Furthermore, the order of the component configurations will not be static like in the current version, but also depend on context information.

Selecting correct component bindings. Syntactical equivalence of provided and required component service is not sufficient, since the provided component servicer could still behave very different, than expected by the component service user. Therefore the semantics of the expected component service behavior need to be considered before binding components. Since we need to decide about the compatibility of components at runtime, formal specification techniques do not help us much (Niebuhr & Rausch, 2007). Instead we follow a test-based approach, where component service users can define test-cases for required component services, which are executed by DAiSI to decide about the compatibility. Since the compatibility may depend on the specific component state and therefore may change at runtime, we enable component developers to specify so called equivalence classes, in which equivalent behavior is assumed. If the component state causes a change in equivalence classes during runtime, DAiSI repeats the test execution and unbinds the components, if these tests fail.

Since we would like to integrate and configure resource constrained sensor nodes as well, we follow the Device Bay approach introduced in the following.

INTEGRATION APPROACH

The Sun SPOT device (Smith, Horan, Daniels, & Cleal, 2006) is used to host components that may query connected sensors. Comparable industrial products are for instance the MicaZ from Crossbow (Homepage of the Crossbow Technology Inc, Wireless Sensor Networks, 2009). Key features of the Sun SPOT device are the wireless ad-hoc communication in self organized networks, the ability to run Java-programs querying connected sensors and the small size of the hardware board. Furthermore a USB-connected basestation exists which acts as part of the sensor network and forwards the communication to a PC-based host. One main problem to address is the limited capability of sensor nodes, for instance the very small memory or the difficult energy supply. Consequently Sun SPOTs cannot provide the environment to implement all layers and provide all infrastructure components of DAiSI. The

middleware layer can only be adopted in a very basic way. This means also the application layer has to be constrained and a specific design for Sun SPOT integration into DAiSI is needed. Our solution is an additional infrastructure component, which is able to integrate resource constrained hardware devices into DAiSI. This component is called Device Bay and is introduced in the next sections. *Generic Device Bay*

The Device Bay maintains the connection between Sun SPOTs and other DAiSI nodes. That means components physically located on Sun SPOTs are integrated into a Dynaptive Systeme by the Device Bay. The Device Bay hosts proxies with provided and contained interfaces. The design is based on (Seidl, 2005) respectively the surrogate architecture (The Jini™ Technology Surrogate Architecture Overview, 2009), referencing to a Device Bay as a computer connected to the application network which is able to integrate several homogeneous kinds of hardware nodes into a network. The main task of the Device Bay is to locate new Sun SPOTs and to set up their component instances. This means that all necessary information for this process has to be stored on the Sun SPOT. This information has to take the dynamic nature of Dynaptive Systems into account, where an arbitrary appearance of different components and even different implementations of the same component service may occur. Therefore the type- and instance view has to be represented in a form that allows the Device Bay to bridge calls to Sun SPOT components and vice versa.

Device Bay Architecture

The design of the Device Bay is divided into a technical and a logical part. The technical part covers communication concerns like un-/marshalling method calls into datagram packets used in Sun SPOT networks. As the reference implementation of DAiSI uses Java and CORBA technology, synchronous Java method calls have to be translated into an asynchronous manner to be sent as datagram packets to the Sun SPOTs. This assures that there is no observable difference between a component located on a Sun SPOT and any other DAiSI application component. In addition there is a component that is responsible for setting up components, that means requesting the information about types and instances of component implementations. The gathered information is used to build an adequate proxy for the component services in order to enable DAiSI's Configuration Component to bind appropriate components.

The logical part reflects the instance view of the component model of DAiSI as depicted on the right side of figure 3. Since the Configuration Component has to determine the available configurations and component service users have to call methods in provided component services, there have to be basic stub implementations. The chosen solution is using a fixed generic implementation of InstanceComponentIf and InstanceComponentConfigurationIf, whereas InstanceComponentServiceIf and InstanceComponentServiceReferenceIf

are specific and must be handled dynamically. As a consequence a Sun SPOT component "tells" which services are provided/needed in which configuration and proxies represented by lean stubs can be loaded dynamically.

Consider that the Casualty Component from figure 2 is placed on a Sun SPOT. The information stored on the node about its component implementation must be transmitted to the Configuration Component via the Device Bay including the following: ComponentId ("Casualty component"), two ConfigurationIds together with their provided services and contained service references denoted by InterfaceIds.

Figure 4 shows the interconnection of two Sun SPOTs implementing the Casualty Component and the Vital Data Sensor Component. The Sun SPOTs communicate with each other and with additional external DAiSI application components using the corresponding proxies on the Device Bay. Thereby the Casualty Component uses the provided component service from the Vital Data

Figure 4. Device Bay containing Proxies for Components located on Sun SPOTs and their Integration into DAiSI

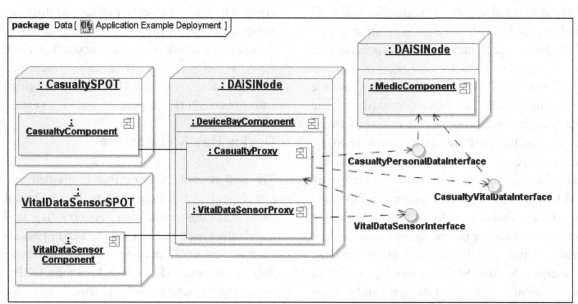

Sensor Component while offering its provided component services to other components.

Dynamic Loading of Stubs and Code Generation

Since a developer of Sun SPOT components does not want to deal with packet transmition and data (de-)multiplexing, a transparent view of components as proposed in the component model is desired. In the context of this model it is possible to generate the proxy stubs automatically. This means the developer specifies the provided component services, for instance as IDL-description and a Java class is generated. This handles all the communication together with the fixed generic part of the implementation and can be loaded dynamically during runtime. In addition it is possible to generate Java-skeletons for the Sun SPOT, too. Thus low-level communication is handled by generic entities on both sides, whereas the developer implements generated function bodies in the Sun SPOT code, "ready to run on DAiSI".

For the Casualty Component this means e.g. generating the VitalDataSensorInterface-stubs

from an IDL-file, which could contain a method like int getPulseRate(). Together with a ComponentId, ConfigurationId and the InterfaceId "VitalDataSensorInterface", this information suffices to build a Java-class that can be loaded dynamically and act as stub for the Vital Sensor Data Component on the Device Bay. Furthermore a Java-function body will be created for the developer, where only the getPulseRate() method has to be implemented. Parameters and return values are fixed and enable generic marshalling of these values. This way the developer can focus on design of a application component without the need to care about technical issues.

Figure 5 presents a sequence diagram with a possible behavior of the Casualty Component. The component may periodically check the vital condition of the casualty and hence must get the current pulse rate. It uses the getPulseRate()-method contained in VitalDataSensorInterface by first sending this request to its casualtyProxy-stub as a packet containing a string, denoted by the method sendPacket(). The request is parsed into a method getPulseRate() invoked at the connected vitalDataSensorProxy. This stub bridges the call

Figure 5. Example showing two Sun SPOT Components communicating

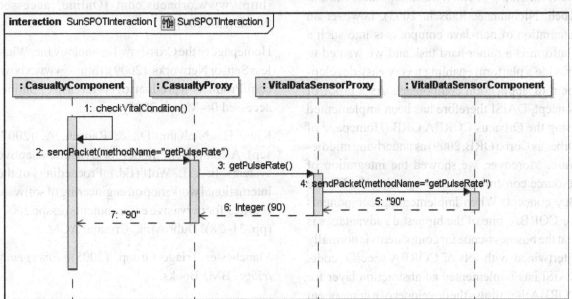

in a similar way to the Sun SPOT implementation vital- DataSensorComponent, which answers with the string "90" in a packet. This string is again parsed into an object from the type Integer representing the value 90 and returned as string to the Casualty Component, which can take further actions.

FUTURE WORK AND CONCLUSION

Due to DAiSI's Configuration Component, it is very easy to start up a Dynaptive System, since we do not have to specify the concrete system binding. Nevertheless during the implementation of the demonstrator described above, some issues remained open. One is the cyclic dependency between components that is needed in some cases. However, allowing cyclic redundancies may cause the whole system to hang up in an endless loop at runtime. Moreover, an Event Component specification is under development within DAiSI. This infrastructure component should enable all application components to communicate not only by remote procedure calls but also using typed events.

In the past we already implemented a similar platform on top of Jini (Anastasopoulos, Bartelt, Koch, Niebuhr, & Rausch, 2005), however an integration of non-Java components into such a platform is a rather hard task and we wanted to provide a platform enabling a very easy development of application components. As a proof of concept, DAiSI therefore has been implemented using the Orbacus CORBA ORB (Homepage of Orbacus Corba ORB, 2009) as underlying middleware. Moreover, we showed the integration of resource constrained nodes by using the Device Bay concept. When implementing components for CORBA, one of the biggest disadvantages is that the business-code for components is normally intertwined with lots of CORBA specific code. DAiSI has implemented an abstraction layer for CORBA that allows the developer of a component

to focus just on the business-code. Our Dynamic Adaptive System Infrastructure therefore enables developers to create components for Dynaptive Systems very easily.

REFERENCES

Anastasopoulos, M., Bartelt, C., Koch, J., Niebuhr, D., & Rausch, A. (2005, Oct). Towards a reference middleware architecture for ambient intelligence systems. In Proceedings of the workshop for building software for pervasive computing. 20th Conference on Object-Oriented Programming Systems, Languages and Applications (OOPSLA).

Bartelt, C., Fischer, T., Niebuhr, D., Rausch, A., Seidl, F., & Trapp, M. (2005, May). Dynamic integration of heterogeneous mobile devices. In Proceedings of the workshop in design and evolution of autonomic application software (deas 2005). ICSE 2005, St. Louis, Missouri, USA.

Bilateral German–Hungarian Collaboration Project on Ambient Intelligence Systems. (2009). (http://www.belami-project.org/ [Online; accessed 06-March-2009])

Homepage of Orbacus Corba ORB. (2009). (http://www.orbacus.com [Online; accessed 06-March-2009])

Homepage of the Crossbow Technology Inc. Wireless Sensor Networks. (2009). (http://www.xbow.com/Products/wproductsoverview.aspx [Online; accessed 06-March-2009])

Klus, H., Niebuhr, D., & Rausch, A. (2007, sep). A component model for dynamic adaptive systems. In A. L. Wolf (Ed.), Proceedings of the international workshop on engineering of software services for pervasive environments (esspe 2007) (pp. 21–28). Dubrovnik, Croatia: ACM.

Manchester Triage Group. (2005). *Emergency triage*. BMJ Books.

Martin Fowler's web page on dependency injection. (2009). (http://martinfowler.com/articles/injection.html [Online; accessed 06-March-2009])

Nehmer, J., Becker, M., Karshmer, A., & Lamm, R. (2006). Living assistance systems: an ambient intelligence approach. In Icse '06: Proceeding of the 28th international conference on software engineering (pp. 43–50). New York, NY, USA: ACM.

Niebuhr, D., & Rausch, A. (2007, sep). A concept for dynamic wiring of components: Correctness in dynamic adaptive systems. In Savcbs '07: Proceedings of the 2007 conference on specification and verification of component-based systems (p. 101-102). Dubrovnik, Croatia: ACM.

Niebuhr, D., Rausch, A., Klus, H., Appel, A., Klein, C., Reichmann, J., & Schmid, R. (2010). Method and apparatus for determining a component conforming to the requirements. Patent pending (Patent Nr. WO 2010/040605 A2).

Niebuhr, D., Schindler, M., & Herrling, D. (2009). Emergency assistance system – webpage of the cebit exhibit 2009. (http://www2.in.tu-clausthal.de/~Rettungsassistenzsystem [Online; accessed 09-February-2009])

Oreizy, P., Medvidovic, N., & Taylor, R. N. (1998). Architecturebased runtime software evolution. In (pp. 177–186).

Sadjadi, S. M., Survey, A., & Exam, P. D. Q. (2003). A survey of adaptive middleware (Tech. Rep.).

Seidl, F. (2005). Development of a device bay architecture for jini federations. Unpublished master's thesis, University of Kaiserslautern.

Smith, R. B., Horan, B., Daniels, J., & Cleal, D. (2006). Programming the world with sun spots. In Oopsla '06: Companion to the 21st acm sigplan conference on object-oriented programming systems, languages, and applications (pp. 706–707). New York, NY, USA: ACM.

Taylor, R. N., Medvidovic, N., Anderson, K. M., Whitehead, E. J., Jr., & Robbins, J. E. (1995). A component- and message-based architectural style for gui software. In Icse '95: Proceedings of the 17th international conference on software engineering (pp.295–304). New York, NY, USA: ACM.

The Jini™ Technology Surrogate Architecture Overview. (2009). (https://surrogate.dev.java.net/doc/overview.pdf [Online; accessed 06-March-2009])

Trapp, M. (2005). *Modeling the adaptation behavior of adaptive embedded systems*. Dr. Hut. Taschenbuch.

ENDNOTES

[1] Abbreviation of Dynamic Adaptive

Chapter 23
Intrusive Evaluation of Ambient Displays

Xiaobin Shen
Monash University, Australia

ABSTRACT

Ambient display is a display, which sits on the peripheral of user's attention. Currently, the research on ambient displays is still in initial stage, so few evaluation styles are available to evaluate ambient displays. Our previous research (Shen, Eades, Hong, & Moere, 2007) proposed two evaluation styles for ambient displays: Intrusive Evaluation and Non-Intrusive Evaluation. In this journal, we focus on the first style by applying two intrusive evaluation case studies. The first case study compares the performance of three different peripheral display systems on both large and small displays. Our results indicate there is a significant difference on a primary task performance and a peripheral comprehension task between large and small displays. Furthermore, we have found that distraction may be composed by display-distraction and self-interruption, and that animation may only influence the display-distraction. In addition, a measurement of efficiency derived from cognitive science is proposed. The second case study focuses on exploring the correct disruptive order of visual cues (animation, color, area and position). Our results show that the correct disruptive order of visual cues in ambient displays is: animation, color, area and position. Furthermore, we also revealed how display-distraction influences the comprehension of ambient display. In addition, this case study further amended the measurement of efficiency, which was proposed in previous case study, to improve its accuracy.

INTRODUCTION

Human vision is composed of two parts: foveal and peripheral. Foveal vision has a narrow angle

DOI: 10.4018/978-1-60960-549-0.ch023

(around ten degrees) but supports higher visual acuity (Peripheral-Vision, 2006). In contrast, peripheral vision covers a wide angle but has lower visual acuity.

In the past thirty years, many research areas have dealt with foveal vision. Examples include

Figure 1. A typical setting for foveal vision

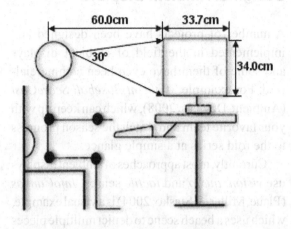

information visualization and human-computer interaction, where almost all research concerns displaying information through foveal vision. On the other hand, few researchers have concentrated on the peripheral vision. The reason is principally that, until recently, a computer user typically had only one screen and foveal vision can cover a large proportion of this screen (see Figure 1).

Figure 1 shows a typical scenario for foveal vision with a single user and a fifteen inch monitor. The largest viewing angle in this scenario is about thirty degrees. The foveal vision of a single person can reach about ten degrees and the user can easily and quickly shift focus from peripheral vision to foveal vision to cover the remaining twenty degrees.

The current trend in displays is to have bigger and bigger screens, but the price of such screens is decreasing. In the near future, the development of technologies (for example, E.INK and Flexible Displays (E.INK, 2006)) will enable information to be displayed everywhere. For example, information can be displayed on the walls, tables, curtains or even clothes. Holmquist and Skog (2003) points out that when information can be displayed on clothes, the computer designer will become a fashion creator. All these new techniques lead to a new world where foveal vision can only cover a small part of the display; this forces user

to engage peripheral vision to retrieve, understand and remember information.

The importance of the peripheral vision to some extent comes from the ubiquitous computing dream. Weiser (1991) first defined a term "Ubiquitous Computing", which proposes a new research area in his journal "The Computer for the 21st Century". Weiser (1991) believes that "the most profound technologies are those that disappear. They weave themselves into the fabric of everyday life until they are indistinguishable from it".

Following his dream, many pioneers of ubiquitous computing have created a number of terminologies (for example, disappearing computing (Russell, Streitz, & Winograd, 2005), tangible computing (Ishii, 2002), pervasive computing (Hansmann, 2003), peripheral display (Weiser & Brown, 1996), ambient display (Wisneski et al., 1998), informative art (Redstrom, Skog, & Hallnas, 2000), notification system (McCrickard, 2006), or even ambient information system (Pousman & Stasko, 2006)). Streitz, Magerkurth, Prante, and Rocker (2005) even divides the Weiser notion of "disappearance" into two trends: *mental disappearance* and *physical disappearance*. Mental disappearance makes users feel that there are no computers, because they integrate into the real life environment smoothly. Physical disappearance actually shrinks the size of computer components (for example, using PDA to replace a normal desktop computer).

In this journal, the first trend of Streitz (that is, mental disappearance) to design and evaluate two ambient display case studies is followed.

RELATED WORK

Research on ambient displays is still immature, and thus there is no universally accepted definition available. Ullmer and Ishii (2002), Matthews et al. (2003), Mankoff et al. (2003) and Stasko et al. (2004) proposed their own definitions but here the definition of Stasko is adapted: "Ambient displays typically communicate just one, or perhaps a few at the most, pieces of information and the aesthetics and visual appeal of the display are often paramount".

Holmquist and Skog (2003) believes the aim of ambient displays is to explore a new way of introducing information in the everyday environment. Mankoff et al. (2003) further points out that the ambitious goal of ambient displays is to present information without distracting or burdening users. In practice, it is difficult to achieve this goal because there are two main limitations on their development:

- *Limitations of current display technologies*: current technology can display dynamically updated data on a high-resolution wall but it still has limitations on showing information everywhere. For example, it is difficult to display real-time information on a highly speed cloud.
- *Limitations of human understanding*: even if the technology required for ambient displays is available, humans still need better ways to interpret and understand this new kind of presentation. Partially, the reason is that no official guidelines exist to guide users on how to read and interpret ambient displays. Also, the existing guidelines in information visualization and human computer interaction cannot be directly used in ambient displays.

The current trend in ambient displays is that many researchers concentrate on the designing of ambient displays but few focuses on the evaluation. On the other hand, evaluation is one of key research challenging in ambient displays. As Mankoff et al. (2003) points out: "Without evaluation, it is difficult to determine which displays are effective and why they are effective. Without this information, it is difficult to improve on existing work".

Design of Ambient Displays

A number of projects have been designed and implemented in the field of ambient displays and some of them have even been commercialized. For example, *Ambient Baseball ScoreCast* (Ambient-Devices, 2008), which can keep up with your favorite team and watch the season progress to the rold series at a simple glance.

Currently, most approaches of ambient displays use *vision*, *audio* and *tactile* senses. *InfoCanvas* (Plaue, Miller, & Stasko, 2004) is a visual example, which uses a beach scene to depict multiple pieces of real-time information. Other similar systems include: *Digital Family Portrait* (Mynatt, Rowan, Craighill, & Jacobs, 2001), *Kandinsky system* (Fogarty, Forlizzi, & Hudson, 2001), *Interactive Poetic Garden* (White & Small, 1998) and *Googleplex* (Google, 2006).

Non-speech audio glance (Hudson & Smith, 1996) represents important properties of a message as a concise sound. Other similar systems include: *Musicbox* (Ullmer & Ishii, 2002) and *Visual Heart Music* (Buccheri, 2005).

Lumitouch (Chang, Resner, Koerner, Wang, & Ishii, 2001) is a tactile example, which can transmit emotional content when the picture frame is touched. Other similar systems include: *Vispad* (Weissgerber, Bridgeman, & Pang, 2004), *Pinwheel* (Dahley, Wisneski, & Ishii, 1998) and *Embrace Wearable Display* (Thomas, 2005).

Evaluation of Ambient Displays

There are few quality evaluations conducted in ambient displays. *Digital Family Portrait, InfoCanvas* and *BusMobile* and *Daylight Display* are four typical evaluations conducted in ambient displays. *Digital Family Portrait* (Mynatt et al., 2001) uses a combination of "Wizard of Oz", interview, and questionnaire to evaluate the designed form, content, and visualization techniques for the portrait. Results from this experiment discovered the categories of information required for day-today awareness of family member, including health, environment, relationships, activity and events.

InfoCanvas (Stasko, McColgin, Miller, Plaue, & Pousman, 2005) conducts an in-depth longitudinal and *in situ* evaluation. The main evaluation techniques are interview and questionnaire, and results from *InfoCanvas* show that it is a useful and informative display. This experiment has demonstrated that it is possible to conduct a successful evaluation by using normal evaluation techniques (for example, questionnaire and interview).

BusMobile and *Daylight Display* (Mankoff et al., 2003) are both evaluated by heuristic evaluation of Mankoff. Results from *BusMobile* proves its usefulness and results from *Daylight Display* shows that users' interests are decreasing as they spent more time in the labs.

INTRUSIVE EVALUATION

Evaluation can be divided into *formative* and *summative* styles from the evaluation time point of view. Also, it can be divided into *laboratory* and *field study* styles from the evaluation environment point of view. Our previous research (Shen et al., 2007) divided the evaluation of ambient displays in *Intrusive* and *Non-Intrusive Evaluation* from user awareness point of view.

Intrusive evaluation is where the user is consciously aware of the evaluation experiment and non-intrusive evaluation is not. Intrusive evaluation often focuses on usability tests in a laboratory environment for a short period. Most such experiments are conducted using well established evaluation techniques in information visualization (for example, questionnaires and interviews).

The relationship between these evaluation styles is that intrusive and non-intrusive evaluation can be conducted in both summative and formative styles. Furthermore, they can also be conducted in laboratory or field study styles.

Theoretically, subjects in intrusive evaluation are *aware* of the experiments. As normal intrusive evaluation requires subjects to conduct some tasks in a laboratory environment within a short period. On the other hand, subjects in non-intrusive evaluation are not continually aware of the experiment. This article focuses on the intrusive evaluation of ambient displays by applying two intrusive evaluation case studies, *moneytree* and *moneycolor*.

INTRUSIVE EVALUATION OF MONEYTREE

Review of MoneyTree

MoneyTree (Shen & Eades, 2004) is a specialized ambient financial display, which only requires subjects to glance at the display for a short time to retrieve meaningful information, while they can still concentrate on their main task (See Figure 2). To make comparable results, two other financial visualization systems, *Digital Data* (See Figure 3) and *Stock Chart* (See Figure 4) are also included. *Digital Data* and *Stock Chart* are probably the two most established financial visualizations, which are commonly available on internet web sites, financial visualization applications and information boards in stock trading centres.

The data used in three systems are received from the ASX (Australian Stock Exchange) server[1], which sends data package as RSS[2] feed every two minutes. Each package includes all trading records within these two minutes. Three specific stock quotes were chosen to be represented in three systems: AMP[3], NCPDP[4] and VCR[5]. For each stock quote, each system focuses on two basic attributes: stock price and volume.

Specifically, *MoneyTree* uses three different types of trees to represent three individual stock quotes and also uses tree length and leaves to represent the trade volume and price respectively (see Figure 2). No visualization history is depicted but image morphing is used to achieve smooth graphical transition from one stage to another.

Figure 2. MoneyTree System

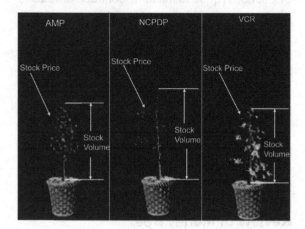

Figure 3. MoneyTree System

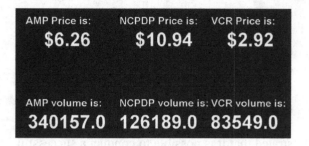

Figure 4. MoneyTree System

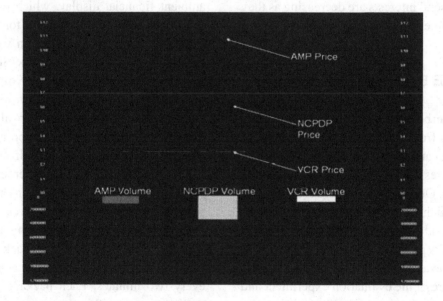

MoneyTree also sets both the data update rate and image change rate as once every two minutes.

Digital Data is a traditional numerical visualization for financial data (See Figure 3), which displays detailed numerical data on three different stock quotes. Specifically, it uses textual display to represent trade price and volume of AMP, NCPDP and VCR. Furthermore, it neither keeps previous trading history nor uses animation during transitions.

Stock Chart is a traditional financial visualization, which combines line and bar chart together (See Figure 4). It uses three different colors to represent three stock quotes; a linear curve represents trade price and a bar chart represents trade volume. Also, it keeps the previous trading history but there is no animation used in transition from one stage to another.

Evaluation of MoneyTree

A brief evaluation of *MoneyTree* was reported (Shen, Moere, & Eades, 2006). Specifically, the detailed evaluation goals of this experiment are twofold:

- To adapt a measurement of efficiency theory from cognitive science to measure the *efficiency* level in *MoneyTree*.
- To discover the difference in the context of *distraction*, *comprehension* and *efficiency* between large and small displays.

Three hypotheses were proposed in this experiment:

H1: Large display performs better than small display in terms of comprehension;

H2: Large display achieves higher efficiency than small display;

H3: The more times subjects shift their focus to the peripheral screen, the more information they will get.

These hypotheses were based on the result of Tan's experiment (Tan, Gergle, Scupelli, & Pausch, 2003), which shows that large display performed better in spatial tasks than small display but there was no significant difference in *comprehension*.

This experiment was conducted in the VIAR [6] room (an information visualization laboratory with multiple screens) at NICTA [7]. Sixteen (8 female) subjects participated in the study. All subjects had normal eyesight. Subject age ranged from 22 to 40 years (average age 28.6 years). Five were master students, nine were PhD students and two were postdoctoral researchers. All of them have little knowledge of ambient displays but none were expert.

Software materials involved in this experiment are primarily consisted of the three evaluation systems: *Digital Data*, *MoneyTree* and *Stock Chart*. Hardware materials are mainly composed of two standard 19 inch desktop monitors; two large rear-project screens; One Dell Precision Workstation 360 [8] and one LogiTech QuickCam Pro 4000 web camera [9].

Specifically, two standard 19 inch desk monitors were used in small display experiment and two large rear-projection screens used in large display experiments. Each of the large screens was 2m (width)*1.5m (height). The same resolution of 1024*768 was set in both experiments. Screen brightness and contrast were adjusted identically. The Dell Workstation was responsible for controlling the information displayed on both large and small displays. Video footage was captured by the web camera and examined by the evaluator to count how many times subjects shifted their focus to the peripheral screen. Figure 5 gave an illustration of the experimental setup.

The desk, chair, keyboard and typing materials were fixed and the mouse was removed from the desk. A reference sheet for the three visualization metaphors was set in front of the keyboard in case subjects forgot the visual mappings.

The experiment consisted two tasks: *primary task* and *secondary task*. The *primary task* of the subjects was to type words on the primary screen for two minutes while an ambient system (that is, *MoneyTree*, *Stock Chart* and *Digital Data*) was displayed on the peripheral screen. The words were derived from the Hamlet (Shakespeare, 1601) and were printed on one side A4 size sheet of paper with a 16 point font. The *secondary task* was to occasionally shift focus to the peripheral screen to fetch information about the three stock quotes.

Specifically, the actual experiment for each subject was composed of four tests:

- **Test 1** – primary task plus *Digital Data*
- **Test 2** – primary task plus *MoneyTree*
- **Test 3** – primary task plus *Stock Chart*
- **Test 4** – primary task only

Figure 5. MoneyTree System

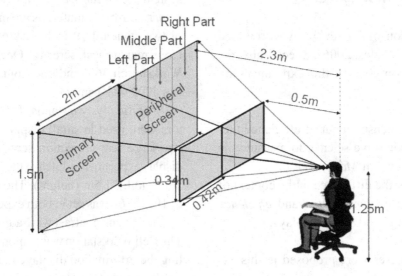

Figure 6. A sample questionnaire in the evaluation of MoneyColor

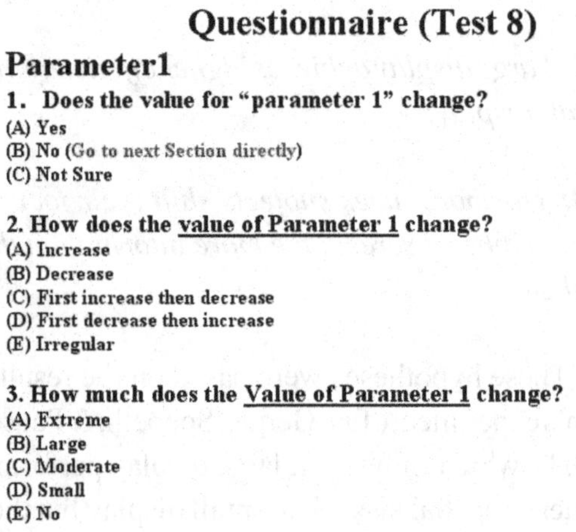

Three parameters were analysed:

- Mean Comprehension Error Rate (MCER) was measured based on the answers in the comprehension knowledge questionnaire (See an example in Figure 6). A larger MCER indicates a worse understanding of each display;
- Mean Words Typed (MWT) was the number of words typed in the primary task. A higer MWT indicates better performance on the primary task;
- Mean Focus Shift (MFS) was the number of focus shifts to the peripheral screen. A lower MFS indicates less distraction;

The computation of *efficiency* was based on Pass and van Merrienboer's *efficiency* measurement theory taken from cognitive science (Pass & Van, 1993). This theory proposes that *efficiency* is the combination of the measurements of mental effort and performance. The rough and ready view was taken that MWT measures performance, and MCER and MFS measure the mental effort. All parameters were calculated in Z Score (Henk, 2004) value. This measure was

Questionnaire (Test 8)

Parameter1

1. Does the value for "parameter 1" change?
(A) Yes
(B) No (Go to next Section directly)
(C) Not Sure

2. How does the <u>value of Parameter 1</u> change?
(A) Increase
(B) Decrease
(C) First increase then decrease
(D) First decrease then increase
(E) Irregular

3. How much does the <u>Value of Parameter 1</u> change?
(A) Extreme
(B) Large
(C) Moderate
(D) Small
(E) No

relatively simplistic, but it was adequate for our purpose.

$$EY = \frac{Z_{MWT} - (Z_{MCER} + Z_{MFS})}{\sqrt{2}} \qquad (1)$$

where, *EY* is the *efficiency* value in Z-Score; Z_{MWT} is the value of mean word typed (MWT) in Z-Score; Z_{MCER} is the value of mean comprehension

Table 1. Paired student's t-Test on MCER between large and small displays; significant different at p<0.05

MCER	Test1	Test2	Test3
Large Display	3.53	2.94	2.54
Small Display	2.67	1.99	1.84
p	0.050	0.012	0.045

Table 2. Paired student's t-Test on MWT in both large and small displays; significant different at p<0.05

MWT	Test1	Test2	Test3
t	-3.63	-2.18	-2.14
p	0.003	0.048	0.049

error rate (MCER) in Z-Score and Z_{MFS} is the value of mean focus shift (MFS) in Z-Score.

Results of MoneyTree

A paired student's t-Test (Siegel & Morgan, 1996) was used to analyze the results and a Z-Score (Gossett, 2006) was applied to calculate the efficiency level. Four results are analyzed in this section and details are described below.

1. **Mean Comprehension Error Rate (MCER):** The results reveal that large displays have a higher MCER than small displays and the difference is significant (see Table 1, where the significant difference p<0.05). This result denies the first hypothesis and shows that *small display performed better than large display in terms of comprehension*. Finer analysis of the results in Table 1 shows a new result: an increasing MCER from the left to the right part on both large and small displays (see Figure 7) in the peripheral screen, which was divided into 3 parts, as shown in Figure 5.
2. **Mean Words Typed (MWT):** Table 2 reveals that large displays achieve lower MWT than small displays in all three tests. Moreover, this difference is significant (p<0.05).
3. **Mean Focus Shift (MFS):** Combining the analysis of the results for MCER and MFS shows that the relationship between them is

in inverse-proportion on both large and small displays (see Figure 8).

This result would seem to deny the third hypothesis and indicates that many focus shifts imply a worse comprehension error rate. However, these results are not significant and need further studies (see Table 3).

4. **Efficiency:** Equation 1 shows that *efficiency* is measured by combining considerations of performance and mental effort. Figure 9 shows the performance in both large and small displays with 95% confidence interval.

Furthermore, Table 4 shows that there is a significant difference (p<0.05) in performance between large and small displays.

Figure 10 shows the mental effort in both large and small displays with 95% confidence interval.

This result denies the second hypothesis but the difference between large and small display is not significant (see Table 5). This result needs further study.

Discussion of MoneyTree

Three issues are to be discussed in this experiment: *Comprehension*, *Distraction*, and *Efficiency*.

1. **Comprehension:** Results in this experiment show that comprehension from ambient displays is affected by relative position of the information in the peripheral screen. The farther the information is from the primary

Figure 7. MCER in both small and large displays with 95% confidence interval

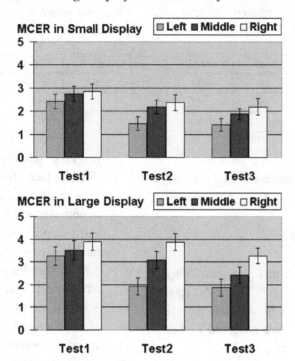

Figure 8. MCER and MFS between large and small displays with 95% confidence interval

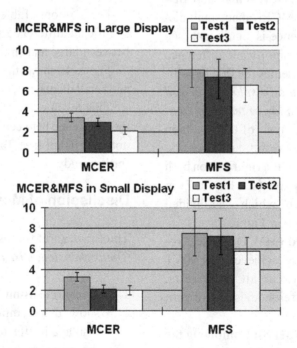

Table 3. Paired student's t-Test on MFS and MCER between large and small displays

	Test1	Test2	Test3
P of MCER	0.050	0.012	0.045
P of MFS	0.272	0.361	0.229

Table 4. Paired student's t-Test on performance between large and small displays

	Test1	Test2	Test3
p	0.003	0.048	0.049

Figure 9. Performance in both large and small displays with 95% confidence interval

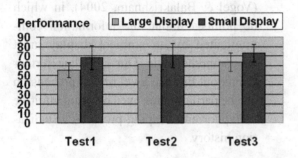

Figure 10. Mental effort in both large and small displays with 95% confidence interval

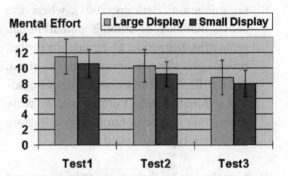

Table 5. Paired student's t-Test on mental effort between large and small displays

	Test1	Test2	Test3
p	0.173	0.162	0.116

screen, the higher the comprehension error rate is (see Figure 7).

This experiment divided the peripheral screen, which is next to the primary screen, into three parts (See Figure 5). The viewing angle to the left part (around 35 degree) of the peripheral screen is less than that to the middle (around 44 degree) and right part (around 53 degree). In the same way, the result of MCER to the left part is less than that to middle and right part in both large and small display experiments.

This result is in agreement with the theory of human vision. An important characteristic of human vision is that acuity outside fovea vision drops rapidly (Peripheral-Vision, 2006). Furthermore, it also extends the Gross (Gross, 2003) site guideline, where he

states that ambient displays is site specific (that is, different sites may affect the design and evaluation of ambient displays). Our guideline also reveals that the position of information on the screen affects the design and evaluation of ambient displays.

Conclusion 1: The most important information in the peripheral display has to be in the close proximity to the primary screen.

2. **Distraction:** Results in this experiment also reveal that the relationship between MCER and MFS is in inverse-proportion (see Figure 8). Further research demonstrates that distraction can be further divided into two parts: *display-distraction* and *self-interruption*. *Display distraction* is caused by the display itself and can be divided into five levels based on different data and tasks (Matthews et al., 2003). *Self-interruption* occurs when subjects decide to look at the peripheral display themselves. *Self-interruption* is

mostly affected by the characteristics of subjects themselves (personality, curiosity). It is difficult to decrease the level of distraction by *self-interruption* because this is under the control of subjects. However, the results in this experiment indicate that it is possible to decrease the *display distraction* by using slow or smooth animation. This result extends the guideline of Bartram on animation (Bartram, 2001), where she shows that slow or smooth animation can reduce the distraction. Our guideline further reveals that slow or smooth animation can reduce *display-distraction* but does not affect *self-interruption*. Furthermore, *display-distraction* can be controlled by adjusting animation type and speed.

Conclusion 2: Distraction can be composed of two parts: *display-distraction* and *self-interruption*. Slow or smooth animation can help to reduce the level of *display distraction* but may not affect the issue of the user's *self-interruption*.

3. **Efficiency:** *Efficiency* is one of the key evaluation concepts in information visualization, but it is seldom used in ambient displays. In this experiment, an efficiency measurement for ambient displays was proposed (see Equation 1). This equation was created to quantify the level of efficiency in ambient displays.
    Results in this experiment show that efficiency in Test 3 is higher than that in Test 2 in both large and small displays (Figure 9 and 10 show that Test 3 has a higher performance and lower mental effort than Test 2). Results from face-to-face interviews indicate that using an intuitive metaphor in ambient display can reduce the mental effort (that is, most subjects have knowledge of stock chart (Test 3) but few have knowledge of *MoneyTree* (Test 2)). Furthermore, results

from face-to-face interviews indicate that keeping the previous visualization history enhances the performance of subjects. A partial reason for this is that the display keeping previous visualization history (Test 3) enables subjects to concentrate better on their primary task than the display that does not keep previous visualization history (Test 2). This result extends the guideline of Vogel (Vogel & Balakrishnam, 2004), in which he points out that the information communicated by an ambient display must be comprehensible. Our guideline further points out that the level of comprehension can be partially improved by using intuitive metaphor and keeping previous visualization history.

Conclusion 3: Using intuitive metaphor and keeping previous visualization history can improve the efficiency of ambient displays.

INTRUSIVE EVALUATION OF MONEYCOLOR

Review of MoneyColor

MoneyColor (Shen & Eades, 2005) is inspired by the art of Hans Heysen (1932), which embeds financial information in an Australian watercolor painting. The data used in *MoneyColor* is also received from the ASX (Australian Stock Exchange) server in RSS[10] format. BHP[11] is the only stock quote used in *MoneyColor*, which also focuses on two attributes: stock price and volume. There are three metaphors in the *MoneyColor* system (see Figure 11):

1. The color of the sky represents the general stock index. The darker the sky, the lower the general stock index.
2. The position of a mountain represents BHP stock price. The higher the position of the

Figure 11. Metaphor of MoneyColor

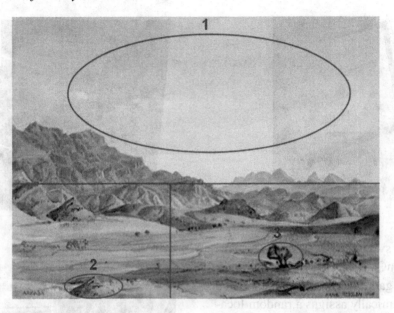

mountain on the image, the higher the stock price.

3. The size of the tree represents stock volume. The larger the tree, the greater the stock volume.

Evaluation of MoneyColor

A brief evaluation of *MoneyColor* was reported in (Shen et al., 2007). Specifically, the general evaluation aim is twofold:

- To explore the correct disruptive order of visual cues (*animation*, *color*, *area* and *position*).
- To further quantify the *efficiency* measurement.

To simplify the measurement, *animation* here refers to the image morphing technique. *Color* refers to the effects of changing color-hue. *Area* refers to the change in the size of the tree and *position* refers to the change of the location of the mountain in *MoneyColor*.

The whole experiment was conducted in the VIAR[12] room at NICTA[13]. Eighteen (nine female) subjects participated in this experiment. Subjects ranged from 21 to 35 years (the average was 26.8 years). Ten were master students, five were PhD students and three were postdoctoral researchers. Seven subjects knew nothing about ambient displays and the remainder had some knowledge; none were experts.

There are two hypotheses for this experiment:

H1: *The disruptive order of visual cues (in descending order) is: animation, color, position and area.*

H2: *There is no direct relationship between comprehension and display-distraction.*

The first hypothesis is based on the results of Cleveland and McGill (1984) on the effective order of visual cue in graphical presentation (demanded full-attention). The second hypothesis is based on our previous case study.

Software materials involved in this experiment are primarily consisted of *MoneyColor* system,

Figure 12. Square-Click

Figure 13. MoneyColor

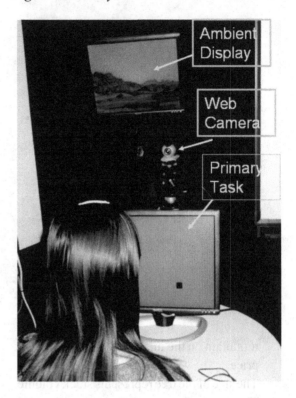

the *Square-Click* system, a driver for a web camera and the OpenCV face detection program[14]. *Square-Click* is a game style system implemented in Java[15]. It dynamically assigns a random location for a black square (size 80*80 pixels) every second. Subjects need to mouse-click the black square within one second of its appearance (see Figure 12). If successful, the black square will be assigned a new random location and scored 1. If not, the black square will be assigned a new location after one second and scored 0. OpenCV is a software used to detect whether subjects look at *MoneyColor* or not.

Hardware Materials used in this experiment include two standard 19 inch desktop monitors with a resolution of 1024*768; one Dell Precision Workstation 360[16]; and one LogiTech QuickCam Pro4000[17] web camera. A mouse is the only input equipment and a desk and chair are fixed in position, as illustrated in Figure 12.

There are two tasks involved in this experiment. The primary task is to play *Square-Click*. Subjects concentrate on the location change of the black square and try to click on the black square within one second of its appearance. The *Square-Click* system lasts two minutes after which it reports the percentage of successful clicks on black squares within one second. The secondary task is to occasionally shift focus to the peripheral screen (e.g.

the *MoneyColor* system) to obtain information. Also, five parameters are analyzed:

- Mean Performance Score (MPS) measures the performance of subjects in the primary task; A larger MPS indicates better performance.
- Mean Comprehension Rate (MCR) measures the answers subjects give in the questionnaire; A larger MCR indicates better understanding of ambient display.
- Mean Self-Interruption (MSI) counts the number of focus shifts to the peripheral screen prompted by the subjects themselves; A larger MSI denotes a more curious/nervous subject.
- Mean Display-Distraction (MDD) counts the number of focus shifts to the peripheral screen caused by display distraction; a lower MDD denotes a calmer ambient display.

Table 6. Mean comprehension rate in each pair of tests

MCR	Test2-3	Test4-5	Test6-7	Test8-9	Test10-11	Test12-13	Test14-15
Animation	0.841	0.667	0.833	0.800	0.600	0.542	0.532
No Animation	0.836	0.646	0.800	0.733	0.583	0.538	0.529
p	0.048	0.043	0.041	0.038	0.049	0.049	0.050

- Mean Degradation of Primary Task (MDPT) measures degradation in the primary task with and without a peripheral screen in place. A lower MDPT indicates a better performance of subjects.

Our previous *intrusive evaluation of Money-Tree* proposed an efficiency measurement, which combined consideration of MWT, MCER and MFS (see Equation 1) but previous results reveal that *self-interruption* did not affect *comprehension* of ambient displays. Therefor, this experiment revises the *efficiency* measurement of Equation 1 to combine MCR and MDD to quantify the *efficiency* level in *MoneyColor*.

$$EY = \frac{Z_{MCR} - Z_{MDD}}{\sqrt{2}} \qquad (2)$$

where, *EY* is the efficiency value in Z-Score; Z_{MCR} is the value of mean comprehension rate (MCR) in Z-Score and Z_{MDD} is the mean display-distraction (MDD) in Z-Score.

The actual evaluation of *MoneyColor* is composed of fifteen tests. Each test lasts two minutes and is followed by a two to five minutes break. The detailed tests are as below:

- **Test 1:** *Square-Click* system only
- **Test 2-3:** *Square-Click* system plus *MoneyColor* (color visual cue with/without animation)
- **Test 4-5:** *Square-Click* system plus *MoneyColor* (position visual cue with/without animation)

- **Test 6-7:** *Square-Click* system plus *MoneyColor* (area visual cue with/without animation)
- **Test 8-9:** *Square-Click* system plus *MoneyColor* (color and position with/without animation)
- **Test 10-11:** *Square-Click* system plus *MoneyColor* (color and area with/without animation)
- **Test 12-13:** *Square-Click* system plus *MoneyColor* (position and area with/without animation)
- **Test 14-15:** *Square-Click* system plus *MoneyColor* (color, position and area with/without animation)

Results of MoneyColor

A within-subject experimental design was used with non-fixed ordering of experimental tests. A paired student's t-Test[18] was used to analyze the results and a Z-Score[19] was used to calculate the values of *efficiency*. Three parameters were analyzed in this section and details are described below.

1. **Mean Comprehension Rate (MCR):** Results in Table 6 show that the value of the mean comprehension rate (MCR) with animation is higher than without animation. Furthermore, this difference is significant (where significant difference is p<0.05).
   A further study of Table 6 reveals that, for the single visual cue, color (Test2-3) has the highest mean comprehension rate (MCR) and position (Test4-5) achieves the lowest.

Table 7. The relationship between MCR and the number of visual cues

	One V.C.	Two V.C.	Three V.C.
MCR	0.771	0.633	0.531
p	0.123	0.081	0.069

The value of mean comprehension rate (MCR) decreases with the increase in the number of visual cues (see Table 7). This result is not significant and requires further study.

2. **Mean Self-Interruption (MSI) and Mean Display-Distraction (MDD):** Our previous intrusive evaluation of *MoneyTree* classifies the distraction into *display-distraction* and *self-interruption*. In this experiment, a combined consideration of mean comprehension rate (MCR), mean self-interruption (MSI) and mean display-distraction (MDD) further

revealed that mean comprehension rate (MCR) is in direct-proportion to mean display-distraction (MDD). However, there is no obvious relationship between mean comprehension rate (MCR) and mean self-interruption (MSI) (see Figure 14). This result denies the second hypothesis proposed for this experiment.

3. **Efficiency:** Results in Table 8 show the value of *efficiency* in the tests with animation is higher than those without animation. However, this result is not significant, and needs further study.

For the single visual cue in Table 8, color (Test 2-3) has the highest *efficiency* and position has the lowest (Test 4-5). The value of *efficiency* also decreases with the increase in the number of visual cues, as illustrated in Table 9. This result is not significantly different and requires further study.

Figure 14. Relationship between MCR, MDD and MSI in MoneyColor

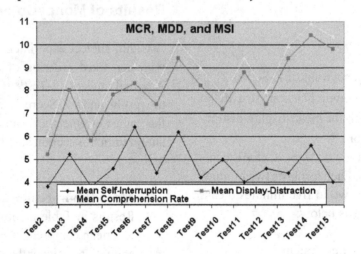

Table 8. Efficiency in each pair of tests

Efficiency	Test2-3	Test4-5	Test6-7	Test8-9	Test10-11	Test12-13	Test14-15
Animation	0.591	0.236	0.314	0.166	-0.030	-0.121	-0.427
No Animation	0.252	0.020	0.154	-0.081	-0.203	-0.363	-0.506
p	0.019	0.027	0.049	0.068	0.085	0.079	0.081

Table 9. The relationship between efficiency and the number of visual cues

	OneVC	TwoVC	ThreeVC
Efficiency	0.261	-0.105	-0.467
p	0.016	0.097	0.102

Discussion of MoneyColor

1. **Order of Visual Cues:** Results in this experiment show that animation is the most disruptive visual cue in the pre-defined visual cue lists (that is, animation, color, position, and area). And, the final order of *disruptiveness* for visual cues is: Animation, Color, Area and Position. This result extends Cleveland and McGill's finding on the order of visual cue in graphical presentations (Cleveland & McGill, 1984), which is that the correct order of disruptiveness for quantitative data is: position, area, color and animation. Our result is different from Cleveland and McGill's finding. This is partly because their effectiveness order demands full-attention, whereas effectiveness order in this experiment demands only partial attention.

    Guidelines 1. The correct disruptive order of visual cues in ambient displays is: animation, color, area and position

2. **Comprehension vs. Distraction:** Results in this experiment also show that the relationship between *display-distraction* and *comprehension* is in direct ratio (the more display-distraction in ambient displays, the better performance in comprehension). On the other hand, there is no obvious relationship between *self-interruption* and *comprehension*. Part of the reason is that *display-distraction* is caused by the change of data source, whereas self-interruption is caused by the personality of the subjects.

Thus, subjects have a better chance of identifying changes in *MoneyColor* by *display-distraction* than by *self-interruption*.

This result extends Matthews' finding on distraction (she called "notification") (Matthews et al., 2003), in which she divides distraction into five levels: *Ignore, Change blind, Make aware, Interrupt* and *Demand attention*. Our result further reveals that different levels of display-distraction may affect the comprehension of ambient displays.

Guidelines 2. Better control of the level of *display-distraction* enhances the level of *comprehension* of ambient displays.

CONCLUSION

In this article, we introduced two intrusive evaluation of ambient display case studies. Results from the first intrusive evaluation of *MoneyTree* indicated that there is a significant difference on a primary task performance and a peripheral comprehension task between large and small displays. Furthermore, we also found that distraction may be composed by *display-distraction* and *self-interruption*. Finally, we also proposed a measurement of *efficiency* derived from cognitive science.

Results from the second intrusive evaluation of *MoneyColor* revealed the correct disruptive order of visual cue in ambient displays is: animation, color, area and position. Furthermore, it also showed that the relationship between *display-distraction* and *comprehension* is in direct ratio, but there is no obvious relationship between *self-interruption* and *comprehension*. Finally, we it further modify the measurement of efficiency, which was originally proposed in previous case study. Our future research includes the running of more experiments to validate results and more *Non-Intrusive Evaluations*.

REFERENCES

Ambient-Devices. (2008). *Baseball scorecast.* http://www.ambientdevices.com/products/sportsCast-Baseball.html

Bartram, L. R. (2001). *Enhancing information visualization with motion.* Phd thesis, School of computing science; Simon Fraser University, Burnaby, B.C.

Buccheri, M. (2005). *Visual heart music.* http://homepages.nyu.edu/ mb1328/thesis/. (Online Resources)

Chang, A., Resner, B., Koerner, B., Wang, X., & Ishii, H. (2001). Lumitouch: An emotional communication device. *CHI'01 extended abstracts on human factors in computing systems* (p. 313-314). New York, NY, USA: ACM Press.

Cleveland, W. S., & McGill, R. (1984, September). Graphical perception: Theory, experimentation, and application to the development of graphical methods. *Journal of the American Statistical Association, 79*(387), 531–546. doi:10.2307/2288400

Dahley, A., Wisneski, C., & Ishii, H. (1998). Water lamp and pinwheels: Ambient projection of digital information into architectural space. *CHI'98 conference summary on human factors in computing systems* (pp. 269-270). New York, NY, USA: ACM Press.

E.INK. (2006). *Electronic paper dsiplays.* http://www.eink.com/. (Online Resources)

Fogarty, J., Forlizzi, J., & Hudson, S. E. (2001). Aesthetic information collages: Generating decorative displays that contain information. *UIST '01: Proceedings of the 14th annual ACM symposium on user interface software and technology* (p. 141-150). New York, NY, USA: ACM Press.

Frischholz, R. (2005). *Face detection.* Online Resources. (http://www.facedetection.com/)

Google. (2006). *Ambient displays in the googleplex.* http://tecfa.unige.ch/perso/staf/nova/blog/2006/06/03/ambient-displays-in-the-googleplex/. (Online Resources)

Gossett, W. S. (2006). *Student's t-tests.* http://www.physics.csbsju.edu/stats/t-test.html. (Online Resources)

Gross, T. (2003). Ambient interfaces: Design challenges and recommendations. *10th international conference on human-computer interaction-HCI'03* (pp. 68-72). Crete, Greece: Lawrence Erlbaum.

Hansmann, U. (2003). *Pervasive computing: The mobile word.* Springer.

Henk, T. (2004). *Understanding probability: chance rules in everyday life.* Cambridge University Press.

Heysen, H. (1932, Accessed on 5 April,). *Hans heysen - the artist.* http://www.hawkersa.info/heysen.htm. (Online Resources)

Holmquist, L. E., & Skog, T. (2003). Informative art: Information visualization in everyday environments. *Proceedings of the 1st international conference on computer graphics and interactive techniques in australasia and south east asia* (pp. 229-235). Melbourne, Australia: ACM Press.

Hudson, S. E., & Smith, I. (1996). Electronic mail previews using non-speech audio. In *Proceeding of the conference companion on human factors in computing systems: Common ground* (pp. 237-238). Vancouver, British Columbia, Canada: ACM Press.

Ishii, H. (2002). *Tangible bits: User interface design towards seamless integration of digital and physical worlds* (No. 3).

Mankoff, J., Dey, A., Hsieh, G., Kientz, J., Lederer, S., & Ames, M. (2003). *Heuristic evaluation of ambient displays* (pp. 169-176). ACM Press.

Matthews, T., Rattenbury, T., Carter, S., Hsieh, G., Dey, A., & Mankoff, J. (2003). *A peripheral display toolkit.*

McCrickard, S. (2006). *Homepage of scott Mc-Crickard.* http://people.cs.vt.edu/ccricks/. (Online Resources)

Mynatt, E. D., Rowan, J., Craighill, S., & Jacobs, A. (2001). Digital family portraits: Supporting peace of mind for extended family members. *Proceedings of the SIGCHI conference on human factors in computing systems* (pp. 333-340). Seattle, Washington, United States: ACM Press.

Pass, F., & Van, M. J. J. G. (1993). The efficiency of instructional conditions: An approach to combine mental effort and performance measures. *Human Factors, 35,* 737–743.

Peripheral-Vision. (2006). *Human peripheral vision.* http://webexhibits.org/colorart/ag.html. (Online-Resources)

Plaue, C., Miller, T., & Stasko, J. (2004). Is a picture worth a thousand words?: An evaluation of information awareness displays. *Proceedings of the 2004 conference on graphics interface* (pp. 117-126). London, Ontario, Canada: Canadian Human-Computer Communications Society.

Pousman, Z., & Stasko, J. (2006). A taxonomy of ambient information systems: four patterns of design. *Proceedings of the working conference on advanced visual interfaces* (pp. 67-74). ACM Press.

Redstrom, J., Skog, T., & Hallnas, L. (2000). *Informative art: using amplified artworks as information displays* (pp. 103-114). ACM.

Russell, D. M., Streitz, N. A., & Winograd, T. (2005, Accessed on 3 April,). *Building disappearing computers* (Vol. 48, pp. 42-48).

Shakespeare, W. (1601). *Hamlet.* http://pathguy.com/hamlet.htm. (Online resources)

Shen, X. (2007). *Design and evaluation of ambient displays.* Phd thesis, School of Information Technology, University of Sydney.

Shen, X., & Eades, P. (2004). Using MoneyTree to represent financial data. *Proceedings of the information visualisation, eighth international conference on (IV'04)* (Vol. 00, pp. 285-289). IEEE Computer society.

Shen, X., & Eades, P. (2005). Using MoneyColor to represent financial data. *In proceedings asia pacific symposium on information visualisation (APVIS2005)* (pp. 125-129). CRPIT.

Shen, X., Eades, P., Hong, S., & Moere, A. V. (2007). Intrusive and non-intrusive evaluation of ambient displays. *Proceeding of Pervasive, 07,* 16–22.

Shen, X., Moere, A. V., & Eades, P. (2006). An intrusive evaluation of ambient displays. *Third international conference on computer graphics and interactive techniques in australasia and south east asia* (pp. 289-292). Dunedin, New Zealand: ACM Press.

Siegel, A. F., & Morgan, C. J. (1996). *Statistics and data analysis: An introduction* (2nd ed.). New York: John Wiley & Sons.

Stasko, J., McColgin, D., Miller, T., Plaue, C., & Pousman, Z. (2005). *Evaluating the infoCanvas peripheral awareness system: A longitudinal, in situ study.*

Streitz, N., Magerkurth, C., Prante, T., & Rocker, C. (2005). *From information design to experience design: Smart artefacts and the disappearing computer* (Vol. 12, pp. 21-25).

Tan, D. S., Gergle, D., Scupelli, P., & Pausch, R. (2003). With similar visual angles, larger displays improve spatial performance. *Proceedings of the SIGCHI conference on human factors in computing systems* (p. 217-224). Ft. Lauderdale, Florida, USA: ACM Press.

Thomas, L. (2005). *Interactive fashionable wearable.* http://interactivefashionablewearable. blogspot.com/. (Online Resources)

Ullmer, B., & Ishii, H. (2002). *Musicbox in tangible bits.* http://tangible.media.mit.edu/projects/musicbox/. (Online Resources)

Vogel, D., & Balakrishnam, R. (2004). Interactive public ambient displays:transitioning from implicit to explicit, public to personal, interaction with multiple users. [ACM Press.]. *Proceedings of UIST, 04,* 137–146. doi:10.1145/1029632.1029656

Weiser, M. (1991, February). The computer for the 21st century. *Scientific American, 265*(3), 66–75.

Weiser, M., & Brown, J. S. (1996). Designing calm technology. *PowerGrid Journal, 1*(1).

Weissgerber, D., Bridgeman, B., & Pang, A. (2004). Vispad: A novel device for vibrotactile force feedback. [IEEE Computer Society.]. *Proceedings of HAPTICS, 04,* 50–57.

White, T., & Small, D. (1998). An interactive poetic garden. *Proceedings of CHI'98: CHI 98 conference summary on human factors in computing systems* (pp. 335-336). New York, NY, USA: ACM Press.

Wisneski, C., Ishii, H., Dahley, A., Gorbet, M., Brave, S., Ullmer, B., & Yarin, P. (1998). *Ambient displays: Turning architectural space into an interface between people and digital information* (pp. 22-32). Springer.

ENDNOTES

[1] http://www.asx.com.au/
[2] Really Simple Syndication
[3] AMP Limited, http://www.amp.com.au
[4] News Corporation, http://www.newscorp.com/
[5] Ventracor Limited, http://www.ventracor.com
[6] Visual Information Access Room
[7] National ICT Australia Ltd.
[8] http://supportapj.dell.com/support/edocs/systems/ws360/smen/index.htm
[9] http://www.logitech.com
[10] Really Simple Syndication
[11] http://www.bhpbilliton.com/
[12] Visual Information Access Room
[13] National ICT Australia
[14] http://www.intel.com/cd/software/products
[15] http://java.sun.com/
[16] http://supportapj.dell.com
[17] http://www.logitech.com
[18] http://www.physics.csbsju.edu/stats/t-test.html
[19] http://www.stat.tamu.edu/stat30x/notes/node34.htmls

This work was previously published in International Journal of Ambient Computing and Intelligence (IJACI), Volume 1, Issue 4, edited by Kevin Curran, pp. 12-31, copyright 2009 by IGI Publishing (an imprint of IGI Global).

Chapter 24
Smart Home Research:
Projects and Issues

Michael P. Poland
University of Ulster, Northern Ireland

Chris D. Nugent
University of Ulster, Northern Ireland

Hui Wang
University of Ulster, Northern Ireland

Liming Chen
University of Ulster, Northern Ireland

ABSTRACT

Smart Homes are environments facilitated with technology that act in a protective and proactive function to assist an inhabitant in managing their daily lives specific to their individual needs. A typical Smart Home implementation would include sensors and actuators to detect changes in status and to initiate beneficial interventions. This paper aims to introduce the diversity of recent Smart Home research and to present the challenges that are faced not only by engineers and potential inhabitants, but also by policy makers and healthcare professionals.

INTRODUCTION

United Nations population demographers predict an increasing number of elderly inhabitants in all societies in the near future, especially in western countries (United Nations, 2008). In Europe, the percentage of the population aged 65 and over in the year 2001 was 17%; it is estimated that by 2035 this figure will have risen to 33% ("Office

of Health", 2008). Ní Scanaill et al. (2006) asserts that eventually the 'Care Ratio' will become unbalanced in that taxes paid by those of working age (usually 16 – 64) will not be sufficient to accommodate a distending older population. They also point out that the situation will be made worse by the fact that apart from infants, elders over 65 are the primary users of a countries healthcare system. The *Public Health Agency of Canada* (2008) has estimated that by the year 2021, 6.7 million

DOI: 10.4018/978-1-60960-549-0.ch024

Canadians will be 65 and over, corresponding to 18% of the population as a whole.

Currently, 16.4% of France's population are 65 and over, a further 8% are over 75 (National Institute, 2006). According to the United Nations Programme on Ageing (United Nations, 2008):

One out of every ten persons is now 60 years or above; by 2050, one out of five will be 60 years or older; and by 2150, one out of three persons will be 60 years or older.

The UN's statistics go even further and state that:

The older population itself is ageing. The oldest old (80 years or older) is the fastest growing segment of the older population. They currently make up 13 percent of the 60+ age group and will grow to 20 percent by 2050. The number of centenarians (aged 100 years or older) is projected to increase 14-fold from approximately 265,000 in 2005 to 3.7 million by 2050.

People generally wish to remain within their own living environment (the research of which is covered in detail in a later section), and therefore this gives researchers the opportunity to deploy assistive technology that will allow those elders to do so. One inevitable consequence of this so called (Ní Scanaill et al., 2006) 'greying population' is the increased prevalence of the symptoms of Dementia among the older generation. Dementia has been described by the Institute of Psychiatry (Albanese et al., 2008) as:

A collection of symptoms, including a decline in memory, reasoning and communication skills, and a gradual loss of skills needed to carry out daily activities. These symptoms are caused by structural and chemical changes in the [human] brain as a result of physical diseases.

Dementia is considered to be one of the main causes of disability in later life, as it renders suffers unable to look after themselves adequately in the performance of daily tasks such as (Nugent et al., 2007) cooking, grooming, dressing, the management of medication and drink preparation. A higher relative proportion of the population now suffer from dementia than have every done so before and the current figure are set to rise over the coming decades (correlating with the statistics on ageing). More people are simply living longer, and this phenomenon can be attributed to better diet and ever improving healthcare. Recent research commissioned by the Alzheimer's Society (Albanese et al., 2008) revealed some facts about dementia which highlight the disease as a growing problem. In 2007 there were 683,597 people with dementia living in the UK (this included over 15,000 young people living with dementia), and this can be taken to represent one person in every 88 of the UK populous as a whole.

The research estimates there will be over 1,000,000 people with dementia in the UK by the year 2025. One third of the population aged 95 and over lives with dementia and 60,000 deaths a year can be directly attributable to the illness (i.e. to delay inception of the illness may save up to 30,000 of these lives per year). Two thirds of people with dementia live in the community i.e. in their own homes; while one third live in residential care homes. 64% of people living in care homes have some form of dementia and the overall financial cost of the disease to the UK is over £17.03 billion a year. Family carers of people with dementia save the UK over £6 billion per year.

The aforementioned report on current dementia statistics in the UK highlights the relatively few numbers of research papers released devoted to dementia and has stated that since 2002 they accounted for only 1.4% of papers i.e. the number of papers released is not relative to the scale of the problem. The top recommendation of the report indicates that addressing the problems associated with dementia should be made a national priority.

With Dementia being such a large problem now, it is easy to see how the problem will become exponentially worse when coupled with aforesaid statistics on ageing from the United Nations (2008). There should now be an urgency to find solutions to a healthcare problem that will be a permanent feature of societies in the Developed World.

This is now a challenge facing those developing assistive technologies and solutions and as such advancements in the area of Smart Homes will be the subject of this review. Smart Homes can be described living spaces facilitated with technology which acts to monitor the patient and intervene in activities of daily living (ADL) usually in a manner which is specific to the needs and illness of the inhabitant. The rest of this review is structured as follows; the next section will cover Smart Home projects presented by region for ease of reference. The following section will highlight various issues that are relevant to the widespread implementation of Smart Homes. The final section will summarize.

SMART HOME PROJECTS

Research conducted in the area of Smart Homes can be found in the Americas, Asia, Australia, New Zealand as well as most European countries. Noury et al. (2003) believe that the first ever attempt to monitor an inhabitant's daily activities can be attributed to Togawa et al. in a paper dating from 1988 (Tamura, Togawa & Murata, 1988). In this early work, quite rudimentary information regarding patient activity was collected and transferred immediately to care staff who would manually interpret the data, taking appropriate action when deemed necessary.

Ní Scanaill et al. (2006) suggest that the first ever system designed to monitor patient mobility can be attributed to Celler et al. dating from 1994 (Celler, Hesketh, Earnshaw & Ilsar, 1994) in which magnetic switches placed in doorways were used to determine presence. This early work also made use of Infrared sensors to pin-point location within a room as well as sensors to detect a range of sound types which had been attributed to common household tasks e.g. washing dishes etc.

Other preliminary research can be attributed to Chan et al. (Chan, Hariton, Ringeard & Campo, 1995) as well as two papers by Richardson et al. (Richardson, Poulson & Nicolle, 1993; Richardson, Poulson & Nicolle, 1993). All of this early research was important in that they attempted to reconcile the need for Smart Homes with the technology currently available; as technology advanced so too did the sophistication of the research projects, with Mozer probably being the first to introduce Artificial Intelligence to the Smart Home problem through the use of a Neural Network (NN) (1998). The following sub-sections outline Smart Home projects by region.

North America

Texas – The MavHome Project at the University of Texas in Arlington (Das, Cook, Bhattacharya, Heierman & Lin, 2002) uses a method of probability known as the *LeZi method* (Bhattacharya & Das, 1999) to learn and predict where an inhabitant is likely to go and which electric appliance they are likely to use based on previous actions and behaviours observed by the system. For example, whenever the patient is mid-way through a sequence of actions the intelligent agent can make several predictions regarding what is likely to happen with the action attributed with the highest probability forwarded as the most likely event. The training of the system in this manner is obviously then specific to the particular individual to which the system has been monitoring over time.

Colorado – In the Adaptive House (Mozer, 1998) the main goal is to balance energy consumption with the requirements and preferences of the patient. The main components to be controlled by the system include thermostats, central heating as well as illumination. The Adaptive House uses a reinforcement algorithm to gather process and predict information within the house.

Florida – The Gator-Tech Smart House by Helal et al. (2005) utilises an Ultrasonic position system to monitor and locate the inhabitant within the environment. This Smart Home is distinctive in that they use common household objects to relay information to the occupant, for instance they use a bathroom mirror to display information. For testing purposes they have also designed a robotic occupant named Matilda to occupy the house (Helal et al., 2003).

Massachusetts – The 'House of the Future' has been created by the Massachusetts Institute of Technology (MIT) (Intille, 2002; Tapia, Intille & Larson, 2004). Here a Bayesian Network model is used to learn patterns of activities from inhabitants which in turn are used to make behavioural predictions. The smart home has been facilitated with a variety of sensors attached to objects and furniture within the environment whilst inhabitants are also equipped with a PDA device, which they are asked to use to input data relating to their actions. Researchers at MIT have voiced disappointment with the results of their project in that whilst they admit that their predictive data has a greater probability than chance, the predictions are not as accurate or as robust as they would have hoped, leaving scope for future research.

Georgia Tech – The Aware Home (Kidd et al., 1999) developed by the Georgia Institute of Technology's main goal is to allow ageing in place for elders. They use several mathematical methods such as Markov Models as well as AI techniques such as Neural Networks to build up a pattern of behaviour of the inhabitant. For instance they use Smart Tiles to study the inhabitant's movements which can then be used to predict future behaviour. They have also used radio frequency identification (RFID) tagging to allow the inhabitant to locate common objects more easily (such as a wallet or keys). The Aware Home also uses audio in order to give inhabitants automatic reminders. Touch screen technology is also utilised to allow the inhabitant to interact with the system. Their Smart Home is quite large covering 5,040 square feet spread out over three floors.

Canada - Mihailidis et al. (Mihailidis, Carmichael & Boger, 2004) have designed a system in Toronto to facilitate 'ageing in place'. The main aim of their smart home is to track hand movements using cameras in order to facilitate the inhabitant with a cue or reminder when appropriate; achieved using intelligent multi-agent architecture, with an agent each being assigned to the roles of 'sensing, planning and prompting.'

Europe

United Kingdom – One of the more well-known UK Smart Home projects was that of the BT/Anchor Trust smart house deployed in England (Barnes, Edwards, Rose & Garner, 1998). The main technologies installed were Infrared (IR) sensors and magnetic switches as well as temperature sensors, all of which are used to build up 'normal' patterns of patient behaviour. The Smart Home could then intervene whenever substantial deviations occur from this usual behaviour which is flagged as abnormal.

Holland – The main goal of the so called 'model house' project from Eindhoven (Vermeulen & Berlo, 1997; Harrington & Harrington, 2000) was to ease and assist the transfer of important data between the 'patient, caregivers and services'. The design of the model house was completed in consultation with the Dutch Senior Citizens Label with sensors collecting information relating to patient activity as well as security systems to alert services of possible intruders. The house is also facilitated with several actuators to control environmental temperature, devices and illumination.

Multinational – A European collaboration undertaking called the 'ENABLE Project' ("ENABLE project", 2008) has partners from Norway, Ireland, Lithuania, Finland and the UK. ENABLE's objective is stated to "investigate whether it is possible to facilitate independent living of people with early dementia and to promote their wellbeing through access to technological systems and products." The project aims at developing a series of products that will assist a patient (specifically suffering from mild dementia) with memory retention by providing them with interactive tasks designed to be practical yet enjoyable. A motto of the project is to 'marry the new with the familiar', with an example of this being the use of a telephone to call relatives simply by pressing a picture of the family member to initiate the call, rather than the inhabitant attempting to recall complex phone numbers.

France – The HIS project (Virone, Noury & Demongeot, 2002) is a smart apartment located in the south eastern city of Grenoble in France. Infrared sensors are again used to monitor and record patient's circadian activity, this information is enriched as physiological data is also collected in order to raise an alarm if necessary.

Spain – A Smart Home development (Guillén, Arredondo, Traver, García & Fernández, 2002) aims at providing a safe environment in which inhabitants are monitored remotely via a medical call centre. Physiological data is collected from patients, which includes blood pressure, heart rate, body temperature and this information is sent to a local PC which in turn transfers the data to the 'health centre'. From there professionals can initiate a video-conference type of communiqué with patients to advice on medicinal prescriptions and well-being, among other interventions. The Smart home is at the testing stage and rather than simply being tested on students; gynaecology and pregnant patients have also been involved in analysing the system's efficiency.

Finland – a Smart Home system developed in Finland named TERVA, which is controlled centrally by a single laptop (Korhonen et al., 1998). Whilst the TERVA system monitors all of the standard bodily rhythms we have come to expect from such Smart Homes, such as heart rate etc. it differs from other smart home projects in that it also attempts to monitor patient mood and

emotional response. It achieves this by measuring the interaction and use of possessions and consumables within the home such as alcohol, tobacco and caffeine; with a correlation being drawn between an increase in usage and a lowering of mood or reaction to a negative event. Therefore the system would measure a very low mood based on the level of interaction detected. The information collected relating to mood is stored in a 'behaviour diary' which can be analysed to make predictive functions.

France – ERGDOM ("Project Ergdom", 2008) (Ergonomic Intelligent Interface in Domotic Functions) is a project from the LAAS research laboratory in France ("LAAS Laboratoire", 2008). The project is an attempt to optimise the cost of heating the smart home environment based on a probabilistic approach to ascertain which room the patient is likely to occupy within the home depending on previously observed movements collected through an indoor IR driven tracking system. The actuators can then intervene to automatically adjust the heating system on behalf of the patient. To achieve this, the system employs the use of an unspecified learning algorithm. Sensors are deployed in a regular pattern thus leaving scope to benefit from research into the optimisation of the sensors within the environment.

Northern Ireland – a Smart Home research laboratory has been implemented at the University of Ulster near Belfast (Nugent, Mulvenna & Hong, in press). The current lab consists of two rooms namely a living room and a kitchen both of which are facilitated with an array of sensors pertaining to several projects running concurrently. Sensors deployed include pressure mats, magnetic switches and RFID tagging. Research lead Prof. Chris Nugent has recently planned to expand this lab to include other household rooms to enlarge the scope of research potential. Projects operating out of this lab include Cogknow ("Cogknow", 2008).

Cogknow aims to assist sufferers of mild dementia in their own homes focusing on the concept of 'cognitive reinforcement' to aid remembering, facilitating social contact, supporting activities of pleasure and the enhancing of feelings of safety (Davies et al., in press). Other research pertaining to this smart lab include the Smart Home Simulator (SHS) which is a virtual testing system modelled on the University of Ulster Smart Home (Poland, Nugent, Wang & Chen, in press). The SHS is used as a preliminary heuristics tool to investigate sensor deployments in virtual reality before they are implemented into the real smart lab at UUJ.

Australia & New Zealand

Sydney – Celler et al. (1995) at the University of New South Wales have pioneered a smart home system that aims at providing effective remote monitoring achieved by:

Continuously monitoring relatively simple parameters that measure the interaction between participants and their environment.

The aims of their project include an attempt to evaluate whether remote monitoring is a viable alternative to institutionalization with regard to Quality of Life (QoL). Other aims include developing data that could assist in pattern recognition for: "morbidity patterns associated with the ageing process". Celler et al. also state that the reliability of the technology is an issue which needs to be evaluated; however, they make no mention specifically to the increased quality of information that would be received from an *optimized* sensor network.

New Zealand – Olaf Diegel at Massey University (2005) has developed a smart system in which a wide array of physiological data is collected from a patient at the same time each day, with data collected ranging from blood sugar to lung capacity. The system contains a learned threshold (based on the data collected each day over a period of time) and when the system 'believes' the patient's physiological signs go beyond this threshold it makes a decision as to whether to

flag an alert. A main outcome of the research is that the system has been proven to improve the medication regimes of inhabitants.

Asia

Japan – Thirteen "Welfare-Techno Houses" (WTHs) (Yamaguchi, Ogawa, Tamura & Togawa, 1998; Tamura, Togawa, Ogawa & Yoda, 1998) have been constructed by the Japanese Ministry of International Trade and Industry to be used as a testing environment for new smart home technologies for which they have amassed a large amount of scientific data. Whilst most Smart Homes are deigned primarily with patients in mind, these WTHs also seek to improve the lives of carers looking after inhabitants. The homes are facilitated with medical devices to record electrocardiogram (ECG) data amongst other physiological signs as well as IR sensors and magnetic switches to record patient movements within the environment.

Japan – Andoh, Watanabe, Nakamura and Takasu (2004) have designed a smart home that specifically monitors physiological patterns associated with sleep. They take particular interest in sleep as they operate under the hypothesis that a correlation can be drawn between decline in sleep and susceptibility to 'physical strength weakening' in elders. They have also developed an algorithm that can analyse and detect the different stages of sleep by accounting for 'bio data' including heart rate, breathing, bodily movements as well as snoring.

Korea – Researchers from Korea (Ha, Lee & Lee, 2006) have deployed 12 PIR sensors in an evenly distributed fashion) in the ceiling of a room measuring 4 x 4 x 2.5 metres. The goal of the location recognition system is to determine lifestyle and 'state of health' of inhabitants. They state that the next step in their research is to develop an algorithm that will have the ability to determine the individual paths of multiple inhabitants of the space concurrently.

Japan – Yamazaki (2006) constructed a smart home called the "Ubiquitous Home", which it is maintained to be superior to other smart home projects for 3 main reasons. Firstly Yamazaki states to have 'enhanced sensor ubiquity'; which simply means that sensors are omnipresent. Secondly, Yamazaki claims to have created a "test bed for specific Japanese services". The litigious advantage of this is not further elaborated on in the literature, whilst the third stated advantage is that he has introduced robotics into the environment to assist the inhabitant with tasks. The environment is quite large in comparison with other Smart Homes which normally only comprise of a few rooms, whilst the Ubiquitous Home encompasses an entire apartment. Cameras and Microphones are contained within each room, as well as floor pressure sensors and IR sensors. They also make use of active and passive RFID systems with information being correlated via the use of tags worn by the inhabitant. Accelerometers are also used in the environment situated underneath the bedroom floor; here they are used for the same purpose as floor pressure sensors, however, they are valued for their higher rate of accuracy. A plasma screen is also used to convey audio-visual information to the inhabitant. The system at present boasts 3 context aware services namely: 'TV Programme Recommendation', 'Cooking Recipe Display' and 'Forgotten-Property Check service'.

Japan – At the University of Tokyo, Noguchi, Mori & Sato (2002) have developed a smart home to monitor activities, record and analyse data. The main goal of the project is defined to sustain the normal daily activities of an inhabitant. Objects, appliances and furniture within the environment are assigned states; with the collective states of these objects being used to define the 'room state'. The system also has the ability to infer in which room the patient currently occupies whilst even being able to detect specific hand movements in certain locations, such as on the kitchen table, which is used to build up a wealthy picture of current activity. Issues within Smart Home Research

ETHICS & SMART HOMES

Several Ethical Issues exist within smart home research and development. Firstly the implementation of Smart Homes may leave recipients with a sentiment of removal of personal choice; much in the same way that many elders may not necessarily wish to be institutionalized in a care home. The reservation to choose whether or not to have assistive technology deployed within a person's home should be respected at all times; even if the choice not to have such technology installed is against the recommendations and/ or wishes of healthcare professionals and care givers. Obviously circumstances for non-consensual intervention on the part of professionals are cases for executive decision. Ní Scanaill et al. (2006) in their *Review of Approaches to Mobility Tele-monitoring* state that:

The decision-making process for selecting a telemonitoring system should be similar to the decision-making process used when selecting a therapy.

This comment highlights the importance and respect that would be attributed to such an assessment.

Research into the acceptability of domotic systems conducted by Peeters (2000) established that elderly people were indeed found to decline the implementation of smart home systems due to an apparent fear than such a system may insinuate to friends and family that their health had deteriorated to a stage whereby they needed to be monitored; they feared this would render them categorized socially as being decrepit and feeble. The abovementioned paper also indicated that seniors were likely to reject such a system in that, due to their operation (relating to location, communication methodology or data gathering practice) inhabitant's may have to alter their daily living patterns or activities (commonly referred to as ADLs or Activities of Daily Living in the literature). This, they feared, would result in them having to 'act' in a certain manner to satisfy the requirements of the system. An example of this may be that a patient may feel they have to follow a strict sequence when taking medication in order for the system to correctly log that the medication has been taken according to the programmed 'rules'. This would place a real or imagined stress on the patient to carry out the operation 'correctly' in order to ensure any alert would not sound. Although this may not be the case, in that the system may be fully capable to deal with such ambiguity, the inhabitant may be unaware of such technical competencies and a taxing preoccupation may develop whereby the patient feels compelled to 'behave in a certain way'.

Another 'fear' from the report (Peeters, 2000) was that of costs (an issue that will be discussed in more depth in a section). Nevertheless, having made these points, it is important to point to other research in which elders have expressed approval for the implementation for smart home technology, as they believe the benefits outweigh the perceived drawbacks.

Brownsell, Bradley, Bragg, Catlin and Carlier (2000) in their paper *Do community alarm users want Telecare?* Surveyed 176 seniors from the United Kingdom who live in the community (mean age 76 years) and found that the majority of respondents approved a system in their home that monitored for falls. Such a system was perceived as an increase in the quality of medical attention currently received by the elders. This evidence was compounded by the fact that 21% of elders who had suffered a collapse in the previous 12 month period prior to the study had inadvertently refused any devices into their home specifically designed to detect falls. Furthermore a similar study on attitudes conducted by Demiris et al. (2006) found that participants expressed an encouraging outlook on the potential of smart home technology; with a main benefit perceived as being the swift post-detection of emergencies and the ability to raise the alarm automatically. The respondents (5 men

and 9 women) however, expressed less enthusiasm for a system that would pro actively collect data to detect deteriorating patterns of behaviour as a tool for predicting adverse events. More sophisticated 'sounding' functions of such a system seemed to be met with an inherent scepticism, possibly a result of the fact that the current old and older old populations still feel disassociated with such high levels of technology; in contrast to how younger generations feel intrinsically at ease encircled by technology in their daily lives and activities.

During the 'e-Health Ethics Summit' which was organized by the Internet Healthcare Coalition in Washington DC in 2000, a code of ethics was unveiled for the first time concerning the area of *eHealth* ("E-Health Ethics", 2008). The document delineates eight main moral areas of eHealth to include accountability, informed consent, professionalism, quality, honesty, openness, privacy and responsible partnering. The code's main goal is for interventionists to obtain explicit informed consent, and whilst any information collected about a patient must be disclosed and traceable to the patient at all times without exception. A copy of the eHealth Code of Ethics can be located at e-Health Code (2008).

PRIVACY

Smart Home technology has the potential to collect vast amounts of information regarding an individual's lifestyle, current health status, potential health status and likes and dislikes. Many industry standards exist whereby organizations have to account for the collection, storage and uses of data obtained about private citizens. Whilst the collection and analysis of sensitive information may be crucial to the successful operation of a smart home; ironically, however, the very same information could "pose the threat of violating inhabitants' privacy" (Babbit, 2006). The area of 'fair information practice principles' has not been entirely overlooked in the literature and several attempts have been made to provide guidelines for the protection of privacy and the control of sensitive information (Federal Trade, 1998; OCED Guidelines, 1980).

Problems that may arise out of the mismanagement of private information could have intrusive and highly detrimental effects to the inhabitant of a smart home. For example in countries that operate a private healthcare system; if information collected via smart home sensor was somehow made available (intentionally or unintentionally) to insurance companies, this data could be used to manipulate or invalidate a patient's level of protection. The consequences of which may include loss of medical cover, inability to obtain cover or the possibility of being 'black-listed' against certain forms of medical protection based on information that was passively collected about an inhabitant in their own home.

Privacy concerns were also voiced by Chan, Estève, Escriba & Campo (2008) who state that:

It is important to verify that the lines of communication are safe and secure, that they ensure perfect confidentially, and that it is impossible for a third party to intercept the data on purpose or by accident. Furthermore data must be flawless and uncorrupted to ensure its correct interpretation and high quality care.

To adequately address these smart home privacy issues Ryan Babbit, at the Iowa State University has proposed a Privacy Management System (PMS) (Babbit, 2006) that gives smart home users a greater level of access and control over information stored about their activities and behaviours. It is envisioned that the modular design of the PMS will allow for its deployment to any smart home regardless of configuration or number of inhabitants. A further privacy model designed specifically for Smart Homes have been designed by Fischer-Hubner and Ott (1998).

LEGAL CONCERNS

The issue of malpractice is a growing concern within Smart Home implementations, especially in the United States, where most aspects of medical care is privatised. Chan, Estève, Escriba & Campo (2008) state that:

[Policy makers should] anticipate the legal conflicts that could arise between recipients and providers of remote care. For example long distance medical personnel might be held accountable for misinterpreting the client's vital signs and symptoms.

The issue can be highlighted with the following hypothetical scenario: an individual refuses institutionalization and instead opts for the implementation of assistive technology within the home on the basis that it will prevent against x, y and z. The smart home is operated as a joint effort between two institutions or organizations, one situated in the recipient's host country with the other situated outside of the recipient's legal jurisdiction in a different country. A situation arises in which the smart home fails catastrophically in preventing x, y or z, or indeed is the actual direct cause of illness or injury. What legal recourse does the recipient have not only to the organization within his/ her country but also to the second organization operating in an entirely different jurisdiction?

It may be because of problems like this that have led researchers such a Cwiek, Rafig, Qamar, Tobey & Merrel (2007) to conclude that the on-the-ground implementation of Smart Homes have been hampered in the USA by the fact that the practice of medical care (and their associated laws) is limited to state borders, with individual states operating in a autonomous fashion from one another. As such sufficient laws do not yet exist that would allow for more geographically flexible deployment of such medical implementations.

Daly (2000) states in his paper *Telemedicine: the invisible legal barriers to the healthcare of the future* that such legal worries regarding Smart Homes are a huge barrier to the progression of Smart Homes into wider society, whilst simultaneously leaving recipients in a legal limbo as to their rights to prosecution or compensation should problems arise. Daly goes on to argue that it is because of reasons such as these, elderly or disabled are ultimately being deprived of the considerable benefits to quality of life that a Smart Home system could provide.

To further exemplify how such legal inadequacies may affect the global development of Smart Homes; In Canada, the practice of Telemedicine is done so in what Chan, Estève, Escriba & Campo (2008) argue is a "legal vacuum", as no laws yet exist to regulate smart home installation or operation. Whilst on the other end of the scale, in Japan there is ambiguity as to whether or not it is actually illegal for a physician to diagnose a patient of an illness via smart home technology as within Japan's 'Doctors Act No. 20' it is law that "diagnosis and treatment should only be provided by examining the patient directly" (Chan, Estève, Escriba & Campo, 2008). It is hoped that policy makers act swiftly and in unison to fill the void that exists between smart home R&D and the legal roadblocks or lack thereof that threaten to impede smart home utilization, especially at a time when such solutions are becoming increasingly forlorn.

SOCIOECONOMIC AND COST ISSUES

"Telemonitoring is a cheaper option that hospitalization, clinical visits, or home help" (Council on Competitiveness, 1996). It is generally undisputed that remote monitoring is more cost effective than caring for individuals in hospitals or care homes, indeed much of the research being conducted concludes that caring for a patient in their own home could provide huge savings in the overall cost of care for the state as well as individuals and their families. For example, Dansky, Thompson and Sanner (2006) showed that patients receiving Telecare had overall lower costs than those in the control group who did not receive Telecare whatsoever, showing that smart home technology reduced medical bills.

In further support of this Bynum, Irwin, Cranford and Denny (2003) showed that in a telehealth project cost savings were achieved at the University of Arkansas for Medical Sciences. The three variables included: Family expenses, days missed at work and travel distance for medical care. The results found that 94% of patients would have to travel in excess of 70 miles for services had it not been for the implementation of Smart Home technology within their living environment. Also without Telecare implementations 84% of carers would miss at least one day at work; all-in-all 74% of families would be required to spend an extra $75 - $150 dollars on medical expenses during the period of study, had it not been for Telecare.

In Croydon, United Kingdom, a study was conducted whereby home visits where replaced by virtual telehealth visits resulted in savings of around £1M per annum (Tang & Venables, 2000). Chan, Estève, Escriba and Campo (2008) extrapolate this figure to conclude that when these savings are spread out over the entire UK population savings can thus be expected to be in the region of £0.2 Billion per annum.

CONCLUSION

The implementation of assistive technology into living environments in the form of Smart Homes may allow individuals suffering from age related illnesses such as mild dementia to remain independent for longer. Indeed it may be argued that interactive assistive systems could potentially slow the progression of the illness by stimulating cognitive function. For individuals suffering from chronic disabilities Smart Homes may offer a new level of autonomy from care givers by tailoring technology for specific needs. Current trends in global demography are mirrored by the explosion of Smart Home research, with these projects increasing in technical complexity and deliverability with successive iterations.

Nevertheless, Smart Homes are a relatively new area of research and as such many barriers relating to their effective implementation remain outstanding.

REFERENCES

Albanese, E., Banerjee, S., Dhanasiri, S., Fernandez, J. L., Ferri, C., Knapp, M., et al. (2007). *Dementia UK: A report into the prevalence and cost of dementia prepared by the Personal Social Services Research Unit (PSSRU) at the London School of Economics and the Institute of Psychiatry.*

Andoh, H., Watanabe, K., Nakamura, T., & Takasu, I. (2004). Network health monitoring system in the sleep. *Proceedings of the SICE Annual Conference* (pp. 1421–1424).

Babbit, R. (2006). Information Privacy Management in Smart Home Environments: Modeling, Verification and Implementation. *Proceedings of the 30th Annual International Computer Software and Applications Conference* (pp. 344-346).

Barnes, N. M., Edwards, N. H., Rose, D. A. D., & Garner, P. (1998). Lifestyle monitoring technology for supported independence. *Comput. Control End. J., 9*(4), 169–174. doi:10.1049/cce:19980404

Bhattacharya, A., & Das, S. K. (1999). LeZi-Update: an information-theoritic approach to track mobile users in PCS networks. *Proceedings of the 5th annual ACM/IEEE International conference on Mobile Computing and Networking* (pp. 1–12).

Brownsell, S. J., Bradley, D. A., Bragg, R., Catlin, P., & Carlier, J. (2000). Do community alarm users want Telecare? *Journal of Telemedicine and Telecare, 6*, 199–204. doi:10.1258/1357633001935356

Bynum, A. B., Irwin, C. A., Cranford, C. O., & Denny, G. S. (2003). The impact of telemedicine on patients' cost savings: some preliminary findings. *Telemedicine Journal and e-Health, 9*(4), 361–367. doi:10.1089/153056203772744680

Celler, B. G., Earnshaw, W., Ilsar, E. D., Betbeder-Matibet, L., Harris, M. F., & Clark, R. (1995). Remote monitoring of health status of the elderly at home. A multidisciplinary project on aging at the University of New South Wales. *International Journal of Bio-Medical Computing, 40*(2), 147–155. doi:10.1016/0020-7101(95)01139-6

Celler, B. G., Hesketh, T., Earnshaw, W., & Ilsar, E. (1994) An instrumentation system for the remote monitoring of changes in functional health status for elderly at home. *Proceedings of the 16th Annual International Conference of the IEEE EMBS, 2*, 908 – 909.

Chan, M., Estève, D., Escriba, C., & Campo, E. (2008). A review of smart homes—Present state and future challenges. *Computer Methods and Programs in Biomedicine, 91*, 55–81. doi:10.1016/j.cmpb.2008.02.001

Chan, M., Hariton, C., Ringeard, P., & Campo, E. (1995). Smart House automation system for the elderly and the disabled. *Proceedings of the IEEE International Conference on Systems, Man and Cybernetics* (pp. 1586-1589).

Cogknow, Helping people with mild dementia navigate their day (2008). Retrieved July 8 2008, from http://www.cogknow.eu/

Council on Competitiveness. (1996). Hi*ghway to Health: Transforming US Health Care in the Information Age*, Washington D.C.

Cwiek, M.A., Rafig, A., Qamar, A., Tobey, C., & Merrel, R.C. (2007). Telemedicine Licensure in the United State: the need for a cooperative regional approach. *Journal of Telemedicine, e-Health, 13*(2)141-147.

Daly, H. L. (2000). Telemedicine: the invisible legal barriers to the healthcare of the future. *Annals of Health Law*, 73–106.

Dansky, K. H., Thompson, D., & Sanner, T. (2006). A framework for evaluating eHealth research. *Evaluation and Program Planning, 29*(4), 397–404. doi:10.1016/j.evalprogplan.2006.08.009

Das, S. K., Cook, D. J., Bhattacharya, A., Heierman, E. O., & Lin, T. Y. (2002). The role of predicting algorithm in the MavHome smart home architecture. *IEEE Wireless Communications, 9*(6), 77–84. doi:10.1109/MWC.2002.1160085

Davies, R. J., Nugent, C. D., Donnelly, M. P., Hettinga, M., Meiland, F. J., & Moelaert, F. (2009). A user driven approach to develop a cognitive prosthetic to address the unmet needs of people with mild dementia. *Pervasive and Mobile Computing, 5*(3), 253–267. doi:10.1016/j.pmcj.2008.07.002

Demiris, G., Skubic, M., Rantz, M., Keller, J., Aud, M., Hensel, B., & He, Z. (2006). Smart Home Sensors for the Elderly: A Model for Participatory Formative Evaluation. *Proceedings of the IEEE EMBS International Special Topic Conference on Information Technology in Biomedicine* (pp. 1-4).

Diegel, O. (2005). Intelligent automated health systems for compliance monitoring. *Proceedings of the IEEE Region, 10*, 1–6.

E-Health Code of Ethics. (2000, May 24). *Journal of Medical Internet Research*. Retrieved July 10 2008, from http://www.jmir.org/2000/2/e9/

E-Health Ethics Summit Releases Code, the Industry Standard (2000). Retrieved July 10 2008, from http://www.thestandard.com/article/0,1902,11564,00.html

ENABLE project. (2008). *Can Technology help people with Dementia?* Retrieved July 7, from http://www.enableproject.org/

Federal Trade Commission. (1998). *Privacy Online: A report to Congress (Part III), Fair Information Practice Principles.* Retrieved Oct 21 2008, from http://www.ftc.gov/reports/privacy3/fairinfo.htm, June 1998.

Fischer-Hubner, S., & Ott, A. (1998). From a formal Privacy Model to its Interpretation. *Proceedings of the 21st National Information Systems Security Conference*

Guillén, S., Arredondo, M. T., Traver, V., García, J. M., & Fernández, C. (2002). Multimedia telehomecare system using standard tv set. *IEEE Biomed. Eng, 49*(12), 1431–1437. doi:10.1109/TBME.2002.805457

Ha, K. N., Lee, K. C., & Lee, S. (2006). Development of PIR sensor based indoor detection system for smart home. *Proceedings of the SICE-ICASE international Joint Conference* (pp. 2162-2167).

Harrington, T. L., & Harrington, M. K. (EDS.) (2000). *Gerontechnology Why and How.* Herman Bouma Foundation of Gerontechnology, Eindhoven, the Netherlands, Shaker Publishing B.V.

Helal, S., Mann, W., El-Zabadani, H., King, J., Kaddoura, Y., & Jansen, E. (2005). The Gator Tech Smart House: a programmable pervasive space. *Computer, 38*(3), 50–60. doi:10.1109/MC.2005.107

Helal, S., Winkler, B., Lee, C., Kaddoura, Y., Ran, L., Giraldo, C., et al. (2003). Enabling location-aware pervasive computing applications for the elderly. *Proceedings of the First IEEE International Conference on Pervasive Computing and Communications* (pp. 531-536).

Intille, S. S. (2002). Designing a home of the future. *IEEE Pervasive Computing / IEEE Computer Society [and] IEEE Communications Society*, *1*(2), 76–82. doi:10.1109/MPRV.2002.1012340

Kidd, C. D., Orr, R. J., Abowd, G. D., Atkeson, C. G., Essa, I. A., MacIntyre, B., et al. (1999). The Aware home: a living laboratory for ubiquitous computing research. *Proceedings of 2nd International workshop on cooperative buildings Integrating Information, Organization, and Architecture* (pp.191 – 198).

Korhonen, I., Lappalainen, R., Tuomisto, T., Koobi, T., Pentikainen, V., Tumisto, M., & Turjanmaa, V. (1998). TERVA: Wellness monitoring system. *Proceedings of the 20th Annual Conference of IEEE Engineering in Medicine and Biology Society, 4,* 1988-1991.

LAAS Laboratoire d'Analyse et d'Architecture des Systémes (2008). Retrieved July 8 2008, from http://www2.laas.fr/laas/2-4257-Home.php

Mihailidis, A., Carmichael, B., & Boger, J. (2004). The use of computer vision in an intelligent environment to support ageing in place, safety, and independence in the home. *IEEE Transactions on Information Technology in Biomedicine, 8,* 238–247. doi:10.1109/TITB.2004.834386

Mozer, M. C. (1998). The neural network house: an environment that adapts to its inhabitants. *AAAI spring symposium on intelligent. Environments,* 110–114.

National Institute for Statistics and Economic studies (2006). *Population Census.* Retrieved June 16 2008, from http://www.insee.fr/en/

Ní Scanaill, C., Carew, S., Barralon, P., Noury, N., Lyons, D., & Lyons, G. (2006). A Review of approaches to mobility telemonitoring of the elderly in their living environment. *Annals of Biomedical Engineering, 34*(4), 547–563. doi:10.1007/s10439-005-9068-2

Noguchi, H., Mori, T., & Sato, T. (2002). Construction of network system and the first step of summarization for human daily action data in the sensing room. Proceedings of the IEEE Workshop on Knowledge Media Networking (pp. 17–22).

Noury, N., Virone, G., Barralon, P., Ye, J., Rialle, V., & Demongeot, J. (2003). New trends in health smart homes. *Proceedings of the 5th International Workshop on Enterprise Networking and Computing in Healthcare Industry* (pp. 118–127).

Nugent, C. D., Davies, R. J., Hallberg, J., Donnelly, M. P., Synnes, K., Poland, M., et al. (2007). HomeCI – A visual editor for healthcare professionals in the design of home based care. *Proceedings of the IEEE EMBC.*

Nugent, C. D., Mulvenna, M. D., & Hong, X. (in press). Experiences in the development of a smart lab. *International Journal of Biomedical Engineering and Technology.*

OCED Guidelines on the Protection of Privacy and Transborder Flows of Personal Data. (1980). *Organization of Economic Cooperation and Development.* Retrieved Oct 21 2008, from http://www1.oecd.org/publications/e-book/9302011E.pdf

Office of Health Economics. (2008). *The Economics of Healthcare.* Retrieved June 23 2008, from http://www.oheschools.org/ohech6pg1.html

Peeters, P. H. (2000). Design criteria for an automatic safety-alarm system for the elderly. *Technology and Health Care, 8,* 81–91.

Poland, M.P., Nugent, C.D., Wang, H., & Chen, L. (in press). *Development of a smart home simulator for use as a heuristics tool for management of sensor distribution.*

Project ERGDOM. (2008). *Ergonomic Intelligent Interface in Domotic Functions.* Retrieved July 8 2008, from http://www.laas.fr/MIS/ERGDOM/Webergdom.htm#Contacts%202

Public Health Agency of Canada. (2008). *Seniors Health*. Retrieved June 23 2008, from http://www.phac-aspc.gc.ca/index-eng.php

Richardson, S. J., Poulson, D. F., & Nicolle, C. (1993). Supporting Independent living through adaptable smart home (ASH) technologies. *Human welfare and technologies: papers from the human service information technology applications (HUSITA) conference on information technology and the quality of life and services* (pp. 87-95).

Richardson, S. J., Poulson, D. F., & Nicolle, C. (1993). User requirements capture for adaptable smarter home technologies. *Proceedings of the 1ˢᵗ TIDE congress* (pp. 244-248).

Tamura, T., Togawa, T., & Murata, M. (1988). A bed temperature monitoring system for assessing movement during sleep. *Clinical Physics and Physiological Measurement, 9*, 139–145. doi:10.1088/0143-0815/9/2/006

Tamura, T., Togawa, T., Ogawa, M., & Yoda, M. (1998). Fully automated health monitoring system in the home. *Medical Engineering & Physics, 20*(8), 573–579. doi:10.1016/S1350-4533(98)00064-2

Tang, P., & Venables, T. (2000). Smart Home and Telecare. *Journal of Telemedicine and Telecare, 6*(1), 691–697. doi:10.1258/1357633001933871

Tapia, E. M., Intille, S. S., & Larson, K. (2004). Activity recognition in the home using simple ubiquitous sensors. *Proceedings of Pervasive, 2004*, 158–175.

United Nations Programme on Ageing. (2008). *The Ageing of the World's Population*. Retrieved June 23, 2008, from http://www.un.org/esa/socdev/ageing/popageing.html

Vermeulen, C., & van Berlo, A. (1997). A model house as platform for information exchange on housing. *Gerontechnology, A sustainable investment of the future* (pp. 337-339). IOS press

Virone, G., Noury, N., & Demongeot, J. (2002). A system for automatic measurement of circadian activity deviations in telemedicine. *IEEE Transactions on Bio-Medical Engineering, 49*, 1463–1469. doi:10.1109/TBME.2002.805452

Yamaguchi, A., Ogawa, M., Tamura, T., & Togawa, T. (1998). Monitoring behavior in the home using positioning sensors. *Proceedings of the 20th Annual International Conference of the IEEE Engineering in Medicine and Biology Society, 4*, 1977–1979.

Yamazaki, T. (2006). Beyond the Smart Home. *International Conference on Hybrid Information Technology, 2*, 350–355.

This work was previously published in International Journal of Ambient Computing and Intelligence (IJACI), Volume 1, Issue 4, edited by Kevin Curran, pp. 32-45, copyright 2009 by IGI Publishing (an imprint of IGI Global).

Chapter 25
Deepkøver:
An Adaptive Intelligent Assistance System for Monitoring Impaired People in Smart Homes

Mehdi Najjar
University of Moncton, Canada & University of Sherbrooke, Canada

François Courtemanche
University of Montreal, Canada

Habib Hamam
University of Moncton, Canada

Alexandre Dion
University of Sherbrooke, Canada

Jérémy Bauchet
TELECOM-SudParis, France

André Mayers
University of Sherbrooke, Canada

ABSTRACT

The chapter presents a novel modular adaptive artful intelligent assistance system for cognitively and/ or memory impaired people engaged in the realisation of their activities of daily living (ADLs). The goal of this assistance system is to help disabled persons moving/evolving within a controlled environment in order to provide logistic support in achieving their ADLs. Empirical results of practical tests are presented and interpreted. Some deductions about the key features that represent originalities of the assistance system are drawn and future works are announced.

DOI: 10.4018/978-1-60960-549-0.ch025

INTRODUCTION

Improvement of life quality in the developed societies has systematically generated an increase in the life expectancy. Nevertheless, the increasing number of elderly person requires more resources for aftercare, paramedical care and natural assistance in their habitats. The situation is further complicated if elders suffer from memory and/or cognitive disorders (Pigot et al., 2008). In this case a permanent assistance is necessary wherever they are. In recent years, some researches (Boger et al., 2006; Mihailidis et al., 2004; Snoek et al, 2008; Tam et al., 2006) proposed intelligent systems to assist elders with cognitive and/or memory troubles to carry out complex daily activities. To maximize their efficiency, such systems require continuous identification of what the impaired person is doing, recognizing its intentions and analyzing the tasks partially carried out; in order to help him/her (if need arise) to achieve and finalize what is already undertaken. However, several specialized works and thematic books (see for example Solie (2004), Beerman & Rappaport-Musson (2008) and Loverde (2009)) underline the difficulties encountered on the human, relational and social planes; also on the communication level between elders receiving aid and those who lend them assistance. A frequently raised key question which always returns is how convincing an elder to comply when s/he flatly refuses? Moreover, things are harder when dealing with stubborn aggressive seniors (Marcell & Shankle, 2001). In other words, how getting an elderly person to listen and make him/her apply optimal sequence of instructions for a safe realisation of activities of daily living (ADLs) without given him/her the impression to command him/her?

This chapter presents *DeepKover*, a novel modular adaptive *artful* intelligent assistance system for cognitively and/or memory impaired people engaged in the realisation of their ADLs.

The goal of this assistance system is to help disabled persons moving/evolving within a controlled environment in order to provide logistic support in achieving their ADLs. The *DeepKover* philosophy is to make the occupier of an intelligent habitat, which is an elderly person (and possibly stubborn and obstinate) feel in a position of leader; i.e., giving him/her the illusion of *"calling the tune"*. Thus, the system becomes user-friendly without showing any dominating or directive behaviour. But this is only an illusion; because for cases considered to be critical where the situation is likely to become alarming, and even dangerous, the system imposes its total control and acts in an authoritative way by refusing to the occupier the achievement of certain tasks and dictating its course of actions. Therefore, *DeepKover* plays a double game: an accompanying adviser for the elder on one hand and a *"partially high-handed"* regulator on another hand. In this sense, the assistance system reveals *"deep cover"* intrigues.

The detection of the undertaken activities (for example, preparing pasta in the kitchen, watching movie in the living room or taking a shower) is based on data that simulate information transmitted by sensors in an intelligent apartment. *DeepKover* calls a Hidden Markov Model (Rabiner, 1989) for the recognition of the activities in progress. A planning module uses Markov Decision Processes (Dietterich, 1998) in dynamic multi-tasks planning to help the elder achieve and finalize ADLs. The remainder of the article is organized as follow. Section 1 presents the modular architecture of *DeepKover* and describes its components. Section 2 is dedicated to the experimental validation where empirical results of practical tests are presented and interpreted. In section 3, we discuss the obtained results and draw some deductions about the key features that represent the originalities of *DeepKover*. We announce our future work in section 4 and in the last section – by way of conclusion – we sum up this research work.

Figure 1. General view of the architecture

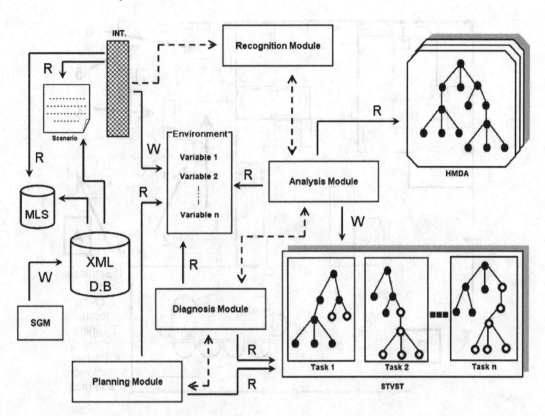

THE MODULAR ARCHITECTURE

The modular architecture is composed of five (5) modules: the scenarios generation module (SGM), the recognition module (RM), the analysis module (AM), the diagnosis module (DM) and the planning module (PM). These modules operate and handle shared data represented in XML structures. The modules communicate by messages. A database gathers randomly generated scenarios (via the SGM) which are used during simulations for the reconstitution of real events. Figure 1 illustrates the general view of the architecture.

The overall environment is an accessible structure. Data in the environment allow the modules to reason in order to properly achieve their functionalities. Modifying the environment is performed via an exclusive write access granted to only one component of the architecture (this detail is clarified below). To make the environment easier to consult, reading (R) is managed by a circular order. This can change if a module notifies another and requests its intervention when detecting anomalies or critical situations. The various modules of the architecture reason on data that are collected by parsing an XML file containing the scenario. As mentioned above, the latter represents a set of events reconstructing simultaneous achievements of several daily activities. Although they are generated randomly, these events are selected according to logical constraints. For example, for the scenario of realizing the *"coffee preparation"* activity, if the events *"coffeemaker alarm is ringing"*, *"coffee cup is full"* and *"sugar bowl is open"* were chronologically generated, then when the event *"coffee cup is clean"* is generated, it will not be accepted in the scenario.

Figure 2. An overview of the smart home

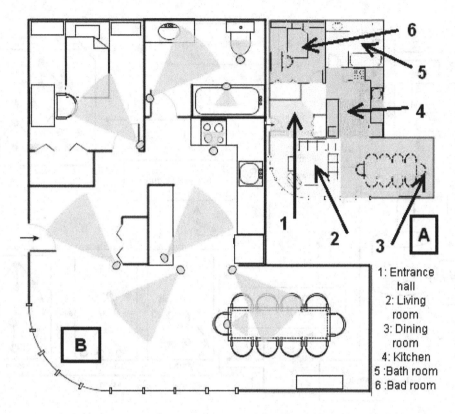

1: Entrance hall
2: Living room
3: Dining room
4: Kitchen
5 :Bath room
6 :Bad room

On the other hand, the event "*holding the coffee spoon*" will be added to the scenario.

An interpreter of scenarios (INT) scans the XML file and – at each temporal unit – sends information relating to one event to the recognition module (RM). Having the exclusive write access (W) on the environment, the interpreter updates it. The environment is a structure that recreates what really occurs in the intelligent apartment thanks to variables which represent all the detectable housing elements (e.g., furniture, kitchen utensils, taps, household electric appliances, etc). In a real context, the state of each detectable element is determined by a set of sensors. Our intelligent assistance system uses an ambient simulator. We have been inspired by *Actirec* (Bauchet & Mayers, 2005), a graphical environment that offers a platform to simulate daily life activities in smart homes. For example, Part A of Figure 2 illustrates an overview of the "*show*" apartment,

Part B illustrates the location of some sensors in the intelligent habitat and Figure 3 shows a partial view of the kitchen (covered by sensor S1) in which an event (e1) representing the opening of a cupboard door is detected (via a sensor embedded in the closet door).

Memorizing Activities

The set of temporary views of started tasks (STVST) constantly informs about the level of progression of each task, in terms of accomplished sub-tasks (recursively, of the sub-sub-tasks of each sub-task). The STVST is updated by the analysis module (AM) and consulted by the diagnosis module (DM). The hierarchical model of the defined activities (HMDA) defines, for each activity, its hierarchical structure, the concerned variables of the environment and their final states when the activity is accomplished. The HMDA also takes

Figure 3. Detection of an event (the cupboard door is open)

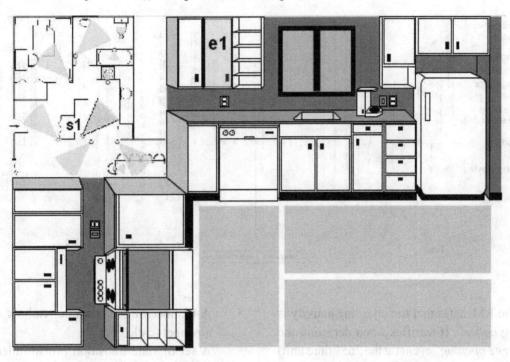

into account constraints of order, sequence and possible mutual exclusivenesses between sub-tasks of an activity.

The Recognition Module

As mentioned before, the recognition of activities is based on data that simulate information transmitted by sensors in the intelligent apartment. At each unit of time and for each sent datum, a Hidden Markov Model (HMM) of the recognition (incorporated into the recognition module) identifies the activity in progress (Rabiner, 1989). This is done by relying on the probability of transitions calculus between the defined states of the HMM. Probabilities of transitions are calculated and refined during the learning phase. This is generally done at the beginning of the simulation. An automatic training of the HMM is carried out by means of typical scenarios stored in the machine learning scenarios database (MLS, in Figure 1). In order to reinforce learning, some generated scenarios of the SGM, that present particular cases, are also

added to the MLS. Once an activity is recognized, the recognition module (RM) notifies the analysis module (AM). The latter examines the sequence of activities regarding the hierarchical model of the defined activities (HMDA) which links up each activity to its sub-tasks. In a recursive fashion, each sub-task is divided into an ordered set of "sub-subtasks". This recursion stops when components of a sub-task represent the perceived events (data from sensors) that are transposed in the environment.

For example, Figure 4 illustrates the recognition of a scenario – as further it advances – where gaps between the RM output (i.e., what RM thinks that is occurring) and the real execution of the scenario appear in dotted lines. Concretely, these differences are fully justifiable. In some cases, the RM identifies an activity and changes decision at the next temporal unit on the base of a new perceived event. Thus, the recognition module briefly misunderstands the situation. For example, as shows in Figure 4, following the "*sink faucet opening*" event detection (at the 263th time

Figure 4. An example of recognition during the execution of a scenario

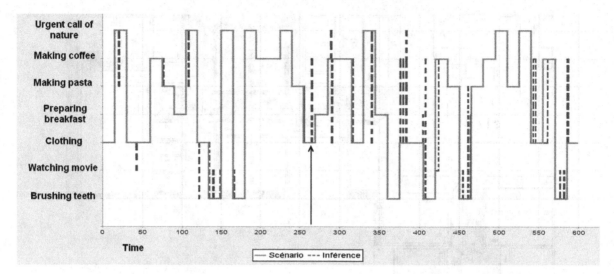

unit), the RM states that the on-going activity is *"making coffee"*. It rectifies when detecting the *"drawer#2 opening"* event (at the 265th time unit) and identifies that the activity which is really undertaken is *"preparing breakfast"*. This hesitation phenomenon is due to the presence of one or more common detectable objects which are shared by at least two activities (here, it is a question of *"sink faucet"*). In this case, the HMM probabilities of transitions and observations (events) come out in favour of the most likely activity.

The Hidden Markov Model

A Hidden Markov Model (HMM) is a finite set of states, each of which is associated with a probability distribution. Transitions among states are governed by a set of probabilities called *transition probabilities*. In a particular state an outcome (called *observation*) can be generated, according to the associated probability distribution. It is only the outcome, not the state, which is visible to an external observer and therefore states are hidden to the outside. An HMM is formally defined as:

- A number of states (called *N*) of the model.

- A number of observation symbols in the alphabet (called *M*).
- A set of state-transition probabilities $A = \{a_{ij}\}$, where:

$$a_{ij} = p\{q_{t+1} = j \mid q_t = i\},\ 1 \le i,j \le N \qquad (1)$$

and q_t denotes the current state. Transition probabilities should satisfy the following constraints:

$$a_{ij} \ge 0,\ 1 \le i,j \le N \qquad (2)$$

and

$$\sum a_{ij} = 1,\ 1 \le i,j \le N \qquad (3)$$

A probability distribution in each state $B = \{b_j(k)\}$, where

$$b_j(k) = p\{o_t = v_k \mid q_t = j\},\ 1 \le j \le N,\ 1 \le k \le M \qquad (4)$$

and where the parameter vector v_k denotes the kth observation symbol in the alphabet *M* and o_t the current observation at *t*. Following constraints must also be satisfied:

Figure 5. A part of the hidden Markov model

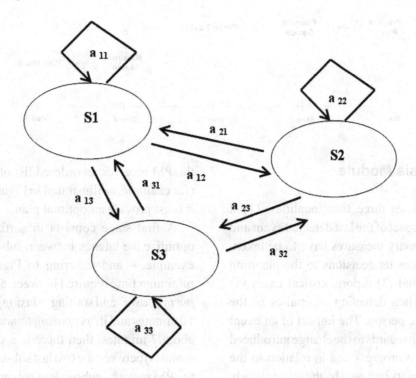

$$b_j(k) \geq 0,\ 1 \leq j \leq N,\ 1 \leq k \leq M \qquad (5)$$

and

$$\sum b_j(k) = 1,\ 1 \leq j \leq N,\ 1 \leq k \leq M \qquad (6)$$

The initial state distribution $\pi = \{\pi_i\}$, where:

$$\pi_i = p\ \{q_1 = i\},\ 1 \leq i \leq N \qquad (7)$$

Therefore, the following compact notation:

$$\lambda = (\Lambda,\ B,\ \pi) \qquad (8)$$

is generally used to denote an HMM with discrete probability distributions.

For example, Figure 5 shows a part of the hidden Markov model where the activity *"making coffee"* is represented by state *S1*. States *S2* and *S3* respectively designate, respectively, *"preparing breakfast"* and *"making pasta"*. Abstractedly, a_{ij} is

the probability of transition from state S_i to sate S_j and a_{ii} is the probably to remain in the same state.

The Analysis Module

The AM works symbiotically and in a bidirectional way with the RM. At each temporal unit, the latter notifies the analyser on a change in an activity in progress or a creation of a new one. The AM consults the environment to update the partial state of the activity. When detecting a new activity, the AM creates a view, initializes it and adds it to the set of temporary views of started tasks (STVST). The analysis consists of (1) scouring the hierarchical structure of the activity – in the HMDA– in a bottom/up way, starting from the leaf nodes (the non-decomposable events) in order to update one STVST partial view and (2) informing the diagnosis module (DM) of the last change.

Figure 6. An example of an ordered list of sub-activities given to the planner in input

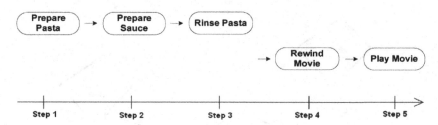

The Diagnosis Module

The DM possesses three functionalities: (1) it evaluates the impact of the last detected event and decides if necessary measures have to be taken, (2) communicates its decisions to the planning module (PM) and (3) reports critical cases via the interface when detecting anomalies in the behaviour of the person. The impact of an event is measured with regards to the change introduced in the activity in progress and in relation to the possible constraints imposed by the other already started activities. A recent event can develop an activity, suspend another, create a new one, bring about its resumption or belong to a set of disparate and singular events that are not defined in the HMDA. The impact is evaluated regarding to the partial states of all started tasks. A critical situation is detected when at least one constraint imposed by an activity in progress is violated. A constraint can be of chronological nature. For example, if the DM notes a time exceeding for tackling a sub-task or for the suspension of an activity. Constraints can also represent relations of sequences dependence. If no critical situation is detected, the DM simply notifies the PM. The latter is depicted in the next section.

The Planning Module

The planning module (PM) takes as input information provided by the analysis module. It aims to maintain the order of the undertaken sub-activities as it is defined in the HMDA. At each unit of time, the PM receives an ordered list of sub-activities (for example, as illustrated in Figure 6) for which it must provide an optimal plan.

A first stage consists in sorting this list to optimize the latency between sub-activities. For example, – and referring to Figure 6 – if the minimum time required between achieving "*preparing pasta*" and starting "*rinsing pasta*" is about 10 minutes and if "*preparing tomato sauce*" takes about 7 minutes, then there is a slack period (3 minutes) between the two last sub-activities. Thus, the PM moves a subsequent sub-activity towards this place to fill the latency (see Figure 7). In this sense, the planner respects the order of the activities undertaken by the occupant but finds the best way of interleaving their achievements. In a real context, this kind of temporal dependence between sub-activities is frequent when realizing activities of the daily living (ADLs). Thus, our hierarchical decomposition of activities allows a more profitable planning in terms of duration of the suggested plan.

The second stage consists in finding an optimal sequence of actions to achieve each sub-activity starting from the current state of the environment (variables' values at a given time t). The planner applies the Value Iteration algorithm (Bellman, 1957) to find a partial plan related to each sub-activity. The Value Iteration (VI) algorithm aims to find the minimal set of actions leading from the initial state of the activity (values of the variables of the environment at t) to a final state. Figure 8 shows the optimal sequence of actions (proposed by the planner) to carry out each one

Figure 7. Interleaving sub-activities thanks to latency optimisation

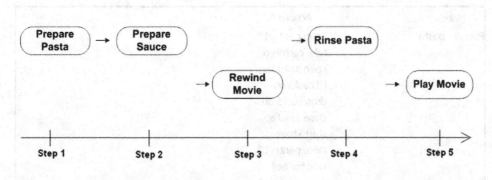

Figure 8. An example of optimal sequence of actions

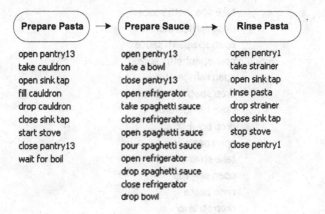

of the sub-activities started by the occupier. The VI algorithm is depicted in the next sub-section.

During the third stage, all the partial plans are assembled to form the total plan. Figure 9 shows the suggested series of actions allowing the elderly person to finish all the started activities. This plan is valid at t, according to the current intentions of the occupier. At $t+1$, the list of the activities, provided to the planning module (by the analysis module) will be modified according to the last action undertaken by the person. This modified list reflects the inferences made by the recognition module on data of the environment to determine the current activity in progress.

Since the occupier of the intelligent apartment is completely free to follow the proposed plan or to ignore it, the system must be reactive and able to be readjusted at any time to provide assistance to the elder. Thus, this malleable planning approach allows real-time monitoring and assisting subjects evolving/moving in the environment. The planner uses Markov Decision Processes (MDPs) in dynamic multi-tasks planning to help memory-impaired elders achieving and finalizing their ADLs already undertaken.

The Markov Decision Processes

To give a definition of MDPs, we take up the introductive proposal of Dietterich (1998) by considering the general AI problem in which an agent interact with an environment. At each time step, the agent observes the environment, chooses and executes an action and receives a real value

Figure 9. The suggested series of actions at t to finish all started activities

Activities	Actions
Prepare pasta	open pantry13
	take cauldron
	open sink tap
	fill cauldron
	drop cauldron
	close sink tap
	start stove
	close pantry13
	wait for boil
Prepare sauce	open pentry13
	take a bowl
	close pentry13
	open refrigerator
	take spaghetti sauce
	close refrigerator
	open spaghetti sauce
	pour spaghetti sauce
	open refrigerator
	drop spaghetti sauce
	close refrigerator
	drop bowl
Rinse pasta	open pentry1
	take strainer
	open sink tap
	rinse pasta
	drop strainer
	close sink tap
	stop stove
	close pentry1

reward. The goal of the agent is to choose actions in order to maximize the sum of these rewards. For the case where the agent can perceive the entire state of the environment and where the actions are stochastic (i.e., the state resulting from an action is a probabilistic function of the previous state and the chosen action), the resulting sequential decision problem is known as a Markov decision process (Puterman, 1994).

A MDP is a 4-tuple $<S, A, P, R>$ where S is a finite set of states, A is a finite set of actions, P is a transition distribution $P: S \times A \times S \rightarrow (0,1)$ such that $P(s,a,s')$ is a probability distribution over

S for any $s \in S$ and $a \in A$; and $R: S \times A \rightarrow IR$ is a bounded reward function. Intuitively, $P(s,a,s')$ denotes the probability of moving to state s' when action a is performed at state s, while $R(s,a)$ is the immediate reward associated with the resulting transition.

Because MDPs provide a very general model of sequential decision-making under uncertainty, they have provided a foundation of much recent work on probabilistic planning where it is assumed that the agent (in an artificial intelligence context) knows the state transition distribution P and the reward function R. Thus, given an MDP, the ob-

Figure 10. The Value Iteration algorithm.

$$V_0(s) \leftarrow 0 \quad \forall s \in \mathcal{S}$$
$$V_1(s) \leftarrow R(s,a) \quad \forall s \in \mathcal{S} \quad \forall a \in \mathcal{A}$$
$$t \leftarrow 1$$
while $\exists s \in S$ such that $|V_t(s) - V_{t-1}(s)| > \epsilon$
    forall $s \in \mathcal{S}$
        forall $a \in \mathcal{A}$
$$Q(s,a) \leftarrow R(s,a) + \gamma \sum_{s' \in S} T(s,a,s')V_{t-1}(s')$$
$$V_t(s) \leftarrow \max_a Q(s,a)$$
$$\pi(s) \leftarrow \arg\max_a Q(s,a)$$
$$t \leftarrow t+1$$

jective is to construct a policy that maximizes the expected accumulated reward over some horizon of interest. In other words, it consists in inferring a policy $\pi: S \rightarrow A$ which indicates for each state $s \in S$ what action $a \in A$ should be performed. The optimal policy π^* maximizes the expected cumulative reward received by the agent. There are many algorithms for finding optimal policies, such as the dynamic programming algorithms value iteration and policy iteration (Puterman, 1994). Most of these algorithms involve computing a function known as the value function $V(s)$ which estimates the expected cumulative reward of starting in state s and following the optimal policy. Formally, the value function is given by the Bellman equation:

$$V(s) := \max_a \sum_{s'} P(s'|s,a)\big[R(s'|s,a) + V(s')\big] \tag{9}$$

A simple variant of the Value Iteration algorithm is expressed by the algorithm illustrated in Figure 10.

EXPERIMENTAL VALIDATION

To validate our approach, we have performed several series of simulations representing dif-ferent sequences of activities that a person can perform. The experimental validation has been made according to two main lines. Seven experiments were conducted to (1) evaluate the efficiency of the recognition process, while two other experiments were achieved for (2) testing the planning approach and quantifying its added value (i.e., the improvement via optimization of latencies). The following sub-sections report on the experimental validation details and interpret the empirical results.

The Recognition Process

In all experiments, the recognition efficiency (RE) was measured. RE denotes the similarity between what RM *thinks* that is occurring and the real scenario execution and thus, allows measuring the efficiency of the recognition technique.

Table 1 shows three experiments with variable levels of complexity (from 1 to 7). The duration of each experiment is 600 units of time. These experiments differ by the manner of carrying out activities. Various ways of making the same activity were synthesized within the HMDA (see section 1.1) and taken into account during the test process. For example, in "*Preparing Breakfast*", the number and the order of the sub-activities in Experiment 1 are different from those in Experiment 2 and Experiment 3. The goal of this series

Table 1. The recognition efficiency regards the number of activities and their ways of realization

Number of Activities (NA)	Recognition Efficiency (%)			Mean (Activities)
	(Experiment 1)	(Experiment 2)	(Experiment 3)	
1	81,41	95,81	82,11	86,44
2	90,33	85,33	88,71	88,12
3	81,76	89,67	83,22	84,88
4	79,21	85,33	91,78	85,44
5	71,33	86,91	91,33	83,19
6	80,17	83,72	78,81	80,91
7	83,06	80,83	84,21	82,71
Mean (Experiment)	81,04	86,81	85,74	**85,18**
Other characteristics: Noise (33%) – No-Observation (10%) – No-Normalization – Time (600)				

Table 2. The recognition efficiency regards the No-Obs variation and the normalisation factor

No-Observations (%)	Recognition Efficiency (%)	
	(Experiment 4) Normalization (No)	(Experiment 5) Normalization (60%)
0	88,31	87,15
5	87,98	91,49
10	87,31	82,97
15	87,98	85,64
20	80,31	82,64
25	82,47	84,64
30	76,63	88,65
35	70,12	84,64
40	69,95	79,63
Mean	81,23	85,36
Other characteristics: Noise (5%) – Time (600) – NA (7)		

Table 2 illustrates two experiments with durations of 600 units of time and a noise probability of 5%. During these tests, the normalization has been disabled for Experiment 4 but enabled for Experiment 5 and its value was fixed to 0.6. In addition, for each value of the No-Observations factor, randomly generated scenarios including 7 simultaneous interlaced activities (NA = 7) were used to measure the recognition efficiency. Here, the goals were (1) to verify if the enabling/disabling of the normalization affects the recognition effectiveness; and if it is the case, (2) to check whether it represents a considerable difference. The No-Observations (No-Obs) phenomenon and the concept of normalization are explained in section 2.3.

Table 3 shows two other experiments with durations of 600 units of time and also involving 7 simultaneous interlaced activities (NA = 7) with a No-Obs coefficient of 0.1 and without normalization. The percentage of noise was varied from 0 to 0.4. In Experiment 6, the fixed period of time (FPT) has been initialized to 10 time-units and has been changed to 15 time-units in Experiment 7. The FPT is the duration exclusively allotted to only one activity during the execution of a scenario. This parameter belongs to the set of variables of the scenario generation module (SGM, see section 1). Note that the RM is unaware of the

of experiments is to measure the efficiency of the recognition (1) by fixing the percentage of noise (33%), that of the No-Observations phenomenon and the enabling/disabling of the normalization (see section 2.3); and (2) while varying the manners of realization of the activities. The noise phenomenon represents disparate unlinked events that are randomly inserted (one by one) in an activity during its realization.

Table 3. The recognition efficiency versus the noise variation and the FPT parameter

Noise (%)	Recognition Efficiency (%)		
	(Experiment 6) FPT (10 time units)	(Experiment 7) FPT (15 time units)	Mean
0	87,31	86,48	86,91
5	86,98	86,23	86,61
10	85,31	84,14	84,73
15	84,47	83,97	84,22
20	83,64	81,81	82,72
25	82,31	79,47	80,89
30	80,63	81,98	81,31
35	81,80	80,63	81,22
40	82,31	82,97	82,64
Mean	83,86	83,07	**83,47**

Other characteristics: No-Observation (10%) – NA (7) No-Normalization – Time (600)

Table 5. The optimized plans duration regards the number of activities after N tests

Number of Activities (NA)	Optimized Plans Duration (T.U.) (Experiment 9)	
	Mean	Standard Deviation
1	4,347	2,564
2	7,758	2,592
3	10,997	2,452
4	14,630	2,701
5	17,653	2,417
6	21,106	2,023
7	24,496	1,553

Noise (33%) – No-Observation (10%) – No-Normalization – N = 250

FPT value. Here, the goal was to verify the following hypothesis: whatever the FPT value, allowed for the execution of an activity during the synthesis of a scenario, the noise percentage variation does not affect the recognition efficiency.

Table 4. The non-optimized plans duration regards the number of activities after N tests

Number of Activities (NA)	Non-Optimized Plans Duration (T.U.) (Experiment 8)	
	Mean	Standard Deviation
1	4,694	2,590
2	9,316	3,411
3	14,175	3,608
4	18,876	3,792
5	23,621	3,113
6	27,917	2,641
7	32,800	1,694

Noise (33%) – No-Observation (10%) – No-Normalization – N = 250

The Planning Process

Table 4 and Table 5 show – respectively – two additional experiments with variable number of activities (NA, from 1 to 7), a noise probability of 33%, a No-Obs coefficient of 0.1 and without normalization. For each complexity level, 250 randomly generated scenarios (N) were run. Table 4 (respectively, Table 5) illustrates means of the non-optimized (respectively, optimized) corresponding plans duration (in time units) and the standard deviations where N = 250 and $1 \leq NA \geq 7$. Table 6 partially takes up data of Tables 4 and 5, and shows the saved time – in time units (TU) and percentage – thanks to the optimization process.

EMPIRICAL RESULTS INTERPRETATION

The Recognition Process

In Table 1, the number of simultaneous activities carried out by the occupant represents the complexity of the whole task. Each activity is decomposed in turn in sub-activities; and so on

Table 6. The time saved

Number of Activities (NA)	Plans Duration (T.U.)		Saving	
	Non-Optimized (Experiment 8)	Optimized (Experiment 9)	Time saved (T.U.)	Time saved (%)
1	4,694	4,347	0,346	7,376
2	9,316	7,758	1,558	16,719
3	14,175	10,997	3,178	22,417
4	18,876	14,630	4,246	22,492
5	23,621	17,653	5,968	25,264
6	27,917	21,106	6,811	24,397
7	32,800	24,496	8,304	25,318
Noise (33%) – No-Observation (10%) – No-Normalization – **N = 250**				

recursively. For each complexity level, activities were chosen randomly. The arithmetic mean of the recognition percentage is respectively 81.04, 86.81 and 85.74 for Experiment 1, 2 and 3. The mean by activity (all experiments joined) was also calculated. This lies between the minimum value of 80.91 and the maximum of 88.12. The absolute mean of the recognition is about 85.18. Figure 1 graphically summarises the data of Table1.

The ability of the Markov model to recognize the activity in progress and to identify the synthesized scenario is strengthened thanks to the learning process that the HMM has undergone and which allow refining the transitions probabilities. Abstractedly, the learning process helps the HMM determine the probable current state with respect to the previous state and to the transition probability following the last observation. The transition probabilities are calculated thanks to the Baum-Welch algorithm (Baum et al., 1970; Welch, 2003). This is a generalized expectation-maximization (EM) technique that computes maximum likelihood estimations for an HMM parameters, when given only observations as training data. The algorithm (1) calculates the forward probability and the backward probability for each HMM state and (2) determines the frequency of the transition-observation pair values.

Both Table 1 and Figure 11 show that the performance of the model relating to the recognition of activities – by taking into account various manners of their achievements – lies in a very acceptable range (88.12% in the best of the cases and 80.91% in the worst).

In intelligent ambient systems and especially those embedded within smart homes, treating and managing latencies are frequent key issues (Courtemanche et al., 2008). These *periods of inactivity* represent durations when the system (by means of sensors) is unable to detect what the occupier is doing; for example, when the person is in a mode unexpected to be detectable. Concretely, if we consider the activity *"Watching a DVD movie"* and during the viewing of the film, if the DVD player is playing, the remote control is near the occupant who is sitting on his sofa and nothing else happens, then the movement sensors and the electromagnetic sensors dissimulated in the living room furniture are not able to inform the system when the occupier asleep seated[1]. Therefore, *"Watching a DVD movie"* contains much time where no observation can be emitted from the smart home to the HMM. This is what we call the No-Observations phenomenon. For example, in our tests, allotting a coefficient of 0.35 for No-Obs amounts to synthesize random scenarios where, for each included activity, 35% of its whole

Figure 11. Recognition percentage variation regarding the number of activities (curve A) and experiments 1, 2 and 3 (curve B)

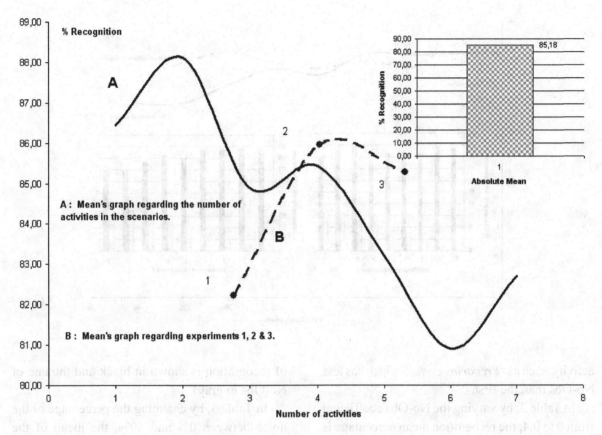

duration will consist of No-Obs (Table 2, Experiments 4 and 5). In a practical context, a high No-Obs coefficient associated with one or several activities gives arise to serious problem for an HMM. Due to the distribution probability B_j *(k)* (section 1.2.1, formula 4) – which privileges high No-Obs activities on the reception of a No-Obs observation, these activities become attractive states within the Markov model. This swindles the HMM to detect the activity in progress. The normalization represents a smart device to overcome this problem.

In probability theory (Feller, 1968), the Bayes' law is often used to compute posterior probabilities given observations. More precisely, the theorem relates that the posterior probability measure is proportional to the product of the prior probability

measure and a likelihood function. Abstractedly, this implies that one must multiply (or divide) by a normalizing factor in order to assign 1 as a value measure of the whole space (Tijms, 2004) (i.e., the sum of all possible observations; which is quiet conform to formula 6 of section 1.2.1).

In our approach, we adopt an equitable probability distribution of No-Obs occurrences over all the activities. For example, a normalization factor (NF) of 0.6 (Table 2, Experiment 5) allots a uniform probability of 60% of No-Obs (B_j*(No-Obs)* = 0.6); i.e., we consider that for any activity, and on each unit of time, there is 60% of chance that the observed event is a No-Obs. Thus, the normalization avoids that an activity such as *"Watching a DVD movie"* – for example – negatively influences the recognition of another

Figure 12. Details of Experiments 4 and 5 (% of recognition vs. % of No-Obs) and the recognition variation in relation to the No-Obs variation, depending on the normalization factor

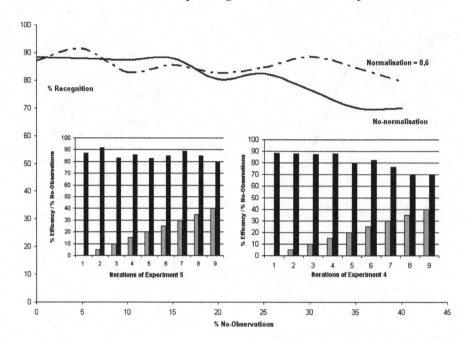

activity, such as "*Preparing coffee*" which has less No-Obs than the first.

In Table 2, by varying the No-Obs coefficient from 0 to 0.4, the recognition mean percentage is 81.23 for Experiment 4 (without normalization) and 85.36 for Experiment 5 (with NF = 0.6). Theoretically, the normalization factor is computed using the probability mass function of the Poisson distribution (Evans, Boersma, Blachman & Jagers, 1988).

Table 2 shows that the HMM performance improves thanks to the normalization (in the best of the cases, by 14% for a No-Obs coefficient of 0.35). Note that even without normalization, the recognition efficiency does not drop beyond 69.95% (for a No-Obs coefficient of 0.4 in Experiment 4). This is due to the pre-tests learning process which takes into account the combination of the training scenarios that represent, as mentioned before, various manners of realizing the activities. Figure 12 shows graphic details of the experiments of Table 2 (where the percentage

of recognition is shown in black and the one of No-Obs in gray).

In Table 3, by changing the percentage of the noise between 0% and 40%, the mean of the recognition percentage is 83.86 for Experiment 6 (with FPT = 10) and 83.07 for Experiment 7 (with FPT = 15). The main remark is that the recognition efficiency (RE) measurements are very close for a given noise coefficient (N). For example, where N = 0.15, RE = 84.47 (with FPT = 10) and RE = 83.97 (with FPT = 15). The greatest variation is about 2.84% (for N = 0.25). The absolute mean is 83.47.

As mentioned before, the goal of these experiments was to verify that whatever the FPT value parameter, the noise percentage variation does not affect considerably the recognition efficiency of our HMM. Indeed, and as shown in Table 3, Figure 13 and Figure 14, the empirical results strongly support the initial hypothesis. As mentioned before, in the worst case (N = 0.25), the variation is lower than 3% (see Figure 14).

Figure 13. Details of Experiments 6 and 7 (% of recognition vs. % of noise) and the recognition variation mean

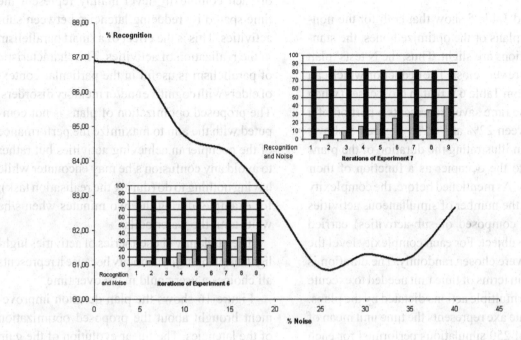

Figure 14. The recognition variation regarding the noise variation depending on the FPT factor

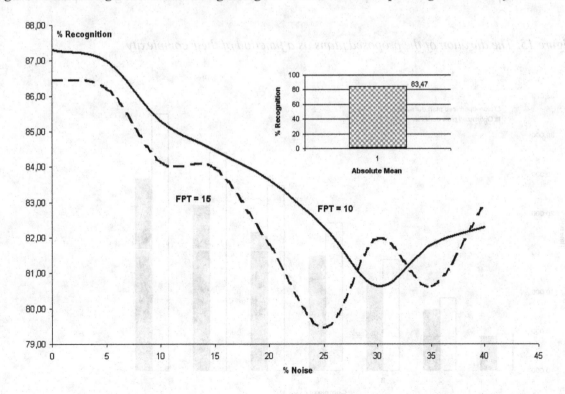

The Planning Process

Table 4 and Table 5 show that both for the non-optimized plans or the optimized ones, the standard variations are slight. Thus, the N tests' plan durations are very close. The deduction which can be made from Table 6 is that in most cases (when $NA \geq 3$) the time saved represents a portion of a value between 22% and 25%. Figure 15 shows the diagram illustrating the duration of the plans proposed to the occupier as a function of their complexity. As mentioned before, the complexity represents the number of simultaneous activities (each one composed of sub-activities) carried out by the subject. For each complexity level the activities were chosen randomly. The duration is expressed in terms of time unit needed to execute each of the multiple actions dictated by the plans. The ordinate axe represents the time unit mean of all series of 250 simulations performed for each complexity level. It enables to appreciate the reduction of plans duration by the optimization

algorithm. The variations between the two columns of each complexity level mainly represent the time spared by reducing latencies between sub-activities. This is the effect of a smart parallelism in the realization of activities. The characteristic of parallelism is useful in the particular context of elders with cognitive and/or memory disorders. The proposed optimization of plans is not computed with the aim to maximize the performance of the occupier in achieving activities but rather to avoid any confusion s/he may encounter while having nothing to do (during the realisation task); for example, during the two minutes when s/he waits until the water boils.

The randomly chosen series of activities highlight the planning dynamicity because it represents all choices a user could make over time.

Figure 16 shows the plan duration improvement brought about the proposed optimization of the latencies. The linear evolution of the gain with regard to the complexity of the plans is also expressed. The amount of gain on plan's duration

Figure 15. The duration of the proposed plans as a function of their complexity

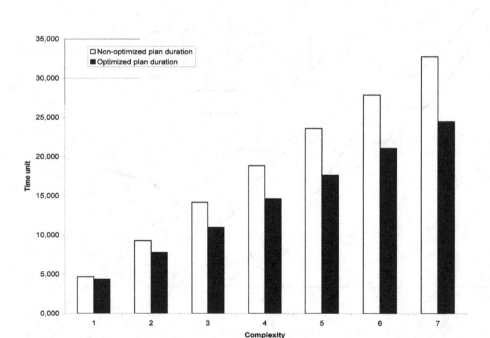

is conceivable as the complexity raises. This is explained by the fact that opportunities to optimize latencies increase with the number of activities (and sub-activities) carried out at the same time by the subject. The more the subject is undertaking activities simultaneously, the more the optimization algorithm is beneficial.

DISCUSSION

An important phase of the *DeepKover* assistance process is the recognition of what really occurs within the habitat; since the system reaction – in term of optimal planning of tasks to be made or terminated – for better assisting the occupier is primarily based on what does *DeepKover* "think" that is happening. This section discusses relations and distinctions between our modular architecture and other related works, mainly regarding recognition and planning. Originalities of *DeepKover* are also addressed.

Recognition via Hidden Markov Models

HMMs have became the method of choice for modelling stochastic processes and sequences in speech recognition (Rabiner, 1989) and handwriting recognition (e.g., Nag et al., 1994). HMMs have also been applied extensively in natural language modelling (ref. Manning & Schütze, 1999) and even in molecular biology (e.g., Kroger et al., 1993; Baldi et al., 1994). Furthermore, HMMs were successfully used to model temporal information on applications such as gesture detection (e.g., Kale et al., 2002), expression recognition (e.g., Lien et al., 2000) and image or video-based face identification (e.g., Chellappa et al., 1995). For example, Samaria and Young (1994) used pixel values in each block as the observation vectors and applied HMM spatially to image-based recognition, Nefian et al. (2002) proposed to utilise DCT (Discrete Cosine Transform) coefficients as observation vectors and a spatially embedded HMM was used for face detection, Liu and Chen (2003) proposed a dynamic adaptive and temporal HMM that performs video-based face recognition.

Figure 16. The plan duration improvement brought about the optimization of latencies

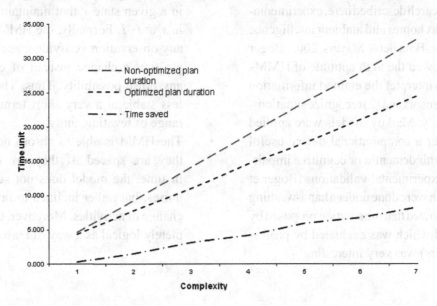

HMMs were also applied to intelligent tutoring systems (ITS), particularly with regard to modelling the behaviour of individual students (e.g., Stevens et al., 2005). In addition, Beal et al. (2007) investigated the idea to model students' action traces using HMM that denotes their engagement level as they work with an ITS. In the latter, modelling the performance of a student was done by fitting the Markov model to the sequence of actions emitted by the learner, with hypothesized hidden states corresponding to a student's engagement level.

Besides the vast number of engineering applications, recent researches in economics revealed that having recourse to Markov models represents a useful way of capturing stochastic nature of many financial variables (e.g., Rydén, Teräsvirta, & Asbrink, 1998; Bulla & Berzel, 2008). By focusing on the methodology based on hidden Markov processes, researchers have developed a practical use of the modelling issues thereby benefiting the field of economics research (Bulla, 2006). This leads to infer that to resort to such techniques in financial economics proves more their effectiveness which has now been recognized even in areas of social science research as well (Bhar, & Hamori, 2004).

Furthermore, within a perspective quite similar to that of the research described here, experimentations led in smart homes and ambient intelligence (see for example, Bauchet & Mayers, 2005; Boger et al, 2006) showed the high aptitude of HMMs to correctly (1) interpret the emitted information from ambient sensors and (2) recognize situations. More particularly, Markov models were applied in order to offer a computational device useful to aid people with dementia or cognitive impairments. Some experimental validations (Boger et al., 2006), which were done under a hand-washing task context, showed that the solution proposed by the model (and which was evaluated by professional caregivers) was very interesting.

In this sense, and as described above, our practical tests (see section 2) show a high efficiency of our HMM in recognizing activities of daily living (ADLs), independently of the variations of different technical parameters (i.e., normalisation, no-observations, activities' duration, noise, number of activities and the fixed period of time). However, the interpretation and analysis of empirical results allow us drawing some deductions which we expose below.

Experiments 6 and 7 illustrated in Table 3 show that:

- The HMM is as tolerant (regarding noise) as the recognition (of a transition between two activities) is differed in time; because rather that interpreting a perceived observation (occurred at time t) as a state change indication, the model can consider it as a disparate event which represents a noise, and thus maintain the same state at t+1.

- The less tolerant the HMM is (regarding noise), the more it oscillates between states (activities) during the recognition process. The model is more sensitive, maybe too much in some cases. Let's consider the condition c where the HMM detects at time t an observation o_i which not very probable in a given state s_i that maintain the model in s_i at $t+1$. Formally, the HMM interprets any observation verifying c as an immediate state's change instead of considering any noise possibility. Thus, The HMM is less stable at a very short term; i.e., on a range of few time units.

- The HMM is able to absorb noises when they are spaced. If they are contiguous in time, the model does not see them as noises, but rather inclined to favour a real change of activities. Moreover, this is completely logical as a way of reasoning.

Here, a dilemma occurs: is it better (1) to react instantaneously and be responsive, sometimes needlessly? or (2) to wait to be sure about an activity change and thus, to have delays in the recognition ? In this case, how much can we tolerate the duration of a delay? In certain critical cases, delays are not acceptable. For example, if the occupier is in the kitchen and get ready for lighting a cigarette whereas the gas valve of the cooker is open. Here, to avoid catastrophic consequences, the HMM must instantaneously recognize the "*Smoking cigarette*" activity. A possible solution consists in varying the sensitivity of the HMM regarding the noise according to the context; i.e., by categorizing all situations that occur. For example, by allotting a *green code* for ordinary situations, an *orange code* for undesirable but non dangerous situations and a *red code* for alarming situations. The recognition module would interact with the diagnosis module to know the current situation code and would vary the parameterisation of the HMM sensitivity.

Experiments 4 and 5 summarized in Table 2 show that:

- Normalisation gives constant weight to No-observations within activities. In other words, the normalisation standardizes the impact of the No-Obs phenomenon regarding the detection results; and therefore, contributes to increase the recognition effectiveness.

Latencies are frequent in smart environments that imply human behaviours (Najjar & Hamam, 2007). As mentioned previously, these latencies negatively influence the HMM's transitions probabilities making the model quiet unreliable during the recognition. Indeed, activities with many No-Obs (e.g., "*Watching a DVD movie*") become attractive states within the HMM. The normalisation provides an acceptable solution which offers a justification for the use of Markov

processes in the recognition of activities of daily living (ADLs).

Planning via Markov Decision Processes

We opt for broaching the planning issue according to three theoretical aspects: the (1) dissection of the *space problem* into partitions, (2) the rebuilding of the plan from the partitioned regions and (3) the optimality of the suggested plan. By way of conclusion, we end this sub-section by addressing some originalities of the planning approach.

The MDP Partitions and Sub-MDPs Connections

In order to solve a planning problem in terms of actions plan, Dean & Lin (1995) propose some techniques of (i) regions' partitioning (where each region represents a sub-problem) and (ii) combination of partial solutions whose each one would result from a partition. These techniques (DTPSD, for Decomposition Techniques for Planning in Stochastic Domains) rest on the use of parameters describing the relation between a partition R (a sub-MDP resulting from the decomposition of the initial problem. i.e. the full MDP) and its neighbours. These parameters are initially defined and remain unchanged since the structure of the problem never changes. Thus, the problem to be solved is seen as a task to achieve (mono-task) which does not take into account the notion of time. In the context of cognitively impaired people, individuals unceasingly make *not logically-structured things* that change the topology of the partitions. In this sense, a *strong-link* technique is impossible to exploit. In our approach, each partition R does not have fixed and predefined neighbours. These will change constantly during the resolution of the problem which, in this case, consists of several concurrent tasks (multi-tasks). The vicinity of a partition is dynamically given according to the interleaving of the various tasks in progress and whose simultaneous achievements progress in time. Whereas our planning approach proceeds chronologically, DTPSD is timeless and static. Partitions in DTPSD share the same variables of environment but they do not share the values of these variables. The coherence of each variable value (for example, *Cupboard#2-Open = True*) for the various partitions is maintained thanks to static transitions (Dean & Lin, 1995). Our dynamic partitioning cannot be possible via this type of transitions. In our case, the DTPSD strong link notion is replaced by a weak connection: the share out by all partitions (sub-MDPs) of a pool of environment variables which allow specifying at any time the internal states of these variables. The coherence of the variables' values is maintained using a general structure – that we call the environment (see Figure 2) – containing the values of all the variables. As these values can change at each unit of time, each partition consults the environment to know in which state the variables are. This lead to assuring the coherence while allowing a dynamic partitioning.

Meuleau et al. (1998) present a technique for approximately computing optimal solutions to stochastic resource allocation problems modeled as MDPs. Their approach exploits two key properties to avoid explicitly enumerating the very large state and action spaces associated with these problems. First, the problems are composed of multiple tasks whose utilities are independent. Second, the actions taken with respect to (or resources allocated to) a task do not influence the status of any other task. Each task is therefore viewed as an MDP. However, these MDPs are weakly coupled by resource constraints: actions selected for one MDP restrict the actions available to others. In addition, the second property makes the approach unusable for a dynamic partitioning with various levels of dependences, in one hand, and prevents the optimization of the latencies, in another hand.

Scheduling Partial Plans

Scheduling partial plans allows developing a total plan which takes into account – intelligently – the various constraints related to the problem. More precisely, in smart homes and in multi-goals planning context, scheduling is used to plan simultaneous realisations of several activities while ensuring that the plan will not be confusing or too complex for a memory or cognitively impaired person. For example, if the two activities to be achieved are *"Watching movie"* and *"Making pasta"*, then it is necessary to avoid a plan which would repetitively send the elderly from one room to another. i.e., *"Turning on the VCR"* → *"Putting on the stove"* → *"Rewinding the video tape"* → *"Taking a cauldron"*, etc. In this sense, the necessity of partial plans is crucial in multi-goals planning and their scheduling makes it possible to benefit from relations between certain goals.

MaxQ (Dietterich, 1998) offers a tree graphical notation for describing the goal/subgoals structure of a task. The MaxQ tree contains two kinds of nodes: Max nodes and Q nodes. Max nodes with no children denote primitive actions. Those with children represent subtasks. The immediate children of each Max node are Q nodes. Each Q node represents an action that can be performed to achieve its parent's subtask. Figure 17 shows a MaxQ graph for the *Taxi Domain* mentioned in (Dietterich, 1998). MaxQ does not consider the scheduling of partial plans, since the approach suppose one total static goal related to the achievement of one task (MaxRoot, in Figure 17). The MaxQ tree never changes. Its corresponding task has always the same fixed sequence of subactivities. Actions represented by the Max nodes (under each Q node) can define the contents of partial plans. However, since the tree is fixed, there cannot be a scheduling of partial plans. In addition, MaxQ is Q-Learning based. This learning technique determines a priori the values of the parameters of each sub-MDP (probabilities of transition and rewards). This is possible only if

Figure 17. The MAXQ graph for the Taxi Domain

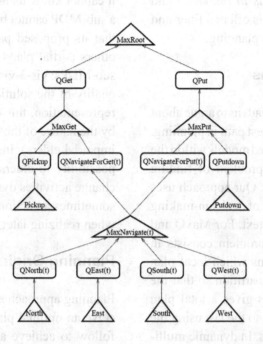

the hierarchy of the Max nodes and the Q nodes is fixed (see (Dietterich, 1998) for more details). If the tree changes in time, then all calculations would have to be started again. This static structure allowing the Q-Learning cannot be applied in multi-tasks planning that requires scheduling of the partial plans.

The tree-based organisation is useful and serves two main goals which are consequently dependent. The first goal is how to give more coherence to the whole plan. The second is about optimizing the plan by managing the latencies. To broach the first goal, let us suppose that the general context of the problem is to spend one ordinary day in an intelligent habitat (approximately a hundred of environment variables which reflect the states of realisation of ten or so activities). This problem is broken up into various partitions. Each one of them is split up in turn in several sub-regions. Finally, this leads to a significant number of partitions. Since the topology of our partitioning is dynamic (i.e., the neighbours of an area change constantly), if we wish to avoid synthesizing

senseless plans (for example, an unreasonable simultaneous achievement of activities) it is necessary to establish temporary link between some partitions (for example, those belonging to the same activity). In this sense, the tree-based structuring of activities is used to solve the problem of the temporal abstraction (Dietterich, 1998). The tree structure is useful to determine which partitions must be dependent between them for a certain time (the reader can refer to (Dietterich, 1998, p.4-6) for more details and explanations). As mentioned above, the second goal consists in optimizing the plan by an effective management of the latencies. Planning the complete realisation of an activity before passing to the achievement of another does not allow benefiting from idle times between sub-activities of the same activity; for example, *waiting for boiling to infuse tea*. We associate a tree to our MDPs in order to add a hierarchical aspect to the topology of the problem decomposition. This aspect enables interlacing the achievements of sub-activities of several activities in progress (for example, to *rewind a video tape* while *water heats in the kettle* and *pasta cook on the stove*). This offers a finer and more intelligent treatment in planning.

The Optimality of Plans

The last addressed key issue leads us to argue about the objective to find the shortest path in planning. MaxQ introduces MDPs-based models within the framework of a stochastic problem of finding the shortest path in planning. Our approach uses MDPs within the framework of decision-making in multitasks realisation context. For MaxQ and DTPSD, the shortest path problem consists in finding by algorithmic means which local plan (policy) to choose for each partition so that the joint of these regional plans gives a total plan going from the first partition to the last using the minimum of possible actions. In dynamic multi-tasks planning where the solution of the problem consists in satisfying a set of goals, the notion of "*from the first partition towards the last*" has less of sense. Here the objective is to provide a total plan allowing the satisfaction of several simultaneous goals. Since the topology of the partitioning varies according to the current states of the subgoals and, hierarchically, according to those of the sub-subgoals, we cannot consider a fixed state space as for DTPSD and MaxQ. Hence, it is necessary to make more flexible the representation of the states[2] (as it is impossible to have variables of transition) what involves in some cases few actions in excess (for example, opening and closing the same cupboard twice). But this is not really disadvantageous, since multi-tasks planning does not have the same objective as the shortest path problem. However, dynamic multi-tasks planning makes more difficult the shortest path search. Each time that a sub-MDP seeks the best sequence of actions to carry out for planning a sub-activity, a part of the set of the beliefs related to the problem is hidden from it. For example, a sub-MDP does not know preconditions of its neighbour sub-MDPs because, due to the dynamic partitioning,

it cannot know its neighbours in advance. Thus, a sub-MDP cannot be able to consider the effects that its proposed partial plan will have on the others partial plans computed by its neighbour sub-MDPs. Vis-à-vis the compromise between the quality of the solution and the flexibility of the representation, this choice seems quiet justified by the nature of the targeted people (cognitively impaired elders). Insofar as we want to give the possibility to elders to interrupt/resume and to change activities dynamically, it is tolerable that sometimes an action involves additional actions when realizing later activities.

Planning Originalities

Planning approaches – as DTSPD – aim to conceive an optimal plan that the user will have to follow to achieve a goal initially defined. Our approach reverses the dependence between the planning and the user. It is the planner who adjusts its suggested plan regarding to the user's needs; and not the opposite. As mentioned before, one of the goals of *DeepKover* is to assist an elder moving/evolving within a controlled environment in order to provide him/her a logistic support in the realisation of activities of daily living (ADLs). Thus, the planning philosophy is to provide a plan which is always a function of the multiple current intentions of the occupier. This latter is *relatively* free to follow or not the step proposed by the planner. If s/he does not do it, then the plan will have to be readjusted according to the choice of the person. This leads to adding new goals and/or changing the order of the realisation of existing sub-goals. In this sense, we think that our approach is innovative in the context of the dynamicity of goals and the flexibility of the planning representation.

Our originality lies in the dynamic goals treatment. The DTPSD planning approach is functional only in a mono-task context. Thus, the key issue of dynamic goals is not addressed. In the MaxQ approach, the structure of the hierarchical tree cannot change without having to start again all calculations. In our approach, it is possible to include new goals (new tasks/activities) in the planning process, to withdraw others and/or to change their order. This is done in real time without need for starting again any algorithms. As mentioned above, we provide a solution to the impossibility of making fixed and predefined partitioning according to a DTPSD-based philosophy in dynamic multi-tasks planning; because the topography (i.e., the repartition of the neighbours regions) is variable. For example – and thanks to the optimisation caused by the effective management of the latencies – a sub-activity, such as "*Boiling water*" can as well be followed by "*Preparing tomato salsa*" or by "*Rewinding a video-cassette*".

FUTURE WORK

In *DeepKover*, the diagnosis module (DM) is able to detect unexpected and undesirable events but do not perform any subsequent treatment. Our current research aims at conceiving mechanisms to deal with this kind of events. As mentioned earlier in the DM section, a critical situation is detected when at least one constraint imposed by an activity (recursively, sub-activity) in progress is violated. Constraints can be of chronological nature or can represent relations of sequences dependence. For example, for a given task T_1, if the achievement of the sub-task ST_{i+1} must absolutely be done following the realization of the sub-task ST_i, then an event which causes the suspension of T_1 and the resumption of another task T_n will not be tolerated. By considering a concrete scenario (example 1), if the occupier – who is in the kitchen – opens a valve of the gas stove (a necessary step to light the cooker) and if the following action would be to open a cupboard, then the DM detects an undesirable situation (called in this case, "*yellow code*"). Because of a dependence pattern defined in the sub-activity "*Opening valve i of the gas stove*"

which indicates that this task must be followed the successive task in the same sub-activity, i.e., "*Activating the electric spark i*" of the ring whose valve is already open. The planner, notified of this situation, must synthesize an optimal plan to cure what just occurred.

In another case (example 2), inspired by the same previous scenario, if the elder (1) had previously open the kitchen cupboard to take his/her cigarettes and lighter (let's suppose that they are presently on the kitchen table) and if, after (2) having opened the valve of the gas stove (to reheat a soup), (3) s/he opens a drawer and take an ashtray, then the DM detects initially a *yellow code* (after the valve opening) followed by a "*red code*" when recognizing that the ashtray is hold. The red code represents an alarming situation which requires a prompt intervention for an urgent remediation. Except for the synthesis of optimal suggested plans by the planning module, the assistance system, thanks to the DM, must raise an alarm in critical situations.

Moreover, yellow codes can automatically switch into red codes after few time units. Indeed, the authorized time for the suspension of an activity whose last accomplished sub-task has a dependence pattern is relatively short. In example 1 (see above), if the occupier would not have properly react following the yellow code (gas-valve open), the assistance system would have eventually raise the alarm; because the situation would be promptly transformed into a red code (gas leakage); and ideally, a control sub-system (possibly, another module which should be added to *DeepKover*) closes the gas-valve and automatically lights the cooker hood to evacuate the gas outside.

From this viewpoint, we are actually preparing *the icing on the cake*, i.e., working on refining the DM functioning so that *DeepKover* will be able to manage both the undesirable and alarming situations. Once this it is done, we plan to begin new experimental tests with subjects put in real situations of realization of ADLs.

CONCLUSION

We have presented *DeepKover*, a modular adaptive *artful* intelligent assistance system for cognitively and/or memory impaired people engaged in the realisation of their activities of daily living (ADLs). The goal of this assistance system is to help disabled persons evolving within a controlled environment in order to provide logistic support in achieving their ADLs. We have also discussed the obtained empirical results of the experimental validation and drew some deductions about the originalities of the assistance system. Other aspects of *DeepKover*'s architecture, such as the diagnosis module, will be refined and deeply detailed in future chapters/papers.

ACKNOWLEDGMENT

DeepKover is a research project in which eleven collaborators have been involved – three professors, one post-doctoral fellow, one PhD student, two Master students and four undergraduate students. The authors want to thank Wojtek Jurewicz, Gilbert Samson, Jonathan Berriault and François Lizotte for their help on the realisation of the modular architecture.

REFERENCES

Baldi, P., Chauvin, Y., Hunkapiller, T., & McClure, M. (1994). Hidden Markov models of biological primary sequence information. *Proceedings of the National Academy of Sciences of the United States of America, 91*(3), 1059–1063. doi:10.1073/pnas.91.3.1059

Bauchet, J., & Mayers, A. (2005). A modelisation of ADLs in its environment for cognitive assistance. Proceedings of the 3rd International Conference on Smart Homes and Health Telematic (ICOST05). Magog, Quebec, Canada. pp. 221-228.

Bauchet, J., Vergnes, D., Giroux, S., & Pigot, H. (2006). A pervasive cognitive assitant for smart homes. Proceedings of the International Conference on Aging, Disability and Independence. St-Petersburg, FL, USA. pp. 228-234.

Baum, T., Petrie, G., Soules, N., & Weiss, N. (1970). A maximization technique occurring in the statistical analysis of probabilistic functions of Markov chains. *Annals of Mathematical Statistics, 41*(1), 164–171. doi:10.1214/aoms/1177697196

Beal, C., Mitra, S., & Cohen, P. R. (2007). Modeling learning patterns of students with a tutoring system using Hidden Markov Models. Proceedings of the 13th International Conference on Artificial Intelligence in Education (AIED), Marina del Rey, CA, USA pp. 238-245.

Beerman, S., & Rappaport-Musson, J. (2008). [The Caregiver's Complete Handbook for Making Decisions. Prometheus Press.]. *Elderly Care*, 911.

Bellman, R. E. (1957). *Dynamic Programming*. Princeton University Press.

Bhar, R., & Hamori, S. (2004). *Hidden Markov Models – Applications to Financial Economics. Advanced Studies in Theoretical and Applied Econometrics*. Princeton University Press.

Boger, J., Hoey, J., Poupart, P., Boutilier, C., Fernie, G. & Mihailidis, A. (2006). A Planning System Based on Markov Model to Guide People with Dementia Through Activities of Daily Living. in IEEE Transactions on Information Technology in BioMedicine. 10(2):323-333

Bulla, J. (2006). Application of Hidden Markov Models and Hidden Semi-Markov Models to Financial Time Series. *Doctoral Dissertation*. University Library of Munich, Germany.

Bulla, J., & Berzel, A. (2008). Computational issues in parameter estimation for stationary hidden Markov models. *Computational Statistics. Springer, 23*(1), 1–18.

Chellappa, R., Wilson, C. L., & Sirohey, S. (1995). Human and machine recognition of faces: a survey. *Proceedings of the IEEE, 83*(5), 705–741. doi:10.1109/5.381842

Courtemanche, F., Najjar, M., Paccoud, B., & Mayers, A. (2008). Assisting Elders via Dynamic Multi-tasks Planning – A Markov Decision Processes based Approach. Proceedings of the ACM International Conference on Ambient Media and Systems (Ambi-Sys '08). Quebec City, Canada. pp:312-321

Dean, T., & Lin, S. H. (1995). *Decomposition techniques for planning in stochastic domains.* Technical Report CS-95-10, Department of Computer Science, Brown University, Providence, Rhode Island, USA.

Dietterich, T. G. (1998). The MAXQ Method for Hierarchical Reinforcement Learning. *Proceedings of the 15th International Conference on Machine Learning.* pp: 118-126

Evans, J. R., Boersma, J., Blachman, N. M., & Jagers, A. A. (1988). The Entropy of a Poisson Distribution. *SIAM Review, 30*(2), 314–317. doi:10.1137/1030059

Feller, W. (1968). An Introduction to Probability Theory and its Applications (Volume I). John Wiley & Sons (Eds.).

Kale, A. N., Rajagopalan, N., Cuntoor, A., & Krueger, V. (2002). Gait-based Recognition of humans Using Continuous HMMs. *Proceedings of the 5th IEEE International Conference on Automatic Face and Gesture Recognition*, Washinton D.C. May 20-21, pp.336-341.

Kroger, M., Wahl, R., & Rice, P. (1993). Compilation of DNA sequences of Escherichia coli. *Nucleic Acids Research, 21*(13), 2973–3000. doi:10.1093/nar/21.13.2973

Krogh, A., Mian, S. I., & Haussler, D. (1994). A Hidden Markov Model that Finds Genes in E-coli DNA. *NAR, 22*, 4768–4778. doi:10.1093/nar/22.22.4768

Lien, T., Kanade, C., Li, C., & Cohn, J. F. (2000). Determination of Hidden Markov Model Topology for Facial Expression Analysis. *IEEE Transactions on Pattern Analysis and Machine Intelligence, 29*(3), 417–428.

Liu, X., & Chen, T. (2003). Video-based face recognition using adaptive Hidden Markov Models. Proceedings of CVPR'03, Madison, Wisconsin. pp: 215-221

Loverde, J. (2009). *The Complete Eldercare Planner - Revised and Updated Edition*. Three Rivers Press.

Manning, C. D., & Schütze, H. (1999). *Foundations of Statistical Natural Language*. Cambridge, MA: The MIT Press.

Marcell, J., & Shankle, R. (2001). *Elder Rage: How to Survive Caring for Aging Parents*. Impressive Press.

Meuleau, N., Hauskrecht, K. E., Peshkin, L., Pack-Kaelbling, L., Dean, T., & Boutilier, C. (1998). Solving very large weakly coupled Markov decision processes. *Proceedings of the 10th conference on Artificial intelligence.* pp:165 – 172.

Mihailidis, A., Carmichael, B., & Boger, J. (2004). The use of computer vision in an intelligent environment to support aging-in-place, safety, and independence in the home. [Special Issue on Pervasive Healthcare]. *IEEE Transactions on Information Technology in Biomedicine, 8*(3), 1–11. doi:10.1109/TITB.2004.834386

Nag, R., Wong, K. H., & Fallside, F. (1994). Script recognition using hidden Markov models. Proceedings of International Conference on Acoustics Speech and Signal Processing. pp:2071-2074.

Najjar, M., & Hamam, H. (2007). Intelligent Environments for Assistance to Elders in Daily Life Activities. Proceedings of the 5th International Conference on Intelligent Multimedia and Ambient Intelligence (IMAI 07). July 15-22, Salt Lake City, Utah, USA. pp:1482-1487.

Nefian, A. V., Liang, X., Pi, X., Liu, C., Mao, L., & Murphy, K. (2002). A coupled HMM for audio-visual speech recognition", the IEEE International Conference on Acoustic Speech and Signal. 31(1):336-347.

Pigot, H., Bauchet, J., & Giroux, S. (2008). *Assistive devices for people with cognitive impairments. The Engineering Handbook on Smart Technology for Aging, Disability and Independence* (pp. 217–236). Wiley & Sons. doi:10.1002/9780470379424.ch12

Puterman, M. L. (1994). *Markov Decision Processes: Discrete Stochastic Dynamic Programming. J.* New York: Wiley & Sons.

Rabiner, L. (1989). A tutorial on Hidden Markov Models and selected applications in speech recognition. *Proceedings of the IEEE, 77*(2), 257–286. doi:10.1109/5.18626

Rydén, T., Teräsvirta, T., & Asbrink, S. (1998). Stylized facts of daily return series and the hidden Markov model of absolute returns. *Journal of Applied Econometrics, 13,* 217–244. doi:10.1002/(SICI)1099-1255(199805/06)13:3<217::AID-JAE476>3.0.CO;2-V

Samaria, F., & Young, S. (1994). HMM-based architecture for face identification. *Image and Vision Computing, 12*(8), 338–349. doi:10.1016/0262-8856(94)90007-8

Snoek, J., Hoey, J., Stewart, L., Zemel, R., & Mihailidis, A. (2008). Automated detection of unusual events on stairs. *Journal of Image and Vision Computing., 18*(3), 112–124.

Solie, D. (2004). *How to Say It to Seniors: Closing the Communication Gap with Our Elders.* Prentice Hall Press.

Stevens, R., Johnson, D., & Soller, A. (2005). Probabilities and prediction: Modeling the development of scientific problem solving skills. *Cell Biology Education, 4,* 42–57. doi:10.1187/cbe.04-03-0036

Tam, T., Boger, J., Dolan, A., & Mihailidis, A. (2006). An Intelligent Emergency Response System: Preliminary Development and Testing of a Functional Health Monitoring System. *Gerontechnology (Valkenswaard), 4*(4), 209–222. doi:10.4017/gt.2006.04.04.005.00

Tijms, H. (2004). *Understanding Probability – A lively introduction to probability theory for the beginner.* Cambridge University Press.

Welch, L. (2003). Hidden Markov Models and the Baum-Welch Algorithm. *The IEEE Information Theory Society Newsletter., 53*(4), 10–24.

ENDNOTES

[1] It would be necessary for that case to incorporate an additional module of recognition of the behaviour based on video sequences of the subject (Kale and al., 2002).

[2] To define the possible states of an activity, our planning approach only uses variables of environment that are relevant to the activity (or even to its sub-activities). Indeed, we cannot define nor make use of concepts such as the border or the periphery of region (activity), as in DTPSD.

Chapter 26
RFID–Enabled Location Determination within Indoor Environments

Kevin Curran
University of Ulster, Northern Ireland

Stephen Norrby
University of Ulster, Northern Ireland

ABSTRACT

The ability to track the real-time location and movement of items or people offers a broad range of useful applications in areas such as safety, security and the supply chain. Current location determination technologies, however, have limitations that heavily restrict how and where these applications are implemented, including the cost, accuracy of the location calculation and the inherent properties of the system. The Global Positioning System (GPS), for example, cannot function indoors and is useful only over large-scaled areas such as an entire city. Radio Frequency Identification (RFID) is an automatic identification technology which has seen increasingly prominent use over the last few decades. The technology uses modulated Radio Frequency signals to transfer data between its two main components, the reader and the transponder. Its many applications include supply chain management, asset tracking, security clearance and automatic toll collection. In recent years, advancements in the technology have allowed the location of transponders to be calculated while interfacing with the reader. This article documents an investigation into using an active RFID based solution for tracking.

INTRODUCTION

Accurate location determination systems have been a luxury for large scientific institutions and military installations for some time, but such systems are much too complex and expensive for use in smaller areas such as schools, clinics and even the common household. Similar systems, available commercially, have limitations that make it difficult to accurately determine the location of an object or person in these areas. Many systems that track subjects in real time have severe limitations when tracking individuals in a smaller area, such as a room, building or garden. GPS devices

DOI: 10.4018/978-1-60960-549-0.ch026

require line of sight with satellites in order to be tracked correctly, meaning devices cannot be tracked indoors or in some areas surrounded by tall buildings. The degree of accuracy to which GPS provides location information is also inadequate for applications that monitor areas with specific boundaries between where an individual is allowed and where they are not. Mobile phone tracking is expensive and works only in more developed areas in range of multiple cell towers. Position estimation, to within an average of fifty metres, is much too inaccurate to track subjects over a small area. Implementing a location determination system using ZigBee received-signal-strength (RSS) has the advantage that the system can work indoors, however the cost of implementation is rather high and the complex network infrastructure may need constant maintenance. Place Lab is an open source solution but since it relies on a centralised list of "landmarks" to work correctly, it would not be suited to smaller areas such as inside buildings (at room level).

Hence, a system that could deliver quick and accurate position information (i.e. to within half a metre) at minimal cost could have many extremely useful applications, such as monitoring the safety of children in school, the whereabouts of patients in a hospital or even tracking inmates in a prison. Radio Frequency Identification (RFID) is an automatic identification technology that is widely used across a multitude of applications, including security, safety and asset tracking. A modulated radio frequency signal is used to transfer data from transponders, attached to people, animals or objects, to a reader in the vicinity. Recently, systems have been developed that can calculate the location of a tag, as well as read the data it contains. This major development in RFID technology could allow for the installation of cheap, accurate and reliable location tracking systems to greatly improve safety in schools, clinics and many other areas.

Technologies that determine the current location of a person or object have very useful applications in many areas, including security, safety systems, location-based information services, mapping and the tracking of people, animals and goods. The first highly successful location determination technology was Radio Detection and Ranging, more commonly known as radar. Many engineers and scientists, including Nikola Tesla, had worked on the principles of radar in the early part of the twentieth century. Several systems were patented in the 1930s in the United States, Germany and France. However, the British were the first to use radar as a defence from enemy aircraft attacks, with Robert Watson-Watt's 1935 patent GB593017. The Second World War brought about a large push in radar research on both the allied and axis sides. Radar systems work by transmitting a very short, high-intensity burst of radio waves at a high frequency. After transmission, the transmitter is disabled and the receiver is turned on. The receiver listens for an echo created by any object (e.g. an aeroplane) within range of the transmitter. The distance of the object from the transmitter can be estimated by measuring the time taken for the echo to arrive. Modern radar systems can also measure the Doppler shift of the echo to estimate the speed of the object. Figure 1 shows the components of a typical radar system.

This article outlines the use of RFID-radar technology to track the location of items or people indoors. The RFID based tracking system allows items/people to be tagged with long-range and short-range RFID tags. An RFID-radar system is used to provide 2D position location with identity, range and tracking information, thus keeping the user informed of each person's location. The user may define areas within the monitored zone as "unsanctioned," and the system alerts the user if any tracked individual enters any of these unsanctioned areas.

Figure 1. A radar system

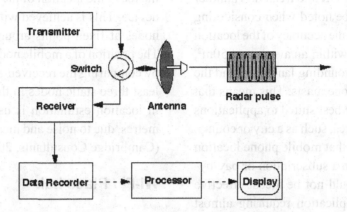

LOCATION DETERMINATION TECHNOLOGIES

There are a number of popular, accessible and versatile technologies available, each with their own advantages and disadvantages for particular applications.

GPS

The Global Positioning System (GPS) is a Global Navigation Satellite System (GNSS), employing a network of twenty-four satellites launched by the United States Department of Defence. Originally intended for military use, it was declared free for civilian use in 1983 by President Ronald Reagan, after Korean Air Lines Flight 007 was shot down by the Soviet Air Force after mistakenly entering Soviet airspace - it was believed that the disaster may have been averted if the flight crew had access to better navigation systems (Pellerin, 2006). GPS satellites circle the Earth twice a day at a very precise orbit. Each satellite contains an atomic clock, and transmits data to the ground at synchronised intervals. The data contains the exact time and the satellite's position in the form of an *ephemeris*. GPS receivers also contain a clock and, since the speed of the satellite signal transmission is a known constant, they calculate the distance to each satellite in range by comparing the transmission time

sent by the satellite to the reception time given by the receiver's clock. Once the receiver knows the distance to and position of at least three satellites, it can calculate its position on the ground using a method known as *trilateration*, similar to triangulation. GPS is used in navigational systems for automobiles, aircraft, ships, spacecraft and even pedestrians, mapping and surveying, geophysics and archaeology, emergency location, location-based games, mobile satellite communications, weather predication, photographic "Geocoding" and social Networking. Military uses include missile guidance, target tracking, troop movement coordination and reconnaissance.

Mobile Cellular Systems

Mobile phones, when switched on, send out a signal to cell towers within its vicinity. By comparing the time for the signal to arrive and relative signal strengths from multiple towers, an estimated location of the handset can be obtained. Some mobile phone companies have begun to offer customers location-based services and applications, such as O2's "Friend Finder" and "Find My Nearest ATM." [1] Commercial products such as that of LocateMobiles.com are also available, which allow users to register online and track a specific handset on any of the UK's four major network operators. The location, accurate to within fifty metres, is plotted on a map of the UK and Ireland. A number of limitations are to be noted when considering this approach. Firstly, the accuracy of the location estimation is only to within an average of 50m^2, depending on the surrounding landscape and the number of nearby phone masts. This means that this method would be best suited to applications that monitor a wide area, such as a city or county. Another limitation is that mobile phone location queries often work on a subscription or pay-by-query basis. This would not be a cost-effective approach for any application requiring almost real-time updates of a subject's current location.

ZigBee

ZigBee is based on the IEEE 802.15.4 standard for Wireless Personal Area Networks (WPANs). The ZigBee standard is regulated by the ZigBee Alliance, a group with over 150 members worldwide. ZigBee is similar in concept to other WPANs such as the well-known "Bluetooth," however it is designed to provide connectivity between small packet devices, while Bluetooth concerns connectivity between large packet user devices such as mobile phones and laptop computers. Thus, ZigBee devices are much less complex than comparable Bluetooth devices and, as such, are a fraction of the cost[3]. ZigBee is ideal for radio-frequency applications that require secure networking, long battery life and a low data rate. ZigBee WPANs have typical communication speeds of up to 250Kbps, and can support up to 255 devices in a single network. ZigBee is also compatible with most common network topologies, such as mesh networks, star networks and peer-to-peer networks. Common applications for ZigBee include heating, ventilation and air conditioning, lighting systems, intrusion detection, wireless smoke detectors, automatic meter reading and medical monitoring.[4] A ZigBee mesh structure can be used to track mobile nodes, effectively giving the real-time location of the carrier of the mobile device. This is achieved with a network of static nodes at fixed points around the tracking area. The position of a mobile node can be triangulated by comparing the received-signal-strengths of at least three static nodes in the vicinity. Accuracy in location estimation is usually to within five metres, due to noise and measurement resolution (Cambridge Consultants, 2006).

Wi-Fi / Place Lab

Place Lab is a collaborative effort between Intel Research Seattle and other academic institutions which relies on the existing wireless network infrastructure. The Place Lab software uses an online database of the coordinates of known wireless base stations, known as landmarks. Components within the software known as "spotters" retrieve a list of landmarks within the vicinity of the device being used. A second component, known as a "mapper," attempts to associate the list of landmarks retrieved by the spotters with entries in the database. A final component, called the "tracker," triangulates the device's position by using the output from the mapper and the relative signal strengths. Experiments show that the accuracy of the position estimation approaches 20m when the device can detect 4 or 5 distinct beacons in a ten second window. Figure 2 shows a computer with Place Lab software detecting nearby beacons A, B and C. The advantage of Place Lab is that it is free to use and the hardware needed is minimal. Place Lab is also a good choice for users concerned with privacy, as their position is calculated client-side. Place Lab, however, requires quite a number of entries in the database for a user's location in order to provide accurate position information over a wide area. Some large cities, such as Seattle, have a large landmark database. It is unlikely, however, to find many landmarks for smaller, less developed areas (McMullan et al., 2007).

Figure 2. A hand-held portable RFID reader [9]

Ubisense

Ubisense is a real-time location system that uses ultra-wideband RF technology to provide positional information accurate to 15cm. The ultra-wideband technology's advantage over conventional RFID and WiFi is its ability to operate in challenging environments by penetrating walls and other obstacles. The system consists of active tags whose ultra-wideband pulses are used in location calculations, a fixed infrastructure of sensors that receive the pulses from the tags and software to process location data and relay it to users and other related systems. Potential applications include determining the location of a pallet of goods in a warehouse where there may be many obstacles, and allowing the association of data read by a barcode reader with the device's location at any point in time.

Ekahau Positioning Engine

The Ekahau Positioning Engine (EPE) is a software-based real-time location system, whose patented algorithm uses signal strength calibration to calculate the location of devices with "floor-, room- and door-level accuracy." EPE is capable of detecting a variety of devices, including Ekahau

Wi-Fi Tags, Laptops, PDAs, barcode scanners, passive RFID scanners and other Wi-Fi-enabled devices[5]. Since EPE is software-based, an existing Wi-Fi infrastructure can be location-enabled with a matter of hours, enabling rapid implementation at an affordable cost. EPE supports all standard 802.11a/b/g access points and a single server can track thousands of assets through multiple buildings. EPE also comes with a Software Development Kit to allow development of custom applications that utilise the EPE system[6].

RADIO FREQUENCY IDENTIFICATION (RFID)

Radio Frequency Identification, is a technology used for the automatic identification and tracking of goods, animals and people. A typical system consists of a three parts – a transponder, a reader, and a controlling application. Transponders hold data on whatever person or object they are attached to, usually containing a unique code used for identification, such as a serial number. When within an appropriate range of a reader, the transponders transmit this data to the reader using radio waves. The reader decodes this radio signal into digital information, which is then relayed to a computer application that makes use of it. RFID technology is extremely widespread, used in many different applications such as security systems, public transport payment systems, the tracking of commercial goods, and livestock identification.

History of RFID

RFID is a relatively old technology, dating back to World War II. Both allied and axis forces had been using Radar technology, which gave an early warning of incoming fighter planes. The problem was that there was no way to identify which of the "dots" on the Radar screen were friendly and which were hostile. German fighters used a crude system where pilots rolled their planes when returning to base. This altered the radio signal reflected back to their base's Radar system, informing the Radar crew that the incoming planes were friendly[7]. The British developed the IFF (Identify Friend or Foe) system, which used transponders fitted to allied planes. These transponders broadcasted a signal identifying the aircraft as friendly when "interrogated" by a coded RADAR signal from base. Commercial applications appeared in the 1960s, such as the popular anti-theft system known as Electronic Article Surveillance (EAS). This system used only 1-bit-capacity tags, but provided a cheap and effective countermeasure against theft. RFID development and research increased dramatically into the 1970s, with notable developments such as *"Short-range radio-telemetry for electronic identification using modulated backscatter"* presented by Alfred Koelle, Steven Depp and Robert Freyman of Los Alamos Scientific Laboratory, Northwestern University. Los Alamos also had teams developing systems for animal tagging and vehicle tracking, in collaboration with other organisations such as the United States Federal Highway Administration. By the late 1980's, RFID systems were becoming quite widespread in a number of applications such as animal tracking, secure personnel access and toll collection. RFID road toll collection systems were first employed in Europe, such as those in France, Spain, Italy and Norway. The United States followed shortly afterwards with a system developed for the Dallas North Turnpike in 1989.

The 1990s saw most toll roads in the United States equipped with RFID. In 1991, the first electronic tolling system that allowed vehicles to pass collection points without the need to slow down was deployed on a highway in Oklahoma. Other notable systems were those of the Kansas turnpike and the Georgia 400, which used multi-protocol readers that were compatible with their own new "Title 21" tags, as well as the older ones of neighbouring systems. Texas Instruments introduced TIRIS (Texas Instruments Registration and

Identification System), initially fitted to vehicles as engine immobilisers. The system was modified for a multitude of different applications, including fuel dispensation and the detection of counterfeit casino chips (Landt, 2001). Nowadays, RFID is a part of everyday life. Millions of workers use RFID tags to gain access into company premises, pay tolls on highways, pay parking fees, borrow library books and even play games. Some critics are concerned that RFID tagging will be so ubiquitous in the near future as to be almost Orwellian in nature (Lomas, 2006).

Components of an RFID System

The following is an overview of the major components of an RFID system.

RFID Tag/Transponder

The tag, or transponder, is the device attached to a person, animal or object containing information used for identification. The vast majority of tags comprise of an integrated circuit and an antenna. The integrated circuit performs a number of functions, including power control, data storage, data processing, and the modulation and demodulation of radio frequency signals. The data stored usually depends on the protocol used for the communication between the tag and the application receiving data from the reader. A typical tag's memory could include a unique tag ID, a security password and a Cyclic Redundancy Check (CRC) code, used for error detection. The integrated circuit is connected to an antenna. The shape and size of the antenna is determined by the application of the RFID tag and its designated frequency. Coiled antennas are used in low-frequency and high-frequency "passive tags," while dipole antennas are employed in Ultra High Frequency tags. The type and design of antenna used is important in balancing the effectiveness and cost of tags. For example, single-dipole antennas are cheaper to produce than dual-dipole antennas, but they rely heavily on their orientation in order to be successfully read by a reader. The integrated circuit and antenna are connected together using a substrate, usually a thin, flexible plastic. An effective substrate is durable and protects the circuit, antenna and their connection from static build-up and physical damage. The substrate and its components are often covered in a type of packaging that offers further protection and allows the tag to be implemented effectively, e.g. casing safe enough for "under-the-skin" implants (Tedjasaputra, 2006).

Three different classes of RFID tags exist, describing the source of the tag's power – *passive*, *active* and *semi-passive*. Passive tags use no internal power supply, and instead capture the tiny electrical current induced in their antennas by the incoming radio signal (or *carrier signal*) in a capacitor, a process called *inductive coupling*. The coiled antenna. The capacitor's stored energy is then used to power the integrated logic circuits and send a modulated response to the reader. Depending on the operational frequency of the passive tag, two methods of modulation are used. In tags that operate on a frequency less than 100MHz, charge from the capacitor is released to the antenna in varying strengths over time, changing the radio frequency emitted. The reader receives the data by demodulating the signal using these variances.

In higher-frequency tags, a method known as *backscattering* is utilised, in which the resistance of the antenna is modified by the tag, causing an RF signal to be emitted. The reader receives the tag's data by demodulating the backscatter signal. The operational frequency and antenna design affects the range within which a passive tag can be read, which can be from 10cm to up to a few metres. Due to their simplistic design, passive tags are inexpensive, long-lasting, and can be so small that they fit inside a sheet of paper[8]. A *contactless smart card* is a special type of passive RFID tag where the data is read when it is in close proximity to a reader. The card does not have to be in contact with the reader in order to be read. Its applications include secure access control and loyalty card systems in retail stores. Active tags contain an internal battery that provides a power source for the integrated circuit and antenna. This gives active tags the following advantages over passive tags:

- Autonomy from the reader - Active tags can transmit their own RF signals, rather than have to backscatter one from a reader.
- Increased range – Active tags can typically be read from hundreds of metres away.
- Increased power of signal – The power source boosts the signal, allowing active tags to be read even when underwater or in metal containers.
- Increased storage capacity – More detailed data can be stored about an object, allowing some tags to give information without having to use a serial number to retrieve data from a database.

However, the addition of a power source gives active tags some disadvantages to passive tags:

- More expensive – Active tags cost a lot more to produce because of the increased complexity of the circuit and component design.
- Increased size – The internal power source increases the minimum size of the tag, which may limit possible applications.
- Shorter shelf-life – Active tags need much more maintenance than passive tags, as the internal batteries lose power eventually, meaning that the tag will cease to work until they are replaced. Today, however, batteries in active tags can provide power for up to ten years.

Semi-passive tags are similar to active tags, in that they both contain internal power supplies. They, however, only use it to supply power to the microprocessor and any sensors the tag uses; it is not used to transmit an RF signal. Signals are backscattered to the reader in the same way as a passive tag. Semi-passive tags, while more expensive, generally have faster response times and greater data storage capacity that passive tags due to the battery-assisted circuitry. The battery also usually lasts longer than one contained in an active tag as it is not used to broadcast signals (Weinstein, 2005).

Reader

The reader can come in many different forms, such as a in a hand-held portable device (as shown in Figure 2), fixed in a "portal" that reads any tags passing through, or mounted on a conveyor belt, reading tags as they pass by. Readers send out a signal that interrogates any tags in its vicinity. This interrogation can be as simple as a request for all data contained in a tag's memory, or it can request specific data from different portions of memory. Some readers can also write data to tags that have writeable memory.

Readers receive a signal back from a tag it has interrogated, demodulates the signal and then decodes it into digital data. This data is then passed onto a computer system for processing. While not precise terms, readers can be classified as either "intelligent" or "dumb." Intelligent readers are those that can operate on different protocols and filter data they receive. They are usually frequency agile, meaning they can read tags functioning on different frequencies at the same time. A dumb reader can usually only read one type of tag on one frequency using a single protocol. Reader collision is a problem that arises when a signal from one reader interferes with the signal of another, due to overlap. A solution to this problem is Time Division Multiple Access (TDMA), which basically tells the readers to read at different times. However, any system using TDMA has to compensate for duplicate tag reads, as both readers will read the same tag at different times. Another method of combating reader collision is to operate in "dense reader" mode, where a reader switches to a differ-

ent channel within a frequency range if it detects another reader in close proximity operating on the same channel as its own[10].

Software

Intelligent readers are often computers in themselves, while more simple readers are networked to a separate computer system. Readers only read data from tags, which would be useless without an application that makes use of it. For example, a reader may pass a serial number of an item onto a database application that retrieves data to display it on a screen, modifies the stock number, sets a "sold" flag as to not trigger a shop's security system, sets a "loaned" flag for a book in a library, etc. Most reader software will also include functions for the direct control of the reader itself, writing data to tags, error correction and the handling of duplicate tag reads.

Types of Memory

Tags incorporate different types of memory, namely *read-only, read-write,* and *write-once-read-many.* Passive tags usually employ read-only memory, which has its data written during the microchip's manufacturing process. Once written, the data cannot be edited or erased, making the chips very secure and tamperproof. The memory capacity of most passive tags is very small, around twenty bits (or more if needed), so the data stored is usually a unique tag identification number. Write-Once-Read-Many (WORM) memory is similar to read-only, except that the programming is left to the user, rather than done during manufacturing. Once the user has programmed the memory, it can be said to be the same as read-only memory. Most active tags contain read-write memory, which is also user-programmable, but allows much more flexibility as data can be read and rewritten at all times. Read-Write memory means that tags can store a lot more detailed information, which can be changed during each stage of the track-

Table 1. Main frequency ranges used for RFID

Frequency	Read Range	Tag Type	Average Tag Cost	Applications
125KHz – 134KHz (Low Frequency)	1 Foot	Passive	£0.50	Car Keys, Animal Identification
13.56MHz (High Frequency)	3 Feet	Passive	£0.25	Smart Cards, Library Systems
915MHz – U.S. 868MHz – Europe (UHF)	30 Feet (pass) 300 Feet (act)	Active and Passive	£0.25	Commercial Goods Tracking
2.45GHz (Microwave)	100 Feet	Active and Passive	£12	Motorway tolling systems

ing process of an item. It also allows tags to be reused for different applications later on. Active tags commonly have a memory capacity from 64 bytes to 32Kb, but some hold as much as 1Mb.

Frequency

RFID systems, because they generate and emit electromagnetic waves, are classed as radio systems. Thus, they are subject to regulation from the national radio regulatory body. They must operate on a frequency that does not hinder or disrupt any other radio devices or services, especially television, radio, mobile phones and the radio systems used by the emergency services. There are four main frequency ranges used by RFID systems, illustrated in Table 1.

When choosing what frequency to use, one must consider the environment in which the system is situated, the range at which the tags are to be read and any materials that the RF signals must travel through. Each frequency has its own merits and drawbacks, depending on the application.

- Low-frequency tags are less power hungry and operate very well in environments containing metals, liquids, dirt and mud. Their read-range, however, is very short, often less than one foot (Scher, 2004).
- High-frequency tags have a better read range, ~3 feet, and they work better on metal objects.[11]

- Ultra-High-Frequency (UHF) tags offer much larger read ranges and data transfer rates than high-frequency and low-frequency tags, but there is a large increase in power consumption and a decrease in penetrative ability through certain materials. Large volumes of UHF tags can be identified at the same time, but tags often require a clear path to the reader to be read correctly (Lahiri, 2006).
- RFID tags using microwave frequencies have faster read-rates than UHF but are much more expensive. Microwaves penetrate non-conductive materials very well, but they are absorbed by water. Signals from microwave tags can usually only be read from a certain direction, depending on where the reader is "pointed" (Scher, 2004).

Standards

Standards in RFID dictate guidelines that must be followed to allow interoperability between different systems. There are standards that deal with the air interface protocol (i.e. the method of communication between tags and readers), data formatting (how data is stored on a tag), and the applications of the RFID systems. Two major organisations involved in creating standards for RFID systems are the International Organisation for Standardisation (ISO) and the Auto-ID Center.

Table 2. ISO standards relating to RFID (RFIDWizards.com, 2007)

Standard	Details	Notes
ISO 11784	Identification of animals	Code structure
ISO 11785	Identification of animals	Technical concept
ISO 14223	Identification of animals	Air interface
ISO/IEC 14443	Proximity ID Cards	1 – Physical Characteristics 2 – Power & Signal Interfaces 3 – Anti-collision & Initialisation 4 – Transmission Protocol
ISO/IEC 15961	RFID for item management	Application Interface
ISO/IEC 15962	RFID for item management	Data encoding rules & logical memory functions
ISO/IEC 15693	Vicinity ID Cards	1 – Physical Characteristics 2 – Air Interface & Initialisation 3 – Anti-collision & Transmission Control
ISO/IEC 18000	RFID for item management	1 – Foundation for all air interface definitions in ISO/IEC 18000 2 – Air interface communications below 135khz (Type A = 125kHz; Type B = 134.2kHz) 3 – Air interface communications at 13.56MHz 4 – Air interface communications at 2.45GHz 5 – Withdrawn 6 – Air interface communications at 860MHz to 960MHz 7 – Air interface communications at 433MHz
ISO IEC TR 18046	RFID device performance test methods	N/A
ISO/IEC TR 18047	RFID device conformance test methods	3 – Test methods for air interface communications at 13.56MHz 4 – Test methods for air interface communications at 2.45GHz
ISO 18185	Electronic seal tags	N/A
ISO/IEC 19762	Automatic Identification & Data Capture techniques	3 – RFID
ISO 23389	Freight Containers	Read-Write RFID

The ISO is a worldwide body made up of representatives from national standards organisations. Table 2 shows a list of ISO standards relating to RFID.

The Auto-ID Center

The Auto-ID Center is responsible for a number of important standards in RFID. They were set up as a research group at the Massachusetts Institute of Technology in 1999 to develop the Electronic Product Code (EPC) and related technologies for the tracking of products through the global supply chain[12]. Their objective was to create a cost-effective RFID system that utilised disposable tags, as manufacturers were unlikely to retrieve any tags they put in their products, and operated in the UHF band, to give a suitable read-range for supply chain applications. In order for the RFID system to be used globally - one company could read another company's tag - the Auto-ID Center developed its own standardised air-interface protocols, namely Class 0 and Class 1.

- The Class 0 standard describes the interface, protocol, operational algorithms, and tag requirements operating at a 900MHz frequency. The tags are read-only and are programmed at the factory.
- The Class 1 standard describes the interface, protocol and tag requirements operating at a frequency of 13.56MHz. The

Figure 3. Example EPC and its components (Brock, 2001)

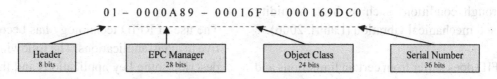

tags are passive and were originally Write-Once-Read-Many (WORM) tags, but most are Read-Many-Write-Many in reality.

In 2003, the Auto-ID Centre split into two separate bodies – Auto-ID Labs, which remained at MIT, and EPCGlobal, which became a subsidiary of the Uniform Code Council (UCC) and Electronic Article Numbering International (EAN). In September of the same year, the Class 0 and Class 1 EPC protocols were handed off to EPCglobal, provided that they would be available to all manufacturers and end-users, royalty-free. The protocols were subsequently ratified by EPCglobal's Board of Governors. In December 2004, the Class 1 Generation 2 protocol was approved by EPCglobal, which had many advantages over the original Class 1, as well as conforming more to ISO standards.

Generation 2 tags' advantages over Class 1 tags include improved tag identification, better equipment compatibility, much faster and more reliable tag reading, better tag security with the ability to lock and kill a tag using a reader, better storage capacity and less expensive. While a barcode will identify the manufacturer and class of a product, the Electronic Product Code uniquely identifies each physical product within this class. Table 3 describes the data components in an Electronic Product Code (Myerson, 2007).

Advantages & Limitations of RFID

RFID systems offer many advantages over a broad range of applications. These advantages include:

Table 3. Data Components in an electronic product code (Myerson, 2007)

Field Name	Field Size	Description
Header	8 bits	Identifies the encoding scheme
EPC Manager	28 bits	Identifies the manufacturer
Object Class	24 bits	Identifies the product class
Serial Number	36 bits	Unique ID for the physical product

- RFID tags do not need to be in any physical contact with the reader in order to be read. This speeds up operation and eliminates wear and tear on the tags and the reader.
- Tags can be read in the absence of line of sight of a reader. Readers can also read tags through certain materials that are "RF-lucent" for the frequency being used.
- Tags with read-write capabilities can have their data rewritten many times. This enables tags to be reused and enhances applications with dynamic tag-writing.
- Tags can have read ranges from an inch to more than one hundred feet, allowing applications to use tags that work within an optimal read range
- The storage capacity passive tags can range from a few hundred bits to a few thousand bytes. Active tags can store any amount of data, as its dimensions are not restricted, provided that the tag is deployable.
- Readers can read multiple tags within a very short period of time
- RFID tags can be equipped with other components, such as sensors, to perform other functions

311

- Many tags are durable enough to survive rough conditions such as heat, humidity and mechanical vibration (Lahiri, 2006).

RFID does suffer from certain limitations and these include:

- Limited penetration of RF signals, even through "RF-lucent" materials;
- Some environments, such as those with RF-opaque and RF-absorbent materials, hinder the technology at certain operational frequencies and, in some cases, prevent it from working at all;
- A bottleneck still exists on the number of tags that can be read within a particular period of time;
- Improper hardware choice and setup can severely hinder an RFID solution. For example, reader collision may occur if multiple readers are not installed correctly;
- Because RFID uses electromagnetic waves, systems can easily be disrupted using jamming devices at the right frequency;
- RFID technology has come into some controversy over privacy. Opponents suggest that RFID, with tags being so small to be barely noticeable, can be used to track individuals without their consent. There are also concerns over the fact that RFID tags attached to products remain functional long after consumer purchase, and can be scanned without their knowledge. Another privacy issue is that if, in future, each retail item is to have its own uniquely-identified tag, every purchased item could be associated with a particular credit card number.
- Even with the cost of some tags being around a few pence each when bought in bulk, RFID is still regarded to be too expensive to implement in many applications, such as item-level stock tracking in retail (Lahiri, 2006).

Modern Applications of RFID

The use of RFID technology has become lucrative in many applications. The following sections describe some key applications and the areas in which they benefit from RFID.

Passports

A number of countries have issued passports containing RFID tags over the past decade. Most RFID tags contain at least 32kb of EEPROM and, to ensure compatibility with different countries, adhere to the ISO/IEC 14443 proximity card standard, among others. Data stored on the tags may include biometric data in the form of facial recognition, fingerprint recognition and/or iris recognition. Tags may also store travel history, i.e. the time, date and place of entries to and exits from each country, unique chip identification number and digital signature to protect the stored data from alteration[13]. This data is used to better authenticate a traveller's citizenship of a country, and also greatly increases the difficulty in producing a counterfeit passport.

Transportation Charges

Many transportation authorities have introduced RFID proximity cards for cashless payment of fares on buses, trains and subways. Most work by allowing the passenger to use cash to "top up" the card at a machine in the station, giving a certain number of journeys. Examples include the Massachusetts Bay Transportation Authority's *CharlieCard* and the *Octopus Card* in Hong Kong. The latter has since evolved to be used for many applications such as payment at vending machines, supermarkets and car parks. RFID tags are also used on many motorways for toll collection, often without the need for the driver to stop or slow down at all. Such systems include the "Eazy Pass" on the M1 Motorway outside

Dublin, Ireland and the DART-Tag on the Dartford Crossing outside London.

Security

RFID security systems are employed at many retail stores to alert staff of the attempted theft of an item. Each item contains an RFID tag, either concealed within the packaging or placed in plain sight, acting as a deterrent to shoplifters. RFID readers act as a "gate" that one must walk through to exit the shop. If these readers detect a tag on an item passing through, an alarm is tripped, indicating the attempted theft. To stop legitimately-bought items from tripping the alarm when customers exit the shop, each items tag is deactivated or "killed" at the counter so it will no longer send any information back to the readers. Similar systems are used in libraries, where a book that hasn't been borrowed at the counter will trip an alarm if it passes through the gates at the exit. However, the tags are not destroyed to allow passage through the gates, as in the retail systems, as the tags need to be reused once the borrower returns the book. Instead, the readers retrieve a unique ID from the tag and consult the library's database server to conclude whether the alarm needs to be triggered[14]. Modern cars are equipped with immobilisers that prevent them from being "hotwired" by allowing the engine to start only when the car's genuine key is being used. Car keys contain RFID tags which store a unique serial number. A reader retrieves this serial number from the car key and compares it to the expected number. If they do not match, the im-

mobiliser is enabled. RFID systems are used by many businesses and organisations to control access to restricted areas, where authorised personnel are given RFID proximity cards. An RFID reader is attached to a system that controls the locking mechanism of a gate or door. The system will only open the lock when a proximity card with a valid ID passes in front of the reader. This type of system allows different levels of security clearance with the same type of card for all personnel.

Supply Chain

Much success has been had with the use of RFID systems in the monitoring of goods as they pass through the supply chain. Figure 4 shows a simple diagram depicting the several stages in the supply chain from the manufacturer to the consumer.

An item can be equipped with an RFID tag to be tracked as it passes through the following points in the chain:

1. At the manufacturer's shipping dock as it is loaded onto a truck;
2. At the receiving dock of the distributor
3. At the distributor's shipping dock as it is loaded onto a truck;
4. At the retailer's as the pallet is unloaded;
5. At the sales counter when a consumer buys the product (Lahiri, 2006)

RFID tags offer a number of advantages over barcodes, another popular method for controlling stock in the supply chain:

Figure 4. Stages in the supply chain

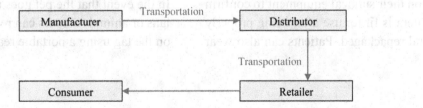

- They do not require line of sight to be read;
- They can be read at any orientation;
- Multiple tags can be read simultaneously;
- They have a larger read range
- They can store more data, e.g. the time and date it arrives and leaves a certain part of the supply chain;
- Less labour is required as reading is more automated (UPS Supply Chain Solutions, 2005).

RFID use is becoming more widespread in the supply chain. Over the past few years, the U.S. retail giant Wal-Mart issued a directive requiring over one hundred of its top suppliers to be compliant with their RFID stock tracking system[15]. These tags are embedded in pallets and cases to be read in warehouses. Many shipping companies also use RFID tags to track trucks, trailers and shipping containers. Some retailers have considered the potential of using item-level RFID tags in-store. This would allow every item in a trolley to be read at once, calculating the total cost in seconds, whereas a barcode reader would take much longer scanning each item individually.

Healthcare

RFID has a number of useful applications in the healthcare and pharmaceutical industries. Pharmaceutical companies can use RFID tags to detect products that are counterfeit, expired or tampered with. They are also useful in clinical trials by improving the tracking of drug usage throughout the testing phase, helping to speed up the approval process by regulatory bodies (UPS Supply Chain Solutions, 2005). Hospitals may make use of RFID tags to keep track of their medical equipment assets, or on their surgical equipment to confirm that each item is fit for use after being properly cleaned and repackaged. Patients can also wear tags (e.g. on wristbands) that contain emergency medical data and also allow them to be tracked throughout the hospital. Some staff may wear RFID tags in order for quick location should an emergency arise (UPS Supply Chain Solutions, 2005). The management of controlled substances and pathogens can be monitored efficiently and safely using an RFID tracking system. RFID tracking can also help to ensure that laboratory specimens, such as blood and biopsy samples, are properly identified (Crounse, 2007).

Animal Tracking and Identification

Many farms use RFID systems to track and identify their livestock, where tags are usually attached to the animal's ear. Each tag contains a unique ID which can then be used to retrieve specific information about the animal from a database, such as the herd it came from, date of birth, inoculations it has had, and blood relations. This becomes especially useful during transportation of the animals, where misidentification of specific animals can have severe financial and health-related consequences. RFID tags are also used to track animal movements, such as the migratory patterns of birds. In 2006, a company named Smart-Tek, based in British Columbia, Canada, successfully completed a test by using RFID to track birds in China, with the objective to map the spread of bird flu (Jones, 2007). A similar system could help prevent the spread of mad cow disease among cattle herds. The state of Colorado in the United States is exploring the possibility of using RFID to track and protect its elk herds (Ou-yang, 2007). Many pet-owners have RFID tags implanted into their pets, which stores the name of the dog, the name of the owner and their contact information. In the event that the pet goes missing, veterinarians or animal rescuers can read the information on the tag using a portable reader.

RFID RADAR AND LOCATION BASED DETERMINATION

RFID has seen widespread use across many different applications. The vast majority of these applications, however, only use the data contained in tags within the reader's zone, rather than the location of the tag at any given time. RFID's potential as a location-determination technology has become increasingly prominent with the development of "RFID-Radar" systems and their installation in places such as prisons, schools and hospitals.

Prisoner Monitoring

Several states in America have employed RFID systems to improve security and automate the monitoring of prison inmates. The Los Angeles County Sheriff Department spent $1.5 million U.S. dollars deploying Alanco Technologies' TSI Prism system at one of their correctional facilities in 2005. The TSI Prism system uses tamper-proof, active RFID tags worn as wristbands by inmates, and RFID readers throughout the jail. Each tag links each inmate to a particular profile in the system, which can be used to restrict them to certain parts of the jail, or keep them away from other particular prisoners. The system alerts prison staff if inmates enter restricted areas or move within a certain range of inmates they are required to stay away from. The ultimate aim is to reduce violence between inmates, deter escape attempts and to monitor their whereabouts at all times[16]. Alanco's TSI Prism system has also been deployed in Minnesota, Michigan, Illinois and Ohio, with other states to follow suit[17].

Child Safety

In 2005, a trial was conducted in Yokohama City, Japan, to monitor the safety and whereabouts of school children as they travelled to and from school. Each participating child wore a 2.4GHz RFID tag complying with the 802.11 Wi-Fi standard. Software known as AeroScout determined the location of the child based on the signal strength of the tag received by Cisco Wi-Fi access points, acting as RFID readers, around the city. The software then used the tag's unique Media Access Control (MAC) address to record the location in a centralised database. The tags could be read up to one thousand feet away, and location estimation was accurate to within ten metres. Each tag also had a call-button which a child could press if they were distressed or in need of assistance. When pressed, the child's parents or guardian received an email notification along with an image of a map showing the location of the child. The system could be set up to notify parents or guardians if their child passed a certain Wi-Fi access point[18]. The *Legoland* theme park in Denmark introduced the "KidSpotter" system in 2004, where young children are fitted with RFID wristbands when they enter the park. The system tracks these wristbands anywhere within the park's boundaries, meaning that parents can be alerted of a child's whereabouts via SMS if their child goes astray.

Alzheimer's Patients

Several tracking systems for patients suffering from Alzheimer's disease and dementia exist in hospitals and nursing homes around the world. These patients wear wristbands containing RFID tags that are detected by readers all around the premises. If a patient tries to leave without being discharged, or enters a potentially dangerous area, staff members are alerted to their whereabouts and are able to facilitate their safe return. Another similar system is that used by Project Lifesaver, an American non-profit organisation that employs search teams equipped with RFID readers to scan for and locate RFID tags contained in wristbands worn by patients that wander away from home[19].

RFID RADAR LOCATION DETERMINATION PROTOTYPE

RFID has seen widespread use across many different applications. The vast majority of these applications, however only use the data contained in tags within the reader's zone, rather than the location of the tag at any given time. Radio Frequency Identification tags can be easily added into most everyday objects. Trolley Scan's RFID-radar (rfid-radar.com, 2007) is an example of an indoor RFID based location determination system that has the accuracy capability of less than fifty centimetres in an area up to one hundred meters deep, however this depends on the tags used and may be as little as ten meters. The system can track up to fifty tags and locate their location within a few seconds. The system has three main components, the reader, the antenna array and the tags. The reader measures the distance of the signals from the tags, the antenna array for energising the tags and finally the tags themselves. Trolley Scan RFID-radar system claims that it can:

- Monitor a zone of up to 100m deep, to an accuracy of less than half a metre
- All tags in reading zone can be scanned within a matter of seconds
- The reader can map out the location of all transponders in the reading zone in one, two or three dimensions and many readers can work in close proximity with minimal interference due to the bandwidth being only 10kHz at UHF frequencies

The reader connects to the computer via an RS232 port. It measures the distance of signals travelling from transponders and provides an energy field to power them. Two or three receiver channels in the reader allow the angle of the signal's arrival to be calculated. The reader's processor can make up to ten thousand range measurements per second and its operational frequency can be set anywhere in the range of 860MHz to

Figure 5. RFID radar screen output

22:45:08	BCBBB0005	21.78	-19.2	-
22:45:08	BCBBB5002	23.53	-0.5	-
22:45:08	BCBBB0026	24.09	31.6	-
22:45:09	BCBBB0004	39.43	-15.5	-
22:45:09	BCBBB0002	11.73	-3.1	-
22:45:09	BBBBB0000	47.88	8.8	-
22:45:09	BCBBB0027	27.01	-22.1	-
22:45:09	BCBBB0026	24.10	32.4	-
22:45:09	BCBBB0002	11.73	-3.0	-
22:45:09	BCBBB0004	39.43	-16.0	-
22:45:09	BCBBB5002	23.53	-2.1	-
22:45:09	BCBBB0005	21.78	-21.5	-

960MHz. The processing module can report the identity, position in 2D or 3D space, and movement at one-second intervals of any tags in the reader zone. Its location accuracy is within half a meter and its pointing accuracy is to within one degree. The tags are passive backscatter Ecotag UHF transponders. The credit-card-sized 200uW EcochipTags have a range of ten meters, while the 5uW stick tags have a maximum operating range of forty meters. The antenna array contains one transmit antenna for energising the passive transponders and one antenna for each receiver, giving a total of three antennas in the array. The system works by measuring the distance the signal travels from each transponder within the reading zone on two receivers. By comparing the ranges on both receivers, the angle of arrival can be calculated, allowing the system to show the range and direction of a tag at the time of reading. By measuring the range many times per seconds, the system can plot the path of moving transponders. Tag location data is streamed to a computer connected to the equipment using an RS-232 port. An example stream, showing data for multiple tags, is shown in Figure 5.

The columns, from left to right in Figure 5, indicate the time of the tag report, the tag ID, the range of the tag in meters and the angle of the tag from the reader's centre-line. The 'P' at the end indicates that the radar has temporarily lost contact with the tag since the last report cycle. Figure

Figure 6. Trolley scan RFID-radar software GUI

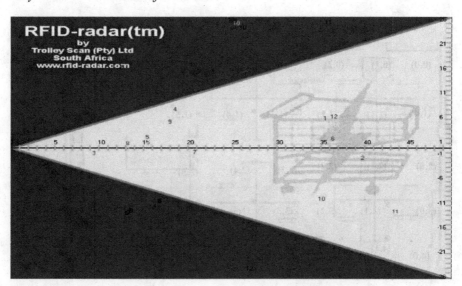

6 shows a graphical representation of the location of the tags in the above data stream, in the demo program supplied with the unit.

We evaluated the base performance of the RFID-radar by comparing the estimated location with the true location of tags in an indoor scenario. Tag Reading range however is affected by goods placed in the path between antenna and tag. The RFID-radar comes with two types of speed tags. The single speed tag they claim can work at up to 51 Kmh and the dual speed tag works at up to 12 Kmh. The RFID reader utilizes an array of adjacent antennas. One transmits an RF constant field to energize the passive transponders, while others depending on the spatial tracking, receive RF signals from transponders. A receiving antenna determines a tag location in one dimension, and two are needed for 2D with three for 3D RFID-radar has two receiving antennas and it determines location in 2D. Dipoles couple to radiation polarized along their axes, so the visibility of a tag with a simple dipole-like antenna is orientation-dependent. Tags with two orthogonal or nearly-orthogonal antennas, often known as dual-dipole tags, are much less dependent on orientation and polarization of the reader antenna,

but are larger and more expensive than single-dipole tags. We tested just single-dipole tags, so the measurements were strictly dependent on their polarization. The antenna was horizontal to the ground and also the tags had to be horizontal to the ground. As the manual refers, when one of the antennas has the wrong polarisation, especially the energiser antenna and the transponder, then no energy is transferred to the transponder and as a result it does not work. The RFID-radar includes three patch antennas in total, which are used to provide a service in close proximity to metal surfaces, but the structure is 2 cm thick, and the need to provide a ground layer and ground connection increases the cost relative to simpler single-layer structures.

The radio frequency environment is a hostile environment for signal strength-based location systems. This is because signal propagation is characterised by reflections, diffractions, and scattering of radio waves caused by structures within the building. Multipath (distortion of a signal due to many different paths to get to the receiver) is an enemy of narrow-band radio. It causes fading where wave interference is destructive. Some UWB systems use "rake" receiver techniques to

Figure 7. Room MG281 with all calibrated locations

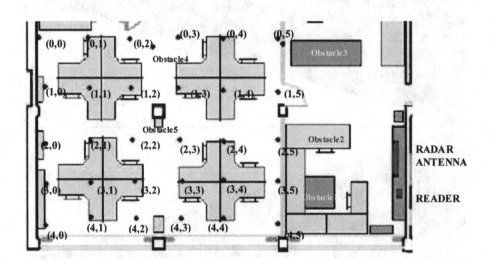

recover multipath generated copies of the original pulse to improve performance on receiver. Other UWB systems use channel equalization techniques to achieve the same purpose. Narrow band receivers as in RFID-radar can use similar techniques, but are limited due to the poorer resolution capabilities of the narrow band systems. Multipath within buildings is strongly influenced by the layout of the building, the construction material used, and the number of people in the building. As the number of people in the building varies, the propagation characteristics of RF signals change as well. This is because the human body is made up of water and water absorbs RF signals. At different times of the day, a different number of humans may be present in the building causing the signal strength at the various locations in the building to vary considerably. As a consequence, a Radio Map created at any one particular time may not accurately reflect the environment at a different time. This can reduce the accuracy of the RADAR system considerably.

For this reason an appropriate indoor test scenario was chosen to test the systems accuracy and we also verified the performance of the system through the following characteristics. With regards

to the actual location estimates, we looked for sufficient precision so that the reported position should be within the range accuracy stated by the maker and systems operation should not interfere with other systems nor crash in active environments. With regard to tracking performance the tracking system should not make jumps that the tracked object would never perform and the trace of the target on screen (or in database) should resemble the actual motion of the target. Additionally, the tracking should show a delay that remains steady and systems operation should not be limited to just a handful of moving nodes and should allow additional nodes to migrate in and fade out. To respect all these constraints, the experiments were carried out in the first floor of MG building in the Magee Campus of the University of Ulster, in a room without humans but containing office furniture (desks, chairs, bookcases and similar). All experiments for the RFID radar were carried out in the same lab as the system could not penetrate walls. Dots on the map in Figure 7 are the calibrated locations.

One design consideration for the evaluation was how the system would translate positional data from the RFID-Radar system to a graphical

Figure 8. Tracking a transponder after calibration

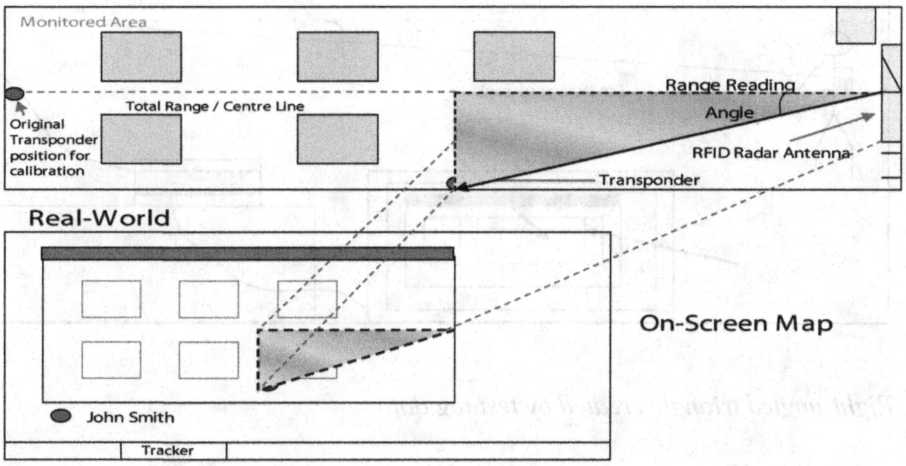

representation shown on our prototype map. The system was "calibrated" for the area to be monitored, by placing a transponder at the far edge of the area and storing its range information. This "total range," shown in Figure 8 was then used in calculations to depict the relative position of transponders to the equipment on the on-screen map. Figure 8 shows the layout of a simple room to be monitored using the RFID-Radar system. A transponder is placed on the far wall, giving the relative location data of the "far edge" of the monitored area. The location data is stored in the program and is assigned to the corresponding edge of the map in the GUI. The transponder used in the calibration process is no longer needed and can be reassigned to an individual to be tracked by the system.

Figure 9 shows how we translated location data from a transponder onto the map in the GUI. It can be seen that a transponder's range and angle reading, together with the centre line, creates an imaginary right-angled triangle. With trigonometric calculations, and the known total range, the triangle could be scaled down so that the icon depicting the tag will appear on the map in the location corresponding to the real tag's location.

Each object (person) to be tracked in the tests was assigned an RFID tag containing a unique ID. The reader in the RFID-Radar system retrieves this ID and calculates the location of the tag. Both the tag's ID and location data were sent to the master computer via an RS232 connection. The monitoring software shows the location of the tag on the map screen using the tag's location data.

Figure 10 shows the imaginary right-angled triangle created by the tag's range and angle reading. The ratio of the X-axis of the tag to the total range is 27.82 / 50, which is 0.556. Therefore, if the on-screen map is 1000 pixels across, the icon representing the tag would appear 556 pixels (0.556 x 1000) across from the left side of the map where Tan (Angle) = Opposite / Adjacent and Opposite = Tan (Angle) * Adjacent therefore the opposite side is equal to: Tan (22) * 556 = 224.6 = 225.

The icon representing the tag should appear 225 pixels above the centerline of the map screen. The calibration distance was set to four meters, and the demo software supplied with the equipment was used to calibrate the system with a stick tag placed four meters in front of the antenna. The demo software then began to stream location data for the tag. Any tag, when it first entered the read-

Figure 9. Overview of system

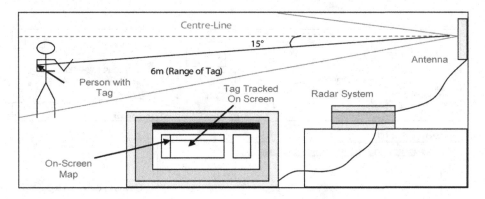

Figure 10. Right-angled triangle created by test tag data

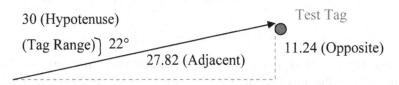

ing field of the equipment, was initially reported with a range of around 60m and an angle of 0°, which was simply not accurate. Each location report for the tag had the same incorrect data for around 45 seconds after the tag entered the field. After around a minute, the reported ranges decreased to a value close to the correct 4m. The associated data is shown in Figure 11.

The angle reports were sometimes erratic, with values fluctuating in a range of 0° - 6°. This was not a major problem at the small test range of 4m as a change of angle that small would not make a very noticeable difference in its mapped location. However, at large ranges, e.g. 30m, even a small fluctuation in the angle value could significantly affect its position on the map. Once the tag's range reports settled on a value near 4m, moving the tag further from or closer to the antenna did not increase or decrease the range. Once the tag was moved, the "RANGE" command had to be submitted to the equipment to recalculate the new range, which took an average of 30 seconds. Sometimes the newly-calculated range was

inaccurate, e.g. increasing from 4m to 9m when moving the tag closer to the antenna.

The main problem unearthed was that the reader was not able to report a correct range or a Tag ID for those locations which were not in line of sight (LoS) with the antennas. LoS is a requirement too restrictive since in a typical indoor environment there are lots of obstacles between the tags and the Antennas. In the room there are some metal obstacles drawn in grey in Figure 12. For static measurements (i.e. objects were not moving), the average error distance of RFID-radar was found to be 4.19m.

Problems for the failure of the reader reporting the range came from Obstacle1 and Obstacle2 (the first one is Lab furniture and the second one a structural vertical building column). Of course in a normal office, there will often be obstacles (objects sizeable compared to the wavelength of the operating frequency, from a couple of centimetres upwards) made of wood or metal. Figure 12 shows the locations in red where the radar failed to log the tag. The bold lines in green high-

Figure 11. Associated data from radar

BCBBB4677^	60.01	007.8	BCBBB4677^	05.89	010.0
BCBBB4677^	60.00	007.8	BCBBB4677^	05.90	010.0
BCBBB4677^	60.00	007.8	BCBBB4677^	05.89	010.0
BCBBB4677^	60.00	007.8	BCBBB4677^	05.87	010.3
BCBBB4677^	60.02	007.8	BCBBB4677^	05.87	010.0
BCBBB4677^	60.01	007.8	BCBBB4677^	05.87	010.0
BCBBB4677^	60.01	007.8	BCBBB4677^	05.87	008.4
BCBBB4677^	60.01	007.8	BCBBB4677^	05.91	009.6
BCBBB4677^	60.03	006.0	BCBBB4677^	05.88	009.3
BCBBB4677^	60.04	006.5	BCBBB4677^	05.91	009.3
BCBBB4677^	60.01	005.8			
BCBBB4677^	05.90	005.8	**RED**	= End portion of Data streamed initially.	
BCBBB4677^	05.90	005.8	GREEN	= Range decreases to a more accurate value.	

*Figure 12. Locations where RFID-radar failed to locate tags in red (Good spots are in **bold green**)*

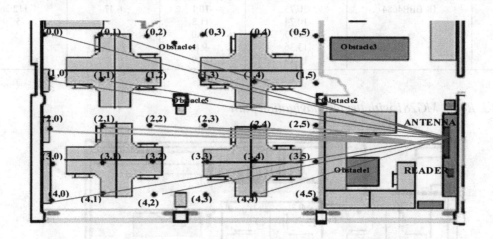

light locations (2,0), (2,1), (2,2), (2,4) and (2,5) where the Radar had good measurements from the tags. Table 4 shows a sample of locations and measurements.

Finally, we tested the ability to track relatively fast moving objects. When the distance of the Tags to the antenna is small, the Accuracy should be high, however when the read range starts increasing uncertainty is introduced into the system. Here we used the single speed Claymore tag. The path navigated for tests shown in Figure 13 was traversed at a very slow walking pace. The average length of each walk was 2 minutes and the sampling rate was 30s. Obstacles caused

the reader to lose the tag thus the accuracy of measurements was poor. We found the radar to require~10-20s to determine the exact position of tags. We found this seriously limiting and would only recommend for static situations where transponders are relatively stationary. However, in reality devices to be tracked are not fixed to a location[21]. Here we found the average error distance for slowly moving devices was 10m.

We noticed an initial delay in reporting a tag's location. These observations may be an indicator that the accuracy of the RFID-Radar equipment is adversely affected in smaller environments where obstacles and interference from other

Table 4. Locations with poor measurements

Location	Tag ID	Range (m)	Angle (grad)	Real Range(m)	AvgRange accuracy(m)
(0,2)	BCBBB4691	12.09	0.0	13.82	(18.17)
		17.63	0.0		4.35
		18.11	0.0		
		24.19	0.0		
		18.84	0.0		
(0,3)	BCBBB4677	11.88	0.0	11.17	(13.95)
		18.44	0.0		2.78
		15.00	0.0		
		15.34	0.0		
		9.12	0.0		
(0,4)	BCBBB4685	12.91	-16.9	9.70	(14.25)
		20.67	-16.9		4.55
		14.47	-13.8		
		12.23	-16.9		
		10.97	-14.8		
(4,5)	BCBBB4684	10.75	-10.1	6.47	(12.26)
		10.74	-11.8		5.79
		13.33	-10.0		
		13.36	-9.8		
		13.15	-10.9		

Figure 13. Room MG281 with the test navigation path

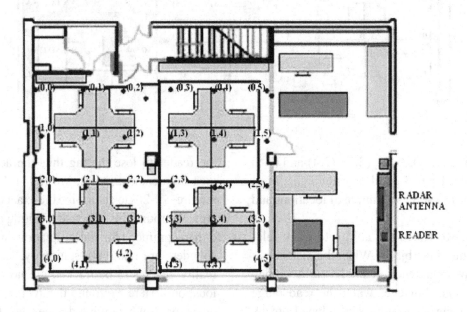

technology may hinder measurement. Range and angle readings often failed to be updated correctly when the tag was moved around. Furthermore, because of frequent fluctuations in the range and angle data supplied by the RFID-Radar equipment, the icons on the map, representing the real-world tags, appeared to "jump" around the point on the map, even if the tag itself was stationary, especially at large ranges.

CONCLUSION

We found the equipment yielded too many inaccurate readings to use the prototype in any practical way. Trolley Scan's RFID-radar transponders were relatively cheap however and the reader can map out the location of all transponders in the reading zone in one, two or three dimensions. Drawbacks were that signals from transponders can be interfered with or may not be read correctly through certain "RF-lucent" materials. For instance, while the claimed reading range of the reader is one hundred meters, the actual range with 5uW passive stick-type transponders is around forty meters. The number of transponders in the reading zone is limited to fifty and only the current range of Ecotag transponders is supported. Finally tags are accurately tracked only when moving under a certain speed and it has to be stated that there is not a strong user-base or development community

Even with accurate tag location data, there is a delay of nearly a minute when calculating the location of a new tag that has entered the radar's field of view, and a similar delay when updating tag data when the tag has moved. These delays would mean that RFID-Radar would be impractical for applications that require accurate real-time locations of moving objects or people over large areas. The RFID-Radar equipment would function best in a large, open environment, with few obstacles and no interference from other RF devices. Suitable applications may include locating stock in an open-plan warehouse, or the location of a parked car in a car park. Delays in updating tag positions would not be critical in these situations, as the tags would most likely be stationary when using the system. RFID technology used in location determination systems may become much more widespread in the future, with new developments such as Ultra-Wideband tags that significantly improve performance and efficiency in indoor environments

REFERENCES

Brock, D. L. (2001). *The Electronic Product Code (EPC)*. Available at http://interval.hu-berlin.de/downloads/rfid/EPC/MIT-AUTOID-WH-002.pdf.

Cambridge Consultants. (2006). *Zonal Location and Asset Tracking with ZigBee Technology (using RSSI)*. Available at http://www.zigbee.org/imwp/idms/popups/pop_download.asp?contentID=9567.

Crounse, B. (2007). *RFID: Increasing patient safety, reducing healthcare costs*. Available at http://www.microsoft.com/industry/healthcare/providers/businessvalue/housecalls/rfid.mspx.

Jones, K. (2006). *Using RFID tags to track bird flu*, EE Times (TechWeb). Online athttp://www.eetimes.com/news/latest/showArticle.jhtml;jsessionid=1K5RGLBMKOARWQSNDBECKHSCJUMEKJVN?articleID=183702439.

Laboratories, R. S. A. (2007). *RFID, A Vision of the* Future. Available at http://www.rsa.com/rsalabs/node.asp?id=2117.

Lahiri, S. (2005). *RFID Sourcebook*. IBM Press. ISBN 0131851373.

Landt, J. (2001). *Shrouds of Time – The History of RFID*. Available at http://www.transcore.com/pdf/AIM%20shrouds_of_time.pdf.

Lomas, N. (2006). *How Orwellian Can You Get – RFID For Air Travellers*. Available at http://networks.silicon.com/lans/0,39024663,39163311,00.htm.

McMullan, C., Cahill, D., & Fry, D. (2007). *Place Lab Geopositioning System*. Available at http://ntrg.cs.tcd.ie/undergrad/4ba2.05/group1/index.html.

Myerson, J. (2006). *RFID In the Supply Chain*. CRC Press. ISBN 0849330181.

Ou-yang, J. (2007). *RFID Will Revolutionize the World*. Available at http://www.cse.ohio-state. edu/~ouyang/RFID%20Technology.htm.

Pellerin, C. (2006). *United States Updates Global Positioning System Technology*. Available at http://usinfo.state.gov/xarchives/display. html?p=washfile-english&y=2006&m=February &x=20060203125928lcnirellep0.5061609.

RFID-Radar.com. (2007). Available at http:// www.rfid-radar.com.

RFIDWizards.com. (2007). *ISO RFID Standards: A Complete List*. Available at http://www.rfidwiz-ards.com/index.php?option=com_content&task= view&id=242&Itemid=174.

Scher, B. (2004). *Understanding RFID Frequencies*. Available at http://www.rfidusa.com/super-store/pdf/Understanding_RFID_Frequencies.pdf.

Stockman, H. (1948). *Communications by Means of Reflected Power*. Proceedings of the IRE (pp. 1196-1204).

Supply Chain Solutions, U. P. S. *RFID In Healthcare* (2005). Available at http://www.ups-scs.com/ solutions/white_papers/wp_RFID_in_healthcare. pdf.

Tedjasaputra, A. (2006). *RFID Tag Attachments*. Available at http://www.rfid-asia.info/2006/12/ rfid-tag-attachments.htm.

Weinstein, R. (2005). *RFID: A Technical Overview and its Application to the Enterprise*. Available at http://ieeexplore.ieee.org/ iel5/6294/32043/01490473.pdf?tp=&arnumber =1490473&isnumber=32043.

Wideman, R. M. (2004). *Project Life Spans in the 1990s*. Available at http://www.maxwideman. com/papers/plc-models/1990s.

ENDNOTES

[1] http://www.o2.co.uk/privacy.html

[2] http://www.locatemobiles.com

[3] http://www.wisegeek.com/what-is-zigbee. htm

[4] http://www.zigbee.org/en/about/faq.asp

[5] http://www.ekahau.com/?id=4500

[6] http://www.ekahau.com/?id=4510

[7] http://www.rfidjournal.com/article/ view/1338/1/129

[8] http://news.bbc.co.uk/1/hi/technolo-gy/6389581.stm

[9] http://www.mobiledataforce.com/Products/ pointsyncRFID_Overview.stm

[10] http://www.rfidjournal.com/faq/19

[11] http://www.rfidjournal.com/faq/17/61

[12] http://www.rfidjournal.com/article/articlev-iew/1335/1/129/

[13] http://travel.state.gov/passport/eppt/ eppt_2788.html

[14] http://www.biblio-tech.com/html/rfid.html

[15] http://www.rfidjournal.com/article/ view/642/1/1

[16] http://www.networkworld.com/ news/2007/061807-us-state-turns-to-rfid. html

[17] http://www.rfidjournal.com/article/ view/1601/1/1

[18] http://www.rfidjournal.com/article/articlev-iew/2050/1/1/

[19] http://www.projectlifesaver.org/public_ html/aboutus.htms

This work was previously published in International Journal of Ambient Computing and Intelligence (IJACI), Volume 1, Issue 4, edited by Kevin Curran, pp. 63-86, copyright 2009 by IGI Publishing (an imprint of IGI Global).

Compilation of References

Abowd, G. D., Atkeson, C. G., Hong, J., Long, S., Kooper, R., & Pinkerton, M. (1997). Cyberguide: A Mobile Context-Aware Tour Guide. *ACM Wireless Networks*, 3(5), 421–433. doi:10.1023/A:1019194325861

Abowd, G., & Mynatt, E. (2002). The humen experience. *IEEE Pervasive*, 1(1), 48–57. doi:10.1109/MPRV.2002.993144

Adamczyk, P., & Bailey, B. (2004). *If not now, when?: the effects of interruption at different moments within task execution*. In CHI '04: Proceedings of the SIGCHI conference on Human factors in computing systems.

Addington, M., & Schodek, D. (2005). *Smart materials and etchnologies for the architecture and design professions*. Elsevier, Architectural Press.

Addlesee, M., Curwen, R., Hodges, S., Newman, J., Steggles, P., & Ward, A. (2001). Implementing a sentient computing system. *IEE Computer*, 34(8), 50–56.

Afsarmanesh, H., Masís, V. G., & Hertzberger, L. O. (2004). Virtual Community Support in Telecare. In *L. Camarinha-Matos & H. Afsarmanesh (Eds.) Processes And Foundations For Virtual Organizations*, 211-220.

Ahmed, A., Ali, J., Raza, A., & Abbas, G. (2006). Wired Vs Wireless Deployment Support For Wireless Sensor Networks. In TENCON 2006 - 2006 IEEE Region 10 Conference (pp. 1-3). Presented at the TENCON 2006 - 2006 IEEE Region 10 Conference, Hong Kong, China.

Åkesson, K.-P., Bullock, A., Greenhalgh, C., Koleva, B., & Rodden, T. (2000). A toolkit for user re-configuration of ubiquitous domestic environments. In *Proceedings of the 15th Annual ACM Symposium on User Interface Software and Technology*, Paris. ACM Press.

Akyildiz, I. F. (2002). Wireless sensor networks: A survey. *Computer Networks*, 38(4), 393–422. doi:10.1016/S1389-1286(01)00302-4

Al–Ali, A. R., & Al-Rousan, M. (2004). Java-Based Home Automation System. *IEEE Transactions on Consumer Electronics*, 50(2), 498–504. doi:10.1109/TCE.2004.1309414

Albanese, E., Banerjee, S., Dhanasiri, S., Fernandez, J. L., Ferri, C., Knapp, M., et al. (2007). *Dementia UK: A report into the prevalence and cost of dementia prepared by the Personal Social Services Research Unit (PSSRU) at the London School of Economics and the Institute of Psychiatry*.

Al-Muhtadi, J., Chetan, S., Ranganathan, A., & Campbell, R. (2004) Super spaces: A middleware for large scale pervasive computing environments. In: *Workshop on Middleware Support for Pervasive Computing (PerWare), PerCom '04 Workshop Proceedings*, Orlando. 198–202

Alonso, R. S., de Paz, J. F., García, Ó., Gil, Ó., & González, A. (2010). HERA: A New Platform for Embedding Agents in Heterogeneous Wireless Sensor Networks. In Hybrid Artificial Intelligence Systems []. Springer Berlin / Heidelberg.]. *Lecture Notes in Computer Science*, 6077, 111–118. doi:10.1007/978-3-642-13803-4_14

Ambient-Devices. (2008). *Baseball scorecast*. http://www.ambientdevices.com/products/sportsCast-Baseball.html

Ames, M., Bettadapur, C., Dey, A., & Mankoff, J. (2003). Healthy Cities Ambient Displays. *In Extended Abstracts of UbiComp 2003*. http://guir.berkeley.edu/pubs/ubicomp2003/healthycities.pdf

Anastasopoulos, M., Bartelt, C., Koch, J., Niebuhr, D., & Rausch, A. (2005, Oct). Towards a reference middleware architecture for ambient intelligence systems. In Proceedings of the workshop for building software for pervasive computing. 20th Conference on Object-Oriented Programming Systems, Languages and Applications (OOPSLA).

Anderson, R. N. (1999). A Method for constructing complete annual U.S. life tables. Vital Health Statistics. *National Center for Health Statistics, 2* (129), 1-28.

Andoh, H., Watanabe, K., Nakamura, T., & Takasu, I. (2004). Network health monitoring system in the sleep. *Proceedings of the SICE Annual Conference* (pp. 1421–1424).

Apel, S., & Böhm, K. (2005). Towards the Development of Ubiquitous Middleware Product Lines. In ASE'04 SEM Workshop, volume 3437 of LNCS.

Arroyo, E., Bonanni, L., & Selker, T. (2005). Waterbot: exploring feedback and persuasive techniques at the sink. Paper presented at the SIGCHI conference on Human factors in computing systems (CHI'05).

Aura (2002) *Distraction-free Ubiquitous Computing.* http://www.cs.cmu.edu/~aura/

Baars, B. J., & Mc Govern, K. (1996). Cognitive views of consciousness, What are the facts? How can we explain them?" In *The Science of Consciousness* (eds.)M. Veldmans Routledge Press, 69.

Babbit, R. (2006). Information Privacy Management in Smart Home Environments: Modeling, Verification and Implementation. *Proceedings of the 30th Annual International Computer Software and Applications Conference* (pp. 344-346).

Bach, K. (1990). Actions Are Not Events, Mind. *Oxford Journals, 89*(353), 114–120.

Bahadori, S., Cesta, A., Grisetti, G., Iocchi, L., Leonel, R., Nardi, D., et al. (2003b). RoboCare: Pervasive Intelligence for the Domestic Care of the Elderly. *AI*IA Magazine Special Issue*.

Bailey, B., Konstan, J., & Carlis, J. (2001). *The Effects of Interruptions on Task Performance, Annoyance, and Anxiety in the User Interface.* In Proceedings of INTERACT '01.

Baldi, P., Chauvin, Y., Hunkapiller, T., & McClure, M. (1994). Hidden Markov models of biological primary sequence information. *Proceedings of the National Academy of Sciences of the United States of America, 91*(3), 1059–1063. doi:10.1073/pnas.91.3.1059

Ballesteros, F., Soriano, E., Leal, K., & Guardiola, G. (2006). Plan b: An operating system for ubiquitous computing environments. In *Proceedings of the Fourth Annual IEEE International Conference on Pervasive Computing and Communications*, pages 126–135. IEEE Computer Society.

Bandara, A., Payne, T., De Roure, D., Gibbins, N., & Lewis, T. (2008). A pragmatic approach for the semantic description and matching of pervasive resources. *International Journal of Pervasive Computing and Communications, 6*(1), 434–446.

Barba, J., de la Fuente, D., Rincón, F., Sánchez, F., & López, J. C. (2010). OpenMax Hardware Native Support for Efficient Multimedia Embedded Systems. *IEEE 2010 International Conference on Consumer Electronics.*(pp. 433-434).

Barnes, N. M., Edwards, N. H., Rose, D. A. D., & Garner, P. (1998). Lifestyle monitoring technology for supported independence. *Comput. Control End. J., 9*(4), 169–174. doi:10.1049/cce:19980404

Bartelt, C., Fischer, T., Niebuhr, D., Rausch, A., Seidl, F., & Trapp, M. (2005, May). Dynamic integration of heterogeneous mobile devices. In Proceedings of the workshop in design and evolution of autonomic application software (deas 2005). ICSE 2005, St. Louis, Missouri, USA.

Barton, J. and Kindberg. T. (2001) *The Cooltown user experience.* Technical report, Hewlett Packard, February 2001.

Bartram, L. R. (2001). *Enhancing information visualization with motion.* Phd thesis, School of computing science; Simon Fraser University, Burnaby, B.C.

Bauchet, J., & Mayers, A. (2005). A modelisation of ADLs in its environment for cognitive assistance. Proceedings of the 3rd International Conference on Smart Homes and Health Telematic (ICOST05). Magog, Quebec, Canada. pp. 221-228.

Bauchet, J., Vergnes, D., Giroux, S., & Pigot, H. (2006). A pervasive cognitive assitant for smart homes. Proceedings of the International Conference on Aging, Disability and Independence. St-Petersburg, FL, USA. pp. 228-234.

Bauer, M., Becker, C., & Rothermel, K. (2002). Location Models from the Perspective of Context-Aware Applications and Mobile Ad Hoc Networks. *Personal and Ubiquitous Computing, 6*(5/6), 322–328. doi:10.1007/s007790200036

Baum, T., Petrie, G., Soules, N., & Weiss, N. (1970). A maximization technique occurring in the statistical analysis of probabilistic functions of Markov chains. *Annals of Mathematical Statistics, 41*(1), 164–171. doi:10.1214/aoms/1177697196

Beal, C., Mitra, S., & Cohen, P. R. (2007). Modeling learning patterns of students with a tutoring system using Hidden Markov Models. Proceedings of the 13th International Conference on Artificial Intelligence in Education (AIED), Marina del Rey, CA, USA pp. 238-245.

Beerman, S., & Rappaport-Musson, J. (2008). [The Caregiver's Complete Handbook for Making Decisions. Prometheus Press.]. *Elderly Care*, 911.

Bellavista, P., Corradi, A., Montanari, R., & Stefanelli, C. (2003). Context- aware middleware for resource management in the wireless internet. *IEEE Transactions on Software Engineering, 29*(12), 1086–1099. doi:10.1109/TSE.2003.1265523

Bellman, R. E. (1957). *Dynamic Programming.* Princeton University Press.

Bergman, E. (2000). *Information Appliances And Beyond, Paperback.* UK: Elsevier Science & Technology.

Beuche, D. (2003). Variant management with pure::variants. Technical report, pure-systems GmbH.

Bhar, R., & Hamori, S. (2004). *Hidden Markov Models – Applications to Financial Economics. Advanced Studies in Theoretical and Applied Econometrics.* Princeton University Press.

Bhattacharya, A., & Das, S. K. (1999). LeZi-Update: an information-theoritic approach to track mobile users in PCS networks. *Proceedings of the 5th annual ACM/IEEE International conference on Mobile Computing and Networking* (pp. 1–12).

Bigioi, P., Cucos, A., Corcoran, P., Chahil, C., & Lusted, K. (1999, August). Transparent, Dynamically Configurable RF Network Suitable For Home Automation Applications. *IEEE Transactions on Consumer Electronics, 45*(3), 474–480. doi:10.1109/30.793529

Bilateral German–Hungarian Collaboration Project on Ambient Intelligence Systems. (2009). (http://www.belami-project.org/ [Online; accessed 06-March-2009])

Blue, P. *IBM project* (2004) http://researchweb.watson.ibm.com/compsci/brochure2001/PlanetBlue.pdf

Blum, J. & Eskandarian, A. (2004). The Threat of Intelligent Collisions. *IT Professional (IEEE Computer Society periodical).*

Boger, J., Hoey, J., Poupart, P., Boutilier, C., Fernie, G. & Mihailidis, A. (2006). A Planning System Based on Markov Model to Guide People with Dementia Through Activities of Daily Living. in IEEE Transactions on Information Technology in BioMedicine. 10(2):323-333

Boldrini, C., Conti, M., Jacopini, I., & Passarella, A. (2007, June). *HiBOp: A History Based Routing Protocol for Opportunistic Networks.* Paper presented in the Proceedings of the WoWMoM 2007, Helsinki.

Bonabeau, E., Dorigo, M., & Théraulaz, G. (1999). *Swarm intelligence: from natural to artificial systems.* Oxford University Press.

boyd, d. (2006). Friends, Friendsters, and MySpace Top 8: Writing community into being on social network sites. First Monday, 11(12).

boyd, d., & Ellison, N. B. (2007). Social network sites: Definition, history, and scholarship. Journal of Computer-Mediated Communication, 13(1), 11.

Boyer, J. (2007). Xforms 1.0 (third edition). Http://www.W3.Org/tr/2007/rec-xforms-20071029/.

Bratman, M. E. (1987). *Intentions, plans and practical reason.* Cambridge, MA, USA: Harvard University Press.

Bratman, M. E., Israel, D., & Pollack, M. (1988). Plans and resource-bounded practical reasoning. *Computational Intelligence, 4,* 349–355. doi:10.1111/j.1467-8640.1988.tb00284.x

Braun, E., & Mühlhäuser, M. (2004, May 25-28). Extending xml uidls for multidevice scenarios. Paper presented at the Workshop on Developing User Interfaces with XML of the Advanced Visual Interfaces Conference, Gallipoli, Italy.

Breejen, J. d., & Deenstra, M. (2007). Ping Pong Pixel.

Brennan, S., & Meier, R. (2007). STIS: Smart Travel Planning Across Multiple Modes of Transportation. In *Proceedings of the 10th International IEEE Conference on Intelligent Transportation Systems (IEEE ITSC 2007)* (pp. 666-671). Seattle, Washington, USA: IEEE Computer Society Press.

Brewer, J. (2004). Factors in Designing Effective Ambient Displays. Poster in Ubicomp 2004.

Brewer, J., Williams, A., & Dourish, P. (2005). Nimio: An Ambient Awareness Device. Paper presented at the European Conference on Computer-Supported Cooperative Work (ECSCW'05).

Brignull, H., & Rogers, Y. (2003). Enticing People to Interact with Large Public Displays in Public Spaces. In Proc. Interact 2003, 17-23.

Brignull, H., et al. (2004). The Introduction of a Shared Interactive Surface into a Communal Space. In Proc. CSCW 2004, 49-58.

Brock, D. L. (2001). *The Electronic Product Code (EPC)*. Available at http://interval.hu-berlin.de/downloads/rfid/EPC/MIT-AUTOID-WH-002.pdf.

Brown, P. J. (1996) The Stick-e Document: a Framework for Creating Context-Aware Applications. In: *Proceedings of Electronic Publishing '96*. Page(s): 259-272

Brownell, B. (2005). *Transmaterial: A Catalog of Materials That Redefine our Physical Environment*. Princeton Architectural Press.

Brownell, B. (2008). *Transmaterial 2: A Catalog of Materials That Redefine our Physical Environment*. Princeton: Architectural Press.

Brownsell, S. J., Bradley, D. A., Bragg, R., Catlin, P., & Carlier, J. (2000). Do community alarm users want Telecare? *Journal of Telemedicine and Telecare, 6*, 199–204. doi:10.1258/1357633001935356

Brumitt, B., Meyers, B., Krumm, J., Kern, A., & Shafer, S. A. (2000). Easyliving: Technologies for intelligent environments. In *Handheld and Ubiquitous Computing, 2nd Intl. Symposium*, pages 12–27.

Brusilovsky, P., Kobsa, A., & Nejdl, W. (Eds.). (2007): The Adaptive Web, Methods and Strategies of Web Personalization. LNCS 4321 Springer, ISBN 978-3-540-72078-2

Buccheri, M. (2005). *Visual heart music.* http://homepages.nyu.edu/mb1328/thesis/. (Online Resources)

Bulla, J., & Berzel, A. (2008). Computational issues in parameter estimation for stationary hidden Markov models. *Computational Statistics. Springer, 23*(1), 1–18.

Bulla, J. (2006). Application of Hidden Markov Models and Hidden Semi-Markov Models to Financial Time Series. *Doctoral Dissertation*. University Library of Munich, Germany.

Bullinger, H.-J., & ten Hompel, M. (Eds.). (2007). *Internet der Dinge*. Berlin: Springer. doi:10.1007/978-3-540-36733-8

Bullivant, L. (2005). *4dspace: Interactive Architecture, Architectural Design*. Wiley-Academy.

Bullivant, L. (2006). *Responsive environments – Architecture, art and design*. V & A Contemporary Publications.

Bullivant, L. (2007). *4dsocial: Interactive Design Environments*. Architectural Design, Wiley-Academy.

Burgess, J., Gallagher, B., Jensen, D., & Levine, B. N. (2006, April). *Maxprop: Routing for vehicle-based disruption-tolerant networking*. Paper presented in the Proceedings of the IEEE INFOCOM, Barcelona.

Burns, B., Brock, O., & Levine, B. N. (2005, March). *MV Routing and capacity building in disruption tolerant networks*. Paper presented in the Proceedings of the IEEE INFOCOM 2005, Miami, FL.

Bynum, A. B., Irwin, C. A., Cranford, C. O., & Denny, G. S. (2003). The impact of telemedicine on patients' cost savings: some preliminary findings. *Telemedicine Journal and e-Health, 9*(4), 361–367. doi:10.1089/153056203772744680

Cai, Y., & Abascal, J. (2006). *Ambient intelligence in everyday life*. Springer-Verlag.

Cai, Y. (2007). Instinctive Computing. In Artifical Intelligence for Human Computing, LNAI 4451.

Calvary, G., Thevenin, D., & Coutaz, J. (2003). A Reference Framework for the Development of Plastic User Interfaces. Retrieved May 20, 2008, from http://iihm. imag.fr/publs/2003/MuiBook03.pdf

Cambridge Consultants. (2006). *Zonal Location and Asset Tracking with ZigBee Technology (using RSSI).* Available at http://www.zigbee.org/imwp/idms/popups/ pop_download.asp?contentID=9567.

Camp, T., Boleng, J., & Davies, V. (2002). A survey of mobility models for ad hoc network research. *Wireless Communication and Mobile Computing Journal, 2*(5), 483–502. doi:10.1002/wcm.72

Capra, L., & Emmerich, W. and Mascolo. C. (2003) Carisma: Context-aware reflective middleware system for mobile applications. *IEEE Transactions on Software Engineering, 29*(10):929 – 45, 2003/10/. doi:10.1109/ TSE.2003.1237173

Capra, L., Emmerich, W., & Mascolo, C. (2001). Reflective middleware solutions for context-aware applications. *Lecture Notes in Computer Science, 2192*, 126–133. doi:10.1007/3-540-45429-2_10

Carbonell, N. (2006). Ambient Multimodality: towards Advancing Computer Accessibility and Assisted Living. *International Journal on Universal Access in the Information Society*, 18-26.

Celler, B. G., Earnshaw, W., Ilsar, E. D., Betbeder-Matibet, L., Harris, M. F., & Clark, R. (1995). Remote monitoring of health status of the elderly at home. A multidisciplinary project on aging at the University of New South Wales. *International Journal of Bio-Medical Computing, 40*(2), 147–155. doi:10.1016/0020-7101(95)01139-6

Celler, B. G., Hesketh, T., Earnshaw, W., & Ilsar, E. (1994) An instrumentation system for the remote monitoring of changes in functional health status for elderly at home. *Proceedings of the 16th Annual International Conference of the IEEE EMBS, 2,* 908 – 909.

Cesta, A., Bahadori, S., Cortellesa, G., Grisetti, G., & Giuliani, M. (2003). The RoboCare Project, Cognitive Systems for the Care of the Elderly. *In Proceedings of International Conference on Aging, Disability and Independence (ICADI'03).* Washington, DC, USA.

Chan, M., Estève, D., Escriba, C., & Campo, E. (2008). A review of smart homes—Present state and future challenges. *Computer Methods and Programs in Biomedicine, 91*, 55–81. doi:10.1016/j.cmpb.2008.02.001

Chan, M., Hariton, C., Ringeard, P., & Campo, E. (1995). Smart House automation system for the elderly and the disabled. *Proceedings of the IEEE International Conference on Systems, Man and Cybernetics* (pp. 1586-1589).

Chang, A., Resner, B., Koerner, B., Wang, X., & Ishii, H. (2001). Lumitouch: An emotional communication device. *CHI'01 extended abstracts on human factors in computing systems* (p. 313-314). New York, NY, USA: ACM Press.

ChaosComputerClub. (2001). Project Blinkenlights.

Chater, N. (2002). Simplicity: A unifying principle in cognitive science. Retrieved November 16, 2008, from http://homepages.cwi.n/~paulv/papers/tcs02.pdf

Chavez, B. R. (2003). Effects of Stress and Relaxation on Time Perception. Masters thesis, Uniformed Services University of the Health Sciences, Bethesda, Maryland.

Chellappa, R., Wilson, C. L., & Sirohey, S. (1995). Human and machine recognition of faces: a survey. *Proceedings of the IEEE, 83*(5), 705–741. doi:10.1109/5.381842

Chen, H., & Joshi, A. (2004). An Ontology for Context-Aware Pervasive Computing Environments, *Special Issue on Ontologies for Distributed Systems. The Knowledge Engineering Review, 18*(3), 197–207. doi:10.1017/ S0269888904000025

Chen, G., & Kotz, D. (2000) A Survey of Context-Aware Mobile Computing Research, *Dartmouth Computer Science Technical Report TR2000-381,* Department of Computer Science, Dartmouth College, November 2000.

Chen, H. (2004) *An Intelligent Broker Architecture for Pervasive Context-Aware Systems,* PhD Thesis, University of Maryland, Baltimore County.

Chen, H. Perich. F., Finin, T. and Joshi. A. (2004) SOUPA: Standard Ontology for Ubiquitous and Pervasive Applications. *Proceedings of Mobiquitous 2004: International Conference on Mobile and Ubiquitous Systems: Networking and Services*, Boston, USA.

Cheverst, K., Davies, N., Mitchell, K., Friday, A., & Efstratiou, C. (2000). Experiences of Developing and Deploying a Context-aware Tourist Guide: The GUIDE Project. In *Proceedings of the Sixth Annual International Conference on Mobile Computing and Networking (MobiCom 2000)* (pp. 20-31). Boston, Massachusetts, USA: ACM Press.

Choi, J., Shin, D., & Shin, D. (2006). Intelligent pervasive middleware based on biometrics. *Lecture Notes in Computer Science, 4159*, 157. doi:10.1007/11833529_16

Churchill, E. F., Nelson, L., Denoue, L., Helfman, J., & Murphy, P. (2004). Sharing Multimedia Content with Interactive Public Displays: A Case Study. *In Proceedings of the 5th conference on Designing Interactive Systems* (pp. 7-16). New York: ACM.

Clear, A. K. Dobson. S. and Nixon. P. (2007) An approach to dealing with uncertainty in context-aware pervasive systems. In: *Proceedings of the UK/IE IEEE SMC Cybernetic Systems Conference 2007. IEEE Press.*

Cleveland, W. S., & McGill, R. (1984, September). Graphical perception: Theory, experimentation, and application to the development of graphical methods. *Journal of the American Statistical Association, 79*(387), 531–546. doi:10.2307/2288400

Cogknow, Helping people with mild dementia navigate their day (2008). Retrieved July 8 2008, from http://www.cogknow.eu/

Consolvo, S., Klasnja, P., McDonald, D. W., Avrahami, D., Froehlich, J., LeGrand, L., et al. (2008). Flowers or a robot army?: encouraging awareness & activity with personal, mobile displays. In UbiComp '08: Proceedings of the 10th international conference on Ubiquitous computing, NY, USA, 2008 (pp. 54–63). ACM.

Context Aware Computing Group Blog, (2006) http://context.media.mit.edu/press/

Conti, M., & Giordano, S. (2007). Multihop Ad Hoc Networking: The Theory. *IEEE Communications Magazine, 45*(4), 78–86. doi:10.1109/MCOM.2007.343616

Conti, M., & Giordano, S. (2007). Multihop Ad Hoc Networking: The Reality. *IEEE Communications Magazine, 45*(4), 88–95. doi:10.1109/MCOM.2007.343617

Conti, M., Crowcroft, J., Giordano, S., Hui, P., Nguyen, H. A., & Passarella, A. (2008). Minema. H. Miranda, L. Rodrigues, & B. Garbinato (Ed.), *Routing issues in Opportunistic Networks.* Springer

Corchado, J. M., Bajo, J., Tapia, D. I., & Abraham, A. (2010). Using Heterogeneous Wireless Sensor Networks in a Telemonitoring System for Healthcare. *Information Technology in Biomedicine. IEEE Transactions on, 14*(2), 234–240.

Corchado, J. M., Pavón, J., Corchado, E., & Castillo, L. F. (2005). Development of CBR-BDI agents: A tourist guide application. *In Proceedings of the 7th European Conference on Case-based Reasoning 2004, Lecture Notes in Artificial Intelligence (LNAI). 3155*, pp. 547-559. Springer-Verlag.

Coronado, E., & Cherkaoui, S. (2007). Secure Service Provisioning for Vehicular Networks. *International Workshop on ITS for Ubiquitous ROADS (UBIROADS).*

Costa-Font, J., & Patxot, C. (2005). The design of the long-term care system in Spain: Policy and financial constraints. *Social Policy and Society, 4*(1), 11–20. doi:10.1017/S1474746404002131

Council on Competitiveness. (1996). Hi*ghway to Health: Transforming US Health Care in the Information Age*, Washington D.C.

Courtemanche, F., Najjar, M., Paccoud, B., & Mayers, A. (2008). Assisting Elders via Dynamic Multi-tasks Planning – A Markov Decision Processes based Approach. Proceedings of the ACM International Conference on Ambient Media and Systems (Ambi-Sys '08). Quebec City, Canada. pp:312-321

Crounse, B. (2007). *RFID: Increasing patient safety, reducing healthcare costs.* Available at http://www.microsoft.com/industry/healthcare/providers/businessvalue/housecalls/rfid.mspx.

Cwiek, M.A., Rafig, A., Qamar, A., Tobey, C., & Merrel, R.C. (2007). Telemedicine Licensure in the United State: the need for a cooperative regional approach. *Journal of Telemedicine, e-Health, 13*(2)141-147.

Czarnekci, K. (2005). Staged Configuration through Specialization and Multi-Level Configuration of Feature Models. Software Process Improvement and Practice, special issue on. *Software Variability: Process and Management, 10*(2), 143–169.

Czerwinski, M., Robertson, G., Meyers, B., Smith, G., & Robbins, D. (2006). Large Display Research Overview. In *CHI '06: Extended Abstracts on Human Factors in Computing Systems* (pp. 69–74). New York: ACM. doi:10.1145/1125451.1125471

Dahley, A., Wisneski, C., & Ishii, H. (1998). Water lamp and pinwheels: Ambient projection of digital information into architectural space. *CHI '98 conference summary on human factors in computing systems* (pp. 269-270). New York, NY, USA: ACM Press.

Daly, H. L. (2000). Telemedicine: the invisible legal barriers to the healthcare of the future. *Annals of Health Law*, 73–106.

Dansky, K. H., Thompson, D., & Sanner, T. (2006). A framework for evaluating eHealth research. *Evaluation and Program Planning, 29*(4), 397–404. doi:10.1016/j.evalprogplan.2006.08.009

Das, S. K., Cook, D. J., Bhattacharya, A., Heierman, E. O., & Lin, T. Y. (2002). The role of predicting algorithm in the MavHome smart home architecture. *IEEE Wireless Communications, 9*(6), 77–84. doi:10.1109/MWC.2002.1160085

Davidson, D. (1963). Actions, Reasons, and Causes. *The Journal of Philosophy, 60*(23), 685–700. doi:10.2307/2023177

Davies, R. J., Nugent, C. D., Donnelly, M. P., Hettinga, M., Meiland, F. J., & Moelaert, F. (2009). A user driven approach to develop a cognitive prosthetic to address the unmet needs of people with mild dementia. *Pervasive and Mobile Computing, 5*(3), 253–267. doi:10.1016/j.pmcj.2008.07.002

de Bruijn, J. (2003). Using ontologies. enabling knowledge sharing and reuse on the semantic web. Technical report, Technical Report DERI-2003-10-29, DERI, 2003.

de Ipiña, D. L., Vazquez, J., Garcia, D., Fernandez, J., García, I., Sainz, D., & Almeida, A. (2006). A middleware for the deployment of ambient intelligent spaces. *Lecture Notes in Computer Science, 3864*, 239. doi:10.1007/11825890_12

Dean, T., & Lin, S. H. (1995). *Decomposition techniques for planning in stochastic domains.* Technical Report CS-95-10, Department of Computer Science, Brown University, Providence, Rhode Island, USA.

Decker, K., & Li, J. (1998). Coordinated hospital patient scheduling. *In Proceedings of the 3rd International Conference on Multi-Agent Systems (ICMAS'98)* (pp. 104-111). IEEE Computer Society.

Demiris, G., Skubic, M., Rantz, M., Keller, J., Aud, M., Hensel, B., & He, Z. (2006). Smart Home Sensors for the Elderly: A Model for Participatory Formative Evaluation. *Proceedings of the IEEE EMBS International Special Topic Conference on Information Technology in Biomedicine* (pp. 1-4).

Denning, P. J., & Metcalfe, R. M. (1998). Beyond Calculation: The Next Fifty Years of Computing, Springer, 83-84.

Dey, A. K., & de Guzman, E. (2006). From awareness to connectedness: the design and deployment of presence displays. In *Proceedings of the CHI'06*, 899–908

Dey, A., & Abowd, G. (2000). Towards a Better Understanding of Context and Context-Awareness. In *the Workshop on The What, Who, Where, When, and How of Context-Awareness, as part of the 2000 Conference on Human Factors in Computing Systems (CHI 2000)* (pp. 1 - 12). The Hague, The Netherlands.

Dey, A.K., Salber, D., Futakawa, M. and Abowd, G.D. (1999) An Architecture to Support Context-Aware Computing. *Submitted to UIST '99.*

Didigo, (2006). Didigo SmartDrive USB Key. Retrieved December 1, 2008, from Ubergizmo, The Gadget Blog Web site: http://www.ubergizmo.com/15/archives/2006/01/didigos_smartdrive_usb_key_with_led_display.html

Diegel, O. (2005). Intelligent automated health systems for compliance monitoring. *Proceedings of the IEEE Region, 10*, 1–6.

Dietterich, T. G. (1998). The MAXQ Method for Hierarchical Reinforcement Learning. *Proceedings of the 15th International Conference on Machine Learning.* pp: 118-126

Dobson, S., Coyle, L., & Nixon, P. (2007). *Hybridising events and knowledge as a basis for building autonomic systems.* IEEE TCAAS Letters.

Dourish, P. (2004). What we talk about when we talk about context. *Personal and Ubiquitous Computing, 8*(1), 19–33. doi:10.1007/s00779-003-0253-8

Dowling, J., Cunningham, R., Harrington, A., Curran, E., & Cahill, V. (2005). Emergent Consensus in Decentralised Systems using Collaborative Reinforcement Learning. In *Post-Proceedings of SELF-STAR: International Workshop on Self-* Properties in Complex Information Systems* (pp. 63-80): Springer-Verlag.

Downie, A. (2008). São Paulo Sells Itself. In *Time Magazine, US Edition*, 172:22. New York: Time Warner.

Ducatel, K., Bogdanowicz, M., Scapolo, F., Leijten, J. and Burgelma, J.C. (2001) *ISTAG:* Scenarios for ambient intelligence in 2010. *ISTAG 2001 Final Report.*

Dusparic, I., & Cahill, V. (2009). Distributed W-Learning: Multi-Policy Optimization in Self-Organizing Systems. In *Proceedings of the Third IEEE International Conference on Self-Adaptive and Self-Organizing Systems (SASO '09)* (pp. 1-10): IEEE Press.

E.INK. (2006). *Electronic paper dsiplays.* http://www.eink.com/. (Online Resources)

Eberhart, R. C., Shi, Y. and Kennedy, J. (2001) *Swarm Intelligence.* Morgan Kaufmann; 1st edition, 978-1558605954

E-Health Code of Ethics. (2000, May 24). *Journal of Medical Internet Research.* Retrieved July 10 2008, from http://www.jmir.org/2000/2/e9/

E-Health Ethics Summit Releases Code, the Industry Standard (2000). Retrieved July 10 2008, from http://www.thestandard.com/article/0,1902,11564,00.html

Eisenhauer, M., Rosengren, P., & Antolin, P. (2009). A Development Platform for Integrating Wireless Devices and Sensors into Ambient Intelligence Systems. *Sensor, Mesh and Ad Hoc Communications and Networks Workshops, 2009. SECON Workshops '09. 6th Annual IEEE Communications Society Conference.*(pp. 1-3).

Eisenstein, J., Vanderdonckt, J., & Puerta, A. (2000). Adapting to mobile contexts with user-interface modeling. In *wmcsa*, page 83. Published by the IEEE Computer Society.

Elliot, K., & Greenberg, S. (2004). Building Flexible Displays for Awareness and Interaction. In *Proceedings of the UbiComp '04 Workshop on Ubiquitous Display Environments*, Nottingham, U.K.

Ellison, N. C. S., & Lampe, C. (2006). Spatially Bounded Online Social Networks and Social Capital: The Role of Facebook. In Annual Conference of the International Communication Association, Dresden, Germany, 2006.

ENABLE project. (2008). *Can Technology help people with Dementia?* Retrieved July 7, from http://www.enableproject.org/

Endres, C., Butz, A., & MacWilliams, A. (2005). A Survey of Software Infrastructure and Frameworks for Ubiquitous Computing. *Mobile Information Systems, IOS Press, 1*(1), 41–80.

Engelbrecht, A. P. (2007). *Computational Intelligence, An Introduction.* John Wiley & Sons.

Engelmore, R., & Morgan, T. (1988). *Blackboard systems.* MA: Addison-Wesley Reading.

Erickson, P., Wilson, R., & Shannon, I. (1995). Years of Healthy Life. *Statistical Notes* (7).

Erman, L., Hayes-Roth, F., Lesser, V., & Reddy, D. (1980). The hearsay-ii speech-understanding system: Integrating knowledge to resolve uncertainty. [CSUR]. *ACM Computing Surveys, 12*(2), 213–253. doi:10.1145/356810.356816

European Commission. (URL accessed in 2008). The KAREN European ITS Framework Architecture.

European Radio Commissions Committee. (2005) Frequencies and Standards. (on-line) http://www.ero.dk/doc98/official/pdf/ REP083.PDF#433050000. Accessed 5th July 2005.

Evans, J. R., Boersma, J., Blachman, N. M., & Jagers, A. A. (1988). The Entropy of a Poisson Distribution. *SIAM Review, 30*(2), 314–317. doi:10.1137/1030059

Fajardo, N., & Vande Moere, A. (2008). ExternalEyes: Evaluating the Visual Abstraction of Human Emotion on a Public Wearable Display Device. Paper presented at the Conference of the Australian Computer-Human Interaction (OZCHI'08), Cairns, Australia.

Federal Trade Commission. (1998). *Privacy Online: A report to Congress (Part III), Fair Information Practice Principles.* Retrieved Oct 21 2008, from http://www.ftc.gov/reports/privacy3/fairinfo.htm, June 1998.

Feller, W. (1968). An Introduction to Probability Theory and its Applications (Volume I). John Wiley & Sons (Eds.).

Ferscha, A. (2007) A Matter of Taste. *Workspace Awareness in Mobile Virtual Teams*, In *Proceedings of the 9th IEEE International Workshop on Enabling Technologies.* Retrieved September 14, 2010 from portal acm.org/citation.cfm?id=1775424

Ferscha, A., Emsenhuber, B., Schmitzberger, H., Thon P. (2006). Aesthetic Awareness

Fischer-Hubner, S., & Ott, A. (1998). From a formal Privacy Model to its Interpretation. *Proceedings of the 21st National Information Systems Security Conference*

Fisher, G. (2008. April 5-10). Challenges and Opportunities fro Distributed Participatory Design (DPD). In *proceedings of CHI 2008*, Florence, Italy, ACM Press.

Flachbart, G., & Weibel, P. (2002). *Disappearing architecture – From real to virtual to quantum.* Birkhäuser.

Fogarty, J., Forlizzi, J., & Hudson, S. E. (2001). Aesthetic information collages: Generating decorative displays that contain information. *UIST '01: Proceedings of the 14th annual ACM symposium on user interface software and technology* (p. 141-150). New York, NY, USA: ACM Press.

Fogg, B., & Iizawa, D. (2008). Online Persuasion in Facebook and Mixi: A Cross-Cultural Comparison. *Persuasive Technology, 2008*, 35–46. doi:10.1007/978-3-540-68504-3_4

Forlizzi, J., Li, I., & Dey, A. (2007). Ambient Interfaces that Motivate Changes in Human Behaviour. Retrieved May 20, 2008, from http://ftp.informatik.rwth-aachen.de/Publication/CEUR-WS/Vol-254/paper02.pdf

Frischholz, R. (2005). *Face detection.* Online Resources. (http://www.facedetection.com/)

Fu, X., & Li, D. (2005). *Haptic Shoes: Representing Information By Vibration.* in *In Proc. Asia Pacific Symposium on Information Visualisation.* Sydney: CRPIT.

Fuentes, L., & Gámez, N. (2008). A Feature Model of an Aspect-Oriented Middleware Family for Pervasive Systems, In Proc. AOSD Workshop on Next Generation Aspect Oriented Middleware, 11-16, Belgium.

Fuentes, L., et al. (2005). An Aspect-Oriented Ambient Intelligence Middleware Platform, In Proc. 3rd Int. Work. on Middleware for Pervasive and Ad-Hoc Computing.

Fuentes, L., et al. (2006). Combining Components, Aspects, Domain Specific Languages and Product lines for Ambient Intelligent Application Development, Proc. of International Conference on Pervasive Computing, Ireland.

Future-Application-Lab. *Informative Art.* http://www.viktoria.se/fal/projects/infoart/. Accessed on 3 April, 2006; Online Resources.

Gaber, J. (2007). *Spontaneous Emergence Model for Pervasive Environments* (pp. 1–4). IEEE Proceedings of Globecom Workshops.

Gaia Project. (2005) *Active Spaces for Ubiquitous Computing* http://gaia.cs.uiuc.edu/

Gajos, K. Z. (2008) "Automatically Generating User Interfaces," In: Ph.D.Dissertation, Retrieved July 30, 2009, from http://www.cs.washington.edu/ai/puirg/papers/kgajos-dissertation.pdf

García-Herranz, M., Haya, P. A., Esquivel, A., Montoro, G., & Alamán, X. (2008). Easing the smart home: Semi-automatic adaptation in perceptive environments. *J. UCS, 14*(9), 1529–1544.

Gaver, W., Bowers, J., Boucher, A., Law, A., Pennington, S., & Villar, N. (2006). The history tablecloth: illuminating domestic activity. In *Proceedings of the 6th conference on Designing Interactive systems* (pp. 199-208). University Park, PA, USA: ACM

Gelernter, D. (1985). Generative communication in linda. [TOPLAS]. *ACM Transactions on Programming Languages and Systems, 7*(1), 80–112. doi:10.1145/2363.2433

Gellersen, H. W., Schmidt, A., & Beigl, M. (1999). Ambient Media for Peripheral Information Display. *Personal and Ubiquitous Computing, 3*(4), 199–208. doi:10.1007/BF01540553

Georgantas, N., Mokhtar, S. B., Bromberg, Y. D., Issarny, V., Kalaoja, J., Kantarovitch, J., et al. (2005). The Amigo Service Architecture for the Open Networked Home Environment, *IEEE Proc. of 5th Working IEEE/IFIP Conference on Software Architecture,* (pp. 295-296).

Georgeff, M. P. (1984). A Theory of Action for MultiAgent Planning, *Proceedings of 1984 conference of the American Association for Artificial intelligence.* (pp. 121-125).

Gerlach, M., Festag, A., Leinmüller, T., Goldacker, G., & Harsch, C. (2007). Security Architecture for Vehicular Communication. *International Workshop on Intelligent Transportation (WIT).*

Ghosh, J., Sumesh J. Philip, & Chunming, Q. (2007, March). Sociological Orbit aware Location Approximation and Routing (SOLAR) in MANET. *ELSEVIER Ad Hoc Networks Journal, 5*(2), 189-209.

Gilad, L., & Croft, C. (2007). *imPulse.* In CHI '07: Extended Abstracts of the SIGCHI conference on Human factors in computing systems.

Golder, S. A., Wilkinson, D., & Huberman, B. A. (2007). Rhythms of Social Interaction: Messaging within a Massive Online Network. In 3rd International Conference on Communities and Technologies (C&T 2007).

Golle, P., Greene, D., & Staddon, J. (2004). Detecting and Correcting Malicious Data in VANETs. *ACM International Workshop on Vehicular Ad Hoc Networks (VANET).*

Gómez, J., Montoro, G., & Haya, P. A. (2008). ifaces: Adaptative user interfaces for ambient intelligence. In *Proceedings of IADIS International Conference Interfaces and Human Computer Interaction*, pages 133 – 140.

Gong, L. (2001). A software architecture for open service gateways. *IEEE Internet Computing, 5*(1), 64–70. doi:10.1109/4236.895144

González-Bedia, M., & Corchado, J. M. (2002). A planning Strategy based on Variational Calculus for Deliberative Agents. *Computing and Information Systems Journal, 10*, 2–14.

Google. (2006). *Ambient displays in the googleplex.* http://tecfa.unige.ch/perso/staf/nova/blog/2006/06/03/ambient-displays-in-the-googleplex/. (Online Resources)

Gossett, W. S. (2006). *Student's t-tests.* http://www.physics.csbsju.edu/stats/t-test.html. (Online Resources)

Greenberg, S., & Fitchett, C. (2001, November 11-14). Phidgets: Easy development of physical interfaces through physical widgets. Paper presented at the 14th annual ACM symposium on User interface software and technology, Orlando, Florida.

Greenfield, A. (2006). *Everyware – The dawning age of ubiquitous computing.* New Riders.

Greenwood, P. et al (2008). Reference architecture. AOSDEurope NoE Public Documents (AOSD-Europe-ULANC-37).

Gross, T. (2003). Ambient interfaces: Design challenges and recommendations. *10th international conference on human-computer interaction-HCI'03* (pp. 68-72). Crete, Greece: Lawrence Erlbaum.

Grossglauser, M., & David, N. C. T. (2002). Mobility Increases the Capacity of Ad hoc Wireless Networks. *IEEE/ACM Transactions on Networking, 10*(4). doi:10.1109/TNET.2002.801403

Grossglauser, M., & Vetterli, M. (2003, March). *Locating nodes with EASE: last encounter routing in ad hoc networks through mobility diffusion.* Paper presented in the Proceedings of the *22nd IEEE Annual Joint Conference of the IEEE Computer and Communications Societies (IEEE INFOCOM 2003)*, San Francisco.

Grossmann, M., Bauer, M., Hönle, N., Käppeler, U.-P., Nicklas, D., & Schwarz, T. (2005). Efficiently Managing Context Information for Large-scale Scenarios. In *Proceedings of the Third IEEE International Conference on Pervasive Computing and Communications (PerCom 2005)* (pp. 331-340). Kauai Island, Hawaii, USA: IEEE Computer Society.

Grosz, E. (2001). *Architecture from the outside – Essays on virtual and real space.* MIT Press.

Gu, T., Pung, H. K., & Zhang, D. Q. (2004) A Bayesian approach for dealing with uncertain contexts", In *the Proceeding of the Second International Conference on Pervasive Computing (Pervasive 2004)*, Vienna, Austria, April 2004.

Guan, R., Pruehsner, W. R., & Enderle, J. D. (2000, April). The Computerized Environmental Remote Control. *Proceedings of the IEEE 26th Annual Northeast Bioengineering Conference* (pp. 147–148).

Guillén, S., Arredondo, M. T., Traver, V., García, J. M., & Fernández, C. (2002). Multimedia telehomecare system using standard tv set. *IEEE Biomed. Eng, 49*(12), 1431–1437. doi:10.1109/TBME.2002.805457

Ha, K. N., Lee, K. C., & Lee, S. (2006). Development of PIR sensor based indoor detection system for smart home. *Proceedings of the SICE-ICASE international Joint Conference* (pp. 2162-2167).

Hallnäs, L., & Redström, J. (2001). Slow Technology: Designing for Reflection. *Personal and Ubiquitous Computing, 5*(3), 201–212. doi:10.1007/PL00000019

Hansmann, U. (2003). *Pervasive computing: The mobile word.* Springer.

Harrington, T. L., & Harrington, M. K. (EDS.) (2000). *Gerontechnology Why and How.* Herman Bouma Foundation of Gerontechnology, Eindhoven, the Netherlands, Shaker Publishing B.V.

Harrison, C., Amento, B., Kuznetsov, S., & Bell, R. (2007). Rethinking the progress bar. In UIST '07: Proceedings of the 20th annual ACM symposium on User interface software and technology, New York, NY, USA, 2007 (pp. 115–118). ACM.

Harsch, C., Festag, A., & Papadimitratos, P. (2007). Secure Position-Based Routing for VANETs. *IEEE Vehicular Technology Conference (VTC-Fall).*

Haya, P. A., Alamán, X., & Montoro, G. (2001). A comparative study of communication infrastructures for the implementation of ubiquitous computing. *UPGRADE. The European Journal for the Informatics Professional, 2*, 5.

Haya, P. A., Montoro, G., & Alamán, X. (2004). A prototype of a context-based architecture for intelligent home environments. In *International Conference on Cooperative Information Systems (CoopIS 2004).*

Hayes-Roth, B. (1985). A blackboard architecture for control. *Artificial Intelligence, 26*(3), 251–321. doi:10.1016/0004-3702(85)90063-3

Hazelwood, W., Coyle, L., Pousman, Z., & Lim, Y.-K. (2008). Ambient Information Systems. In

Hazlewood, W. R., & Knopke, I. (2008). Designing Ambient Musical Information Systems. In Proceedings of the *8th International Conference on New Interfaces for Musical Expression* (pp. 281-285) Genoa, Italy: ACM

Heer, J., & boyd, d. (2005). Vizster: Visualizing Online Social Networks. In IEEE Symposium on Information Visualization (InfoVis 2005). Minneapolis, Minnesota, October 23-25.

Heiner, J. M., Hudson, S. E., & Tanaka, K. (1999). *The information percolator: Ambient information display in a decorative object.* In *Proceedings of the 12th Annual ACM Symposium on User Interface Software and Technology.* ACM Press.

Heinzelman, W. B. (2004). Middleware to support sensor network applications. *IEEE Network, 18*(1), 6–14. doi:10.1109/MNET.2004.1265828

Helal, S., Mann, W., El-Zabadani, H., King, J., Kaddoura, Y., & Jansen, E. (2005). The Gator Tech Smart House: a programmable pervasive space. *Computer, 38*(3), 50–60. doi:10.1109/MC.2005.107

Helal, S., Winkler, B., Lee, C., Kaddoura, Y., Ran, L., Giraldo, C., et al. (2003). Enabling location-aware pervasive computing applications for the elderly. *Proceedings of the First IEEE International Conference on Pervasive Computing and Communications* (pp. 531-536).

Hemmert, F. (2009). Life in the Pocket. *International Journal of Ambient Computing and Intelligence (IJACI)* on Ambient Information Systems 2009.

Hemmert, F., Joost, G., Knörig, A., & Wettach, R. (2008). *Dynamic knobs: shape change as a means of interaction on a mobile phone.* In CHI '08: Extended abstracts on Human factors in computing systems.

Henk, T. (2004). *Understanding probability: chance rules in everyday life.* Cambridge University Press.

Henricksen, K., Indulska, J., McFadden, T., & Balasubramaniam, S. (2005) Middleware for Distributed Context-Aware Systems, *Proc. of the International Symposium on Distributed Objects and Applications (DOA '05)*, Cyprus, October 2005, *Lecture Notes in Computer Science*, LNCS 3760, Page(s): 846-863.

Hewlett-Packard. (2002). *Understanding Wi-Fi*. Hewlett-Packard Development Company.

Holmquist, L. E. (2004). Evaluating the Comprehension of Ambient Displays. Paper presented at the Conference on Human Factors in Computing Systems - Extended Abstracts (CHI'04), Vienna, Austria.

Holmquist, L. E., & Skog, T. (2003). Informative art: information visualization in everyday environments. In Proceedings of the *1st international Conference on Computer Graphics and interactive Techniques in Australasia and South East Asia* (pp. 229-235) Melbourne, Australia. ACM, New York, NY

Homepage of Orbacus Corba ORB. (2009). (http://www.orbacus.com [Online; accessed 06-March-2009])

Homepage of the Crossbow Technology Inc. Wireless Sensor Networks. (2009). (http://www.xbow.com/Products/wproductsoverview.aspx [Online; accessed 06-March-2009])

Hommel, B., Musseler, J., Aschersleben, G., & Prinz, W. (2001). The theory of event coding (TEC): A framework for perception and action planning. *The Behavioral and Brain Sciences*, 24(5), 849–878. doi:10.1017/S0140525X01000103

Hong, X., Gerla, M., Bagrodia, R., & Pei, G. (1999, August). *A group mobility model for ad hoc wireless networks*. Paper presented in the Proceedings of the ACM International Workshop on Modeling, Analysis and Simulation of Wireless and Mobile Systems (MSWiM), Seattle, Washington.

Hönle, N., Käppeler, U.-P., Nicklas, D., Schwarz, T., & Grossmann, M. (2005). Benefits of Integrating Meta Data into a Context Model. In *Proceedings of the 2nd IEEE PerCom Workshop on Context Modeling and Reasoning (CoMoRea 2005)* (pp. 25-29). Kauai Island, Hawaii, USA: IEEE Computer Society.

Hopper, A. (1999). The cliord paterson lecture: Sentient computing. Philosophical Transactions of the Royal Society of London, 358(1773), 2349-2358.

Hsieh, G., & Mankoff, J. (2003). A Comparison of Two Peripheral Displays for Monitoring Email: Measuring Usability, Awareness, and Distraction. UC Berkeley, EECS Department. Technical Report No. UCB-CSD-03-1286.

Huang, E. M., & Mynatt, E. D. (2003). Semi-public displays for small, co-located groups. In Proc. CHI 2003, 49-56.

Huang, E. M., et al. (2008). Overcoming Assumptions and Uncovering practices: When Does the Public Really Look at Public Displays? In Proc. Pervasive 2008, 228-243.

Hubeaux, J.-P., Capkun, S., & Luo, J. (2004). *The Security and Privacy of Smart Vehicles*. IEEE Security & Privacy Magazine.

Hudson, S. E., & Smith, I. (1996). *Electronic mail previews using non-speech audio*, in *Proceeding of the Conference Companion on Human Factors in Computing Systems: Common Ground* (pp. 237-238). ACM Press: Vancouver, British Columbia, Canada.

Hudson, S. E., & Smith, I. (1996). Electronic mail previews using non-speech audio. In *Proceeding of the conference companion on human factors in computing systems: Common ground* (pp. 237-238). Vancouver, British Columbia, Canada: ACM Press.

Hui, P., Crowcroft, J., & Yoneki, E. (2008, May). *Bubble rap: Social-based forwarding in delay tolerant networks*. Paper presented in the Proceedings of the 9th ACM international symposium on Mobile ad hoc networking & computing (MobiHoc'08).

Human-Resource-Committee (2008). *National statement on ethical conduct in research involving humans: Part 18-Privacy of information.* accessed on 10 Oct.

Hydra (2009). Hydra Feature Modelling. http://caosd.lcc.uma.es/spl/hydra

Hyman, J. (2006). Three fallacies about action. *In Proceedings of the 29th International Wittgenstein Symposium.* (pp. 137-163).

IEEE. P1609.2 (2006) - Standard for Wireless Access in Vehicular Environments - Security Services for Applications and Management Messages. IEEE 802.11p (status of the project), IEEE Task Group TGp, http://grouper.ieee.org/groups/802/11/Reports/tgp_update.htm

Intel, *Intel Open CV,* www.intel.com/research. Accessed on 11 August, 2008, Online Resources.

Intille, S. S. (2002). Designing a home of the future. *IEEE Pervasive Computing / IEEE Computer Society [and] IEEE Communications Society, 1*(2), 76–82. doi:10.1109/MPRV.2002.1012340

Ishii, H. (2002). *Tangible bits: User interface design towards seamless integration of digital and physical worlds* (No. 3).

Ishii, H., & Ullmer, B. (1997). Tangible Bits: Towards Seamless Interfaces between People, Bits and Atoms. In *Proceedings of the Conference on Human Factors in Computing systems* (pp. 234-241). New York: ACM.

Ishii, H., Wisneski, C., Brave, S., Dahley, A., Gorbet, M., Ullmer, B., et al. (1998). Ambientroom: Integrating ambient media with architectural space. Paper presented at the Conference on Human Factors in Computing Systems (CHI), Los Angeles, US.

Jafarinaimi, N., Forlizzi, J., Hurst, A., & Zimmerman, J. (2005). Breakaway: an ambient display designed to change human behavior. In *CHI '05 extended abstracts on Human factors in computing systems* (pp. 1945-1948). Portland, OR, USA: ACM.

James, D., & Drennan, J. (2005). *Exploring Addictive Consumption of Mobile Phone Technology.* In Proceedings of ANZMAC 2005.

Jayaputera, G. T., Zaslavsky, A. B., & Loke, S. W. (2007). Enabling run-time composition and support for heterogeneous pervasive multi-agent systems. *Journal of Systems and Software, 80*(12), 2039–2062. doi:10.1016/j.jss.2007.03.013

Jennings, N. R., & Wooldridge, M. (1995). Applying agent technology. *Applied Artificial Intelligence, 9*(4), 351–361. doi:10.1080/08839519508945480

Johan, R., Skog, T., & Hallnäs, L. (2000, January 22-24). Informative art: Using amplified artworks as information displays. Paper presented at the Designing augmented reality environments, Elsinore, Denmark.

Jones, K. (2006). *Using RFID tags to track bird flu,* EE Times (TechWeb). Online at http://www.eetimes.com/news/latest/showArticle.jhtml;jsessionid=1K5RGLBMKOARWQSNDBECKHSCJUMEKJVN?articleID=183702439.

Kakihara, M., & Sorensen, C. (2002). Mobility: an extended perspective. In *Proceedings of the 35th Annual Hawaii International Conference on System Sciences* (pp. 1756–1766).

Kale, A. N., Rajagopalan, N., Cuntoor, A., & Krueger, V. (2002). Gait-based Recognition of humans Using Continuous HMMs. *Proceedings of the 5th IEEE International Conference on Automatic Face and Gesture Recognition,* Washinton D.C. May 20-21, pp.336-341.

Kaye, J. (2004). Making Scents: aromatic output for HCI. *Interaction, 11*(1), 48–61. doi:10.1145/962342.964333

Khedr, M., & Karmouch, A. (2005). ACAI: agent-based context-aware infrastructure for spontaneous applications. *Journal of Network and Computer Applications, 28*(1), 19–44. doi:10.1016/j.jnca.2004.04.002

Kidd, C., Orr, R., Abowd, G., Atkeson, C., Essa, I., & MacIntyre, B. (1999). The aware home: A living laboratory for ubiquitous computing research. *Lecture Notes in Computer Science,* 191–198. doi:10.1007/10705432_17

Kikin-Gil, R. (2006). Buddybeads: techno-jewelry for non-verbal communication within teenager girls groups. *Personal and Ubiquitous Computing, 10*(2-3), 106–109. doi:10.1007/s00779-005-0015-x

Kim, J. H., Lee, W. I., Munson, J., & Tak, Y. J. (2006). Services-Oriented Computing in a Ubiquitous Computing Platform. In *Proceedings of the Fourth International Conference on Service Oriented Computing (ICSOC 2006)* (pp. 601-612). Chicago, USA: Springer Verlag.

Kindberg, T., & Fox, A. (2002). System software for ubiquitous computing. *Pervasive Computing, IEEE, 1*(1), 70–81. doi:10.1109/MPRV.2002.993146

Kjaer, K. E. (2007) A survey of context-aware middleware SE'07: *Proceedings of the 25th conference on IASTED International Multi-Conference* 2007.

Kjeldskov, J., Howard, S., Murphy, J., Carroll, J., Vetere, F., & Graham, C. (2003). Designing TramMateña Context-Aware Mobile System Supporting Use of Public Transportation. In *Proceedings of the 2003 Conference on Designing for User Experiences* (pp. 1-4). San Francisco, California, USA: ACM Press.

Klus, H., Niebuhr, D., & Rausch, A. (2007, sep). A component model for dynamic adaptive systems. In A. L. Wolf (Ed.), Proceedings of the international workshop on engineering of software services for pervasive environments (esspe 2007) (pp. 21–28). Dubrovnik, Croatia: ACM.

Kolarevic, B. (2003). *Architecture in the digital age – Design and manufacturing.* Taylor & Francis.

Kolarevic, B., & Malkawi, A. (2005). *Performative Architecture – Beyond instrumentality.* Spon Press.

Komissarov, D. (2006). plusminus design: flashbag. Retrieved December 1, 2008, from plusminus design by Dima Komissarov Web site: http://www.plusminus.ru/flashbag.html

Korhonen, I., Lappalainen, R., Tuomisto, T., Koobi, T., Pentikainen, V., Tumisto, M., & Turjanmaa, V. (1998). TERVA: Wellness monitoring system. *Proceedings of the 20th Annual Conference of IEEE Engineering in Medicine and Biology Society, 4*, 1988-1991.

Krakowiak, S. (2003) *What is Middleware?* http://middleware.objectweb.org/

Kranz, M., Holleis, P., & Schmidt, A. (2006). Ubiquitous presence systems. In *SAC '06: Proceedings of the 2006 ACM symposium on Applied computing*, 1902–1909.

Kreller, B., Carrega, D., Shankar, J. P., Salmon, P., Böttger, S., & Kassing, T. (1998). A Mobile-Aware City Guide Application. In *Proceedings of ACTS Mobile Communications Summit* (pp. 60-65), Rhodes, Greece.

Krishna, A. (2006). Context-Specific Middleware Specialization Techniques for Optimizing Software Product-Line Architectures. *ACM SIGOPS Operating Systems Review, 40*(4), 205–218. doi:10.1145/1218063.1217955

Kroger, M., Wahl, R., & Rice, P. (1993). Compilation of DNA sequences of Escherichia coli. *Nucleic Acids Research, 21*(13), 2973–3000. doi:10.1093/nar/21.13.2973

Krogh, A., Mian, S. I., & Haussler, D. (1994). A Hidden Markov Model that Finds Genes in E-coli DNA. *NAR, 22*, 4768–4778. doi:10.1093/nar/22.22.4768

Krueger, C. W. (2007). Biglever Software Gears and the 3-tiered SPL Methodology. In OOPSLA '07: Companion to the 22nd ACM SIGPLAN conference on Object oriented programming systems and applications companion, 844–845, New York, NY, USA, ACM.

LAAS Laboratoire d'Analyse et d'Architecture des Systémes (2008). Retrieved July 8 2008, from http://www2.laas.fr/laas/2-4257-Home.php

Laboratories, R. S. A. (2007). *RFID, A Vision of the Future.* Available at http://www.rsa.com/rsalabs/node.asp?id=2117.

Lahiri, S. (2005). *RFID Sourcebook.* IBM Press. ISBN 0131851373.

Landt, J. (2001). *Shrouds of Time – The History of RFID.* Available at http://www.transcore.com/pdf/AIM%20shrouds_of_time.pdf.

Lanzola, G., Gatti, L., Falasconi, S., & Stefanelli, M. (1999). A Framework for Building Cooperative Software Agents in Medical Applications. *Artificial Intelligence in Medicine, 16*(3), 223–249. doi:10.1016/S0933-3657(99)00008-1

Le Gal, C., Martin, J., Lux, A., & Crowley, J. (2001). Smartoffice: Design of an intelligent environment. *IEEE Intelligent Systems*, 60–66. doi:10.1109/5254.941359

Lee, D., & Meier, R. (2007). Primary-Context Model and Ontology: A Combined Approach for Pervasive Transportation Services. In *Proceedings of the First IEEE International Workshop on Pervasive Transportation Systems (IEEE PerTrans 2007)* (pp. 419-424). White Plains, New York, USA: IEEE Computer Society.

Lee, D., & Meier, R. (2009). A Hybrid Approach to Context Modeling in Large-Scale Pervasive Computing Environments. In *Proceedings of the Fourth International Conference on COMmunication System softWAre and middlewaRE (COMSWARE 2009)* (pp. 1-12). Dublin, Ireland: ACM Press.

Lee, K., et al. (2002). Concepts and guidelines of feature modeling for product line software engineering. Number 2319 in LNCS, 62–77. Springer-Verlag.

Lee, W., et al. (2007). Product Line Approach to Role-Based Middleware Development for Ubiquitous Sensor Network, In Proc. 7th IEEE Int. Conf. on Computer and Information Technology, 1032-1037, Japan.

Leguay, J., Lindgren, A., Scott, J., Friedman, T., & Crowcroft, J. (2006, September). *Opportunistic content distribution in an urban setting.* Paper presented in the Proceedings of the 2006 SIGCOMM Workshop on Challenged Networks (CHANTS 2006), Pisa, Italy.

Lehmann, O., Bauer, M., Becker, C., & Nicklas, D. (2004). From Home to World - Supporting Context-aware Applications through World Models. In *Proceedings of Second IEEE International Conference on Pervasive Computing and Communications (Percom'04)* (pp. 297-308). Orlando, Florida: IEEE Computer Society.

Li, K. A., Baudisch, P., Griswold, W. G., & Hollan, J. D. (2008). *Tapping and rubbing: exploring new dimensions of tactile feedback with voice coil motors.* In UIST '08: Proceedings of the 21st annual ACM symposium on User interface software and technology.

Lien, T., Kanade, C., Li, C., & Cohn, J. F. (2000). Determination of Hidden Markov Model Topology for Facial Expression Analysis. *IEEE Transactions on Pattern Analysis and Machine Intelligence, 29*(3), 417–428.

Lindgren, A., Doria, A., & Schelen, O. (2003, July). Probabilistic routing in intermittently connected networks. *ACM SIGMOBILE Mobile Computing and Communications Review, 7*(3), 19–20. doi:10.1145/961268.961272

Liu, X., & Chen, T. (2003). Video-based face recognition using adaptive Hidden Markov Models. Proceedings of CVPR'03, Madison, Wisconsin. pp: 215-221

Lomas, N. (2006). *How Orwellian Can You Get – RFID For Air Travellers.* Available at http://networks.silicon.com/lans/0,39024663,39163311,00.htm.

López de Ipiña, D., & Lai Lo, S. (2001, September 17-19, 2001). Sentient computing for everyone. Paper presented at the The Third International Working Conference on New Developments in Distributed Applications and Interoperable Systems, Krakóow, Poland.

Loughran, N., et al. (2008). Language Support for Managing Variability in Architectural Models. Proc. of the 7th International Symposium on Software Composition, LNCS 4954:36-51, Budapest.

Loverde, J. (2009). *The Complete Eldercare Planner - Revised and Updated Edition.* Three Rivers Press.

Lum, W., & Lau, F. (2002). A context-aware decision engine for content adaptation. *IEEE Pervasive Computing / IEEE Computer Society [and] IEEE Communications Society, 1*(3), 41–49. doi:10.1109/MPRV.2002.1037721

Lund, A., & Wilberg, M. (2007). Ambient displays beyond conventions. Paper presented at the British HCI Group Annual Conference.

Manchester Triage Group. (2005). *Emergency triage.* BMJ Books.

Mankoff, J., & Dey, A. K. (2003). From conception to design: a practical guide to designing ambient displays. In Ohara, K., & Churchill, E. (Eds.), *Public and Situated Displays.* Amsterdam: Kluwer.

Mankoff, J., & Dey, A. K. (2003). From conception to design: a practical guide to designing ambient displays. In *K. Ohara & E. Churchill* (eds.), *Public and Situated Displays.* Kluwer. Retrieved November 15, 2008, from http://www.intelresearch.net/Publications/Berkeley/072920031038_155.pdf

Mankoff, J., Dey, A. K., Hsieh, G., Kientz, J., Lederer, S., & Ames, M. (2003). Heuristic Evaluation of Ambient Displays. In *Proceedings of the Conference on Human Factors in Computing Systems (CHI 2003)* (pp. 169-176). New York: ACM.

Manning, C. D., & Schütze, H. (1999). *Foundations of Statistical Natural Language.* Cambridge, MA: The MIT Press.

Marcell, J., & Shankle, R. (2001). *Elder Rage: How to Survive Caring for Aging Parents.* Impressive Press.

Marcus, A. (1998). Metaphor design for user interfaces. In *Proceedings of - CHI 98 – the ACM conference on Human factors in computing systems.* ACM Press. doi:10.1145/286498.286577

Margolis, L., & Robinson, A. (2007). *Living Systems – Innovative materials and technologies for landscape architechture*. Birkhäuser.

Marin-Perianu, M., Meratnia, N., Havinga, P., de Souza, L., Muller, J., & Spiess, P. (2007). Decentralized enterprise systems: a multiplatform wireless sensor network approach. *Wireless Communications, IEEE, 14*(6), 57–66. doi:10.1109/MWC.2007.4407228

Martin Fowler's web page on dependency injection. (2009). (http://martinfowler.com/articles/injection.html [Online; accessed 06-March-2009])

Mascolo, C., & Musolesi, M. (2006, July). *SCAR: Context-aware Adaptive Routing in Delay Tolerant Mobile Sensor Networks*. Paper presented in the Proceedings of the Delay Tolerant Mobile Networks Symposium of Int. Wireless Communications and Mobile Computing Conference (IWCMC 2006). Vancouver, Canada.

Materio (2007). *Material World 2: Innovative Materials for Architecture and Design*. Birkhäuser.

Matthews, T. (2003). *A peripheral display toolkit. EECS Department*. Berkeley: University of California.

Matthews, T. L. (2007). *Designing and evaluating glanceable peripheral displays*. PhD Thesis. University of California at Berkeley.

Matthews, T., Dey, A. K., Mankoff, J., Carter, S., & Rattenbury, T. (2004). A toolkit for managing user attention in peripheral displays. Paper presented at the Symposium on User Interface Software and Technology (UIST'04), Santa Fe, US.

Matthews, T., et al. (2004). A toolkit for managing user attention in peripheral displays. In *Proceedings of the 17th annual ACM symposium on User interface software and technology*. 2004: ACM.

Matthews, T., Rattenbury, T., Carter, S., Hsieh, G., Dey, A., & Mankoff, J. (2003). *A peripheral display toolkit.*

McCarthy, J., et al. (2001). UniCast, OutCast & GroupCast: Three Steps Toward Ubiquitous, Peripheral Displays. In Proc. Ubicomp 2001, 332-345.

McCrickard, D., & Chewar, C. (2003). *Communications of the ACM 46, 3 (March. 2003)*. Attuning Notification Design to User Goals and Attention Costs.

McCrickard, D. S. (2003). A model for notification systems evaluation-assessing user goals for multitasking activity. *ACM Transactions on Computer-Human Interaction, 10*(4), 312–338. doi:10.1145/966930.966933

McCrickard, D. S., Chewar, C., Somervell, J. P., & Ndiwalana, A. (2003). A model for notification systems evaluation- assessing user goals for multitasking activity. *ACM Transactions on Computer-Human Interaction, 10*(4), 312–338. doi:10.1145/966930.966933

McCrickard, S. (2006). *Homepage of scott McCrickard*. http://people.cs.vt.edu/ccricks/. (Online Resources)

McCullough, M. (2004). *Digital Ground – Architecture, Pervasive Computing, and Environmental Knowing*. MIT Press.

Mcluhan, H. M. (1967). *Understanding Media: The Extension of Man*. New American Library.

McMullan, C., Cahill, D., & Fry, D. (2007). *Place Lab Geopositioning System*. Available at http://ntrg.cs.tcd.ie/undergrad/4ba2.05/group1/index.html.

Mehin, A., Rosen, T., & Glaister, C. (2004). *Open Source*. Retrieved December 1, 2008, from Afshin Mehin's Design Portfolio Web site: http://afshinmehin.com/open_source.htm

Meier, R., Harrington, A., Beckmann, K., & Cahill, V. (2009). A Framework for Incremental Construction of Real Global Smart Space Applications. *Elsevier Pervasive and Mobile Computing, 5*(4), 350–368. doi:10.1016/j.pmcj.2008.11.001

Meier, B., Zimmermann, T., & Perrig, W. (2006). Retrieval experience in prospective memory: Strategic monitoring and spontaneous retrieval. *Memory (Hove, England), 14*(7), 872–889. doi:10.1080/09658210600783774

Meier, R., Harrington, A., & Cahill, V. (2005). A Framework for Integrating Existing and Novel Intelligent Transportation Systems. In *Proceedings of the 8th International IEEE Conference on Intelligent Transportation Systems (IEEE ITSC'05)* (pp. 650-655). Vienna, Austria: IEEE Computer Society.

Meier, R., Harrington, A., & Cahill, V. (2006). Towards Delivering Context-Aware Transportation User Services. In *Proceedings of the 9th International IEEE Conference on Intelligent Transportation Systems (IEEE ITSC 2006)* (pp. 369-376). Toronto, Canada: IEEE Computer Society.

Meier, R., Harrington, A., Termin, T., & Cahill, V. (2006). A Spatial Programming Model for Real Global Smart Space Applications. In *Proceedings of the 6th IFIP International Conference on Distributed Applications and Interoperable Systems (DAIS 06)* (pp. 16-31). Bologna, Italy: Springer-Verlag.

Meuleau, N., Hauskrecht, K. E., Peshkin, L., Pack-Kaelbling, L., Dean, T., & Boutilier, C. (1998). Solving very large weakly coupled Markov decision processes. *Proceedings of the 10ᵗʰ conference on Artificial intelligence.* pp:165 – 172.

Meunier, J. A. (1999). A Virtual Machine for a Functional Mobile Agent Architecture Supporting Distributed Medical Information. *In Proceedings of the 12th IEEE Symposium on Computer-Based Medical Systems (CBMS'99).* IEEE Computer Society, Washington, DC.

Mignonneau, L., & Sommerer, C. (2008). Media Facades as Architectural Interfaces. In Sommerer, C., Lakhmi, C., & Mignonneau, L. (Eds.), *The Art and Science of Interface and Interaction Design* (pp. 93–104). Berlin, Heidelberg: Springer. doi:10.1007/978-3-540-79870-5_6

Mihailidis, A., Carmichael, B., & Boger, J. (2004). The use of computer vision in an intelligent environment to support ageing in place, safety, and independence in the home. *IEEE Transactions on Information Technology in Biomedicine, 8,* 238–247. doi:10.1109/TITB.2004.834386

Miksch, S., Cheng, K., & Hayes-Roth, B. (1997). An intelligent assistant for patient health care. *In Proceedings of the 1st international Conference on Autonomous Agents (AGENTS'97)* (pp. 458-465). California, USA: ACM, New York. n-Core: A Faster and Easier Way to Create Wireless Sensor Networks. (2010). Retrieved October 15, 2010, from http://www.n-core.info

Montoro, G., Haya, P. A., Alamán, X., López-Cózar, R., & Callejas, Z. (2006). A proposal for an xml definition of a dynamic spoken interface for ambient intelligence. In in Computer Science (LNCS), L. N., editor, *International Conference on Intelligent Computing (ICIC 06),* volume 4114, pages 711–716.

Morais, Y., et al. (2009). A Systematic Review of Software Product Lines Applied to Mobile Middleware, In Proc. 6th Int. Conf. on Information Technology: New Generations, USA.

Moran, E. B., Tentori, M., González, V. M., Martinez-Garcia, A. I., & Favela, J. (2006). Mobility in hospital work: Towards a pervasive computing hospital environment. *International Journal of Electronic Healthcare, 3*(1), 72–89. doi:10.1504/IJEH.2007.011481

Motorola (2008) Motorola Inc, Payment Trends and Emerging Technologies for Retailers, Whitepaper, USA, 2008

Moustafa, H., Bourdon, G., & Gourhant, Y. (2006). Providing Authentication and Access Control in Vehicular Network Environment. *International Information Security Conference (IFIP SEC).*

Moya, F., Villa, D., Villanueva, F. J., Barba, J., Rincon, F., Lopez, J. C., & Dondo, J. (2007). Embedding Standard Distributed Object-Oriented Middlewares in Wireless Sensor Networks. *Wireless Communications and Mobile Computing Journal, 12*(3), 315–327.

Moya, F., & Lopez, J. C. (2002). SENDA: An Alternative to OSGi for Large Scale Domotics. *In proceedings of IEEE Networks Conference.* (pp. 165-176).

Mozer, M. C. (1998). The neural network house: an environment that adapts to its inhabitants. *AAAI spring symposium on intelligent. Environments,* 110–114.

Muller, M., Blomberg, J., Carter, K., Dykstra, E., Halskov, K., & Greenbaum, M. (1991). Participatory design in Britain and North America: responses to the "Scandinavian Challenge. In *Proceedings of CHI'91 - the SIGCHI conference on Human factors in computing systems: Reaching through technology.* ACM Press.

Müller, K., Rumm, P., & Wichert, R. (2008). *PERSONA – ein EU-Projekt für Unabhängigkeit und Lebensqualität im Alter.* Berlin: Proceedings Ambient Assisted Living.

Munson, J., & Tak, Y. J. (2007). The XVC Framework for In-Vehicle User Interfaces. In *Proceedings of the First IEEE International Workshop on Pervasive Transportation Systems (IEEE PerTrans 2007)* (pp. 435-442). White Plains, New York, USA: IEEE Computer Society.

Musolesi, M., & Mascolo, C. (2006). *A Community Based Mobility Model for Ad Hoc Network Research.* Paper presented in the Proceedings ACM/Sigmobile Realman.

Musolesi, M., Hailes, S., & Mascolo, C. (2005, June). *Adaptive Routing for Intermittently Connected Mobile Ad Hoc Networks*. Paper presented in the Proceedings of the 6th International Symposium on a World of Wireless, Mobile, and Multimedia Networks (WoWMoM), Taormina - Giardini Naxos.

Myerson, J. (2006). *RFID In the Supply Chain*. CRC Press. ISBN 0849330181.

Mynatt, E. D., Back, M., Want, R., & Frederick, R. (1997). Audio aura: light-weight audio augmented reality. In *Proceedings of the 10th annual ACM symposium on User interface software and technology* (pp. 211-212). Banff, Alberta, Canada: ACM.

Mynatt, E. D., Rowan, J., Craighill, S., & Jacobs, A. (2001). Digital family portraits: Supporting peace of mind for extended family members. *Proceedings of the SIGCHI conference on human factors in computing systems* (pp. 333-340). Seattle, Washington, United States: ACM Press.

Nag, R., Wong, K. H., & Fallside, F. (1994). Script recognition using hidden Markov models. Proceedings of International Conference on Acoustics Speech and Signal Processing. pp:2071-2074.

Najjar, M., & Hamam, H. (2007). Intelligent Environments for Assistance to Elders in Daily Life Activities. Proceedings of the 5th International Conference on Intelligent Multimedia and Ambient Intelligence (IMAI 07). July 15-22, Salt Lake City, Utah, USA. pp:1482-1487.

National Institute for Statistics and Economic studies (2006). *Population Census*. Retrieved June 16 2008, from http://www.insee.fr/en/

Nealon, J. L., & Moreno, A. (2003). *Applications of Software Agent Technology in the Health Care domain* (Vol. 212). (A. Moreno, & J. L. Nealon, Eds.) Basel, Germany: Birkhäuser Verlag AG, Whitestein series in Software Agent Technologies.

Neely, S., Stevenson, G., & Nixon, P. (2007). Assessing the Suitability of Context Information for Ambient Display. In Workshop on Designing and Evaluating Ambient Information Systems at Pervasive 2007.

Nefian, A. V., Liang, X., Pi, X., Liu, C., Mao, L., & Murphy, K. (2002). A coupled HMM for audio-visual speech recognition", the IEEE International Conference on Acoustic Speech and Signal. 31(1):336-347.

Nehmer, J., Becker, M., Karshmer, A., & Lamm, R. (2006). Living assistance systems: an ambient intelligence approach. In Icse '06: Proceeding of the 28th international conference on software engineering (pp. 43–50). New York, NY, USA: ACM.

Nelson, H., & Stolterman, E. (2003). *The Design Way: intentional change in an unpredictable world*. Educational Technology Publications.

Nguyen, H. A., & Giordano, S. (2007, September). *PROSAN: Probabilistic Opportunistic Routing in SANETs*. Paper presented in the Proceedings of the ACM MobiCom/SANETs, Montreal.

Nguyen, H. A., & Giordano, S. (2008, June). *Spatiotemporal Routing Algorithm in Opportunistic Networks*. Paper presented in the Proceedings of the IEEE WoWMoM/AOC, California.

Nguyen, H. A., Giordano, S., & Puiatti, A. (2007, June). *Probabilistic Routing Protocol for Intermittently Connected Mobile Ad hoc Networks (PROPICMAN)*. Paper presented in the Proceedings of the IEEE WoWMoM/AOC 2007, Helsinki.

Ní Scanaill, C., Carew, S., Barralon, P., Noury, N., Lyons, D., & Lyons, G. (2006). A Review of approaches to mobility telemonitoring of the elderly in their living environment. *Annals of Biomedical Engineering, 34*(4), 547–563. doi:10.1007/s10439-005-9068-2

Niebuhr, D., & Rausch, A. (2007, sep). A concept for dynamic wiring of components: Correctness in dynamic adaptive systems. In Savcbs '07: Proceedings of the 2007 conference on specification and verification of component-based systems (p. 101-102). Dubrovnik, Croatia: ACM.

Niebuhr, D., Rausch, A., Klus, H., Appel, A., Klein, C., Reichmann, J., & Schmid, R. (2010). Method and apparatus for determining a component conforming to the requirements. Patent pending (Patent Nr. WO 2010/040605 A2).

Niebuhr, D., Schindler, M., & Herrling, D. (2009). Emergency assistance system – webpage of the cebit exhibit 2009. (http://www2.in.tu-clausthal.de/~Rettungsassistenzsystem [Online; accessed 09-February-2009])

Noguchi, H., Mori, T., & Sato, T. (2002). Construction of network system and the first step of summarization for human daily action data in the sensing room. Proceedings of the IEEE Workshop on Knowledge Media Networking (pp. 17–22).

Noury, N., Virone, G., Barralon, P., Ye, J., Rialle, V., & Demongeot, J. (2003). New trends in health smart homes. *Proceedings of the 5th International Workshop on Enterprise Networking and Computing in Healthcare Industry* (pp. 118–127).

Nugent, C. D., Mulvenna, M. D., & Hong, X. (in press). Experiences in the development of a smart lab. *International Journal of Biomedical Engineering and Technology*.

Nugent, C. D., Davies, R. J., Hallberg, J., Donnelly, M. P., Synnes, K., Poland, M., et al. (2007). HomeCI – A visual editor for healthcare professionals in the design of home based care. *Proceedings of the IEEE EMBC*.

OCED Guidelines on the Protection of Privacy and Transborder Flows of Personal Data. (1980). *Organization of Economic Cooperation and Development*. Retrieved Oct 21 2008, from http://www1.oecd.org/publications/e-book/9302011E.pdf

Offenhuber, D. (2008). The Invisible Display - Design Strategies for Ambient Media in the Urban Context. In *Proceedings of 2nd Workshop on Ambient Information Systems*. Colocated with Ubicomp 2008, Seoul, South Korea 2008.

Offenhuber, D. (2008). The Invisible Display - Design Strategies for Ambient Media in the Urban Context. Paper presented at the International Workshop on Ambient Information Systems, Colocated with Ubicomp 2008, Seoul, South Korea.

Office of Health Economics. (2008). *The Economics of Healthcare*. Retrieved June 23 2008, from http://www.oheschools.org/ohech6pg1.html

Office-of-the-privacy-commissioner. *Privacy in Australia*. http://www.privacy.gov.au/ Accessed on 20 Dec., 2008, Online Resources.

Oh, Y., Schmidt, A. and Woo, W. (2007) Designing, Developing, and Evaluating Context-Aware Systems, *MUE2007, IEEE Computer Society*, 2007, Page(s): 1158-1163.

OMG (2008). OMG Data Distribution Service (DDS) for real-time systems, v1.2.

Oosterhuist, K. (2007). *iA #1 Interactive Architecture*. Paperback, Episode publishers, Rotterdam.

Open GIS Consortium Inc. (1999). *OpenGIS Simple Features Specification for SQL, Revision 1.1* (OpenGIS Project Document 99-049,).

Oreizy, P., Medvidovic, N., & Taylor, R. N. (1998). Architecture based runtime software evolution. In (pp. 177–186).

OSGi Alliance. (2006). OSGi Service Platform: Core Specification, version 4.0.1, www.osgi.org.

Ou-yang, J. (2007). *RFID Will Revolutionize the World*. Available at http://www.cse.ohio-state.edu/~ouyang/RFID%20Technology.htm.

OWL. (2008) *Web Ontology Language Primer* http://www.w3.org/TR/owl-ref/

Oxygen, M. I. T. Project (2004) *Pervasive Human Centered Computing*, http://oxygen.csail.mit.edu/Overview.html

Papper, R. A., Holmes, M. E., Popovich, M. N., & Bloxham, M. (2005). Middletown Media Studies II: The media day. Muncie, IN: Ball State University Center for Media Design (report available online www.bsu.edu/cmd/insightandresearch).

Pass, F., & Van, M. J. J. G. (1993). The efficiency of instructional conditions: An approach to combine mental effort and performance measures. *Human Factors, 35*, 737–743.

Patel, D., & Agamanolis, S. (2003). Awareness of life rhythms over a distance using networked furniture. In *Adjunct Proceedings of UbiComp 2003*. Habitat.

Paternó, F., & Santoro, C. (2002). One model, many interfaces. In Kolski, C., & Vanderdonckt, J. (Eds.), *Computer-Aided Design of User Interfaces III* (pp. 143–154). Dordrecht: Hardbound. CADUI, Kluwer Academic Publishers.

Pecora, F., & Cesta, A. (2007). Dcop for smart homes: A case study. *Computational Intelligence, 23*(4), 395–419. doi:10.1111/j.1467-8640.2007.00313.x

Peeters, P. H. (2000). Design criteria for an automatic safety-alarm system for the elderly. *Technology and Health Care, 8,* 81–91.

Pellerin, C. (2006). *United States Updates Global Positioning System Technology.* Available at http://usinfo.state. gov/xarchives/display.html?p=washfile-english&y=2006 &m=February&x=20060203125928lcnirellep0.5061609.

Peltonen, P., Kurvinen, E., Salovaara, A., Jacucci, G., Ilmonen, T., Evans, J., et al. (2008). It's Mine Don't Touch!: Interactions at a Large Multi-Touch Display in a City Centre. In *Proceeding of the 26th Annual SIGCHI Conference on Human Factors in Computing Systems* (pp. 1285-1294). New York: ACM.

Peripheral-Vision. (2006). *Human peripheral vision.* http:// webexhibits.org/colorart/ag.html. (Online-Resources)

PERSONA EU Consortium. (2008), www.aal-persona. com, 2008. Furfari, F.; Tazari, M.-R. (2008) Realizing Ambient Assisted Living Spaces with the PERSONA Platform ERCIM News, 74, July 2008.

Pervasive (2003). Centre for Pervasive Computing. http:// www.pervasive.dk.

Phillips, B. (1999). *Metaglue: A Programming Language for Multi-Agent Systems.* PhD thesis, MIT.

Pigot, H., Bauchet, J., & Giroux, S. (2008). *Assistive devices for people with cognitive impairments. The Engineering Handbook on Smart Technology for Aging, Disability and Independence* (pp. 217–236). Wiley & Sons. doi:10.1002/9780470379424.ch12

Plaue, C., Miller, T., & Stasko, J. (2004). Is a picture worth a thousand words?: An evaluation of information awareness displays. *Proceedings of the 2004 conference on graphics interface* (pp. 117-126). London, Ontario, Canada: Canadian Human-Computer Communications Society.

Pohl, C. et al (2007). Survey of existing implementation techniques with respect to their support for the practices currently in use at industrial partners, AMPLE Project deliverable D3.1.

Pokahr, A., Braubach, L., & Lamersdorf, W. (2005). Jadex: A BDI Reasoning Engine, R. *Multi-Agent Programming, 3*(3), 149–174. doi:10.1007/0-387-26350-0_6

Pokahr, A., Braubach, L., & Lamersdorf, W. (2003). Jadex: Implementing a BDI-Infrastructure for JADE Agents. *In EXP - in search of innovation (Special Issue on JADE),* 76-85.

Poland, M.P., Nugent, C.D., Wang, H., & Chen, L. (in press). *Development of a smart home simulator for use as a heuristics tool for management of sensor distribution.*

Ponnekanti, S. R., Lee, B., Fox, A., Hanrahan, P., & Winograd, T. (2001). Icrafter: A service framework for ubiquitous computing environments. *Lecture Notes in Computer Science, 2201,* 56–77. doi:10.1007/3-540-45427-6_7

Pousman, Z., & Stasko, J. (2006). A taxonomy of ambient information systems: four patterns of design. In *Proceedings of the working conference on advanced visual interfaces,* 67-74.

Preece, J., Sharp, H., & Rogers, Y. (2002). *Interaction Design: Beyond HumanComputer.* 3rd edition ed. John Wiley & Sons Ltd.

Preuveneers, D., Jan, V. B., Wagelaar, D., Georges, A., Rigole, P., & Clerckx, T. (2004). Towards an Extensible Context Ontology for Ambient Intelligence. *In proceedings of second european symposium in ambient. Intelligence,* 148–159.

Primer, R. D. F. (2008) *Resource Description Framework* http://www.w3.org/RDF/

Prior, S., Arnott, J., & Dickinson, A. (2008) Interface metaphor design and instant messaging for older adults. In *CHI '08: CHI '08 Extended Abstracts,* 3747–3752.

Proceedings of the 2nd Workshop on Ambient Information Systems. Colocated with Ubicomp 2008, Seoul, South Korea.

Project, E. R. G. D. O. M. (2008). *Ergonomic Intelligent Interface in Domotic Functions.* Retrieved July 8 2008, from http://www.laas.fr/MIS/ERGDOM/Webergdom.htm#Contacts%202

Public Health Agency of Canada. (2008). *Seniors Health.* Retrieved June 23 2008, from http://www.phac-aspc.gc.ca/index-eng.php

Puterman, M. L. (1994). *Markov Decision Processes: Discrete Stochastic Dynamic Programming. J.* New York: Wiley & Sons.

Rabiner, L. (1989). A tutorial on Hidden Markov Models and selected applications in speech recognition. *Proceedings of the IEEE, 77*(2), 257–286. doi:10.1109/5.18626

Rao, A. S., & Georgeff, M. P. (1991). Modeling rational agents within a BDI-architecture, *Proceedings of the 2nd International Conference on Principles of Knowledge Representation and Reasoning (KR'91)*.10 (3), (pp. 473-484).

Raya, M. & Hubaux, J.-P. (2007), Securing Vehicular Ad Hoc Networks. *Journal of Computer Security (JCS) - special issue on Security on Ad Hoc and Sensor Networks.*

Raya, M., & Hubaux, J. (2005). The Security of Vehicular Ad Hoc Networks. *A CM Workshop on Security of Ad Hoc and Sensor Networks (ACM SASN).*

Rayner, J. (2007). Aquascript - Information Waterfall.

Rayner, M., Lewin, I., Gorrell, G., & Boye, J. (2001). Plug and play speech understanding. In *Proceedings of the Second SIGdial Workshop on Discourse and Dialogue-Volume 16*, pages 1–10. Association for Computational Linguistics.

Reas, C., & Fry, B. (2003). Processing: a learning environment for creating interactive Web graphics. In SIGGRAPH '03: 2003 Sketches & Applications, NY, USA, 2003 (p. 1). ACM.

Redstrom, J., Skog, T., & Hallnas, L. (2000). *Informative art: using amplified artworks as information displays* (pp. 103-114). ACM.

Reenskaug, T. (1979). Thing-model-view-editor, an example from a planningsystem. 12.

RFID-Radar.com. (2007). Available at http://www.rfid-radar.com.

RFID Wizards.com. (2007). *ISO RFID Standards: A Complete List.* Available at http://www.rfidwizards.com/index.php?option=com_content&task=view&id=242&Itemid=174.

RFSolutions. (2006) *RTFQ1 Data Sheet.* (on-line) http://www.rfsolutions.co.uk/acatalog/DS069-7.pdf

Richardson, S. J., Poulson, D. F., & Nicolle, C. (1993). Supporting Independent living through adaptable smart home (ASH) technologies. *Human welfare and technologies: papers from the human service information technology applications (HUSITA) conference on information technology and the quality of life and services* (pp. 87-95).

Richardson, S. J., Poulson, D. F., & Nicolle, C. (1993). User requirements capture for adaptable smarter home technologies. *Proceedings of the 1st TIDE congress* (pp. 244-248).

Richtel, M. (2003). The Lure of Data: Is It Addictive? Retrieved December 1, 2008, from The New York Times Web site: http://query.nytimes.com/gst/fullpage.html?res=9502E3D81E3AF935A35754C0A9659C8B63

Rivera, J., & Len, T. (2002). Get ready for xforms. Http://www.Ibm.Com/developerworks/xml/library/x-xforms/.

Robertson, T., Mansfield, T., & Loke, L. (2006, August). Designing an immersive environment for public use. In *Proceedings Participatory Design Conference*, Trento, Italy, ACM Press.

Roman, M., Hess, C., Cerqueira, R., Ranganathan, A., Campbell, R., & Nahrstedt, K. (2002). Gaia: A Middleware Infrastructure to Enable Active Spaces. *IEEE Pervasive Computing / IEEE Computer Society [and] IEEE Communications Society, 1*(4), 74–83. doi:10.1109/MPRV.2002.1158281

Román, M., Hess, C. K., Ranganathan, A., Madhavarapu, P., Borthakur, B., Viswanathan, P., et al. (2001). Gaiaos: An infrastructure for active spaces. Technical Report UIUCDCS-R-2001-2224 UILU-ENG-2001-1731, University of Illinois, Urbana-Champaign.

Russell, D. M., Streitz, N. A., & Winograd, T. (2005, Accessed on 3 April,). *Building disappearing computers* (Vol. 48, pp. 42-48).

Ruyter, B., & Aarts, E. (2004). Ambient intelligence: visualizing the future. In *Proceedings of AVI '04 - the working conference on Advanced visual interfaces*. ACM Press.

Ryan, N., & Pascoe, J. (1998) Adding Generic Contextual Capabilities to Wearable Computers. In: *Proceedings of 2nd International Symposium on Wearable Computers*. Page(s) 92-99

Rydén, T., Teräsvirta, T., & Asbrink, S. (1998). Stylized facts of daily return series and the hidden Markov model of absolute returns. *Journal of Applied Econometrics, 13*, 217–244. doi:10.1002/(SICI)1099-1255(199805/06)13:3<217::AID-JAE476>3.0.CO;2-V

Sadjadi, S. M., Survey, A., & Exam, P. D. Q. (2003). A survey of adaptive middleware (Tech. Rep.).

Salavon, J. (2008). Jason Salavon. Shoes, Domestic Production 1960 - 1998.

Salber, D., et al. (1999). Designing for Ubiquitous Computing: A Case Study in Context Sensing. GVU, Technical Report GIT-GVU-99-29, July 1999.

Samaria, F., & Young, S. (1994). HMM-based architecture for face identification. *Image and Vision Computing, 12*(8), 338–349. doi:10.1016/0262-8856(94)90007-8

Sancho, M., Abellán, A., Pérez, L., & Miguel, J. A. (2002). *Ageing in Spain. Second World Assembly on Ageing*. Madrid, Spain: IMSERSO.

Santiváñez, C. A., Ramanathan, R., & Stavrakakis, I. (2001, October). *Making link-state routing scale for ad hoc networks*. Paper presented in the Proceedings of the 2nd ACM international symposium on Mobile ad hoc networking & computing, Long Beach, CA, USA

Santos, A. L., et al. (2008). Automated Domain-Specific Modeling Languages for Generating Framework-Based Applications. Proc. of the 12th Int. Software Product Line Conference, Limerick.

Sarangapani, J. (2007). *Wireless Ad hoc and Sensor Networks: Protocols, Performance, and Control* (1st ed.). CRC.

Scher, B. (2004). *Understanding RFID Frequencies*. Available at http://www.rfidusa.com/superstore/pdf/Understanding_RFID_Frequencies.pdf

Schilit, B., Adams, N., & Want, R. (1994) Context-Aware Computing Applications. *1st International Workshop on Mobile Computing Systems and Applications*. Page(s): 85-90

Schilit. B. and Theimer. M. (1994) Disseminating active map information to mobile hosts. *IEEE Network*, Page(s):22–32.

Schmidt, A. (2005). Interactive Context-Aware Systems Interacting with Ambient Intelligence. In Riva, G., Vatalaro, F., Davide, F., & Alcaniz, M. (Eds.), *Ambient Intelligence, The Evolution of Technology, Communication and Cognition, Towards the Future of Human-Computer Interaction* (p. 164). IOS Press.

Schoch, O. (2006). My Building is my Display. In *Proceedings of the 24th Annual eCAADe Conference* (pp. 610-616).

Schön, B., O'Hare, G. M., Duffy, B. R., Martin, A. N., & Bradley, J. F. (2005). Agent Assistance for 3D World Navigation. *Lecture Notes in Computer Science, 3661*, 499–499. doi:10.1007/11550617_50

Segura, D., Favela, J., & Tentori, M. (2008). Sentient displays in support of hospital work. Paper presented at the UCAMI, Salamanca, Spain.

Seidl, F. (2005). Development of a device bay architecture for jini federations. Unpublished master's thesis, University of Kaiserslautern.

Sellen, A., Eardley, R., Izadi, S., & Harper, R. (2006). The whereabouts clock: early testing of a situated awareness device. In CHI '06: extended abstracts on Human factors in computing systems, New York, NY, USA, 2006 (pp. 1307–1312). ACM.

Sengers, P., et al. (2004). Culturally Embedded Computing. *Pervasive Computing, 3*(1).

Shadbolt, N. (2003). Ambient intelligence. *IEEE Intelligent Systems, 18*(2), 2–3. doi:10.1109/MIS.2003.1200718

Shafer, S., Brumitt, B., and Cadiz, J. (2001). Interaction issues in context – aware intelligent environments. *Human – Computer Interaction*.

Shah, R. C., Roy, S., Jain, S., & Brunette, W. (2003, May). *Data MULEs: Modeling a three-tier architecture for sparse sensor networks*. Paper presented in the Proceedings of the IEEE workshop on Sensor Network Protocols and Applications (SNPA), 2003.

Shakespeare, W. (1601). *Hamlet.* http://pathguy.com/hamlet.htm. (Online resources)

Shami, D., Leshed, G., & Klein, D. (2005). Context of Use Evaluation of Peripheral Displays (CUEPD). *In INTERACT 2005, LNCS*, 579-587.

Shen, X. (2006). Design and Evaluation of Ambient Displays. In *School of Information Technology*. Sydney: University of Sydney.

Shen, X., Eades, P., Hong, S., & Moere, A. V. (2007). Intrusive and non-intrusive evaluation of ambient displays. *Proceeding of Pervasive, 07*, 16–22.

Shen, X., & Eades, P. (2004). Using MoneyTree to represent financial data. *Proceedings of the information visualisation, eighth international conference on (IV'04)* (Vol. 00, pp. 285-289). IEEE Computer society.

Shen, X., & Eades, P. (2005). Using MoneyColor to represent financial data. *In proceedings asia pacific symposium on information visualisation (APVIS2005)* (pp. 125-129). CRPIT.

Shen, X., et al. (2008). An Evaluation of Fisherman in a Partial-Attention Environment. In *Proceedings of ACM CHI'08 BELIV workshop*.

Shen, X., Moere, A. V., & Eades, P. (2006). An intrusive evaluation of ambient displays. *Third international conference on computer graphics and interactive techniques in australasia and south east asia* (pp. 289-292). Dunedin, New Zealand: ACM Press.

Siegel, A. F., & Morgan, C. J. (1996). *Statistics and data analysis: An introduction* (2nd ed.). New York: John Wiley & Sons.

Sivaharan, T., Blair, G., Friday, A., Wu, M., Duran-Limon, H., Okanda, P., et al. (2004). *Cooperating Sentient Vehicles for Next Generation Automobiles.* Paper presented at the The First ACM International Workshop on Applications of Mobile Embedded Systems (WAMES'04), Boston, Massachusetts, USA.

Skog, T., Ljungblad, S., & Holmquist, L. E. (2003). Between Aesthetics and Utility: Designing Ambient Information Visualizations. Paper presented at the Symposium on Information Visualization (Infovis'03).

SmartSwim. (2008). SmartSwim UV Intensity Bikini. Retrieved December 1, 2008, from Impact Lab: A laboratory of the future human experience Web site: http://www.impactlab.com/2008/10/02/smartswim-uv-intensity-bikini/

Smith, K. S., & Ziel, S. E. (1997). Nurses' duty to monitor patients and inform physicians. *AORN Journal, 1*(2), 235–238.

Smith, M. K., Welty, C., & McGuinness, D. L. (2004). OWL Web Ontology Language Guide [Electronic Version]. *W3C Recommendation*. Retrieved 2008.

Smith, R. B., Horan, B., Daniels, J., & Cleal, D. (2006). Programming the world with sun spots. In Oopsla '06: Companion to the 21st acm sigplan conference on object-oriented programming systems, languages, and applications (pp. 706–707). New York, NY, USA: ACM.

Snoek, J., Hoey, J., Stewart, L., Zemel, R., & Mihailidis, A. (2008). Automated detection of unusual events on stairs. *Journal of Image and Vision Computing., 18*(3), 112–124.

Solie, D. (2004). *How to Say It to Seniors: Closing the Communication Gap with Our Elders.* Prentice Hall Press.

Somervell, J., et al. (2002). An evaluation of information visualization in attention-limited environments. In *Proceedings of the symposium on Data Visualisation 2002*. Barcelona, Spain. Lau, A., & Moere, A. V. (2007). Towards a Model of Information Aesthetics in Information Visualization. In *Proceedings of the 11th International Conference Information Visualization*. 2007. Ambient-Device. (2008). *Ambient Device Information at a glance*. Accessed on 18 Dec., 2008 http://www.ambientdevices.com/cat/index.html, Online Resources.

Souchon, N., & Vanderdonckt, J. (2003, June 4-6). A review of xml-compliant user interface description languages. Paper presented at the International Conference on Design, Specification, and Verification of Interactive Systems, Funchal, Portugal.

Sousa, J. P., & Garlan, D. (2002) Aura: An architectural framework for user mobility in ubiquitous computing environments. In WICSA 3: *Proceedings of the IFIP 17th World Computer Congress - TC2 Stream /3rd IEEE/IFIP Conference on Software Architecture*, pages 29–43, Deventer, The Netherlands, The Netherlands, 2002. Kluwer, B.V.

Sparacino, F. (2008). Natural interaction in intelligent spaces: designing for architecture and entertainment. *Multimedia Tools and Applications, 38*, 307–335. doi:10.1007/s11042-007-0193-9

Spiller, N. (2002). *Reflexive architecture. Architectural Design*. Wiley-Academy.

Spillers, F. (2008). *Synch with me: Rhythmic interaction as an emerging principle of experiential design*. Paper presented at the 6th Conference on Design & Emotion 2008.

Spyropoulos, T., Psounis, K., & Raghavendra, C. S. (2005, August). *Spray and wait: Efficient routing in intermittently connected mobile networks*. Paper presented in the Proceedings of the ACM SIGCOMM workshop on Delay Tolerant Networking (WDTN), Philadelphia, PA.

Spyropoulos, T., Psounis, K., & Raghavendra, C. S. (2007, March). *Spray and Focus: Efficient mobility-assisted routing for heterogeneous and correlated mobility*. Paper presented in the Proceedings of the IEEE PerCom Workshop on Intermittently Connected Mobile Ad Hoc Network, NY.

Sriskanthan, N., & Tan, K. (2002). Bluetooth Based Home Automation Systems. *Journal of Microprocessors and Microsystems, 26*, 281–289. doi:10.1016/S0141-9331(02)00039-X

Stallings, W. (2002). *Wireless Communications and Networking*. New Jersey, USA: Prentice-Hall.

Stan's_Cafe. (2008). Of all the people in all the world.

Stasko, J., McColgin, D., Miller, T., Plaue, C., & Pousman, Z. (2005). Evaluating the InfoCanvis Peripheral Awareness System: A Logitudinal, In Situ Study. Technical Report GIT-GVU-05-08, GVU Center/Georgia Institute of Technology, Atlanta, GA, USA

Stasko, J., Miller, T., & Pousman, Z. Plaue, C., & Ullah, O. (2004). Personalized peripheral information awareness through information art. In *Proceedings of UbiComp '04*, 18–35.

Stevens, R., Johnson, D., & Soller, A. (2005). Probabilities and prediction: Modeling the development of scientific problem solving skills. *Cell Biology Education, 4*, 42–57. doi:10.1187/cbe.04-03-0036

Stockman, H. (1948). *Communications by Means of Reflected Power*. Proceedings of the IRE (pp. 1196-1204).

Stolpan (2008) StoLPaN EU Consortium., www.stolpan.com, Budapest, 2008.

Streitz, N. A., Rocker, C., Prante, T., Alphen, D. V., Stenzel, R., & Magerkurth, C. (2005). Designing Smart Artifacts for Smart Environments. *Computer, 38*(3), 41–49. doi:10.1109/MC.2005.92

Streitz, N. A., Röcker, C., Prante, T., Stenzel, R., & van Alphen, D. (2003). Situated interaction with ambient information: Facilitating awareness and communication in ubiquitous work environments. In *Tenth International Conference on Human-Computer Interaction (HCI International 2003)*, 133–137.

Streitz, N., Magerkurth, C., Prante, T., & Rocker, C. (2005). *From information design to experience design: Smart artefacts and the disappearing computer* (Vol. 12, pp. 21-25).

Strimpakou, M. A., Roussaki, I. G., & Anagnostou, M. E. (2006). A context ontology for pervasive service provision. In *Proceedings of the Twentieth International Conference on Advanced Information Networking and Applications (AINA'06)* (pp. 1-5). Vienna, Austria: IEEE Computer Society. U.S. Department of Transportation. (URL accessed in 2007). The National ITS Architecture Version 5.0. from http://itsarch.iteris.com/itsarch/index.htm

Subramonian, V., & Xiang, G. (2004). Middleware Specification for Memory-Constrained Networked Embedded Systems, *In proceedings of IEEE Real-Time and Embedded Technology and Applications Symposium (RTAS)*. (pp. 306-313).

Supply Chain Solutions, U. P. S. *RFID In Healthcare* (2005). Available at http://www.ups-scs.com/solutions/white_papers/wp_RFID_in_healthcare.pdf.

Tam, T., Boger, J., Dolan, A., & Mihailidis, A. (2006). An Intelligent Emergency Response System: Preliminary Development and Testing of a Functional Health Monitoring System. *Gerontechnology (Valkenswaard), 4*(4), 209–222. doi:10.4017/gt.2006.04.04.005.00

Tamura, T., Togawa, T., & Murata, M. (1988). A bed temperature monitoring system for assessing movement during sleep. *Clinical Physics and Physiological Measurement, 9*, 139–145. doi:10.1088/0143-0815/9/2/006

Tamura, T., Togawa, T., Ogawa, M., & Yoda, M. (1998). Fully automated health monitoring system in the home. *Medical Engineering & Physics, 20*(8), 573–579. doi:10.1016/S1350-4533(98)00064-2

Tan, D. S., Gergle, D., Scupelli, P., & Pausch, R. (2003). With similar visual angles, larger displays improve spatial performance. *Proceedings of the SIGCHI conference on human factors in computing systems* (p. 217-224). Ft. Lauderdale, Florida, USA: ACM Press.

Tandler, P. (2004). The beach application model and software framework for synchronous collaboration in ubiquitous computing environment. [Special issue: Ubiquitous computing.]. *Journal of Systems and Software, 69*(3), 267–296. doi:10.1016/S0164-1212(03)00055-4

Tang, P., & Venables, T. (2000). Smart Home and Telecare. *Journal of Telemedicine and Telecare, 6*(1), 691–697. doi:10.1258/1357633001933871

Tapia, D. I., & Corchado, J. M. (2009). An Ambient Intelligence Based Multi-Agent System for Alzheimer Health Care. *International Journal of Ambient Computing and Intelligence, 1*(1), 15–26. doi:10.4018/jaci.2009010102

Tapia, E. M., Intille, S. S., & Larson, K. (2004). Activity recognition in the home using simple ubiquitous sensors. *Proceedings of Pervasive, 2004,* 158–175.

Tapia, D. I., Bajo, J., & Corchado, J. M. (2009). Distributing Functionalities in a SOA-Based Multi-agent Architecture. In *7th International Conference on Practical Applications of Agents and Multi-Agent Systems (PAAMS 2009)* (pp. 20-29).

Taxén, G. (2004). Introducing participatory design in museums. In *Proceedings Participatory Design Conference 2004*, Toronto, Canada.

Taylor, R. N., Medvidovic, N., Anderson, K. M., Whitehead, E. J., Jr., & Robbins, J. E. (1995). A component- and message-based architectural style for gui software. In Icse '95: Proceedings of the 17th international conference on software engineering (pp.295–304). New York, NY, USA: ACM.

Tchepnda, C., Moustafa, H., Labiod, H., & Bourdon, G. (2006). Securing Vehicular Communications: An Architectural Solution Providing a Trust Infrastructure, Authentication, Access Control and Secure Data Transfer. *IEEE AutoNet - Global Communications Conference (Globecom).*

Tchepnda, C., Moustafa, H., Labiod, H., & Bourdon, G. (2008). Performance Analysis of a Layer-2 Multi-hop Authentication and Credential Delivery Scheme for Vehicular Networks. *IEEE Vehicular Technology Conference (VTC-Spring).*

Tedjasaputra, A. (2006). *RFID Tag Attachments.* Available at http://www.rfid-asia.info/2006/12/rfid-tag-attachments.htm.

Tentori, M., & Favela, J. (2008). Activity-aware computing for healthcare. *IEEE Pervasive Computing / IEEE Computer Society [and] IEEE Communications Society, 7*(2), 51–57. doi:10.1109/MPRV.2008.24

The Jini™ Technology Surrogate Architecture Overview. (2009). (https://surrogate.dev.java.net/doc/overview.pdf [Online; accessed 06-March-2009])

Thomas, R. (2000, September). Remote Control IR Decoder. *Everyday Practical Electronics, 29*(9), 698–701.

Thomas, L. (2005). *Interactive fashionable wearable.* http://interactivefashionablewearable.blogspot.com/. (Online Resources)

Tijms, H. (2004). *Understanding Probability – A lively introduction to probability theory for the beginner.* Cambridge University Press.

Tolmie, P., Pycock, J., Diggins, T., MacLean, A., & Karsenty, A. (2002). Unremarkable computing. In *Proceedings of the SIGCHI conference on Human factors in computing systems: Changing our world, changing ourselves* (pp. 399-406). Minneapolis, Minnesota, USA: ACM.

Tomitsch, M., Kappel, K., Lehner, A., & Grechenig, T. (2007). Towards a Taxonomy for Ambient Information Systems. In *Workshop at Pervasive 2007: Designing and Evaluating Ambient Information Systems. 5th International Conference on Pervasive Computing* (pp. 42-47). Toronto, Canada.

Tomitsch, M., Kappel, K., Lehner, A., & Grechenig, T. (2007). Towards A Taxonomy For Ambient Information Systems. Paper presented at the Pervasive 2007 Workshop on the Issues of Designing and Evaluating Ambient Information System, Toronto, Canada.

Törpel, B. (2005). Participatory design: a multi-voiced effort. *In Proceedings of CC '05 - the 4th decennial conference on Critical computing: between sense and sensibility*. ACM Press.

Trapp, M. (2005). *Modeling the adaptation behavior of adaptive embedded systems*. Dr. Hut. Taschenbuch.

Truong, B. A. Lee. Y. K. and Lee. S. Y. (2005) Modeling uncertainty in context-aware computing. *Fourth Annual ACIS International Conference on Computer and Information Science*, 2005. Volume, Issue, 2005 Page(s): 676-681

Ullmer, B., & Ishii, H. (2006). *Musicbox in tangible bits*. Accessed on 15 January, 2006 http://tangible.media.mit.edu/projects/musicbox/, Online Resources.

Ullmer, B., & Ishii, H. (2002). *Musicbox in tangible bits.* http://tangible.media.mit.edu/projects/musicbox/. (Online Resources)

United Nations Programme on Ageing. (2008). *The Ageing of the World's Population.* Retrieved June 23, 2008, from http://www.un.org/esa/socdev/ageing/popageing.html

Vahdat, A., & Becker, D. (2000, April). *Epidemic Routing for Partially Connected Ad hoc Networks* (Tech. Rep. CS-200006). Duke University.

Vallgårda, A., & Redström, J. (2007). Computational composites. In *Proceedings of CHI '07 - the SIGCHI conference on Human factors in computing systems*. ACM Press.

van Dantzich, M., Robbins, D., Horvitz, E., & Czerwinski, M. (2002). Scope: Providing awareness of multiple notifications at a glance. In *Proceedings of AVI 2002*, 157–166.

van Woerden, K. (2006). Mainstream Developments in ICT: Why are They Important for Assistive Technology? *Technology and Disability*, *18*(1), 15–18.

Vande Moere, A. (2008). Beyond the Tyranny of the Pixel: Exploring the Physicality of Information Visualization. Paper presented at the IEEE International Conference on Information Visualisation (IV'08), London, UK.

Vazquez J.I., López de Ipiña D. and Sedano I. (2007) SOAM: A Web-Powered Architecture for Designing and Deploying Pervasive Semantic Devices. *International journal of web information systems - ijwis*, 2007.

Vermeulen, C., & van Berlo, A. (1997). A model house as platform for information exchange on housing. *Gerontechnology, A sustainable investment of the future* (pp. 337-339). IOS press

Viegas, F. B. boyd, d., Nguyen, D. H., Potter, J., & Donath, J. (2004). Digital artifacts for remembering and storytelling: posthistory and social network fragments. Proceedings of the 37th Annual Hawaii International Conference on System Sciences, IEEE Computer Society.

Viegas, F. B., Golder, S., & Donath, J. (2006). Visualizing email content: portraying relationships from conversational histories. In CHI '06: Proceedings of the SIGCHI conference on Human Factors in computing systems, New York, NY, USA, 2006 (pp. 979–988). ACM.

Villa, D., Villanueva, F. J., Moya, F., Rincon, F., Barba, J., & Lopez, J. C. (2006). Embedding a Middleware for Networked Hardware and Software Objects. *In proceedings of Advances in Grid and Pervasive Computing.*(pp. 567-576).

Villa, D., Villanueva, F. J., Moya, F., Rincon, F., Barba, J., & Lopez, J. C. (2007). Minimalist Object Oriented Service Discovery Protocol for Wireless Sensor Networks. *In proceedings of Advances in Grid and Pervasive Computing.* (pp. 472-483).

Villanueva, F. J., Villa, D., Moya, F., Rincon, F., Barba, J., & Lopez, J. C. (2007). *Lightweight Middleware for Seamless HW-SW Interoperability, with Applications to Wireless Sensor Networks, In proceedings of IEEE Design* (pp. 1042–1047). Automation and Test in Europe.

Villanueva, F. J., Villa, D., Moya, F., Santofimia, M. J., & Lopez, J. C. (2009). A Framework for advanced home service design and Management. *IEEE Transactions on Consumer Electronics*, *55*(3), 1246–1253. doi:10.1109/TCE.2009.5277984

Virone, G., Noury, N., & Demongeot, J. (2002). A system for automatic measurement of circadian activity deviations in telemedicine. *IEEE Transactions on Bio-Medical Engineering*, *49*, 1463–1469. doi:10.1109/TBME.2002.805452

Vogel, D., & Balakrishnan, R. (2004). Interactive Public Ambient Displays: Transitioning from Implicit to Explicit, Public to Personal, Interaction with Multiple Users. In *Proceedings of the 17th Annual ACM Symposium on User Interface Software and Technology* (pp. 137-146). New York: ACM.

Walker, K. (2003). Interactive and Informative Art. In *D. Duncan Seligman* (eds.), *Artful Media. IEEE Xplore.* Retrieved November 12, 2008, from http://ieeexplore.iee.org/stamp/stamp.jsp?arnumber=1167916&isnumber=26330

Wang, M. M. (2008). Middleware for wireless sensor networks: A survey. *Journal of Computer Science and Technology.*, *23*(3), 305–326. doi:10.1007/s11390-008-9135-x

Wang, X. H., Dong, J. S., Chin, C., & Hettiarachchi, S. R. (2004). Semantic space: an infrastructure for smart spaces. *IEEE Pervasive Computing / IEEE Computer Society [and] IEEE Communications Society, 3*(3), 32–39. doi:10.1109/MPRV.2004.1321026

Wang, Y., Jain, S., Martonosi, M., & Fall, K. (2005, August). *Erasure-Coding Based Routing for Opportunistic Networks*. Paper presented in the Proceedings of the ACM SIGCOMM WDTN-05, Philadelphia, PA.

Watkins, J. (2007, November). Social Media, Participatory Design and Cultural Engagement. In *proceedings of OzCHI 2007*, Adelaide, Australia.

Watkins, J., & Russo, A. (2005, April 12-15). Digital Cultural Communication – Designing co-creative new media environments. *C & C '05*, London, UK.

Webb, J. (2002). *Developing Web Applications With Microsoft Visual Basic. Net and Microsoft Visual C#. Net*. Washington, USA: Microsoft Press.

Weber, W., Rabaey, J. M., & Aarts, E. (2005). *Ambient Intelligence*. Springer-Verlag New York, Inc.doi:10.1007/b138670

Weinstein, R. (2005). *RFID: A Technical Overview and its Application to the Enterprise*. Available at http://ieeexplore.ieee.org/iel5/6294/32043/01490473.pdf?tp=&arnumber=1490473&isnumber=32043.

Weiser, M., & Brown, J. S. (1995). Designing calm technology. *PowerGrid, 1*(1), 10.

Weiser, M., & Brown, J. S. (1995). *Designing Calm Technology*. Xerox PARC.

Weiser, M. (1991, September). The computer of the 21st century. *Scientific American, 265*(3), 66–75. doi:10.1038/scientificamerican0991-94

Weiser, M. (1994). The world is not a desktop. *Interaction, 1*(1), 7–8. doi:10.1145/174800.174801

Weiser, M., & Brown, J. S. (n.d.). Designing calm technology. *PowerGrid Journal, 1*(1), 1-5.

Weissgerber, D., Bridgeman, B., & Pang, A. (2004). Vispad: A novel device for vibrotactile force feedback. [IEEE Computer Society.]. *Proceedings of HAPTICS, 04*, 50–57.

Welch, L. (2003). Hidden Markov Models and the Baum-Welch Algorithm. *The IEEE Information Theory Society Newsletter.*, *53*(4), 10–24.

Wenger, E. (1998). *Communities of Practice – Learning, Meaning, and Identity*. Cambridge, UK: Cambridge University Press.

Werb, J., & Lanzl, C. (1998). Designing a positioning system for finding things and people indoors. *IEEE Spectrum, 35*(9), 71–78. doi:10.1109/6.715187

Werner, J., Wettach, R., & Hornecker, E. (2008). *United-pulse: feeling your partner's pulse*. In Mobile HCI 2008: Proceedings of the 10th international conference on Human computer interaction with mobile devices and services.

White, J., & Schmidt, D. C. (2008). Model-Driven Product-Line Architectures for Mobile Devices, Proceedings of the 17th Annual Conference of the International Federation of Automatic Control, Seoul.

White, T., & Small, D. (1998). An interactive poetic garden. *Proceedings of CHI '98: CHI 98 conference summary on human factors in computing systems* (pp. 335-336). New York, NY, USA: ACM Press.

WHO. (2007). *Global Age-friendly Cities: A Guide*. World Health Organization.

Wideman, R. M. (2004). *Project Life Spans in the 1990s*. Available at http://www.maxwideman.com/papers/plc-models/1990s.

Widmer, J., & Le Boudec, J. (2005, August). *Network coding for efficient communication in extreme networks*. Paper presented in the Proceedings of the ACM SIG-COMM 2005, Workshop on Delay Tolerant Networking (WDTN 2005), Philadelphia, PA.

Williamson, J., Smith, R., & Hughes, S. (2007). *Shoogle: excitatory multimodal interaction on mobile devices*. In CHI'07: Proceedings of the SIGCHI conference on Human factors in computing systems.

Winograd, E. (1988). Some observations on prospective remembering. Practical aspects of memory: Current research and issues, 1, 348–353.

Wisneski, C., Ishii, H., Dahley, A., Gorbet, M. G., Brave, S., Ullmer, B., et al. (1998). Ambient Displays: Turning Architectural Space into an Interface between People and Digital Information. In Proceedings of the *First International Workshop on Cooperative Buildings, Integrating Information, Organization, and Architecture* (pp. 22-32).

Wolff, J. G. (1982). Language acquisition, data compression and generalization. *Language & Communication, 2,* 57–89. doi:10.1016/0271-5309(82)90035-0

Wolff, J. G. (2006). Information Compression by Multiple Alignment, Unification and Search as a Unifying Principle in Computing and Cognition. Retrieved 16 November 2008, from http://www.citebase.org/fulltext?format=application/pdf&identifier=oai:arXiv.org:cs/030705

Wong, W. S., Aghvami, H., & Wolak, S. J. (2008). Context-Aware Personal Assistant Agent Multi-Agent System. In *Proceedings of the 19th IEEE International Symposium on Personal, Indoor and Mobile Radio Communications (PIMRC 2008)* (pp. 1-4).

Wooldridge, M., & Jennings, N. R. (1995). Intelligent Agents: Theory and Practice. *The Knowledge Engineering Review, 10*(2), 115–152. doi:10.1017/S0269888900008122

Wooldridge, M. (2000). *Reasoning about Rational Agents. Intelligent robotics and autonomous agents series 16.* The MIT Press.

Wyche, S. P. (2007). *2007, 2771-2776*. Exploring the Use of Large Displays in American Megachurches. In Extended Abstracts CHI.

Yamaguchi, A., Ogawa, M., Tamura, T., & Togawa, T. (1998). Monitoring behavior in the home using positioning sensors. *Proceedings of the 20th Annual International Conference of the IEEE Engineering in Medicine and Biology Society, 4,* 1977–1979.

Yamazaki, T. (2006). Beyond the Smart Home. *International Conference on Hybrid Information Technology, 2,* 350–355.

Yang, X., Liu, J., Zhao, F., & Vaidya, N. (2004). A vehicle-to-vehicle communication protocol for cooperative collision warning. *International Conference on Mobile and Ubiquitous Systems (MobiQuitous)*.

Zarki, M., Mehrotra, S., Tsudik, G., & Venkatasubramanian, N. (2002). *Security Issues in a Future Vehicular Network*. European Wireless.

Zhang, W., et al. (2007). Product Line Enabled Intelligent Mobile Middleware, In Proc. 12th IEEE Int. Conf. on Engineering Complex Computer Systems, 148-160.

Zhao, Q. A., & Stasko, J. T. (2002). What's Happening?: Promoting Community Awareness through Opportunistic, Peripheral Interfaces. In Proc. AVI 2002, 69-74.

Zhao, W., Ammar, M., & Zegura, E. (2004, May). *A Message Ferrying Approach for Data Delivery in Sparse Mobile Ad Hoc Networks*. Paper presented in the Proceedings of the 5th ACM International Symposium on Mobile Ad Hoc Networking and Computing (MobiHoc), Tokyo, Japan.

Zhou, C., Frankowski, D., Ludford, P., Shekhar, S., & Terveen, L. (2007). Discovering personally meaningful places: An interactive clustering approach. [TOIS]. *ACM Transactions on Information Systems, 25*(3).

ZigBee. (2006). *ZigBee Specification Document 053474r13*. ZigBee Standards Organization. ZigBee Alliance.

Zingerle, A., Wagner, T., & Heidecker, C. (2006). *Atem-Raum*.

About the Contributors

Kevin Curran BSc (Hons), PhD, SMIEEE, MBCS CITP, MACM, MIEE, FHEA has made significant contributions to advancing the knowledge and understanding of computer networking, evidenced by over 350 publications. He is a regular contributor to BBC radio & TV news in Northern Ireland and is listed in the *Dictionary of International Biography,* Marquis *Who's Who in Science and Engineering* and by *Who's Who in the World.* He has chaired sessions and participated in the organising committees for many highly-respected international conferences and workshops. He is on the editorial boards of a number of journals and he is Editor in Chief of the International Journal of Ambient Computing and Intelligence. Dr Curran has also served as an advisor to the British Computer Society in regard to computer industry standards.

* * *

Xavier Alamán got his PhD in Computer Science (Universidad Complutense de Madrid - 1993), MSc. Artificial Intelligence (Univ. California Los Angeles - 1990), MSc. Computer Science (Universidad Politecnica de Madrid - 1987), MSc. Physics (Universidad Complutense de Madrid - 1985). He has served as the Dean of the School of Engineering, Universidad Autónoma de Madrid, from 2000 to 2004. He got the tenure in the same university in 1998, as professor of Computer Science. He previously was an IBM researcher for 7 years. His research interests include Ambient Intelligence, Knowledge Management cooperative tools, and multimedia systems. He has been main researcher in several R&D projects in these areas. He has contributed with more that 50 publications in journals, books and conferences.

Ricardo S. Alonso is a PhD. student at the University of Salamanca (Spain). He obtained an Engineering in Telecommunications degree in 2008 at the University of Valladolid (Spain) and an MSc in Intelligent Systems at the University of Salamanca (Spain) in 2009. He has also been a co-author of several papers published in recognized workshops and symposiums.

Jérémy Bauchet received a Ph.D. in Computer Science from the University of Sherbrooke (Canada) in 2008. His main research interests are the application of pervasive computing to cognitive assistance and human-machine interaction. He is a research engineer at the Institut Telecom Sud-Paris (France).

Mike Bennett is a PhD scholar in the School of Computer Science & Informatics in University College Dublin Ireland, where he researches Human-Computer Interaction and Interaction Design. He is particularly interested in the question "How can we enrich human experience and augment human abilities by enabling people to create and shape their own user experiences?". Previous to joining UCD he was a research associate in MIT Media Lab Europe.

Gustavo Berzunza is a graduate student in computer science at CICESE. His research interests include context-aware computing, internet technologies and software engineering. He received his BS from the Universidad Autónoma de Yucatán (UADY), Mexico.

Gilles Bourdon has graduated from Telecom SudParis and started to work for Vodafone-Airtouch in California before joining Orange Labs in 1999, now managing a team of experts in AAA technologies. After several years contributing to the IETF in the fields of AAA, VPN and IP routing, he also participates to the broadband networks evolution within the Broadband Forum (ex-DSL Forum) with a focus on IP sessions. His research interests are focussed on network operator security architectures for ad-hoc networks.

Liming Chen is a lecturer at the School of Computing and Mathematics, University of Ulster, UK. He received the BSc and MSc degrees from Beijing Institute of Technology, China, in 1985 and 1988, respectively. He obtained the PhD degree in Artificial Intelligence from De Montfort University, United Kingdom, in 2002. His current research interests include the semantic technologies, ontology enabled knowledge management, intelligent agents, information/knowledge fusion and reasoning, semantic sensor networking, assistive technologies and their applications in smart homes and intelligent environments.

Juan M. Corchado received a PhD. in Computer Science from the University of Salamanca in 1998 and a PhD. in Artificial Intelligence (AI) from the University of Paisley, Glasgow (UK) in 2000. At present he is the Dean of the Faculty of Computer Science and Director of the BISITE Research Group (http://bisite.usal.es). He has leaded several Artificial Intelligence research projects sponsored by Spanish and European public and private institutions. He has been president of the organising and scientific committee of several international symposiums and co-author of more than 250 books, book chapters, journal papers, technical reports, etc. published in recognized journal, workshops and symposiums.

François Courtemanche received his B.Sc. (2006) and M.Sc. (2008) degrees in Computer Science from the University of Sherbrooke (Canada). He is currently a Ph.D. student in Computer Science at the University of Montreal (Canada). His research focuses on Cognitive Modeling, Human-Computer Interactions, Affective Computing and Machine Learning. He has also a Minor in Philosophy from the University of Sherbrooke (2006).

Lorcan Coyle currently holds an SFI funded Post-Doctoral Fellowship at University College Dublin. He was conferred with his PhD at Trinity College Dublin in 2005. He also holds a Bachelors degree in Computer Engineering from Trinity College (B.A.I. 2001). His research interests include Pervasive and Ubiquitous Computing, Context-Aware Systems, Machine Learning, Personalization technologies, and Electronic Voting. Dr Coyle has published at a number of international journals and conferences including Knowledge Engineering Review, the journal on Knowledge-Based Systems, Artificial Intelligence Review, the International Conference on Pervasive Services (ICPS), and Intelligent User Interfaces. Dr Coyle serves as general co-chair at the 20th Irish Conference on Artificial Intelligence and Cognitive

Science (AICS 2009); served as volunteers chair at Pervasive 2006; and as Publications Co-Chair at Pervasive in 2007. He is a member of the editorial board for the International Journal of Ambient Computing and Intelligence and serves or has served on a number of Internationally peer reviewed symposia and workshops in the area of context-awareness and ubiquitous computing, including the International Symposium on Location and Context Awareness, the International Conference on Autonomic and Autonomous Systems, the IEEE International Symposium on Ubiquitous Computing and Intelligence, the International IEEE Workshop on Management of Ubiquitous Communications and Services, the International Workshop on Modelling and Reasoning in Context, and the International Workshop on Ubiquitous Systems Evaluation. He has also served as reviewer for the Knowledge Engineering Review, as well as many of the premier venues for Ubiquitous Computing, including Ubicomp, PerCom, Pervasive, CHI, IUI, and the Internet of Things conference.

Alexandre Dion received a M.Sc. in Computer Science from the University of Sherbrooke (Canada) where his research project was on modeling cognitive errors in daily activities. He is currently a software engineer working on ASP.Net at Microsoft Corporation (USA).

Peter Eades obtained a PhD in Mathematics from the Australian National University in 1978. He holds the Chair of Software Technology at the University of Sydney. Previously, he has held academic positions at the University of Queensland (1978 - 1991) and the University of Newcastle (1992 - 2000), as well as visiting positions at the University of Louisiana, Fujitsu Research Laboratories, McGill University, and the University of Limerick. Peter's main research interest is algorithms for network visualisation, and other geometric algorithms.

Noel Evans received the B.Sc. degree in 1973 and the M.Sc. degree in 1974 from the Queen's University of Belfast, Northern Ireland, UK. He obtained a Ph.D. degree from Queen's in 1977 for work on programmable transversal filters built using intracell charge-coupled devices. Following further research into narrow-gate CCDs at Queen's, he taught analogue electronics and communications at the University of Ulster from 1980-2006. Here he also developed research programmes into biomedical instrumentation, human and animal physiological signal acquisition using radio frequency techniques, and electromagnetic wave propagation at frequencies extending across the HF-UHF bands. He now works as an independent consultant in communications and telemetry.

Lidia Fuentes received her M.Sc. degree in Computer Science from the University of Málaga (Spain) in 1992 and the Doctor degree in 1998 from the same University. She is an Associate Professor at the Department of Computer Science of the University of Málaga since 1993. Her research interests deal with the application of advanced Software Engineering Technologies such as Aspect-Oriented Software Development (AOSD), Model Driven Development (MDD), Software Product Line (SPL) and Software Agents, mainly to Ambient Intelligence and Embedded Systems. She has participated in several conferences as a member of the program committee (e.g. OOPSLA, AOSD, UCAMI, GPCE, etc.) and the organizing committee (e.g. ECOOP). Her most significant publications can be found in international journals such as IEEE Transactions of Software Engineering, IEEE Internet Computing, ACM Computing Surveys, Computer Journal or Software Practice and Experience. She is actively participating in several European research projects about AOSD, MDD and SPLs (e.g. AOSD-Europe, AMPLE, etc.).

Jesus Favela is a professor of computer science at CICESE, Mexico, where he leads the Mobile and Ubiquitous Healthcare Laboratory and heads the Department of Computer Science. His research interests include ubiquitous computing, medical informatics, and computer-supported cooperative work. He received his BS from the Universidad Nacional Autónoma de México (UNAM) and an MSc and a PhD from the Massachusetts Institute of Technology. He is a member of the ACM and the Mexican Computer Science Society, of which he is former president.

Alois Ferscha was with the Department of Applied Computer Science at the University of Vienna at the levels of assistant and associate professor (1986-1999). In 2000 he joined the University of Linz as full professor where he heads the Excellence Initiative "Pervasive Computing", the department of Pervasive Computing, the Research Studio Pervasive Computing Applications (as Part of the Research Studios Austria, Salzburg) and RIPE (Research Institute of Pervasive Computing). Ferscha has published more than a hundred technical papers on topics related to parallel and distributed computing. Currently he is focused on Pervasive and Ubiquitous Computing, Embedded Software Systems, Wireless Communication, Multiuser Cooperation, Distributed Interaction and Distributed Interactive Simulation. He has been a visiting researcher at the Dipartimento di Informatica, Universita di Torino, Italy, at the Dipartimento di Informatica, Universita di Genoa, Italy, at the Computer Science Department, University of Maryland at College Park, College Park, Maryland, and at the Department of Computer and Information Sciences, University of Oregon, Eugene, Oregon, U.S.A. He has been the project leader of several national and international research projects. Some of his recent involvements in projects are InterLink (funded by IST FET), BEYOND THE HORIZON (funded by IST FET), CRUISE NoE – Creating Ubiquitos Intelligent Sensing Environments (IST FP6), SPECTACLES (Autonomous Wearable Display Systems) in cooperation with Silhouette International, INSTAR (Information and Navigation Systems Through Augmented Reality) (2001-2003), Siemens München, AG, CT-SE-1, BISANTE, EU/IST, Broadband Integrated Satellite Network Traffic Evaluation (1999-2001), Peer-to-Peer Coordination (2001–), Siemens München, AG, CT-SE-2, Context Framework for Mobile User Applications (2001–), Siemens München, AG, CT-SE-2, WebWall, Communication via Public Community Displays, Connect Austria (2001-2002), VRIO, Virtual Reality I/O, with GUP JKU, IBM Upper Austria (2002-2003), MobiLearn, Computer Science Any-Time Any-Where, (2002-2004), Mobile Sports Community Services, (SMS Real Time Notification at Vienna City Marathon 1999, 2000, 2001, 2002; Berlin Marathon 2000, 2001, 2002), etc. He has served on editorial boards of renowned international scientific journals (e.g. Pervasive and Mobile Computing (Elsevier), Transactions of the Society for Computer Simulation), on steering and programme committees of several conferences like PERVASIVE, UMBICOMP, ISWC, WWW, PADS, DIS-RT, SIGMETRICS, MASCOTS, MSWiM, MobiWac, TOOLS, Euro-Par, PNPM, ICS, etc. to name a few. His activities and recognition in the parallel and distributed simulation community is expressed by his being the General Chair of the IEEE/ACM/SCS 11th Workshop on Parallel and Distributed Simulation (PADS'97), has served on the committees of several conferences, the Program Committee chair for the PADS'98, Program Committee chair for the Seventh International Symposium on Modeling, Analysis and Simulation of Computer and Telecommunication Systems (MASCOTS'99), and recently the 12-th IEEE International Symposium on Distributed Simulation and Real Time Applications (DS-RT 2008).

Nadia Gámez received her M.Sc. degree in Computer Science from the University of Málaga (Spain) in 2007. She is a PhD student at the University of Málaga since 2008. Her main research interests are

Middleware platforms for Ambient Intelligence and Embedded Systems and Software Product Lines. She has participated in the AOSD Network of Excellence and the AMPLE (Aspect-Oriented Model-Driven Software Product Line Engineering) project. Currently, she is participating in the Spanish Ministry Project RAP and the Junta de Andalucía regional project FamWare. Her work has been published in international journals as JUCS, IJACI or ISSE and conferences like AD-HOC NOW, UCAmI, IWAAL or MOMPES. Also, she has participated as programme committee in several symposiums and workshops as UCAmI, IWAAL, WMUPS or CLEI.

Javier Gómez is researcher at the UAM-Indra Ambient Intelligence Laboratory (AmILab) of the School of Engineering of the Universidad Autónoma of Madrid (U.A.M.). His current research projects focus on middleware layers and adaptive interfaces for ambient intelligence. He got the Electrical Engineering degree from U.A.M. Contact him at Amilab, EPS-UAM, C. Fco. Tomas y Valiente 11, 28049 Madrid Spain; jg.escribano@uam.es.

Manuel García-Herranz is a doctoral candidate and researcher at the UAM-Indra Ambient Intelligence Laboratory (AmILab) of the School of Engineering of the Universidad Autónoma of Madrid (U.A.M.), where he is also a teacher assistant. His current research projects focus on Human Computer Interaction over Intelligent Environments. He received the Engineer in Computer Science degree from U.A.M. Contact him at Amilab, EPS-UAM, C. Fco. Tomas y Valiente 11, 28049 Madrid Spain; manuel.garciaherranz@uam.es.

Silvia Giordano holds a PhD. from EPFL, Switzerland. She is currently the head of the Network Lab (NetLab) in the Institute of System for Informatics and Networking (ISIN), and as direction member of ISIN, at the University of Applied Science - SUPSI in Ticino, Switzerland. She is teaching several courses in the areas of: Networking, Wireless and Mobile Networking, Quality of Services and Networks Applications. She is co-editor of the book "Mobile Ad Hoc Networking" (IEEE-Wiley 2004). She has published extensively on journals, magazines and conferences in the areas of quality of services, traffic control, wireless and mobile ad hoc networks. She has participated in several European ACTS/IST projects and European Science Foundation (ESF) activities. Since 1999 she serves as Technical Editor of IEEE Communications Magazine, and is currently editor of the series co-editor of the new Series on Ad Hoc And Sensor Networks of the IEEE Communication Magazine. She is also editor of Ad hoc networks journal by Elsevier, Ad Hoc & Sensor Wireless Networks journal, Ocpscience, Journal of Ubiquitous Computing and Intelligence (JUCI) and Journal of Autonomic and Trusted Computing (JoATC) both by American Scientific Publishers (ASP), and Mediterranean Journal of Computer and Networks, SoftMotor. She was already co-editor of several special issues of IEEE Communications Magazine and Baltzer MONET and Cluster Computing on mobile ad hoc networking and QoS networking. She will be general chair of WoWMoM 2009, program co-chair of IEEE PERCOM 2009, was program co-chair of IEEE VTC-Fall 2008, IEEE MASS 2007, workshop chair of IEEE WOWMoM 2007, tutorial chair of MobiHoc 2006, general chair of IEEE WONS 2005, organizer of IEEE Persens 2005-2009 workshop, IEEE AOC2005-2009 workshop and ACM Mobihoc SANET workshop 2007-2008 and is/was on the executive committee and TCP of several international conferences, and serves as reviewer on transactions and journals, as well as for several important conferences. Prof. Silvia Giordano is a member of

IEEE Computer Society, ACM and IFIP WG 6.8. Her current research interests include wireless and mobile ad hoc networks, QoS and traffic control.

Habib Hamam is a Canada Research Chair holder on Optics in Information and Communication Technologies. He leads research in biomedical engineering, wireless hybrid systems and waveguide based therapeutic methods. He is a full professor at the Faculty of Engineering of the University of Moncton (Canada).

Pablo Haya is a full--time teacher in the School of Engineering of the U.A.M. and a researcher of AmILab. His research interests currently focus on Human Computer Interaction over Intelligent Environments. He received his PhD in Computer Science and Telecommunications from the Universidad Autónoma of Madrid. Contact him at Amilab, EPS-UAM, C. Fco. Tomas y Valiente 11, 28049 Madrid Spain; pablo.haya@uam.es.

William Hazlewood is a PhD student in the School of Informatics at Indiana University Bloomington focusing on Human-Computer Interaction and Design. His research interests center around the design, use, and evaluation, of ambient information technologies, particularly those that are not specifically task-based, and are situated in everyday living. William has hosted a series of workshops in order to develop a strong research community around the study of such technologies. His current advisers include Kay Connelly and Erik Stolterman at Indiana University, as well as Yvonne Rogers from the Open University in the UK.

Rosaleen Hegarty BSc (Hons) is a PhD student researching in the area of Ambient Intelligence in the School of Computing and Intelligent Systems, Faculty of Computing and Engineering at the University of Ulster, Magee College.

Fabian Hemmert is a PhD candidate in the Design Research Lab at Deutsche Telekom Laboratories, Berlin. Having a background in computer science and interface design, his PhD research is concerned with embodied interaction.

Seok-Hee Hong obtained a PhD in Computer Science and Engineering from Ewha University in Korea, 1999. She is Associate Professor and Principal Research Fellow at the University of Sydney. Previously, she has held academic positions at the University of Newcastle and Ewha University, as well as visiting research positions at IPK (Germany), JAIST and Kyoto University. Seok-Hee's main research interest is Graph Drawing, Information Visualisation and Visual Analytics.

Germán Insua is originally from Galicia, Spain where he studied Superior Professional Formation on Computer Systems for two years. He set up his own business as Computer Consultant in 2000. Meanwhile, he started studying Bachelor Degree in Computer Science at the Spanish University of Distance Education heading for a BSc degree by 2009. In summer 2008 took up a position with the Odysseus summer programme (ODCSSS at University College Dublin), where he worked on "Ambient Jewelry: Be part of your friend's desktop" with Prof. Paddy Nixon and Mike Bennett. Today he is living in Tokyo (Japan), working at the Embassy of Spain in charge of their I.T. Department.

Eugene Kenny is an undergraduate student in the School of Computer Science and Informatics at University College Dublin (scheduled to graduate in summer 2009). He was awarded a place in the Online Dublin Computer Science Summer School (ODCSSS) in Ireland in summer 2008 where he was supervised by Ross Shannon and Dr. Aaron Quigley on research themed around technologies for social connectedness. The paper presented here describes many of the outputs of this research.

Holger Klus holds a Diploma in computer sciences and is a PhD student at the Software Systems Engineering chair at Clausthal University of Technology. His main research interests are mobile and context-aware applications. He gained experiences in this area by developing middleware solutions and applications in several research projects and together with industrial partners. Currently he works in the OPEN project (http://www.ict-open.eu/), a project which is funded by the European Union. It aims to develop an environment, which provides people with the ability to continue to perform their tasks when they move about and change their interaction device.

Houda Labiod is an Associate Professor at Department INFRES (Computer Science and Network department) at Telecom ParisTech (previously named ENST) in Paris (France) since 2001. In 2005, she obtained her HDR (Habilitation à diriger les recherches). Prior to this, she held a research position at Eurecom Institute, Sophia-antipolis, France. She obtained her PHD thesis from the University of Versailles Saint-Quentin-en- Yvelines (France) in 1998. Her current research interests include mobile ad hoc networks, wireless LAN networks, sensor networks, wireless mesh networks, NEMO networks, Vehicular communications, QoS service provisioning, performance evaluation, modeling and security of large-scale distributed systems, cross layer design in wireless networks and link adaptation mechanisms. Dr. LABIOD has published four books and many research papers in these areas. She is a Founder of NTMS Conference, on New Technologies, Mobility and Security (NTMS2007). She served as an Associate Editor and is on the Editorial Board for COMNET journal.

Karen Lee BSc (Hons) is a PhD student researching in the area of Ambient Intelligence in the School of Computing and Intelligent Systems, Faculty of Computing and Engineering at the University of Ulster, Magee College. Her research interests include hybrid web applications and mobile computing.

Deirdre Lee is a Research Associate in the eGovernment Unit at the Digital Enterprise Research Institute (DERI), National University of Ireland, Galway. Her research interests include eGovernment, eParticipation, data interoperability, the Semantic Web, collaborative environments, context-aware mobile and pervasive computing systems, and web services. She has worked on European Commission projects in the Sixth Framework Programme, the Competitiveness and Innovation Framework Programme (CIP), eParticipation Preparatory Action, and the Lifelong Learning Programme. Lee received a B.A. in Information and Communication Technology (ICT) and a M.Sc. in Computer Science from Trinity College Dublin, Ireland in 2004 and 2007 respectively. She has also worked as a research assistant in the IBM Research Lab, Zurich, Switzerland from 2004 – 2006. Contact her at Deirdre.Lee@deri.org.

Juan Lopez received the MS and PhD degrees in Telecommunication (Electrical) Engineering from the Technical University of Madrid (UPM) in 1985 and 1989, respectively. From Sep1990 to Aug 1992, he was a Visiting Scientist in the Department of Electrical and Computer Engineering at Carnegie Mellon

University, Pittsburgh, PA (USA). His research activities center on computer-aided design of integrated circuits and systems. His work is focused on algorithms for automatic synthesis, co-design and embedded computing. From 1989 to 1999, he has been an Associate Professor of the Department of Electrical Engineering at UPM. Currently, Dr. Lopez is a Professor of Computer Architecture and Dean of the School of Computer Science at the University of Castilla-La Mancha.

Tom Lunney BSc (Hons), MSc, P.G.C.E, PhD, MIEEE, MBCS received his degrees from Queen's University Belfast, and is now a Senior Lecturer in Computer Science in the University of Ulster. His research areas include concurrent and distributed systems, artificial intelligence and multi-modal computing. He has presented papers at a range of International Conferences and participated in the organising committees for a number of international conferences and workshops. He has taught at other educational institutions including Queens University, Belfast and The University of Pau, France. He is currently Course Director for postgraduate masters programmes in the University of Ulster.

Katrin Müller joined Motorola Labs in 1999, where she championed Motorola's Design for Environment activities and sustainable development in cooperation with many business units. In this function she was also responsible for product assessment, life cycle information management, and product service development as well as training of engineers and suppliers on DfE. Since 2005 she is driving research in sensing solution for seamless mobility in Europe. She has established the new research area on Ambient Assisted Living and is managing several European funded research projects under the growth program.with special focus on system and application development, data fusion and feedback. Katrin Müller earned her Doctor degree in Mechanical Engineering and Production Technology and managed an interdisciplinary research team in a special research program on recovery of resources at the Technical University in Berlin. She holds the Motorola Six Sigma Green Belt and mastered a business improvement project for cycle time reduction. She demonstrated technology thought leadership in over 30 presentations and publications, got 3 patents successfully filed and serves as technical reviewer in Motorola's things-to-things patent committee.

André Mayers (PhD) is a full professor of computer science at the University of Sherbrooke and the director of a research group about Intelligent Tutoring Systems, mainly focused on knowledge representation structures that make easier the acquisition of knowledge by students, the identification of their plans during problem solving activities and the diagnosis of their knowledge acquisition level. He is also a member of a data mining research group.

René Meier is a Lecturer in Computer Science at Trinity College Dublin. His interests as a researcher in distributed systems cover a variety of overlapping areas related to very large-scale, context-aware mobile and pervasive computing systems as well as to self-organizing systems. These include middleware for highly mobile and location-aware applications, context-aware services, self-organizing peer-to-peer systems, and the application of middleware architectures to smart cities, with a particular focus on intelligent transportation systems. He has served as editorial board member for the Mobile and Pervasive computing community of the IEEE- Computer Society's first on-line magazine, IEEE Distributed Systems Online. Currently, he serves as associate editor for the IGI International Journal of Ambient Computing and Intelligence (IJACI) and for Springer Wireless Networks - The Journal of

Mobile Communication, Computation and Information (WINET). Contact him at Rene.Meier@cs.tcd. ie or www.cs.tcd.ie/Rene.Meier.

Andrew Moere is a Senior Lecturer in Design Computing at the Design Lab of the Faculty of Architecture, Design and Planning of the University of Sydney. He studied Architectural Engineering at K.U.Leuven, Belgium, and received his Ph.D. from ETH-Zurich, Switzerland. His research interests include data visualization and visual design, from traditional screen-based media to more explorative and innovative applications ranging from electronic fashion to media architecture. His teaching comprises interaction design, physical/wearable computing and 3D real-time multimedia. Andrew is also the sole author of a weblog called "information aesthetics" (http://infosthetics.com), a daily updated online repository collecting intriguing and creative forms of information representation.

Germán Montoro received his PhD in Electrical and Computer Engineering (Universidad Autónoma de Madrid - 2005) and currently is full-time teacher at Universidad Autónoma de Madrid. He has been an invited researcher at the University of Miami and University of Ulster. His research interests are spoken dialogue systems and adaptive interfaces, focussed on ambient intelligence.

Hassnaa Moustafa obtained her MSc. degree in Parallel and Distributed Systems from the University of Paris XI (Orsay), France. In December 2004, Hassnaa obtained her Ph.D. degree in Computer and Networks from the Ecole Nationale Superieure des Telecommunications (ENST)-Paris. Since then she is a Research Engineer at France Telecom R&D (Orange Labs), where she is involved in many research activities including Security, Authentication, Authorization, and Accounting (AAA), Services Access Control and IP Autoconfiguration. Hassnaa is the scientific responsible of an integrated French national project, on advanced services for ad hoc networks, with academic and industrial participants and is involved in some standardization activities, mainly within the IETF.

Francisco Moya received his MS and PhD degrees in Telecommunication Engineering from the Technical University of Madrid (UPM), Spain, in 1996 and 2003 respectively. From 1999 he works as an Assistant Professor at the University of Castilla-La Mancha (UCLM). His current research interests include heterogeneous distributed systems and networks, electronic design automation, and its applications to large-scale domotics and system-on-chip design.

Maurice Mulvenna received his degrees from the University of Ulster, where he is a Professor of Computer Science. He researches artificial intelligence and pervasive computing and serves on many program committees, including IEEE Pervasive Computing, IEEE Pervasive Computing and Applications, Pervasive Systems and Computing and IEEE-ACM Web Intelligence. He is a senior member of both the IEEE and Association for Computing Machinery (ACM), and is a chartered member of the British Computer Society (BCS).

Mehdi Najjar is a research scientist at the Canadian Space Agency. He received his Ph.D. in artificial intelligence from the University of Sherbrooke (Canada), where he was also a lecturer at the Department of Computer Science. His research interests are related to smart homes & ambient intelligence, to human-computer interaction and to intelligent learning environments.

Hoang Nguyen is a PhD candidate at the Network Lab, Information System and Networking Institute (ISIN), University of Applied Sciences (SUPSI), Switzerland. He holds an MSc degree in Computer Science from Institut National Polytechnique de Toulouse (INPT), France. He is currently working on context-based routing protocols in opportunistic networks.

Dirk Niebuhr holds a Diploma in computer sciences and is a PhD student at the Software Systems Engineering chair at Clausthal University of Technology. His main research interests are means to provide dependable dynamic adaptive systems. A middleware designed especially for these systems - the Dynamic Adaptive System Infrastructure DAiSI - has been developed under his lead. He carried out the technical lead of the middleware workpackage within the BelAmI project (http://www.belami-project. org/). Furthermore he has been responsible for the tailoring aspects during the development of the V-Modell XT (http://www.v-modell-xt.de/).

Paddy Nixon is the Professor of Distributed Systems and head of the Systems Research Group (SRG) in the Department of Computer Science in the University College Dublin Ireland. His funding of €2.5 million from the SFI is helping to seed the formation of the SRG with an initial core activity in Secure and Predictable Pervasive System.

Stephen Norrby BSc (Hons) is a graduate in Computer Science from the University of Ulster, Northern Ireland. He is currently working within industry and his interests include web systems, security and location based services.

Chris Nugent received a Bachelor of Engineering in Electronic Systems and DPhil in Biomedical Engineering both from the University of Ulster. He currently holds the position of Professor of Biomedical Engineering within the School of Computing and Mathematics at the University of Ulster. His research addresses themes of Technologies to Support Independent Living, Medical Decision Support Systems and the development of Internet based healthcare models.

Dietmar Offenhuber studied Architecture at TU Vienna and Media Art and Sciences at the MIT Media Lab. From 1995-2004 Dietmar worked at the Ars Electronica Futurelab as a designer, exhibition developer and curator, most recently as Key Researcher for interactive spaces. In 2004, Dietmar was a Japan Foundation Fellow at the IAMAS institute in Gifu, Japan, followed by a professorship at the University of Applied Sciences in Hagenberg. From 2006 to 2008 he worked as Research Assistant at the MIT Media Lab. Since 2008 he is Professor at the Art University Linz and Key Researcher for information visualization at the Ludwig Boltzmann Institute for Media Art Research.

Michael Poland received a Bachelor of Science in Interactive Multimedia Design from the University of Ulster in 2006. After a short period in Industry he returned to University of Ulster to undertake a PhD. Michael's current research interests include Artificial Intelligence, Sensor Distribution Optimisation and Machine Vision for Smart Homes.

Aaron Quigley is an academic staff member of the School of Computer Science & Informatics in the Complex and Adaptive Systems Laboratory, University College Dublin. Aaron's research interests include pervasive computing, software engineering, information visualisation, human computer interaction, graph drawing, location and context awareness, peer-to-peer computing, surface interaction and network analysis. He has published over 70 peer reviewed publications and is the program co-chair for LoCA 2009, the workshop co-chair for Pervasive 2010, the conference co-chair for I-HCI 2009 and the tutorials co-chair for the IEEE Tabletop and Interactive Surfaces conference 2009.

Umar Rashid is a PhD student in School of Computer Science & Informatics, University College Dublin, Ireland. He received his BS in Computer Systems Engineering from GIK Institute, Pakistan and MS from Gwangju Institute of Science & Technology, South Korea. His research interests include software engineering and human-computer-interaction in context-aware pervasive computing environments. He is particularly focused on design and evaluation of collaborative pervasive computing systems, with emphasis on personalization and privacy management.

Fernando Rincon completed his graduate studies in Computer Science at the Autonomous University of Barcelona in 1993. In 2003 he obtained the PhD degree from the University of Castilla-La Mancha, where he is currently an Assistant Professor. His research interests include System-On-Chip integration, Hw run-time reconfiguration and Heterogeneous Distributed Systems.

Pablo Sánchez is a Senior Lecturer at the Universidad de Cantabria, Spain. His principal research interests are in Aspect-Oriented Software Development, Model-Driven Development and Software Product Lines. His PhD thesis was about a model-driven development process for the development aspect-oriented executable UML models. He has been an active member of the AOSD Network of Excellence and the AMPLE (Aspect-Oriented Model-Driven Software Product Line Engineering) project. His work can be found at conferences like MODELS, ECMDA, ECSA or SLE and international journals such as Information Software and Technology or Journal on Object Technology. He has been a member of the programme committee for events like the series of workshops for Aspect-Oriented Modeling or for Model-Based Methodologies for Pervasive and Embedded Software (MOMPES). He has also reviewed articles for journals such as Transactions on Aspect-Oriented Software Development or Software and System Modeling (SoSym).

Maria Santofimia received the degree of Technical Engineer in Computer Science in 2001 from the University of Córdoba (Spain); the Master's degree on Computer Security from the University of Glamorgan (Wales, UK) in 2003; and the degree of Engineer in Computer Science in 2006 from the University of Castilla-La Mancha (Spain). She is currently working towards her PhD as a member of the Computer Architecture and Networks Research Group (ARCO) at the Univeristy of Castilla-La Mancha. She is an assistant professor in the School of Computer Science in Ciudad Real.

Jose Santos obtained his Electronic Engineering Degree from the Universidad Simon Bolivar in Caracas, Venezuela in 1998, his Ph.D. in Electronic Engineering from the University of Ulster, Northern Ireland, UK in 2002, and a Pg.Cert. in Higher Education Teaching from the University of Ulster in 2003. He is a Lecturer in the school of Computing and Intelligent Systems at the Magee Campus of the University of Ulster since 2002. He is also a member of the Ambient Intelligence Research Group which is part of the Intelligent Systems Research Centre (ISRC) at the University of Ulster. His research interests lien in the area of Ambient Intelligence, RF and Wireless Systems, Sensor Networks, biotelemetry and biomedical systems.

Andreas Schaller joined Motorola in 1995. Since 1998 Andreas is working for Motorola Labs, PRRC-Europe, based in Taunusstein, Germany. Currently he is managing the Motorola Labs research area 'Short Range RF Communications' in Europe. Andreas has a Motorola Six Sigma Black Belt and holds several patents. Prior to joining Motorola, Andreas received an MSc Degree in Manufacturing Engineering from the University of Erlangen-Nuremberg, Germany.

Daniela Segura is a graduate student in computer science at CICESE. Her research interests include mobile and ubiquitous computing, human-computer interaction and software engineering. She received her BS from the Instituto Tecnológico de Tepic (ITT), Mexico.

Ross Shannon is a PhD student in the Systems Research Group in the Complex and Adaptive Systems Laboratory, University College Dublin. His research focuses on the temporal aspects of information visualisation in applications like social networks, communication networks and pervasive systems.

Xiaobin Shen obtained his PhD "Design and Evaluation of Ambient Displays" in School of Information Technology, University of Sydney in 2007. He is a software leader in Australian National Data Service, Monash University, Australia. Previously, he was a research fellow (Australian Postdoc Fellowship Industry) at the University of Melbourne. Xiaobin's main research interest is Information Visualization, Bioinformatics and Visual Analytics.

Dante I. Tapia received a PhD in Computer Science from the University of Salamanca (Spain) in 2009. He obtained an Engineering in Computer Sciences degree in 2001 and an MSc in Telecommunications at the University of Colima (Mexico) in 2004. At present he is a full-time researcher at the BISITE Research Group (http://bisite.usal.es) of the University of Salamanca (Spain). He has been member of the organising and scientific committee of several international symposiums and co-author of more than 50 papers published in recognized journal, workshops and symposiums.

Christian Tchepnda obtained his engineer degree in computer science from the Algiers Sciences and Technologies University (USTHB) in 2004. He also obtained a M.S. degree in communication networks from the Paris Pierre & Marie Curie University (UPMC) in 2005. At the end of the same year, he joined Orange Labs and Telecom ParisTech as a research engineer and as a PhD candidate respectively. His areas of research include many aspects of infrastructure, ad hoc, mesh and hybrid wireless networks with a main focus on security, authentication and access control architectures for IP services.

Monica Tentori is a doctoral student in computer science at CICESE and a lecturer in computer science at the Universidad Autónoma de Baja California (UABC), Mexico. Her research interests include ubiquitous computing, human-computer interaction, and medical informatics. She received her MSc in computer science from CICESE. She is a student member of ACM-Sigchi.

David Villa received his MS degree in Computer Engineering from the University of Castilla-La Mancha in 2002. Since then he works as a Teaching Assistant at the University of Castilla-La Mancha (UCLM). He is currently pursuing the PhD degree in Computer Science from UCLM. His current research interests include heterogeneous distributed systems, and distributed embedded system design. Jesus Barba received the Computer Engineering Diploma from the University of Castilla-La Mancha (UCLM), Spain, in 2001. In 1998 he joined the Computer Architecture and Networks Group at UCLM where he is working as Teaching Assistant with the Department of Information and Systems Technology from 2001. He is currently pursuing the PhD degree in Computer Science from UCLM. His research interests include SoCs, HW/SW integration and embedded distributed systems.

Felix Villanueva received the Computer Eng. Diploma from the University of Castilla-La Mancha (UCLM) in 2001. In 1998 he joined the Computer Architecture and Networks Group at UCLM where he is now working as Teaching Assistant. He is currently pursuing the PhD degree in Computer Science from UCLM. His research interests include wireless sensor networks, ambient intelligence and embedded systems.

John Wade graduated from the North West Institute of Further and Higher Education (N.W.I.F.H.E.) in 2001 with a B.Tec HND in Electrical and Electronic Engineering. John is the holder of a first class honours degree in electronics and computing, with diploma in industrial studies (DIS), which he obtained from the University of Ulster in 2004. In 2005 he obtained an Msc in computing and intelligent systems from the University of Ulster. John is currently undergoing a Ph.D in Intelligent systems at the University of Ulster's Intelligent Systems Research Centre (ISRC) where he is focusing on developing a biologically inspired training algorithm for spiking neural networks. As well as neural networks John's main areas of interest are, wireless communications, and intelligent systems.

Bernhard Wally received his BSc from the University of Applied Sciences (FH) Hagenberg in Media Technology and Design focusing on image processing and computer vision in 2004. He subsequently received his MSc in Digital Media in 2006, again from the FH Hagenberg, with his master thesis about homogenization of heterogeneous network technologies and respective devices in the home automation industry. He had been with the Department of Pervasive Computing at University Linz, before he joined the Viennese office of the Research Studio Pervasive Computing Applications where he is currently project manager of and key contributor to the working group pervasive display systems. During his time at University Linz, Bernhard Wally worked on several industrial and scientific projects on tangible user interfaces, context technologies and energy management systems. He also held courses at the FH Hagenberg in programming and interaction design for the Bachelor and Master programmes in Mobile Computing. In his current affiliation he is pursuing his PhD by investigating media façades, explicit and implicit interaction metaphors for public displays as well as sensor systems for display-centric presence recognition.

Hui Wang received his BSc (computer science) and MSc (artificial intelligence) from Jilin University of China in 1985 and 1988 respectively, and PhD (artificial intelligence) from University of Ulster in 1996. He worked at University of Ulster as a lecturer from 1996 to 2002, a senior lecturer from 2002 and a reader from 2007. His research interests include machine learning, data/text mining, uncertainty reasoning, spatial reasoning, and information retrieval. He has authored or co-authored over 90 scientific articles in these areas in journals and conferences, and edited a special issue of Decision Support Systems Journal. He is an associate editor for IEEE SMC-B (from 2009) and Journal of Software (from 2009).

Mikael Wiberg, PhD is an associate professor at the department of Informatics at Umeå university in Sweden. Wiberg is also Research Director at UID - Umeå Institute of Design at Umeå university. In his research, mostly focused on mobile interaction, the emerging interaction society, interaction design and interactive architecture, he has published his work in a number of international journals, including e.g. ToCHI, BIT, IEEE Network, IEEE Pervasive computing, etc. and he has also published his work in books, encyclopedias, and in international conference proceedings including e.g. CHI, HCI, Group, etc.

Index

A

AAL technology 89
Absolut 169, 170
Absolut ICEBAR 169, 170
abstract connection layer (ACL) 90
acceptability 116
ACE system 139
active attack 46
activities of daily living (ADL) 33, 34, 35, 36, 37, 38, 261
actuators 259, 262, 263
adaptive house project 261
admin agent 21, 22
aesthetics 127, 128, 148
ageing in place system 262, 271
Alzheimer's disease 260
ALZ-MAS 17, 18, 19, 20, 21, 22, 23, 24, 25, 26, 27
ambient awareness device 128
ambient communication experience (ACE) 139, 141, 142, 143, 144
ambient computing 166, 178
ambient display 127, 128, 130, 131, 240, 241, 250, 252, 255
ambient display design 242
ambient display evaluation 240, 242, 243, 245, 246, 249, 250, 251, 253, 254, 255, 256, 257
ambient display evaluation, intrusive 240, 243, 250, 255, 257
ambient display evaluation, non-intrusive 240, 243, 255

ambient displays 31, 32, 33, 34, 36, 41, 95, 120, 125, 135, 147, 155, 240, 241, 242, 243, 245, 247, 249, 250, 251, 253, 255, 256, 257, 258
ambient football scorecast 148
ambient furniture 135
ambient information systems (AIS) 94, 95, 96, 97, 98, 99, 100, 101, 102, 103, 128, 139, 145, 241
ambient information technology 157
ambient intelligence (AmI) 17, 18, 19, 20, 24, 27, 28, 29, 30, 32, 33, 40, 56, 57, 71, 72, 73, 74, 76, 77, 78, 80, 81, 82, 205, 206, 219, 220, 229, 230, 238
ambient intelligence environments 205
ambient interaction 96, 99, 101
ambient jewelry 134, 135, 136, 137
ambient life 105, 106, 107, 109
ambient middleware framework for context-awareness (AMiCA) 223, 224
ambient umbrella 148
ambient visualization 128, 130
AmI-based system 18
AmI environments 32
AmI software applications 71
APIs 72, 74, 75, 76
application engineering 78
application responsive 139
applications driven features 73
application units (AUs) 45
Asia 261, 264
asset tracking 301, 302
assistive technology 260, 265, 267, 268
AtemRaum 107, 110
augmented area 4